Europe in the
High Middle Ages
1150–1300

A GENERAL HISTORY OF EUROPE

General Editor: Denys Hay

For many years the volumes of Denys Hay's distinguished *General History of Europe* have been standard recommendations for university students, sixth formers and general readers. They offer broad surveys of European history, in which the detailed discussion (on a regional or continent-wide basis) of social, economic, administrative and intellectual themes is woven into a clear framework of political events. They set out to combine scholarship with accessibility in texts which are both attractively written and intellectually vigorous. Now the series is being revised and refreshed again, with many of the books being relaunched – reset, redesigned, and in a larger, more reader-friendly format.

Currently available:

A.H.M. Jones, *The Decline of the Roman World*

Christopher Brooke, *Europe in the Central Middle Ages 962–1154* (Third Edition)

John H. Mundy, *Europe in the High Middle Ages 1150–1300* (Third Edition)

Denys Hay, *Europe in the Fourteenth and Fifteenth Centuries* (Second Edition)

H.G. Koenigsberger, George L. Mosse, and G.Q. Bowler, *Europe in the Sixteenth Century* (Second Edition)

D.H. Pennington, *Europe in the Seventeenth Century* (Second Edition)

M.S. Anderson, *Europe in the Eighteenth Century* (Third Edition)

Franklin L. Ford, *Europe 1780–1830* (Second Edition)

Harry Hearder, *Europe in the Nineteenth Century 1830–1880* (Second Edition)

J.M. Roberts, *Europe 1880–1945* (Second Edition)

A GENERAL HISTORY OF EUROPE

Europe in the High Middle Ages
1150–1300

THIRD EDITION

John H. Mundy
Columbia University

An imprint of **Pearson Education**

Harlow, England · London · New York · Reading, Massachusetts · San Francisco · Toronto · Don Mills, Ontario · Sydney
Tokyo · Singapore · Hong Kong · Seoul · Taipei · Cape Town · Madrid · Mexico City · Amsterdam · Munich · Paris · Milan

Pearson Education Limited

Edinburgh Gate
Harlow
Essex CM20 2JE
England

and Associated Companies around the world

Visit us on the World Wide Web at:
www.pearsoneduc.com

First published under the Addison Wesley imprint 1973
Second edition 1991
Third edition 2000

ISBN 0 582 36988 6 CSD
ISBN 0 582 36987 8 PPR

British Library Cataloguing-in-Publication Data
A CIP catalogue record for this book can be obtained from the British Library.

Library of Congress Cataloguing-in-Publication Data
A catalog record for this book can be obtained from the Library of Congress.

10 9 8 7 6 5 4 3 2 1
04 03 02 01 00 99

Typeset by 35 in 9.5/12.5pt Stone Serif
Produced by Pearson Education Asia Pte Ltd.
Printed in Singapore

To Charlotte Williams Mundy

Contents

List of maps

Abbreviations

AA.SS	*Acta sanctorum*
BIMA	*Bibliotheca iuridica medii aevi*, ed. Augusto Gaudenzi *et al.*, 3 vols. (Bologna 1888–1901)
BGPM	*Beiträge zur Geschichte der Philosophie des Mittelalters*
BuF	*Briefsteller und Formelbücher des eilten bis vierzehnten Jahrhunderts*, ed. Ludwig Rockinger, 2 vols. (Munich 1863–64)
CICan	*Corpus iuris canonici*, ed. Emil Friedberg, 2 vols. (Leipzig 1879–81)
CICiv	*Corpus iuris civilis*, ed. Mommsen, Krüger *et al.*, 3 vols. (Berlin 1912–20)
MGH	*Monumenta Germaniae Historica*
Const.	*Constitutiones et acta publica*
Epp. sel.	*Epistolae selectae*
LL	*Leges*
Ldl	*Libelli de lite*
SS	*Scriptores*
FIG in usum scholarum	*Fontes iuris germanica antiqui in usum scholarum*
SS in usum scholarum	*Scriptores rerum Germanicarum in usum scholarum*
Staatschriften	*Staatschriften des späteren Mittelalters*
PL	*Patrologia latina*, ed. J.P. Migne (Paris 1844–64)
RIS	*Rerum italicarum scriptores*, new edition 1900 onward
Rolls Series	*Rerum britannicarum medii aevi scriptores*
TUJ	*Tractatus universi juris*

Preface

This history is written for college and university students, especially those who hope to acquire rather more learning than most of their peers. Young people understand everything that their elders can, but also differ from the old. Innocent or perhaps ignorant, they comprehend more rapidly than older persons because, burdened by experience and learning, the latter often peer in order to judge instead of merely looking in order to understand. This difference has long excited comment. It is probably true that the old, as Giles of Rome phrased the commonplace, 'are naturally skeptical and ungenerous; the young generous and credulous.'[1] Aside from this, all adults, young and old, are intellectually equal. A history addressed to pupils is therefore also addressed to the wider audience of their parents and teachers.

The text of this book has been interlarded with quotations from primary sources because they alone convey the colour of the period. Occasional Latin technical terms have also been retained. This reminds readers of something easily overlooked in today's age of national languages. The Europe treated here was a region mainly divided between the Latin-speaking peoples and the German-speaking ones. Although the latter had invaded and subjected the Romans, the latter's Mediterranean culture had in turn conquered them. Western Europe's universal language had become Latin, and French, a language of Latin stock, was the most widespread literary and legal vernacular. In spite of the importance of the Germanic and Nordic peoples (and, for this volume, the lesser weight of the Celts, Greeks and Slavs), Latin and its derivatives so dominated Europe's cultural life that the single adjective best qualifying the idea of 'western Europe' for this period is 'Latin'. This term cleanly distinguishes 'the West' from Greek, Slavic and Arabic Europe, Near East and Africa.

Many primary sources cited here derive from printed editions, but recourse is sometimes had to documents and tracts cited in other writers' books. Citations from books by modern authors are sometimes used even when I have read the original text, because the discussion around the passage quoted in the modern book is so illuminating. No matter what the source, however, the translations of Latin and medieval vernacular texts (but not Greek and Hebrew) are my own.

---

[1] *De regimine principum* 1 1 2 (Rome 1607) 7.

The method of citing primary texts has been simplified. Literary texts were usually divided into books and chapters, and sometimes into other subdivisions. The first number given in this book is that of the book and the second that of the chapter, with the other subdivisions following thereafter. None of these divisions is signalled here, because a reader who looks up the source can easily divine where to look. In addition, the reader is provided with the page number of the text edition or modern book wherein the cited text was found. Technical citations of law are eschewed here because non-specialists do not know them. Justinian's *Codex*, for example, is cited as *Code*, not as *C.*, and canon law citations are also simplified. Occasional exceptions to these rules will be signalled.

Footnotes have been made as succinct as possible. Most references to secondary works are taken from books listed in the general bibliography, which is itself divided into groups, one for each part of this history, where the full titles may be found. Other texts or editions are given full references the first time they appear, but are thereafter abbreviated. If texts are cited, the authors' names and the titles of their works may be found in the general index.

To make the first names mentioned in this book seem as familiar as possible, they have been anglicized, if at all possible. Names nevertheless pose difficulties. One person cited below is 'Petrus Johannis Olivi' – 'Peter', that is, 'son of John Olivi'. Following traditional scholarship, however, he will be referred to as 'Peter John Olivi'. Another example is Remigio, son of Girolamo, in whose case the Italian style of 'Remigio de'Girolami' will be used.

For the various editions of this work, Joan Ferrante, Beatrice Gottlieb, Jocelyn N. Hilgarth, Julius Kirshner, Kimberly Lo Prete, Domenico Maffei, Ronald G. Musto, Leah L. Otis, Peter N. Riesenberg, Zephira E. Rokeah, Kenneth M. Setton, Sir Richard W. Southern and Kennerly M. Woody are thanked for useful references to primary sources.

John Mundy
New York, 1999

Chapter 1

Introduction

The subject matter

The view of the past advanced by historians is often obscured by fogs or mists specific to each historical period. Those of medieval history are because Europe's culture was then ecclesiastical, whereas today's is secular. Secular thinkers seek to find the origins of the institutions and thought that they applaud, and hence when looking for today's ancestors vault back over the Middle Ages to Greek and Roman antiquity. Their opponents, modern folk who go to church, are in a sense impoverished because they experience only a subculture dominated by secularism. One result is that they dote on the Middle Ages, an age that becomes for them a weapon with which to attack the present. After the disasters of recent European history, one understands their doubts about secularism, but their Middle Ages is too full of idealized persons and institutions to be real.

Modern research has defined the differences between classical, medieval and modern times, and contrasted the otherworldly emphasis of late antique and medieval thought with the thisworldly emphasis of moderns and of their predecessors in antiquity. This truthful distinction has, however, encouraged some to go too far. To them, today's thisworldly thought promotes rational propositions, those within reach of demonstration, whereas yesterday's otherworldly thought was religious, beyond, that is, the reach of the same. Institutions are confused with ideas: the Church becomes religion, so to speak, and the state and other secular institutions embody reason. This overlooks the fact that, although there are many differences between the two ways of thinking, they have something in common, namely their love of propositions that transcend human reason. Many convictions of today's secular thinkers about, for example, human free will, moral potential, the necessity of personal freedom for social and economic advancement and humanity's central role in the cosmos are as fanciful as any mystery found in Christianity, Judaism or Islam.

Using the ideas expressed by the words 'religious' or 'rational' to describe motives for human action is both traditional and valid. To reject either one of them in favour of the other, however, is to misuse them. Some say, for example, that a person or group acted only for religious motives; others

1

counter that they were solely animated by rational, economic or material motives. One wonders what such definitions mean. Men and women play games: they turn prayer wheels, recite God's names, make music, work on puzzles or perform calculations. When done by a man or woman alone, these have little to do with the society in which the person lives, but seem instead to be means of testing his or her harmony with the nature of things. When they play with others or before an audience, however, play becomes a way of competing or joining with other men and women. What prompted the game in the first place is that many, indeed most, feel that there is a natural order into which they can fit themselves, or of which they can make use. This desire is tied to society, but transcends – much as play does – the specific social world in which individuals live. One reason is that the problems that engender this feeling are uniform throughout history: birth, for example, growth, sickness and death, and also humanity's ever-exuberant hope for freedom and love. These are expressed by a mixture of rational and religious passions and ideas. The desire to avoid death, for example, causes humanity both to people the other world with possibly imaginary souls and to work rationally to prolong life in this one.

The characteristics of particular periods especially attract historians because they distinguish one age from another. They also bulk large in the sources for historical study, probably because humans spend little time being born, loving or dying but a great deal in life's routines. Only sleep takes more time than these. Experience nevertheless teaches that the primal activities are more consequential, because humans are basically moved by the need to discover and use the right order of things to attain love and retain life. Historians are therefore obliged to recognize the similarities of human desire in the many languages, secular or ecclesiastical, technical or commonsensical, scientific or mystic, lent to them by transient institutions, philosophies and religions. One recalls, for example, a debate as to whether the ideas of Karl Marx were mainly drawn from the thought of his time or instead arose within himself, having few or no outside sources. This debate really rehearsed arguments about free will and determination, ones as far beyond demonstration as the old scholastic ones pitting innate natural capacity against the need for an infusion of divine grace. Once, moreover, the intrinsic similarities of some modern and medieval propositions about humanity's role in the deity's providence or in natural history are perceived, one begins to understand why people are addicted to propositions beyond demonstration.

This addiction presumably derives from need. Will the cancer kill me? Or, am I really loved? All that can be done to answer such questions is to hope and play games; besides, although recourse to propositions beyond proof often inhibits human freedom, history also shows that it sometimes helps it. Most institutions have been built on humanity's reasonable and demonstrable needs for health, material welfare and a measure of freedom in the disposition of talents and goods. In late Rome, however, these normally healthy drives and their concomitant institutions were so overwhelmed by internal disruption and external attack that the people found them inordinately oppressive, and therefore turned to the other world, the world beyond demonstration. Rome's inhabitants rejected Greco-Roman earth-centred reason, religion and society and gave loyalty instead to religious mysteries. Christianity's obscurantism was not only a failure of nerve but also a liberating secession from service to state and society and from the self-defeating race for wealth, learning and well-being.

The institutional precipitate of this revolutionary attitude was the medieval Church. Starting from late Rome's state church, an evolution of some six centuries led to a new structure of governmental and social power. Empowered by society, ecclesiastical authority headed by the Roman pontiffs was raised to counterbalance lay power, thus making practical liberty a matter of choosing between secular and ecclesiastical authority, institutions and patterns of thought, by using one against the other. If one seemed unduly inhibiting, men and women could and did turn to the other. Great though it was, this balance between the two powers was only temporary and lasted from about 1000 to 1400. During the period of clerical leadership, of which the central century is treated in this volume, the disruption of this medieval synthesis was announced. Called on to direct the world's practical life as well as to sing religion's anthems, the clergy itself began to turn from theology to philosophy, from mystery to reason, from the other world to this one.

These considerations lead this author to assume that few or no human activities lack a religious dimension, an appeal to, or a use of, propositions beyond demonstration, nor to call on what can be projected to be reasonably likely on the basis of human experience in nature. The genesis of heresy (belief differing from that of the majority), for example, has been ascribed by some to religious belief and by others to social or economic motives. In this book there is no dichotomy: the medieval believer, doubter or heretic is described as both a religious and an economic person.

There are also divergent ways of viewing the relationship of nations, classes, groups and sexes. Many feel that the powerful always abuse the weak, the warlike the pacific, the rich the poor, and men women. Conjecturing that societies based on violence are bound to lack solidarity's cement, others instead assert that the mutually profitable use of one by the other has held society together throughout history. Although lamenting servitude, for example, some modern writers – Marx among them (when talking about Greek slavery) – have asserted that without it, there would have been no culture. Still, all that can really be shown is that labour is necessary for civilization, and that coerced work sometimes has advantages over free. Greco-Roman civilization was spread towards the Rhine and Danube valleys from the shores of the Mediterranean in part by a temporary increase of servitude, but that does not mean that coercion was necessary. History only seems to say that oppression sometimes helps humankind and harms it at others.

Some contemporaries have been so sickened by past human savagery that they discern no profit in history because, to them, it merely provides models for bad behaviour. This position is odd: to deny hideousness suppresses much of real living and all of dying. Others, too numerous to cite, love selectively, explaining away evil and emphasizing the good. Their past is read in terms of their present: good institutions and good people have led to today's fulfilment. In the view of some, the medieval attempt to extirpate heresy and attack Islam and Judaism was unhappy, but also necessary because the Church created and defended European culture. Again, the subordinate place of women and the exploitation of peasants by townsmen and lords were functional because without their labour there would have been no monuments of art or letters. It is nevertheless likely that medieval men and women were of two minds: Jews and Muslims were detested, but intellectually admired; serfs scorned, but also emancipated; women brutalized, but also loved as equals.

Some hope to teach a moral lesson by asserting that the exploitation of others is always self-defeating and hence destroys the unjust. Like the mad, individuals and societies undoubtedly often repeat actions to excess, persisting in behaviour that causes defeat. But is there a necessary link between self-destruction and the unjust? One can surely exist without the other, as the long duration of awful empires attests, not to speak of the lengthy lives of some appalling persons. Someone might nevertheless object that all empires have fallen; but then all individuals have died, and surely not because of self-destruction.

In a sense, death is independent of humanity and its institutions and, because of the fear it inspires, precipitates both human invention and destruction. Having given life, nature launches all into a race from oncoming death. Children, men and women are the runners, who combat their neighbours, young against old, men against women, debtors against creditors, families, provinces, nations and races, one against the other. But it is also true that, from the brief commerce of these racers, new life derives to run yet further distances, as do exchanges of information, momentary but fond solidarities and relatively long-lived institutions and cultures. In addition, fear for their own futures make the actors worry about what they do to others, but, given the rapidity of death's approach, only hasty and partial restitution can be made. The history of individuals and societies further shows that excess is wrong or self-defeating. But, overborne by death's rush and the hordes driven before it, who can know when he or she has passed the limit? An historian of such vertiginous scenes had best avoid moralizing, and instead imitate Benedict Spinoza, who pleaded for objectivity:

4

When I apply my mind to history, I intend . . . to deduce from human nature nothing outrageous or unheard of but instead those things that best fit experience. I will inquire into the things pertaining to this science with the same freedom of spirit one is accustomed to use in mathematics, and will sedulously take care not to laugh at, lament or execrate, but rather understand human actions.[1]

The tendency to read modern experience back into history must also be resisted. One example is the notion that economic expansion is necessarily accompanied by growing human freedom. This opinion is surely mistaken, because Europe's early modern expansion was accompanied by a great increase in slavery. Again, reflecting the 'triumph of the bourgeoisie' in the French Revolution, some historians believe that merchants were progressive, but that churchmen, nobles and peasants were backward. This view is both irrational and also overlooks the prohibition of usury, which, along with technological change, made all the difference between medieval and modern economic individualism or capitalism. Lastly, many of the same scholars, however much they otherwise disagreed, claimed to have found an essential and original difference between northern urbanism and that of the Mediterranean. Serving as capital of a province and housing rural landowners, the ancient city was said to have lived again in medieval Italy, whereas the northern city created a new urbanism led by a bourgeoisie free from the trammels of rural society. This medieval bourgeois city was consequently the foundation of the progressive modern and capitalist mercantile and manufacturing city; an original creation, then, of northern European, perhaps of German, culture. This book argues instead that, in origin though not in development, northern and southern medieval towns were fundamentally similar.

Today's Church seeks autonomy, claiming a sphere exempt from the omnipresent power of the secular state. This urge is understandable, but it has also inspired not a few to maintain that medieval papal assertions of what seem like expressions of political will and power really dealt only with moral or spiritual questions. Sometimes useful, this position is usually mistaken because most churchmen and pontiffs wanted to 'reform' political institutions in order to support a church that, in their view, taught humanity how to attain heaven. Again, the opinion that, by failing to reform in this period, the papal Church invited its overthrow during what Protestants call 'the Reformation' is surely doubtful. It is wholly unlikely that the reforms envisaged by modern Christians would have prevented that great transformation.

A final and personal note: I much regret that the political and social history of Scandinavia, the Iberian peninsula, south Italy and Sicily, Slavic Europe and Greek and Saracen areas are hardly touched on in this book. The decision to neglect these subjects is partly because one book cannot treat

---

[1] *Tractatus politicus* 1 4 in *Opera* (ed. Carl Gebhardt, Heidelberg 1925) 274.

everything and partly because I fear writing about societies whose languages I cannot read. Readers may nevertheless remember that institutions in Scandinavia, Hungary and the nearby Slavonic states were similar to those seen earlier in Italy and the west of Europe during the Carolingian period. Another deficiency is that this book barely touches on the history of art, architecture, music and literature, but a justification is that these are specialized subjects best left to the technicians who work on them.

History, biography and poetry

The large majority of the primary sources cited in this book derive from charters containing contracts, testaments, local customs and other economic and constitutional materials. To these may be added legal treatises written by canonists (specialists in church law) and civilians (those teaching law, especially Roman, in the schools) and by government officers in monarchies or republics. In addition, churchmen, especially academics, and an occasional layman produced literature dealing with government and the relations of Church and state, forms of political and social organization as well as theology, both dogmatic and moral. These materials will be described in the later chapters of this book.

More fascinating to many readers are texts that allow them to see how successful the individual actors on history's stage were, whether they foresaw the future or were able to understand their present. Although a natural desire because life requires models, this urge easily becomes a cult of human fame, a partial equivalent of medieval canonization, and – even about today's personalities, when sources are abundant – gives rise to questionable work. The difficulty is that, even when honourable persons or biographers explain motives, their revelations suffer from a natural reluctance to disclose interests. Besides, very few medieval texts describe the intentions (whether false or true) of actors or depict their intimate feelings and conduct. Some do, however, even pieces close to saints' lives. The so-called autobiography of Peter, the hermit of Monte Morrone, who became Pope Celestine V (pope 1294, d. 1296), gives a relatively frank view of its hero's milieu. Similarly, the life of the canonized king of France, Louis IX, issued by John, lord of Joinville, in 1309, sketches, with unusual realism, aspects of the king's behaviour and qualities, as well as those of his courtiers and clergy. On the whole, however, biography and autobiography were rarer in medieval than in modern or contemporary history. This lack is not crippling. If most of the texts reporting the lives and feelings of Abelard and Heloise are late, for example, they clearly show what contemporaries believed to be their institutional and mental contexts. If, then, specific persons are rarely fully seen, what people thought about, their ways of acting and their plans for living are easily perceived. Apart from treatises on theology, philosophy, law and government and contemporary illumination, painting and sculpture, the two most instructive types of sources are the many histories and literary pieces composed in this period.

Although the elegance of an Otto of Freising (d. 1158) was not surpassed in the period with which this volume deals, universal history was well represented. Other than the English historians mentioned below, good examples are the *Pantheon* of Godfrey of Viterbo (d. 1191) and the *Historical Mirror* of the Dominican encyclopedist Vincent of Beauvais (d. *circa* 1259). Similar in tradition was William of Nangis (d. 1300), a monk in the royal monastery of St Denis that, from about 1274, began to produce the semi-official annals of the French monarchy, the *Great Chronicles*. There were also specialized histories with a large chronological range like Martin of Troppau's (d. 1278) papal and imperial history, a version of which was finished by 1258.

Partly because their treatment of antiquity and the earlier Middle Ages was usually distilled from earlier sources, historians were more original (although not less biased) when dealing with their own times. Among the best were England's prolific chroniclers William of Newburgh (d. 1198), Roger of Hoveden (d. 1201) and the great Matthew Paris (d. 1259), a monk of St Albans, who also illustrate how information could be transmitted with accuracy and detail from one part of Europe to another. Each significant event evoked its historians. An example is the German monk Helmhold's (d. 1177) history of the conquest of the Baltic Slavs. Among the best chroniclers of the crusades in the Near East was William, archbishop of Tyre (d. *circa* 1186), gifted in Arabic and Greek, who also wrote a lost, although much cited, account of the oriental states.

Some events were covered thoroughly by contemporaries. The Albigensian crusade of 1209 and the introduction of the inquisitors into Languedoc in the 1230s, for example, were recorded in the general French and English chronicles. Local and specific histories also expressed every possible point of view, save that of the Cathar church. Peter of Vaux de Cernay, a Cistercian who accompanied the Crusaders (1212–18), wrote a detailed polemical history, full of propaganda and miracles. A rhymed vernacular history composed by two authors, now called the *Song of the Crusade*, expressed the attitudes of the southerners, the first half being that of those on the side of the Crusade and the second of those resisting it. Although intolerant, a cool account of the spread and repression of Catharism was given by a later chaplain of the counts of Toulouse, William of Puylaurens, in the 1270s. He enlivened his record with natural wonders, but put miracles aside. A brief but remarkably accurate history of the early repression of Catharism was penned by the Dominican William Pelisson (d. 1268), an inquisitor whose enthusiastic pursuit of Cathars embarrasses modern Catholics. Lastly, a history of the Dominican order was composed by Bernard Gui (d. 1331), who paid special attention to Languedoc and Toulouse, where he, as an inquisitor, spent much time in his order's mother house.

The term history did not mean what it means today. *Oriental History*, by the famed preacher James of Vitry (d. 1240), is an historical guidebook to the Holy Land and adjacent regions, and his *Occidental History* treated the orders, structure and sacraments of the Latin Church. His were manuals for parish priests, preachers and clergy on pilgrimage or missions. Above all, history was a moral discipline. Moralizers all, historians favoured parties or interests; Matthew Paris, for example, being hostile to both Rome and the monarchy of Henry III. Although informative and often very perceptive, history was primarily partisan and polemical, and therefore even more openly biased in favour of contemporary causes than is academic history today, if such can be imagined.

Gui was one of several authors from the new mendicant orders who recorded the glories of their founders, the lives of their saints and their learned men, the latter replete with the titles of, and details about, their works. Related to this genre was the history by Salimbene of Parma (d. *circa* 1290), perhaps the most astonishing document of all. This friar outlines the history of the Franciscan order from the death of its founder, its internecine struggles and battles with other orders and the papacy. He wove a history of his life in the order into an account of the wars between the Italian republics and the Hohenstaufen Empire from 1167 to 1287, spicing everything with perceptive, if intolerant, details on every divergent religious sect and political party. Hoping to improve church government, he also included a tract *On Prelates*.

Town and provincial history was an early speciality of laymen. A notable example in this period was the history of the March of Treviso written by the son of a notary, the grammarian Rolandino of Padua (d. 1276). To this may be added a literature in praise of individual cities. The one cited in these pages is the oddly statistical praise of Milan by Bonvesino of Riva of about 1282. Since lay literacy in Latin was widespread in Italy, these were in that language. As seen above anent the Albigensian crusade, vernacular history had also begun to make an appearance. An outstanding example was the history of the Fourth Crusade and of the Latin Empire of Constantinople by Geoffrey of Villehardouin, marshal of the Champagne and of Romania (d. *circa* 1213).

As in Otto of Freising's and his continuator's *Deeds of Frederick* (I Barbarossa), biography was close to history. Capetian ideology coloured a life of Philip II Augustus of France by William the Breton (d. *circa* 1224–26). Princely lines were also interested in recording the histories of their families and famous ancestors. The canon Breton of Amboise's (*fl.* 1155–73) history of the counts of Anjou and lords of Amboise and that of the lords of Ardres and counts of Guines by the clerk Lambert of Ardres (*fl.* 1194–1203) exemplify this genre. A chaplain composed a vernacular verse biography of William, marshal of England and earl of Pembroke (d. 1219), a work that, if not always accurate, is veracity itself about the milieu of his hero. By the thirteenth century, laymen were in this business themselves, writing both biographies and autobiographies in the vernacular. Among the most celebrated of these were the memoirs of Philip of Novara (d. 1261–64), a great lord, jurist and historian of Cyprus and 'Overseas France'. Joinville's biography of Louis IX, mentioned above, is another.

Career and advancement attracted society's elite, and literature reflected it. Heroes who taught lessons were what was wanted. Some of these, like the twelfth-century *Ralph of Cambrai*, preached the virtue of moderation and the unhappy fate of those ruled by excess. Others, like the earlier *Song of Roland*, provided a hero whose Christlike sacrifice provided a popular model of how to win fame by arms and whose victory, to speak institutionally, recorded monarchy's triumph over that of the aristocratic family. There were also caricatures, replete with anti-heroes without a shred of virtue. The religious counterpart of the acquisition of fame by soldiers was the attainment of sanctity by the saints, the Church's heroes. Saints' lives were becoming increasingly historical in this period and large collections designed for the use of preachers were appearing. A celebrated example was James of Voragine's (Varazze, d. 1298) collection of semi-biographies called the *Golden Legend*. Related to this literature were such exemplarist semi-historical books as the *Dialogue of Miracles* by the Cistercian Caesarius of Heisterbach (d. 1240), designed to explore the hazards and models of the religious life ostensibly for the benefit of novices.

A spate of increasingly specialized tracts on the 'ages of man', manners, chivalry and social and political theory was written by laymen such as Novara mentioned above, Brunetto Latini (d. 1294–95) and the polymath Raymond Llull (d. *circa* 1315). These authors wrote in the vernacular, thus showing that they were the second generation in lay letters because verse initially predominated. In poetry, the individual or individual choice was the central subject. Influenced by religious thought, themes of moral ascent or progress were outlined in poems such as *Perceval*. This subject was easily joined to that of love. In his *Erec and Enide*, Christian of Troyes (*fl.* 1150–80) – a poet admired by Dante – taught that true love flourishes only among those who strive to advance in the world. The tests to be overcome by lovers were investigated in Arthurian literature by means of figures such as Lancelot and Queen Guenievre. Troubadour verse especially explored longing or being in love, a condition as yet not satisfied, or never to be. There was an enormous literature on the subject, some of it playful and earthy. In 1184–86 Andrew the Chaplain wrote his *On Love*, a witty socio-philosophical encyclopaedia of the topic.

Vernacular writing, moreover, had begun to transcend history, war's heroics and love. Mentioned above, Raymond Llull joined love to theology. Yet another writer in the vernacular was the famous poet Dante Alighieri (d. 1321), who began work on his *Divine Comedy* about 1307. During the ten

9

or more years he spent on this vernacular verse encyclopaedia, he took time off to compose in Latin a political and ecclesiological tract *On Monarchy* (*circa* 1313). Widely circulated, the larger part of the *Romance of the Rose* was written in French somewhere between 1270 and 1285 by John Clopinel of Meung, presumably a clerk and a major translator of Latin texts. Not only a lively description of love, of the war between woman and man and of manners, John's *Romance* was also an encyclopaedia of philosophy and theology, based especially on the Cistercian theologian, Alan of Lille (d. 1202). These great vernacular works show how high the culture of the lay elite was around 1300.

The relationship of the clergy and the laity that has been touched on here will be sketched in more detail in the next chapter.

Part One

EUROPE

Chapter 2

Social frontiers: clerks and laymen

The two peoples

Western Europeans elevated the Church to lead Latin society during the Gregorian Age, a period of intermittent internal warfare extending from about 1050 until 1130. During this slow revolution, a new structure of social and governmental power came into being and remained to characterize western Europe's apogee in the twelfth and thirteenth centuries. This structure differed from that obtaining in the earlier Middle Ages as well as from that appearing in early modern times. Before the revolution, Europeans had been governed – except on the local and familial levels – by empires and quasi-national states, aided by often rebellious but always subordinate churches. After 1300, larger units of political and social power were growing into nation-states or other substantial units of government, such as the expanding Italian and German republics and principalities. The secular power in these centres was rising to rule a subordinate clergy, eventually, indeed, to replace them in large part by lay levites, the philosophers of modern times.

During the period treated in this book, although great early medieval monarchies lingered on, and although, as shall be seen, some states were already beginning to evolve into modern nations, most power was entrusted to the ecumenical authority of the Roman Church and to the local governments of town and countryside. The latter, whether urban or rural, lordly or republican, achieved a degree of freedom from central government that they never again enjoyed. From the days of the Gregorians until the turmoil of the fourteenth and fifteenth centuries, Europe was led by an inadvertent but real alliance between the rural and urban well-to-do and the churchmen under the See of Peter.

The Church embodied the cultural identity of the 'Christian republic'. Although war persisted, Christendom's only easily justified wars were the Crusades, waves of expansion at the expense of neighbouring cultures and religions. The needs of this imperialism encouraged plans designed to realize a peaceful Christian society at home, the military being restrained there by the law of just war and the peace or truce of God. Just price and the condemnation of usury were employed to protect Crusaders and police the marketplace. Propaganda for economic brotherhood helped build a social corporatism with which to try to tie the grasping hands of the rich and mighty. In every activity, the expansion of the penitential system and of the courts of canon law testified to the willingness of the people to allow the clergy to regulate and harmonize life on earth.

Not always harmoniously, the secular clergy were aided by the monastic orders. Indeed, around 1100, the monks often led the rest. Cistercians were famed for clearing forests and marshes, Europe's best soldiers served in the ranks of the military orders, and new quasi-monastic foundations appeared everywhere to house the aged, the sick, the destitute and the fallen. The thirteenth century saw the fulfilment of earlier efforts in education: the building of a university system and parish schools. Monks and parish clergy combined to enhance the role of sacerdotal authority by proclaiming the miracle of the mass and expanding penitential police. In regard to the mass, the cup having been withdrawn from the laity during the Gregorian age, the priestly miracle of transubstantiation was finally codified at the fourth Lateran Council in 1215 and the Corpus Christi feast spread by papal edict in 1264. The role of the priest in the miracle of the mass and as judge in the court of conscience fortified a confident sense that a direct link existed between God's eternal ordinance and human institutions, one tying heaven and earth together.

Circumstances seemed to justify this sanguine attitude. Growing populations, newly cleared fields, new towns, expanding personal freedom and the conquest of foreign lands made nature seem beneficent and earthly institutions fit to help humanity achieve a happy end. Still, difficult adjustments on the part of Christians were required, ones precipitating basic changes in the behaviour and attitudes of the Church. Many were still attracted by what had once given freedom in the days of Rome and the state-dominated churches of the earlier Middle Ages: the accent on the other world – the world of heaven against earth, of spiritual against material values, of things felt but beyond demonstration against things demonstrable. To educate for heaven, however, the clergy increasingly turned to examine and manipulate the world in which they lived. The receptiveness to Aristotelian and Arabic natural philosophy was an expression of this change. Another was a heightened interest in both the ideal and practical forms of ecclesiastical and secular government. Clerical and lay utopians tried to remake the world on the model of the supernal Jerusalem, to make a heaven on earth. Around 1200, this movement attracted such varied groups as the teachers at Paris headed by Peter Cantor (precentor of Nôtre Dame, d. 1197) and the humble craftsfolk brigaded in the popular movement of the Italian Humiliati.

The Austin Friar Giles of Rome (d. 1316) said that government's main objective was to educate men and women to attain heaven. For this, the people must be at peace, possess the material means of living well, and enjoy the prospect of a suitable education:

14

Kings should see that the study of letters flourishes in their kingdoms, and that many learned men and scholars are there. Where wisdom and letters flourish, surely the whole will thence draw a measure of learning . . . Indeed, if rulers do not promote education and do not wish their subjects to be learned, they are not kings but instead tyrants.[1]

Work in the world led to a gradual shift not only of values but also of clerical institutions. When the state dominated the Church, the monk's contemplative and cloistered life seemed more consequential than the active life. This conviction never wholly died. To the abbot Rupert of Deutz (d. 1135) the apostles had been monks, and the Saviour did not have them preach, baptize or perform miracles but instead exalt themselves by exemplifying virtue and humbling themselves before others, a teaching that still attracted Francis of Assisi (d. 1226). On the other hand, the new mendicants, even the Assisan's, strove to animate the Church's mission by preaching and stimulating penance at the world's crossroads. Their programme had earlier been previsioned by Peter Cantor, who likened teaching and preaching to a house. Its foundation is study and reading; disputation and discussion compose its walls; 'preaching . . . is the roof protecting the faithful from the heat and tempests of the vices'.[2]

Preaching provided instruction for the Christian republic. Bernard of Clairvaux's (d. 1153) tours to southern France, the Rhineland and elsewhere illustrate how famous preachers were sought after by the local clergy. Around the turn of the century the university replaced the cloister as the training ground for the pulpit, and Paris produced many successful preachers whose sermons were collected for the use of others. Among these were the revivalist Fulk (d. 1202), a parish priest of Neuilly and student of Peter Cantor; Robert of Curzon (d. 1218), professor at Paris and cardinal; Stephen Langton (d. 1228), professor there and later archbishop of Canterbury; and James of Vitry, who died in 1240 as cardinal and archbishop of Acre. The mendicants picked up this torch in the thirteenth century. Local chroniclers exaggeratedly claimed that a Franciscan spellbinder, Berthold of Regensburg (d. 1272), attracted crowds 100,000 strong.

Scripture and Bible history were basic sources for this ministry. An example of the latter is the *Scholastic History* of a one-time chancellor of Paris, Peter Comestor (d. *circa* 1179), recounting the bible story with legendary accretions. Scripture was given its great or ordinary gloss by commentators from Anselm of Laon (d. 1117) to Gilbert the Universal, a canon of Auxerre and later bishop of London (d. 1134). Thereafter followed commentaries or postils on specific parts of the Bible. Much was done in Paris, where the work of two

---

[1] *De regimine principum* 3 2 8 (Rome 1607) 417. The Latin *industres* is translated as *sages hommes* in the French *Li livres du gouvernment des rois* (ed. S.P. Molenaer, New York 1899) 314.
[2] *Verbum abbreviatum* 1 in *PL* CCV 25.

canons regular of St Victor, Hugh (d. 1141) and Andrew (d. 1175), was later advanced by the circle of Peter Cantor mentioned above. In the thirteenth century, leadership passed to the mendicants, who added much traditional Jewish commentary, especially that of Rashi of Troyes (Solomon, son of Isaac, d. 1105). Including postillators as radical as Peter John Olivi (d. 1298), the Franciscans produced the greatest commentator of all, Nicholas of Lyra (d. 1340). These studies prompted dissatisfaction with the sacred text itself. Always swinging wide, another Franciscan, Roger Bacon (d. 1292), attributed the imperfections of the contemporary Bible to the fact that the Paris book-makers were laymen, and married ones at that!

The pulpit led to penitence and the court of conscience. The Franciscan Alexander of Hales (d. 1245) and the Dominican Thomas Aquinas (of Aquino, d. 1274) together expounded the doctrine of the treasury of the saints, a reservoir of superabundant grace on which to draw for the forgiveness granted to the fallible. Developing the idea of purgatory, churchmen were convinced that the punishments and pardons that they assigned penetrated into death beyond life. Penitential practice was reinforced by the requirement published at the Lateran Council of 1215 that Catholics perform at least one annual confession to a priest. Manuals of casuistry appeared, starting with that of the Cistercian Alan of Lille in the later twelfth century. At about the same time, Peter Cantor issued his *On Sacraments and Advice to the Soul*, the third book of which was devoted to cases of conscience. Similar to a collection of legal opinions was the standard *Summa of Penitential Cases* written between 1220 and 1234 by the Dominican Raymond of Penyafort (d. 1275). This literature branched out to produce epitomes and specialized tracts. A brief compilation called *Rules for the Merchants of Toulouse* concerning usury was culled by a Dominican named Guy from the much larger *Confessors' Summa* of John of Freiburg (d. 1314), written in the 1290s.

The clergy needed manuals to understand their world. John of Salisbury's (d. 1189) *Policraticus* touched on all subjects regarding the relation of the faith to secular life and government, but in too elegant a way to appeal to a wide audience. More successful were the *Sentences* by Peter Lombard (d. as bishop of Paris in 1160), a textbook treating questions of theology and Church organization, a manual 'canonized' at the Lateran Council in 1215. Becoming encyclopaedic, this effort reached its apogee between 1247 and 1259 in the Dominican Vincent of Beauvais's *Great Mirror*, a work subdivided into three ample parts: one on nature, another on doctrine and a third on history.

Converting the world into a school or foyer for heaven, the clergy began to absorb the intense sense of vocation that had once marked the withdrawn religious. This inner asceticism and progress in self-discipline were explored by the Franciscan Bonaventure (John of Fidanza, d. 1274) in his *Itinerary of the Mind*. Although spiritual withdrawal still attracted, physical retirement into the cloister came to lack the appeal of active engagement in the world's life, and those fighting evil were soon called superior to the monks in their cloisters. Robert of Curzon claimed that a teacher explaining scripture deserved a higher reward than a Cistercian. The canonist Hostiensis (Henry of Susa, cardinal of Ostia, d. 1271) referred to 'just judges leading the active life without duplicity, a life which, if well conducted, is more fruitful than the contemplative'.[3]

These attitudes exemplify the paradox of Church leadership: the more the clergy led, the more they came to respect the world's professions. Some even admitted that soldiers were needed more than monks. Gregory VII complained in 1079 to Abbot Hugh of Cluny, who had received a Burgundian duke into the cloister when the papacy wanted allies against the Empire: 'you have received the duke into Cluny's quiet and thereby deprived a hundred thousand Christians of a protector'.[4] And canon lawyers were flattered to hear Boncompagno of Signa (d. before 1250) borrow from Roman law to liken them to soldiers in arms.

Perhaps the clergy could have provided all of these functions themselves, and to some extent they did, as in the military orders. Directing the world, however, was only part of their ambition. They also wanted to protect the liberty of the ecclesiastical order by gaining freedom from secular authority. Dominant though churchmen seemed after the Gregorian age, they remembered earlier subjection and, to avoid lay oppression, wished to be their own judges. Because princes and magistrates wanted those active in the world to be accountable in their courts, freedom required clerks to withdraw from secular office and professions involving them in lay affairs. Paradoxically, then, the Gregorian desire for freedom from lay power not only resulted in Rome leading Europe, but also encouraged a reforming laity and clergy to eradicate the old clerical cadres holding secular office. This effort helped create or revive the secular literate or clerical professions during the Gregorian troubles. Not a few early jurists and scribes were onetime clerks who had been married or charged with simony and, fleeing to the world, helped build lay literacy and the secular professions there.

The extent of this change should not be overstated. Lay literacy in Latin had never entirely vanished. That princes should be literate had always been urged, and there were lay notaries and lawyers in parts of Italy long before the Gregorian age. These exceptions, however, almost prove the rule. As the Premonstratensian Philip of Harvengt (d. 1182) said, the word 'clerk' meant 'churchman', and charters, even those written by secular notaries, often referred to the clergy simply as 'literate persons'.

Although the separation of the spheres of lay and clerk was long obscured by a lack of trained laymen and by persisting old state-dominated churches,

---

[3] His *Summa Aurea* cited in Kantorowicz, *The King's Two Bodies* 122n.
[4] *Registrum* 6 17 in *MGH Epp. sel.* II 351.

a start had been made and ecclesiastical legislation pointed in two directions. Starting early in the twelfth century and continuing to the fourth Lateran Council of 1215, churchmen were forbidden to serve as officers, lawyers and notaries for lay governments and persons. Church law also sought to limit clerical education for secular pursuits. By 1163 monks were prohibited from studying civil law and medicine, and in 1219 this prohibition was extended to parish rectors and other full-time officers. Lower clerical grades were left free to learn the secular professions except surgery, but clerks were not usually permitted to exercise them except in the military orders, within the Church itself or, if need be, to help the poor in emergencies.

Letters, professions and laicism

The relationship between the clergy and laity was never easy. Repeating canonists such as Stephen of Tournai (d. 1203), the civilian Alberic of Rosate (d. 1354) summed it up around 1300: 'There are two peoples, one of the clerks and the other of laymen . . . and they are two types of diverse nature, one superior and the other inferior . . . There are therefore two governors in Milan, the archbishop who rules the clerks and the temporal lord who rules the laity.'[5] The literate professions inhabited the disputed frontier between the ecclesiastical and lay nations.

The first secular professions were medicine, law and scribal services. To these were soon added the teachers of the liberal arts, such as grammarians, and of the sciences like mathematics. Related to these was a wide range of tradesfolk and artisans such as builders, druggists, surgeons or barbers and the stationers and bookcopiers who sprang up around the universities. Because many were in lower clerical orders and because middle-aged persons frequently moved into clericature, the frontiers were never clear. The history of the mason Gerhard of Rile, 'master of the fabric' of the cathedral at Cologne begun in 1248, is a case in point. In 1257 Gerhard became a canon and his wife entered a Cistercian house. By 1268 this master mason had attained the priesthood and four of his adult children had followed him into the Church.

Lawyers soon expressed lay professional self-consciousness. Roman law maintained that the Empire and its law were sacred, postulating that judges who repressed crime shared this quality. Text appended to the twelfth-century code called *Peter's Excerpts* expressed the idea: 'The sacred is partly human, like the laws, and partly divine, like the Church. Some priests are therefore divine . . . and others human, like magistrates, who are neverthe-less called priests because they administer something sacred, that is, the

---

[5] *De statutis* 2 2 17 in *TUJ* II 29a.

laws.'[6] A later jurist attributed to Alberic of Rosate the self-congratulatory fancy 'that judges who judge justly are not only to be called priests, but even angels of God, and deserve more than monks'.[7] Circumstances also obliged the Church to admit the equality of lay jurists. As early as 1252, the layman Giles Fuscararius (d. 1289) taught canon law at Bologna, and not a few judges sitting in the papal court and those of the bishops were laymen. And others trod on the lawyers' heels. If lawyers could be called priests, so also could soldiers, a notion found in Raymond Llull's *Order of Chivalry*, the most popular manual of knighthood and nobility of the age.

The lay spirit went beyond professionalism and added a sense of vocation taken from the cloistered religious. The spread of the monastic ethos to the lay world, at first in the Gregorian age and then again during the mendicant movements of the thirteenth century, will be treated in later chapters. Here it may be noted that this combination of the priesthood of the active life with the monastic contemplative life had begun to give laymen a growing sense of equality with the clergy. Besides, however much they led, clerks often confessed that, in God's eyes, all men and women were equal. Gerhoh of Reichersberg (d. 1169) opined that, rich or poor, noble or servile, merchant or farmer, everyone who has renounced the devil, 'even if he never becomes a clerk or a monk, can be shown to have renounced the world . . . Every man has his place and every profession without exception has a rule in the Catholic faith and apostolic doctrine suitable to its quality, under which, by fighting well, a man can attain the crown.'[8] Laymen belong to orders, said James of Vitry, just as do monks:

> We do not judge only those who renounce the world and enter an order to be monks, but instead . . . all faithful Christians who serve the Lord under evangelical rules and live ordained under the one highest abbot [Jesus] . . . There is an order of the married, of the widowed and of virgins. Soldiers, merchants, farmers, artisans and all the other multiform types of men have rules peculiar to each.[9]

Spiritual equality would have meant little without literacy, especially in Latin. The principal conduits of lay Latin literacy were the professions of medicine, law and the public scribes. Just as the academics had borrowed their black robes from the clergy, so had they taken their language of learning and law. Spread among jurists, notaries and grammarians, a simplified Latin emerged as a juristic and literary vehicle, finding a place between high Latinity and the rising vernaculars beneath. What this meant is easily seen.

---

[6] *Petri Exceptionum appendices* 1 95 in Herman Fitting, *Juristische Schriften des früheren Mittelalters* (Halle, 1876) 164.

[7] Kantorowicz, *The King's Two Bodies*, 122n.

[8] *Liber de aedificio dei* 43 in PL CXCIV 1302d.

[9] *Historia occidentalis* 34 (ed. J.F. Hinnebusch, Fribourg, 1972) 165–66.

Around Toulouse in Languedoc, for example, scribal Latin improved, driving the vernacular out of the documents as the professional notariate penetrated villages and small towns in the decades after 1200. In the same region, furthermore, ordinary businessmen habitually collected their own files of Latin documents and could surely read them. In Italy, Boncompagno remarked that 'merchants do not need elegant diction because almost all correspond with each other either in their vulgar tongues or corrupt Latin'.[10]

The proponents of this Latin were aware of its character. Introducing his history of the March of Treviso, the grammarian Rolandino of Padua explained why he chose Latin instead of the vernacular: 'I write prose because I can say what I want more clearly in it than in verse . . . [and many] prefer to discover in Latin the sufferings and labours of modern men than to hear of the deeds of the noble ancients in the vulgar.'[11] The relationship of this Latin to the classical language is expressed by Boncompagno of Signa, who detested the authority of the ancients, especially what he thought was Cicero's needlessly obscure style: 'In [Tully's] rhetorical works, the construction is inept and the position of words intricate, whereby he most clearly contradicted his own instructions, because he there stated that the narrative should be brief and lucid.'[12] Wildly off base, this notary opined that Ciceronian Latin would never regain its place because students no longer studied it. Who, he asked, obeys the professors of rhetoric with their artificial Latin composition? Only an idiot would address a fellow named Pope as 'Mr Servant of God's Servants'.

The currency of this vulgar Latin was wide because most literature between 1200 and 1300 was written in it. Not only was it used by jurists and notaries, but it was also the language of the clergy and their schools. As the examinations recorded in Odo Rigaud's register of visitations in his archdiocese of Rouen from 1248 to 1269 show, rural clerks were not always very literate, and vulgar Latin was easier to learn than classical discourse. Partly because of its flexibility, this Latin was also eminently suitable for technical discourse in philosophy and theology, and it therefore caught on in the schools, in spite of John of Salisbury's lamentation about the decline of standards.

An assessment of taxes in the upper and lower towns of Carcassonne for the Flemish war in 1304 affords a glimpse of a modest city's professional services. Estimated on the basis of four persons per taxable hearth, the population was around 9,500 souls. Including nine parish rectors, some 260 clerks lived there. This figure incorporates priests, monks, friars, the canons etc. of the cathedral chapter and lesser folk, such as hospital workers and inmates,

---

[10] *Boncompagni Boncompagnus* in *BuF* I 173.
[11] *Cronica in factis et circa facta marchie Trivixiane (AA 1200–62)* in *RIS* (ed. 1905) VIII i 7–8.
[12] *Rhetorica novissima* Prologue in *BIMA* II 252.

schoolteachers and domestics. The legal professions were represented by 43 public notaries (solicitors) and 15 advocates (barristers), while 12 Lombards and 30 Jews offered economic services. Lastly, 43 nobles and 40 other military inhabited or were stationed in this administrative capital.

Because business required correspondence, Lombard merchants were probably literate in the Latin in which their contracts were written. Most Jews were literate in the vernacular and Hebrew, but few in Latin. That notaries and advocates were literate in Latin goes without saying, but there were differing degrees of competence. Representing clients before the bar, lawyers in the Midi were all university trained; notaries, on the other hand, had probably been taught letters in parish or monastic schools and then apprenticed to others in the profession. In a university town like Bologna, notaries usually also went through the faculty of arts.

Nine medical doctors were also counted in Carcassonne. There, because of the town's proximity to the medical faculty at Montpellier, most medical doctors were physicians (*physici*), those who had studied Aristotle's physics at a university. These undoubtedly knew Latin. Farther north, it is likely that most doctors were medicos (*medici*), men trained by practitioners, just about the same as surgeons who had little Latin. The matter was almost one of geographical distribution. Although, as Bonvesino of Riva records for Milan, physicians were common enough in Italy's urbanized areas, there were few in the north, even in the Low Countries, where they were largely to be found among the clergy who did not practise for laymen. Along with the legal and medical elites at Carcassonne went the clergy, especially those who had taken higher orders, many of whom had seen the inside of a university and were titled 'master'. Lastly, urban patricians often had competence in vulgar Latin letters.

Most gentlemen were literate only in the vernacular. This also goes for certain groups in the Church, such as the female religious and even secular canons, those whose birth was so elevated that they, like the canons of St Mark's of Venice, were damned if they would learn Latin. This does not mean they were uncultivated. The poetry of the age – vernacular literature was at first primarily poetic – treated almost every theme of interest to an alert mind. Gentlemen of means usually had clergy and scribes in their households to whom they dictated their letters and who read aloud at dinner or other times. An extravagant example is Baldwin, in 1169 count of Guines and lord of Ardres, towns near Boulogne in north France. The count's secretary was a layman who collected romances and heroic songs. He also translated parts of scripture, sermons, a commentary on the mystical sense of the *Song of Songs*, Alfred's life of St Anthony, 'a great part of the physical art', Solinus's *On the Nature of Things* and selections from Augustine, Denis the Areopagite and Thales of Miletus (!) for his patron's edification. Dinner, when reading often took place, must have been a heavy affair up there in Guines.

Vernacular letters grew during the thirteenth century. Vegetius's late Roman *On War*, a basic text for soldiers, was widely circulated in the original Latin, but parts were paraphrased and incorporated in Spain's vernacular 'mirror' of government called the *Book of the Laws* (*Siete Partidas*) of 1260. Vegetius's text was translated into French by John of Meung, whose other translations also testify to the audience for vernacular works: Boethius's *Consolation of Philosophy*, the *Calamities* and letters of Abelard and Heloise, Ailred of Rievaulx's *Spiritual Friendship* written about 1160, and Gerald of Wales's *Topography of Ireland* of about 1188.

'An illiterate king is a crowned ass.' This tag spread to nobles and patricians during the time studied in this book. There was schoolteachers' special pleading here: could one be a soldier and also an amateur of letters? Writing the history of the counts of Anjou, the canon Breton of Amboise defended Fulk the Good, who had celebrated mass in clerical garb on the feast of St Martin of Tours, by saying that: 'although expertly instructed in letters and the grammatical art as well as in Aristotelian and Ciceronian reasoning, this intelligent man was considered the best among the more vigorous knights'.[13] Gerald of Wales (d. 1220) later claimed that the more a man knew the liberal arts the better he was as a soldier, a point proved by adducing Greece under the Macedonians, Rome under the Caesars and Frankland under the Carolingians! By the time John of Meung wrote his *Romance of the Rose*, the idea that a gentleman should be as lettered as he was expert in arms was a commonplace. The wide circulation of Dante's poetic and vernacular works reminds one of Italy's many literate patricians and gentlefolk. As significant was the penetration into legal documentation of the vernacular. Generalized everywhere by about 1300, vernacular documents testify to the literacy of the business classes and even of some artisans. In Tuscany, Brunetto Latini wrote a vernacular rhetoric in Ciceronian style for the use of town notaries and chancellors. In addition, many of those who wrote for laymen were clergy. A number of troubadours, for example, were clerical or ended their lives in clerical garb or as oblates.

Most layfolk, nevertheless, were illiterate. Dated no later than 1324, a manual for parish priests shows a way to reach them: 'the literate can have knowledge of God from Scripture, but ignorant ones must be instructed by books designed for laymen, that is, by pictures'.[14] If many could not read, they could be read or sung to, and hence evidence of the popularity of literary themes is seen everywhere. A Bolognese statute of 1288 ordered singers of French songs not to perform in public places when preaching was underway. Writing on business morality, a Dominican named Guy wagged his

---

[13] *Chronique des comtes d'Anjou et des seigneurs d'Amboise* (ed. Louis Halphen and René Poupardin, Paris, 1913) 40.

[14] *Speculum humanae salvationis*, Prologue (ed. J. Lutz and P. Perdrizet, Leipzig, 1907) 2.

finger at Toulouse's shopkeepers and artisans: 'I advise each of you to read or at least to listen to [my *Rule for Merchants*] in place of the useless fables and romances customarily read in workshops and stores.'[15]

The audience of lay letters was therefore far larger than the number of the literate, and reached far below gentlemen and patricians. Modern imagination does a disservice to medieval popular culture by using terms such as 'courtly love'. It is true that the stories are usually aristocratic in tone, but who would think of public notaries or medical technicians as ideal lovers? Soldiers, especially gentlemen, were better: by risking their lives in war, they showed ability to risk love with all its loyalty and difficult tests. The beloved was also a lady. Never mentioned in the literature, her risk was childbirth, but neither she nor her lover is ever seen changing the children's nappies.

Although lovers in poetry (save a few) were both handsome and rich, there was no necessary class affiliation among those who loved them. Nor can one assign to different classes the genres of love literature, from the courtly fancies of Arthurian romance to the earthiness of the *fabliaux*. The lives of the troubadours compiled in the fourteenth century show that not a few of the most courtly poets were burghers, merchants and even artisans. At Toulouse, the two greatest poets were Peter Vidal (*fl.* 1180–1206), the son of a furrier, and the rougher William Figueras (*fl.* 1215–45), a barfly and son of a tailor. Nobles, moreover, both enjoyed and wrote earthy verse. The early troubadour William IX, duke of Aquitaine (d. 1127), composed some of the raunchiest stuff on record. The chronicler William of Malmesbury (d. *circa* 1143) reported with mock horror that the duke had a mistress 'whom he so loved that he had the girl's picture painted on his shield, often saying that he wished to bear her in battle as she bore him in bed'.[16]

The effects of the invasion of what had once been their near monopoly sometimes upset the clergy. Because their best were better trained than layfolk, their doubts about the competence of laymen in philosophy and theology were partly justified. Their reaction was nevertheless greater than the cause justified, showing a desire to put the genie back in the bottle. Besides, intellectuals have biases. Churchmen, for example, shared a prejudice against lawyers. Giles of Rome observed:

> all jurists are political idiots. For, just as laymen and plebeians are called dialectical ignoramuses by the Philosopher ... because they do not argue with artifice and dialectical skill, so lawyers, because they speak of politics narratively and without reason, may be called political ignoramuses. It is obvious how much more highly those who know the political and moral sciences are to be regarded than those who merely know law.[17]

---

[15] Cited and discussed in my *Society and Government at Toulouse in the Age of the Cathars* 113–14.
[16] Bezzola, *Les origines et la formation de la littérature courtoise en occident* II, ii, 272.
[17] *De regimine principum* 2 2 8 (Rome, 1607) 309.

In almost the same words, this opinion was repeated by the Franciscan Roger Bacon. Although inviting wonder about how people often make their knowledge into the universe's only yardstick, these conflicts between lay and clerical intellectuals are good evidence of the power of secular intellectualism at this time.

In fine, before and in the period with which this volume deals, churchmen led western Europe. Turning towards the world that they believed they ruled, they tried to discover what composed it and to create agencies to make it better. In so doing, they helped build lay literacy and the lay spirit, both of which were to reduce clerical power and authority later on. In the meantime, however, the two peoples, clerical and lay, were relatively harmoniously balanced. The scales were to tip decisively to secular authority only later, during what Protestants call 'the Reformation' and the rise of Europe's secular nations.

Chapter 3

Cultural frontiers:
France, Italy and Europe

France

France and Italy's leadership of Latin Europe around 1200 was recent. Until the latter eleventh century, the Germans and their Empire seemed preponderant, and the memory of this circumstance influenced the perceptions of those living later. Frederick I Barbarossa, the Hohenstaufen emperor (d. 1190), asserted that Europe's other kings were kinglets in comparison with him. Only in 1268, with the extinction of the Hohenstaufen imperial line, did such an opinion seem absurd because, by that time, contemporaries were finally aware of the power of France and Italy. The rapid expansion of the Capetian monarchy, the invasion of much of Europe by papal power and its affiliated Lombard merchant bankers and the defeat of the Hohenstaufen had driven the lesson home. Still, the foundations of French and Italian success had been laid much earlier. What drove it was the early revival of Mediterranean commerce, the victory of the papacy over the Empire, the rise of Italian commercial and industrial power and the emigration of French people and culture from about 1050 to 1150; in short, during the Gregorian age. Curiously, the grandeur of the French had no sooner been realized than it began to fade. In Florence around 1300, the Dominican Remigio de'Girolami asserted without fear of contradiction that all Europe's other monarchs were mere kinglets when compared to France's, whose prince was paradigmatically the King, just as Aristotle was the Philosopher and Mary the Virgin. Barely half a century after he died in 1319, even a loyal Frenchman would have smiled sadly on hearing such a remark.

For a time, however, French greatness was assured. Along the northern frontier with the Empire, French speech entered maritime Flanders at the expense of Flemish, French culture penetrated into Luxembourg, and Capetian political influence was dominant from the royal province of Flanders to the Lorraines by 1300. To the east, the absorption of the county of Champagne into the royal domain in 1284 bounded a province whose princes had often looked towards the Empire. By 1245 the old imperial territory of Provence had fallen to the house of Anjou, a Capetian cadet line. The occupation of

Lyons by France in 1312 completed the possession of the Saône valley, and French influence penetrated the Burgundies and Lorraines and into the Rhineland and Swabia. Pope John XXII (d. 1334) believed that King Philip IV the Fair (d. 1314) of France had a good chance of being elected emperor. There were limits, however: the loyalty of Flanders was doubtful, Walloon regions like the Namurois and the Liègeois were not part of the kingdom, and other French-speaking areas such as Savoy and parts of the Lorraines and Burgundies lay beyond Capetian control.

The history of the Iberian frontier is similar. From Carolingian times Catalonia was part of France and, until the 1220s, some public scribes there dated their documents by French regnal years. In the decentralized Midi, a loose confederation under the house of St Gilles-Toulouse had reached from western Provence on the Rhone river to Agen on the Garonne, and began to break up in the late twelfth century. It looked as if the Catalans and Aragonese (who joined under one dynasty in 1162) would take over from Provence through maritime Languedoc to the Pyrenean counties, and that the rest would fall to the Poitevin Aquitanians, a group joined to the Plantagenet (or Angevin) Atlantic French and English monarchy in the reign of Henry II (d. 1189).[1]

The Plantagenets lost most of their French domains, including Poitou, during the reign of Philip II Augustus (d. 1223), and were thereafter powerless. Beginning with the Albigensian Crusade launched in 1209, northern French Crusaders and eventually the Capetians themselves intervened in Languedoc. Already failing in Provence, the Catalan–Aragonese hold there was erased by the crusader Simon of Montfort (d. 1218), who killed King Peter II of Aragon on the battlefield of Muret in 1213. Although Languedoc and the mountain counties were restive throughout the fourteenth century and Montpellier was not lost to Catalonia–Aragon until 1349, by 1300 most of the Midi had been absorbed by the Capetians. In the meantime, however, a treaty signed at Corbeil in 1258 had split this once unified linguistic and cultural area. The Catalans renounced claims to Provence, Languedoc and the counties on the northern slopes of the Pyrenees, while France surrendered its ancient claim to Catalonia. The only breach of the Pyrenean frontier in favour of France came about as a result of the union of Navarre with Champagne in 1235, because the Capetian collected this kingdom in 1284 along with the northern inheritance of the counts of Champagne.

Rivalled only by the Italians, the French were Europe's greatest crusaders, a leadership that implied excellence in warfare. Certainly, others also exemplified martial vigour. Although the imperialist Alexander of Roes granted the French pre-eminence in learning, he reserved for the Germans the capacity

---

[1] Plantagenet is here used for the English Angevines, in order to avoid confusion with the cadet line of the Capetians in Anjou, active from Provence to Italy and Hungary.

to conquer others. Famed for naval warfare, the Italians were also not bad on land and, during the late twelfth century, popularized the crossbow, whose penetrating bolts prompted the introduction of horse and plate armour. By about 1300, indeed, warfare's future course could be dimly discerned in the successful combination of bowmen and men-at-arms by the English in their Scottish wars and in a seemingly fortuitous defeat of Habsburg chivalry by Swiss footmen in 1295.

For the time being, however, chivalry ruled the battlefield, and French chivalry, especially that of northern France, was Europe's best. William of Newburgh reports that Richard Coeur de Lion believed that French knights were 'sharper' than the English because of exercise in frequent tournaments. 'English knights', the king said, 'should learn the art and use of war [in tournaments] so that the Gauls should not insult them, as being rude and less expert.'[2] The finest soldiers of the age, the Templars and Hospitallers, were largely recruited in France, and northern France produced the two most famous soldiers of the age, Richard Coeur de Lion (d. 1199) and Simon of Montfort (d. 1218). Exceptions apart, the military orders in Spain and Germany followed the rule of the Temple, itself inspired by the Cistercians; and the Teutonic Order (founded 1190; military in 1198) derived its military rule from the Temple and that for its hospitals from the Hospitallers.

Along with soldiers went emigrants. The great age of French emigration precedes the time treated in this book and lies between 1050 and 1150. Soldiers and settlers flooded from Poitou, Aquitaine, Languedoc and the Burgundies into Spain. Many Spanish towns had French quarters in the twelfth century. In 1118 the king granted Toledo's citizens their customs, describing them as Castilians, Mozarabs and French. In successive waves, Cluniac monks and then Cistercians also penetrated everywhere so that many southern French monasteries had affiliates south of the Pyrenees. The first major victory over Spain's Arabs and Berbers won by Spanish arms without direct French participation was Las Navas de Tolosa in 1212.

Much the same was true on the German frontier: the earlier age witnessed the deeper penetration, although some migration naturally continued. In 1253–55, for example, at the Mongol capital at Quaraqorum in central Asia, the Franciscan missionary William of Ruysbroek met three French-speaking persons swept up in the Mongol raid on Hungary of 1242, a Lorrainer, a Parisian and a Londoner. French settlement in Hungary's nascent towns, however, had reached its peak around 1100. German towns had also admitted these immigrants, especially French Jews. The school of Rashi of Troyes, the celebrated Talmudist and biblical commentator, influenced the rabbis of Mainz, Worms and Speier, and French Jews settled in the Rhineland, the upper Danube valley and also eastern Saxony. Even in the thirteenth century,

---

[2] Gauthier, *La chevalerie*, 675.

French was still occasionally spoken by German Jews, leaving traces in Jewish speech from Cologne to Regensburg.

England was part of the German nation, but the conquest of 1066 made it a province of French culture. Led by Normans who clung to a Nordic identity setting them apart from the other French, the invasion drew volunteers from all the north-east, from Brittany to the Liègeois. After the conquest, the Anglo-French indifferently referred to themselves as 'Normans' or 'Frenchmen'. Nor did French pressure cease at that date or even at the accession in 1154 of the Plantagenets from Anjou. Although declining, settlement continued into the thirteenth century. The last, unsuccessful French invasion was that of Philip Augustus's son in 1215 at the end of John's turbulent reign, but a lighter French penetration persisted, as shown by the importation of officers from as far away as Provence and Savoy into royal service under Henry III (d. 1272). The French were sure that they had conquered the English. Abbot Suger of St Denis (d. 1151) reasoned in his life of Louis the Fat that William Rufus of England failed in his attempt to invade France because 'it is not right or natural for Frenchmen to be subject to Englishmen, but only for Englishmen to be subject to Frenchmen'.[3] A little over half a century after 1274, when this sentiment was incorporated into the vernacular *Great Chronicles of France*, it appeared absurd as the English began the invasions of the Hundred Years War.

Populous Italy received fewer French. The earlier movements of the Burgundians and Savoyards were followed by that of a modest number of Normans and other French, who helped build the Norman kingdom of Sicily and the mainland principalities around Naples in southern Italy from about 1060 to 1091. The only other penetration of importance was that of the Angevins in the thirteenth century, a subject treated later. Although their language, manners and literature were eagerly adopted in Italy, French success was greatest further to the east. In the Near Eastern Crusader states, the French nearly monopolized the lordly ranks and rivalled the Italians in urban settlement, especially in the Holy Land, Cyprus and parts of mainland Greece. Everyone knew of their role there. When the Latins were threatened by a Greek and Bulgar attack in 1224, Pope Honorius III (d. 1227) asked aid from France for Robert of Courtney, emperor of Constantinople. God, he said, 'has given into the hands of the Gauls the empire of Romania . . . and there a New France, as it were, has recently been created'.[4]

French was the language of the Crusaders and, with its long domestication in the Near East, soon became a *lingua franca* for many in an arc from Greece to Egypt. Much later on, a Cypriot told the truth when he wrote that 'after

---

[3] *Vita Ludovici grossi regis*, Prologue (ed. Henri Waquet, Paris, 1864) 10–12.
[4] *Odorico Rinaldi Annales ecclesiastici ab anno MCXCVIII ubi desinit Cardinalis Baronius auctore Odorico Raynaldo* (ed. J.D. Mansi, Lucca, 1747) I 536a–b.

the Lusignans conquered the island, we began to speak French and Greek became barbaric'.[5] An example of the advance of French at the expense of a Germanic tongue is to be seen in England. Although Latin also played a role, French suppressed a lively Germanic administrative and literary dialect there until well into the thirteenth century. Once it had gained full recognition beside Latin in the ever-conservative language of law, French held its place in England for ages. Praised by Fortescue in the fifteenth century, by Coke in the seventeenth, its recent demise was still mourned by Blackstone in 1758.

Latin apart, French was also Europe's premier literary language. Although in debt to earlier literature, Arabic, both Muslim and Jewish, early German and Celtic, as in the *Matter of Brittany*, and to classical letters, the French undoubtedly led the Latin world in this period. Few poets equalled Christian of Troyes, Bertrand of Born (d. 1208/10), Bernard of Ventadour (*fl.* 1180s), William of Lorris (d. *circa* 1240) and John of Meung. The Burgundian Humbert of Romans (d. 1277) remarked that Dominicans given to 'celestial' speech had trouble speaking about mundane things, 'just as Frenchmen . . . cannot easily replace their speech with another because of the nobility of both their language and fatherland'.[6] No matter what their origins, authors who sought wide audiences wrote in French. In his *Treasure* of 1260–66, Brunetto Latini remarks: 'were anyone to ask, since I am Italian, why this book is written in Romance, in the French tongue, I reply that it is for two reasons, one, that I am in France, and the other, that this language is the most delectable and widespread of all tongues'.[7]

Not that vernacular literature other than French did not exist. Both Spain and Germany boasted native tongues, which, indeed, were widely used by rural and urban scribes rather earlier than was the case in Italy or France. In both regions also, although about 50 years behind France, poets such as Wolfram of Eschenbach (d. *circa* 1225), Walter von der Vogelweide (d. 1240) and Alphonse the Wise of Castile (d. 1284) wrote in the vernacular and, however much they owed to French authors, were assuredly their equals. In Italy, easy Latin helped retard the development of Italian, and French, both Provençal and northern, quickly became the language of courts and urban aristocracies. Still, a popular vernacular poetry persisted to burst out in famed verse with the Tuscans Guido Cavalcanti (d. 1300/01), Cino of Pistoia (d. 1336) and Dante. England's literature was still partly suppressed by French in the period treated here, but there were limits to English Gallicism. Philip of Rémi, lord of Beaumanoir (d. 1296), poked fun at the insular speech of his Anglo-French employers in his youth. As early as the 1260s, middle English

---

[5] The fifteenth-century Leontios Mahkairas, cited in Grousset, *L'empire du Levant*, 379.
[6] *De eruditione praedicatorum* 7 39 in ed. J.J. Berthier, *Opera de vita regulari* (Rome, 1888) II 465.
[7] *Li livres dou tresor* I 129 (ed. Carmody) 126.

romances appeared, and the author of *Of Arthour and Merlin* remarked that he knew many nobles who spoke no French.

Music was closely related to poetry, much of which was sung. Although little secular music has been disinterred, except for a few tunes, ecclesiastical music is better known. In that area, the French led in introducing polyphony into plainsong. Leadership in this quasi-secularizing of Church music was seen at St Martial in Limoges until about 1150 and thereafter at Nôtre Dame of Paris in the latter twelfth century, with Leoninus (*fl.* 1160–70) and Perotinus (*fl.* 1190–1200). By the mid-thirteenth century, the Rhineland and France's eastern counties were forging ahead and English polyphony was seen *circa* 1275.

France was also the home of the arts of sensibility: manners, style and elegance of dress. Frenchmen lived well in the relatively peaceful thirteenth century. Latini complained that Italians, warring among themselves, built crabbed country houses enclosed by walls and towers, but the French 'build grand and ample houses with large decorated rooms to have joy and delight without war and disturbance', homes surrounded by lawns and fruit trees.[8] No wonder that John of Salisbury called France 'the most gentle and civil of all nations'.[9] Envy combined with anger to caricature French arrogance. At the time of the conflict over Maimonidean ideas, a rabbinical correspondent warned against the conservative French rabbis. 'Watch out for the French,' he said, 'because they think their best chance of knowing God is when they eat beef marinated in a wine and garlic sauce . . . Most of them anyway have two women and their thoughts are incessantly on intercourse.'[10]

There was more to it than comfort and chic. French styles and engineering dominated architecture, both military and civil. Among the most inventive monuments of castramentation were the Hospitallers' Krak des Chevaliers in Syria, completed around 1205, and Richard Coeur de Lion's Gaillard des Andeleys in Normandy. Better known is the invention of Gothic, probably in the Ile de France, a style and engineering technique that spread throughout northern France and the Plantagenet domains on either side of the Channel during the late twelfth century. Replacing or refurbishing older monuments, Gothic began to penetrate Languedoc and Italy around 1220 and Germany by 1263. If Peter of Montreuil, the probable designer of the Ste Chapelle, busied himself largely around Paris, his relative Eudes accompanied his patron Louis IX to Cyprus and there designed several churches. Villard of Honnecourt, author of an architectural sketchbook, was employed from Hainault to Hungary. In 1287 Stephen of Bonneuil left Paris for Sweden

---

[8] Ibid. I, 129 (ed. Carmody) 126.

[9] Letter 225 in *PL* CXCIX 253.

[10] *Güdemann Geschichte des Erziehungswesens . . . der Juden* I 73. The letter was attributed to Maimonides!

with a team of builders. John des Champs brought Gothic to Toulouse and Narbonne and, in 1266, Peter of Agincourt accompanied Charles of Anjou to southern Italy, where, after introducing the French style, he was knighted.

Love of learning was often described as a French characteristic. A German commonplace gave the university to the French, assigning the Empire to its own people and the Church to the Italians. Paris was the great centre of scholastic study. Few spoke about French legal studies, because what the French exported in this sphere was essentially their highly developed seigniorial institutions, sometimes called feudal. These influenced England, penetrated western Germany, were imported into southern Italy under its twelfth-century Norman kings and became predominant in the Latin colonies along the coasts of the eastern Mediterranean and Aegean Seas. There a notable monument was the *Assizes of Jerusalem and Cyprus*, a collection of laws and tracts on government, one of whose authors was Philip of Novara, an active memoirist, soldier and statesman of 'overseas France'.

Italy

Italy did not lag behind France: her fleets swept the Mediterranean and her sons and daughters joined the French settling along that sea's eastern shores. When Constantinople fell in the Fourth Crusade of 1204 and the Latin Empire was established in Greece and the Aegean, a quarter of the territory was given to Baldwin of Flanders, the French emperor, and the rest was divided equally between the principal Crusaders and the Venetians who had provided the fleet. This effectively gave the latter the upper hand in Bosporan and Greek commerce. The Piedmontese house of Monferrato, moreover, was granted the major fief of the new Latin emperor, the kingdom of Thessalonica. More lasting was the settlement of Italians along the coasts of the Mediterranean and Black Seas, where they enjoyed privileges of extra-territoriality and self-government.

Italian armies never gained overseas victories comparable to those of the French, however, largely because they were employed at home to defeat the traditional power of the Empire in the peninsula. Although imperial suzerainty never wholly disappeared there, it gradually became an idea significant in diplomacy and political thought, as in Dante's *On Monarchy*, but of modest significance in the practical politics of Italy's principalities and republics. As the jurists, including the French Peter Dubois (d. 1312), recognized, these little states admitted 'no superiors in the world'. Their victory over transalpine power was won for Lombardy with the defeat of Frederick I Barbarossa at Legnano and the subsequent Peace of Constance in 1183. The north Italian maritime cities profited from the struggle over the succession between the Guelfs and the Hohenstaufen after the death of Henry VI in 1197 to weaken southern Italy, the new and powerful imperial ally. Although

German intervention continued, the great wars of the age of Frederick II were mainly those of monarchic southern Italy against the Guelf republics of north and central Italy, who, with French aid, won a crushing victory.

Although Italy might have done better unified under the Apulian or Sicilian Hohenstaufen, contemporary Italians felt no sense of failure. Their freedom was what impressed foreigners, and hence James of Vitry described them as:

> Circumspect in council, diligent and zealous in managing their governments, prescient and tenacious in regard to future affairs, refusing to be subject to others, defending before all else their liberty, issuing their own laws and customs under one common captain whom they elect and observing them faithfully.[11]

Moreover, if Italy's maritime enterprise ruled the eastern Mediterranean by the end of the twelfth century, the next century saw it rise in the western part of that sea and penetrate into the Atlantic as far north as Bruges in the period between 1271 and 1317. As later chapters will show, the penetration of Italian merchant bankers and moneylenders north and west of the Alps also marked the economy of the thirteenth century.

Gaining both liberty and profit, Italy's republics allied with the papacy against the emperors. By 1200, during the pontificate of Innocent III, the Roman Court became the diplomatic capital of the Latin West, and by 1300 western princes were well advised to retain ambassadors there. Many of these representatives were also officers of the Italian merchant-banking houses, especially Florentines. Playing on the classical division of Europe into four great nations, the French, Germans, Italians and Spaniards, Boniface VIII once looked around his court and observed that the Florentines constituted a 'fifth nation'. Besides, the papacy was itself Italian. From the death of the Englishman Adrian IV in 1159 until the accession of Urban IV in 1261, the popes were all Italians and so were most of the curial personnel. Two of the four larger mendicant orders of the thirteenth century were Italian in origin, including the Franciscan, the largest of all. Again, if the French seemed to contemporaries to exemplify intellectual life with their university of Paris, Italian mendicants invaded that institution's faculty of theology. The first Dominican to teach there was Roland of Cremona (d. 1250), and the names of John of Fidanza (Bonaventure) and Thomas of Aquino speak for themselves.

Although rivalled by the graduates of Montpellier and, in Mediterranean regions, by the Jews, Italians were also pre-eminent in medicine. If France had philosophy, Italy had law. Schooling in Roman law had been revived in Bologna and other centres not long before 1100, but there was more to it than that. 'Modernizing' Roman law, the professors created the most influential secular common law of the age. As indicative of Italian leadership

---

[11] *Historia orientalis* 67 (Douai, 1596) 124.

were those who taught canon law, Latin Europe's other great common law. Mediterranean in origin, this law was most studied in north Europe before 1100, but by 1150 this had changed: the great canonists now learned their business in Italy. The earlier collections of law issued by the bishops Burchard of Worms (*circa* 1015) and Ivo of Chartres (*circa* 1115) were replaced by the standard textbook, that of the Italian monk Gratian, of which a first version was prepared between 1139 and 1150. A lesser but still significant legal tradition was Lombard law. Significant for fiefs and homage and systematized by professors trained in Roman law, this became a normative code by 1300, being accepted directly within the Empire and indirectly elsewhere. Lastly, these learned studies rested on a foundation of practical legislative and judicial experience. The statutes and codes of Italy's urban republics constitute the largest body of constitutional materials to be found anywhere in western Europe in the thirteenth and fourteenth centuries. Although moderns have lamented Italy's much divided state, her small republics and monarchies were already models for Europe's later states. The theologian William of Auvergne (d. 1249 as bishop of Paris) noted with astonishment that her republics' heralds were divided into grades for diplomatic purposes, *ambassadores* in livery for significant matters and *legati* or *nuncii* for lesser ones.

Although still under transalpine and French influence, Italy's arts were beginning to evolve independently. What fired her artists were, first, reaction against the Germans who dominated the peninsula, and then, after a honeymoon in the first half of the thirteenth century, a backlash against the invading French. Italians sought inspiration that did not come from beyond the Alps. For a time Byzantine art sufficed, but, in the long run, the most fruitful source was classical antiquity. Already discerned in the 1100s, the renewal of classicism is seen in the spacious independence of the buildings in the cathedral complex of Pisa, for example, as well as in specific works, such as the reliefs in the cathedral and baptistery of Parma executed by Benedict Antelami in 1198. Ancient models reappeared: the equestrian relief of Oldrado of Tresseno, *podestà* in 1233, that graced the Palazzo delle Ragione in Milan. In the baptistery pulpit of Pisa, completed in 1260, the Apulian architect and sculptor Nicolas Pisano employed classical models for the figures decorating a Gothic monument. Giotto of Bondone, later city architect for the republic of Florence, was a well-known painter and sculptor by 1300.

However, Italians did not come by their classicism without borrowing. An example is the history of Latin style. In the twelfth century, the best Latin was usually written north of the Alps, as John of Salisbury attests. Shown by the *dictatores* of Orléans, an elegant if sometimes affected Latinity marked composition there until well into the thirteenth century. Influenced by the practical needs of the legal profession and the notariate, Italians generally favoured simpler styles and found their counterparts north of the Alps only among the academic theologians and scholastics whose lack of style

33

had so annoyed John of Salisbury. An illustration of this practical spirit is Boncompagno of Signa's hostility to Ciceronian Latin. In the long run, as remarked above, his suit against classicism was lost. The growing use of the vernacular for legal documents irreparably weakened the base of popular Latin culture. Almost as damaging was the influence of transalpine Latinity, so useful for the pomp of prelates and princes. Lawyers did not appreciate this new development and never quite gave in to it. The Bolognese professor Odofredo (d. 1265) referred scathingly to those who wish to 'speak obscurely and in a pompous style as do the most exalted doctors and also Peter of Vinea', chancellor of the emperor Frederick II.[12] Still, the self-conscious style of many of Italy's rhetoricians and intellectuals in the late thirteenth century shows that they were about to make classicism their own. The Latin elegance of Petrarch (d. 1374) and Boccaccio (d. 1375) had had a long gestation, it seems, and one of its parents was not Italian.

Europe

To sum up, France and Italy led Europe during the twelfth and thirteenth centuries. Their pre-eminence seems odd when their internal constitutions are examined. During this time when French law spread far beyond her frontiers, France herself boasted no monarchy or state comparable to that of England, Norman southern Italy or even the declining Empire. To illustrate the machinery of French government, or lack of it, a few wagons containing all the archives and treasury of the Capetian monarch were captured on the battlefield of Fréteval by Richard Coeur de Lion in 1194. The typical Italian state that produced Europe's common (Roman) law and published its most elaborate statutes was an urban republic, tiny when compared to the states of Spain and England and to Germany's provinces, not to speak of the Empire.

Size was not, however, the principal criterion. Having implanted Latin civilization in north and east Europe, the great states and quasi-national kingdoms that ruled Europe from the days of the Carolingians weakened in the eleventh and twelfth centuries. The age of empires was over. In spite of the Hohenstaufen revival, the Empire was irreparably shaken by the alliance of the Roman Church with German local princes and Italian towns in the time of Gregorian enthusiasm. Another example is to be seen in Iberia. Conquering the Moors with French aid, but wishing to be free of their allies, Castile's princes tried to advance a Spanish idea of empire. In 1139 Alfonso VII was styled emperor, ruling in New Castile, Leon, Aragon, Navarre, Castile, Galicia (Portugal), Catalonia and Provence; in 1159, the northern *Annals of Cambrai*

---

[12] Wieruszowski, *Vom Imperium zum nationalen Königtum* 67n.

spoke of three empires: the Byzantine, the German and that of Galicia (St James of Compostella). Defeated by geography and by papal and French encouragement of separatism in Portugal, Catalonia-Aragon and elsewhere, this reminiscence of Spanish unity soon faded, however. What remained was Spain's insistence on its independence and equality with France and the Empire. Writing in 1210–12, Vincent Hispanus, chancellor of Portugal, reversed Charlemagne's victory recorded in France's *Song of Roland* by averring that when 'Charles with the French wished to enter Spain, the Spaniards met them at Spain's gates, conquered them in battle and killed the twelve peers . . . Spanish prowess alone obtained the empire'.[13]

The princes of Europe's peripheral powers, from the Kiraly (king, from Charles = Charlemagne) of Hungary to the kings of Norway, governed quasi-national states that still resembled Carolingian Frankland in governmental and social institutions. Although their churches were invaded by Rome and their civil institutions transmuted by French institutions and immigration, England, the states of inland and western Iberia and northern and eastern Germany had, and partly retained, an identity and unity that marked them off from France and Italy. While conquered by the French, England never disappeared as a nation.

Significant though these quasi-Carolingian retentions were, it was in France and Italy and the parts of Europe hard against their frontiers that the institutions most characteristic of the medieval epoch reached their apogee in this time. On the local level, these were the lordships of the countryside and the 'collective seigniories' of the towns, both jealously seeking a measure of independence from regional princes or kings. Both types of community were generally governed by persons of wealth, both new and old, of lineage, both newly ascending and traditional, and of experience in government. To simplify complex social structures, the local well-to-do had combined with ecumenical popes to weaken Europe's emperors, kings and regional princes.

The harmony of northern and Mediterranean power typical of this period was instanced by the largely amicable relationship of France and Italy. The peoples in these quasi-nations combined during the Crusades to penetrate the Near East at the expense of Greek and Saracen. Although torn by conflicting parties and although her kings were not always the allies of the popes, France – the 'refuge of the popes' was the commonplace – usually buttressed Roman policies, and Rome in turn represented the interests of the Italians, especially that of the northern republics. After 1250 this once loose alignment gradually became more rigid, as the Capetian house rose to rule the larger part of France and its cadet line of Anjou entered Italy to help the popes destroy the Hohenstaufen. After this, France's kings and Rome's popes were often considered to be Europe's greatest princes, a fact lamented by a

---

[13] Post, *Studies in Medieval Legal Thought* 486 and 490.

German such as Alexander of Roes. When Rabban bar Sauma, a Nestorian Christian from Peking, was sent by Persia's Mongol khan to bring the Latins into an alliance against Muslim power, he first visited the Roman pontiff. He then went to Paris to see the king and, on his way back to Rome in 1288, stopped off briefly at Bordeaux, a town he thought to be England's capital. And of the two princes, few doubted that the pope was the greater. To Rabban, he was Europe's king of kings, a notion common among Europe's Jews. In 1321, Todros, son of Isaac, remarked that the year of the rising of the Pastoureaux was 'when the lepers were suppressed and evil men appeared before the pope, the king of nations, demanding he destroy the true law'.[14]

The French and Italians did not advance because of power and wealth alone; they were also blessed by circumstances. One reason that their neighbours accepted leadership so easily was that Europe's frontiers were expanding. The Spaniards fought the Muslim kingdoms to the south, their crusades and military orders remaining in the peninsula. The English were busy along the Celtic fringe, their gallicized nobility being far less enthusiastic about the Crusades to the Holy Land than were their brothers across the Channel. England's greatest Crusader, Richard Coeur de Lion, was the most French of all her kings. Although Swabian and Alpine Germans looked to the south, Germany's northern and eastern inhabitants fought their wars on their own frontiers. If the Teutonic Knights began in the Holy Land, they won their fame on the Vistula and beyond. Europe's centre therefore profited because, in this expansionist age, her peoples looked outside Latin culture for advancement, not within. It was there, on their frontiers, that English, Germans and Spaniards confessed that they emulated the French. Around 1108, an archbishop of Magdeburg summoned troops against the Slavs:

> Wherefore, O most famous Saxons, Franks, Lorrainers and Flemish, conquerors of the world, here you can both save your souls and . . . acquire and settle a beautiful land. [God], who has summoned the French to set out from the furthest reaches of the west to triumph by the virtue of their arms against his enemies in the furthest east, will give you the will and power to subjugate these nearby inhuman gentiles.[15]

---

[14] His commentary on the tractate Nazir cited in Baron, *A Social and Religious History of the Jews* XI 251.

[15] Rudolph Kötzschke, *Quellen zur Geschichte der ostdeutschen Kolonisation* (Leipzig and Berlin, 1912) 10, No. 3.

Chapter 4

Crusades and missions

Crusades and European expansion

Holy wars against non-Christians and especially Muslims in Spain and the Mediterranean had begun in the eleventh century, and what has been called the First Crusade was launched against the Near East in 1092. Themes justifying these grand aggressions were the superiority of the Catholic faith and the recuperation of lands usurped by Saracens from the Christian Roman Empire in earlier times; hence a French lawyer, Peter Dubois, called his Crusade tract *The Recovery of the Holy Land*. For a similar reason, the Iberian Christian war against the Muslims was called a 'reconquest'. Canon lawyers justified the Crusade, Innocent IV (d. 1254) sharing the views of Hostiensis who wrote:

> On Christ's coming all honour, principate, dominion and jurisdiction... was removed from infidels and given to Christians... whence we firmly state that infidels should legally be subject to Christians and not vice-versa... We nevertheless concede that those who recognize the dominion of the Church are to be tolerated... and [that they] can have possessions, Christian dependent farmers and even jurisdictions... Other infidels who do not recognize the power of the Roman Church... we judge unworthy of kingdom... and all dominion, and those who occupy the Holy Land or other [once-Christian] regions ought to be attacked by authority of the Church.[1]

Earlier times had seen great military success. The first European overseas empire had been built by the conquest and European settlement of parts of Palestine and Syria. Fate intervened, however, and the latter twelfth century witnessed the first of many local counterattacks. Greek attempts to recover central Anatolia from the Seljuk Turks failed when the Emperor Manuel was defeated at Myriokephalon in 1176. Further south, a unified Syria and Egypt under Nureddin and Saladin took Jerusalem in 1187 and threatened the rest of the Holy Land. In the western and central Mediterranean, the rigorist sect of the Almohades rallied Muslims. Moving east from Morocco, these Berbers regained by 1160 the coast from Bone to Tripoli, once dominated by the Norman kings of Sicily. Profiting from Christian divisions, the movement

---

[1] *Commentaria in quinque libros decretalium* (2 vols., Venice, 1581, rprt.) II 128ra–29vb.

momentarily rallied the Iberian Muslim princes and administered a severe defeat to the Castilians as late as 1196.

The Saracen counterattack then halted and the Christians advanced again. Already slowed by five recently created Christian military orders and frequent French crusades, Almohade progress in Spain was arrested and a grand Christian alliance crushed their host at Las Navas de Tolosa in 1212. By 1238, the subordination of Minorca and the loss of Valencia had breached Muslim control of the central reaches of the western Mediterranean. By 1287, all the Balearics had fallen to Catalonia–Aragon. Portugal had taken the Algarve by mid-century, and half-empty Cordova, populous Seville and Cadiz fell in 1265 to Castile. Italians began to penetrate North Africa economically, and missionaries and merchants from France and Italy were active from Senegal on the Atlantic to Tunis near Sicily. Europe's geographical knowledge grew apace. In 1291, the Genoese merchant corsair Benedict Zaccaria (d. 1307) joined with others to equip two ill-fated galleys that set out past Gibraltar, perhaps to circumnavigate Africa. Known since 1270, 'the parts of the newly discovered islands commonly called the Fortunate Islands' (the Canary islands) were given to a Majorcan chartered company for occupation and government in 1342.[2] The Azores islands were marked on a portolan chart of 1350.

In the east, the Latins turned aside to shatter the Greeks. Beginning with Cyprus's loss to Richard Coeur de Lion in 1191, Latin arms moved to the Bosporus. A Franco–Venetian crusade captured Constantinople in 1204, creating a Latin empire that, although it lasted on the Bosporus only until 1261, left durable French and Venetian possessions in mainland Greece from Thessaly and Attica to the tip of the Peloponnesus. Some of the Aegean islands and Rhodes, Crete and Cyprus lasted as Latin dominions into modern times. Westerners had not gained so much eastern territory since the days of the First Crusade. In Syria and the Holy Land, the deterioration of the Latin position was arrested partly by the efforts of Coeur de Lion. Thereafter, in spite of defeats such as the Egyptian campaign of Louis IX in 1249, Christian expeditions and the civil wars between the Ayyubid dynasts of Saladin's Kurdish line kept the frontier more or less stable. Threatening war, Frederick II Hohenstaufen recovered the administration of Jerusalem in 1229 and held it until 1244, six years before he died.

Christian frontiers were also stabilized by the Mongol irruption into the Near East. Although these powers worked together only in Armenia, the Mongols conquered Iran, took Baghdad in 1258, ruined Irak and raided Syria and the Seljuk principalities of Anatolia. The unification of central Asia and China under the Mongol aegis offered opportunities for trade. The khans also ruled their heterogeneous domains with foreigners, and hence Marco

---

[2] David Abulafia, *A Mediterranean Emporium: the Catalan Kingdom of Majorca* (Cambridge, 1994) 110.

Polo plausibly claimed that he took service at the Mongol court in 1275 as a provincial governor and ambassador. The khans also favoured religious heterogeneity and encouraged Latin missions. From 1245 until 1340, missionaries were despatched eastward. An example is the Apulian Franciscan John of Monte Corvino in 1294, who translated the New Testament into the Mongol tongue, erected a monastery and two churches in Peking and delighted the khan by buying 150 boys to chant the Latin mass. In 1307, Clement V named him archbishop of Peking.

Fifty years after the Polos, the Franciscan Odoric of Pordenone reported that the *fondaco* for Christian merchants in the Chinese port of Amoy contained a public bath-house and church. The fastest route to China ran from the Genoese towns in the Crimea–Azov region of the Black Sea across the Caspian Sea and thence through Tatary. Writing early in the fourteenth century, Francis di Balducci Pegolotti, a director of the Bardi firm of Florence, reported that the route to Peking was safely open. Italians were also busy in Iran, then controlled by a friendly Mongol khanate. About 1321, a Dominican observed that Genoese merchants sailed vessels from the Persian Gulf to India and Ceylon, recruiting local sailors and Abyssinian marines. Noting that Egypt was the Christians' main enemy, around 1313 the friar William Adam from Languedoc suggested stationing a squadron off Aden to intercept Red Sea traffic.

After 1300, however, these alluring prospects vanished because Mongol power faded rapidly: Persia returned to the Muslims and China to a native dynasty. The Muslim people, destined to play a major role during modern times, was already showing its muscle, an Ottoman Turkish force having crossed the Dardanelles to Europe in 1300. To the south the Mamluks, erecting a government built around an elite of slave soldiers, replaced the Ayyubids in Egypt and Syria. Their commander Baybars repulsed the Mongols in the 1260s and re-established the Abbasid caliphate in Cairo. His successors went on to expel the Latins from their coastal holdings in Cilicia, Syria and the Holy Land, where Acre was the last town to fall, in 1291. Islam also advanced in the western Mediterranean where a new Moroccan dynasty, that of the Berber Merinids, unified the North African coast, repulsed the Franco-Italian attack of Louis IX on Tunis in 1270, and reinforced the Muslim frontier kingdom of Granada in Spain by raids from 1261 to 1285.

Turning to Europe's north and east, there too momentary retreat had marked the late twelfth century. In Hungary, for example, the Byzantines made and unmade kings at the height of the Comnenian dynasty and even briefly diminished the hold of the Latin Church. After the death of the Emperor Manuel in 1180 and the subsequent collapse of the Greek Balkan empire, Greek and Slavic Christianity retreated everywhere. In Russia, the Mongol assaults of the 1230s and 1240s all but obliterated the southern principalities from Kiev to the Carpathians, and subjugated all Russia save northern Novgorod. Nor did these eastern Christians win much sympathy from the Latins: Roger Bacon coolly wrote off the Ruthenians as 'schismatics' who practised the Greek rite.

The Germans profited, partly because there was no strong state to resist them. Once-powerful Hungary weakened throughout the thirteenth century and was not pulled together again until the accession of a Neapolitan–Angevin dynasty in 1308. Poland was divided and did not unify until well into the fourteenth century and, of the pagan peoples near the Baltic, only the Lithuanians showed signs of creating a state. Even the disasters afflicting these regions helped the Germans. Mongol raids on Poland and Hungary from 1241 on increased their princes' need to import Germans to build cities and modernize courts and armies on the model of western chivalry.

German penetration of eastern Europe was often peaceable, but where the populations remained staunchly pagan it was different. Wars against the Wends came early when the Germans resumed the push over the Elbe. By the thirteenth century they were settling the Vistula valley and had thrown outposts along the Baltic shore as far north as Riga, founded in 1198. From 1208 on, the Teutonic Knights took leadership, absorbing two military orders already active in Livonia and Prussia. Around the Baltic and North Seas – a northern Mediterranean as it were – the forerunners of the Hanseatic merchants were appearing. From towns as far apart as Cologne or Utrecht in the west and Reval in the east, the merchants of the Gothland Society dominated the once Scandinavian port of Wisby and, by 1229, had settled in Russian Novgorod with rights similar to those of a Mediterranean *fondaco*. Led by Lübeck's merchants, Germans established other *kontore* in Bruges, Bristol, London and England's east-coast ports by the 1260s. By 1293, Lübeck's leadership in north Germany had been recognized and the Hanseatic League was just around the corner. After a victory by German cavalry in Scania in 1134, Scandinavian princes hastened to modernize, importing knights and modelling local institutions on German ones. The last Danish maritime empire succumbed to German attack in 1227, and Scandinavia was thereafter partly opened to German exploitation.

With the exception, then, of what may be called German Europe, where expansion continued, Latin Europe halted before or around 1300 and began to retreat. This inspired redeployment. The Grand Master of the Teutonic Order, for example, remained at Acre to 1291 and then retired through Venice to Prussian Marienburg in 1308. Chivalry partly followed this movement, and Prussia became the magnet for Crusaders. On the whole, however, the failure of the Latin effort against Near Eastern Christians and Muslims disturbed Europe deeply.

Renascent Saracen power had profited from changes within Latin Europe. In the past, war had moved towards the frontiers. French culture and arms, for example, invaded England until the early thirteenth century, and the

Anglo–French expanded at the expense of Britain's Celtic fringe. From 1152 onwards the English penetrated Ireland, conquering Leinster and the Pale and raiding throughout the island, and by 1284 the remnant principality of north Wales had been irrevocably crushed. By 1307, England's attack on the curious Anglo–Celtic and even quasi-French power called Scotland seemed about to result in the annexation of that kingdom.

A shift ensued, however. If Henry III's campaigns in France were flops, they nevertheless secured Capetian recognition by 1258 that Guienne and adjacent areas were fiefs legitimately held by the English king, thus halting the Capetian conquest of the Plantagenet continental domain. From the 1290s, the English again began to intervene in Flanders. Steps towards the Hundred Years War, the intermittent combats from 1292 through the 1330s were hardly English victories because the county of Flanders remained French long after these skirmishes. By the Peace of Athis in 1305, in fact, the French had acquired Douai, Béthune, Lille and St Omer, and avenged their earlier defeat at Courtrai in 1302 by crushing the Flemish townsmen at Cassel in 1328. But France's hope of incorporating the rest of Flanders into the royal domain was forever finished. In sum, although the English had yet to invade the continent and lay claim to the French crown, Capetian France had ceased expanding.

In the British Isles the English had themselves been set back. If Wales was too far gone to raise its head, Ireland was not and, in spite of several major efforts, English holdings gradually shrank in the later thirteenth century. Scotland's first war of independence, initially successful, lasted from 1296 to 1328 and Robert Bruce's victory at Bannockburn in 1314 ended the hope of uniting the two kingdoms, in spite of a long period of English intervention in a much more destructive war from 1334 to 1346.

Despite conflicts at home such as those between the German emperors and the Italian towns, or the Plantagenets and Capetians over France's Atlantic provinces, furthermore, Europe's great war before 1200 had been the Crusade. This may be seen in the numbers of effectives in the field. Richard Coeur de Lion won his spurs in France and lost his life there, but won his laurels as a captain in the eastern Mediterranean, where he commanded armies two or three times the size of those he led at home. By 1200, however, the largest armies were to be found in Europe, especially Italy, during the Hohenstaufen wars. War had come home to roost.

In 1150 Italian navies had swept the waters of the eastern Mediterranean, and largely French Crusaders occupied its easternmost shores. Between Italy's maritime cities and the Holy Land had lain two powers, the Greeks at the height of the Comnenian revival and the Norman state of southern Italy and Sicily, whose mutually destructive battles over Epirus, Macedonia and Antioch were unremitting. The first of the two powers to fall was Byzantium, beset not only by the Seljuk Turks in Anatolia, but also, from 1186, by the

41

Balkan revolts of the Bulgars. At about the same time, the Latins began to attack the Greeks, an attack culminating in the catastrophe of the Fourth Crusade in 1203–4, from which Byzantium never fully recovered. About the same time, Italian maritime republics aided a Hohenstaufen invasion of southern Italy and Sicily, profiting from the ensuing wars from 1190 to 1215 to win substantial trade concessions and rights of extra-territoriality. During the thirteenth century, the struggle between the more urbanized north and centre of Italy against southern Italy – a Latin state with remnant Greek and Muslim components – intensified. The victory went to the north, resulting not only in the defeat of the Hohenstaufen in 1268, but also in Sicily's secession from the mainland part of the south Italian state in wars from 1282 to 1302.

The victory of the popes and their Lombard allies was at the cost of increased foreign intervention in Italy. Beset at Rome, Innocent IV fled to Lyons on the Rhone. Although he later returned and his successors usually resided in Italy from 1245 to 1312, the general councils that had formerly been summoned to the Lateran were held in the Rhone valley. Northern Italian strength having proved insufficient to defeat the Apulians, Sicilians and the German imperialists, Innocent invited the French to settle the question. From 1261 – the year in which the French pope Urban IV (the first after 11 Italians starting in 1159) was elected – to 1268, the Angevins spearheaded the final assault on Hohenstaufen Italy.

Nor were the French Italy's only invaders. As the Germans failed, others filled Ghibelline ranks. A weak Castilian intervention preceded the entry of the Catalans and Aragonese at the time of the Sicilian revolt in 1282 against the Angevin French, known as the Vespers. These interlopers did not stop in Sicily but pushed on into the Aegean, establishing themselves at Thebes and Athens in 1311. The struggles between Italy's maritime powers intensified, further weakening Latin power in the Near East. The Greeks retook Constantinople in 1261, partly because of Genoese hostility to Venice's monopoly of Bosporan commerce, and the combat between these two republics helped cause the loss of the Syrian and Palestinian coasts. Only the largest naval powers could hope to compete any longer. Genoa crushed Pisa's fleet at Meloria in 1284 and devoured her commercial empire thereafter. Marseilles' flourishing trade suffered the same fate during the Angevin and Catalan struggles over Sicily.

In brief, by fighting among themselves, the Latins helped the non-Latin peoples of the Mediterranean halt western expansion by the end of the thirteenth century. This was accompanied by a change in ideas formulated during the Gregorian age about Christendom and the Crusade. On the defeat of the Empire, the conception of membership in a Christian republic rose above that of a secular state. When Urban II launched the war to 'recover' Jerusalem from infidel hands in 1092, he also weakened the justification for wars within

Europe, even surrendering or relaxing the sanctions against 'heretics' and 'schismatics' that had marked the Gregorian wars in the Empire and against lay domination of the Church. Urban's step seemed to be a compromise, even a retreat, but it enabled the papacy to assume the leadership of Europe's expansion after the Gregorian civil war. Not that holy war was only applicable outside of Europe. Abbot of Cluny, Peter the Venerable (d. 1156), wrote to Pope Eugenius III that his local enemies were 'false Christians . . . worse than Saracens', who 'were to be fought with Christian arms'.[3] His position was not inventive. The popes used the Crusade indulgence against Roger II of Apulia-Sicily in 1135, Ireland in 1152 and the king of Leon in 1197, and a war launched in 1199 against the Markward of Anweiler, Hohenstaufen regent in Sicily, was also a crusade. The historian Matthew Paris even assumed that the campaign of the French prince Louis against John of England in 1213 was a papal holy war. But all this was secondary: the true holy war was the Crusade against Islam and other non-Christian peoples.

Around 1200, holy war began to turn back in earnest into Europe. The Fourth Crusade of 1204 against the 'schismatic' Greeks was first deplored by the pope, but soon applauded because of hope for the union of the churches. Much more popular was the crusade launched in 1209 against the Albigensians, a war of the northern French against the Midi. The return to the Gregorian pattern of religious wars at home awaited the final struggle between the popes and the Hohenstaufen from 1240 on. Innocent IV then prohibited preaching the Crusade for Jersualem in Germany in order to draw troops to the Italian front. The Angevin attack on the Hohenstaufen was declared a Crusade, as were the successive Capetian and Angevin wars against the Catalans and Sicilians from 1282 on. The popes became so used to calling their wars crusades that Boniface VIII launched one in 1297 against his enemies among the cardinals and in the papal states, including the Colonna family. Dante derided him as 'the prince of the new Pharisees, whose every enemy was Christian, waging war near the Lateran, not with Saracens or Jews, only with Christians'.[4]

Dante's complaints against the 'misuse' of the Crusade were not unique. Matthew Paris accused Innocent IV of sabotaging Louis IX of France's Crusades to advance his Italian policy. In 1265, when in France, an archbishop of Tyre observed that it was bad when the pope redirected to Sicily those pledged to the Holy Land, but worse when money raised for Jerusalem went to support Angevin wars in Italy without the consent of the donors. The popes nevertheless wanted the Crusades resumed, but believed that the Hohenstaufens had first to be defeated in order to stop Europe's internecine wars.

---

[3] Norman Housley, 'Crusades against Christians: their Origins and Early Development, c. 1000–1216' in *Crusade and Settlement* (ed. Peter W. Edbury, Cardiff, 1985) 24.
[4] *Inferno* 27 85.

The failure to defeat the Saracens encouraged an oft-expressed belief that corruption and sin impeded the Christians. Peter Cantor argued that sin could not be eradicated by conquering others, only by purifying one's own soul and society. Doubts about their leadership made some believe that, to succeed, the cause must be entrusted to the 'just' or the poor in spirit. Already evident in the First Crusade, this idea eventually took on all sorts of forms, of which the most egregious was the Children's Crusade of 1212. Initially designed to stir faith, popular preaching from the Loire valley to that of the Rhine evoked a curious youth march towards Jerusalem. Greeted by Innocent III (d. 1216) and others as praiseworthy, because fervid youth shamed the indifference of age, the movement petered out, leaving several thousand displaced persons and with charges that merchants or Jews had sold them into Muslim slavery.

Similar ideas about the force of innocence were expressed by the Pastoureaux, who rose to crusade for Louis IX during his captivity in Egypt in 1251. Initially encouraged by authorities such as the queen mother, these Holy Innocents were not children but rather 'the poor'. They also remained at home, roughing up townsmen, the well-to-do and Jews. Movements of this type had been known in the west before, an example being the Capuciati of Puy in 1182. Also initially encouraged by the pope, this group was organized to defend the peace threatened by unemployed soldiers and lordly bandits when fighting ended between the Capetians and Plantagenets. Like the Pastoureaux, the Capuciati got out of hand and were suppressed. One difference between the two movements, however, is worth underlining. The Capuciati tried to restore peace, the necessary counterpart of the Crusade: God's peace at home, God's war abroad! The Pastoureaux and those who merged into the peasant and artisan revolutionaries of the fourteenth century differed: theirs was God's war at home.

Finding scapegoats was no monopoly of the poor; all of society played that game. Blaming the fall of Acre on the misbehaviour of its defenders was a case in point. The Templars were especially chosen for obloquy because their houses served as treasuries for kings, for example, whereas the rival Hospitallers ran hospitals. The real reason that the Templars were singled out, however, was that, as the earliest and greatest military order, they symbolized Christendom's defeat. Most of their members were to be found at home, it was charged, not at the front. The prestige of the order had been falling consistently, and the French crown had begun to attack it in 1287. Serious persecution started in 1306, the order was abolished in 1312 and the grand master and his staff were executed in 1314. Like other victims of escapism, the knights were charged with everything: heresy, materialism, sorcery and sodomy with man and beast. The abolition of the Templars was the first successful attack by lay power on a religious order.

Secular princes found popular support for taking command of the Crusades from the popes. As the head of what seemed Europe's greatest power and heir of Louis IX, canonized in 1297, the French king thought himself Latin Europe's natural leader. Philip IV's councillors wished to unify the military orders, make their prince grand master, assume the crown of Jerusalem and lead a united Europe in a great crusade. They also came to believe that France's interests were identical with those of the Holy Land and the faith, and hence the notion that the secular nation is the Holy Land was being born.

Missions and toleration

Opposition to crusades always existed, because religion was held to be voluntary, not to be imposed by force. Some even thought that religion and secular government were so far apart that not only did infidels enjoy natural rights, but pagan dominion over Christians was also justifiable. As the Crusades failed, these themes were reinvigorated during the thirteenth century. Franciscan radicals, Salimbene said, were happy when their prophecy of Louis IX's failure was fulfilled in the disaster of Damietta in 1249. Roger Bacon argued that crusades involved the Church in secular wars, proving his point by the French Crusade against Catalonia–Aragon. Even when unbelievers are beaten, moreover, Christians lack troops to hold the conquest. Infidels and pagans:

> are not converted by war, but instead slain and sent to hell . . . [Those] labouring for their conversion, especially the Teutonic Knights, really wish to reduce them to slavery, as Dominicans, Franciscans and other reliable men throughout Germany and Poland have clearly ascertained. The pagans therefore defend themselves, not because they have a better religion, but because they resist violence.[5]

Missions seemed the better way. Francis of Assisi preached in Palestine and perhaps in Egypt in 1219. After his conversion in 1265, the Majorcan Raymond Llull lectured everywhere to encourage missions and language studies. He was at Vienne in 1311 when the council vainly recommended that Oxford, Paris, Bologna and Salamanca teach Arabic, Greek, Hebrew and Syrian. He visited Armenia, Cyprus and North Africa, and was believed to have been martyred in Algeria in 1315. Raymond of Penyafort, general of the Dominicans, urged Thomas Aquinas to write his *Against the Gentiles* in 1261/64 for use in missions, asked Spanish kings to finance language schools and echoed a decision of the order's general chapter of 1250 that Arabic, Greek and Hebrew should be taught. Careers were built around missions. The Dominican Raymond Martin was employed in Aragon investigating Jewish texts in 1264. In that year and again in 1269 he preached against Islam in Murcia and Tunis, and retired as lector in Hebrew at his order's

---

[5] *Opus maius* 3 3 13 and 4 2 1 (ed. J.H. Bridges, Oxford and London, 1897–1900) II 121 and 200.

school in Barcelona in 1281. The Preachers created a Society of Missions in 1312 which – together with the United Brethren, a group of sympathetic Greek Basilians – ran missions in Persia and Armenia in the early fourteenth century. Hopes for voluntary conversion were vibrant. The reunification of Christendom also seemed about to be attained. Part of the Armenian church joined Rome in 1198, and Latin influence in the Balkans rose to culminate in a momentary unification of the Bulgar church with the Roman in 1204. The greatest achievement of all came when Constantinople united with Rome at the second Council of Lyons in 1274.

The movement failed, one reason for which being that the Latins twisted the arms of those they wished to bring to the 'way of truth'. They were sometimes open about it. A pagan fort on Germany's eastern frontier was summoned in 1227, for example, in this way: 'If you want peace, renounce idolatry and receive the true peace, which is Christ.' The defenders of another replied: 'We know your God is greater than ours because he has forced us to worship him by conquering us. Whence we beg that, sparing us, you mercifully impose on us . . . Christ's yoke.'[6] Normal for pagans, such ideas were even applied to Greek Christians. Arguing against some Germans who objected to levying the Crusade against Christians, Hostiensis contended: 'if you assert it meritorious to preach the overseas crusade for the . . . recuperation of the Holy Land, all the more is it worthy to preach the cross against schismatics to preserve the unity of the church!'[7]

Motives were sometimes hidden. When Constantinople fell in 1204, Thomas Morosini replaced the Greek patriarch of that city and, importing Venetian canons, planned to replace all Greek prelates with them. Although initially appalled, Innocent III himself forced the Greeks to subscribe to Latin beliefs – so vigorously that soon only one bishop remained in his see – and fostered the entry of Latin missionaries, at first Cistercian, then mendicant. What could happen to Greek churches, moreover, is seen in Cyprus after the Lusignan dynasty was established in 1192. By 1220 all Greek clerks swore oaths of obedience to Rome, and two years later the island's four Greek prelates were ordered out of town to live in the countryside. A Latin attack led to papal 'arbitration' in 1260 in which the pope abolished the Greek metropolitan, entrusting his functions to the Latin archbishop of Nicosia, and assigned the clerical tithe to the Latins. No wonder Constantinople's union with Rome lasted only eight years!

Nor could relations have been different, because religion was what defined citizenship. Rooted in unbelief or indifference towards religion, tolerance nevertheless existed. In the Holy Land, French rural lords were more tolerant than newly arrived Crusaders. Saladin was something of a hero to western

---

[6] The chronicle of Livonia in *MGH SS in usum scholarum* 48 and 80.
[7] *Summa Aurea* (Lyons, 1537, rprnt.) 178va, No. 19.

gentlefolk, and Dante reserved him a pleasant place in hell. In Wolfram of Eschenbach's romance *Parzifal*, the heathen Feirefiz fully equals the hero in chivalry; besides, they are blood relatives! Moved by a desire to purify the Latins, Peter Cantor praised Muslim absorption in prayer, monotheism, detestation of idolatry, lack of 'images' and 'sacrifices' in their 'temples'. He also praised their sobriety, noting that Saladin scorned drunken Christians, and encouraged the giving of alms to an indigent pagan or Jew rather than a Christian who could get by.

Tolerance was not widespread, however. Alan of Lille called Muslims 'pagans'. Responding to allegations that the Christian Trinity was polytheist, lawyers such as Innocent IV and Hostiensis asserted that Islam was itself idolatry and polytheism. Dante repeated an old story that Islam derived from Judaism and Christianity, but this made it worse, because it was a heresy. James of Voragine, archbishop of Genoa, states that a Jacobite archdeacon or Nestorian monk converted Mohammed from idolatry into Christian heresy. Gerald of Wales explained why Saracens eschewed pork: they were judaizing! Wine was also prohibited because Mohammed, 'when drunk, since he had preached filth . . . fell . . . in the street and was bitten by pigs'.[8] Both Jews and Saracens thought that clerical celibacy exposed boys and girls to risk, which, in turn, made William of Auvergne, professor and bishop of Paris, claim that Muslims 'used or abused male slaves and even many animals'.[9] Occasional toleration aside, the relationship of Christians and Muslims was always difficult. The chancery of Pope Eugene III (1145–53) drafted a letter to a Muslim prince, thought so elegant that it found a place in a German formulary book:

Eugene bishop etc. to a king or sultan of the Saracens. We do not greet you, not because we do not wish your health, but because you do not believe in the true health, that of Christ Jesus crucified for the salvation of humankind, and because you do not cease injuring those who profess Christ.[10]

As if diplomacy were not difficult enough!

Matters often got out of hand. Even among inhabitants of the Holy Land where live and let live was the rule, an assembly at Nablus in 1120 proposed castrating Christian and Saracen males who miscegenated. A woman merely lost her nose! If captured in war, furthermore, Christians and Saracens often enslaved each other. James of Vitry described what happened when Damietta fell in 1220. Four hundred rich captives were exchanged for Christians; the rest were sold as slaves, James himself buying the children for conversion to Christ. In events stretching from 1287 to 1335, the Christian conquest of the Balearic islands witnessed the enslavement of many common folk.

---

[8] *De principis instructione* 1 17 in *Rolls Series* LXXXI viii 68.
[9] *De universo* in Paris National Library MS. lat. 15756 84r a–b.
[10] *Baumgartenberger Formularius* in *BuF* II 731, dated *circa* 1302.

Facing religion's pressures, the tolerance or indifference of secular monarchy was weakened. Conqueror of Toledo in 1085, Alphonse VI of Castile described himself as emperor of the 'two religions' when addressing Muslims, and a successor, Ferdinand III (1217–52), had Arabic, Castilian, Hebrew and Latin inscribed on his tomb. In the code called the *Usages of Barcelona*, the prince undertook to defend the rights of all citizens, Christian, Saracen, Jew and 'heretic' (those, perhaps, adhering to the Mozarabic rite). Such attitudes were seen when Christians invaded Spain's Arabic areas and were aided by rebellious Muslim and Jewish populations. 'Divide and rule' is good counsel for a monarch, and minorities, moreover, provided useful officers and troops. Alphonse VIII of Castile (d. 1214) was criticized by Innocent III for paying Muslim officers with church tithes. Similar censure fell on Andrew II of Hungary (d. 1235) for employing Ismaelites (Asiatic Muslims) to suppress magnate opposition, and this was repeated against his successors of the Arpad dynasty. Frederick II Hohenstaufen's Saracen military colony at Lucera in the Capitanata infuriated Rome.

Overcoming princely resistance, laws barring Muslims from public office, from owning Christian slaves or domestics, against publicity for their cult and social intercourse with Christians spread from the late twelfth century, inspired by the Roman pontiffs. By the early fourteenth century, similar legal impediments were imposed on Greek 'schismatics' in Sicily by the Catalan Frederick III (d. 1337). This law or what was behind it affected everything. Alphonse X of Castile's poetry and even his *Book of the Laws* were remarkably intolerant compared to earlier Spanish letters.

In fine, like Greeks, Muslims living under Latin rule rightly viewed missionaries as agents of a persecution to which they were about to be subjected. In the past, Saracens had often summoned Latins to help solve internecine squabbles; by 1300, however, they had learned better – for a time.

War and missions

The great Majorcan Llull thought of himself as a missionary to the Muslims, and learned Arabic for that purpose. But the context of his mission was clearly defined by the canonists Hostiensis and Innocent IV, the latter stating that, although Muslims may not be converted by force, the pope can nevertheless order them to admit 'preachers of the Gospel in their lands because every rational creature is made to praise God . . . [and] they sin if they prohibit preachers'. Nor was this a two-way street, because 'they are in error but we are on the "via veritatis"'.[11] By the time he outlined his last plan in 1308 – one owing much to a book of about 1291 by Fidenzio of Padua, a Franciscan

---

[11] *Commentaria super libros quinque decretalium* 429vb, Nos. 8 and 10, in that order.

in the Holy Land – Llull recommended a crusade to assure a 'fair hearing'. The canonists Hostiensis and Innocent IV had in fact opined that Muslims contravened natural law by refusing free entry to Christ's 'good news'. Some therefore favoured outright conquest. In his materialist *Recovery of the Holy Land* of 1306, Peter Dubois urged this course because it would be vastly profitable. He thought that spices, and so on, would be cheaper after the conquest. Educated young westerners would intermarry with Saracens, showing them how good it could be. The Mamluks' Egyptian subjects, especially women, were enslaved and would revolt when freedom's banner was waved. A reformed church was to educate young women and men for eastern settlement. Political unity under the king of France, a European congress and permanent international arbitration, with the Roman pontiff as final arbiter, would eradicate war in Europe. Others played war games. In 1321, the Venetian senator Marino Sanuto proposed unifying Europe under both pope and French king. He also hoped for an alliance between the Tatars and Latins to attack the strategic base of Near Eastern power in Egypt, and looked forward to dominating the Indian Ocean.

These schemes all shared the notion that the faith required coercion. History, indeed, had shown that, apart from Mongol Asia, missions succeeded only where the Latins ruled. Even the momentary union of Constantinople and Rome in 1274 was prompted by the emperor Michael VIII Paleologus's fear of Charles I (d. 1285) of Naples's plan to restore the Latin empire on the Bosporus. The Sicilian Vespers of 1282 and resultant loss of Sicily to the Catalans enabled or obliged the emperor Andronicus II to drive the unionists out and withdraw obedience from Rome. Marsiglio of Padua (d. 1342) summed up this failure:

> It cannot be shown from sacred Scripture that an infidel can be forced to confess the Christian faith . . . and it follows that, if an overseas expedition is made to force infidels to do so, such an expedition should not be considered meritorious. If it is made, however, to force infidels to obey civil commands of the Roman prince and people and pay taxes as they are supposed to by law, such an expedition, I think, should be thought meritorious because its objective is the peace and tranquillity of all citizens.[12]

Marsiglio had not only junked holy war, he had inadvertently pointed the way to Europe's secular colonial empires.

That hostility to one's enemy stimulates is shown by the great fruit born by the knowledge that Christians obtained of Muslim writings. Llull modelled his hero Blanquerna on Muslim mystic hermits or *sufis*. The *Mir'ag* or *Ladder*, a mystic voyage by Mohammed into heaven and hell, was translated into

---

[12] *Defensor minor* 7 3 (ed. C.K. Brampton, Birmingham, 1922) 18–19. This work of 1342 summarized the *Defensor pacis* of 1324.

Castilian by a Jewish doctor at the court of Alphonse X, and into Latin and French in 1264 by Bonaventure of Siena. Bonaventure did so that Christians might 'know that rash assaults against Christ by Mohammedans were as wrong-headed as they were ridiculous, and that, when compared with such lies, the truth of the Christian faith will seem all the more appealing'.[13] Without this and other pieces of Saracen popular piety, however, Dante's *Divine Comedy* might not have had its distinctive architecture. Even in retreat, then, Latin Europe still hungrily devoured the wisdom of other cultures, thus preparing a renewed eruption that would astonish the world in early modern times.

At this time, however, the Latin retreat was real; indeed, it was sometimes a rout. There was more to the failure of Christian missions than is stated above. In 1332–33 those (largely Italian) attending a service in the Franciscan church of Tabriz in Persia heard a radical friar, George of Adria, describe Pope John XXII as the Antichrist. The Latins were exporting not only their faith but also their civil wars, and these show that, at home as abroad, the Church's mission was faltering. Aspects of this are examined in the last three chapters of this volume.

---

[13] Francesco Gabrieli, 'New Light on Dante and Islam' in *East and West* IV (1953) 175a.

Chapter 5

The Jews

Divisions and education

Other than a few Muslims, the Jews were the only people in the Latin West normally permitted to hold a faith other than Christian, and the law dealing with them was an adaptation of late Roman and Visigothic legislation. Although massacres of Jews in the Rhineland marked the early Crusades and Muslim Spain in the first half of the twelfth century, these ceased, and around 1200, both in northern and Mediterranean regions, Europe's Jews flourished as never before. The greatest centres of Jewish life were found outside of the Latin West in Byzantine and Arabic areas, but this was changing, partly because Sicily and most of Spain had been conquered, and partly because Saracen power was fading. Europe's Jews were few in number, the heaviest populations being along the Mediterranean frontier. In 1343 the Jews in Palma (90 per cent of those on Majorca) were a trifle over eight per cent of the town's population. Up north, hardly more than 3,000 lived in England in the late thirteenth century, a well-to-do group drowned in a total population of five or so million.

Jews had long been richer than the peoples among whom they lived. As intermediaries between Islam and Christendom, they helped transmit Mediterranean culture. Although this function was fading and western Jewry was itself becoming parochial, Jews were more literate than most of their Christian neighbours, thus confirming their sense of cultural superiority. They had also found a way of living with the Latins. An example was the abrogation of polygyny by the ruling of Gershom of Mainz (d. 1028), one echoing the ban on polygyny for Roman citizens. Surrendering a basic social practice, however, they held all the more firmly to religion.

Mediterranean Jews probably enjoyed an ampler culture than northern ones. From the south – one thinks of Maimonides (d. 1204), an Andalusian who mostly lived in Cairo in Egypt – came an influential Aristotelian natural philosophy. French and German rabbis condemned this thought. In Italy, Languedoc and Spain, things were different, although intellectual battles took place there too. The history of philosophy was paralleled by the practical art of medicine. Whereas Jewish doctors were rare in the north, they were busy in Spain and Languedoc, and Italy's popes and southern princes employed them.

Mediterranean Jews were also more given to messianism and mystical thought. Although Eleazar Rokeah (son of Jehudah, d. 1223–32) of Worms produced an encyclopaedia of quietist ethics, messianic numerology, folk-lore and superstition called the *Book of the Devout*, he was from the Italian family of the Kalonymides active in Speyer, Mainz and Worms. Besides, if German or Ashkenazic Jewry vaunted its Hasidic mysteries, Spanish or Sephardic rabbis, along with those of Languedoc, led in the similar tradition of the Kabbalah. The author of the *Zohar*, Moses son of Shemtob (d. 1305) of Leon, lived in Guadalajara and, although he voyaged all over the Mediterranean from Syria to Italy, the prophetical messianist Abulafia (Abraham son of Samuel, d. after 1291) was raised in Saragossa and Tudela. Abulafia also represents a special messianic and prophetical tradition. Although northerners speculated about the date of the Messiah's coming, they usually put it off; in the south, they brought it nearer. In 1263, the Kabbalist Nahmanides (Moses son of Nahman or Rambam) of Barcelona and Gerona stated in a debate with Paul Christiani, a Dominican apostate from Judaism: 'When the end of time comes, the Messiah will go to the pope at God's command and ask him to liberate his people.' Perhaps this tradition was what urged Abulafia to plead Jewry's case before the pope in 1280.[1]

Jews were not intellectually sealed off from Christians. There was a Jewish minnesinger, Süsskind of Trimberg. As soon as Walter of Metz had finished his verse encyclopaedia *Image of the World* in 1245, the Londoner Deulecresse (Chaim son of Deulecret) translated it into Hebrew. Mediterranean Jews were especially open minded. They created a secular love poetry that influenced Christian verse, as Muslim poetry did. Writing on ethics in 1278, the Roman Jehiel son of Jekutiel cited not only Scripture and the *Talmud*, but also the philosophers Aristotle and Porphyry and a saying of Frederick II Hohenstaufen. In the early 1300s, Leo Romano (Judah son of Moses, b. 1292), a courtier of the Angevin Robert I (d. 1343), not only translated Arabic texts, but also produced a Hebrew version of selections from Augustine, Albertus Magnus and Aquinas. Intelligent Jews, he said, 'believe that true knowledge is going to other peoples, especially Christians'.[2] Leo's older cousin Immanuel son of Solomon (grandson of Jekutiel of the Roman Zifroni family, d. 1330) was a poet in Hebrew and Italian, a friend of men in the circle of Dante and Cino of Pistoia. He also wrote a mystical commentary on the *Song of Songs* and a collection of satirical verses on religion, love and Jewish life called the *Mehabberoth*. He is a bad Jew, he says, but not thereby a Saracen or Christian. Take the best from each faith: Christian eating and drinking are good, Moses required few fasts and one can debauch with Mohammed. Love is the only complete lordship, knowing no law, no mass, no prophet.

---

[1] Scholem, *Jewish Mysticism* 128.
[2] Güdemann, *Geschichte des Erziehungswesens . . . der Juden* II 157.

Jewish synagogues were schools. Most youths left school either at the age of thirteen, the age of religious majority, or sixteen. Many dropped out before, as is seen in the *Hukke ha-Torah* of Languedoc where, if a pupil is weak, the teacher is to take him to his father and say: 'God may enable your son to do noble things, but, for learning, he's too stupid.'[3] Although a few girls were trained by rabbinical fathers, no provision was made for women. From the age of five, boys began with languages (the local vernacular, Hebrew and Aramaic), examples being drawn from the Bible, itself studied in subsequent years. From ten to sixteen, parts of the *Mishnah* were read. After that, during seven years in which the pupils lived with their teacher, material from the whole *Talmud* – that is, both the *Mishnah* and the *Gemara* – and rabbinical commentaries were studied.

The *Hukke ha-Torah* has led some to think of Jewish universities. The fact that most rabbis came from rabbinical families or married into them, however, shows that Jews were educated in the homes of learned men. Standard in Arabic culture, this educational method was also normal in Christendom, where apprentices (*discipuli*) were sent to live with master artisans, and young gentlemen learned manners, arms and sometimes letters in the courts of local magnates. What made the university different from Islamic, Jewish and Latin lay education was ecclesiastical celibacy. This partly freed the life intellectual from family bondage, and so strong was its impress that it even marked studies in secular law and medicine in which many teachers were married.

Formal education among Jews was limited to scripture and the *Talmud*, but philosophy and natural science flourished, especially among Jews in Arab lands. Like that of some Muslim philosophers, however, Maimonides's attempt to graft philosophy on to the law, as in the *Mishneh Torah* of 1180, was not well received. The situation was different among the Latins where, by 1300, university students had formal instruction in Aristotelian thought. In Jewish education, then, everything centred on the law, and hence the tone of rabbinical literature was analogous to that of Latin legal writing. Abraham of Posquières (son of David or Rabad, *fl.* 1150–70) from Montpellier glossed five of the *Mishnah* tractates as well as 24 of the *Talmud*, and pioneered commentary on the *Midrashim*. He also published responses on particular questions and, of course, criticized Maimonides's *Mishneh Torah*.

Abraham seems narrow until one remembers that an encyclopaedia like the *Talmud* contained not only law and observances, but also examples of ethics, magic, prophecy, indeed all sorts of subjects. The unification of such heterogeneous material into texts like the *Talmud* suited an Arabic Mediterranean society divided into national–religious 'castes', and was also of use to Jews as a European minority. The urge towards unity contrasted sharply with

---

[3] Ibid. I 96: 'schwer von Begriff'.

the Latin bent in the opposite direction. Although Raymond Llull attempted to join all knowledge into one grand scheme, a united body of learning, tradition and law never emerged in Latin Christianity, probably because religion did not there define a nation or a people. There were many nations under its aegis and, within these, the separation, even mutual hostility, of church and state encouraged institutional autonomy. Hence, as they grew, the different disciplines – theology, law and grammar – became specialities, creating special faculties.

Government and economy

Jewish communities enjoyed a limited autonomy, limited because the Christian community insisted on the superiority of its morality and religion. Although relatively tolerant, for example, Innocent IV was certain that 'the pope can judge Jews if they do anything contrary to evangelical law'. Thus, although Jews in Muslim areas remained polygynous, they were restricted to monogyny among the Latins, as noted above. This rule and certain religious restrictions aside, self-government was the norm. Their own judges, the *dayanim*, normally settled civil litigation among Jews. Civil cases between Jews and Christians usually went to the defendant's court, although in England and north France these were often arbitrative panels, half Jewish, half Christian. In some Italian statutes and John of England's legislation of 1201, criminal cases involving the shedding of blood came before Christian courts. This meant intrusion into the Jewish community, even in a case of adultery between Jews, specified by a law of Cologne in 1252.

The institutions of Jewish self-government were similar to those of Christian guilds and small communities. Government by elders was the rule, and these councillors frequently chose their own successors. In theory, however, the adult male members of the synagogue chose the rulers. Writing to the Jews in Saragossa in 1264, Rashba (Solomon son of Adret) of Barcelona remarked that a community is not legally bound to choose either the wise or rich for its canonical seven councillors. Constitutions varied, he said, there are 'places where business is run by the elders . . . Others where . . . [they] can do nothing without consulting the people and obtaining their consent, and still others where individual leaders can do as they see fit'.[4] Such councillors were to raise the taxes required by government, and here too practices differed. Answering a query from Montpellier, Rashba remarked that the senior community sometimes dominated, but that elsewhere, as at Tarragona, Villafranca and Montblanch, the larger centre was obliged to consult the lesser ones when assigning taxes.

---

[4] Haim Beinart, 'Hispano–Jewish Society' in *Cahiers d'histoire mondiale* XI (1968) 227.

According to lawyers trained in Roman law, Jews were citizens but, from the days of Christian Rome and Visigothic Spain, they were prohibited from holding public office and land. In regard to land, exceptions were admitted. Encouraged to lend money, they were granted the right to use or rent land pledged to them for debt. In 1239, Frederick II Hohenstaufen allowed the Jews from the island of Gerbi (settled in Palermo to introduce indigo and henna) a portion of the royal date groves – few Arabic-speaking town dwellers lacked a date palm – and the right to rent lots for houses with leases of from five to ten years. Save in Spain or Italy, however, Jews never became farmers or landlords, but instead leased vineyards, dairies and other facilities, largely for domestic and ritual consumption.

Jews usually served Christian princes. In England, Sicily and Spain, they were the possessions – 'special serfs of our treasury' in Sicily, 'chattels' in England – of the kings, who jealously guarded their monopoly. In the mid-twelfth century, the *Laws of Edward the Confessor* reported that 'all Jews ... must be under the guardianship and protection of the king; and may not be subject to a "richman" [baron] without the king's licence, because Jews and all their property are the king's'.[5] In centralized monarchies, princes appointed leaders for the Jews – as Frederick II acceded to the request of the Palermitan Jews and ordered his governor to appoint an elder from among them – or even appointed a head of the nation's Jews like the 'Jews' bishop' in England, an officer sometimes replaced by a synod. England's community was ordered in 1241 to choose delegates to meet at the Worcester parliament to negotiate a subsidy to the king.

Where political power was decentralized, as in France, Jews fell under local lords. In 1235, a count of Boulogne blandly willed to 'his' people the property of 'his' Jews in reparation for 'his' sins. A Capetian effort to claim them all met great resistance and, from 1198 to 1230, the crown settled for treaties with the counts of Champagne and those of Saint-Pol and Nevers. The parties prohibited luring Jews from another's Jewry, stipulating the return of those who moved. Small wonder that, writing in the late twelfth century, Isaac son of Samuel of Dampierre referred enviously to the fact that elsewhere than in France 'Jews have the right to reside wherever they wish, like nobles'.[6] The Empire was not yet so decentralized. Although Frederick II gave rights over Jews to the princes, he nonetheless issued a general privilege for them in 1236 and, until late in the century, Germany's Jews insisted that they were not citizens of local communities, but instead of the Empire or at least of a substantial principality. A rabbi who had served all over Germany, Meier son of Baruch (d. 1293), claimed that the Jews 'are not dependants

---

[5] *Gesetze der Angelsachsen* (ed. Felix Liebermann, Halle, 1901) I 650.
[6] Baron, *A Social and Religious History*, XI, 18–19.

obliged to pay taxes wherever they happen to be, as gentiles are, but are like nobles'.[7]

Both princes and republics profited from 'their' Jews because they were usurers. Typically, although his celebrated *Liber Augustalis* of 1231 called it a 'public crime', Frederick II Hohenstaufen expressly exempted Jews from the law, arguing that 'their usury is [not] illicit and prohibited by divine law . . . because they are not subject to the law instituted by the blessed fathers'.[8] And the emperor, like other public authorities including canon law judges (who used the sanction of excommunication), obliged debtors to pay up. Jewish transactions, in short, were registered, enforced and taxed by Christian government. A threat of confiscation sometimes replaced this traditional income by obligatory loans or ransoms. Hard pressed by war with the Plantagenets, Philip II Augustus first ransomed 'his' Jews and then drove them out in 1182. This expedient failed because they migrated to France's greater feudatories and enhanced the revenues of the Capetian's rivals; they were therefore re-admitted 16 years later. Jews were used or abused, in short, according to need. Matthew Paris's wisecrack about the pledging of the Jews by Henry III of England to his brother Richard of Cornwall in 1255 is an illustration: those whom the king had skinned the count would eviscerate.

In spite of such attitudes, princes had no desire to kill the geese laying golden eggs and rarely initiated attacks on the Jews. Until systems of general taxation based on wealth had been widely introduced (they begin towards the end of the period treated in this book), Jewish loans were a sure source of princely revenue because, being based on actual transactions, they grew with the economy. Their permitted usury therefore had a public function, because government, although often both defrauded and defrauding, siphoned some of the lucre into the treasury in return for protection and enforcement. As a result, Jews were dependent on their princely or republican masters. If popular hatred exploded uncontrollably, however, the authorities usually bowed before the storm but tried to reap a last-ditch profit of confiscation.

The opponents of princes hated Jews. England's baronial opposition attacked them from Magna Carta in 1215 until the expulsion of 1290. The expulsion from France in 1315 coincided with the nobles' league of France and the Champagne against arbitrary royal government. Towns also attacked their Jews when rising against their lords. Otto of Freising reports that Bernard of Clairvaux in 1146 silenced a wandering monk at Mainz who stirred up popular revolts by attacking the Jews. Once princely or seigniorial power was reduced and urban aristocracies built oligarchies, however, they made peace with the Jews. It was then the people's turn and, as the plebs gained a measure of political power around 1300, Jewry's trials began again.

---

[7] Ibid.

[8] *Historia diplomatica Frederici secundi* 4 pt. 1 (ed. J.L.A. Huillard-Bréholles, Paris, 1844) 10–11.

Even in the expanding economy of the twelfth century, Christian merchants drove Jews out of commerce except in the Mediterranean and along Europe's eastern frontiers. Paced by maritime Venice, north Italy's towns led the world in exclusionary legislation. At Perugia in 1279, a newly elected *podestà* took oath to refuse entry to Jews. Without commerce and denied land ownership, Jews were obliged to specialize in moneylending. The ecclesiastical attack on Christian usury may have had something to do with the increase of hostility towards Jews. The fourth Lateran Council of 1215 required Jews to restore 'grave and immoderate usuries', because 'the more the Christian religion curbs the taking of usury, the more does Jewish perfidy become used to this practice, so much so that, in a short time, Christian wealth will be exhausted'.[9] Local anti-Jewish movements were often headed by the clergy, especially its radicals. The Franciscan John Peckham (d. 1292), archbishop of Canterbury, spearheaded a petition of 1283 asking Edward I to demand restitution of usury from the Jews and urged their expulsion in 1290. Other churchmen were wiser, but also knew that moneylending invited popular hatred. Abelard (d. 1142) had his fictional Jew repeat what Jews themselves often stated, namely that, not being permitted to own land, 'what remains to us is usury, that we sustain our miserable lives by taking interest from others, which makes us hateful to them'.[10]

Moneylending was not enthusiastically engaged in by all: it was forbidden among Jews, and taking usury from Christians was also actively debated. Some justified the practice: around 1204 Moses of Paris (son of Jehiel, grandson of Mattathiah) permitted it because the brotherhood of Jew and Christian had been sundered, an opinion dismissed by Joseph the Zealot (son of Nathan Official) of Sens. Still, just as some Christians allowed usury taken from Saracens, Maimonides permitted usury to defeat the enemies of the faith. In 1246, Meier son of Simon of Narbonne adopted what will be seen to be a familiar expedient among Christians, namely calling usury interest. Many Christians, including Thomas Aquinas, claimed the practice to be immoral. When asked why Jews, since they had no other way of making a living, should be punished for usury, he coolly replied that they ought not to be allowed to profit from crime.

And Jews were indeed moneylenders. Notarial registers from Perpignan in Roussillon in the late thirteenth century contain a total of 14 acts showing Jews active in commerce and local trade, as against 1,643 lending money to Christians. Of the 220 Jewish adults mentioned in these acts, at least 80 per cent were moneylenders and, of those mentioned twice, 93 per cent were in the business. Perpignan, however, corrects a widespread misapprehension about usury, namely that loans were only made to the poor or improvident institutions or individuals. Perpignan was a new town at that time, and most

---

[9] *Liber extra* 5 19 18 in *CICan.* II 816.
[10] *Dialogus inter philosophum, Judaeum et Christianum* in *PL* CLXXVIII 1618.

Jewish loans there were to successful businessmen. One concludes that Jews were welcome in underdeveloped areas, and hence accompanied the Germans in their drive to the east. Once a region had been built up, however, Christians – such as the Lombards in France and England – replaced Jews in the big money. Then Jews were forced into humble trades and petty usury or pawnbroking which, although profitable and necessary, evoked popular hostility. Roussillon is an example. Although suits against Jewish usurers were brought into ecclesiastical courts from about 1261, Catalonia's princes stoutly protected their right to lend at usury and took their traditional cut. In the early fourteenth century, however, popular and judicial actions began a systematic attack on the Jewish community, leaving it impoverished by the next century.

The Jews' greatest enemies were the people and churchmen. This was because churchmen were the ideologues who voiced the passions of the age, and because the people, the humble many, suffered poverty more than others and hence their feelings were virulent. Rescinding the expulsion of 1306, the French crown readmitted the Jews in 1315 and tried to protect them. This policy failed because of the popular movement of the Pastoureaux from 1319 through the early 1320s that, beginning in Languedoc, swept all France. Shouting utopian slogans, mobs of deracinated workers, farmers and others, massacred Jews as well as lepers before turning against the rich and towards inevitable repression. Such was the backdrop for the royal expulsion of the Jews in 1322.

To judge from their early expulsion from England and northern France, Jewish torment also had to do with the growth of centralized states. The gradual institution of general taxation weakened princely links to this minority. Jews were not needed as much as in the past, and attacking them not only eased the introduction of new taxes but also provided a one-time profit from their expulsion or impoverishment. And, even without a wish to harm, princes, like others, enjoy doing what they cannot help but do.

The attitude of princes towards Jews is therefore worth examining. Few publicly defended their relationship with the Jews, but instead they either argued that things are necessarily imperfect in this world, or asserted – as did Otto III, duke of Burgundy, in 1205 – that papal law against employing them in public office was an invasion of the secular sphere. Exponents of Christian brotherhood and utopia had harsh words for them because they profited from Jews. By allowing Jews to take usury from Christians, some said, the prince was the real usurer. Aquinas claimed that, even if they lost in doing so, princes should 'make Jews earn their living by working, as in Italy, rather than allow them to live idly enriched by usury'.[11] The idea appealed to

---

[11] *De regimine iudaeorum ad ducissam Brabantiae* 2 in *Opuscula philosophica divi Thomae Aquinatis* (ed. R.M. Spiazzi, Turin, 1954) 250a.

England's King Edward I, among others, and in 1275 he tried to abolish usury and open real property to Jews. But even where, as in parts of Italy, Jews were often artisans, so abrupt an economic dislocation and impoverishment of the well-to-do could not really be effected. James of Vitry thought that he knew the ideal when he urged Latins to emulate the Muslims:

> Saracens . . . hold [Jews] in greater hatred and contempt than do Christians. For while the detestable avarice of Christian princes supports them for material profit, permits them to have Christian servants and allows them to despoil their Christian subjects by immoderate usuries, they are allowed to live among the Saracens only when they work with their hands at the most abject and vile professions, are servants and slaves of the pagans and live in the lowest possible condition.[12]

When princes went over to the popular side, as they sometimes or eventually did, it was a bad day for Jews. Forwarding the canonization of Louis IX of France, the dead king's chaplain, William of Chartres (d. *circa* 1280), praised his hero:

> As hateful to God and man, Jews he so detested that he could not even see them, nor did he want to turn their property to his own use, saying that he did not want their poison and that he did not want them to exercise usury, but instead gain their livelihood in licit professions or commerce . . . When many of his councillors tried to persuade him to the contrary, asserting that the people could not live without loans, cultivate land or exercise professions or commerce, and that it was better that the Jews, who were already damned, should perform this damnable function than Christians who would, for this very reason, oppress the people with even heavier usuries, he answered as a Catholic, saying: 'Concerning the Christians and their usuries, that pertains to the prelates of the Church, but those of the Jews pertain to me, because they are under the yoke of my servitude . . . Let the Jews give up usury or leave my land!'[13]

Although Christian and Jew often lived at peace, Abelard knew how Jews felt and had his spokesman say: 'we are thought worthy of such contempt and hate by all that whoever injures us believes that action to be the highest justice and the greatest sacrifice to his God'. After sleepless nights, Jews arise and go fearfully among enemies, and even the princes 'who rule us and from whom we buy protection at such cost desire our deaths because it is then more permissible to seize our possessions'.[14] Social relations were always difficult. Jocelyn of Brakelonde's history of Abbot Samson of St Edmunds recorded that, in the late twelfth century, a sacristan of Bury St Edmunds:

> was called father and patron [by the Jews], who delighted in his guardianship, having free entry and egress, often going about the monastery by the altar and reliquary while solemn masses were being celebrated. They put their money in our

---

[12] *Historia orientalis* 82 (Douai, 1596) 160.

[13] *De vita et actibus . . . Ludovici noni* in *Historiae Francorum scriptores* (ed. François Duchesne, Paris, 1636) V 471.

[14] *Dialogus inter philosophum, Judaeum et Christianum* in *PL* CLXXVIII 1617.

treasury under the protection of the sacristan, and, even more absurd, their wives and children were received in our almshouse during wartime.[15]

There were times when relations were impossible. The fiscal and constitutional crisis shaking England's monarchy in the late thirteenth century prompted a round-up by the beleaguered monarch of Jews and others for economic 'crimes' such as coin clipping. In the period 1278–79, about 600 Jews were brought for trial to the Tower of London. Anywhere from 280 to 293 of them, just under ten per cent of all England's Jews, may have been executed!

Conversion and persecution

To judge from Abelard and Raymond Llull, even sympathetic Christians believed that the Jews were punished for the Saviour's fate. Asking whether a people must defend a person unjustly condemned, Peter Cantor answered that it was not that they had killed Christ, but rather that, as Augustine of Hippo had said, they had not tried to save him. Augustine wrote: 'The Jews sinned mortally in allowing Christ to be crucified because they blanched . . . when their numbers protected them. They could have rescued him.' And Peter concluded: 'Christ would not have been crucified had that people united to oppose it.'[16] As punishment, God made them a people without a prince, everywhere humiliated and oppressed. Having refused the Lord's 'my yoke is easy and my burden light' (Matthew 11:30), they were left bearing the heavy burden of an old law, one superstitious (taboos on food, menstrual blood, etc.) and materialist (circumcision *vs* baptism). Abelard's Jew says: 'the precepts of [our] law are so tangled with difficulties that we are crushed as intolerably by its yoke as by the oppression of other men. Who, for shame and pain, does not abhor or fear to receive this sacrament of our circumcision?'[17]

Although subordinate to religious and social themes, racist concepts reinforced this hostility. These abounded, and colour and appearance were much commented on. Blond, white and blue-eyed are the usual heroes and heroines of medieval literature. What appear like black Carthaginians made the final attack on the martyr Roland, and even so open a man as the raconteur Marco Polo, who was entranced by Chinese women, described black Africans as demonic looking. Caesarius of Heisterbach's book for novices in the Cistercian order several times refers to the Jewish 'stench', which, however, can be washed away by baptism.

---

[15] *Cronica Jocelini de Brakelonda de rebus gestis Samsonis, abbatis monasterii Sancti Edmundi* (London, 1951) 10.

[16] *Liber casuum conscientiae* No. 340 in *Summa de sacramentis et animae consiliis* III 2a (ed. J.-A. Duugauquier, Louvain and Lille, 1963) 417–18, and Augustine's *Enarratio in Psalmos* 81 4, carried in the *Glossa ordinaria*.

[17] *Dialogus inter philosophum, Judaeum et Christianum* in PL CLXXVIII 1618.

That Jews hated them was a common Christian suspicion, as was the notion that malevolent envy was a Jewish characteristic. New expressions of these ideas appeared during the Gregorian and crusading periods, when Europe's sense of Christian citizenship was strengthened. Around 1141 the story of the Christian boy, a holy innocent, murdered by the Jews makes its appearance. So popular was this fiction that, in 1181, Abbot Samson of St Edmunds managed to conjure up his own boy martyr. In 1255, England's justiciars said that the murder of Hugh of Lincoln – a fabrication – implicated all Jewry. Written for a king of a partially Jewish society whose forebears had been notably tolerant, the *Book of the Laws* of Alphonse X of Castile blandly noted that it was said that Jews crucified Christian boys on Good Friday.

Paralleling a desire for a more exact definition of civil and social status among Christians themselves, legislators and jurists separated Jews and Christians ever more sharply. Borrowing from late Roman and Visigothic legislation, the Church led in formulating this new law during the pontificates of Alexander III (d. 1181) and Innocent III, especially in the Lateran Council of 1215. The intention was partly protective: the Jews' right to keep faith and property was asserted by Calixtus II (d. 1124) and repeated by pope after pope. The anti-Jewish tale of the ritual murder of Christian boys was repeatedly attacked, especially by Innocent IV in 1247 and 1253. In Rome, where the pope was prince, each pontiff issued a constitution enshrining Jewish liberty on accession.

The other objective was to keep Jews in 'their place'. It was customary at Rome for them to exhibit their scrolls of the law during the pope's solemn parades, a custom also emulated by secular princes. Saluting the law, the pope observed aloud that the Jews, by not cleaving to Christ, had failed to obey it! The theme of Jewish servitude surfaced in a papal letter of 1205 reminding Alfonse VIII of Castile that, by appointing Jewish officers, he was putting the handmaid before the mistress. In the same year, Innocent III requested France's princes to repress the 'excesses' of the Jews, 'lest they presume to lift up their necks, submitted to the yoke of perpetual servitude, against the reverence due the Christian faith'. By 1215 a battery of laws prohibited relations between Jews and Christians, employment of Christian servants, building of new synagogues and holding public office. Imitating Islamic law on this point, they were also to be visible: 'Jews and Saracens of either sex . . . should wear clothing to distinguish them from Christians, and not go out in public on Easter'. In 1215, as has been seen, notorious Jewish moneylenders were required to restore usuries under pain of an 'indirect excommunication' designed to break commercial links between Jews and Christians, first mentioned in a papal letter of 1198.[18]

---

[18] The three canon law citations are *Liber extra* 6 6 13 and 5 6 14 in *CICan* II 776, and ibid. 5 9 12 and 18 in ibid. 814–16.

As missions rose in importance, Judaic texts were studied with greater care. Two years before his death in 1239, Gregory IX was enraged because the *Talmud* and rabbinical commentaries had passages hostile to Christianity. In 1240, a debate between Nicholas Donin, a convert to Christianity, and some rabbis took place at Paris before the queen mother. The latter were only permitted to answer charges against their faith and, two years later, several wagon-loads of their books were burned. Although, as his biographer Joinville tells us, Louis IX would have preferred to run the Jew through, he ordained in 1254 that they should cease from usury, blasphemy and sorcery and that their books should be burned. Even silence was held against them. Robert of Criklade (d. *circa* 1161), a Benedictine at Oxford, said that the ancient Josephus's silence about Christ was a Jewish plot to hide the evidence that condemned them.

In Catalonia–Aragon, Paul Christiani of Burgos, a converted Jew and Dominican, petitioned Clement IV against the *Talmud* and, in 1267, the pope requested the king to establish a commission. The commission 'corrected' but did not burn this and other Jewish texts because the missionary friar Raymond Martin said that they were useful for Christ's cause. A 'debate' took place in Gerona in 1263, one similar to that in Paris mentioned above. The intellectual quality of these events is indicated by the fact that the Jewish leader at Paris, Rabbi Jehiel, and his peer at Gerona, Nahmanides, fled to Palestine shortly after the exchanges. In 1242, furthermore, the crown of Aragon obliged its Jews and Muslims to hear Christian missions and, in 1263, gave preachers access to mosque and synagogue. Still, secular princes disliked exposing these profitable subjects to forced conversion during popular riots. In 1296, James II of Aragon limited access to Jewish quarters to preachers with retinues of no more than ten and prohibited the conversion of those under age. Ecclesiastical authority favoured preaching: in 1278 the popes granted the Dominicans the right to preach in all Lombard communities. Himself a missionary, Raymond Llull said that princes who forbade such preaching 'lest [their profitable] Jews and Saracens flee into other countries' preferred this world to 'God's honour and the salvation of their neighbours'. Knowledge of the other's beliefs, it seems, had increased the hostility of the two religions.

Anti-Jewish ideas influenced areas such as Germany where they had not been generalized before. Written sometime between 1215 and 1235, Eike of Repkow's law code, the *Saxon Mirror*, does not mention the conception of Jewish servitude, but the Swabian *Mirror* of 1274/5 speaks of it at length. Jews had usually been treated like Christian merchants in older law, but now things changed. Promulgated in 1265 by the archbishop of Mainz, the statutes of a group of rural lords and towns on the Rhine, Main and Lahn rivers stated that the peace must be upheld for all inhabitants, adding 'even for Jews'.[19]

---

[19] *MGH Constit.* II 612 No. 444.

Although protecting Jews against townsmen, Frederick II, outdoing the pope because he was at war with Rome, may have been the first to introduce the notion of Jewish servitude into imperial law. Confirming Vienna's liberties in 1237, he excluded Jews from holding public office 'since, from earliest times, imperial authority has proclaimed perpetual servitude to be the punishment of the Jewish crime'.[20] In Germany as elsewhere, however, secular law only reluctantly followed ecclesiastical. If churchmen derived Jewish servitude from Christ's death, secular law preferred another explanation for slavery's origin: they were defeated in war when the emperor Titus captured Jerusalem.

That Jewry law became ever more hostile is exemplified by the statutes of Avignon in the early fourteenth century. Jews were locked in the *Juzataria* on Christian holy days and not allowed outside when Christ's body was being paraded. No 'Jews or whores may dare touch fruit or bread exposed for sale; if they do, they must buy what they have touched'.[21] Race crime was revived. A passage on treason, adultery and arson in the English lawbook called *Fleta* included the following: 'Apostate Christians, witches and others of that kind are to be drawn and burned. Those cohabiting with Jews and Jewesses, those engaged in bestiality and sodomites are to be buried alive.'[22] A provincial council at Avignon in 1337 listed cohabitation with Jews, Muslims or beasts among the crimes that confessors could not absolve without episcopal consent.

Not surprisingly, living on the same street or in the same quarter of a town became more advisable, indeed obligatory, for Jews. This change was not radical because, except for the rich who liked more spacious places, ordinary folk had usually lived near their work and synagogue. Besides, Arabic society provided models for separate town and village quarters, which, if not common, were also known in western countries. Northern Spanish towns had French quarters with their own law, and Slavs and Germans rarely lived together. The French Jews invited to settle in Speyer by the prince archbishop in 1084 were delighted by the walled enclosure that he provided. German Jews settling the valleys of the Oder and Warta rivers were not offended by the insistence of a provincial council of Gniezno held in Breslau in 1267 that they live apart. Relations had nevertheless worsened. The fathers at Breslau expressly kept the Jews separate to preserve Christians from 'corruption'. Earlier in 1084, the bishop of Speyer had wanted them protected from the 'animal herd' of 'his' Christian subjects. Coercion made a quarter into a ghetto.

In the late thirteenth century, Jewish conditions varied widely. In Spain and other Mediterranean regions, notably its islands, they were protected

---

[20] *Historia diplomatica Friderici secundi* (ed. J.L.A. Huillard-Bréholles, Paris, 1852–62) V pt. I 57.

[21] *Coutumes et règlements de la république d'Avignon* (ed. M.A.R. de Maulde, Paris, 1879) 200 tit. 137.

[22] *Fleta* 1 35 in *Selden Society* LXXII (London, 1955) 90.

because they were one of several religious minorities, Muslim and sometimes Greek. In east Europe, where their economic services were much in demand, they were not only protected but also privileged. There, serfs were subject to particular lords but Jews, like nobles and some burghers, held of the prince alone. Eastern town law was sometimes beneficent. In 1297 the Brandenburger lord of the town of Stendal ordered that 'Jews shall enjoy the common law of the city and are to be treated by the [town councillors] like their own burghers'.[23] In England, France and north and central Italy, however, they were impoverished, as in Italy, or expelled, as from England in 1290 or royal France in 1306 and again in 1322. As expropriation pushed the Jews from central regions towards Europe's frontiers, the distinction between northern Jewry and that of the Mediterranean was further reinforced.

The slow deterioration of their position evoked varied reactions among Jews. One was rage, and hence, although the polemic of the two faiths was always crude, it plumbed new depths at this time. Compiled from earlier French sources, especially the work of Joseph the Zealot in the 1260s, the anonymous German *Nizzahon vetus* of around 1300 exemplifies this. The apostle Peter is there called Peter the Ass, a teaching not unknown among Christians, where Peter, who represented the active life and the Roman hierarchy, was sometimes portrayed as a bumbler in contrast to John, the apostle of contemplation, apocalyptic understanding and intellectualism. Few Christians, however, enjoyed the notion that Christ was a common criminal, the Hanged One, or the story of his illegitimacy from the whore Mary, referred to throughout as Haria, from the Aramaic 'ordure'. Not, again, that such was unheard of among Christians. According to the French jurist and publicist Peter Dubois, Boniface VIII, when dying, was urged to give his soul to the Virgin. He replied: 'Silence fool, I don't believe in that she-ass or her foal.'[24]

Bad in a Christian's mouth, this was unforgivable in a Jew's. As they learned how Jews doubted the Saviour, mocked the Virgin, the Trinity, etc., inquisitors not only went after the *Talmud* but all sorts of books. In his manual of 1323–24, Bernard Gui recommended destroying works by Rashi of Troyes, Maimonides and the rationalist polemist David Kimhi son of Joseph (*fl.* 1160–1235) of Narbonne. This deterioration led Spain's Jews to reverse their stand of the early twelfth century, and instead to praise Saladin for liberating Jerusalem in 1187, and Europe's community generally favoured Islam thereafter. The Jews also wanted to go 'home', to Palestine, the land from which they thought Rome had expelled them. Fleeing persecution, Nahmanides went to Jerusalem, finally settling in Acre where he died in 1267. He believed that the Messiah would come when the Jews returned home, and that the land would then bloom anew: 'nowhere in the world is a once good and

---

[23] Otto Gierke, *Das deutsche Genossenschaftsrecht* I (Berlin, 1861) 261.

[24] Text No. 34 in Etienne Baluze, *Vitae paparum Avenionensium* (ed. Mollat, Paris, 1917) III 162.

prosperous land now so desolate. Since we were exiled, it has accepted no nation or tongue, and, though all try to dwell in it, none succeed.'[25]

Defencelessness also inspired self-hatred. By failing to teach the law, making irreverent noise in synagogue and so on, said Isaac of Corbeil in 1277, the Jews had brought it on themselves:

> We must learn from the Christians who, although they have the wrong faith, stand silent in their houses of prayer . . . Our fathers have told us and our own eyes have seen that many synagogues have been destroyed or changed into churches because we did not treat them with due respect.[26]

A parish priest would have been struck dumb by this observation. According to Berthold of Regensburg's Lenten sermons, Christians really made noise, upsetting the elevation of the host with flirting and gaming.

Some Jews converted voluntarily, but their erstwhile community reacted strongly against them and helped those converted by force to escape. Because the converted not infrequently relapsed, laws for heretics were soon applied to them, and by 1271 inquisitors were charged with hunting them down. Around 1280, the law doctors of Pavia, Bologna and Ferrara recommended that those who aided or promoted an escape were liable to the death penalty. Those providing food or shelter were to be fined, exiled or excommunicated. So lively was this question that in 1278 Nicholas III reissued a Visigothic conciliar canon of 633 stating that 'Jews cannot be forcibly converted, but if they are however unwillingly, they must retain it . . . lest God's name be blasphemed'.[27] As the treatment accorded to the numerous new Christians in the kingdom of Naples shows, however, conversion was no easy answer. A royal decree of 1311 required the Jews to leave their quarters and integrate with Christians. Later legislation reversed this, ordering them to live apart because they might Judaize Christians. One suspects that, although names change easily, habits and economic functions do not, especially in a competitive economy.

Given this history, it seems strange that the often astute Roger Bacon lamented:

> an infinite number of Jews among us have perished because no one knew how to preach to them or to interpret the Scriptures in their tongue, or to dispute with them . . . O! ineffable loss of souls, when it would be so easy to convert innumerable Jews.[28]

---

[25] Arye Grabois, 'The Idea of Political Zionism in the 13th and early 14th Centuries' in *Festschrift Rëuben R. Hecht* (Jerusalem, 1959) 68.

[26] Güdemann, *Geschichte des Erziehungswesens* I 84–85.

[27] *Decretum* D 45 dictum ante c. 5 (Friedberg 2 161) and Canon 57 of the IV Council of Toledo.

[28] *Opus maius* 3 13 (ed. Bridges) III 120.

This Franciscan surely shared his fantasies with the people, but the poor in movements such as the Pastoureaux were impatient. Urged by material poverty and oncoming death, these humble eschatologists looked for signs of coming bliss and, if the Jews had to be converted to provide them, they would see to it that they were. Members of a tiny minority domiciled among a hostile majority whose solidarity was based on separatism, however, few Jews were willing converts. When threatened they rarely converted, and the consequent persecutions set in motion a rhythmic cycle of pogroms, expulsions and impoverishment that tormented late medieval Jewry. At one time Latin Crusaders had gone to fight unbelievers abroad; they now chased Jews around at home.

To conclude, toleration of Jews was rare, and the level of discourse even between intellectuals was rarely high. Thomas of Cantimpré, for example, claims that, in the 1250s, a nameless prelate and royal councillor persuaded the king of France not to burn Jewish books. For this God killed him with a sudden stomach 'flux'. The Dominican went on:

> Note, dear reader, that all oriental Jews think that Jews who, against Moses' law and the prophets, receive and copy the book called the *Talmud* are heretics and excommunicates. And nevertheless this archbishop of Christ's law had defended such books![29]

Cantimpré's barbarism was not shared by many Latin intellectuals. If northern European rabbis did not often read Maimonides's *Guide for the Perplexed* of 1190, Thomas Aquinas wrestled with it and the Dominican Neoplatonist Master Eckhart (d. before 1329) swore by it, and the authoritative rabbi Rashi of Troyes influenced biblical studies through the work of Nicholas of Lyra. Typically, the work of both authors had been condemned by the inquisitor Bernard Gui, but his opinion did not carry far.

---

[29] *Bonum universale de apibus* 1 36 in Paris National Library MS lat. 3585 5v.

Part Two

ECONOMY

Chapter 6

Foundation and growth

The land

Agriculture moved into high gear in the early twelfth century and continued expanding through the thirteenth century, accompanied by an improvement in traction, the spread of water- and windmills and the extension of the three-field system. The people of this age diffused a technology bequeathed to them by their fathers: only horses for ploughing and windmills were new.

Growth was especially marked on the frontiers from Spain to Slavdom. Partly settled earlier, central Spain's high plateaux were still filling up. The eastward push in Germany was resumed after the wars of the Gregorian age. Led or accompanied by Dutch and Flemings, Germans crossed the Saale and Elbe valleys, going toward Transylvania and the Tatra range. Settlement stood still in the Lusatias, central Brandenburg and Mecklenburg up to about 1200; then, to the north of Bohemia and Moravia, it moved forward through Pomerania, into Silesia and the north Vistula valley. Tidal marshes were drained along the North Sea and Baltic coasts. Although Holland and the Zuyder Zee were untouched by 1300, cultivation at the mouths of the Rhine, Meuse and Scheldt rivers had advanced at the expense of the sea almost as far as today. The monasteries were pioneers: over two-thirds of the Abbey of the Dunes' land at Hulst in the Scheldt estuary consisted of land reclaimed from the sea. River valleys were opened: the Milanese diked and cleared the central Po valley by about 1300. Clearing valleys both increased the culti-vated area and converted swampy streams into navigable rivers.

Although the Alps, Pyrenees and other mountains bordering the Mediter-ranean basin had important stands of timber, Europe's great forest lay to the north. There, bounded by Arctic seas and tundras and southern mountains and steppes, a vast wood extended from England into Russia. By 1300 the western reaches of this belt had been split into large segments. England's king claimed that the whole county of Essex lay within his forest. Partly cleared of trees, the region between the Rhine and Loire rivers, especially Flanders and Brabant, had become north Europe's most urbanized part, an early example of a sizeable inland urbanism not located on irrigated river valleys. This region was also the centre of the most widely spread national culture of this age, the French.

So well had nature endowed the northern plain that one wonders how the Mediterranean basin could equal it. The south's dry climate and light soils supported less cereal production, and land could not be used as intensively as up north, where a system of using two-thirds of the arable annually was commonly adopted. Northerners were also beginning to use horses for ploughing because, although they cost more than oxen, they were faster. Morocco, Lombardy and the Castilian plateaux were famous for horses, but only the damper northern soils could feed enough of them for agricultural use. Horses were not even much employed for transportation in the south, asses, supplemented by mules, being normal. Besides, except in favoured areas such as Lombardy and alluvial valleys in southern France, central Italy and Catalonia, nature's wealth enabled northern farmers to live in larger villages than those of the south.

Northern advantages were not fully realized, however, until modern times. Too many forests remained to be thinned, too many swamps to be drained. Intensive agriculture had only penetrated the alluvial soils of northern France and parts of western Germany. In England, the three-field system had spread only to heavy soils of the south and east and plough horses were not used everywhere. The Mediterranean held its own against the still underdeveloped north, moreover, partly because of geography. Northern transportation was chiefly overland, whereas the indented coasts of the Mediterranean's many peninsulas and islands offered cheap sea transportation. In addition, inadequacy of food storage and the need for dietary variety aided Mediterranean agriculture. The north depended on southern dried fruits, rice and sugar, and preservative spices came across the inland sea.

Mediterranean techniques were also highly developed. Dry soil irrigation was common in the Near East, Africa and Spain, where Valencia's canals were famous. Lacking summer moisture, Milan's upland plain was irrigated by the waters of the Ticino, brought about 40 miles in the canal called the Muzza built between 1179 and 1257. Ranching in the Mediterranean's savannahs produced horses, beef and wool. In Castile from the 1260s, the *Mesta*, an organization of landlords, shepherds and merchants, functioned under royal sponsorship. Forty years later its wool competed with England's and Burgundy's in both Tuscany and Flanders. Because its urban population was not heavy, the Mediterranean area still supplied its needs for agricultural products, with the exception of timber. Sicily and Apulia produced enough cereal to help feed northern Italy's mercantile and industrial towns, Apulia exporting nearly 690,000 bushels in good years during the early fourteenth century.

As markets grew, so did specialization. The Italian Salimbene was astonished to see that farmers around Auxerre in 1245 raised nothing but wine, exporting it to buy food. Although most regions produced some wine, the Bordelais, Poitou, Burgundy and the valleys of the Moselle and Rhine were famous by 1300. Regional specialities involved international relationships. Wine sold in Flanders came from the Rhineland, the Bordelais and Poitou. Although wool for the cloth manufactured in Flemish shops came partly from Flanders itself, England, Brabant, Burgundy and Spain also contributed. Woad, the blue dyestuff used there, came from the Rhineland and Picardy, and also, by 1300, from the Garonne valley from Agen to Toulouse. In short, England, Flanders and the Rhine and Garonne valleys had strong economic links, a reason for the struggle over Flanders between England and France.

Desiring to supply themselves, regions and towns favoured mixed production. Townsfolk often cultivated a field or two for vegetables or wine for the household, and the rich had substantial farms providing produce, storage facilities, summer recreation and countinghouses for rural usury. Agriculture was regulated. Around 1300, Mantua's magistrates tried to stabilize their county's 9,000 acres: 60 per cent in arable and pasture, 30 in vineyard and fruits and six in timber. Because the town could make do with its own, Messina's magistrates prohibited the importing of wine in 1272 and 1294.

Walter of Henley in the early thirteenth century, Robert Grosseteste (d. 1253), bishop of Lincoln, and the Bolognese lawyer Peter Crescenzi early in the fourteenth century wrote tracts on farming. Agronomy was still in its infancy: Crescenzi was mainly interested in law, his agronomy a bare epitome of the ancient Columella, and Grosseteste really wrote about household management. Even the practical Walter of Henley was mainly interested in estate management: plough horses he wrongly thought useless 'because the malice of ploughmen will never allow a team of horses to go faster than oxen'.[1]

Agriculture supported a substantial population. Loose estimates – all that are available – for the decades around 1300 indicate densities not materially surpassed until the agricultural and industrial revolutions of modern times. The area within modern France's frontiers may have contained around 20 million souls. Agriculturally rich, England supported around five million in 1300. Italy boasted about eight million, of which about two and a half were in the south and Sicily. Some heavy populations are seen. In 1281, the town and county of Padua contained about 90,000 souls, with about a third in the town. Town and country had about 100 per square mile, the countryside alone about 65. In 1255, the region of Pistoia supported about 114 people per square mile. Parts of Flanders surely surpassed these figures.

This population rested on a fragile base. Fertilization was primitive, crop alternation rare and metal tools in short supply, as was animal traction. Even in crowded Italy, a team of oxen could equal the value of a small farm. One

---

[1] *Le dite de Hosebonderie* (ed. Elizabeth Lamond, London, 1890) 10.

result was that yield per acre was often low. Cereal production on the lands of the bishop and chapter of Winchester, for example, was about five times higher around 1914 than in the thirteenth century. Still, modernity itself admitted wide variations, an acre in the Po valley producing about 26 bushels of grain around 1900, a sharp contrast with Sicily's 12. In 1879, the yield of grain per acre in the region around Mantua had no more than doubled since the thirteenth century. Around Marseilles in 1812, the return on seed grain planted over a ten-year period was about four and a half to five, only a trifle higher than that expected by the Hospitallers there 500 years earlier. Yield per acre, moreover, was not so important at the earlier time because farm-yard fowl, small beasts and garden crops plus the hunt weighed more in the balance than today. Nor was the need for exports as great, because the town population was relatively small.

A study of famines in western Germany and the Low Countries shows that, while the twelfth century suffered about five general crises, only local diffi-culties were experienced for a century after the hardships of 1215–16, them-selves alleviated by importing eastern German grain. Not that shortages did not strike. England underwent six years of them in this period, three of them falling together from 1257 to 1259 to make a famine. Difficulties aside, west Europe's climate was markedly benign through the thirteenth century, and food stocks increased until around 1300. French hospital regulations provided for meat three times a week and eggs or fish on other days. Workers building a bell tower at Bonlieu in Forez in 1300 were provided liberally with bread, beans for soup, eggs, cheese, meat and wine. The well-to-do canons at Maroeuil in Artois in 1244 received bread, three eggs and three herrings or a portion of salt meat daily.

Eating well, however, is not enough. In spite of spicing, salting and smok-ing, food storage was in its infancy. The cold wave of the early fourteenth century showed how much humanity could suffer from a reduction of food production for more than a year. Moreover, full stomachs do not alone determine health; medical care is also needed. Excepting minor cures, good diet and some surgery, medicine helped little until modern times. The death rate was high, especially among the lower classes. Statistics from Winchester indicate that in 1245 the life expectancy of a 20-year-old rural worker who had escaped the high mortality of childhood was 24 years. The age distribu-tion was also quite unlike today's. Although longevity was not rare, infants and children died like flies.

Population pressure became acute before 1300 and untilled land of good quality was rare. This threatened forests. In heavily settled north France during the thirteenth century, landlords protected their woods from overcut-ting and abrogated villagers' rights to pasture their beasts there. By 1300, the mountains around the Mediterranean were losing their forests. From Eng-land to Italy grain had been planted in marginal soils. Villages were bursting at the seams. In 1241, the inhabitants of Origgio near Milan cultivated 55 per cent of their land; by 1320, only 16 per cent was left untilled. The population of nine villages near Nice rose from 414 households in 1263 to 722 in 1315. Subdivision of farmland is seen at Weedon Beck (Northants) where the number of tenants rose from 81 to 110 between 1248 and 1300. Larger holdings also suffered, an inheritance of about 240 acres at Rozoy in the Ile de France being subdivided into 78 parcels. Excessive subdivision blocked rational use of the land and impeded the implementation of new technology. Government regulation grew apace in urbanized Italy, whose republics regulated labour, crops, contracts and marketing. Population pressure, paralleled by increasing litigiousness within communities, led to social troubles like the Pastoureaux of France and the rising of the 1280s in the Low Countries that foreshadowed the social wars of the fourteenth century.

Although agrarian growth was slowing, that population increased after a drop in the early fourteenth century until the disaster of the plague makes it probable that contemporaries were unaware of it. Their expectations were those of earlier ages. In addition, the turn of the century showed signs of continued progress. Germany continued to expand. Pomerania was settled in the thirteenth century, and heavy settlement in East Prussia and adjacent regions did not begin until after 1280. Opened to colonization in the late thirteenth century, by 1350 Silesia boasted around 1,500 new settlements. Rounding out also kept alive a feeling of growth, even in areas of older settlement (Figure 6.1 illustrates a mix of old and new planning styles). In northern France the twelfth century witnessed an enormous implantation of new villages. In the south, as emigration to Spain from the valleys of the Garonne and its confluents ceased, a new village movement got under way. From around 1230 until 1350, over 400 planned towns and villages were founded (for example, see Figure 6.2), though some failed to grow.

The town

The medieval town reached its apogee in the 1320s. It was not large, a population of 5,000 being substantial. Bigger towns existed even in northern Europe, however, especially in and around Flanders. A rather small area, this county had many towns with 10,000 or more souls. The population of Ghent may have reached 60,000, Bruges was possibly 35,000 and Ypres 15,000 to 20,000. Between the Rhine and Loire valleys and extending over the Channel to southern England there were other important towns. Cologne had perhaps 30,000 inhabitants. Set among modest towns and surrounded by rich plains, Paris may have reached 80,000 in 1328. Although, as in early modern times, wealthy England had no other large towns, London was a real metropolis, housing anywhere from 60,000 to 80,000. Using the poll taxes, London's share of England's wealth has been estimated at from three and a half per cent in 1307 to just over two in the famine year of 1315. Readers are reminded that all these figures are rough estimates.

Lombardy, Liguria, western Venetia, the Romagna and Tuscany probably constituted Latin Europe's most urbanized region. Venice's population reached about 90,000 in 1338 and Milan was almost the same magnitude, Genoa being somewhat smaller. The patriotic chronicler John Villani estimated Florence's population at 90,000 before the plague. Pisa had 50,000 in 1315. Like Flanders, what made Italy impressive were the many substantial towns in small areas (for example, see Figure 6.3). Other than Florence and Pisa, for example, Tuscany boasted four solid towns: Siena, Lucca, Pistoia and Arezzo. This contrasts with other Mediterranean regions where occasional large cities such as Naples and Palermo (50,000 inhabitants) and the metropolises of Alexandria and Constantinople focused economic life in spaces without other important centres.

A hub of communications and a manufacturing centre, a town's relations to the countryside were many faceted and included government, defence, education and transportation. Princes planted towns to 'build the region', as the founding charter of Jüterbog in Brandenburg said in 1174. At Leipzig in 1160, burghers immigrating to Posen were urged to acquire and exploit rural properties. Poland's grand duke valued towns so highly that in 1253 he gave Posen jurisdiction over seventeen nearby villages. When L'Aquila was founded in the Abruzzi around 1254, its episcopal prince provided 'that a city of one body be constructed from outlying villages and lands, which, as dispersed members . . . were unable to resist the attacks of our enemies by affording each other mutual aid'.[2]

Town and countryside were not rigorously separated in this period. Many town dwellers either worked the land or invested in it. In 1187/88 the wives of two landed notables divided an inheritance that included twenty-six contracts recording payments of interest or rents by free and dependent families in an area around Toulouse reaching nearly fifty kilometres from Isle-Jourdain in the west to Verfeil in the east. After 1250, almost two-thirds of the new loans by Jews to Christians in Perpignan were made to countryfolk and, in the late thirteenth century, Lombards lent money in rural France from Normandy to the Lorraines and Hainault to Dauphine. Even large cities were somewhat rural. Florence's industrial proletariat worked seasonally in the fields and nearly a third of the debts occasioned by the crash of the Peruzzi merchant bankers in Florence in 1347 were paid by selling landed property. Typical was the Champagne town of Provins, which in the early fourteenth century had a population of 8,000–10,000 in the town and eight villages outside. In a plebiscite, townsmen cast sixty-four per cent of the votes and

---

[2] Lousse, *Société d'ancien régime* 208–09.

villagers thirty-six; about a third were in textile industries and nearly a fifth in agriculture.

If towns were somewhat rural, villages were somewhat urban. Mining was a village industry, as was woodwork for export. Besides, restrictions imposed by artisan guilds could impede urban industry, driving new processes into the less organized countryside. In the thirteenth century Flanders' export woollens were manufactured not only in cities but also in small centres like Dixmuiden and Poperinghe. Combined with geography, technology sometimes even benefited villages more than towns. In the late twelfth century the introduction of water mills into England weakened urban fulling, moving it to Yorkshire and Wales, areas with ample waterpower. Castelfigline near Florence boasted a guild of tailors, and in 1350 Fabriano in the March of Ancona was famed for quality paper. Villagers sometimes made fortunes acting as part-time moneylenders and merchants, as members of merchant guilds in England's towns. Around 1180, the lord obliged the tavern keepers of Ferrières in the Gâtinais to shut their shops during his 'banal' wine sale because they were brokers for foreign buyers.

Nevertheless, innovation was more frequent in town because, living at a communications hub, townsfolk were in contact with other areas and heard of their inventions earlier. Townsfolk were more informed and talkative than rustics and lived more interesting lives. In 1202, when the burghers of Tournus in Burgundy requested the abolition of the marriage tax (*formariage*), they did so 'because it appeared infamous and strange to foreigners'.[3] The countryside was invaded by town moneylenders, lawyers and notaries; in spite of rural monasteries, the clergy was concentrated more heavily in town; and secular government also had its seat there. Most tournaments, litigation, festivals, clerical synods and so on were held in or near towns. When nobles inhabited villages – and they often moved to town in wintertime – their horizons were broad because they travelled. Chivalry's poet, Christian of Troyes, introduced Erec and Enide at a duel in a bourg, and had them complete their ascension to royal crowns in a city.

Townsfolk battled countryfolk, each seeking maximum gain. In urbanized Italy and Flanders towns victoriously reduced the countryside to subservience, but elsewhere they did not. A vexing question was that of tolls on bridges, rivers and overland routes. Often designed to fund transport facilities, tolls were rarely voluntarily abolished and easily multiplied in this decentralized society. Those along the Rhine increased from about 19 in 1200 to about 54 in 1300. The urban desire for untrammelled trade is only one side of the picture, because, just as did rural lords, towns imposed their tolls. Besides, tolls siphoned off profits from interregional commerce to advance

---

[3] Duby, *La société aux XIe et XIIe siècles dans la région Mâconnais* 400.

local interests and, inadvertently, protected local industries and even independence. The consuls of Toulouse waged war against twenty-three lordships
and communities from 1202 to 1204. They fought not only to abolish tolls,
but also to subject the villages and small towns, to open them to exploitation. Italy's urban republics did the same, as well as seeking to make sure
that the 'county' provisioned the town cheaply.

Such conflicts should not be overemphasized, because economic growth
cushioned rivalries, expanding areas of mutual interest. If town moneylenders hurt villagers, they also aided their search for freedom from their
lords. Moreover, this was no simple struggle between town and countryside
because great cities, modest towns, villages and hamlets had differing interests. By 1300, commercial growth and the revival of the centralized state had
created a pattern of expanding capitals, while middling towns stabilized or
shrank, villages amalgamated and small hamlets withered.

Friction also existed between areas of heavy urban development and
those of light. Sometime after 1200 most north Italian towns were forced to
regulate grain supply, and by 1300 most of them had permanent bureaux
fixing prices and distributing grain. Siena's bureau dates from the early
thirteenth century and precedes by about fifty years the first such agency in
Flanders' Ghent. In 1261, 2,200 tons of Sicilian grain entered the port of Genoa
alone. By the early fourteenth century, a grain merchant opined that her
'county' could feed Florence for only five months of the year and, in 1320,
the republic owed the Acciajuoli firm 40,000 gold florins for Sicilian grain.
The Hohenstaufen and Angevin wars saw a radical change in the relationship of south to north Italy. In the late twelfth century, Apulia–Sicily was
an active maritime power; some of her industries, such as silk, were widely
reputed; and her state was the grandest in Italy. By 1300, all had changed.
Sicily and Naples had been divided between the Catalans and the French,
and the sea had been wholly lost to the northerners. Luccan and Florentine
silk was better known than that of Palermo, and northern townsfolk ate
Sicilian and Apulian grain and meat.

It comes as a shock to realize just how small the largest towns were. No
western city in 1300 came near the size of ancient Rome (from 300,000 to
1 million). In ancient and medieval times, furthermore, both the Near East
and China boasted centres with perhaps as many as a million inhabitants.
Technology's relationship to geography plays a role here. Ancient and medieval alike, great cities were either seaports or located in irrigated valleys like
the Nile, and the inadequacy of overland transportation prevented their rise
in inland areas until the age of the railroad. Still, neither geography nor
technology explains the smallness of the medieval town. In 1300, Venice
and Bruges were great ports, but neither equalled ancient Rome.

Another comparison is useful here. In 1500, Paris was over three times as
large as it had been in 1300, yet France's overall population was probably

smaller. This ability to support larger urbanism was not primarily caused by technological progress. Although Atlantic traffic had increased, carting was more common and canals had just begun to supplement medieval river routes, basic techniques were not greatly advanced. Innovations such as gunpowder and printing were not related to living standards, and the improved sailing vessels that were eventually to change it had little effect as yet. It is likely, in fact, that the Frenchman of 1500 lived scarcely any better than had his forefather of 1300.

The inventions mentioned above announce a change, however. They were all connected with warfare and the growth of government. The existence of a great state also explains why the Romans had been able to maintain huge cities in spite of their backward technology. Expanding states and the concomitant concentration and mobilization of resources and manpower were what made the great city of modern times possible, and their absence wholly explains the small size of the medieval town.

Industry and commerce

At its peak around 1300, European manufacturing was especially devoted to textiles, and this remained true until late in modern times. Wool cloth was the biggest export commodity and linen came second. In 1313, 92,500 seals were stamped in the town of Ypres to be affixed to bolts of woollen cloth. Initially importing cotton from Syria, a cottons industry began in central Italy in the early fourteenth century. To these export industries may be added leather and furs. Something like heavy industry also existed. With around 30,000 inhabitants, Toulouse produced 1,000 mail coats, 3,000 gorgets, 3,000 helmets and 600 crossbows for the crown in 1295. In the mid-fourteenth century, Ghent boasted about 5,200 weavers and fullers out of a population of around 60,000. In 1292 Paris, a capital and consumer-centred city, had about 130 regulated professions divisible into the following categories:

27 per cent in clothing and personal furnishings
17 per cent in metallurgy
17 per cent in textiles and leather goods
14 per cent in food and consumptibles such as firewood
8 per cent in furniture
4 per cent in building and related arts
2 per cent in medicine and sanitation
2 per cent in banking, brokerage, bookmaking and the public baths.

The smaller town of Poitiers registered only nineteen guilds in the early fourteenth century. Represented by three organizations, riding equipment and harnesses constituted the most developed industry. There were also ropemakers, locksmiths and tinsmiths. Four guilds prepared leather goods and textiles. No fewer than six sold foodstuffs and fuel, to which may be added two guilds of publicans and innkeepers. Doubling as bankers or moneylenders, goldsmiths led the financial life of the town.

Substantial industry required a lively commerce in basic commodities. In some years around 1300, England exported up to 15 million pounds of raw wool, and a year's export of about 25 million gallons of wine from the Garonne valley was recorded. French wine went everywhere. In 1229 it found a market in Saracen Tunis (!), and in 1291 quantities were shipped to the Genoese towns on the Black Sea. Exotic commodities were moved in bulk. Preparing for a wake, a princely family bought from a Hanseatic merchant at Stockholm in 1328 one and a half pounds of saffron, 12 pounds of caraway, 90 pounds of almonds, 105 pounds of rice and four of sugar, all from the Mediterranean, especially Spain and Italy. Asia contributed four and three-quarter pounds of ginger, a pound of cinnamon and three pounds of galingale, while Africa provided half a pound of grains of paradise, good for hot toddies. The shopping list included three large barrels of wine, one from the Rhine and two from Bordeaux. Having sourly described the mock grief of his Italian compatriots at funerals, Boncompagno of Signa remarked that Englishmen and other northerners 'mix drink with their tears until they're drunk, and thus are consoled by being happier than usual'.[4]

Growing commerce sparked improvements in transportation. Mediterranean sailors adopted northern Europe's rudder and square sail in the late twelfth century, and Alexander Neckham mentioned the navigational use of the compass by 1187. Portolani sea guides accurately 'mapped' the Mediterranean coast. Point-to-point sailing was frequent in that sea, but, as was true until very recently, most shipping hugged the coast. Until the great galleys of the fourteenth century, ships were small, although the Italian marine boasted a ship (*nave*) 110 feet long with a cargo capacity of 630 tonnes. Contact by sea between the Baltic and North Sea area and the Mediterranean was sporadic in the twelfth century. Exemplifying Italy's rise, her mariners first voyaged to northern waters in 1277, and by about 1314 regular sailings to Flanders and England from Genoa and Venice were scheduled. Along with this, Italians began to take service in Spain and France and hence diffused Mediterranean maritime law and lore.

Inland transportation was partly based on rivers, especially downstream; with exceptions such as Milan and Florence, few inland cities not on navigable rivers grew large. France's major inland towns were all blessed with navigable rivers – Paris, Rouen, Orléans, Lyons and Toulouse. Farmers around Auxerre shipped wine to Paris via the Seine, and those just north of Toulouse

---

[4] *Boncompagnus Boncampagni* in *BuF* I 141–42.

used the Garonne to get their wine, wool and woad into the Atlantic market. German rivers flow from south to north and, when combined with the Baltic Sea, drew eastward-moving immigrants to the north. The indifference of Germans in these regions to the affairs of the Empire on the Rhine and in Italy was partly caused by this geography.

Medieval roads were rarely paved, save in town where there was heavy pedestrian traffic. This remained true of Europe until very recently, a primary reason being the use of horses and asses, whose hooves need no paving. The thirteenth century witnessed a growing use of cartage, the four-wheeled wagon with pivoted front axle supplementing the two-wheeled cart from about 1250. Cartage, however, had a long way to go. Even the famous Septimer pass in the Alps was unsuitable for carts until after the mid-fourteenth century. Year-round cartage in some areas, nevertheless, had already resulted in planking or paving muddy stretches. The highway between Florence and Pisa was paved in 1286, and embanked to avoid spring floods. An engineering feat was the opening of the St Gotthard pass in the Alps in 1237, a route soon eased by a stone bridge. Villages, towns and princes legislated concerning roads, even providing for shade trees. Bridges were often financed by ecclesiastical institutions; builders sometimes formed temporary fraternities and, as 'pious places' in canon law, received donations in private testaments. Used for maintenance, bridge tolls also often supported hospitals associated with and sometimes built on them.

Overland transport had improved enough since antiquity to make the urbanization of west Europe's inland reaches possible. In Roman times overland bulk haulage doubled the price every hundred miles; in the thirteenth century, loose figures estimate the increase to have been about a third. Shipping naturally remained cheaper. In 1283, for example, the San Niccolo carried grain from Sicily to Pisa, increasing the original price at only about eight per cent per hundred miles. Transport and travel were nevertheless relatively slow. Ten miles a day was common for pack trains and 18–20 miles for mounted parties. In season, the length of the Mediterranean could be traversed in one to two months. These estimates do not illustrate maximum speed. Heavy specie was brought from York to the army at Stirling in Scotland in the summer of 1304 in two carts, each pulled by five horses, in seven days, over 30 miles a day. A galley is said to have gone from Pisa to Sardinia averaging a hundred miles per day in 1313. Around 1300 overland couriers of Tuscan merchant-banking firms counted five days from Avignon to Paris, eight to Bruges, 13 to Venice and ten to Valencia. In short, all of Europe could be informed of an event in about a month.

Transport and travel were seasonal. On unpaved roads, what could be carted in summer had to be sledded in winter. Storms all but shut the North and Baltic seas for three months yearly. The Mediterranean was easier: Marino Sanuto, a Venetian senator, thought of stationing a squadron off Alexandria to intercept that port's year-round commerce. Venetian statutes in 1284 nevertheless forbade the state convoys sailing from December 1 to March 1. Commerce generally slowed during the winter, and this rhythm was also reflected in regional fairs: Toulouse's ran from mid-Lent to early December. Even the fairs of Champagne and Brie, where the Lombards met the rest of Europe's merchants to exchange commodities and thrash out a primitive balance of payments, submitted to the same rule. The fairs successively held in Troyes, Provins, Bar on the Aube and Lagny on the Marne petered out from November to January. Only commercial centres like Genoa and Venice were active year round, though even there the tempo slowed.

Planning, building and living standards

Most homes and workshops were humble and small, rarely over two storeys, and usually not made of stone. In timber-rich regions they were built of wood or wood and stucco, often being roofed with straw. Brick and adobe were common in the Mediterranean. What first struck the eye, however, were a town's towers and spires. Monuments of jealously guarded independence, town and village walls cost heavily. Monumental stone or brick architecture was another huge investment, most of the major western churches having been built by the early fourteenth century. By then Toulouse, a town of around 30,000, boasted five great churches, one the size of Chartres, not to speak of many less significant monuments. So decorated were these communities that King Henry II of England (d. 1189), witnessing the burning of his natal city of LeMans, cried out that, since God had stolen from him the place he loved most in the world, 'I'll pay you back as much as I can by taking from you what you most love in me!' – namely, his soul.[5]

Building exalted the arts. John Pisano and Giotto were architects and also painters and sculptors. Virtuosity was rewarded: a master mason of Bologna was acclaimed a 'noble and famous architect' in 1234 and a Florentine who undermined the walls of Poggibonsi in 1220 was exempted from taxes. When Orvieto employed Lawrence Maitanis in 1310, it gave him 12 gold florins annually, the right to have apprentices, citizenship for self and family, 15 years' exemption from military service and taxes, and a noble's right to bear arms. Art had been assimilated to letters in Italian towns, because Maitanis's privileges were those granted professors of the liberal arts. A contract in 1294 provided that the apprentice residing with a Florentine master painter would 'zealously perform whatever the said master ordered him to do in the theory or practice of the said art'.[6]

---

[5] Gerald of Wales, *De principis instructione* 3 24 in *Rolls Series* XXI iii 283.
[6] Published in Braunfels, *Die Staatsbaukunst in der Toskana* 225.

Specialization did not prevent disaster. The choir of Beauvais Cathedral collapsed in 1284. It rose to a height of 150 feet, the world's highest hall until steel construction, and took nearly 40 years to rebuild. Building was often slow, but rapid work was not unusual. Richard Coeur de Lion constructed Gaillard des Andeleys in just over a year in 1197–98. Even though the castle fell in 1204, it justified his boast: 'By God's throat, if that castle were built of butter and not of iron and stone, it would defend me against [the king of France] and all his power.'[7] In 1159 the Genoese built a wall of 5,520 feet including four towers in 53 days.

Village and town statutes accented cleanliness and orderliness in the disposition of rainwater, garbage and ordure. Slaughterhouses and some industries were either placed outside town or downstream. San Gimignano had two street sweepers for each quarter. Public service was owed by property holders, and duties in town and country differed. The custom of Milan in 1216 obliged rustics to maintain public roads, irrigation canals and the like; townsfolk were to busy themselves paving, illuminating streets and digging cesspools. Impure air, it was thought, induced illness: in 1237 the *podestà* ordered all Florence's streets paved to be 'cleaner, more beautiful and healthier'. Similar motives inspired Philip Augustus for Paris in 1198, though with few immediate results. In Siena the first street map for planning purposes is heard of in 1218, and the first building code was dated 1262. Like the law on highroads, this legislation was modelled on Roman law but grew to surpass its model, determining the width of streets, uniformity of facades, etc. Old laws destroying buildings as punishment for crime were questioned. Urging that 'so noble a city should not be deformed by ruins, especially since men and not property have sinned', the count of Toulouse petitioned Pope Gregory IX to have the law rescinded anent condemned heretics, but was refused in 1236.[8] A more enlightened Luccan statute of 1309 read: 'Lucca's appearance should not be deformed by the destruction of houses and towers.'[9]

Social class affected town planning. In Tuscany, for example, Ghibellines were lukewarm about it, being satisfied with their own commodious townhouses, of which the towers of San Gimignano are reminders. Because humbler folk passed more time in the streets, the popular, or Guelph, party busied itself enlarging public squares and ecclesiastical and public buildings. Men of this political complexion also wrote books praising their cities, an example being that by the schoolteacher Bonvesino of Riva about Milan in 1288.

In old communities planning was limited to ameliorating existing centres, but new ones and enlargements were formally laid out. In the new city added to Hildesheim in 1216–20, the rectangular street grid contrasts sharply

---

[7] Gerald of Wales, *De principis instructione* in *Rolls Series* XXI viii 290.

[8] *Register* II 1245 No. 4758.

[9] Braunfels, *Staatsbaukunst in der Toskana* 45.

Figure 6.1 Aachen, like most medieval towns, was fitted to its geography. The central rectangle is the Carolingian 'palatium'. Striped parts show built-up areas which, nucleated by a twelfth-century wall enclosing c. 50 ha., grew natural tentacles as seen in the 175 ha. enclosed by the second wall of 1300–1350. François L. Ganshof, *Etude sur le développement des villes entre Loire et Rhin au moyen âge* (Paris and Brussels, 1943), Map No. 2.

with the often unplanned older town. The most popular plan was the simple rectangular or square grid, often adapted to an irregular exterior wall for reasons of defence, as in Neubrandenburg in 1248. Roman planning favoured hexagonal or octagonal circumferences for defence, and this is seen in not a few gridded centres, for example the lower town added to Carcassonne in 1247. Planned cities took time: Aigues Mortes was begun in 1244 but its walls were still being built in the 1270s. In 1290, when the king and the Cistercians planned Grenade on the Garonne (named after Spain's Grenada), the fortifications were laid out, the layout gridded and places set aside for a central market, church and public hospital.

Figure 6.2 Florence exemplifies remnant ancient Roman planning. Note also the dots showing the many houses with towers by the end of the fourteenth century. Sketched from the map in Leonardo Benevolo, *Storia dalla cittá* (Rome, 1975), 439.

Town planning was not a profession. The sculptor John Pisano served as town planner in Siena and Pisa. Clergy, knights, notaries and simple burghers directing settlement in east Germany planned towns and villages and published customary laws. Nor was there a distinction between village and town. Although jurists distinguished between cities housing episcopal sees (*civitates*), towns or villages (*ville*) and fortified villages (*castella*), *villa* was also a generic term describing any community, big or small. Further-more, since settlers wanted urban amenities, founders preferred to advertise towns (*ville* and *burgi*) and accorded them urban privileges; in east Germany and Poland, some were even grandly called *civitates*. Many a new town in hilly Cornwall was smaller and had fewer conveniences than old villages in the rich plains of East Anglia. An example of this planning is Revel, near Carcassonne. Founded in 1342, this gridded and hexagonal little town was to have public mills, a prison and a square, arched and colonnaded, on which the town hall was to be located.

Planning gave attention to public health. In the early fourteenth century, Lucca published a statute book of sanitary regulations, and village custumals

Figure 6.3(a) Pruno in the Apennines near Lucca, a hilltop shoulder village first seen in a charter of 804. Its parish church is the hall that overlooks the valley near the tower. Eduardo Detti, 'Urbanistica medievale minore, 2', *Critica d'Arte* (1958) fasc. 25–6, pp. 74–5.

Figure 6.3(b) Revel, a 'bastide' (small town or village), founded and chartered in 1342 and settled by 1345, to the north-west of Carcassonne, with a planned colonnaded market square and a church in a marginal square to the south; the terrain was 'centuriated' both within and without the walls. Reproduction from Dillon's map of the Canal du Midi of 1771, published in Gustave Doumerc, *Histoire de Revel en Lauragais* (Toulouse, no date), facing p. 128.

Figure 6.4 Carcassonne, showing the contrasting types of layout extant in 1300. To the right, the late Roman hilltop Old City housing the cathedral fitted to the site for defence, re-fortified by 1300 (restored 1855–79), mapped in 1866. On the left, the new town ('bastide') founded in 1247 to the west across the Aude River. Formal planning with hexagonal fortifications, mapped in 1729. A. Mahul, *Cartulaire et archives des communes de l'ancienne diocèse et de l'arondissement administratif de Carcassonne* (6 volumes in 7, Paris 1857–82), 5 (1859) facing p. 716 and 6.2 (1871) preceding p. 1. Photograph inset of showing relationship of Old City to the new town, *Atlas aérien de la France* 3, Fig. 112.

Figure 6.5 Hildesheim in Saxony illustrates typical urban facilities and a characteristic mixture of old layout and new planning styles in a given community. Map adapted from Jürgen Köppke, *Hildesheim, Einbeck, Göttingen und ihre Stadtmark im Mittelalter* (Hildesheim, 1967). Its divisions and monuments are:

A. The Old City. Walling from 1167; 'Universitas civium' 1171, seal 1217, 'consules' 1236. Size and population c. 60 ha and c. 6,000 in 1450.

B. The New City first seen in a document of 1221. Covering c. 20 ha and 2,000 inhabitants in 1450, it was joined to Old City in 1583.

C and D. The Bruelh and Damm suburbs unfortified in 1300.

1. The cathedral founded in 814 and its bourg fortified c. 1000.
2. The Old Market, the original ribbon village.
3. Jews' Street and synagogue. 28 households in 1386, expelled in 1457.
4. Two Benedictine cloisters and two of canons dating from c. 1000 to 1133.
5. The Dominicans, Franciscans and Magdalene Sisters' cloister from 1220 to 1235.
6. Beguinages from c. 1200 on.
7. Parish churches starting with St Andrew's in the eleventh century to 1333.
8. Three hospitals and a leper house from 1133 to 1320.
9. Town halls in the Old City and the New City.
10. The ravenstone for displaying the bodies of executed criminals.

often included similar provisions. Public bathing was part of this: twenty-six bath-houses were listed in the tallage of Paris in 1292. As important was the attack on sickness, old age and burial costs. Revel's planners did not neglect charity: 'The consuls and university of the said town may construct ... two houses of piety [hospitals] in suitable places wherever they see fit, each containing a half arpent of land in which the poor of Christ shall be received.'[10] Protected by canon law, hospitals were diverse in organization, some being attached to monasteries or cathedral chapters and others being private or municipal. Leper houses and private old folk's homes were often self-governing. Although military, the Hospitallers and Teutonic Knights were famed for hospitals, and even the Templars housed pensioners (corrodians). The Trinitarians, founded in 1198, devoted a third of their budget to repurchasing captives from the Saracens and the rest to hospitals. A papal bull of 1291 listed 99 Trinitarian Holy Ghost hospitals. Centred on the Mediterranean, 43 of these were in north and central Italy and 17 in the south, a similar number in south France and Spain, and only 22 elsewhere.

Save for leproseries, hospitals did not usually specialize, although some did, such as Metz's maternity hospital of the early fourteenth century. Characteristic of many, however, is St Catherine's in Esslingen in 1232, where the poor, passing strangers, needy women in labour, orphans and sick were received. Many hospitals for the aged were small, housing the apostolic number of thirteen inmates. Some were larger: Strasbourg's St Leonhard's had fifty prebends for the aged, besides offering other services. Nürnberg's Holy Ghost housed about 250 patients in 1341. Towns sometimes had considerable facilities. With a population of fewer than 30,000 in 1262, Toulouse had seven leper houses and fourteen or fifteen hospitals. One hospital contained fifty-six beds, another was surely larger, but most housed a dozen or so aged folk. Villages were not far behind. In 1210, Isle Jourdain near Toulouse possessed two small hospitals and a leper house. Larger Jewish communities also had hospitals, one in Regensburg in 1210, for example, and another in Cologne.

Given the state of medical knowledge – in 1308, suddenly taken ill, Albert I of Habsburg was hung up by his feet! – care consisted of rest, bathing and wholesome diet. Roger of Molins's Hospitaller statutes proposed in 1181 that pork or mutton was to be served three days a week, with chicken for those dieting. Diagnosis was provided by lay doctors: Molin's rules stated that a doctor 'who knows the quality of excrements, the diversity of the sick and can administer the remedy of medicines should be hired in each hospital'.[11] Private help was supplemented by the state: in Milan around 1300 town

---

[10] J. Ramière de Fortanier, *Chartes des franchises de Lauragais* (Paris, 1939) 576.
[11] Léon Le Grand, *Statuts d'hôtels-Dieu et de leproséries* (Paris, 1901) No. 1, 12.

doctors were paid to give care to the poor. Hospital staffs of clerical and nursing personnel often formed chapters with voting rights. In 1220 the Hôtel Dieu of Paris was staffed by four priests, four other clerks, twenty-five sisters and thirty lay brothers. Ideally, hospital staffs treated the sick and poor as Christ. The Hospitallers called their patients 'sick lords' and the statutes of the hospital of Aubrac in 1162 told its staff to 'take care that . . . the poor always precede as lords, while you follow as serfs'.[12]

Hospitals and religious houses also provided services to young and old oblates. At Toulouse, those wanting care and residence when sick or old acquired retirement plans: in 1233 a man entered the hospital as a permanent resident, receiving bread and water as a brother. He was to be kept 'well dressed and shod, including Stamford cloth, and equipped with breeches and shirts in summer and winter' for life.[13] A cutler, presumably sick, retired into the hospital in 1242, leaving two houses and other property to his heir, a minor son. Under the guardianship of fellow craft members, the boy was to reside at the hospital for ten years to be educated in letters. The estate was to pay for teachers, books and clothing, and a hundred shillings if the young heir ceased study or left the order at the term's expiration. So extensive a system explains why Raymond Llull mistakenly crowed in 1308 that 'Christians build hospitals to receive the poor, the sick and travellers, and have one, two or even three in each city, but I never heard that Saracens have more than two hospitals, one at Tunis and the other at Alexandria'.[14]

Expanding economies brought a better standard of living. Economic growth, however, is rarely uniform among social classes, and criticisms of new wealth abounded around 1200, the commonplace being that gold dictates every-thing. Writing in the 1220s, the biographer of William the Marshal of England contrasted the spartan beginnings of his champion – he travelled with two servants! – with the luxury of the lowest squire of his own times, voyaging with a pack animal laden with clothing and creature comforts. Tears as big as crocodile eggs ran down Prior Geoffrey of Vigeois's face when he asserted around 1184 that:

> our barons used to wear common cloth, so that the [bishop] and the viscount . . . when travelling wore lamb skins and fox furs that an artisan would be ashamed to wear today. Since then, rich vestments of divers colours have been invented, strangely cut in spherical figures with little pendant tails and tassels . . . Now boots, once rare and reserved for gentlefolk, are worn by anybody. Once, men shaved their heads and grew beards; now peasants and workers grow long hair and shave their beards.

---

[12] Ibid. 17.

[13] My 'Charity and Social Work in Toulouse' in *Traditio* XXII (1966) 263–64n.

[14] *Disputatio Raymundi christiani et Hamar saraceni* 2 25 in *Beati Raymundi Lulli opera* IV (Mainz, 1729, rprt.) 474b–75a.

As Merlin remarked, the walk of women has come to resemble a serpent's undulations because of the mad length of their trains . . . Cloth and furs cost twice what they used because nowadays humble folk wear clothing suited to the greatest lords of past times. [In contrast] the old-timers daily found something left on their tables with which to nourish the numerous poor . . . Today, these onetime hosts of the castles are often obliged to go about begging themselves.[15]

Both the poor and the old rich found a common enemy in the new rich, and the *nouveaux* were often townsmen. Around 1200, John of Flagy's romance *Hervi* records the marriage of the daughter of a duke of Lorraine – the father had silenced her plaints lest he lose his debt-ridden lands – to a rich bourgeois of Metz. The author saw to it that the issue of this union had nothing to do with trade but preferred hunting, fighting and love, as became a gentleman.

The people of the recent past had experienced periods of economic crisis. From the 1170s through to the mid-1220s the economy faltered, with the usual accompaniment of wars and shortages. After 1250 a series of difficulties culminated in a downturn from 1278 to 1285. Surely related to a change in climate, renewed and severe troubles appeared just before 1300 and were not exorcized until 1319. These setbacks, however, were repaired and nobody could have dreamed what the disasters of the 1340s would bring. All over Europe new village emplacements and town walls were planned to absorb the projected population increase. Experience had misled the planners, however: those walls were not filled until the eighteenth century.

It was also hard to judge: what seemed decline was sometimes growth. An instance is the rapid withering of the fairs of Champagne and Brie during the early fourteenth century. Although hurt by the French wars in Flanders, these fairs mainly failed because of economic growth. The meeting place for Europe's two main urban areas – that centred in Flanders, and that in north Italy – the Champagne was admirably located as long as the main commercial route was the Rhone valley. As seen above, however, the sea route between Italy and Flanders came into use in the late thirteenth century and new Alpine passes also multiplied routes from Germany to Italy. Once Italian merchants visited the Champagne, but by 1300 they were residing permanently in all important northern cities, including Paris, a town that absorbed much Champagne business. The decline of the fairs of Champagne and Brie, in fine, was really a sign of economic maturity.

---

[15] *Chronique* I 73 in *Recueil des historiens des Gaules et de la France* XII 450.

Chapter 7

Organization

Rural enterprise

The manor, or great farm, required a balance of labour and land. Excluding forests, pastures and commons, a manor's territory was divided into strips or fields assigned the demesne, and those held by tenants (*see* Figures 7.1 and 7.2). The demesne was the main farm, and those who worked it were the landlord's 'family', a household ranging from gentlemen agents to servile domestics, and the tenants, free or servile, paid by land allotted to them by the lord in return for labour on the demesne. In Bavaria, a typical lord assigned tenants three or four times more land than he retained in demesne. Even great manors were rarely self-sufficient. Many essential commodities – salt, metalware, millstones, stock animals, etc. – were imported. Autarchic landlords disliked buying commodities from outside, but enjoyed selling. In the thirteenth century, Glastonbury, Peterborough, Ramsey and other large English monasteries pushed the export of wool and grains. The farmers of Ramsey Abbey near Ely performed carting services as far south as London and Canterbury.

The great farm was not universal in Europe, and manors always varied widely in size. Those englobing whole villages were few, even in the parts of Germany or England famed for manorial exploitation. Over half the villages of Leicestershire contained more than one manor, and one had as many as five. Besides, small farms always existed, and much of Europe's geography was inimical to the community farming of the manorial system. Mediterranean dry soils did not require the heavy ploughs and community traction was needed on the rich but heavy northern soils. Although large estates with dependent farmers existed in the south, open fields were rarer than in the north and demesne less important for landlords. Mountainous and hilly areas, broken terrain and recently drained areas favoured independent more than community farming. Certain types of crops – dyestuffs, wine and olives – did not lend themselves to manorial farming.

For many reasons, some discussed below, the great farm was undoubtedly declining. In Bavaria, monastic and seigniorial demesnes were breaking up into a number of smaller units rented to lesser knights or estate bailiffs, some of whose farms were substantial. A second stage occurred during the later

Figure 7.1 Heiteren near Neubreisach in Alsace, a 'villa' in 768. A road or 'ribbon' village with Roman field gridding ('centuriation') modified by medieval farmers. August Meitzen, *Siedlung und Agrarwesen der Westgermanen und Ostgermanen, der Kelten, Römer, Finnen und Sklaven* (3 vols, Berlin, 1895), 3, Map 44.

Figure 7.2 Much Wymanley in Hertfordshire, England, in 1803. Accommodated to the terrain, strips in a three-field manor founded on a Roman 'villa', with the lord's strips heavily marked. Meitzen, *Siedlung, etc.* 3, Map No. 96.

thirteenth century, when wealthy yeomen exploited farms averaging about fifty acres. A similar process had taken place in France, where modest knights, substantial bailiffs, burghers and well-to-do farmers built semi-independent farms. Change was gradual. On eight manors of the bishop of Winchester, thirty-seven per cent of the land was in demesne in the second half of the thirteenth century; about twenty-four per cent in the early fourteenth century.

Although many farms were composed of strips and parcels of land mixed among the allotments of the villagers in large, open fields, others were concentrated, especially in cleared land. Parts of the north European plain began to look modern. During the thirteenth century in Burgundy, gentlefolk left the villages inhabited by their parents, building modest manor houses in the midst of their own farms or 'domains'. These small farms were less self-sufficient than large manors. Handicrafts played a smaller part and, to pay for industrial goods from nearby towns, crops were tailored to fit market needs.

Landlords increasingly relied on salaried labour and, being less necessary, tenants' work was either commuted into rents or sold. At Pasignano near Florence, for example, the monastery housed fourteen monks and the demesne was farmed by nearly forty lay brethren, the equivalent of a lay landlord's 'family'. The rest of the cloister's land was rented to sixty-nine tenants, whose labour services were of so little value that the abbot alienated them all in 1242. Elsewhere such services were long retained. Although the Alsatian monastery of Marmoutier had replaced field work by rents early in the twelfth century, transport services and help at harvest and hay making were required until well into the thirteenth century. This change transformed the relationship of tenant and landlord. Save for jurisdictional rights and commutation charges for old services, a landlord's right was best expressed in terms of land rent. Documentation changed: registers balancing allotments given to tenants against service were replaced by current leases, to be discarded when new ones were issued. As long as rent was not lost, it mattered little who used the land, the replacement of tenants even being welcome because mutations were taxed. Instead of being community planners, landlords were becoming rentiers.

Old manors often briefly regained ground. In the thirteenth century, England's larger monasteries, assured of grain and wool markets, resumed the direct management of their lands, expanded demesnes and even increased the labour owed by their peasants. The late thirteenth century, however, witnessed renewed decline. Although sales and other contracts relaxing tenurial restrictions were widespread in England, they were more common in recently settled areas and around towns than in the manorial regions of the Midlands. *Meierrecht* and types of tenure evidencing the disintegration of old manors were common along the Rhine, but began to penetrate north-west Germany only during the late thirteenth century. The difference between the later and earlier ages was one of degree, not of kind. The great manor had never entirely dominated rural life, and the smaller units still partly relied on manorial service owed by tenants.

Like semi-independent farms, flexible land tenures gradually spread, ranging from England's burgage tenure to Languedoc's commoner's fief. The same was also seen east of the Elbe river, where field labour was not required of settlers from the mid–twelfth century on. Because town and village were not far apart, many of England's boroughs were mere villages, just like 'new towns' across the Channel. An example in the Low Countries was Herenthals, founded by the duke of Brabant in 1209, settled by farmers called 'burghers' owing hereditary rents and minimal services.

Frontier settlement together with urbanization have been held to explain the appearance of semi-independent farms and the weakening of the manor's community enterprise. The argument is partly correct. Trans-Elbian Germany was free of manorial services until the late thirteenth century, and urbanization encouraged a division of labour between town and countryside. Village workshops slowly surrendered industrial production to towns, and farmers raised commodities designed for the markets of a slightly urbanized world. One aspect was the use of money (gained in exchange for export crops) by countryfolk. In 1245, ordinary cultivators on farms of the Bavarian monastery of Baumberg paid 58 per cent of their charges in money, while those with vineyards paid 98 per cent.

Urbanization and the frontier, however, effected change only in favourable circumstances. Eastern German settlement was channelled through newly founded towns, and manorial services and tenures did not penetrate there at first. Things changed later as economic growth halted and then retreated. Like those of early modern Spanish America, eastern Europe's cities of around 1300 served a pre-manorial function, that of encouraging settlement. Too precocious to last, the towns, save for some ports, were then reduced in early modern times by the rise of the rural great manor with its semi-industrial workshops. During economic growth, however, matters evolved differently. In early medieval western Europe, the spread of the manor, heir to Rome's fading urbanism, constituted a pre-urban stage. In the later stage, the high point of which is being treated in this book, towns moved to the fore and both manor and village industry declined.

Nor did – or does – economic growth, the settlement of new lands and urbanization necessarily lessen coercion. They did not when the manorial system spread into north-west Europe, a great economic advance for regions beyond Rome's frontiers. Nor did they always in antiquity (the post-Punic Roman republic) or modern times (Europe's colonial expansion), when slavery accompanied the settlement of new lands, economic growth and urbanization. The question is therefore why coerced labour did not grow in this age of rapid economic growth and urbanization.

One reason was that circumstances and institutions opposed a rational use of humans as machines: oppression existed but slavery was not practicable at this time. Churchmen insisted on individual responsibility; hence, slave or free, all women and men owed charity to Church and society and had the right to marry and have issue. Although this did not prevent servitude, it impeded the efficient use of human labour. Similarly, political particularism drew lords towards martial and governmental functions and away from a purely economic use of their farms and dependants. England's brief renewal of manorialism in the thirteenth century, for example, was partly because the king's near monopoly of government encouraged lords to exploit the economy more vigorously. In such a context, seigniorial decentralization meant a measure of freedom for serfs.

Slavery also requires plentiful recruits. Unlike conquering Rome and early modern Europe, entrepreneurs at this time had no easy way to replace superannuated humans. The Church forbade enslaving Christians and, except for some Baltic peoples who were in any case being rapidly converted, Europe had no large reservoirs of non-Christians. Such were found around the Mediterranean, but were protected by Near Eastern and North African states still holding their own against the Latins. Apart from a few bonanzas such as the fall of Damietta in 1219 and the conquest of the Balearic Islands, a thin trickle of largely female slaves from Africa and the Black Sea was all that Europeans got their hands on. Selling slaves was profitable, however, and the Genoese penetrated the Black Sea trade from Kaffa in the Crimea in the late 1260s.

If slavery was relatively unprofitable, selling freedom was not because, in an expanding economy, farmers were willing to pay for liberty. Commutation of services into money spelled freedom, because the real value of money shrank in the normal price rise. The change was gradual: in 1181, of the twenty patrimonial manors of St Paul's of London, six offered dues in kind, eight in kind and money and six wholly in money. Slowly, a landlord's own farm began to outweigh the dues and rents collected from dependants. In 1267, a lord's demesne near Mâcon in Burgundy provided an annual income of about a hundred pounds; villagers holding tenures contributed only five. Farmers favoured hereditary rights. In 1233 at Pasignano in Tuscany, of the sixty-eight families holding of the monastery, eight knights and town patricians may be excluded. Of the remaining tenants, six were non-hereditary, while fifty-five were tenants paying fixed quit-rents for farms, both hereditary and alienable at will. Ideally, farmers wanted freeholds. Although known in Frisia and Scandinavia where manors were rare, this ambition was not often fully realized. Around towns, especially Italy's urban republics, the abolition of lordly rights and depreciation of rents enabled farmers to free their farms.

Even if commutation of services into money meant eventual loss for landlords, it was profitable. In a growing economy where land remained to be cleared, alert lords wanted capital, and money rent received from old parcels could help develop new lands from which little had come in the past. Landlords, in fact, often insisted on money payments and farmers, short of cash, were often unhappy about it. New exploitations had many advantages beside rent. During the late thirteenth century, farmers settling in eastern Germany usually paid an entry fee. Fees collected for the use of mills, wine presses and other common facilities built by lords were profitable. In brief, as long as land remained for settlement or more intense exploitation, rent fixing and the commuting of rents and services into money was a means of selling old investments in order to buy new. Nevertheless, while many landlords profited, some lost out. In the mid-twelfth century Cluny's houses, committed to old contracts, suffered crisis, while new Cistercian ones flourished.

As rents were increasingly fixed, rent value sank in comparison to the real value of land. Long-term rent contracts were described as sales, and possession or use-right came to be nine-tenths of the law. Not that rents were meaningless, because, although slowly declining, they were steady investments for rentiers. Active entrepreneurs and landlords, however, often acquired the use-right in order to lease it again for sums representing a true return. In 1281, only fourteen per cent of the revenues of St Peter's monastery in Ghent came from hereditary leases, eighty-six from short-term ones. Land was also leased to be improved, to have tenants plant new crops and, if labour was plentiful, landlords favoured short-term sharecropping leases. Rural and urban investors also provided herdsmen with animals or ploughmen with oxen or horses and shared the profits.

At Pasignano in Tuscany in the early thirteenth century, most villagers held of the monastery paying hereditary quit-rents and some services. By 1300, the situation had altered radically. Already weakened in 1242, services disappeared altogether when Florence abolished them in 1289. Meanwhile, the monks tried to acquire the use-right to their lands. Of about fifty farms, half had been largely lost to them, being leased perpetually at fixed rent. The other half, however, was held by farmers on short-term leases who paid as much as half their grain crop. In this and other regions, agriculture had moved far from the manors of the past. The relationship of lord to dependant had turned into one of investor to worker. More free than before, farmers got seed, animals and capital, but they were more exposed to the vagaries of the market. When economic growth slowed around 1300, the deleterious side of the farmworker's relationship to the capitalizer became apparent. No longer inhibited by manorial laws, division among heirs also split the peasant's farm, making it less viable in an increasingly competitive economy.

As new land ran out and few new technologies improved productivity, crisis became general. In parts of France and south-west Germany, obligations reminiscent of manorial servitude were reimposed. Generally, however, entrepreneurs in areas of dense settlement pushed farmers off the land. In this circumstance, serfs with quasi-hereditary land were disinclined to buy liberty. Up to about 1300, France's kings were slow to free their serfs. Enfranchisement was expensive: the serfs of Pierrefonds paid Louis IX (d. 1270) five per cent of the value of their real property; those of Paray ten per cent of the value of their movables. During the Aragonese and Flemish wars from the 1290s on, the crown stepped up its efforts to sell liberty. Under Louis X (d. 1316) it even tried to force farmers to buy their freedom. Serfs in the Toulousain, from whom the treasury hoped to get a third of the value of their goods, held back. The best that the government got was six to thirteen per cent, and even then many refused to buy freedom. Liberty was too costly if it cost a tenancy.

As the thirteenth century' aged, landlord and tenant relations were less and less happy. Competitiveness, however, still stimulated invention more than social war. Rural credit mechanisms, for example, changed radically. In the past, a form of mortgage was common: those wanting capital pledged property for loans, surrendering the income of the pledge as interest on the loan. Since real property was thereby risked, this contract was practical only when land was cheap. As land became dear, circumstance joined with ecclesiastical censure of this frankly usurious contract to push the mortgage out. Capital, one soon discovered, could be obtained without usury: rents on land or means of production and labour could be sold, giving creditors anywhere from five to fifteen per cent annually. First seen in the twelfth century, the flexible 'census' contract gradually spread. What could not be foreseen was that, in later difficult economic circumstances, rents could also become crushing perpetual burdens.

Commerce

Commerce was at once universalist and particularist. Merchants were inhabitants of particular communities, not Italians so much as Luccans or Pisans. When harmed by foreigners and refused redress, their fellow citizens granted them the right to exact reparation from any denizen of the other town or region. Although rare in quasi-national England or the royal lands of France, marque and reprisal was known in Italy's independent cities. The jurist Alberic of Rosate remarked that, although opposed to natural law, it had currency where there was no superior government. It was also used in towns like Toulouse in Languedoc, Arles in Provence and Cologne in the Rhineland, where political decentralization required communities to protect their own interests. Overlapping authority sometimes made trade a chancy affair. In 1303, a Milanese merchant on his way to Flanders was seized by a Rhenish lord because the emperor, sovereign of both, owed him money!

Communications being what they were, few merchants were sedentary. Lombards travelled to Flanders and Germans to Barcelona in the course of a season. Once out of their home regions, merchants were among foreigners. Around 1300, a rich noble like Benedict Zaccaria of Genoa owned industrial shops in Genoa and Florence, raised mastic on Chios, mined alum in Phocaea and, as merchant and corsair, ranged from England to the Holy Land. He could look after himself, but ordinary merchants needed protection against rampant localism.

Protective institutions had therefore appeared. Foremost were fairs, times and places under special law designed to protect merchants. Merchants from warring communities abode together under the fair's peace, marque and reprisal being in abeyance. Bartholomew of Exeter's (d. 1184) penitential records papal legislation censuring those who harassed pilgrims and merchants, even those molesting the latter with unwarranted tolls. By threatening exclusion from the all-important fairs of Champagne and Brie, the counts of that region and their successors, France's kings, issued efficacious safe-conducts to Lombards and others coming to the fairs.

Lombards visiting the Champagne fairs usually voyaged in caravans and well-travelled arteries spawned special associations. In the early fourteenth century, the *hanse* of the Loire river consisted of twenty-two guilds, towns and rural lords. Others were designed to control particular trades. By the early thirteenth century, the London *hanse* included fifteen Flemish towns whose merchants imported English wool. Another *hanse* united those of seventeen cities handling the sale of manufactured cloth at the Champagne fairs. Italians at those fairs created a society to prohibit members from suing each other in foreign courts. The Pisans captured by the Genoese in the naval battle off Meloria in 1284 formed a 'university' with its own seal. When domiciled in the Near East and Egypt, Latins lived in jurisdictional enclosures analogous to ghettos. The two large Venetian settlements in Mamluk Alexandria enjoyed self-government but were locked at night from the outside. Established in 1261, the Genoese community of Pera across the Golden Horn from Constantinople soon outstripped the capital itself. Self-governing, it offered citizenship in Genoa's overseas empire to Greek, Near Eastern and Latin applicants. Similar but smaller institutions were seen in the west. Around 1300, Lucca had consulates (merchant hotels, really) in London, Bruges, Paris, Montpellier, Avignon, Genoa, Venice, Rome and Naples. Similar were those of the Germans in London and Bruges, where they won extra-territorial rights in 1250 and 1252.

Common economic interests bred leagues of cities. Such were the Cinque Ports in England, with their commonly elected mayor and councillors, whose authority was confirmed by the crown in 1278. Leagues were more free-wheeling where central power was weak, the most famous being the Teutonic Hanseatic League. This began around 1230 with an agreement between merchants from Hamburg and Lübeck. By 1265 other towns agreed to adopt the latter's maritime code, and in 1293 twenty-six communities met at Rostock to expand this agreement. By 1300, the *hanse* dominated commerce in the North and Baltic seas.

In the thirteenth century commerce weakened the contrast between universalist and particularist elements. Prizing the profits to be made from foreigners, townsfolk protected them. Inns were regulated to assure pilgrims and merchants of honest treatment. Innkeepers mediated between foreign and native businessmen, and soon brokers emerged, appearing in south Germany, the Rhineland and Flanders during the first four decades of the thirteenth century. Italy was more advanced: a schedule of brokers' fees was published in Genoa in 1204, and in 1233 Pisa counted over 165 such specialists. It also became possible to run a business from a distance; to be, in short, sedentary. A courier service created by Lombards at the Champagne fairs helped. Italian merchant-banker firms established networks. The Florentine Acciajuoli had forty-one factors abroad in 1341, mostly in Italy, but others were stationed from London to Nicosia and Tunis. The great Peruzzi boasted

150 factors spread even more widely through Europe, North Africa and the Near East.

Growing trade led to uniform commercial law. By the late twelfth century, Italian codes had so influenced each other that one may speak of a common Mediterranean maritime law. Derived from Byzantine and Italian models, Barcelona's code influenced law in much of Europe. The Plantagenets spread the *Rolls of Oleron* from the Bay of Biscay to the narrow seas, a source for later Flemish sea law. Lübeck's code ruled the North and Baltic seas, a version with 250 articles being sent to the Teutonic Order in 1254. These codes fought particularism. The ancient law of salvage gave finders the profits of storm or navigational error, sometimes even allowing shipwrecked foreigners to be ransomed, an affront to Christian brotherhood militated against by papal conciliar decrees from Gregory VII to the third Lateran Council of 1179. By 1200, the law of wreck and wrack had been mitigated in the Mediterranean, save on the frontier between Muslim and Christian. In the north progress was slower, and Gerald of Wales found it apposite to contrast English barbarity with Roman civility. The Hanseatic towns were granted exemptions from wreck and wrack by treaties with England in 1228 and Flanders in 1253.

Although marque and reprisal continued, it had lost its sting in Italy, the individual's right having become so hedged about by treaties between the republics that it had come to resemble modern international reprisal. Something similar took place north of the Alps. In 1271, Deventer asked Cologne to abrogate personal marque and reprisal lest an individual's malice upset trade. Magdeburg's twelfth-century code legislated against reprisal, and its law was adopted in Brandenburg, the March of Lausitz, Silesia and Pomerania.

Reinforcing this were dual citizenship and domiciliary rights, both reflecting frequency of contact. In 1249, Cologne and Trier agreed to be 'one people' to promote wine sales. Dual citizenship, usually non-political, was common in Italy and elsewhere. Similar was the right to reside and trade, an example being the Lombard privilege. Although Italians – or Lombards, as others usually called them – had begun settling in France early in the thirteenth century, the privilege was not seen until the latter half of the century. In Germany the oldest was that of Trier in 1262 and, reflecting the fading of the Champagne fairs, the first Flemish one dates from 1281. By about 1325 most Rhenish, Swiss and south German towns accorded Italians residence rights. In the tallage roll of 1292, Lombards were the wealthiest Parisians: two had taxable incomes nearly twice that of the richest local patrician clan. The French crown still claimed foreigners' inheritances so that when Gondolfo, Paris's greatest Lombard, died in 1300, it took four years before his heirs freed what remained of the fortune from royal custody.

The Lombards invaded Europe's economy in the thirteenth century. This was partly due to Italy's location in the centre of the Mediterranean basin, midway on the axis of trade running from Flanders to the Middle East.

Italian industry, moreover, equalled that of the north. A further stimulus was the link of Italian, especially Tuscan, merchant bankers to the papacy, serving as its main collectors and creditors. A partial schedule published by Martin IV (d. 1285) assigned Tuscany and Liguria to the Buonsignori of Siena. England, Scotland and most of Germany and Slavonia went to eight Florentine houses; Portugal and parts of Spain to three firms from Pistoia and Lucca; and the Squarcialupi of Lucca drew the consolation prize, the northern islands, including Greenland, where hides and whalebone served in lieu of currency.

Italians replaced the Jews in providing credit, making their expulsion from England and France possible. In the visitations of Odo Rigaud, archbishop of Rouen, from 1248 to 1269, most monasteries' creditors were still Jews. Rigaud himself borrowed from Lombards, however, and by 1300 most French monasteries were in debt either to local moneylenders or Lombards. By 1291, resident Lombards paid the French crown twice the revenue that it received from Jews. Even on the lower levels of moneylending, Lombard usurers were busy in France. In 1260, three Luccan merchants, capitalized by three sleeping partners, opened a pawnshop in Poigny near Troyes. These usurers were careful about the natives, ordering their factors 'in the said store not to sleep with the servant who lives with them'.[1] The distinction between petty usury and big business was recognized in Italy's mature economy. Pistoia and Florence taxed petty moneylenders but never touched their great merchant bankers, who were, as John Villani (d. 1348) called them, 'the columns of Christianity'.[2]

The Italians did not win everywhere. Jews remained economically powerful in the Iberian peninsula and in eastern Europe. Active in England and Flanders, Italians never penetrated the Germans' northern seas. By 1300, the frontier between German and Italian mercantile enterprise had been fixed in Flanders, where it remained for centuries. Elsewhere the emergence of local businessmen hurt the Lombards. By 1300, local moneylenders, aided by the Lombards' debtors in France, enabled, or possibly compelled, the crown to expropriate and expel them. Such actions were sporadic – 1268–69, 1274, 1277, 1291 – and soon rescinded, but show the start of a desire to do without foreigners; the Pastoureaux hated Lombards almost as much as they did Jews. Local society had begun to arm itself against medieval universalism, paralleling the beginning of the national state and the decline of papal authority in Latin Europe.

In the meantime and for long, Lombards were useful. An example is to be seen in the Florentines Albizo and Musciatto, sons of Guido, who, together

---

[1] Thomas W. Blomquist, 'Luccan Bankers in the Champagne' in *Journal of European Economic History* 14 (1985) 531.

[2] Armando Sapori, 'Compagni mercantili toscane' in *Studi in onore di Enrico Besta* (Milan, 1937) II 136.

with their brother Niccolo, entered French royal service in 1289, where they helped modernize the fiscal administration. It was Biche et Mouche, as the French called them, who raised the florins from the Peruzzi firm with which were hired Raynald of Supino's soldiers, who attacked Boniface VIII at Anagni in 1303.

Business, credit and industry

A marriage of labour and capital, business created many types of contracts. Modernized by Italy's jurists, Roman law was the prime source for these, providing a 'common law' normative everywhere in a divided world. Another source, evidenced by terms such as 'risk', was Mediterranean Islamic and Jewish practice. Lastly, basic contracts derived from early agrarian practice.

Many argue that land is retrograde, inhibiting economic individualism and imposing hereditary right as a norm. Not all landed contracts were heredi-tary, however, and benefices or fiefs were a kind of salary not necessarily based on land. When money was available, fiefs were paid in cash. Writing on Italian government in the 1240s, John of Viterbo called the pay given to public officers a 'salary or fief'.[3] This use of 'fief' was seen everywhere, and England's king bought allies in the thirteenth century with cash pensions or 'money fiefs'.

In rural contracts, the party providing land and equipment was termed the 'lord', and the tenant was to deliver a share of the crop to the lord's home or shed, there to be weighed. An industrial parallel is seen in clothmaking statutes from Toulouse in 1227. The raw wool supplier was described as 'lord or lady', to whose house finished goods were to be delivered for weighing. Issued before the building of textile guilds, these statutes favoured entrepren-eurs by regulating the putting-out or domestic system in their favour.

The partnership or 'society' joined capital to labour, the partners sharing profits and risk. Sharecropping was described by Italian jurists as a 'quasi-society', risks being shared because a tenant was insured against loss caused by weather and warfare. Other contracts were similar, an example being a contract whereby investors put money or animals with a farmer or shepherd to share the profit. Lordly rights could also be shared. Most new towns and villages founded by the count of Toulouse in Languedoc after 1250 were partnerships with local lords. In 1198, conflict between the bishop of Viviers and the same count over the silver mines of Largentière ended in a partner-ship. Family communities were also known and even frequent in some places.

How close these forms were to each other is seen in Beaumanoir's cus-toms of the Beauvaisis issued around 1283, where commercial and political

---

[3] *Liber de regimine civitatum* 21 in *BIMA* III (Bologna, 1901) 225.

partnerships, family societies and even the community of man and wife are all lumped together in a chapter on 'companies'. If Italian jurists were beyond that stage, they still discussed the Lombard communitarian family and always insisted that a commercial 'society' was a brotherhood. Jurists such as Azzo (d. *circa* 1230) and Accursius (d. 1260) also found in Roman law a 'law of brotherhood' making all partners brothers, equally responsible and exposed to risk. Lacking this quality, societies or contracts were termed 'leonine', reflecting the tale of the lion who ate the shares of the beasts with whom he had agreed to hunt.

In Toulouse, the cathedral canons sued the armed guards of a farm in 1191 for breach of 'society' because they had lost it to an enemy. In 1218, a dying father put capital bequeathed to a minor son in a company for a term of seven years, ordering his executors to receive yearly accounts from the active partners. Most partnerships were small, but some were large. Among the latter were maritime societies which financed their expensive ships and cargoes by dividing them into shares. As early as 1197, a Venetian vessel was capitalized by a hundred shares. Mines were financed by shares, those of the Swedish copper mine of Stora Kopparberg being first mentioned in 1288. Large-scale business enterprise used the same methods. Although the average number of partners in a Tuscan merchant-banking firm was around five, some had five times as many. External capitalizers were also employed here. In 1331, the capital of the Florentine Bardi consisted of fifty-eight shares, of which about thirty-six per cent was held by six family members and the rest by five outsiders.

Most partnerships were short-lived. Maritime ventures were often for one voyage, and even great merchant-banking societies were constellations of transitory partnerships. Large-scale milling or mining, however, required companies of longer duration. The Bazacle water mills in Toulouse were operated separately, each being owned by a group of partners, some millers and some investors, clerical or lay. The operators gradually joined to face lawsuits and carry out common designs, in 1177 combining to build a barrage across the Garonne river to channel the flow. In 1193, a spokesman acted for all Bazacle partners in a lawsuit, thus beginning a company that lasted until 1925. Continuity was also lent by family tradition, as in merchant-banking firms. When the Florentine Scali crashed in 1326, they had been in business for over a century.

Functional specialities appeared everywhere. In 1307, the Florentine Alberti merchant bankers gave branch partners maintenance, a share of profit and a salary. Practical business required a combination of partnerships, contractual relationships and hired labour. Florence's Peruzzi both employed managers all over Europe and invested in sixteen industrial and commercial companies. A rough capitalist, John Boine Broke (d. 1286 or 1287) of Douai, joined partnerships for merchant ventures, put his wool out for manufacture and ran his own dye works and drying house with hired labour. Salaried workers are heard of at the Bazacle mills in 1291. In 1388 – a time when business was not as good as fifty years earlier – the Strozzi–Credi wool workshop in Florence employed about fifty persons, of whom a quarter were permanent, fifteen per cent apprentices and the rest dayworkers.

Brotherhood sometimes resisted specialization. The shareholding miners of the Tuscan silver mine at Massa Marittima together elected masters to direct the pits, and a partner who neither worked nor sent a replacement was to surrender his share in the company. Similar restrictions were imposed on investors by millers at Douai and elsewhere. It was, however, already normal in mines and mills for one partner to provide capital and another labour. When, in 1294, the abbot of Admont held shares in Steiermark iron, he was obviously not a miner or smelter.

The distinction between active and inactive partners was adopted early in maritime companies because the capital needed exceeded that possessed by the merchants or seamen aboard the vessel. Shares were sold to sleeping partners, investments that could be sold, pledged, willed and divided like other property. In large family merchant-banking firms, investors were often partners for profit, having nothing to do with management. This stretched the fabric of the 'society' because partners were responsible for the actions of their associates. In small companies, partners were protected from loss because they knew its members well. In 1256, Rolandino Passaggeri's notary's manual tells that a partner must agree 'not to contract debts or give credit without the consent of the other partners, and to show, see and give accounting of the partnership whenever the other partners require it'.[4] In large companies, lesser partners needed and demanded a voice.

When, after a period of difficulty, the Buonsignori rebuilt the Great Table of Siena in 1289, the seniors pledged to conduct the business in line with the decisions 'of the majority of [the family] and of the other partners of the said firm'.[5] As firms became larger and directors separated from the investing partners, stronger controls evolved. Jurists came to describe them as fictive persons, and hence distinguished between the capital of a company and the private fortunes of its partners. In 1301, the Florentine wool guild or Calimala provided that a creditor of an insolvent partner could not attack the firm itself, merely take the debtor's shares. In 1298, the Buonsignori junior partners petitioned the republic to intercede at the papal court, to grant a moratorium on payments, and asked that 'no partner . . . be obliged to pay the debts of the said company above or beyond his share of the capitalization'.[6] Initially rejected, the principle was accepted by 1310.

---

[4] *Summa artis notarie* 1 6 (Venice, 1583) I 141v.

[5] Sapori, 'Compagni mercantili toscane' in *Studi . . . Enrico Besta* II 126.

[6] Ibid. II 127.

After 1250, government regulation grew rapidly in Italy. Founded in 1234 or 1235, the Maona of Ceuta, a Genoese chartered company, assembled investors to arm a fleet in return for sharing booty. By 1346 the Maona of Chios-Phocea – a huge chartered 'society' divided into 2,013 shares valued at a hundred pounds each – gave the government of the conquered islands to the shareholders. The Venetians preferred government management. The senate ordered its merchants in Alexandria in 1283 to corner the cotton and pepper trade and, before 1300, sponsored the building of great galleys and instituted a convoy system for them. Given a monopoly of carrying spices, silk and other light and valuable goods, these vessels were increasingly owned and operated by the government.

Chartered companies were near relatives of the *montes* created by governments to raise money. Heard of from the 1160s, *montes* derived partly from the assignment of public revenue to pay debts owed to its creditors and partly from the forced loans characteristic of urban and seigniorial public finance. In Genoa in 1164, a *mons* of seven shares was created by assigning revenues for eleven years, the shares being divided among six creditors, who purchased anywhere from two full shares to a quarter of a share, each alienable and negotiable. The system underwent huge expansion. Shares in harbour duties, the state salt monopoly, indeed all revenues were assigned to raise money. By about 1180 they were assigned in perpetuity and became heritable, though government retained the right to repurchase and regulate the rate of return. Towns advertised the annual return paid on these formally forced loans, and investors clamoured for them. In 1262, Venice consolidated all debts and *montes* into a state-managed fund paying five per cent annually; in short, a funded debt. Love of free enterprise led Genoa to differ from Venice. By 1323, her companies had become autonomous with directors elected by the shareholders. Whatever the form, the state's emergence as a major economic operator shows the superiority of Italian fiscal techniques. No northern ruler established a *mons* in the thirteenth or early fourteenth centuries, and even the largest northern towns had only begun to sell shares of municipal income. Government-regulated or managed companies and funds also reinforced the idea of limited liability, because investors in government debts or companies risked no more than they had invested.

Another way of capitalizing was an outgrowth of depositing money or valuables in safekeeping. Churches and monasteries, especially Templars and Hospitallers, were traditionally used for this purpose. Worried about secular lawsuits, in 1198 the pope's rule for the Trinitarians prohibited this order from receiving specie in deposit. Templars and Hospitallers were allowed to, but could not pay interest. The lay banker's great advantage was that he enticed clients by offering not only protection but also profit on deposits. In 1215, Boncompagno of Signa listed the kinds of deposits:

Some deposit property with the religious, others with laymen who are believed good, others with innkeepers of whom they have heard report or with whom they are staying, and still others with merchants or moneychangers. Some then deposit only for safekeeping and others for both safekeeping and profit.[7]

Deposit contracts soon became ordinary investments for widows, gentlefolk and ecclesiastical institutions. In Perpignan in 1286, a businessman was given money by a noblewoman in deposit:

in order to do business with the said money together with my own, either person-ally or by agents in France, Flanders or elsewhere, from this date for a year or more as it pleases both of us, and I will faithfully give you three parts of the profit . . . retaining the fourth . . . for my labour.[8]

Depositors also entrusted their means to the Italian merchant-banking firms at rates that were known in the market.

Deposits had many advantages. Although not free of ecclesiastical censure, they were not looked on with the disfavour of outright usury. In civil courts, investors did not share responsibility for the actions or debts of those with whom they deposited: if depositees failed, depositors became their creditors. Deposit for gain was so flexible that during the thirteenth century it replaced loans and various kinds of partnerships. The meaning of this for capitaliza-tion is illustrated by the larger Tuscan companies. From 1300 to 1303, over a million gold marks were deposited with the Spini firm by the papacy. In 1318, the assets of the Florentine Bardi were over ten million gold marks, a sum eight times larger than the firm's original capital. Nearly as grand was the Scali of Florence who, as noted above, failed in 1326. According to the Florentine historian John Villani, a partner in the Buonsignori firm who intentionally hid their malfeasance, the total liability of the Scali after bank-ruptcy was 400,000 florins, a sum that slightly surpassed the revenue of Edward II of England in 1323. A Genoese lawsuit of 1200 shows that busi-nessmen had 'call' deposits, ones where depositors received no interest but could withdraw at will, the banker meanwhile investing the capital. Bankers soon encouraged reputable depositors to overdraw, hence investing in loans, short and long term. Lacking figures, the quantity of credit created cannot be estimated, but it must have been huge.

Even though guilds and governments combined to produce banks, they were not yet highly specialized. Tuscan firms were only partly banks, being principally mercantile houses investing in commerce, industry, land and government finance. Smaller operators on the local level were what the Tuscan merchant bankers were on the universal. Possibly once a serf, Arnold of

---

[7] *Boncampagnus Boncompagni* in *BuF* I 173.
[8] Emery, *The Jews of Perpignan* 194–95 No. 147.

Codalet became one of Perpignan's richest men in the period from 1276 to 1287. He invested in trading ventures from Seville to Flanders, and speculated in local lordly and ecclesiastical revenues. He received both call deposits and investment deposits from local businessmen and rentiers, thus serving as a one-man banking and investment house.

Interest rates were high around 1300. In Catalonia, the legal maximum was twelve and a half per cent for Christians and twenty for Jews. On commercial credit, Genoa permitted twenty-five per cent and Venice set the maximum at twenty, as did the Champagne fairs in 1311. For what moderns would describe as consumer credit, higher rates were allowed. Under the Flemish Lombard Privilege of 1281, Italians were permitted forty-three per cent, and moneylenders exacted appalling rates from the poor. In 1289, a Lombard at Nîmes was charged with having extorted 202 per cent. State finance also sometimes involved staggering rates. Losing the war, Frederick II promised to pay his Roman bankers anywhere from thirty-six to forty-eight per cent.

Moderate returns on investments were common, however, and overall rates of profit were not great, perhaps because the high cost of capital was partly compensated for by the high rate of gain. Around 1300, land rents brought annual returns of anywhere from five to ten per cent. Those who deposited for gain with businessmen in Perpignan wanted about ten per cent. The government debt of Genoa offered subscribers from seven to ten per cent, while Florence's gave anywhere from five to fifteen. After paying off the seven or eight per cent owed on depositors' investments, the Peruzzi partners averaged a profit of just under sixteen per cent in the prosperous period from 1308 to 1324. The usual percentage on deposits with mercantile firms in Florence ranged from six to ten per cent yearly and, to judge from the books of the Del Bene firm, the return of partners in the wool industry oscillated between seven and fifteen per cent.

Business required ancillary agencies, of which some were ecclesiastical, although, as seen above, the direct participation of the Church was fading. The Languedoc hearth tax raised by the pope in the Albigensian crusade in 1212 had been deposited with the Templars. The French crown used the Paris Temple as a treasury until 1295, but the Tuscans had taken this business by mid-century. Although the decline of the Temple was related to the failure of the crusade, Tuscan merchant bankers also won out because they offered better service. They served as revenue collectors, employed bills of exchange, essential instruments in a decentralized economy, and deposits placed with them yielded a return. They also operated on as grand a scale as the Temple. Whereas the Scoti of Genoa had aided Simon of Montfort modestly during the Albigensian crusade, by 1266 a combine headed by the Buonsignori of Siena advanced Charles of Anjou 160,000 pounds of Paris, a sum larger than the total debt owed by the French crown to the Temple in 1286.

Specie, moreover, no longer had to be transported. Improving on the methods of the Templars, merchant bankers devised paper transfers. A primitive bill moved credit from Genoa to Alexandria in 1155. Papal collectors in London used bills of exchange issued by the Bardi to carry credits to Rome. Non-negotiable promissory notes were generalized, a collection of 7,000 for the period from 1249 to 1291 being discovered in the archives of Ypres alone. As early as 1200, interbank transfers were common in Italy, and by mid-century Italian merchants at the Champagne fairs normally used them. When embargoing the export of goods and money to Italy during the conflict with Boniface VIII in 1301, Philip the Fair took care to prohibit credit transfers by merchants' letters and deposits.

Coinage became more uniform and stable as commerce grew and the state developed economic power. By 1300 England had reduced the number of mints from over forty to twelve, and even France, initially burdened by almost three hundred, cut this to thirty by 1315. Coin values increased and various types corresponded to Europe's principal economic areas. Before 1200 the English minted the great silver penny (sterling), which became a standard in the Hanseatic North and Baltic seas. In 1192 the Venetians issued the great penny, whose weight and style, only slowly received in Venice itself, were adopted by many towns in the peninsula and also replaced Norman south Italian coinage. Italian-style coinages spread everywhere. The great penny of Tours imitated an Italian model in 1266, and was itself copied by many coinages in the Rhineland by 1300. At about that time the king of Bohemia invited Florentine mintmasters to introduce their models in his realm.

Gold coins, the first since Carolingian times, made their appearance. In 1149 the Genoese stamped a few gold coins that never caught on, and even the Emperor Frederick II's *augustales* had only modest economic significance. The Florentine florin of 1252 and the Venetian ducat of 1284 really established gold coinage. Writing in the late thirteenth century, the Dominican preacher Remigio de'Girolami praised his city's coin:

> The [florin's] nobility is shown in three ways: first, by its metal, because the gold in Sicily's *tarena* is good, that in the *augustalis* better, but that in the florin best; second by its engraving, because on one side it has the lily, a thing of great excellence . . . and third, by its currency, because it circulates throughout the world, even among Saracens.[9]

All was not bliss, however. Although the economy continued to flourish, public finance was shaky around 1300. Trying to extend their authority without adequate support from a still decentralized society, princes ran into debt,

---

[9] C.T. Davis, 'An Early Florentine Political Theorist: Fra Remigio de'Girolami' in *Proceedings of the American Philosophical Society* CIV (1960) 688.

sometimes ruinously. By 1290 Guy of Dampierre, count of Flanders, owed the Lombards a sum equalling nearly a quarter of the annual take of the French royal treasury, and his resulting powerlessness invited France and England to intervene in industrial Flanders. Weak public finance gradually affected all the economy. Undertaken for profit, the mutation of 1295 was the first significant breach of the stability of France's royal coinage since the start of the century. In spite of howls of rage by those whose savings had been wiped out, and protestations by the clergy in 1303–4 and nobility in 1314 and 1316, devaluation of coinage soon became normal government policy in France and in much of Europe. In short, a crisis reflecting undeveloped national public finance preceded the general economic difficulties of the fourteenth century.

Chapter 8

Usury and corporatism

The prohibition of usury

Churchmen were of two minds about the economy because scripture enjoined: from each according to his means, to each according to his needs.[1] In the aftermath of the Gregorian age, utopians tried to make the world into a Christian society where men, like monks of old, lived in brotherhood without private property. This teaching paralleled the rise of nascent guild hostility to economic individualism around 1200 and the gradual secularization of the monastic idea. A student of Peter Cantor, Cardinal Robert of Curzon, professor at Paris and papal legate in 1213, wrote:

> So many evils cannot be purged unless a general council of all bishops and princes is convoked under the lord pope, where the Church and princes together will instruct all, under penalty of excommunication . . . to work either mentally or physically, and eat only their own bread, that is, the bread won by their own labour, as the apostle commanded, and that there be no idle or pushing fellows among us. Thus would all usurers, factious men and robbers be removed; thus would charity flourish and the fabric of the churches be restored; and thus would all be brought back again to its pristine state.[2]

Many doubted the ideal. Robert of Curzon's legatine mission to France was ended abruptly by Innocent III in 1216 because the king opposed his attack on usury, the clergy disliked the utopian rhetoric of his councils and the well-to-do detested his preaching the crusade to the poor, children and even the sick.

If common possession was sanctified in divine and natural law, Gratian's *Decretum* admitted that society is forced to choose between two evils, that of private property or the greater evil of violence or anarchy. Caesarius of Heisterbach knew how to trim it. He praised Ensfrid, dean of St Andrew's in Cologne, because he took from the rich to feed the poor. Others, however, should not do so because 'the saints are allowed many things not permitted to those not holy. Where God's spirit is, there is liberty!'[3] If the poor were

---

[1] Acts of the Apostles 4:32–35.

[2] 'Le traité "De usura" de Robert de Courçon' 33, ed. Georges Lefèvre in *Travaux et Mémoires de l'Université de Lille* 10 (1902), and 2 Thessalonians 3:10–12.

[3] *Dialogus miraculorum* 6 5 (ed. Joseph Strange, Cologne, 1851) I 352.

aided, private property was permitted and, indeed, some justified it more than others. It was only postlapsarian to Duns Scotus, but Aquinas found it even in the state of innocence. Giles of Rome rehearsed Aristotle's arguments against Plato's communism: we have an incentive to do well with what we ourselves own, and brothers often fight over common inheritances. Still, it is a pity because 'had men not corrupt appetites . . . and were they not prone to evil, it would be good . . . to have property in common, because the more in common it is, the more divine it is . . . As things are now, however, it is useful for a community's citizens to have private property, because . . . men are not normally perfect.'[4]

Some also confessed that merchants performed necessary social functions. A passage by Honorius (*fl.* early twelfth century) defines their honour: 'You minister to all nations because you bring what they need through the perils of roads, rivers, thieves and the dangers of solitude. All men are your debtors to render prayers for your labour.'[5] Giles of Rome's schedule of salaries 'for labour' includes gains from special knowledge, and this Austin friar even lauded the dubious case of the ancient philosopher who cornered olive presses in the off season to rent them at high rates when needed.

Compromise aside, the clergy viewed those in other social orders sourly, probably because moral censoriousness is the usury that the religious mind exacts from others of the world's inhabitants. Carried in Peter Lombard's *Sentences*, a passage from a council at Rome of 1078 conveys this attitude:

> If a soldier or trader or one devoted to any profession that cannot be exercised without sin should come to penitence when snared in serious sin . . . , he should know that he cannot perform true penitence by which to obtain eternal life unless he leaves business or gives up his profession . . . That he should nevertheless not despair, we urge him to do whatever good he can in the meantime that omnipotent God may light his soul to penitence.[6]

The final sentence shows how the clergy opened the door to forgiveness or penitential casuistry.

Ecclesiastical legislation expressed the churchman's hope for economic brotherhood and willingness to press hard on laymen. Following the law of brotherhood, Christians were not to lend at usury to other Christians. As Gratian put it: 'Usury exists when more is asked than is given; for example, were you to give ten shillings and seek more, or one measure of grain and require something more.'[7] *La Somme le Roi*, a vernacular tract of 1279, lists as

---

[4] *De regimine principum* 2 3 6 (Rome, 1607) 361–62.

[5] *Speculum ecclesiae, Sermo generalis ad mercatores* in *PL* CLXXII 865. Honorius may have been from Autun, Canterbury or Regensburg.

[6] *Decretum* 2 33 3 de penitencia 5 6 in *CICan* I 1241.

[7] *Decretum* 2 14 3 4 in *CICan* I, 735, and Deuteronomy 24:19–20.

usurers moneylenders, mortgagers, heirs who refuse restitution of usury by penitents, helpers of Jews, businessmen taking advantage of buyers and debtors.

Exceptions were made for the poor and minors, that is, wives and widows. The consuls of Genoa's chamber of commerce were not too bold when they promised to uphold all sentences rendered by the archiepiscopal court except those 'concerning usury given to minors from money . . . that guardians have placed to advantage'.[8] In a decretal often cited to justify the deposit contract, Innocent III instructed the archbishop of the same town to permit a poor citizen to invest his wife's dowry with a merchant to sustain matrimony's burdens. The Church itself was also the pauper. As will be seen, when mortgages were forbidden, churchmen were expressly allowed to use them to redeem church property from lay hands. This exception was soon extended to include the recuperation of patrimonies wrongly lost to lay families.

The law on usury did not spring up overnight. The principle was known in antiquity and had spread during the early Middle Ages, but did not seriously invade the lay world until the Crusades. The need to protect Crusaders from creditors then elicited papal and conciliar legislation. Following the introversion of the Crusade itself, the accent began to shift. Churchmen, exemplified by Robert of Curzon at the Council of Paris in 1212–13, moved from protecting Crusaders to converting the whole world into a truly Christian society. This affected both secular business and clerical practice. Although mortgages were always suspect because creditors collected the fruits of pledged property as interest or usury, monasteries, military orders and chapters as well as layfolk had regularly invested in these contracts. After their condemnation by the pope in 1180, they did so only in exceptional cases. When in 1163 Alexander III wrote to an archbishop of Rheims asking him to protect a debtor against immoderate usury, it seemed that, as in Roman law, moderate usury was tolerated. After the Lateran Council of 1215, however, that excuse could be pleaded only by Jews.

The Church developed new enforcement agencies. Episcopal tribunals changed in the late twelfth century from synodal bodies of laymen and clergy to courts under professional judges called officials, and the new courts actively prosecuted usurers. At the Council of Toulouse in 1229, testaments not witnessed by churchmen were declared suspect, thus indirectly insisting on deathbed restitution of usury. At the Council of Lyons in 1274, notorious usurers were denied Christian burial until restitution was made. At that of Vienne in 1311–12, the canon *Ex gravi* crowned the edifice by condemning princes or magistrates who protected or permitted usury, declaring heretical those pertinaciously defending this sin.

---

[8] B.N. Nelson, 'Blancardo the Jew' in *Studi in onore di Gino Luzzato* (Milan, 1949) I 115n.

This law changed business practice. In the twelfth century lawyers frankly mentioned usury. The code called *Peter's Excerpts*, widely used in southern France and Italy, regulated the relationships of creditor and debtor in a chapter called 'If anyone owes a sum to his creditor, that is, capital and usuries, and pays any part of the debt, he may choose at the time of payment whether he wishes it to count for the usuries or for the principal'.[9] Writing in 1215, Boncompagno of Signa casually recorded a letter form requesting intercession to obtain a loan at usury, which included the following promise: '[the debtor] will give satisfactory security to the creditor . . . for both capital and usury'.[10] Again, an easy interpretation of business partnerships was current. The glossator Alberic of Porta Ravennate (d. early 1190s) proposed that a *societas* where one partner bore the risk and the other shared the profit was licit. If the great canonist Hostiensis echoed Alberic's argument later on, his had become a minority voice. Contemporary practice is shown in Rolandino Passaggeri's treatise for notaries, where he warns them not to condone usury by writing partnership documents 'in which only gain and not both the gain and loss are mentioned'.[11]

By this time, jurists rarely mentioned usury save to condemn it, and town statutes, like those of St Gilles in 1233, warned notaries to avoid it. Sometimes, as at Toulouse, the change occurred with dramatic rapidity. A common contract, the usurious mortgage, vanished in the 1190s. Usurious loans disappeared during a period of factional strife within the town when, from 1206 to 1215, Bishop Fulk, once a merchant and troubadour in Marseilles, created a White Confraternity to evoke popular support for a crusade against both heretics and usurers. Although the heretics were scarcely touched and the White was speedily countered by a Black Confraternity, Fulk was successful against usury. During this time testamentary restitution became normal and loans vanished from documents. The speed and intensity of this law's reception varied widely from place to place. Fast at Toulouse, it was slow in the mercantile centre of Marseilles where it was introduced only after *Ex gravi* was published in 1318.

As the prohibition of usury became prominent, so also did penitential restitution. The practice was old and tied to the Church's view of the rich, whom, Honorius warned:

> God wanted to be the fathers of the poor. Remember, you came naked into the world, and naked you will leave it. Because you must leave your riches to others, hasten now to build up heavenly treasures by the hands of the poor . . . Decorate churches with books, robes and other ornaments, restore those destroyed or

---

[9] *Exceptiones Petri* 2 29 and 31 and also 1 5 in ed. C.G. Mor, *Scritti giuridici preireneriani* (Milan, 1938) II 115 and 54.

[10] *Boncompagnus Boncampagni* in *BuF* II 167.

[11] *Summa artis notarie* 1 5 (de locatio et conductio) (Venice, 1583) I 123v.

deserted, enlarge the prebends of God's servants . . . Build bridges and roads thus preparing your way to heaven, and provide lodging, food and clothing for the poor, sick and wandering, thus buying eternal riches for yourselves.[12]

Systematic testamentary restitution, however, did not begin much before the 1180s, but thereafter spread rapidly. Rolandino listed the various types under the following rubrics, of which the first three are *certa* and the fourth *incerta*:

1. Open or public restitution to known persons.
2. 'In fear of infamy', covert restitution by the penitent's confessor to known victims whose names are listed in a closed codicil externally authenticated by two witnesses.
3. General restitution by the penitent's executors to those who can prove usury against him.
4. Distribution of a sum of money by the executors to pious causes for the souls of those whom the usurer has harmed.

Obviously open to abuse, the latter distributions 'are to be made only with the consent of high authority, such as pope or bishop'.[13] Everyone knew of the problem. In his biography of Louis IX of France, John of Joinville complained that the devil invented restitution in order to corrupt the clergy.

Restitution was a rendering of accounts by an individual in the sweat of the deathbed; gifts for salvation (*pro anima*) during a life of crime could not replace it, and hence what moderns call philanthropy was condemned as one of the seven deceptive types of restitution by a council at Ravenna in 1317. Such gifts could not be rejected, however, because few confessors could deprive of hope those who expressed an intention of healing the wounds they had dealt the pauper or Christ. In 1310, when the capital stood at £147,000, the Peruzzi gave £2,500 for pious causes. The partners of this merchant-banking firm were not thereby excused from deathbed restitution, at least not in theory, but it must have come close to this. In 1254, for example, a pope gratified the Austin Friars of Todi:

Inclining to your prayers, we permit . . . you to receive for the erection of your church up to £500 . . . from those of . . . Todi who have extorted usuries or acquired other things illicitly and cannot discover to whom restitution should be made. Nor do we wish that those who have given you the said usuries should be held to make other restitution for them.[14]

Writing between 1254 and 1262, the Franciscan Claro of Florence asked whether those who invested in town revenues bought during a war and

---

[12] *Speculum ecclesiae, Sermo generalis ad divites* in *PL* CLXXII 864.
[13] The *Flos testamentorum* in his *Summa artis notarie* I 226v–27r.
[14] *Bullarium OESA* No. 116 in *Augustiniana* 13 (1963) 499, referring only to 'usurae incertae'.

profited tenfold in the subsequent peace were obliged to restitution. 'They are to be excused,' he says, 'because of their risk and danger and are not held to make restitution to the town, but nonetheless ought to give very fat charities from their profits.'[15]

The growth of moral rigorism requires explanation. Although labour was sometimes permitted, ecclesiastics were forbidden economic activity except as rentiers. This was reinforced, if not imposed, by the division between the two peoples, clerical and lay, that compelled ecclesiastics to surrender functions for which they could be held responsible by civil power. Rentiers, however, are disadvantaged in burgeoning economies. Churchmen therefore looked for ways of eliciting lay charity, and moral rigorism combined with social utopianism was a way of sharing economic growth. Hence restitution and obligatory charity made the medieval town into a jewel box by building 'pious places', churches, cloisters and bridges. The expansion of parish and university education and hospital care for the sick and aged was financed by the same. The attack on usury, moreover, may not have slowed economic growth. Rent sales (*census*) replaced the mortgage and, being simple sales, were not formally usurious. They also, relative to the ever-mounting value of land, reduced the price of capital. The banning of the loan with usury stimulated the use of business partnerships and the deposit contract. This suited a time when the price of capital tended to diminish as risk declined.

These economic benefits, however, were unintended by churchmen, and rigorists did not favour easy escape. Henry Goethals of Ghent (d. 1293) declared rent sales usurious, and the deposit contract was even more frequently attacked. The lengths to which rigorists went is shown by the canon *Naviganti* of 1236, wherein Gregory IX refused any profit to those who lent money to merchants even if they shared the risk. Although laxists like Cardinal Geoffrey of Trani in 1245 argued that this law referred only to maritime loans, rigorists used it against any and all business. Still, the opinion earlier advanced by Peter Cantor may have been the more probable one: 'Were [one] to invest money and share both the loss and the pain . . . that would not be usury.'[16]

The banishment of usurious contracts from public records did not mean that moneylending ceased. The contracts were converted into loans without usury. Innocent III in 1206 permitted a debtor to gratify a creditor with a gift, as long as there was no intention of cheating. Roman law's distinction between usury (a creditor's profit on a loan) and interest (a loss to the creditor by a debtor's non-fulfilment of contract) was especially useful and, in canon law, a putative penalty could be spelled out in loan contracts. Raymond of Penyafort believed that 'if the penalty is . . . placed in the contract by the

---

[15] *Casus conscientiae Fr. Clari de Florentia* 30 in Bibl. Naz. Flor. MS B. VII. 1166 (Conv. Soppr.) 3Sr. Julius Kirshner kindly gave me a xerox copy of the original MS.

[16] *Liber casuum conscientiae* 3 3 III 2a (ed. Dugauquier) 181 Paragraph 213.

common consent of the parties, to the effect that, through fear of it, the debt will be paid on a certain day, usury is not committed, so long as the intention is good'.[17]

Two interpretations of interest allowed casuistry about intention to enter the equation. Typical of twelfth-century civil law, the code called *Peter's Excerpts* allowed a deceived party to 'recuperate the price together with the interest, that is, the loss he has suffered because of the sale, and the gain he could have made with his money'.[18] To some, like Hostiensis, damaged parties could only recuperate their loss and not the putative gain that they might have made. Noting that entrepreneurs lending to towns or persons thereby forwent a probable profit, however, Peter John Olivi suggested compensation. He argued that:

since money or property . . . is put to work for a certain probable gain, it not only has the simple quality of money or goods, but, beyond that, a certain seminal quality of generating profit, which we commonly call capital, and therefore not only does the simple value of the object itself have to be returned, but also an added value.

Forthrightly rejecting Aristotle's 'barren money' theory, this Franciscan noted that the added value was created 'by the industry of merchants; and hence derives not from the money itself but instead from its owners' industry'. Departing further from the censorious attitudes of other scholastics who insisted that the intrinsic value of a commodity determines its just price, he instead improved on the opinion of Albertus Magnus to find that prices are determined by the market because different individuals, moved by different needs, set different values on things. Besides, 'if no increase of price [is allowed], the common good will be harmed because those having commodities will not promptly sell or provide them to those wanting and needing them'.[19]

The examination of intention took place in the court of conscience, where the market's hot urges were cooled by the rigour or fanned by the laxity of confessors. A Franciscan, Olivi was sure that a penitent's desire to avoid punishment was enough for forgiveness (unlike Dominicans who held that true contrition was necessary), but that did not mean that he tried to obviate the doctrinal prohibition of usury and its attendant penitence and restitution for usury. He nevertheless shows that confessors and judges were informed

---

[17] *Summa de poenitentia et matrimonio cum glossis Ioannis de Friburgo* 2 de usuris 5 (Rome, 1603, rprt.) 231.

[18] *Exceptiones Petri* 2 15 (ed. Mor) II 108 and *Digest* 7 47 1 2.

[19] Olivi's opinions are cited from his *Tractatus de emptionibus et venditionibus, de usuris, de restitutionibus* in Joel Kaye, *Economy and Nature in the Fourteenth Century: Money, Market Exchange, and the Emergence of Scientific Thought* (Cambridge, 1998) 119 and 124.

by community consensus, and that the size of the interest or penalty was partly set by the market.

The Church's penetration of the marketplace reflects the weakness of secular government in the post-Gregorian epoch. As the state renewed its powers, however, conflicts arose. In 1205, for example, Philip Augustus of France questioned the right of church tribunals to prosecute usurers without royal consent. He had a motive: for 30,000 shillings Louis VII had promised not to punish the burghers of Tours in 1143 'for usury, ill-gotten gain or other multiplication of money'.[20] This attitude enraged Peter Cantor. Christian usurers licensed by princes are rightly called Jews, he said, 'because princes . . . do not permit them to be charged with any crime, saying, "These are our Jews."' But they are worse than Jews 'because Jews are permitted by scripture to take usury from a foreigner, but not from a brother, which is what Christian usurers do'.[21] Towns were equally frank. Magistrates at Bologna in 1250 described their town's debts as being 'owed both to usurers and others'.[22]

Some princes and lords, however, favoured the Church's stand. With undeveloped tax systems and a special relationship with their Jews, they settled for a share of the take. The *Exchequer Dialogue* and the tract on England's laws attributed to Glanville (d. 1190) show that England's kings quickly received church law, surrendering the prosecution of living usurers to the Church but claiming the inheritances of dead and unrepentant ones for the crown. In France reception was slower, but, if the code named after St Louis represents actual practice, the rewards were more widely shared: 'When a usurer is found in the territory of a baron or elsewhere, and it is proven against him, his property goes to the baron. His sin is then punished by Holy Church.'[23]

No more usurious than rural millers, estate bailiffs and rich landlords, townsfolk were nevertheless especially disturbed by the law on usury because, although moved by the hope for economic brotherhood, investment was their livelihood. The interplay of economics and republican government was curious because the well-to-do generally ran the government. Although the poor obviously lent both commodities and money, what preserved them for virtue was their incapacity for vice on a sufficient scale. Although many with old wealth were also usurers, their interest in public office and hostility to the new rich veiled their economic aggression. Censure was therefore mainly directed against the new rich, those involved in usury that invited the

---

[20] Heinrich Büttner, 'Frühmittelalterliches Städtewesen in Frankreich' in *Studien zu den Anfängen des europäischen Städtewesens* (Lindau, 1958) 186.

[21] *Verbum abbreviatum* 50 in *PL* CCV 158 and Deuteronomy 23:19.

[22] Philip Jones, *The Italian City-State from Commune to Signoria* (Oxford, 1997) 398.

[23] *Etablissemens de St Louis* 1 91 (ed. Paul Viollet, Paris, 1881) II 148–49.

description 'manifest and notorious usurers'. An archbishop of Pisa in 1323 defined such individuals as 'notorious in law because they have confessed or have been condemned for usury, or notorious in fact because they have given evidence of involvement in this business in a way which no subterfuge can hide, as when they have a counter or table ready for this business'.[24] Usury was therefore political, and its repression led to violence, as in Toulouse during the Albigensian crusade and frequently in Italian cities. Although nobody dared question the canons, governments necessarily applied them reluctantly. If rigorists often berated Italian merchant bankers, their republics protected them; and if moralizers questioned their debt societies (*montes*), subscribers were protected by claiming that these were forced loans.

Because both state and society require investment, the law appeared irrational to some. In his influential *Summa of the Confessors*, the Dominican John of Freiburg followed Hostiensis in saying that, where laws contradict each other, the more humane or rational ones are to be preferred. As the commonplace went, God demands nothing impossible. Elaborating on arguments earlier expressed by Azzo, Cino of Pistoia commented that 'the emperor who rules . . . the world sees that men are not as charitable as they ought to be, and the poor consequently suffer hunger . . . Because, as I have said, divine law is to be interpreted by human law which allows an evil to avoid worse, he thought it equitable for usury to be asked.'[25] Moderate theologians joined lawyers in this position. Thomas Aquinas opined that practical needs (especially of the poor) made concession necessary. The principle was: 'Sometimes practical law permits something unjust lest the community bear greater inconvenience, just as God sometimes permits evil lest the good He knows will derive from evil be impeded.'[26] Nevertheless, usurers, Jewish or Christian, are to restore their usuries if the wronged debtors are known. Most debtors, however, are unknown or, as they said, 'uncertain'. For uncertain debtors, Aquinas went on, a prince may tax the Jews for the common good – in effect, government may license usury and profit from it. The learned professor then added: 'And what has been said of the Jews is to be understood of . . . all others who busy themselves in usurious pravity.'[27] It may be concluded that a secular magistrate or prince who permitted usury was not heretical so long as he did not assert that his action was without sin.

Rome's church was Latin Europe's greatest government and, although utopian voices were heard in it, money outshouted them. What that meant in

---

[24] Emilio Cristiani, 'Note sulla legislazione antiusuraria Pisana (secolo XII–XV)' in *Bollettino storico pisano* XXII (1953) 13.

[25] From his *Super codicis* cited in T.P. McLaughlin, 'The Teaching of the Canonists on Usury' in *Mediaeval Studies* 1 (1939) 92–93.

[26] *De malo* 13 4 6 in *Opera omnia* XXIII (Rome and Paris, 1982) 256b.

[27] *De regimine Judaeorum* 3 in *Opuscula philosophica* 250b.

the forum of conscience is easy to see. In 1297, Boniface VIII addressed the Florentine Franzesi merchant bankers, noting that:

> because . . . much . . . property is known to have come into your hands by means of usury and evil and illicit contracts . . . we, benignly considering that you are un-covering your guilt in this matter by a humble and spontaneous confession for the exoneration of your consciences, and wishing . . . to provide for you of the great clemency of the apostolic see, remit and concede to you that . . . you may licitly and freely have and retain all you have acquired in this way.[28]

And among the Franzesi were the Mouche and Biche who harmed Boniface so greatly in the conflict with the French king!

Luke 6:35 is hard indeed to obey: 'Love your enemies, do good and lend, hoping for nothing therefrom'! Commenting on Dante's *Comedy*, Benvenuto of Imola (d. 1387/88) stated the problem succinctly: 'He who practises usury goes to hell; he who does not, to poverty.'[29]

Economic corporatism

That the mortgage and loan with usury were driven out of circulation is puzzling. Some have explained it by saying that these contracts provided capital for consumption, loans being made mainly to the poor, improvident gentlefolk or declining monasteries. This is doubtful. Jewish loans at usury in Perpignan in the 1290s went to members of all classes and successful busi-nessmen were among the borrowers. At Toulouse before the Albigensian crusade, income from mortgages (*pignora*) constituted a substantial part of a normal landed family's wealth, and towns everywhere borrowed at usury. Such contracts were so necessary that, when banned, substitutes soon re-placed them and, where they could not be replaced, gained a half-life as licensed usury. Would it not have sufficed to police these functional con-tracts by means of the just price?

Clerical moral rigorism alone could not have imposed this inconvenience on an unwilling society. Lay adherence was linked to the Crusades, where debt protection was among a Crusader's privileges, and in 1214 Innocent III told Philip Augustus that these aggressions could not be mounted unless usury was suppressed. The clerical programme's propaganda of brotherhood and social utopia also appealed mightily to the newly rising trade and craft guilds. A result was that the denigration of private property characteristic of the monks momentarily spread to lay society.

Guilds were free from such censure and also reflected the desire of crafts- and tradesfolk to pool strength to protect and increase labour's rewards. There

---

[28] *Registres de Boniface VIII* I 627 No. 1661.
[29] H.-J. Gilomen, 'Wucher und Wirtschaft im Mittelalter', *Historische Zeitschrift* 250 (1990) 265.

was little uniquely medieval about this, nor was it limited to economics. Charity was maximized by organization and also crime: Tours had a beggars' guild in the late twelfth century and gangs or clubs were common in Italian towns. It is worth recalling, moreover, that the guild movement was to be long lived: the associations described below were the forerunners of a corporatism that grew in France through the seventeenth century and, although weakening because of factory production, dominated German labour as late as the revolution of 1848.

Guilds were usually new in the late twelfth century. In 1200, Paris had a powerful merchant guild and four or more trade and craft organizations. From 1261 to 1270, the town's *Book of the Professions* registered the statutes of 101 trades and crafts. In 1292 there were 130, and in 1313 no less than 157. The rapidity of this expansion gave guildsmen a sense of adventure that never again marked Europe's corporate structures.

In northern Europe, association was first expressed in brotherhoods providing protection to traders and others whose itinerant occupations placed them outside of ordinary communities. In 1200, the Danish guild of Flensburg even obliged brethren to aid the flight of a member who had slain a stranger. Merchant guilds or *hanses* soon combined economic functions with jurisdictional or governmental ones. In the late thirteenth century, membership in the merchants' guild of Bedford, near London, was tantamount to community citizenship. Most northern towns, however, had gone beyond this stage. As they appeared, craft and trade guilds took their places beside the merchants and, as a result, political functions were separated from economic, the merchants' association becoming only the 'first among equals'. It was not without power, however: Paris came closest to self-government when her merchants' association farmed the royal office of provost in the late twelfth century. In Italy and adjacent regions the situation was different. There merchant associations had also played a role, but by the early thirteenth century they had become analogous to modern chambers of commerce with economic police powers. In the custom of Milan of 1216, the chamber of commerce had jurisdiction over the town mint and markets, and its statutes and judicial decisions were read annually in the citizens' general assembly.

Guild domination of urban political life sometimes built oligarchy. In 1240 at Bruges, the plutocratic and patrician entrepreneurs of the wool industry monopolized high public office via their 'Hanse of London'. Much the same may be said about Florence's entrepreneurial associations of the wool and silk guilds and that of the bankers. The difference between these later associations and earlier primitive ones is that, although political office was sometimes limited to their members, town citizenship was not confused with guild membership.

All owed service to prince or community. In 1158, the tanners of Toulouse promised to build siege artillery in wartime, and twenty years later the stonemasons of Nîmes served the artillery, receiving 100 shillings for each wall breached. During the Albigensian war, Toulouse's butchers were to accompany the militia and sell meat at fixed prices on credit. The Garonne boatmen stated in 1231 that they owed the count river transport services. Florentine construction guilds helped the republic draft building codes and inspect buildings, and provided engineers and artillerymen for the army at Montaperto in 1260.

Particular trades or crafts organized and, as industrial specialization grew, their guilds split apart. In 1227, for example, Toulouse's woollens had one association; shortly before 1300, five guilds shared the industry, each with a different speciality. Scission took place because the small-scale machinery available at this time made household workshops compatible with efficient production. In addition to sleeping or capitalizing partners, these workshops contained a master or owner, wife and children, several day workers and a few apprentices – seven to a dozen. Mining and water-milling surpassed these limits, as did textiles, an industry to be explored below.

In brief, the crafts and trades vision of economic heaven was an independent shop with a small staff and family participation. Guilds tried to make the mean the norm of the profession and often prohibited members owning more than one or two tables or shops. In England's Beverley around 1200, the weavers excluded members who became rich enough to qualify for the drapers' or merchants' guild. Meticulous regulation of raw material purchases, production methods and prices show that mutual suspicion is the price of economic brotherhood. Guilds were monopolistic, excluded foreigners and early exhibited a trend towards hereditary membership. In the late twelfth century, Parisian butchers limited ownership of tables to families already in the guild. Similar motives multiplied training stages, accentuating the 'mystery' or 'mastery' of a craft. The crown of that edifice was the obligatory masterpiece, which was not general in Paris until the fourteenth century. Technical conservatism was also normal. In France and England, old hand-mill guilds waged a futile struggle against water-powered fulling mills. Just before 1300, German cloth guilds fought the introduction of the spinning wheel. In addition, when economic growth slowed, the relation between master and worker worsened because the latter had no chance of becoming a master with a shop.

Guild technological conservatism and monopoly excited resistance by consumers and import–export interests. Governments refused to exclude immigrants and fought guild attempts to regulate the sources of raw material and prices of finished goods. By the end of the thirteenth century guilds had won their place in the sun, but were falling under ever more intense scrutiny. At the same time, the appearance of state-chartered companies, the spread of protectionism (for example, Pisa in 1303 prohibited the import of semi-finished woollens to protect local industry) and the enactment of navigation acts, such as that of Barcelona in 1286, were compatible with guild corporatism. As long as its cartel impulse was subordinated to the common good, the guild was a means by which society mobilized itself for economic battle. Especially around the Mediterranean basin, the economic structure being limned around 1300 was that of the later mercantilist state.

Guild scission was not simply a response to technology, it was also caused by the resistance of small owners and craftspeople to exploitation by the wealthy. The issues between entrepreneurs and artisans were many, and centred around partnerships and putting-out contracts. Capitalists also supplied equipment and town statutes prohibited artisans from pledging tools to secure loans. Legislation also protected imprisoned debtors: Beaumanoir proposed that, if debtors 'have nothing, he who keeps them in prison must give them bread, wine and soup as much as they can use at least once a day'. His maximum term was forty days, longer ones being 'contrary to humanity'.[30]

Masters and dayworkers often battled. A burgomaster of Provins was slain in 1281 when journeymen clothworkers protested about an increase in hours, and twelve years later laws against their associations were again promulgated. Entrepreneurs' associations fought those of artisans. At Leicester, weavers and fullers formed guilds in 1264 and 1275 to bargain with the drapers of the guild merchant. In the late thirteenth century, London's merchants claimed that the weavers had raised prices without notice, cut the number of looms, engaged in a slowdown and, in effect, gone on strike by extending Christmas holidays through January.

Similar conflicts also afflicted larger industries, those resembling capitalist industrial organization. By 1291 personnel at the Bazacle water mills of Toulouse were divided into shareholders, a legal and managerial staff and workmen who, in that year, were forbidden to form a guild. In the Florentine wool industry around 1200 one heard only of weavers, dyers and finishers. In those early days, also, even big entrepreneurs rarely thought in terms of factories, but instead capitalized others' shops or manufactured indirectly by putting out. Although no true factory system appeared, it has been seen above that some productive units were quite large. More significant were industry-wide entrepreneurial organizations, especially in textiles. By the 1290s two such guilds were in place, the *Arte di Calimala*, specializing in importing unfinished cloth, and the *Arte della Lana*, whose members imported raw wool. Under the *Lana* were no less than fourteen different crafts, some in guilds, like weavers and finishers, and others, dyers and carders, employed by putting out. In regard to the latter, *Lana* entrepreneurs both provided raw material and equipment and had police authority. The workers tried to organize, and

---

[30] *Coutumes de Clermont-en-Beauvaisis* 51 1539 (ed. Am. Salmon, Paris, 1900) II 279–80.

struggle was continual. 'Moral' regulator of the marketplace, the Church was involved: bishops generally favoured the *Lana* and Franciscan popular preachers the workers.

The *Lana* also policed entrepreneurs because, by using workers not under its control, members and interlopers could profit from substandard labour. This also touched the countryside because villages provided 'black market' labour. Matters became very casuistic indeed. Preaching in 1304, the friar Jordan of Rivalto excoriated the bishop's attack on peasants weaving illegal cloth in order to aid the poor. This Franciscan, however, inadvertently comforted the most voracious entrepreneurs. Since Florence's merchant bankers dealt in both international finance and *Lana* partnerships, this corporation's struggles affected all of Europe. Conversely, France's embargo on exporting raw wool and commercial paper to Italy during the battle between Philip the Fair and Boniface VIII affected Florentine political stability.

In the north, Flemish patricians had long battled artisans and labourers. Strikes, although prohibited, were frequent and, as early as 1242, patrician-ruled towns combined to prevent the emigration of workers seeking better conditions. From the 1280s into the early fourteenth century social and political troubles, both rural and urban, shook the whole area. The crafts tried to take over town government, thus annoying France, Flanders's overlord. Opposed by his independent town patricians, the count allied with the people and the English. A shortage of English raw wool in 1297 sparked risings in Douai and Bruges that toppled patrician government and led to the victory over the French at Courtrai in 1302. Although French authority was soon re-established, these conflicts began the persistent social combats that marked late medieval Flanders. In 1300, this was not yet perceived because, occasional violence aside, prospects looked good. If government increasingly intervened in the economy, the guilds invaded government, thus giving artisans a larger part in managing their communities.

Although usually designed for masters, guilds sometimes benefited journeymen. According to the Parisian *Book of the Professions*, swordmakers were judged by six craft guardians, four masters and two journeymen. Journeymen officers among the bronzeworkers were two out of five. Journeymen fullers were still better off: two of the four guardians were journeymen, and in annual elections journeymen chose the guardian masters and masters the journeymen. At Douai, the issues disputed by merchant drapers and the highly trained shearers were settled in 1229. The shearers agreed to forgo strikes but kickbacks were prohibited and pay for work done was fitted to prices by a simple device. When prices rose, the shearers were to petition town-appointed inspectors to present their case to the town council; were they to fall, the merchant drapers were to do the same.

Craftsfolk tried to reduce working hours, and their efforts were modestly successful. Paris's *Book of the Professions* forbade night work in all but eighteen of the 101 crafts registered, citing lighting and the need for repose. Holidays multiply in any society, and in Paris by about 1300 obligatory religious holidays had risen to twenty-eight or thirty, giving, when Sundays are counted, about eighty days of rest annually. To this can be added anywhere from twenty to thirty half-holidays for lesser feasts and the Saturday half-holiday, favoured by the clergy as preparation for Sunday's observances. Crafts also had traditional holidays: the shearers at Arras took four days at Christmas, eight at Easter and eight at Pentecost. The average work week in the region from Paris to Artois has been estimated at four to five days. The year 1300, however, was not labour's time of bliss. Work ran from dawn to dusk, with perhaps an hour off for meals. Hours varied seasonally, from seven or eight in winter to fourteen in summer, salaries being adjusted accordingly: Brussels' wool spinners earned twopence halfpenny a day in winter, three in spring and autumn and four in summer.

Guilds fostered banquets, parades, the induction of new masters and gifts to charity. Subventions were given for members' funerals and free training was given to sons of impoverished masters. Such services were tailored to particular needs. Some of Modena's smiths were wandering tinkers, and their statutes in 1244 therefore state that 'if anyone of the said association falls sick from the Alps to the Po and from Bologna to Parma, guild officers must bring him home . . . at the expense of the profession'.[31] The ordinances of the Parisian furriers of vair in 1319 required an entry fee of one shilling and sixpence plus monthly dues of a penny. For this, sick members received three shillings weekly, three on convalescence and three more on returning to work.

Guild social service was supplemented by burial societies. Linked to the Church, these charities resisted entrepreneurial pressure better than guilds: when, in the late thirteenth century, the Florentine dyers' guild was quashed by the *Lana*, their charitable confraternity still remained. The Church's attitude toward these sodalities was mixed: it supported them in the early twelfth century; fifty years later it often questioned them. A council at Rouen in 1189 complained that churches were crowded with their altars. Similarly, those who made apostolic poverty into a labour ideology, like the Humiliati in north Italy, were sometimes suppressed, as in 1178. By 1201, however, papal policy supported these and similar groups. Propagating Christian utopianism, the Humiliati were successful for a time, and at Florence in 1239 they had a community of brothers and sisters in the cloth industry. About the same time, semi-industrial communities of female Beguines and male Beghards spread like wildfire through Flemish, French and Rhenish towns. In 1250, Cologne boasted about a thousand Beguines.

---

[31] P.S. Leicht, *Storia del diritto Italiano: Le Fonti* (2nd edn, Milan, 1943) 322.

In time, these movements weakened. Lay artisans objected to their competition, and the growth of secular guilds removed part of their reason for being. Although the mendicants favoured economic corporatism and aided charitable agencies helping artisans and labourers, the Church was not wedded to any one social group. Besides, if the humble got charity, the rich played a role in the confraternities, being there in order to dominate. The utopian labour movement had outlived its usefulness, and was often driven out of business. Lay guilds obliged a synod at Arras in 1275 to prohibit Beguines from weaving, dyeing cloth and cobbling, and two years later the Florentine Humiliati retired from industry. Although Beguinages persisted in the Rhineland and Low Countries well into modern times, they had become economically marginal. A petition of 1295 to the town council by the Brussels Beguinage requested the same return for their labour as that given to the members of secular guilds.

Princes also responded to the rising power of artisans and shopkeepers, and often encouraged guild creation, so much so that some towns in backward regions had more developed corporate structures by the mid-thirteenth century than great urban republics. A reason was that princely officers were often recruited from the nobility, a group suspicious of the new rich. To Joinville, a very rich noble, the oppression of the poor by the rich amply justified Louis IX's removal of the provostship of Paris from the merchant guild and its assignment to a royal officer, Stephen Boileau. This action was also applauded by crafts and trades who had fought the patricians since 1250, and they were rewarded by Boileau's publication of their guild ordinances in the *Book of the Professions* of 1261. Princes also often espoused the corporate principle, extending it into the political order. In 1257, the king of Aragon gave the crafts and trades the lesser half of Barcelona's great council's two hundred seats, the same percentage as that given to the patricians, a lesser but swing vote being entrusted to the merchants. Urban republics were reluctant to grant these elements such extensive representation.

Princes, being opportunist, were not actuated by love of the poor. When aristocracies dominated towns, they supported the people; when the situation was reversed, they favoured the rich. When the commons seemed about to take over Barcelona in 1285, the king of Aragon crushed them. At this time, however, kings usually supported guilds because patricians had led towns seeking independence. The merchant guild's loss of the right to farm the provost's office obliterated what little self-government Paris had enjoyed.

In urban republics guilds advanced more slowly, but eventually attained the same heights and, in fact, their corporatism became the constitutional basis of the state. By 1282, the Florentine government was run by the seven greater guilds: the medical and legal professions, bankers, and entrepreneurs' associations of the silk and wool industries. By 1292 middling guilds, butchers and masons, and even some lesser ones had entered, only dyers, carders and other proletarians being excluded. The time was not propitious for further democratization, however, because around 1300, the majority of the people had obtained much of what they desired. A significant minority, however, sometimes swollen by immigration from the countryside, remained deprived of economic and political fulfilment. Over a hundred years of intermittent social war passed before these latecomers, inspired by the earlier, century-long success of ascending lesser social groups, abandoned hope. Add a tightened economy to this friction, and some characteristics of the unhappy but inventive fourteenth century may be glimpsed.

Part Three

SOCIETY

Chapter 9

Women and men

Marriage and love

At Toulouse, married women of all classes were often addressed in documents as 'mistress' (*domina*). Such was not the case with men: few, save notables, were called 'mister' (*dominus*). Women's ability to give life made husband and wife equal in theory and, like a man, a woman was free to choose her mate. Marriage therefore required no more than the free and voluntary agreement of a pair along with consummation. Nuptials were customarily blessed in church, celebrated by a feast and a priest's blessing of the pair in bed, the place of birthing. Around 1300 the doctors of law at Toulouse were asked: was a young woman legally married if she played, when tipsy and half coerced, the 'game of man and wife'? No, they found, because she had been tricked. In the Pauline texts glossed by churchmen, if a husband owned his woman, a wife owned her man. According to a Franciscan active around Paris, equality was required in marriage. Gilbert of Tournai (d. 1270) urged couples not to marry for profit, beauty or lust:

> They should live together happily and honestly honouring God and generating children to serve Him . . . When they are equals, they live in peace, but when they marry for a dowry or property, they always fight. If you wish to marry, marry an equal . . . This is a social love . . . because the pair are equal partners.[1]

Because wives usually outlived husbands, marriage gave women a time of power, namely widowhood, when, unless she had grown sons, a woman acceded to authority over family, property and means of production. From noble to serf, however, everything depended on the liberties won from prince or lord. Limitations aside, powerful middle-aged women appear in every class. A royal example is Blanche of Castile (d. 1252), mother of Louis IX of France, whose long widowhood and regency were acclaimed a great success. However, she had a weakness: she so dominated her son that he hardly dared lend his body to his wife.

Women also healed or, rather, nursed. And risk was attached to that. A knight's widow from Puylaurens testified about the fall of Montréal near

---

[1] D'Avray and Tausche, 'Marriage Sermons', 47 (1980) 114–15.

Carcassonne in 1240. When the French assaulted the place, Ermengarda and 'other noblewomen' were carrying stones for the defenders' artillery. A clamour arose: the French had broken in. The women dashed to take refuge in a house but, 'just as [Ermengarda] sat down, she heard it cried out in the square that her brother Isarn had been wounded. [She] straightway went out, hunting about until she found him.'[2] Although never university-trained physicians, women worked as midwives, having a near monopoly of child-birth. In hospitals women were almost as active as men, partly because physicians were not on hospital staffs and also because hospitals were like monasteries, run by administrators, nurses and sometimes even inmates. A marriage contract involved the hospital of St Antoine at Toulouse in 1202:

> I John the Hospitaller, marry you Sibil; and I, Sibil, marry you John and give my body to . . . the hospital to serve God and the poor . . . I Raymond Calvet [master of the hospital] receive the said Sibil as sister and participant in the said hospital . . . [pledging] to receive no man or woman in the said hospital without their consent, and that John and . . . Sibil are to be the masters of the said house after my death and that of my wife Ricarda.[3]

Women have always been loved, but much depended on age and class. In the 1180s, Andrew the Chaplain recommended wasting no time on farming girls; just push them over. Adam de la Halle (d. 1286/88) disagreed: his heroine was Marion, a peasant maid endowed with natural reason, courtesy and taste who rejected a rough knight in favour of her rustic Robin. Moralizers hastened to channel sex. Philip of Novara tells of a handsome young woman (twenty to forty years old in his scheme) who collected jewelled knives from her success-ive lovers. In middle age (forty to sixty) she began to buy love by surrender-ing the knives until none were left. Others were shrewder: sex and love were not enough for a happy marriage. Christian of Troyes' *Erec and Enide* linked love to friendship and career to make a fulfilling marriage.

Christian's age created a positive cult of love in which lovers were truly equal. Iseult is as competent in woman's work such as healing as Tristan is in hunting and making war. She sacrifices as much and commits as many crimes for love as does he. Aucassin believed a commonplace that men love particu-lar women while women love any useful man, but Nicole showed him he was wrong: women's fidelity equals men's. Erec and Enide are made to rebuild mutual respect and love in their marriage by means of accomplish-ment. Enide undergoes tests of loyalty, courage and social wisdom just as her husband does.

Love's cult was so mighty that it almost pushed sex aside. Perhaps echoing clerical ideas, the troubadour's 'love from afar', like humanity's love of God,

---

[2] My *Men and Women at Toulouse in the Age of the Cathars* 120.
[3] My 'Charity and Social Work in Toulouse' in *Traditio* XXII (1966) 248n.

expressed an overwhelming longing for the unattainable. In *Tristan and Iseult* the lovers have no home on earth, only in heaven. Captivated by love's magic, they violate all social canons: marriage, friendship, family and loyalty to Church and king. This argument was refuted in *Aucassin and Nicolete* where the lovers triumph over family, religion (Nicolete being Saracen in origin) and society to build anew true love, family and society. In its easy way, the poem echoed mystical teaching wherein the ability to love with the flesh gave evidence of a capacity to love spiritually.

Focused by monks, male ambivalence towards women was experienced as rarely before or after. The charm of a girl's figure and the lilt of her voice tempted both Peter Damian (d. 1072) and Peter, the hermit of Monte Morrone (the later Celestine V canonized in 1313), and both converted their attraction into scatological anger. Philip of Novara was cooler. Carnality led older men, prompted by fear of death, to seek 'all sorts of unnatural perversions. Just as pride is the vice of the poor and covetousness that of the rich, so is lust the vice of the old.'[4]

Male complaints about women were sometimes plaintive. *Mahieu's Lamentations* argued before 1292 that marriage is harder than celibacy. Women are impossible: they talk too much. Why did the Saviour first show himself to women after resurrection? Because he wanted everyone to know about it fast. Why did Jesus not marry? He knew better. Celibates concocted the prohibition of divorce. Mahieu asked the Lord: your daughter Eve betrayed you; can you imagine what your wife would have done? The law is unfair: the Saviour ordered what he himself did not dare. Capitulating, the Lord avows that married men will have a higher place in heaven because they have suffered more. He adds that he had sanctified the married state by allowing his mother to marry, 'but I did not tonsure the monks or constitute any monastic order'.[5]

Mixed feelings about the flesh were well-nigh universal, shared by both men and women. They ranged from flagellation to a cult of the body, the laity leaning towards the latter and the religious towards the former. James of Voragine believed it edifying to report that, when asked why he had not healed his daughter Petronilla, the apostle Peter replied that she was too beautiful to live. Still, physical beauty counted: by lifting her skirts, the virgin Nicolete miraculously made a sick man leap up off his bed. The clergy castigated the banners and shining armour of the knights, but Dante's *Convivio* urged men and women to dress well and cultivate beauty of body as well as of mind. The clergy themselves wrote much of the romantic literature of the time, but were of two minds about it. Surely hopelessly, a penitential of Peter Cantor's school distinguished between two types of public entertainers: 'Those

---

[4] *Des quatres tenz d'aage d'ome* 4 (ed. Marcel de Fréville, Paris, 1888) 95.
[5] Langlois, *La Vie en France au moyen-âge* II 277–83.

frequenting drinking bouts and lascivious parties singing dirty songs are damnable . . . Others . . . singing the deeds of princes and lives of saints, and solacing men in sickness and distress . . . can surely be borne, as Pope Alexander says.'[6]

And clerks were of two minds. Writing for layfolk, the chaplain Andrew's *On Love* and John of Meung's later continuation of the *Romance of the Rose* flatly asserted the natural impossibility of celibacy. The layman Peter Dubois, John's contemporary, opined that celibacy had been instituted in antiquity by the old and decrepit. Besides, clerks were not as white as the driven snow. In Andrew's intentionally humorous dialogue between a lady and a gentleman (who happens to be a clerk), the latter argues that heavy petting is better than copulation because it is less likely to cause pregnancy. Both are forgivable, however, being 'natural' since love alone inspires virtue. 'I'll prove to you,' he says, 'that a clerk is a better lover than a layman because he is more prudent.' Unbelievable, replies the lady: clerks are disfigured by tonsure and 'as though clothed in female dress'. They can't even give lovers' gifts, she adds, because they shouldn't have anything to give. Who wants stolen goods?[7]

Peter Damian charged that heterosexual carnality led to homosexuality. Perhaps so, but one way of avoiding women is to be homosexual, and love among males is decidedly ventilated in the sources. Just after 1300, the inquisition of the bishop of Pamiers, who died as Benedict XII in 1342, discovered a gay 'defrocked' Franciscan and hanger-on at the newly founded 'university' in the small town of Pamiers and the young scholars with whom he had relations. This 'looser' also pimped for a prior and canon of St Sernin of Toulouse, a dignitary who used his book porters to meet intimate needs from time to time. The same testimony records a cobbler in Pamiers and a squire of the same persuasion in the nearby countryside. Perhaps the adepts of this minority divergence were obliged to congregate, hence come to town, for reasonably frequent contacts.

Judging from this, homosexuals also gravitated to educational institutions, where celibacy obtained; but celibacy did not necessarily inspire homophilia. Sometime in the 1260s, testimony was recorded about forty-two of the monks in the monastery of Lézat, south of Toulouse. Almost half were said to have been, or to be, sexually active. Three were merely defamed of having had relationships with women, three were said to have favoured female religious from a nearby house, and specific women were named in no less than fourteen cases. Eleven were said to have had issue, six being charged with having had specific children by specific women. Only two were described as given over to 'sodomy', a practice clearly considered a 'fault'. According to one monk, the charge that Prior Hugh 'was a sodomite was repeated secretly . . . and was

---

[6] Gauthier, *La chevalerie* 656.
[7] *De amore* 1 6 G (ed. E. Trojel, Munich, 1964) 189–90.

said out of envy and a desire to harm him'.[8] Weighty canonists nonetheless seemed to believe that sodomy was the paradigmatic unnatural offence. Observing that the Saviour came for all humanity, Christian and non-Christian, Innocent IV stated: 'I believe that if a gentile . . . contravenes the law of nature, the pope may licitly punish him following Genesis 19 where it states that the Lord punishes sodomites who sin against nature's law.'[9]

To return to men and women, childbearing, highly prized though it was, inhibited women. The exposure of unwanted children was prohibited and voluntary abortion was not only forbidden, but risky and largely inefficacious. Birth control was effectively reduced to being a function of the ages at which union took place, modes of sexual intimacy between the sexes and the mistreatment by parents and servants of the very young, especially, to judge from later evidence, females. A second hardship for women was accidents in birthing and childbed fever, which may have resulted in higher death rates among adult females than among men in spite of war, hunting, heavy labour and riding.

Childbearing also tied women to property and family. In farming populations, the need for labour encouraged trial marriage to see if a pair were fertile. Especially among the wealthy, marriages were arranged by parents. Family solidarity and property impeded the freedom of lovers, of men almost as much as women, especially when a family was rich, noble or princely. Although the sources say very little about the private lives of kings and princes until Joinville wrote about Louis IX of France, the will to win drove a prince as mighty as Henry II of England to marry Eleanor of Aquitaine (d. 1204). Although she bore him eight children, this princess was ten years older than her spouse and they were anything but a happy couple.

Another impediment to attaining the ideal was imposed by servitude and service. While accenting uterine succession and hence reminiscent of women in servile families, dependency impeded freedom because no serf could marry without a lord's permission. Within the nobility the same was often true. When, after long service to both Henry II of England and his son Henry, William the Marshal's suit was pleaded before Richard Coeur de Lion on the grounds that his father had given William the heiress to the county of Pembroke, Richard exclaimed: 'By God's legs, he did not give her to him! He only promised to. But I'll give her to him all free, both the machine [the woman] and the land!'[10] Peter Cantor denounced such practices because they contradicted scripture, notably 1 Corinthians 7:39: 'If any woman wishes to marry, let her marry in the Lord' – freely, that is.

---

[8] My *Men and Women at Toulouse in the Age of the Cathars* 51.
[9] *Commentaria super libros quinque decretalium* (Frankfurt, 1570) 430rb. No. 4.
[10] *Histoire de Guillaume le Maréchal* (ed. Paul Meyer, Paris, 1891–1901) v. 968ff.

A final impediment was that women often married older men. Men of middling means waited until they had acquired or inherited property or businesses before marrying. Established older men, furthermore, were unlikely to marry women their own age, and therefore many women married spouses ten or twenty years their senior in first marriages. The disparity in age also helps explain why women – teenaged children – were subjected to physical discipline by their husbands, but it was not all bad. Unattractive or insecure young women did better in the market of the overaged than in that of the young. The marriage of a young woman to a failing older man at the peak of his wealth could lead to a kind of equality, especially if a propertied widowhood soon came to pass.

This kind of union did not attract poets or most young women and men. No romance has lovers who are not exquisitely young. There was fear here too: an old man will be cuckolded by a young wife, a theme seen as early as the eleventh-century poem *Ruodlieb*, where an old spouse sits in a privy watching his wife and a young man through a knothole. More elegantly, Philip of Novara disliked this kind of marriage, 'for if [the male] has the desire, he certainly does not have the capacity'. Even marriage between old folk disgusted him: 'Two rotting bodies in one bed are simply unbearable.'[11]

Lack of freedom prompted theft and, joined to the religion of love described above, adultery was central. To Andrew the Chaplain true love could not exist in marriage and marriage was no excuse for not making love. Here, however, all depends on luck and especially wealth. No poet bothered to count Iseult's children, and what may be passed off as love among the rich is bare adultery among the poor. Or was (is) it? In Italian towns, the people often loved the French, their songs, their manners and loose ways, and so did young knights and patricians who 'lived nobly'. Those whom 'Gallicism' offended, even though they too had heard the siren songs, were lesser gentlefolk, burghers and substantial farmers, those whose modest property pricked social ambition. These worthies drew up laws against sumptuous clothing and conspicuous consumption and especially looked askance at adulterous love.

Being rich, nobles were often more broadminded than the middle classes, but there were limits because careers were more important than love. In spite of professional ambition, Abelard (d. 1142) finally bit the bullet and married Heloise (d. 1164), but they could not sustain the relationship. We know little about the child of this famous pair, but he was raised back home in Brittany by Abelard's sister, and vanished into history saddled with a didactic poem by his father and the awful name of Astrolabe. Adultery was always punishable in law and husbands were sometimes allowed to slay lovers caught in

---

[11] *Des quatres tenz d'aage d'ome* 4 (ed. Fréville) 95.

the act. Relationships involving a wife heading a household or court with juniors disrupted social order and precipitated exemplary punishment. Not long before 1296, a Toulousan apprentice was condemned to death for this offence, although as a minor below twenty-five years of age he was not executed. In 1314, King Philip IV of France imprisoned for life the reportedly adulterous wives of two of his sons (both later crowned) and executed their lovers! In southern France and elsewhere, adulterers were often forced to 'run the town', nude amid the howling crowd. It was nevertheless the Toulousan town fathers who hobbled the prince's right to confiscate property by making it difficult to prove flagrancy.

Lovers were not what these magistrates loved; property was. And they surely also knew that love was fraught with ambivalence. Two of chivalry's greatest heroes, Lancelot and Tristan, were the lovers of their kings' wives. The *Romance of Sidrac*, translated from the Arabic, averred that 'the hottest woman in the world is colder than the coldest man', and that wives had been unfaithful before and still brooks bubble and flowers bloom.[12] A southern French vernacular romance exhibits similar 'wisdom'. Because the king paid attention to his wife Flamenca, Archibald fell into a jealous rage. Constantly watched, the young wife was allowed out only to go to church. There she ran into a secular canon, literate, martial in bearing and background, polite and deeply sympathetic. Busy at the gate watching the king, Archibald had failed to guard the postern. One day, however, the lover blithely rode off to war, and this study of the inefficacy of rage came to a happy end.

Means, literacy and religion

In the areas influenced by Roman and canon law, most brides came with a dowry from their family and received a smaller marriage gift from their bride-groom or his parents. These two parts together made up a marriage portion, which, after the death of the husband, provided for the care of the widow. The administration of the portion was entrusted to the husband who, how-ever, could act only with the consent of his spouse and her friends. After the husband's death, a widow was often appointed manager of the estate until the children reached majority. To recuperate her portion, she had precedence over all other creditors of an estate.

In this system, a family owed a daughter with male siblings no other endowment than her dowry. Real property, means of production and pro-fessional preference went to male heirs and, once the economy was monet-ized in the eleventh century, the daughter's portion was paid in money. The lord of Isle Jourdain in Gascony, west of Toulouse, inserted a passage in his

---

[12] Langlois, *La Vie en France* III 250.

testament of 1200 designed to limit the number of heirs to his properties. With the express consent of his lord, the count of Toulouse, who was present at the rendering of the will, the baron testated that 'if there is a legitimate male son, no woman or daughter will ever again have any portion of the said heredity, but instead the daughters will be married with money'.[13] Not only did magnates follow this not necessarily unfair practice, so did members of every class, both high or low. The poet and lawyer Cino of Pistoia put it succinctly:

> In almost all Italy customs and statutes state that sisters with brothers do not succeed. Their fathers or brothers are therefore obliged to dower them according to the family's dignity and wealth.[14]

Once married, a daughter, like a son, was emancipated, as the custom of Montpellier said in 1204. The system of dowries for brides, together with marriage gifts brought by their young spouses, had one advantage: pairs were endowed when young instead of waiting for their parents' deaths. Besides, parental power was limited and burdened with responsibility. The duty of parents to support and educate children was almost sacred. Jurists agreed that magistrates could adjust the details of both divine and natural law, but could not change essences. A pope, the commonplace went, could never dispense from scripture, nor a legislator from the duty of parents, especially fathers, to raise and educate children. In regard to daughters, parental duty was to see them married or placed, at smaller cost, in a religious order.

However sound the system, marriage portions did not suffice. At Toulouse, examination of about 136 extant marriage charters and testaments from the first half of the thirteenth century shows that a third to a half of the women would have had to do something to eke out widowhood. And because at least thirty per cent of the women listed there were either noble or patrician, the percentage of those whose dowries and gifts were insufficient was surely far higher. Although the value of women declined with age, remarriage could handle lack of means. Work was best, however. According to the Parisian mid-century *Book of the Professions*, widows of trades- or craftsmen carried on their deceased husbands' professions, if they did not remarry out of the craft. In marriage contracts, working women arranged to have their share of joint acquisitions returned on their husbands' deaths. Evidence from later times shows that women were a significant part of the labour force. In 1179–82, the 'brothers and sisters' had equal rights in the turners' guild at Cologne. Parisian guild statutes indicate that some crafts were wholly female and that women, especially widows of craftsmen, could be admitted to the mastership in some woollens guilds. Where guilds participated directly in town

---

[13] My *Men and Women at Toulouse in the Age of the Cathars* 29.
[14] *De nuptiis* in Mayali, *L'exclusion des filles dotées* 47.

government, women even played a minor role in political life. In Provins in the mid-fourteenth century, twelve per cent of the voters in a political plebiscite were women.[15]

Although women's work in field, barn and garden is to be added to the above, their labour failed to persuade contemporaries that they were equal to men. Bodily different, women did not normally plough, hunt or do heavy metalwork or building, and hence crowded into less profitable labour. They also rarely went to war except to urge men on, help them plan for it and lament or rejoice in their departure. Maiming and killing were what war was about, and size counted. Some women were nevertheless suited to it. Although guildswomen usually provided substitutes for watch and ward, Wismar on the Baltic in 1292 boasted one *domina* Adelaide, who pledged herself 'to serve watch as long as she lives just like any other citizen'.[16] However, soldiering was not usually women's business: giving life was, not giving death.

Male size also helps explain why husbands beat wives. Beaumanoir had thrice heard of wives slain by their husbands for adultery, and recommended that, if a woman misbehaved or refused to obey a 'reasonable command . . . a husband may chastise her reasonably'.[17] That a wife might chastise her husband did not occur to him, but it did, however, to Gilbert of Tournai, who believed that a man could correct his wife 'and she should receive it out of love', but then added '*et e converso*'. The normal inequality of the sexes was firmly underpinned by tradition. Giles of Rome took from Aristotle the sentiment that men dominate beasts, males females and adults young. Women were ruled because they 'normally lack men's prudence. There are some who are more intelligent than men, but that is rare . . . and hence women ought naturally be subject to men.'[18] Women were also believed to be more inclined to flinch than men. Writing on criminal law, Albert of Gandino (d. 1310) remarked about judicial torture that, if it is to be applied to a family, 'begin with the child in the sight of the father, because the latter will then speak up more quickly . . . Likewise, first torment women . . . because, being of greater constancy, men will confess more slowly, but women are quicker because their hearts are momentary and unstable.'[19]

In banking and moneylending, physical strength meant little. Since women were in business, once restitution for usury was enforced, women's testaments restoring 'ill-gotten gains' appear. Even in these fields, however, women were

---

[15] Félix Bourquelot, 'Un scrutin du XIVe siècle' in *Mémoires de la société nationale des antiquaires de France* XXI (1852) 455ff.

[16] Wachendorf, *Die wirtschaftliche Stellung der Frau in den deutschen Städten* 32.

[17] *Coutumes de Beauvaisis* No. 1631.

[18] *De regimine principum* 1 2 7 (Rome, 1607) 65.

[19] *Tractatus de maleficiis* 12 in ed. Hermann Kantorowicz, *Albertus Gandinus und das Strafrecht der Scholastik* (Berlin and Leipzig, 1926) 158.

disadvantaged. Law discriminated against them, adjudging their testimony inferior to that of men, and businesswomen had to pay for legal counsel to speak for them in court. Besides, women were rarely as literate as men and were therefore treated in law as dependants, almost as children. Some were literate, nevertheless, often because, although excluded from sacred orders, they were active in both orthodoxy and heterodoxy. Between 1245 and 1251, no less than thirty-two female convents were incorporated into the Dominican Order in the German province alone. At Strasbourg in 1257, twelve cloisters housed about three hundred sisters, and many laywomen were associated with the new mendicant orders. Convents, although inspected by male clergy, were self-governing institutions with elected abbesses. Even at their peak, however, there were far fewer female religious than male. Unlike monks who usually had Latin, moreover, nuns often had only the vernacular, though some were distinguished in Latin letters. Dying in 1179 as abbess of Rupertsberg, Hildegard of Bingen was not only famed for visions but was also an indefatigable traveller and correspondent with theologians, emperors and popes.

The clergy were of two minds about women's intellect. Giles of Rome remarked that, because of their weak endowment with reason, they surrendered to their passions more easily than men. This Austin friar would surely have enjoyed the opinion of Humbert of Romans. Glossing the apostle Paul, this Dominican put it thus:

> I do not permit women to preach for four reasons. First is their lack of intelligence which they have in smaller quantity than men; second is the subjection imposed on them; third is that, if a woman does preach, her appearance will provoke lust . . . and fourth is the memory of the first woman who . . . taught but once and turned the whole world upside down.[20]

Literate or not, laywomen were to stay out of religious debates. Esclarmunda, sister of a count of Foix, widow of a lord of Isle Jourdain, witnessed a legal document in 1198, something never done by those of her sex. But even this exceptional princess, when speaking up during a discussion between the orthodox and heterodox at Pamiers in 1207, was abruptly told by a monk to be quiet and look to her spinning.

To others, however, the picture was different. Addressing the nuns of Godstow, Archbishop John Peckham of Canterbury repeated the worn sentiment that the more fragile their sex, the more worthy their virginal penitence. Some still did not condescend, and knew that there was iron in women. Does not scripture report that weeping women adhered to the crucified Christ more firmly than his fleeing disciples? This quality had inspired Robert of

---

[20] *De eruditione praedicatorum* 2 12 (ed. Berthier) II 406 and 1 Timothy 3:4.

Abrissel (d. 1117) to found the order of Fontevrault (rule adopted in 1115). There, the abbess supervised two convents of professed religious, one female and the other male, as well as two houses of lay sisters for those sick in body (lepers) and sick in mind (fallen women!).

Saints' lives and clerical biographies show that mothers frequently pushed their sons towards the ecclesiastical life. Saying that women heard sermons more regularly and went to confession more willingly than men, the Franciscan preacher Berthold of Regensburg told no secret. Everybody knew that women were more devoted to saints' cults and more credulous in regard to miracles than men. Humbert of Romans loved the 'flaky' quality of female devotion. Decrying clerks who refuse to study scripture because they make no sense of it, this Dominican urged them to imitate:

> matrons and devout women who do not cease from daily reading the psalms merely because they do not understand them. Indeed . . . sacred scripture, even when not understood by readers, has power against spiritual wickedness, just as do the words of enchantment against the serpent, even if the enchanter does not understand them.[21]

Men led the Church, but the true believers were especially women, sometimes embarrassingly so, as Dominicans along the Rhine felt when their female houses and tertiaries multiplied enormously.

Like the clergy, however, women were famed not only for belief but also for manipulativeness. Belief's function is therefore to be examined. Perhaps women profited from, and even stimulated, the hostility of the two worlds of men with which they dealt: the clergy and the laity. Exercised over women, a layman's power was immediate, sexual, deployed in greater physical strength, and practical because it involved property and the maintenance or abandonment of children. The clerk's authority was at a remove, rarely sexual and, in regard to the relationship of women to husbands and lovers, idealistic. It was even unreal, as when it insisted on those Pauline texts that proclaimed the freedom of women to choose their mates and, within marriage, asserted their equality with their husbands. Clerical judgement, in fact, often affronted practical experience. It is therefore no surprise that women peopled the clerical order with chosen sons and enthusiastically seconded their erstwhile children's practice of winning their battles with the laity by means of sentimental obfuscations or appeals to the miraculous. To force the argument a trifle, women were never more practical than when they were at their most credulous.

The Latins were convinced that their women were better off than their Islamic and Jewish sisters. A theme well represented in Caesarius of

---

[21] *Expositio regulae Beati Augustini* Ch. 142 (ed. Berthier) I 429.

Heisterbach's often brutal stories was that Jewish girls – to him, incidentally, frequently very pretty – wished to marry Christian boys or have them as lovers. In his scheme for conquering the Near East, Peter Dubois argued that Muslim men would be entranced by that superior product, the educated western girl, and claimed that eastern women, held in the bondage of poly-gyny and purdah, would welcome crusaders. Others proudly claimed that divorce on a husband's initiative was impossible among Christians, asserting also that women did not attend mosque or synagogue and that no attention was given to their education. These spokesmen were warriors in the long battle between Heleno-Roman monogyny and Near Eastern polygyny, an institution that had spread widely in late antiquity and the early Middle Ages, and was only in this period again beginning another decline.

The daughters of gentlefolk and patricians often learned vernacular letters at home or in convents. According to the Dominican Jordan of Saxony (d. 1237), Dominic Guzman (d. 1221) founded his first house at Prouille in 1206 partly because the gentry in the Midi could not pay for orthodox convents and sent their daughters to the Cathars for education. In 1320, four of Brussels' ten lower schools were for girls. It is therefore not surprising that Mary of France, who wrote her *Lays* at the Plantagenet court from 1165 to 1190, was a major poet, and that biographies of female poets were among those of the troubadours published in the late thirteenth century.

For layfolk in general, however, learning was a waste of time in view of women's duties around the crib and the hearth (not to speak of the field and workshop); duties that, except among the rich, were far more onerous than today. Women were also excluded from the literate professions, partly because these had evolved out of the clerical order and were for long celibate. And exceptions prove the rule. When sick, the canonist John Andreae (d. 1348) is said to have had his daughter Novella lecture his students, but had her veiled from them by a curtain. Female teachers of vernacular letters are heard of in towns, as are scribes, but women did not attend the university and guilds of notaries excluded them.

A sure proof that women were less considered is that they were poorer on average than men. A tax list for Toulouse dated 1335 shows that women formed 8.7 per cent of the heads of household, but that their share of the wealth was only 6.3 per cent of the total. They were not equal even in leperhouses. In the Grand Beaulieu at Chartres in 1264, the allowance for male inmates was ten shillings for wool cloth and four for linen; women were given eight and three. Relatively illiterate and poor, women, especially those of the lower classes, thus survived not only by work but also by using their attractiveness. Concubinage was common. In the countryside south of Toulouse in the 1240s, one even sees an unmarried woman describing her lover as her 'male concubine'. Still, it is obvious that most concubines were female and both poorer and younger than their men. Rural gentlemen had mistresses from the families of their farmers and town patricians from among the humble. An example is Berengar Astro of Toulouse, who had two legitimate children by his wife and a son by his mistress Saussia, with whom he lived. Late in life, Saussia was married off to a man of modest class and had two legitimate daughters by him. Named John, Berengar's natural child used his father's family name, married a wealthy widow and died around 1246.

A yardstick of a concubine's position is the treatment of natural children. John Astro came from a clan whose women were dowered with 1,000 to 1,500 shillings; his father left him only 500, a sum paid by his legitimate half-brother only when dying. It is true that on the highest level natural children did well, especially female ones, perhaps because they could be dowered without affecting family office and property. Male illegitimates were excluded from inheritances, but it was not always easy. In late 1259, litigation erupted between a lord of Isle Jourdain and his cousin-german, the lord asserting that the latter had no right to inherit 'because you are not a legitimate heir of the barony. You are the son of a subdeacon who was prior, canon and archdeacon in the cathedral of Toulouse.'[22] What is odd about this long-drawn-out case is that the mother of the noble lord of Isle was the much respected India, natural daughter of Count Raymond VI of Toulouse (d. 1222). Lastly, in some regions, perhaps all, illegitimacy reflected poverty. To use under-reported figures, at Halesowen near Birmingham in England between 1270 and 1348 five per cent of the females from wealthy farming families were adjudged to have fornicated as against eleven per cent of the middling and sixteen per cent of the poor.[23]

Prostitutes obviously suffered more discrimination than concubines. Statutes against ostentatious lewdness, prostitution, gambling and other street disorders are seen everywhere. Wishing to outdo the clergy in this matter, Louis IX and his brother Alphonse of Poitiers (d. 1271) were hard on the profession. The latter even sacrificed a little when he rescinded his right in Poitiers to protect prostitutes in return for a fee and, when doing so, gratuitously called the women 'stupid'. Social need, however, led princes and magistrates to listen to Augustine's warning: every palace has its cesspool, and whores are necessary lest men fall into even 'worse vices'. A lawsuit at Montpellier of 1285 noted that the town's prostitutes had often been harassed by their neighbours. Acting on the advice of the town council, the royal governor ordered that:

> the said women should reside on the [outlying] street commonly called Hot Street . . . [and he also promised] to the advocate standing for Guirauda of Béziers and Elys of Le Puy there present in the court, and to each and every prostitute now living or

---

[22] My *Men and Women at Toulouse in the Age of the Cathars* 78.

[23] Zvi Razi, *Life, Marriage and Death in a Medieval Parish: Economy, Society and Demography in Halesowen 1270–1400* (Cambridge, 1980) 66.

wishing to live in this town, that the said women . . . will remain now and always under the protection of the lord king and his court.[24]

Once permitted, prostitution had to be regulated and the retirement of personnel provided for. Innocent III thought it meritorious of laymen to marry one-time prostitutes, and a number of orders appeared specializing in them, like the German sisters of Mary Magdalene (founded 1225). Usually associated with hospitals where the 'reformed' women worked, these 'repentant sisters' were part of state-regulated prostitution in the late Middle Ages.

To conclude, although women were obviously often happy, they were subordinate. Repeating Ambrose of Milan, Gratian roundly declared that 'a woman has no power, but submits in everything to the rule of her husband'.[25] And the judges who wrote the code called by Bracton's name borrowed a truism from the Italian jurisconsult Azzo, who had flatly stated: 'Women differ from men . . . because their condition is worse than theirs.'[26]

---

[24] A. Germain, 'Statuts inédits des Repenties du couvent de Saint-Gilles de Montpellier' in *Mémoires de la Société archéologique de Montpellier* 5 (1860–69) 124–26.

[25] *Decretum* C. 33 5 17 (Friedberg 1 1255), the word 'rule' translating *dominium*.

[26] *De legibus et consuetudinibus Angliae* Introductio (ed. S.E. Thorne, Cambridge, MA, 1968) II 32, citing Azzo's *Summa* on the *Institutes*.

Chapter 10

Workers and farmers

Farmers

Latin Europe's social orders were often described simply. There were three – clergy, warriors and labourers – sourly described in a later Dutch saying

> I pray for you,
> I fight for you,
> I lay eggs for you.[1]

Poverty and malice – preached the Franciscan Berthold of Regensburg – made peasants into 'naked' fish devouring each other. Some thought farmers little more than 'stinking serfs', as the poet and lord Bertrand of Born said. The French version of Raymond Llull's manual casually stated that nobles defend 'society because, for fear of being destroyed, the people . . . cultivate the land and, terrified of knights, fear kings and princes'.[2] The Italian prelate Giles of Rome likened rustics to 'barbarians, quasi-forest folk, who do not know how to govern themselves and are therefore natural slaves'.[3]

Rural folk were not always disparaged. In the early twelfth century, Honorius praised them: 'What about farmers? Most will be saved because they live simply and their sweat feeds God's people'; a sentiment later repeated by the Dominican Vincent of Beauvais.[4] The poet Adam de la Halle's *Robin and Marion* has a knightly bully defeated in love by a gentle peasant boy. The theologian Peter Cantor asked who is wise, the rich, lawyers or men of letters? None of these; the wise man is the farmer. But this wisdom rested on a very fragile base.

Farmers ranged from free to slave, and the origins of this inequality interested contemporaries. In his *Customs of the Beauvaisis*, Beaumanoir catalogued the causes of servitude. Poverty or the incapacity to bear arms had caused some persons to be given to saints and the Church, and others to be oppressed by the powerful. Some slavery resulted from capture in war, a belief that rang true in a time when captured Muslims were normally enslaved. These ideas came from Roman law where people were either slave or free, but the

---

[1] Lousse, *La société d'ancien régime* I 103.
[2] *Livre de l'ordre de chevalerie* (ed. V. Minervini, Bari, 1972) 130.
[3] *De regimine principum* 2 3 15 (Rome, 1607) 385.
[4] *Elucidarium* 2 18 in *PL* CLXXII 1148–49.

English author of *Fleta* remarked that, although Roman theory was true 'in law', it was not so 'in fact'. Less legalistic, Beaumanoir stated that servitude had many conditions, hard, light, sometimes personal and sometimes attached to tenure.

This fuzziness reflected social organization. Since late Rome, free and slave had been coming closer. The ideal was a regulated society in which rich and powerful, poor and humble were all bound to service, each person having a function or duty and an appropriate remuneration. The Church advocated this sociology, its spokesmen paralleling heaven's hierarchies with those of the world, saying that true liberty was service to God, Church, prince and people. In 1103, for example, Cluny's monks called their serfs 'rustics who, liberated from the yoke of servitude, have been bound to the service of the blessed Peter'.[5]

In many of Europe's central regions the basic political unit was the lordship, a small state ranging in size from a village to one or several towns. Lords usually had rights over common woods, mills and winepresses. Nominating their clergy, they 'protected' community churches, and exercised justice, both civil and criminal. Relative independence canonized a sometimes brutal lordly power. A Catalan assembly at Cervera in 1202 declared that 'if lords mistreat rustics or take their property, they do not answer to the king unless they hold their fiefs of him', and England's judges blandly opined in 1244 that lords 'may legally sell their rustics like oxen or cows'.[6] In the 1240s, inquisitors hunting heretics near Toulouse tripped over these petty monarchs' rustic concubines.

The lordship or seigniory partially erased the line between slave and free because lords governed all inhabitants, no matter from whom they held their land or to whom they were bound. Words like 'rustics' and 'labourers' and phrases such as Beaumanoir's 'men of the lordship', embracing both free and servile elements, replaced older vocabularies delineating particular tenurial or personal situations. Although this levelling eradicated ancient slavery, it confounded all villagers in a common servitude. Everything was done to abridge the mobility of the inhabitants of what were in effect petty states. Marriage was controlled and taxed to restrict social mobility (*formariage*) and emigration was allowed only on surrender of real and other property, even after the lord had been bought off by means of redemption payments (*remensa* in Catalonia). In parts of England, fines were levied on unmarried women for fornication (*leyrwyte*) and for natural children (*childwyte*). Although somewhat shared by all classes, these demeaning penalties characterized rural life. An imperial peace ordinance for Bavaria in 1152 denied rustics,

---

[5] Duby, *La société . . . dans la région Mâconnais* 248.
[6] Bonnassie, *From Slavery to Feudalism in Southwestern Europe* (Cambridge, 1991) 256, and Hyams, *Kings, Lords and Peasants* (Oxford, 1980) 3.

free or servile, recourse to judicial duels, ordered their clothes to be grey or black and reserved wine for nobles. Taxes, like the lord's tallage and labour services, were generalized, and all were obliged to sue in the lord's courts, losing the right to appeal to royal or provincial ones. In France, the term 'villein' soon designated any village inhabitant, free or servile. In England, where lordship was not so independent, it referred only to manorial dependants.

Western European communities were anything but uniform. Class differences based on wealth were always present, dividing farming folk both in terms of what they experienced and what they anticipated At Halesowen near Birmingham in the early fourteenth century, for example, the well to do had an average of 5.1 children, the middling farmers 2.9 and the poor 1.8.[7] Social divisions were omnipresent. In Scandinavia and sections of northern Germany, where the seigniorial system was as yet hardly seen, the free were numerous and independent but slavery still persisted. In intermediary zones such as England and much of Germany, slaves had vanished, but deep servility marked peasants in villeinage. Parading young rustics for the lord to pick domestic servants was an annual event in English manors. On the other hand, England's monarchy arrested the decline of the free, who customarily attended the hundred court, one at least formally royal. The same obtained in parts of Germany, but the weakened Empire permitted rural lordships to spread in the west and south. Around 1163 the Alsatian monks of Ebersheim divided their dependants into three 'families', knightly (*familia ministerialis*), rent payers (*familia censualis*) and serfs (*familia servilis*).

Even where lordly authority was deeply rooted, however, community membership rarely embraced a whole village, some inhabitants being servile and others free. Administrative officers, often recruited in the village, formed a group apart and so did clergy and the knights or soldiery. Nowhere, however, were the classes wholly separated. Craftsmen were deemed so valuable that they were sometimes held in dependency after ordinary farmers were freed, and around 1200 both craftsfolk and soldiers on Bohemian ecclesiastical lordships were of ministerial status. When the Bohemians accompanied Frederick Barbarossa to Italy in 1158, Vincent, a canon of Prague, remarked that 'not only did noble youths but also many popular folk rejected picks and ploughs and outfitted themselves with swords, spears and other weapons'.[8] Nevertheless, a Bavarian peace ordinance of 1244 allowed rustics to bear arms only when 'defending the fatherland', pursuing criminals or parading on the village's patron saint's day. Ordinary farmers, servile or free, were in fact an 'unarmed multitude' in comparison with a soldiery defined

---

[7] Razi, *Life, Marriage and Death in a Medieval Parish . . . Halesowen* 86.
[8] Wolfgang H. Fritze, *Früzeit zwischen Ostsee und Donau. Ausgewählte Beiträge zum geschichtlichen Werden im Östlichen Mitteleuropa vom 5. bis zum 13. Jahrhundert* 169.

by wealth whose higher ranks were becoming a nobility. This weakness probably explains Beaumanoir's cool description of the rights gained by some as 'what they have of freedom'.[9] England's *Exchequer Book* was even more condescending, and attributed theft, homicide, adultery and other crimes to the English rustics' habitual drunkenness.

Prompted by the general economic growth of the age, greater lords profited from granting freedom to those in the bondage of lesser ones, and France's kings, for example, sold liberty. It is difficult to say how extensive this freedom was, but farmers everywhere wanted it. Stirred by franchises won by the town of Laon and five villages in the nearby commune of Bruyères, fourteen villages grouped around Anizy le Château owned by the bishop and chapter took advantage of an episcopal vacancy in 1174 to buy a commune on Laon's model from the king. The newly elected bishop revoked this grant, and a war ensued in which the town of Laon, a royal monastery and the villagers were defeated by the bishop and local barons. The king then sequestered the bishop's temporal. Fearful for the balance of power, England's king and his allies in Hainault obliged France to revoke the commune in 1179. Similar events transpired in 1185, when Philip Augustus granted the right to a new commune. After much peasant emigration, Anizy won her liberties in the mid-thirteenth century, and several other villages of the group theirs shortly thereafter.

That France's kings were not disinterested lovers of liberty is shown by their grudging grants in the royal domain. A lengthy legal battle between Ste Geneviève of Paris and the inhabitants of Rosny sous Bois began in 1178, when the chapter bought a royal charter asserting the farmers' servile status. Rosny carried its suit to the higher authority of Rome, and over the years no fewer than five popes supported it. Too remote to be efficacious, papal power failed, and the farmers 'voluntarily' disavowed free status in 1226. Such were the times, however, that by 1246 the village was freed in exchange for an annual tallage of £60.

Similar attitudes are found elsewhere. Italy's urban republics wanted villages to share their way of government, and their imagery was generous. When Bologna freed the remaining rustics of her county in 1256–57, six thousand names were inscribed in the citizens' registry called the *Book of Paradise*. Reality was more nuanced. A motive for general rural enfranchisements like those of Vercelli in 1244 and Florence in 1289 was that townsfolk wanted to rupture lordly jurisdictions, impeding their rule of the countryside. Townsfolk were also reluctant to free their own serfs, and lavished little love on farmers. Giles of Rome recalled Aristotle's saying that the wise should govern the stupid:

---

[9] *Coutumes de Beauvaisis* 45, No. 1451 (ed. Salmon) II 233.

[Rustics] lack intelligence and hence are to be ruled by others. . . . Following this opinion, [town] citizens, being more prudent and intellectual, have the right to wage just war against rustics if they refuse to be subject.[10]

Small towns and villages were sometimes able to wring concessions from their lords. Near Toulouse in 1123, testamentary restitution for the 'violence' and 'wicked usages' inflicted on Baziège was given by a lord, and in 1208 a baron's will confirmed his predecessors' grants of 'liberties and customs' to repair the 'injuries, violence and cruelties' that he had wreaked on his small town of Isle Jourdain. Liberty was most advanced in parts of France and Italy where the seigniory was solidly rooted because, although nobles banded together against superiors, lords were jealous little monarchs trying to multiply the number of their citizens. Old communities were weakened by freedoms offered in new ones and, although old ones wished to recover fugitives, the new defended them. A Franconian Rhineland peace ordinance of 1179 provided that a lord 'claiming a man as his serf . . . must plead before the judge of the village' where the fugitive resides.[11] In short, competition among lords made the old saw 'town law makes free' almost as true of the village as the town.

Countryfolk also wanted to limit what they owed. In 1208, new settlers at Nôtre Dame of Paris's village of Braye were 'like other villagers, to have suitable equipment to go with the lord of Braye or his sergeants on campaign . . . with this proviso, that they return home each night'.[12] They also tried to fix or abolish fiscal charges. Among these were fines of justice, especially the lord's right to confiscate property. Taxes or inhibitions on transmitting property were also aimed at. Typical was mainmort at Orly near Paris, where it originally meant the ecclesiastical lord's right to dispose of a peasant's property at death. Mainmort had become a tax on inheritance and, by 1252, a witness testified that it meant that 'if anyone were to die without an heir of his body, his property would go to [the lord], otherwise not'.[13] The ultimate liberty was mobility: to marry freely and leave a community. A clause in the liberties of St Bauzeil near Foix in 1281 reads:

If an inhabitant wishes to leave the said town in order to reside elsewhere, unless he has committed a manifest crime . . . we give him free power and licence to go wherever he wishes with all his property.[14]

Lords were reluctant to grant such privileges, however, because they weakened or even destroyed their little states. In 1258, a lord of Montgaillard

---

[10] *De regimine principum* 2 3 7 and 15 (Rome, 1607) 365 and 385.
[11] Heinrich Mitteis, 'Stadtluft macht frei' in *Festschrift Stengel* (Münster, 1952) 352.
[12] Verriest, *Institutions médiévales* I 157.
[13] Bloch, *Rois et serfs* 30.
[14] Verriest, *Institutions médiévales* I 226.

near St Gaudens provided that 'we enfranchise and manumit all our serfs living in the said village as long as they remain in it. If, however . . . they leave, by that act they revert to their pristine servitude.'[15] In Lorraine, Austria and Bavaria, lords of overcrowded communities encouraged serfs to move to nearby towns or villages in return for annual remitments, but were reluctant to let the free go. When founding new villages, moreover, lords sometimes prohibited farmers from their other communities from settling there.

Franchises were usually recorded in customs or charters, whose publication became common in regions like north Italy, Provence, parts of France and the Low Countries during the twelfth century. Customals were relatively rare in Germany between the Rhine and the Elbe and in England even in the next century, although many newly planted chartered towns were really villages. Each area experienced different rhythms. In the Seine basin near Paris, new communities gained them during the twelfth century, but older communities only benefited from 1245 to 1275. The movement was strong around towns and in areas of new settlement, such as eastern Germany. In the mountainous and lightly populated county of Comminges, sixty villages won charters between 1202 and 1300. Franchises were not home grown because many, if not most, emulated town constitutions. Between 1160 and 1303, the laws of Louvain were adopted by many villages in south-east Brabant and, in their respective areas, the laws of Liège, Douai, Namur and St Pol had the same success. Although inspired by urban models, some were products of princely legislation. Such were the liberties of Lorris of 1155, adopted by royal foundations in the Ile de France, and those of Beaumont en Argonne of 1183, issued by the archbishop of Rheims and eventually adopted by about five hundred villages, mostly in the Champagne.

Within communities, some, both groups and individuals, rose faster than others. Villeneuve le Roi had been granted the free custom of Lorris in 1163, and one is tempted to believe that it was a free community. Louis IX nevertheless found 326 rustics to free there in 1246. In 1233, in the village of Pasignano near Florence, of the seven gentlemen holding of this monastic seigniory, five were knights and of these the most consequential was the 'noble knight Mister Tolosano'. His family was first seen in 1130, when his grandfather, a smith, acquired property in freehold. By 1156 the cash rent of his holdings had been fixed, and in 1202 the abbot enfranchised Tolosano's father. In 1233 his relatives in Pasignano included a smith and several humble farmers, and at nearby Poggibonsi there was a lawyer cousin. Nor was this unique. Durand Blanot, whose brother was a peasant, was a sergeant serving Cluny's monks at Voranges in the Mâconnais. His first son enfeoffed land to a knight and educated a son at Paris. This boy became a master and

---

[15] Ibid.

canon of Nôtre Dame, finishing his career as judge for the archbishop of Lyons from 1274 to 1287. Born *circa* 1220, Durand's second son went to read law at Bologna, returning to enter the duke of Burgundy's service. Knighted by the duke, he acquired the liege fief and seigniory of Uxelles in 1268, thereby replacing a fading baronial family.

Although labour and moneylending were the bottom rungs on the ladder of rustic advancement, arms, law and the Church came next. England's church boasted at least three prelates of peasant origins: Robert Grosseteste, bishop of Lincoln (d. 1253), Robert de l'Isle of Durham (d. 1283) and John Peckham, primate of Canterbury. To Philip of Novara clergy and chivalry were the most worthy and profitable professions. Through arms, one could rise to empire and 'by clergy it has often happened . . . that the son of a poor man becomes a great prelate, and is rich and honoured, and becomes the father and lord of him who was lord of him and his; and rules and governs everyone, and can even become pope, and be father and lord of all Christendom'.[16] Some hated this. Werner der Gaertner, a monk of Ranshofen around 1250, described a peasant named Meier Helmbrecht who was corrupted by war, grew his hair long like a noble, drank wine and wore a sword. Pride went before Meier's fall.

In an age when it was profitable to free men and women, however, clerks often relegated doctrines of service to second place, hunting instead for texts to prove the usefulness of liberty. Some were found in Roman law, where the basic notion was that, in nature, equality and freedom ruled. Paraphrasing his Stoic texts, Ulpian had said: 'In the law of peoples, slaves are considered as nothing, but not so in natural law, because in natural law, all men are equal', a text echoed by medieval lawyers.[17] Some were confident that humanity's pristine liberty could be restored. A prologue to an emancipation in Castel-sarrasin in 1268 reads:

> In nature all men are free, but the law of peoples made some slaves. Because a thing easily returns to its nature, however, learn that we, moved by piety . . . freely manumit our serf.[18]

Using Roman law, Rolandino Passaggeri has a master grant his dependants 'all right of patronage, restoring their ancient birthright and freedom in law, calling them Roman citizens and finally returning them to the primeval law in which all men were born free'.[19]

In both Bracton and *Fleta*, the law of peoples had not destroyed humanity's natural freedom, only obscured it. Boncompagno of Signa also used this

---

[16] *Des quatres tenz d'aage d'ome* 15 (ed. Fréville) 10.
[17] *Digest* 50 17 32, ibid. 1 1 4 and *Institutes* 1 2 2. The phrase 'law of peoples' translates the Latin *ius gentium*.
[18] Bloch, *Rois et serfs* 150.
[19] *Summa artis notarie* 1 7 (Venice, 1583) I 157v, a gloss on *Digest* 1 1 4.

commonplace: 'No one is said to confer liberty but rather to strip off a veil of servitude by which freedom is cloaked.'[20] But enfranchisement was more than restoration; it was also innovation. When the Florentines removed traces of servitude in their county in 1289, the harangue of the act began:

> Because liberty, in which the desire of each man depends on his own will and not on that of another, and by which cities and peoples are defended from oppression and their laws improved, and because freedom is much honoured by natural law, we, therefore, wishing not only to maintain but also to increase it, declare . . .[21]

In both England and Florence, liberty's definition came from *Digest* 1 5 4: 'freedom is the natural faculty of each person to do what he [or she] wants'.[22]

When the priors of Florence spoke of an increase in liberty in 1289 they were referring to the notion of progress, the 'renovation to the better' seen in the mass. In the *Saxon Mirror*, Eike of Repgow dismissed as worthless attempts to find a biblical justification for slavery, concluding 'that man belongs to God and anyone who takes possession of him sins against the power of the Omnipotent. In fact, servitude had its origin in unjust captivities, threats and injuries, [becoming] durable customs which men desire to claim as if they were legal'.[23] In 1311 the king of France enfranchised the bondsmen of the Valois, observing that 'as beings formed in the image of our Lord, men ought generally to be free by natural law'.[24] Two years previously a royal scribe copied a model manumission from a monastery in Soissons:

> Since our Redeemer . . . wished to assume human flesh so that, by divine grace . . . he could restore us to our pristine liberty, it is right that those whom nature created free in the beginning and the law of peoples placed under the yoke of servitude should be restored by the benefit of manumission to the liberty in which they were born.[25]

To these ideas may be added pride of nation or race. Many peoples claimed descent from Rome's founders, Aeneas and the Trojans, and both the French and Germans asserted that they were Franks. Claiming Lyons for France in 1307, the lawyer Peter of Belleperche (d. 1308) opined that it had been the ancient capital of the Gauls, a people who changed their name to Franks when they threw off the yoke of Roman servitude. A royal ordinance of 1315 began:

> According to natural law all men are born free, but by certain usages and customs long introduced and maintained to the present in our kingdom, and perhaps because

---

[20] *Boncompagnus Boncompagni* 5 BuF II 155–56.

[21] Villari, *I primi due secoli della storia di Firenze* 190.

[22] 'Libertas est naturalis facultas eius quod cuique facere libet, nisi si quid vi aut iure prohibetur.'

[23] *Sachsenspiegel* 3 42 (ed. C.W. Gärtnern, Leipzig, 1732) 409.

[24] *Ordonnances des Rois de France de la troisième race* XII 387.

[25] Bloch, *Rois et serfs* 154, derived from Pope Gregory I's Letter VI 12 in *MGH Epp. sel.* I 390.

of their predecessors' crimes, many of our common folk have fallen into the bondage of servitude . . . which much displeases us, we, considering that our realm is called the kingdom of the French, desiring that the fact truly accord with the name . . . have ordered that . . .[26]

Emancipation accompanied economic growth and seigniorial competition and, being paid for the liberty they gave, emancipators profited. A count of Joigny freed a family in 1328 'in remuneration and pure guerdon of good and agreeable services, gentilities and kindnesses that they have given . . . and still assiduously do daily without ceasing . . . in pure and special grace, by God and in pure charity and piety . . . and for the sum of 200 pounds in cash'.[27] Money is not everything, however: 'tis heaven to see others happy when one is happy oneself.

Earlier chapters noted that increasing friction marked the relationship of landlord and tenant around 1300. Lords grasped their remaining prerogatives more firmly, enlarging them whenever possible. All rural populations were affected, but not all equally. Some villages had been so completely freed that lordly authority could not be restored and, within others, individuals had risen too far to be reduced. Such divisions exacerbated social divisions in areas where the rural lordship had once brought about a measure of social fusion.

The new distinctions rigidified, partly because those already free wanted to distinguish themselves from their less fortunate brethren. An illustration is the term 'bourgeois'. Often employed earlier to describe settlers in new villages, it was now restricted to village notables, notaries, merchants or especially well-to-do farmers. Intellectual formalism also bred rigidity, jurists trying to fix each man and woman into the systems they created. They expatiated on Rome's indelible servitude and used Roman phrases like 'men of the body' for those owing service. Even a governor little touched by the schools like Beaumanoir divided the rural population into three groups: gentlemen, the free of the lordship and serfs.

The schools' influence was not wholly baleful. *Fleta* notes that, according to the *ius gentium*, masters had the right of life and limb over slaves, but that Roman law had deprived them of this. The custom of Burgundy allowed those in 'servile servitude' to disavow their lords if threatened with death or lack of maintenance. Not that serfs had it easy. A Freising lawbook of 1328 tells us that masters who killed serfs with swords or clubs were to die, but flogging was different. If a man died the same day, the master was liable; thereafter he was not, because people were rarely whipped to death and, besides, terror was needed to get work out of serfs.

---

[26] *Ordonnances des Rois de France* I 583.
[27] Bloch, *Rois et serfs* 136.

A further beneficial result of the study of law was the formulation of distinctions between 'liberate servitude', 'servile servitude' and slavery. Beaumanoir defined the serf's 'estate':

> There are several states of servitude. Some serfs are so subject that lords can take whatever they have . . . and, rightly or wrongly, imprison them as long as they wish, being held to answer only to God. Others are treated more gently because . . . lords can require nothing except the taxes of their servitude unless they misbehave.[28]

The taxes were rent, tallage, inheritance dues and fees for marriage. Beaumanoir then observes that these happy serfs are to be found in France, especially in the Beauvaisis; the others in foreign lands. His embarrassed comments were not inventive. Robert of Curzon had earlier contrasted serfs in France with the slaves of Apulia and Sicily who were, he said, bought and sold like cattle. Derived from the Latin *sclavus* for Slav (a people often enslaved in the ninth and tenth centuries), the word 'slave' to define this rare social category was being adopted by Italian and French jurists during the thirteenth century.

Lastly, legal definitions of servitude were perhaps not a major preoccupation. Although town patricians invested heavily in rural serfs, the author of the standard commentary on the custom of Toulouse in 1296 closed a dismissive treatment by saying that 'it would be more laborious than useful' to go into detail. Lawyers, he thought, should instead consult a southern Italian treatise by Roffredo of Benevento (d. *circa* 1243).[29] In short, as today, poverty and wealth probably counted more. Almost everywhere, poor farmers lived in poorer housing, married later, were survived by fewer children and were more likely to be or to be considered criminal than substantial ones.

Townsfolk

Townsfolk were not free of servitude. Early in the thirteenth century around Namur they were never called 'free', a term there restricted to nobles, and the same was true earlier in much of north France. A reason was that trading and manual labour were thought inferior to administrative, martial and clerical activities. When England's William the Marshal accosted a runaway monk with a noble damsel, he was not perturbed by their irregular liaison, but confiscated their money on learning that they were going to town to put it out at usury. The *Treasury Dialogue* said that a freeman who wanted to trade or lend money became nothing but a merchant. Such a 'degenerate knight or other freeman should be punished by another than the common law of the free'.[30]

---

[28] *Coutumes de Beauvaisis* 45 Nos. 1451–53 (ed. Salmon) II 233–36.
[29] *Coutumes de Toulouse et leur premier commentaire* (ed. Henri Gilles) 272–73.
[30] *Dialogus de scaccario* 2 13 (ed. A. Hughes, C.G. Crump and C. Johnson, Oxford, 1902) 146.

Key words like 'burgher' and 'citizen' designated not only towndwellers but villagers as well. Urban battles for liberty were similar to those of villages, and rivalry between lords helped towns advance. In 1152, a monk lamented that the citizens of Vézelay, 'abjuring their legitimate lord [the abbot], allied with a tyrant [the count of Nevers] . . . to create an execrable commune . . . casting the yoke of ecclesiastical liberty from their necks'.[31] Both townsmen and villagers tried to lessen charges, tallage and forced loans, quartering, hospitality rights, inheritance taxes, marriage fees and military service. In 1277, the inhabitants of the small town of Aurillac protested at being called 'men of the lordship' (*potestas*), asserting that they were 'free bourgeois, free and exempt from all servile status'. Their lordly abbot agreed: free they were, but they also owed 'many taxes and services . . . that smack of servitude and are contrary to liberty'.[32]

Like those of a village, Lübeck's inhabitants of 1163 were to defend the town but were excused from outside expeditions. In 1223, the countess of Nevers surrendered mainmort to her subjects of Auxerre so 'that their heirs and successors . . . should possess . . . their parents' inheritances without trouble or tax'.[33] If the principle of 'town air makes free' was upheld more vigorously in towns than villages, it was restricted there also. In 1191, a lord confirmed the liberties of Landrecies, but specified that his own serfs should not be admitted there. Meeting at Daroca in 1228, an Aragonese parliament listed 180 deputies, fourteen from Lerida, twelve from Saragossa, and so on down to one or two. The larger communities' representatives were called worthies (*probihomines*) and the smaller simply *isti*. Not that all were peasants, because 'knights and footmen' (*milites et infanzones*) stood for one small place.[34]

Town and village nevertheless differed, and profoundly. Money was more common in towns. The annual tallage paid by each villager at Busigny in 1201 consisted of a measure of oats, a loaf of bread, a hen and sixpence; in 1191, the citizen of Landrecies gave a shilling for his burgher right and fourpence for the lord's tolls. Everything was on a larger scale in town. Fishing villages provided smacks for service; towns offered warships. In 1191, the crown of Sicily allowed Gaeta to cut its military assessment from two galleys to one, save for the general defence of the kingdom. What was social in a village became political in town. In Burgundy, a maltreated serf could abjure his lord. In 1282, the federated towns of Stendal, Tangermunde and Oster-burg in Saxony gained the right to seek another lord if harmed by theirs.

---

[31] Guilhermoz, *L'origine de la noblesse* (1902) 385.

[32] Roger Grand, *Les 'paix' d'Aurillac* (Paris, 1945) 59.

[33] Verriest, *Institutions médiévales* I 223.

[34] Thomas N. Bisson, *Medieval France and her Pyrenean Neighbours: Studies in Early Institutional History* 35–6.

Townsfolk's liberties were won more rapidly and were greater than those of villagers.

Distinctions between town and countryfolk gradually sharpened. By the thirteenth century the word 'labourers' had lost its inclusiveness, being now applied only to farmers. The term 'burgenses' spread widely to describe townsfolk, being restricted in villages to those professional or rich persons who did not live like farmers. When the jurist Alberic of Rosate posed the question 'who are to be called citizens and who rustics?', he answered: 'They are called citizens who were born in a city [or town]; . . . they are called rustics who were born in a village, hamlet or castle.'[35]

Most towns initially consisted of several nuclei, a princely, comital or episcopal walled town, for example, an often recent merchant settlement and one or more agglomerations near monasteries outside the centre. Sometimes aided by princes who wished to weaken enclaves of independent lordly authority, townsmen gradually integrated these more or less independent segments. Once a community sense had emerged, however, princes and lords often changed their minds. Fearing Parisian unity under its merchants' guild, France's kings supported the independence of no less than five jurisdictional areas in town and suburb, including those of the monastery of St Germain des Prés and the Temple.

The formation of a social community created a measure of equality and common membership. Citizenship was obtained by birth and retained by sharing tax and defence burdens. It was also extended to newcomers, after a suitable wait, who participated in common duties. Communities also exiled persons for crime or politics. Citing the glossator Accursius, Alberic of Rosate defined exile as a 'kind of expulsion from the common good; hence, in a certain sense, a secular excommunication'.[36]

Equality was rarely complete. Leaving aside clergy, most towns began with at least three social elements: a martial and administrative cadre rarely averse to trade; merchants privileged, as were Jews, to travel; and tradesmen, artisans and workers, even agricultural ones, who were sometimes in manorial servitude. All owed service to prince and community, knights being better remunerated than others, and artisans less than merchants. In the early twelfth century, the old relation of artisan to merchant could still be seen in Germany. Merchants there often derived liberties from, and owed service to, higher lords, even the emperor, in comparison to artisans, who depended on a local lord or church. The unification of merchant and artisan was therefore expressed by the latter acquiring the liberties, especially the mobility, possessed by the former. In 1120, the founding charter of Freiburg in Breisgau specified that all inhabitants were to be merchants and enjoy the merchant

---

[35] *De statutis* 2 177 17 in *TUJ* II 49ra.
[36] *De statutis* 4 1 9 in *TUJ* II 66ra.

power. Although this use of the term 'merchant' persisted from time to time, especially on Europe's frontiers, it was usually replaced by either 'citizen' or 'burgher', words referring to all members of the community, mercantile or not.

Common citizenship was accepted in regions of rapid urbanization around 1150, but elsewhere the struggle for a unified social community still went on. The lord included in the liberties of Auxerre granted in 1223 a passage reading:

> I manumit altogether and perpetually those other citizens of Auxerre . . . who are not of free condition, so that, the opprobrium of servitude being wholly removed, they may freely leave and return whenever they wish.[37]

Few western towns of any size, however, contained many inhabitants in seigniorial servitude. Some citizens were wealthy, of course, and others poor, but this did not vitiate the principle of equality before the law, any more than it does today. A provision in the statutes of Avignon in the 1240s provided that 'the condition of the good carpenters of this city is no worse than that of any others'.[38] The phrase 'good men' (*boni-* or *probihomines*), used in the early thirteenth century to designate individuals in any social group, elevated or humble, reflects this measure of social equality.

More difficult to assimilate than the humble were the prince's or lord's officers. Before 1100, such servitors everywhere lived in town, and ranged from toll collectors to sergeants, knights and even substantial notables, such as viscounts. They also often combined different functions. The 'proud knights' of Puy in central France, whose towers were levelled by the bishop and people in 1102, operated the town mint; an elite, in short, both military and monetary. Such service groups gained freedom at different times, and some evolved into nobilities. At Worms in 1190, the town council consisted of twenty-eight burghers and twelve ministers. By the thirteenth century, the latter semi-servile officers had become knights or nobles. Some ministerial groups became burghers. At Cambrai, the ministers claimed that their offices and emoluments were hereditary, and in 1135 the dispute between them and their episcopal lord was arbitrated. Those who held fiefs or benefices as salaries were given them hereditarily; those without became burghers forthwith. By 1205, even the superior ministerial group had moved towards the bourgeoisie, being termed 'sergeants of the bishop of Cambrai who are merchants'.[39]

As Salimbene of Parma remarked, nobles in north France lived in the countryside, whereas in Italy they lived in town. He was right, but modern

---

[37] Verriest, *Institutions médiévales* I 223.
[38] *Coutumes et règlements d'Avignon* 208 No. 158.
[39] Ritter, *Ministérialité et chevalerie* 86. 'Minister' translates the Latin *ministerialis*.

historians have elevated this observation into a difference of essences between northern or Germanic towns and Mediterranean or Italian, the latter supposedly being 'classical'. Even in this Franciscan's time, however, matters were more complex. In Italian Savoy and Sicily, few towns boasted noble citizens, and such were also rare in Castile and western Iberia. Nor was the northern frontier clear. Many Rhenish and southwestern German towns counted knights among their citizens. Zürich's council was composed in 1127 of 'ministers and citizens' and 'knights and citizens' in 1225, and Oppenheim's in 1287 was evenly divided between knights and burghers. Although knightly citizens were rare in Flanders, north France and the Low Countries, nobles exempted from town jurisdiction often resided in cities. Sometimes, as in St Quentin or Bourges, they lived in the old nuclei, thereby showing that they had once been part of the community.

Thinking that nobles were citizens when towns were large and powerful is tempting. Size alone, however, was not enough. In southwest Germany and Languedoc, urbanization was relatively light, yet knights were citizens. In Flanders, where great cities lay thick, nobles did not often live in town and, when they did, were rarely citizens. What helps explain such differences is the capacity of princely government in the period up to 1200. Weak little states were found in south and east France, and political control was feeble in a wide belt reaching from north Italy up the Rhone and the adjacent Alpine areas to the valleys of the Meuse and Rhine. Princely policy was based on the principle 'divide to rule'. When nobles lived in town, princes often bolstered distinctions that separated them from the other denizens. The Emperor Henry VI's privilege to Florence in 1187 surrendered much but insisted on the knights' exemption from communal taxes, and a similar provision was included in a Capetian privilege given to Noyon in 1181. Princes tried to prevent knights from living in town or serving as citizens. In the statutes granted to Abbeville in 1184, the count of Pontivy stipulated that 'the bourgeois . . . may not receive in their commune any of my vassals or anyone having a free fief in my domain'. Nor were rural lords allowed to join communes, as they often wished to. In 1179, the count of Troyes expressly ordered that 'no castellan living near Meaux may join that commune save with my permission'. Frederick Barbarossa's edict for Trent forbade its citizens to force anyone to reside in town or compel 'those who live outside in open or fortified villages to be subject to their power and jurisdiction'.[40]

Where towns grew rapidly and central government deteriorated, these inhibitions failed. The best examples are found in Italy, in Lombardy, Venetia, the Romagna and Tuscany, although other regions boasted some success. Knights there domiciled in town profited from the faltering of the emperor's

---

[40] All three of these passages are in Ennen, *Frühgeschichte der europäischen Stadt* 257 and 261.

power to lead their communities to political freedom. Cities also often obliged rural lords to join. At Reggio in 1169, a rural magnate and numerous lesser knights confessed themselves citizens, pledging to reside in town for four months each year in wartime and two in peace. A Sienese statute of 1262 listed a hundred county families obliged to maintain domiciles in town. In short, even though knightly groups long retained privileges, they were being integrated into the community. In 1164, when the Lombard League was formed against the emperor, town ambassadors pledged the support of all inhabitants, excepting only clerks, criminals, madmen, the mute and the blind.

Where towns were weaker or local princes retained more authority, townsfolk reacted differently. Unable to assimilate nobles domiciled in town or oblige rural ones to live there, town fathers sought either to exclude them altogether or restrict them to certain parts of the town. All domiciled at Noyon in 1181 save clerks and knights owed taxes and military service, hence knights were too privileged to be citizens. In the midst of his French wars, England's King John (d. 1216) promised Rouen's citizens that knights would not spend more than one night in town except at the king's express command or because of illness. The founding charter of Freiburg in Breisgau of 1120 proposed that 'no ducal minister or knight will live [there], except with the inhabitants' consent'.[41] Cityfolk even made a virtue of necessity by prohibiting intermarriage between themselves and nobles, as in the founding charter of Lübeck in 1163 and the custom of Cologne. Although the exclusion of nobles in parts of north Europe reflected the weakness of urban political power there, it also created a bourgeois self-consciousness of great significance later on in modern times.

Once attained, town unity began to weaken. One reason was the rise of the 'people' and social corporatism. In the thirteenth century, class, guild and professional affiliation began to replace old individual citizenship. At Toulouse, constitutional documents had usually referred to the citizens simply as the 'good men of the City and Bourg', the two parts of the town. In 1226, however, an edict described the citizenry as knights, burghers 'and other good men', and a contemporary poem as 'the knights, bourgeois and commonalty' or 'the knights, bourgeois and artisans'.[42] These distinctions penetrated private documents around 1250: before that, knights and burghers were not identified as such; after that, notaries were careful to do so. Demarcating function, style of life and wealth, social position became all important. Vital of Canyellas, a Bolognese trained jurist recommended for the see of Huesca in 1235 by Raymond of Penyafort, made 'burghers' sound just like modern 'bourgeois':

[41] Ennen, op. cit. 260.
[42] My *Toulousan Society in the Age of the Cathars* (Toronto, 1997) 107–8.

Citizens are those who live in cities or towns equal to cities; of which group those are called burghers who, although they have masters and workers through whom they exercise professions, do not work with their own hands. There are, however, some who use their hands but are not excluded from the order of the burgesses, such as cloth merchants and moneychangers, and especially lawyers, medical doctors, or surgeons, and others equal or superior to these.[43]

Well-to-do townsmen believed that trade or work with the hands was demeaning, but the worthy did not have it all their way. When the 'people' rose in Italy and the Low Countries, artisans were proud of their blue nails and rarely lost an opportunity of maligning those they called 'the idle'. Besides, nobles like Raymond Llull looked down on the bourgeois:

Almost all crafts- and tradesmen want to be burghers or want their children to be. But there is no estate so perilous as that of the burgher, nor that lasts so short a time . . . No man lives so short a life. And do you know why? Because he eats too much and does not exercise enough . . . No man is so annoying to his friends as a poor burgher, and in no man is poverty quite as shameful as in a burgher. No man gains so little merit or enjoyment from the charity he gives as does a burgher.[44]

Nobles not only scorned them, they also feared them. James of Vitry told townsfolk that their 'communities or rather conspiracies . . . oppress their neighbours violently. If thieves and usurers are held to restitution, how much the more should these violent and pestiferous communities be held to it because they . . . weaken neighbouring knights and steal the jurisdiction of their men from them.'[45]

As towns grew, a quasi-noble patriciate emerged from the burghers. Businessmen, they acquired rural properties and intermarried with the nobility, from whom, indeed, some of their ancestors had sprung. They built lineages contrasting sharply with modest middle-class and artisan families, whose substitute was their guilds. An Avignonese document of 1251 described them as 'honourable burghers who are accustomed to live as knights' and noted that they went to war armed as such.[46] Such were found not only around the Mediterranean, but also in the Low Countries, north France and west Germany. In Metz in the late thirteenth century, eight dominant lineages (defined by blood and alliance or adoption) were divided into about 220 individual families totalling about a thousand members. Such wealthy clans had poor relations. A cloth finisher was a son-in-law of the distinguished Colon house and a daughter of the knight Gervase of Lessy married a baker.

---

[43] *Los fueros de Aragón* (ed. Gunnar Tilander, Lund, 1937) 380.

[44] *De doctrina puerili* cited in Langlois, *La vie en France au moyen âge* IV 353.

[45] *Sermo II ad burgenses* in A. Giry, *Documents sur les relations de la royauté avec les villes de France* (Paris, 1885) 146.

[46] *Coutumes et règlements d'Avignon* 269 No. 16.

As noted above, the urban rich were not only businessmen, but also acquired land, the most secure of all investments. In north and central Italy, the acquisition of farms by burghers or town knights served to tie country-side to city. Elsewhere, where towns had only extended their power over limited regions, this ambition hurt them. Having rural properties, patricians often withdrew from citizenship and, while continuing business in town, contributed no taxes and service to the community whence their wealth derived. The financial stringency afflicting north French cities in the late thirteenth century was partly caused by this problem, but it existed earlier. In 1197 the crown granted Roye 'that townsmen who . . . acquire fiefs, thereby becoming noble, and are not knights should either become members of the commune or vacate the town'.[47]

Facing more marked social differences as time went on, a judge's problem was no longer to make the punishment fit the crime, but instead to make it fit the status and means of the criminal, a matter rehearsed later when examining law. Just as growing social complexity had produced some far above the average burgher's standard of living, so it had also created a proletariat. Composed of youths, recent immigrants and other marginal folk, this group was only slowly and never completely absorbed into the structure of trades, industries and professions. Such persons grew in number during the economic tightening around 1300, posing a threat of delinquency or civil violence. Corporal punishment was therefore lavished on these 'vile' or 'base persons' lacking regular employment and of bad habits.

Paradoxically, growth had created such diversification of social status and wealth that the old vocabulary of equal citizenship no longer suited the town. The demise of equality, furthermore, signalled the weakening of the community solidarity that had enabled towns to win so many victories over reluctant princes.

---

[47] Ennen, *Frühgeschichte der europäischen Stadt* 257.

Chapter 11

Nobles and the military

The military

In city militias, soldiers were of two kinds, horse and foot. In Latin (not the vernacular) the word for soldier (*miles*) had come to mean horseman by this time, showing that mounted troops were more valuable than footmen. Because the military also headed secular government, their ample range embraced all of the titled hierarchy. Beneath nobles such as counts and viscounts came Flanders' and England's barons – sometimes called 'rich men' – Castle's 'rich men', Limousin's 'princes', Burgundy's 'castellans' and Lombardy's 'captains'. And beneath these were the *milites*, a term that was only winning its aristocratic tone in this period. This was a wide-ranging group. At Toulouse in 1128/35, the value of the war-horses given to the Temple by a group of worthies ranged from 1200 shillings to 240, with an average of 528. In fine, cavalry in the early twelfth century ranged from heavy to light in terms of mounts and equipment. Another estimate is seen when Catalonia's early twelfth-century *Usages* casually remarked that knights, unlike rustics, ate white bread.

Two rough estimates show what contemporaries believed were the relations of this group to the various other social classes.[1] Listing compensation payments, Catalonia's *Usages* shows that around 1100 the lowest grade of the nobility was estimated to be from seven to ten times more valuable than a simple farmer, but also that ordinary knights were only two or three times more. In 1212, about a century later, figures in the *Statutes of Pamiers* issued by Simon of Montfort record fines for crimes against property or government in the region around Carcassonne and Béziers. These give the impression that barons were ten to twenty times richer than farmers, knights five to ten times and burghers two to five.

As is obvious, society was evolving and the martial elements were markedly divided by social grades. To be termed 'noble' initially meant to be 'free', and relatively few members of the martial order were nobles. In the 370-odd

---

[1] The first set (mostly taken from the *Usages* of Barcelona) is found in Bonnassie, *La Catalogne du milieu du xe à la fin du xie siècle* 908, and the second in the *Statutes* published in the *Histoire générale de Languedoc* (ed. Devic and Vaisette) 8 No. 165.

villages of the county of Namur in the mid-twelfth century, only about twenty families were noble. However, starting in the eleventh century, first in France and Italy, magnates and afterwards knights gradually became free. This meant that individuals held their salary (sometimes called benefice, later fief) hereditarily and paid no taxes except 'aids': ransom for a lord, dower for his daughters and for knighting his sons. Judged by peers, they also limited the court or military service they owed, in north France the usual obligation being forty days of free military service. Well into the twelfth century, however, past memories were alive. When Louis VI freed his sergeants (the word initially meant 'servants') in Laon in 1129, he specified that they were free to become clerks, knights or burghers. In the 1180s the book named for Glanville still claimed that a peasant, when emancipated and knighted, was free only *vis-à-vis* his master and other farmers, but not those of any other social order. The compilation named after Bracton in the next century maintained the contrary.

Past servitude still meant much to knights. They owed an expensive and sometimes dangerous service and, like farmers under manorial law, were not usually allowed to alienate the property held as salary for their labour. Young men of military family, moreover, were attached for training to the courts of princes and barons from about the age of fourteen, becoming members of the magnate's household. Great princes had large households. In a tournament at Lagny on the Marne in 1180, young King Henry, son of Henry II of England, fielded twenty-seven Normans, twenty French, twenty Flemings, fourteen English and six Angevins. Baronial households were smaller. In 1166, Walter Waleran of Wiltshire owed the king twenty knights, eight of whom were household. Composed of young men trying to please their masters to get brides and lands, households were the elite of the medieval militia. Just as lesser knights did on them, great nobles still depended on kings for the transmission of their fiefs in spite of hereditary right. The ameliorations they wanted are seen in England's *Great Charter* of 1215. After a general statement on ecclesiastical liberty, the next seven rubrics dealt with wardship and inheritance, inheritance taxes, suitable guardianship for minor heirs and shielding widows against forced remarriage.

Strong though the service ethos was, all Italian, French and English knights were noble or free in the period with which this book deals. Ideologically, the Peace of God and the Crusade helped this improvement in knightly status, because churchmen insisted on the soldier's dignity, one enhanced by the creation of the military orders. In Brabant, nobles only assumed the knightly title after the Temple and Hospital entered the duchy around 1175. Enfranchisement also resulted from the decentralization or devolution of government. During that long process, princes, faced by restive magnates, built personal followings of quasi-servile soldiers. At the same time, they encouraged their magnates' followers to seek for themselves the liberties that their masters were winning. The battle between magnates and princes gave simple soldiers the opportunity to advance.

The armed militia's salaries became hereditary and privileged. In urban republics, to compensate for expensive armour and horses, nobles were exempt from some taxes. In Arles in 1205, knights paid only the tithe on their property, others both tithe and tallage; in Pistoia they paid the usual town taxes, but their rural holdings were exempt from the hearth tax. When, moreover, their fiefs and salaries had become heritable, they tried to extend this protection to all family property, no matter how acquired. By the late twelfth century, therefore, law began to forbid alienating real property to knights.

Nobles, including knights, came under the protection of their own law, the 'law of the camp' as the Romans had put it. In Italian republics, litigation between military families was settled in courts of their peers. In princely and baronial courts, assessors chosen from among the litigants' peers arbitrated most lawsuits in the twelfth century, decisions being guaranteed by the relatives of the parties and often described as a 'peace' or 'pact'. Powerful family alliances imposed their will on the state, upholding customs such as compurgation, oaths taken by clan members asserting a member's veracity, and the judicial duel. Beaumanoir's chapter on war largely concerns private war or vendetta, another mark of this martial group.

Family and marital alliances set the social tone of nobles and princes. Wars, like those between Plantagenets and Capetians in France or between the Welfs (Guelphs) and Weiblinger (Hohenstaufen or Ghibellines) in Germany and Italy, were viewed as conflicts between rival families. Poetry treated the conflict of family and state. Charlemagne was slow to proceed against the traitor Ganelon for Roland's death because his mighty family swore for him, and divine judgement in trial by battle was called on to settle the matter. Bernier's vassal's duty to his lord, Ralph of Cambrai, was in conflict with his love of his blood family, the latter's mortal enemies.

Family size and cohesiveness varied vastly and rested on two pillars: siblings sharing common interests and marriage linking patrilineal families. Noble and patrician clans were therefore constellations built around the patrilineal nuclei of the two spouses. That the system could mobilize numbers is seen in 1273 at Tournai, when a patrician renounced his son before the town fathers because the youth had breached a truce. Seventy co-jurors of his lineage and associated groups joined him, as did fifty-three of his wife's. The system, however, was not rigid. In Ralph of Cambrai, two combatants withdrew from combat because they realized that they were insufficiently related to the principals.

Because of the attraction of money and consequent clientage, more than blood counted. In places as far from each other as Lorraine and Tuscany, families formed associations partly of blood and partly of social alliance. Referring to the tower societies of noble or patrician lineages, Boncompagno of Signa's *Cedar* reports that clubs or gangs were common in urban Italy, their names reflecting elevated aspirations: the Falcons, the Lions, the Round Table. A Florentine clan in 1180 linked thirty male heads of family with seven different surnames to build a tower in Por Santa Maria. The Corbolani of Lucca in 1287 embraced a minimum of sixteen households with an elected governing council. As in Italian skyscraper cities like San Gimignano, towers characterized the noble and patrician style. Such towers were larger and higher in towns possessing political liberty: princes did not like them because they were disturbed by independent great families.

The military emancipation was not complete in Germany, where, in spite of the blows dealt to the Empire during the Gregorian age, a quasi-servile soldiery dependent on the emperor or his greater ecclesiastical and secular vassals was still in place. In the mid-twelfth century, to be noble meant to be free; to be a minister or soldier implied servility and often peasant origins. A *Freiherr* was the lowest free noble; a *ministerialis* (translated here as 'minister') was a semi-servile soldier, owing military and court service as well as tallage and servile marriage taxes. As late as 1263 Sophia of Velturns, daughter of a great Swabian minister, was enfranchised to marry a free lord and, although her eldest son was to share her husband's freedom, subsequent ones were to be ministers. Although ministerial offices and benefices were not hereditary, some ministers, especially imperial ones, rose high. Werner of Bolanden served the Hohenstaufen from 1160 to 1190 in wars with the prince prelates of Mainz and Trier. At his peak he governed seventeen castles and towns, almost 1100 knights owed him service and he held lands from forty-six different lords. Another great minister was the Markward of Anweiler, on whom the Emperor Henry VI conferred 'freedom in 1195, and invested him with the duchy of Ravenna, the Romagna and the march of Ancona'.[2] The Markward died in 1202 as regent of Sicily and guardian of the future Emperor Frederick II.

An Englishman, Gervase of Tilbury (d. after 1211), served the Empire as marshal of the kingdom of Arles in the late 1190s. He reports that Henry VI changed the German system, and adopted that of the English and French, thus making knightly fiefs hereditary. Just before and after 1200, a basic change did occur in much of the Empire. In Repkow's *Saxon Mirror* of the early thirteenth century, an enfranchised minister was not noble; in the *Swabian Mirror* (1274/75), he was. The change is also seen around Namur, where in the mid-twelfth century to be a noble was everything. By the mid-thirteenth century knights had so appreciated that, in lists of witnesses, they preceded nobles. Once only nobles were called mister (*dominus* or *messire*), but from about 1220 knights were so addressed. This was gradually

---

[2] The *Ursberger Chronicle* in Bosl, *Reichsministerialität der Salier und Staufer* (Stuttgart, 1950–51) I 593.

accompanied by the acquisition of hereditary right to fiefs or salaries, and the withering of servile restrictions.

Practice and nomenclature varied from region to region. Reinforced by French influence, the knightly title stood above that of the minister in the Rhineland. In parts of Swabia, however, ministers ranked higher because of their close connection with the Hohenstaufens, and in Austria a minister was a great lord. Only around 1240 did lesser knights start to become free, and some became burghers or even yeomen farmers. Variations marked even small areas: knights were ahead in Brabant and Liège, but ministers around Namur. At Namur around 1200 only nobles and prelates had seals, symbols of jurisdiction and legal capacity. The ministerial cadres began to adopt them in the 1220s, and the first extant example of a knight's seal is of 1249.

The freedoms gained posed problems. Servile holdings were less divisible than free, because lords wanted viable economic entities. Partition therefore affected free farmers, and the same was also true of knights. As long as service was ministerial, subdivision was not a threat; as freedom spread it was, but was also cushioned by economic expansion until the *rallentando* after 1300. War and natural loss also helped by pruning heir groups. Of the seven sons of a castellan of Bourbourg near Guines, two entered the Church, two died accidentally and a fifth was blinded in a tournament. The two brothers who successively acquired this inheritance produced no male heirs surviving beyond 1194, when the lordship fell to a granddaughter. Long-continued subdivision weakened families, however, and knights sometimes became farmers with tastes too elevated for their means. In 1287, ten men and women gave homage to the bishop of Clermont Ferrand for the castle of Murat de Barrès.

To diminish the number of heirs, daughters with male siblings were given dower money – once money became current in the eleventh century – to marry or enter the Church, but no real property. The governments' desire to retain knightly militia service, as in England and France from the 1180s, also helped limit heir groups. Methods of single succession to an inheritance, sometimes primogeniture, were widely adopted in the thirteenth century. In his testament of 1202, a Gascon lord proposed that the oldest male was alone to inherit the main family property, the town and barony of Isle Jourdain. Around 1200, the great castellans in the Mâconnais began to adopt single succession, especially primogeniture, and knights soon imitated them. Nobles also insistently pressed offspring into the clergy and careers in law and arms, another reason for their contentiousness.

Difficulties aside, Europe's martial order had reached the point where knights were usually both noble and free, and to be knighted meant to be ennobled. Kings and princes now vied to enter knighthood. In 1248, the year of his election as emperor, William of Holland was knighted by the king of Bohemia with these words: 'I ordain you knight and joyfully accept you as a member of our college.'[3] Although knighting normally took place around the age of twenty-one, princes were often dubbed earlier: Henry III of England at age nine, for example.

Knighthood

To churchmen, the duties of the martial order were similar to those of princes, themselves warriors. Honorius addressed them:

> Soldiers! You are an arm of the Church, because you defend it against its enemies. Your duty is to aid the oppressed, refrain from rapine and fornication, repress those who impugn the Church with evil acts and resist rebels against the priesthood.[4]

And the clerks were censorious. Alan of Lille said that nowadays knights 'are not soldiers, but rather robbers and ravishers; not defenders but rather invaders'.[5] Burghers were usurers and nobles plunderers, went the common-place, and soldiers certainly fought for money and plunder. Bertrand of Born, enemy of Richard Coeur de Lion, poet and lord in Limousin, gloried in spring because war began again. Barons, he thought, were generous when war forced them to enlarge their households. Tournaments were training for soldiers and could be awful: a meet between Burgundians and Englishmen at Châlons in 1274 was fought with war's ferocity. Violence was lessened by favouring single and small-group combats instead of large engagements, but they were still anathema to clerical rigorists, the first Lateran Council in 1139 having denied Christian burial to those who died in them. The law was unenforceable, however, because tourneys also gave young nobles a chance of gaining reputation and money, since victors got prizes. Having begun his career in this way, England's William the Marshal came to the deathbed and a chaplain there intoned that, to attain heaven, what has been taken by force must be returned. The marshal turned to a squire:

> Henry, the clerks are too hard on us; they shave us too closely. I took five hundred knights whose weapons, harnesses and horses I kept. If God's kingdom is closed to me for that, nothing can be done, for I can't give them back . . . Either their argument is false or no man can be saved.[6]

The master of the Temple witnessed William's agony and the archbishop of Canterbury delivered his funeral oration!

Philip of Novara said that 'good knights, by renown, valour and deeds, often attain great wealth and conquest'.[7] An Italian treatise on government

---

[3] Gauthier, *Chevalerie* 291.
[4] *Sermo generalis ad milites* in his *Speculum ecclesiae* in PL CLXXI 865.
[5] *Summa de arte praedicatorum* 40 in PL CCX 186.
[6] *Histoire de Guillaume le Maréchal* (ed. Meyer) v. 18480ff.
[7] *Des quatres tenz d'aage d'ome* 15 (ed. Fréville) 11.

of around 1220 stressed fame. A young knight there asserts that 'the memory of those whom fame reports worthy in arms lives long after their passing, and, as poets' histories and eulogies in French clearly show in books long since spread throughout the world, their names are not lost to posterity'. His older opponent in the town council lamely replies: 'I'd rather be worthy in learning than in arms.'[8]

Churchmen urged knights to eschew earthly glory and seek heaven's. Philip of Novara fits his doctrine of profit and fame to the idea that, like St George, soldiers are Christ's holy martyrs, arguing that a saint's fame outlasts an emperor's because of the yearly feast in the ecclesiastical calendar! One clerical idea, however, appealed to soldiers. In 1128, the Templars swore: 'I will imitate the death of my Lord, because as Christ laid down his life for me, so am I prepared to lay down my life for my brethren.'[9] The brotherhood of arms was lauded by John of Salisbury, indeed by everybody.

Burghers also questioned the martial order. What offended them was the nobility's pride or indifference to ordinary morality. The speed with which gentlemen rode through the crowded streets of Italian towns provoked protest. And what about Geoffrey of Bruyères, lord of Karytaina in Morea, who, just when the Byzantines rose against the Latins in 1252, went off to Italy with the wife of the lord of Catavas, the prettiest woman in all Romania? Whatever others thought, Geoffrey's peers cheered him when he returned. Boncompagno of Signa tells why nobles fell into debt:

> Frequent hospitality for reason of courtliness, standing as guarantors for their friends' debts, gifts given in praise of war, seditious plots, lawsuits, tournaments, marriage settlements, love making, dicing . . . borrowing at usury, gluttony, drunkenness, negligence, violent contentiousness and improvidence.[10]

Rich lords rivalled each other in ostentation. An exaggerated report of a 'court' or meet held by Raymond VI of Toulouse at Beaucaire on the Rhone in 1174 claimed that one lord used wax candles for cooking, another drove twelve ox teams to sow the fields with 30,000 shillings and yet another burned thirty horses. In the *Romance of the Rose*, John of Meung has the lover's army assault the castle of maiden chastity. Merely literary fancy? In 1214, local gentlefolk assembled in Treviso. Armed with golden crowns and jewellery, the maids and ladies defended a fortress whose walls were cloth of gold, scarlet silk and velvet. With fruit, spices, perfumes and flowers, the gentlemen began the assault. Unfortunately, the banner of St Mark was knocked to the ground when the Venetians and Paduans began to brawl entering the first gate, thus fuelling the already lively animosity between the two cities.

---

[8] *Oculus pastoralis* 6 1 in ed. L.A. Muratori, *Antiquitates Italicae medii aevi* (Arezzo, 1776) IX 840–42.
[9] *La règle du Temple* (ed. Henri de Curzon, Paris, 1886) 63, and 1 John:3, 16; John 15:13, etc.
[10] *Boncompagnus Boncompagni* in *BuF* I 166.

Gentlemen wanted to have their way and were easily angered when they did not. A French preacher reports that humble folk lavished affection on their children until their hands were suddenly put to the plough. Gentlefolk differed. They rarely saw their issue, gave them over to servants and then sent them to serve in a notable's household. When ready for war or marriage, however, they were raised on high. Although other classes also went to war, nobles experienced more of it. The mendicant theologian Giles of Rome asserted that the fear of being cut up in combat was more intense than any other. In his lawbook, Beaumanoir discusses permissible and impermissible flight, asserting that those who flee are more likely to be slain than those who stand. Contrariwise, the popular *Romance of Sidrac* observed that 'a good flight is better than a bad remaining'.[11] And some of them knew what war was about. Joinville's description of the rout of Louis IX's first 'battle' at Mansurah in 1249 and the king's counterattack is a model.

To repeat what the Romans said, the soldiery was a militia or profession. The clergy, especially the monastic, was also a militia. As society matured, other militias also appeared. Of these the most significant were the lawyers and masters of law, those whom Placentinus (d. 1192), a jurist who taught at Bologna and Montpellier, called 'a militia of unarmed soldiers, militating in letters'.[12] This echoes Justinian's *Code* and *Institutes*, where majesty was said to be not only decorated by arms but also armed by laws, victorious over enemies abroad and injustice at home. These familiar texts were also enshrined in the English codes named after Glanville and Bracton. Alfonso X of Castile's jurists also used them, and his *Book of the Laws* went on to divide society's orders into 'nobles, knights, masters, citizens, artisans and labourers', adding that 'knowledge of law is another manner of knighthood'.[13]

Jurists of the 'literate' or 'robed militia' even claimed precedence over the 'armed militia'. When Azzo read in the *Code* that those devoted to letters for twenty years were accorded the ex-vicarial dignity, he said it meant that the grammarian Master John and the jurist Accursius should be ranked as counts or dukes on retirement. Albert of Gandino's treatise on criminal law (1286–1301) argued that, although lawyers and judges were exempt from legal torture, knights were not, unless in actual service. Bartolo of Sassoferrato (d. 1357) blandly summarized juristic tradition in 1355: '[The *Code*] says that, as soldiers do in arms, lawyers militate in laws and are more necessary for a republic than soldiers.'[14] In Bologna, fountainhead of legal studies, a town statute of 1301 provided that parades were to be headed by the city's elected

---

[11] Langlois, *La Vie en France au moyen-âge* III 261.
[12] Fitting, *Das castrense peculium* 551.
[13] *Las siete partidas* 1 10 3 (Madrid, 1807) II 90.
[14] Fitting, *Das castrense peculium* 551.

officers, followed by the judges and doctors of law, after whom trailed the knights and commonalty.

Rivalries aside, the military welcomed professionalism because they were career minded. In the romance *Erec and Enide*, Christian of Troyes taught that marriage, making love, wealth and high lineage were not enough; one must also make one's way in the world. The poet borrowed the divisions of 'practical philosophy', namely self-government (ethics), the government of groups (economics) and the government of society (politics). Hence his married hero and heroine first learn self-respect or self-love, then friendship and love of others and finally love of society, at which point they are crowned king and queen.

War's increasing complexity during the twelfth century also stimulated growing professionalism. Introduced from Italy, crossbows, followed soon by improved ordinary bows, made horse armour and reinforcement of chain mail with plate advisable. At Grasse in Provence, a notable estimated in 1214 that 'a knight and armoured horse equalled two knights without horse armour or eight sergeants'.[15] More specialized and riding heavier horses, knights still ruled the field of battle, but needed ancillary formations. A force sent to Agen in 1221 during the Albigensian crusade consisted of twenty knights, thirty sergeants and ten crossbowmen, all mounted. A Genoese mercenary company in 1255 had three hundred knights, each with a pack animal and two squires, twenty mounted crossbowmen and one hundred archers on foot. In the 1270s, Giles of Rome likened knights:

> to the masters and doctors of other sciences. Masters in any branch of learning must be instructed and examined, and none should be promoted to the knightly dignity unless . . . competent in war's work . . . Although foot and cavalry who are not knights wage war, knights ought to be the masters and organizers of the others in battle.[16]

A learned literature on war appeared, initially mainly consisting of versions of Vegetius's late Roman *Epitomy*. True to his time, Salimbene remarked about a *podestà* of Parma that he was 'a brave knight and learned in war'.[17]

Competition between the professions revived definitions of nobility. Was it blood, wealth or virtue? In the mid-1180s, Andrew the Chaplain's lady argued the case of blood. Scarlet dye held better in English cloth than in Italian, and virtue is found more often in nobles than plebeians. Besides, gentlemen are more handsome, nor would God have instituted different social orders without reason. Andrew's contemporary, the abbess Hildegard of

---

[15] *Recueil des actes des comtes de Provence appartenant à la maison de Barcelone* (ed. Fernand Bênoit, Monaco and Paris, 1925) II No. 18.
[16] *De regimine principum* 3 3 1 (Rome, 1607) 558–59.
[17] *Cronica fratris Salimbene de Adam, ordinis minorum* in *MGH SS* XXXII 98.

Bingen, had earlier explained why she admitted only noblewomen. God had instituted a natural order and man should not try, as had Satan, to vault above his natural place. Who would stable cattle, asses, sheep and goats pell-mell together in a barn? As there is a heavenly hierarchy, so also is there an earthly one: God loves all equally, but all are not equal here below.

That most writers were jurists or clerks, whose blood often left something to be desired, denied such sentiments universal plaudits. Blood has little intellectual appeal: all, taught the *Roman de Sidrac*, are sons of Adam, and Dante laughed at the debate about whether Adam was or was not noble. Earlier, the chaplain Andrew remarked that virtue had ennobled men in the past, and 'there are many deriving from these first nobles who are wholly degenerated. And, if you reverse the proposition, it's equally true.'[18] Historian of the house of Anjou Thomas of Loches (d. 1168) explained its humble origins by observing that the Emperor Charles the Bald elevated commoners because:

> there were men of old stock and many family portraits who boasted about their forefather's deeds, not their own, and who, when given office, employed someone from the people to instruct them in their duty, so that those whom the king ordered to command others sought another commander for themselves.

Much of this comes from Sallust's *Jugurthine War*, showing that the arguments against nobility of blood were antique. Thomas also remarked that the humble origin of the Angevin line was of no moment, 'for we have often read that senators formerly lived on the land and emperors were torn from the plough', a point substantiated by scripture's shepherds Saul and David.[19] The poet Wace, a canon at Bayeux *circa* 1161–71, remarked on human equality in his widely read *Roman de Rou*.

Dante had discussed Aristotle's maxim, repeated by the Emperor Frederick II, that nobility was old wealth combined with virtue. He rejected the first part of the proposition because of wealth's three imperfections: 'first, the wantonness of its acquisition; second, the moral danger of its increase; and third, the harmfulness of its possession'.[20] But wealth surely meant something. In Andrew's *On Love*, a plebeian suitor tells a noble lady that he makes money only to spend it, thus defending 'the nobility of my behaviour and virtue. Had I not honest profits, poverty would keep me in obscurity so that I could not perform noble acts, and thus my nobility would rest on nothing but my word, a type of courtliness and nobility no one believes.'[21] Reciting a commonplace from St Jerome, a Parisian Dominican about 1265 saw

---

[18] *De amore* 1 6 (ed. Trojel) 17–18.

[19] *Gesta consulum Andegavorum* in *Chroniques des comtes d'Anjou* (ed. Halphen and Poupardin) 25 and 27. The reference to Cincinnatus is from Cicero's *De senectute* 16 56.

[20] *Convivio* 4 1 3.

[21] *De amore* 1 6 2 (ed. Trojel) 46.

nothing in nobility, 'except that nobles are constrained by a certain need not to degenerate from the virtue of their parents'.[22]

For some, neither blood nor money counted. Since, says the Chaplain, 'virtue is more to be praised in a plebeian than in a noble', a commoner is to be preferred as a lover.[23] Dante's teacher, Brunetto Latini, states in his popular *Treasure* of 1260/66 that 'they commonly say that courtesy comes from lordship, or that its cause is riches or nobility of blood, but the wise say that the only reason a man is worthy of being a prince or lord is intrinsic virtue'. To be 'of mean spirit and high lineage is like being an earthen pot covered outside with fine gold'.[24] Cino of Pistoia expressed similar ideas in his lectures on the *Code* in 1312/14:

> Whoever deserves nobility by virtue is more worthy of being called a noble than he who descends from a noble family, because no one is noble by race . . . He is to be commended for what he has wrought for himself rather than from what he has from his parents.[25]

And Dante concluded that 'nobility comes from virtue; not virtue from nobility'.[26]

In spite of this, blood was popular. James of Voragine's *Golden Legend* described most saints as of high origins, enhanced, of course, by virtue. And many weaselled. The Castilian *Book of the Laws* averred that nobility derived 'first, from lineage, second, from knowledge [as of law] and, third, from excellence in arms, customs and manners'. Still, if 'lineage is a noble thing, virtue surpasses it; and whoever has both may be really called a noble, because he is rich by lineage and rounded out by virtue'.[27]

Chivalry and war

Knighthood and nobility did not escape change. Of forty-three knightly families around 1100 near Cluny in Burgundy, six had vanished by 1200, being replaced by three new ones, one of peasant origins. The tempo then began to accelerate: by 1240, sixteen new knightly lines appeared. Seven of these were branches of old ones, two rose from being bailiffs and one from the peasantry. What goes up can also go down. By the early thirteenth century, about three-fifths of the old nobles around Namur had sunk to the level of ordinary knights. A new and higher nobility called the 'peers of the castle of Namur' appeared during the second half of the century and contained about

---

[22] Pseudo-Thomas's *De eruditione principum* cited in Berges, *Die Fürstenspiegel* 11n.

[23] *De amore* 1 6 4 (ed. Trojel) 76–77.

[24] *Li livres dou Tresor* 2 29 and 54 (ed. Carmody) 199 and 230.

[25] Fitting, *Das castrense peculium* 552.

[26] *Convivio* 4 1 19.

[27] *Las siete partidas* 1 9 6 and 1 21 2 (Madrid, 1807) II 63 and 197–98.

five of the older families. To some, knighthood seemed so unprofitable that they exchanged it for economic advantage. In 1238, the chapter of St Cunibert of Cologne conceded land to one 'who does not intend to become a knight ... Furthermore, be it known that, if the said Otto should become one, he must sell the said property within the year but not to a church, knight or son of a knight who wishes to become one.'[28]

Subdivision of inheritances hurt some military families, and others whose condition was static were affected by the increased expense of warfare caused by the specialization mentioned above. One result was that nobles were busy making ends meet. The poem *Siegfried Helbing* describes Austria's lesser knights. Tournaments were not for them; they wanted to increase their cows' yield of milk. Instead of drinking, they sold the wine that they raised. War had best be over by harvest because these farmers then had to go home. Since knights' privileges were justified by service, however, the statutes of Fréjus in 1235 state that, if a knight spends all his time 'ploughing, digging, carting... or doing other agricultural labour, he should not have the knight's liberty'.[29] Had he not assumed knighthood's duties by the age of thirty, he would have to pay the count of Provence's tallage. Writing in the 1270s, Raymond Llull recommended that poor squires should forgo the golden belt and spurs; they would otherwise become 'thieves' – mercenaries!

Because wealth tended to concentrate and warfare became more demanding, the character of armies was changing. Old terms for knights in south France, such as *caballarii*, vanish early in the thirteenth century, showing that in the past some had only been light horse who swelled the formations of more heavily armed knights. A 'company' seen at Limoux in the early 1230s represents the new style. It consisted of four knights, four mounted crossbowmen and some squires on foot, a configuration close to the later 'garnished lance'. The numbers of knights owing service from given localities clearly diminished. Simon of Montfort required only one well-accoutred knight from Verfeil in 1214, but in 1229, the count of Toulouse was owed fifteen and even thirty-three from comparable places such as Fanjeaux near Carcassonne and Montégut near Albi. Such persons must have been like the 'sergeants and crossbowmen' who, after the knights, took oath to a new count of Toulouse in 1249. In fine, the numbers of fully armed knights seems to have been declining, and sharply. Around 1350, just under four per cent of the population was noble in Provence and under one and a half per cent in Clermont and Amiens in central and north France. Parts of western Europe evolved more rapidly than others. Maritime Brittany and Iberia generally, especially the Basque lands and Castile, had many nobles, but the great contrast was with eastern Europe. In early modern times, nobles in Poland were

---

[28] Guilhermoz, *Origines de la noblesse* 379.
[29] Published in Giraud, *Essai sur l'histoire du droit français* II 12.

ten per cent and more of the population, whereas in the west they usually ranged from one to four per cent.

Town patricians went to war with knights' equipment. The fusion of nobles and patricians was most advanced in Italy, where cities were relatively independent of princes. Since ministerial dependency was not permitted in urban republics, Italian and other towns early developed the practice of knighting any likely person. In the mid-twelfth century, the historian Otto of Freising complained that:

> to oppress their neighbours, [the Milanese] are not ashamed of allowing young men of low condition, artisans of contemptible or mechanical arts, whom other peoples would reject like the plague from honourable and liberal pursuits, to assume the knight's belt . . . and hence far excel all other cities in wealth and power.[30]

Italians answered in the *Entry into Spain*, averring there that the Lombards with Charlemagne at the siege of Pamplona were all free, all knighted without regard to birth and privileged to carry bared swords before the king.

Republican knighthood developed an almost modern quality. Although Accursius's *Ordinary Gloss* of 1220–34 repeated Roman law's prohibition of soldiers being merchants, Florentine and other merchant bankers were usually noble. In 1312–14, Cino of Pistoia sourly remarked that 'nowadays knights rarely give up mercantile pursuits or business, and not a few exercise common crafts and are ignorant of how to arm themselves'.[31] For these, Cino comments, golden spurs and honorifics are enough; they need no other privileges. Knighting became so common a recognition of civic worth that in 1322 the Florentine government ordered that no corpse could be dubbed! Patricians being like knights and knights like patricians, all knights, squires and commoners wealthy enough to 'live nobly' were to serve the republic as knights, either personally or by substitute. Knightly service was equated with a certain level of personal taxes throughout north Italy by the mid-thirteenth century. As a result, the right of knights to judgement by their peers and exemption from taxes slowly faded. A Florentine statute of 1289 defined nobles as members 'of a house where there is a knight, or where there was one within the last twenty years, or as those who, in common parlance, are normally held to be or are called notables, nobles or magnates'.[32]

As the popular parties rose in Italy, magnates were deprived not only of privileges but even of the right to hold public office. This threat prompted four nobles of Putignono to petition Pisa to become commoners in 1322, claiming that 'although they . . . have the name of nobles, they were

---

[30] This passage from the *Gesta Friderici* is cited everywhere, but see Salvemini, *La dignità cavalleresca* 355.

[31] Fitting, *Das castrense peculium* 559.

[32] Salvemini, *La dignità cavalleresca* 398.

nevertheless always effectually commoners and supporters of the Pisan people, and always intended to be so'.[33] Such being the case, ambitious persons no longer wanted knighthood if it implied nobility, and consequently 'popular' knighthood appeared. Bartolo of Sassoferrato (d. 1357) remarked in his commentaries on the *Code*: 'We observe here in Perugia, that if a plebeian is knighted, he becomes noble; but if in Florence, remains a commoner.'[34] The first systematic treatise on heraldry was Bartolo's posthumously published *On Insignia and Arms*. This famous jurist was so indifferent to nobility that he blandly compared coats of arms to watermarks, trademarks and the signs of commercial companies, opining that anyone could have them.

Popular knighthood on this scale is not found outside of Italy, but the fusion of patricians and nobles was known elsewhere. The consuls of Avignon in 1243 ordered that 'according to the ancient liberty of this city, every knight and burgher . . . may aid lords and friends in a vendetta'.[35] In 1303 at Toulouse, 'feudal persons, noble or non-noble' having a hundred pounds (of Tours) annually were to appear with horse and arms. Other 'nobles' having less than this were to appear as best they could.[36] England's 'distraint' of knighthood was somewhat similar. It began in 1224, when those with fiefs worth twenty pounds a year were ordered to be knighted or else pay a fine. In 1225, the king addressed 'all earls, barons, knights and freemen who are not merchants', showing that he was thinking in Roman law's terms seen above. By 1241, distraint was extended to anyone with property worth that amount, whether or not the owner was of knightly stock. When repeated in 1256, Matthew Paris, the historian of St Albans, observed that the law was enacted 'to reinforce knighthood in England as it was in Italy'.[37] Princes everywhere wanted to use the knightly militia, so much cheaper than mercenary companies, and tried to reinvigorate it. Raymond VII of Toulouse (d. 1249) knighted perhaps as many as two hundred 'nobles and others' in 1248 and Edward I of England (d. 1308) dubbed three hundred in a ceremony in 1307. If few soldiers were found, they could help fill their treasuries by fines for non-service.

As did republics, princes found knighting or ennobling useful for rewarding service. To a prince, nobility was won by virtuous individuals and virtue was service to himself. What this meant for social levelling was already understood: Rudolph of Habsburg in 1276 greeted all subjects, from peasant to great noble, as 'my ministers'.[38] Since this rational absolutism meant little

---

[33] Cristiani, *Nobilità e popolo nel commune di Pisa* 114–15.

[34] Salvemini, *La dignità cavalleresca* 399.

[35] *Coutumes et règlemens d'Avignon* (ed. Maulde) 190 No. 112.

[36] January 1303 in my *Society and Government in Toulouse* 102.

[37] *Chronica majora* in *Rolls Series* LVII v 560.

[38] Ritter, *Ministérialité et chevalerie* 105.

even where it was propounded, knighting was used to ennoble people for service. Nor was the service always military. Seen above, an architect was dubbed by Charles I of Naples and a jurist by a duke of Burgundy. Another example is a chamberlain of a count of Namur, who was in office in 1289, became a squire in 1300 and knight in 1305, from his age hardly an ideal soldier.

Again like republics, princes tried to monopolize knighting, but the tradition was that any knight could dub. In France, with semi-independent provinces – Brittany, Flanders, England's Guienne and Gascony – royal monopoly was long in coming. In 1298, the crown confessed that in the seneschalcy of Beaucaire, from time immemorial 'burghers assumed the knight's belt from nobles, barons and even archbishops without the licence of the prince'.[39] But royal knighthood slowly began to win out. A lord of Isle Jourdain, whose predecessor had been dubbed by the count of Toulouse in 1248, styled himself in 1280 'knight of the illustrious king of the French'. An example of royal ennoblement is a charter of 1295:

> Because . . . our dearest father manumitted master John of Taillefontaine, clerk . . . we, approving this liberty, allow . . . him to acquire noble fiefs and assume the belt of knighthood, and, by that act . . . enjoy . . . perpetual nobility.[40]

The mix of function and privilege characterizing the military well-to-do had changed. Until about 1200 – and later in Germany, not to speak of Scandinavia and Slavic lands where knighthood was only being introduced – function had been accented; thereafter the hereditary privilege of those of knightly stock was what counted. In 1226 the emperor wrote to the 'knights' of the Rhenish-Franconian town of Oppenheim; in 1269 he greeted the 'knights and sons of knights'; and in 1275 Rudolph of Habsburg addressed 'all knights, their sons and grandsons at Oppenheim possessing the military right', the latter phrase referring to the privileges accorded to soldiers in Roman law. Unknighted gentlemen from knightly lines were therefore considered nobles. Up to about 1260 around Namur, non-knighted military were generally called sergeants, a term with servile connotations in that area; thereafter, they were called squires and considered noble. The result of this evolution is witnessed by a charter of 1293 emanating from Manosque in Provence, adverting to questions raised between 'the knights and military persons whose names are [so-and-so] knights, and [so-and-so] squires or military on one hand, and the good men and popular persons on the other'.[41]

In France, knighthood became gradually rarer, being replaced by the claim to belong to a noble line. Of the sixty nobles of forty-three families in

---

[39] Gauthier, *La chevalerie* 249.
[40] Guilhermoz, *Origines de la noblesse* 478.
[41] The passages on Oppenheim and Manosque are found in ibid. 479 and 482.

the county of Forez near Lyons who leagued together against royal taxes in 1314–15, four were widows, twenty-nine knights (two of whom had lately been bourgeois) and twenty-seven squires, one of peasant origin. Of the squires, eleven died as such, six were knighted before the age of forty, five before fifty, four before sixty, and one in his sixties. Gone were the days when one was dubbed at twenty-one or shortly thereafter. In fine, although nobles still paid the 'tax of blood' in defence of prince and community, privilege especially typified them.

This social context makes it understandable why the late thirteenth century saw a recrudescence of literature defending hereditary nobility. The most famous voice was Raymond Llull, whose *Order of Chivalry* of 1274–75 was vastly popular. To Llull, a knight who has children by a plebeian wife honours neither gentility nor knighthood, and a knight's wife bearing a child by a villein destroys 'the antiquity of chivalry and the noble confraternity of noble lineage'. He even asserted that commoners cannot be knighted, but soon grudgingly contradicted himself. Unlike beasts, humans are rational, he observed, and so, 'by many noble habits and deeds and by being ennobled by a prince . . . an occasional man of new, honourable and gentle lineage is admitted into chivalry'. Sure that judges should be chosen only from chivalry, he at least believed they should be trained in law as well as war.[42]

This didactic literature added to the romances about war that usually served as soldiers' textbooks, works that Humbert of Romans likened to the clergy's scripture. Books of manners began to appear, urging gentlemen to learn music, chess and suitable sports. Finding that letters and arms go together, John of Meung urged that they be literate. The first evidence of family heraldic dates from the thirteenth century, glorifying lineage with handsome banners and so on. During this period the titles used by noblemen in modern times came into general use: at least in documents knights were 'noble and puissant'. With all its pomposity, so useful an impediment to totalitarian social organization was the irrational principle of noble blood's intrinsic freedom, that no medieval government could bind its citizens to a common servitude. Nor did the state do so until both princes and nobles had bowed off history's stage.

From ancient times, governments had summoned all citizens to arms when the fatherland was endangered, and so sonorous was this call that feudal and urban limitations on service became inane when this trumpet sounded. The most precocious development of this idea was seen in Italy's republics, whose wars, however aggressive, were all called defensive because their citizens had voted for them. This totalitarian vision spread to the larger pre-national units of Latin Europe in the late thirteenth century. By the early fourteenth

---

[42] The two passages cited in this paragraph are from his *Livre de l'ordre de chevalerie* 3 and 7 (ed. Minervini) 176 and 535b.

century, all France owed service or compensatory taxes based on wealth and status, a matter examined later.

The militia service for the 'defence of the fatherland' was not especially efficient. England's successful conquest of Wales was largely the work of professional soldiers. It was also shown for England at Bannockburn against the Scots in 1314 that, to echo Vegetius, multitudes of unpractised soldiers serve only to perplex and embarrass. Similar policies in France led to the log-jam of the crusade against Catalonia–Aragon in 1284–85 and the uncontrollable mob at Courtrai in 1302 arrayed against Flanders' militias. Both of these defeats foreshadowed the disasters of the Hundred Years War. In that later great combat, England's advantage was that her knightly militia could not be mobilized for overseas service, and the crown therefore hired individual magnates and their quasi-professional households and French or English mercenary companies. Although Charles of Anjou's successful intervention in the Italian war against the Hohenstaufen had been carried out with such troops, France's defence against England was based on the noble militia, the invasion having justified calls for the 'defence of the realm'. By virtue of numbers, militias of occasional soldiers can sometimes defeat professionals, but they require social solidarity, a quality especially lacking in France in the later fourteenth century. Impeded by chivalry, it took generations of disaster before professionalism triumphed and the militia principle atrophied in France. Until that occurred, the nobility could not really be called a 'privileged order'.

Chapter 12

Ecclesiastics

Clerical types

In his *Golden Summa* of 1251–52, Hostiensis saw the Trinity reflected in the Church's three orders: layfolk, regular and secular clergy. Clergy in the seven or eight orders were the core of the Church. Major orders were priests, deacons and subdeacons; minor ones acolytes, exorcists, readers, porters and psalmists. Jurists – but not theologians – often elevated the episcopate into a ninth, paralleling the nine orders of the church militant with the nine angelic ones of the church triumphant. Tonsured persons below the grade of subdeacon could marry; around 1300, about a tenth of Rheims's inhabitants were clerical, and hence largely exempt from tax and military service. One result was that clerical numbers multiplied beyond need, as a bishop of Olmütz complained to the Council of Lyons in 1274.

Numbers are hard to estimate. Around 1300, clerks in major orders were perhaps one in ninety of England's population, parish rectors being rare enough to be like belted knights among the laity. In Carcassonne in the early fourteenth century, nine parish rectors equalled the nine university trained physicians in this community of about 9,500 souls, and there were upwards of two hundred other persons under canon law. The latter number included a bishop, cathedral canons, monks and friars, and persons almost wholly lay in oblature serving hospitals and schools, making a very high three per cent of the population. Layfolk under canon law protection performed many duties in cathedrals, parishes and hospitals. Those trained as lawyers or notaries did well. The new bishop's judges or officials, first seen in north France about 1178, were often lay, as were many notaries and judges at the papal court. Another half-lay, half-clerical group consisted of students in parish and monastic schools and universities.

The second principal segment of the clergy was the religious. Some were canons. Some canons were regular, and some of these lived in independent houses such as those of the Premonstratensian order (founded 1120). Other regular canons were in cathedral chapters, although some chapters were composed of secular canons. If the latter, they often remained in lower orders, were assigned a living, inhabited individual houses and had private means. Canons regular were like monks, cloistered and bound by profession to a rule or order, especially Augustinian (Austin canons, founded 1059). Monks were defined by their submission to a rule and also by celibacy, enclosure in the cloister and community of property. Once monks were usually lay, but most took holy orders by this time. Male religious were often divided into three groups. The first, the choir monks, were those who had professed; the other two were the lay brethren and oblates.

Significant in orders such as the Cistercians (founded 1098), lay brethren did not live in the monks' cloister or enter holy orders; theirs was the duty of manual labour. Ideally, the lay brother was Martha, sister of Mary Magdalene and Lazarus, whose labour supported Mary's contemplation. The sisters did not always get on. Disputes between monks and lay brethren were frequent where, as in the order of Grandmont (founded early twelfth century, rule 1143), the latter administered the monastery. According to James of Vitry, the issue was that, when raising money, lay brethren wanted monks to attract lay donors by singing masses for dead donors and the Virgin, but the monks liked the old routines. Orders mostly composed of lay brethren had no troubles. The Hospitallers (founded 1099, military brothers admitted before 1160) and the Templars (founded 1118) got on well with their priestly chaplains.

The lay brother's grade was fading at this time, perhaps because recruits came from an increasingly free world, and both Benedictines and Cistercians were replacing them by salaried domestics. Franciscan lay brethren were titled brothers or friars and, like those in holy orders, belonged to the First Order (founded 1209, given rules in 1221 and 1223), the Second being the nuns of the Clares (founded 1215) and associated layfolk the Third or Tertiaries. They also called their male Tertiaries lay brethren, although they lived in the world.

Lacking vows and tonsure, oblates were the third group. These shaded insensibly into purely lay groups, such as teachers in the schools of monasteries or chapters, children entrusted to them for education, pensioners with corrodies, even old soldiers pensioned by secular patrons. In a mid-century trial of the abbot of the Benedictine house of Lézat, his enemies paraded thirty-six witnesses. Of these the house provided twelve monks (of whom nine were priests) and ten oblates or *donati*. Although four of these lay pensioners held no office there, three were *clerici*, two were public notaries and one was a knight. In addition, a noble widow is known to have been a pensioner together with her nubile daughter and young son. Aged, leprous and sick hospital inmates, hospital and educational staffs and male and female recluses or hermits (who often lived in town) had similarities with the religious. When one adds to this minestrone layfolk who banded together to emulate the life of the religious while remaining in the world, such as Humiliati, Franciscan Tertiaries and Beguines (female) and Beghards (male), one understands why contemporaries were astonished by the variety of such groups. They obscured the line between oblates and converses – Beguines were often called both – and confused the professed religious with layfolk.

Individual religious houses were not large. At its peak around 1150, the mother house of Cluny is said to have had three hundred monks as well as Europe's largest basilica. A little later, England's Cistercian Rievaulx had one hundred and forty monks and six hundred lay brothers; in 1286, Bury St Edmunds had eighty monks and one hundred and twenty-two domestics. These were big houses. An affiliate of Cluniac Moissac, the house of Lézat south of Toulouse, had a minimum of forty-two choir monks in the 1260s. The visitations from 1248 to 1269 of Odo Rigaud, archbishop of Rouen, show many small priories and granges housing two to five religious. Regular or secular, French cathedral chapters ran from thirteen to eighty-four canons, Beauvais having thirty-nine in 1267.

On the other hand, the number of houses was huge. In 1316, a Franciscan assembly at Naples estimated 1,017 male houses in Germany, France and Italy and those of St Clare's nuns at 285. Dominicans (founded 1215) were fewer, 582 male convents and 149 female being listed in 1303. Two other major mendicant orders, the Carmelites (brought to Europe from the Holy Land in 1242 and made mendicant by 1245) and the Austin Friars (Augustinian Eremites, founded 1256) and at least six smaller orders appeared before 1300, all with associated lay groups. By 1300 the Franciscans boasted 250 Tertiary societies, and a provincial council at Colmar in 1303 gathered 150 friars greeted by 300 local Beghards. In 1288, Bonvesino of Riva tells us that in Milan, 'there are fully 220 houses [like private homes] of the second order of the Humiliati of both sexes in our city and county in which a copious number lead the religious life by labouring with their hands'.[1]

To review, two great surges of the religious recast Christendom, the first occurring in the Gregorian age before this book begins, and the other around 1200. Both began with waves of enthusiasm that, though initially repressed, eventually broke free. The Premonstratensian Anselm of Havelberg (d. 1158) reported that the calumniators of the earlier new devotions asked:

> Why are there so many innovations in God's Church? Why do so many new orders rise up? Who can even count the many orders of clerks? Who is not astounded by the many types of monks?[2]

Although Cistercians and Carthusians sometimes settled in the wilderness, the new canons regular were habitual towndwellers, and sought to reinvigorate the secular clergy, build hospitals and educational institutions. An anonymous Premonstratensian tract divided the religious: 'Wholly separated from the crowd, some lead a peaceable life in God . . . Others, located

---

[1] *De magnalibus urbis Mediolani* 3 7 in ed. Francesco Novati, *Bullettino dell'istituto storici italiano* XX (1898) 81–82.

[2] *Liber de una forma credendi et multiformitate vivendi a tempore Abel justi usque ad novissimum electum* in *Dialogi* 1 1 in *PL* CLXXXVIII 1141.

next to men in town or in villages, are sustained by charity from the faithful and by incomes from churches and tithes.' Canons largely lived in towns: 'some are separated as much as possible . . . from the crowd; others are placed next to men; and yet others live among men, and hence are called secular'.[3] Few occupations were as resolutely worldly as those of the Templars and Hospitallers. The later mendicants were largely urban in origin, as befitted an age when towns reached their peak; if they began in cities, they soon spread to quite small towns. Another similarity between the two 'reform' waves was that both lost impetus, partly because, once established, the new orders joined with old ones to brake expansion. Restrictions were finally summed up by papal law prohibiting monks in the houses of old orders from leaving to join ones considered to be more 'rigorous'. Secular clerks also did not want them intruding in their parishes. The Premonstratensian cited above reported that 'I have heard priests . . . muttering that those who have left the world should remit the care of it to secular men, as though [monks] were unsuited to deal with secular business'.[4]

Cluny's and Cîteaux's monks and the canons regular nevertheless remade the secular clergy by inculcating standards of literacy and celibacy. Priesthood was also exalted by the withdrawal of the eucharistic cup from the laity and the teaching of transubstantiation with its priestly miracle of the mass. Joined to the Peace of God and the Crusade, penitential ideas, once mainly monastic, also invaded the world to furnish the court of conscience presided over by secular priests. In the late twelfth century, the schools of the canons of the cathedral, of St Victor and Mont Ste Geneviève created the University of Paris. Peter Cantor, grand chanter of Nôtre Dame, taught there and his works on ecclesiastical discipline and penitence were widely influential. Peter's student James of Vitry, canon regular of Oignies in Brabant, was a spell-binding preacher and in contact with the new Humiliati and Franciscans. In 1216 he won papal approval for the Beguine movement, begun earlier around the Premonstratensians in the Low Countries and enlivened by his 'spiritual mother' Mary of Oignies (d. 1213), famous at Liège. Cistercian monks were chosen by the popes for missions in Greece after the Latin conquest of Byzantium in 1204. They also mounted the first preaching tours against Catharism, and the pontiffs chose them to head the armed incursions of 1178 and 1181 in the Midi and the Crusade in 1209.

In the forefront of intellectual life until just before 1200, the monks thereafter fell behind. Robert Grosseteste, bishop of Lincoln and patron of England's Franciscans, warned the friars that, unless they studied at the university, 'it will surely happen to us as it has to other religious who we see,

---

[3] *Liber de diversis ordinibus et professionibus* 2 and 5 in *PL* CCXIII 814 and 827.
[4] Ibid. 2 in *PL* CCXIII 836.

alas! walking in the shadows of ignorance'.[5] Stephen of Lexington, abbot of Clairvaux, tried to rectify this by founding St Bernard's College at Paris in 1245–46, and Cluny's Benedictines followed in 1260 with theirs. The Cistercians did the same at Toulouse at about the same time.

The new orders seized leadership because they were designed for work in the world. After some hesitation, the pope recognized the working-class Humiliati in 1202, and thereafter the mendicant flood began. Famous for public begging (from which their name came), the mendicants were privileged by the popes. Save for the Franciscans, however, no new order was permitted to have a rule of its own, new rules being prohibited by the Lateran Council of 1215. The Dominicans erected study centres in their convents, and sent the first mendicant master, Roland of Cremona, to teach at Toulouse and Paris in 1229. They enriched the liturgy, Thomas Aquinas composing the order of service for the Corpus Christi feast in 1264. They specialized in penance, and their jurist Raymond of Penyafort issued a basic manual of casuistry in 1234. They were also leading preachers. General of the order from 1254 to 1263, Humbert of Romans remarked that the Saviour celebrated only one mass and was not known to have heard confession; his life was spent in prayer and preaching, to the latter of which he gave most of his time. Preaching explains why Dominicans laid out some churches with a central colonnade separating women from men.

The religious, in fine, twice invaded and twice remade the Church. During the two interventions they themselves changed. In the earlier age, they wanted the world to withdraw into the hermitage. Peter Damian reported that Romuald, founder of the Camaldolese monks about 1012, 'wished to convert the whole world into an hermitage and join the whole multitude of the people into the monastic order'.[6] Later on, they wanted the hermitage to invade and restructure the whole world. The abbot Joachim of Fiore (d. 1202) dreamed of a society to suit the coming age. Five oratories of monks were to inspire the faithful. An oratory of priests and clerks was to perform divine offices, visit and heal the sick and teach Latin and scripture to the young. The final and largest oratory was to be that of the married 'living the common life with their children, using wives for procreation rather than libidinousness'.[7] The married folk were to live by labour, sharing their fruits in common after providing for the clergy and monks. Joachim proved to be a bad prophet. Sacerdotal and teaching duties almost wholly absorbed the

---

[5] Thomas of Eccleston, *De adventu fratrum minorum in Angliam* 15 (ed. A.G. Little, Manchester, 1951) 91.

[6] *Vita beati Romualdi* in ed. Giovanni Tabacco, *Istituto storico Italiano per il Medio evo: 'Fonti per la storia d'Italia'* XCIV (1957) 78.

[7] *Dispositio novi ordinis pertinens ad tercium statum ad instar superne Jerusalem* in Grundmann, *Neue Forschungen über Joachim von Fiore* 120–21.

utopian and eremitic drive of the new orders. By invading both the secular clergy and laity and having nearly converted the streets and marketplaces of the world into monasteries, however, the religious may be thought to have been victorious. The victory was self-defeating, however. If all men and women were gradually becoming monks, what future was there for the cloistered religious?

Clerical freedom

Following 1 Corinthians 7:32–33 and Acts 4:32–37, monks hoped to live like the apostles: from each according to his means and to each according to his need. So essential was the common life that Peter Damian asserted: 'those only are fit for preaching who have no gain from earthly riches, and who, having nothing individually, have everything in common'.[8] The popes encouraged the creation of lay communities devoting themselves to the common life, Urban II in 1091 saying of such a group 'it is worthy of perpetual conservation because it is stamped in the form of the primitive Church'.[9] Praise of the life apostolic was incorporated in Gratian and was thence cited by later ideologues: 'Most unsuitably does he teach who announces the poor man Christ with a fat belly and rubicund cheeks.'[10]

Nor should learning be misused: John of Salisbury said it was for man's betterment and God's glory. It could corrupt, however, and Francis of Assisi urged: 'Care not about books and knowledge, only good works . . . Learning puffs up but love builds!' He told a novice wanting a psalter: 'After you get that, you'll want a breviary. And when you have that, you'll sit in your chair like a prelate, and say to your brother: "Fetch me my breviary!"'[11] Besides, learning is not enough. Ever sententious, Bernard of Clairvaux was right:

> Believe one who knows: you will discover some things more fully in forests than in books. Trees and rocks will teach you what you cannot hear from schoolteachers.[12]

A special kind of freedom is what monks wanted. When St Paul said: '"I wish you to be without care", he was speaking about the solicitude of house and family incumbent on those who have wives'.[13] But freedom from care also drew others, especially lovers. Preferring to be Abelard's 'strumpet', Heloise at first refused to marry her middle-aged professor. Even married folk

---

[8] *Contra clericos regulares proprietarios* 5 in *PL* CXLV 490.
[9] Letter 56 in *PL* CLI 336.
[10] Jordan of Saxony, *Liber vitas fratrum* 3 8 (ed. Rudolph Arbesmann and Winfred Humpfner, New York, 1943) 346, adapted from Gratian's *Decretum* 1 35 4 in *CICan* I 131, taken from Jerome.
[11] *Speculum perfectionis* 4 7 and 9 in ed. Paul Sabatier, *Le Speculum Perfectionis ou Mémoires de Frère Léon* (Manchester, 1931) II 13–14, stories dated about 1311–12, and also 1 Corinthians 8:1.
[12] Letter 106 to Henry Murdach in *PL* CLXXXII 242.
[13] Jordan of Saxony, *Liber vitas fratrum* 3 8 (ed. Arbesmann and Humpfner) 345.

longed for freedom. In 1254, a well-to-do Toulousan smith willed his bed to be kept in his house 'wherein a poor man may lie to remit my sins'.[14] His pauper was Christ, his sins the angers and excesses occasioned by family and business.

Carelessness sometimes eased fear. Told of his oncoming death, Francis of Assisi called Angelo and Leo, 'and when these brothers, full of grief, had come to him they sang with many tears the Song of Brother Sun and those of all the other creatures the saint had written'. Francis then added a verse: 'Be praised, our Lord, for our Sister Bodily Death from whom no man can escape.'[15] And carelessness was sometimes strained. When the anchorite St Macarius, James of Voragine recorded, had 'killed a flea that stung him, and much blood came out of it, he blamed himself for having avenged an injury, and hence remained naked for six months in the desert, whence he returned [to die] torn by wounds and bites'.[16]

Work in the world impeded freedom, and Jerome provided the commonplace: monks do not have the duty of teaching but rather of grieving, of lamenting themselves and the world. 'Practical' monks, however, knew they had to teach and serve those in the world. Before 1141, the Cluniac Orderic Vital lauded a Norman priory because local knights not only worked with the monks but also received instruction, so that the convent became 'a school for the living and a refuge for the dying'.[17] Schools require book learning, as Geoffrey of Breteuil (*fl. circa* 1173) put it: 'a cloister without a library is like a fortress without an arsenal'.[18] Overriding the founder's eremitical bent, the Franciscans therefore educated themselves and built churches in which to preach. Earthly fame, moreover, tempted all: 'Nothing appears wiser to me for a man striving for glory', said John of Salisbury, 'than the favour of honest writers'.[19]

Charity and parish care were supposed to be free, but customary fees to make them predictable had appeared. A dispute between the parish priests of Toulouse and their parishioners just before 1251 or 1255 over testaments, burial, marriage and other fees illustrates the problem, as do those among churches over burial rights. Popular preachers such as James of Vitry won plaudits by saying that the religious gave little to the poor in order to gain much for themselves, and John of Salisbury sourly remarked that the Hospitallers sucked up to the rich instead of embracing the pauper Christ. John of Flagy's *Romance of Garin the Lorrainer* comments:

[14] My 'Charity and Social Work in Toulouse' *Traditio* XXII (1966) 209–10n.
[15] *Speculum perfectionis* 12 123 (ed. Sabatier) I 345–46.
[16] *Legenda aurea vulgo Historia Lombardica dicta* (ed. Th. Graesse, Bratislava, 1890) 102.
[17] *Historia ecclesiastica* 2 5 22 in *PL* CLXXXVIII 447.
[18] Philippe Delhaye, 'L'organisation scolaire' *Traditio* V (1947) 237.
[19] *Policraticus* 8 9 (ed. C.C.J. Webb, Oxford, 1909) II 280.

When a noble lies sick abed in great fear of death, he does not look to his brother or son, nor to his relatives . . . he gives his lands, rents and mills to St Benedict's black monks, and neither daughter nor son gets anything.[20]

Charity's economy was a problem. With money, property or rents, layfolk bought pensions or care in old age or illness and provided education for children. Mutually profitable, over time these corrodian contracts resulted in accumulating property and thus provoked anger against the wealth of the Church. Besides, although military pensioners, young and old male and female corrodians, and children learning letters give evidence of the social usefulness of monastic establishments, all also disrupted the quiet of the cloister. Fundraising, moreover, harassed the rich who, then as now, disliked having to give. The Dominican William of Abingdon delighted his audiences until he began to build the order's house. Henry III of England then remarked: 'Brother William, you used to speak so spiritually; now all you say is "Give, give, give!"'[21]

Attractive to some, the sparse communitarian life repelled others. Around 1200, Guiot of Provins's *Bible* discussed the religious. Cistercians in outlying granges lived well but the rest starved. The abstinence of sick Carthusians from meat was little more than suicide, and recluses or hermits were simply mad. Happy were Augustinian canons, who ate, drank and dressed well; Guiot would like to suffer with them. Moderation – even ease, in fact – was needed by celibate brotherly communities. Robert Grosseteste remarked that:

three things are needed for earthly health: food, sleep and play. He enjoined a penance on a certain melancholy brother, namely to drink a cup of good wine, and, when he had drunk it, although most unwillingly, said to him, 'Dear brother, if you had such a penitence frequently, you'd have a much better ordered conscience.'[22]

The ascetic urge posed problems, especially concerning priestly marriage. As canon law called it, clerical concubinage was attacked in the Gregorian age, providing an issue with which to mobilize lay support – make the teacher suffer! Although provoking change in clerical practice, one observed with stunned disapproval by Muslims and Jews, old ways were hard to uproot. The distinguished Ailred, who died as abbot of Rievaulx in 1166, was the son, grandson and great-grandson of rural priests. Clerical concubinage remained customary in northern England, Scandinavia, parts of Germany and Iberia, and was not infrequent in France and Italy. Of 700 priests visited by Odo Rigaud, archbishop of Rouen, twelve per cent were denounced to him for this 'fault'. In 1238, Castile's King Ferdinand III (the Saint) licensed Guadalajara's clergy to leave property to their children, and his son Alphonse in 1271 did the same for several places in the dioceses of Osma and Burgos.

---

[20] Schreiber, 'Cluny und die Eigenkirche' in *Gemeinschaften des Mittelalters* 117n.
[21] Thomas of Eccleston, *De adventu fratrum minorum in Angliam* 10 (ed. Little) 46.
[22] Ibid. 15 (ed. Little) 92.

In one semester of 1335, of the over two hundred papal dispensations for illegitimacy to allow entry into holy orders, over seventy per cent were granted sons of priests. Below the priestly level, clerical concubinage was even more widespread. Peter Cantor's circle at Paris vainly proposed releasing subdeacons and deacons from the prohibition, partly because they corrupted themselves so easily by buying papal dispensations.

Medieval clerks were more open about sex than religious men are today. Clement VI (d. 1352) is said to have explained his relations with women by saying that he had picked the habit up in youth, and engaged in it now only on doctors' orders. To quiet murmurs, he produced 'a small black book in which he had written the names of . . . incontinent popes, showing from the deeds written there that they governed the Church better than others who were continent'.[23] They also described the pricking of the flesh with great fidelity. The strange 'autobiography' of the hermit Peter of Monte Morrone who became Pope Celestine V records that, for him, God's kindest miracle was to ease his conscience about wet dreams.

Living in a society where class distinctions were overlaid by ostensibly functional orders, men and women chose ways of life because of the roles inherent in them. The courtliness, eruptive romance and angers of gentlefolk contrasted sharply with the bookish and sometimes maudlin emotionalism of the clergy. Few, however, were wholly fulfilled or contained by the choice of order that they, their families and circumstances made for them. Francis of Assisi was the son of an ambitious cloth merchant, and his flight from the countinghouse led him to seek to shine in chivalry. Defeated there, he then turned to poverty's wonders, and there instilled the sacrifice, humility, freedom, psychic ostentation and self-love of the religious life into a migratory community of like souls.

Although hearty bachelors were also attracted, the Church, especially monasteries, offered a way to men who had a larger share than most of motherly qualities. A plan for a Franciscan hermitage read:

> Two of [the hermit friars] should be mothers and they should have two sons . . . The two mothers should imitate the life of Martha and the two sons that of Mary [Magdalene] . . . And the brothers who are mothers should strive to remain remote from all persons and . . . guard their sons . . . so that no one may speak with them. Nor should the sons speak to anyone except their mothers.[24]

Womanly warmth in male communities does not mean that homosexuality was general. In the 1260s, four monks reported on forty-two Benedictines of

---

[23] From the chronicle of Melas cited by Haller, *Vier Kapitel zur Geschichte des ausgehenden Mittelalters* I 121.

[24] Ed. Heinrich Boehmer, 'Analekten zur Geschichte des Franz von Assisi' in *Sammlung ausgewählter kirchen- und dogmengeschichtlicher Quellenschriften* IV (Tübingen, 1961) 46.

the monastery of Lézat. Other than simony, retention of property, working in the fields with members of their families, eating meat and other occasional offences, almost half the inmates were reported to be or to have been sexually active. Seventeen specific women, including sisters at the Fontevrault house of Longages, were named, and eleven monks were charged with having had specific children. Only two, however, were charged with homophilia. About one of these, a witness said that he rather doubted the truth of the allegations, and another suspected that his informants were moved by a desire to harm the monk. In fine, here to the south of Toulouse, the 'vice of sodomy', as they described it, was decidedly ill considered, at least when talking to the police, so to speak. On the other hand, the religious habitually practised both mutual and self-flagellation. Although the lash was used by layfolk for corporal punishment, penitential whipping remained monastic until the spread of the religious vocation in the mid-thirteenth century. It then appeared openly among the laity, an early example being the large-scale flagellant movement that swept wartorn Italy in 1259.

Although otherworldly, the faith reflected the world's variety. On one hand, it was monotheistic; on the other, to speak like a Muslim, polytheistic: three divine persons, the Virgin and local saints' cults, both male and female. The faith penetrated daily living, and earthly life emulated heavenly. Eight knights and four sergeants elected the grand master of the Temple, twelve 'in honour of the twelve apostles. The twelve brothers should together elect a brother chaplain to hold the place of Christ Jesus and keep the brothers in peace . . . And so there will be thirteen brothers.'[25] According to the theological masters appointed to examine the writings of Peter John Olivi in 1319, this Franciscan believed that, just as the Synagogue had been propagated by twelve patriarchs and the Church by twelve apostles, 'so the final Church of the remaining Jews and gentiles is to be propagated by twelve evangelical men. Whence Francis had twelve associates or sons, through whom and in whom was founded the evangelical order.'[26] The world was also a comic mirror of heaven. To Boncompagno of Signa, the invalidation of contracts was prefigured in paradise because, when the Lord asked: '"Adam, where are you?" – [Adam] straightway proposed the objection of fraud, saying: "The wife you gave me deceived me"'.[27]

Spiritual and material were inseparable. The archbishop of Cologne pillaged the relics of the Magi (!) from fallen Milan in 1162, and the Crusaders looted Constantinople's rich trove of relics in 1204. James of Vitry hung a finger of Mary of Oignies encased in silver on his necklace, giving it to Pope Gregory IX 'to carry against the vice of swearing by which he was atrociously

---

[25] *La règle du Temple* (ed. Curzon) 210.
[26] In Etienne Baluze, *Miscellanea sacra* (Lucca, 1761) II 271b.
[27] *Rhetorica novissima* 1 14 in *BIMA* II 254a.

tempted'.[28] Countess Theodora, Thomas Aquinas's sister, shocked nobody when she asked the abbot of Fossanuova for her brother's right hand:

> Although fourteen years in the earth, being unable to pull it off the body, [the abbot] had to cut it off with a knife, and it gave off a wonderfully sweet odour to those venerating it.[29]

The incarnation was treated in much the same fashion. In 1178 Peter Maurand, a Cathar at Toulouse, recanted and was obliged to swear that the consecrated wafer in the mass was 'not only a symbol but also the true body and blood of our lord Jesus Christ, and actually and not only symbolically, but in very truth, is handled and broken by the hands of priests and ground by the teeth of the faithful'.[30] Peter was repeating the oath exacted from Berengar of Tours in 1059 about transubstantiation, a text carried by both Gratian and Peter Lombard. This miracle was awkward, however. Because their intention is evil or lacking, the latter remarked, neither heretics nor excommunicates can confect a sacrament and an animal cannot eat the host. Thence arises a question: 'What then does a mouse take or chew?' And an answer: 'Only God knows.' And why did the Lord choose this particular miracle? 'Lest the mind abhor what the eye perceives, because we are not in the habit of eating raw flesh or drinking blood . . . and lest the Christian religion be mocked by unbelievers.'[31] God was being tactful but. according to Roger Bacon and others, Jews and Muslims both continued to charge the Christians with covert cannibalism.

Clerical rivalries

Secular clerks came to terms with the world in which they worked. In spite of efforts to separate God's things from Caesar's, the things remained tightly linked, providing targets for rigorist monks and mendicants. Archetypal, the prince-archbishop of Mainz rode in full armour with bared sword borne before. A clerk at the University of Paris joked that he could believe anything save that German bishops could be saved:

> Almost all wield both swords, spiritual and material. Judging blood cases and waging wars, they care more about paying soldiers than about saving souls.[32]

---

[28] *Les lettres de Jacques de Vitry* (ed. R.B.C. Huygens, Leiden, 1960) 1n and 72.

[29] A life added to James of Voragine's *Legenda aurea* (ed. Graesse) 919, reflecting Chapter 11 of William of Tocco's life in *AA.SS.* March 1 678A–B.

[30] My 'Une famille Cathar: Les Maurand', *Annales: ESC* (1974) 1222–23.

[31] Both quotations are from *Libri IV sententiarum* 4 10 and 13 in *PL* CXCII 863 and 868.

[32] Caesarius of Heisterbach, *Dialogus miraculorum* 2 27 (ed. Strange) I 9.

Ecclesiastical and secular careers overlapped. An example is that of the financial officer Richard Fitzneale, treasurer and presumed author of the *Exchequer Dialogue*. Richard was a second-generation crown servant who died as bishop of London in 1198 and whose father, then bishop of Ely, had bought him the treasury office in 1169. Mixing war and clericature was common. True of institutions, such as the military orders, the mixture was also seen in individual careers. One Englishman, Gervase of Tilbury, was raised in Italy, studied and perhaps taught at Bologna and served as a chancery officer in England, Sicily, and for the archbishop of Rheims before becoming military commander of the kingdom of Arles for Emperor Otto IV (d. 1218). Although he married in Provence, he may have retired as a secular canon in England. In 1215, France's army at Bouvines was marshalled by Garin, one-time canon and Hospitaller, then bishop of Senlis and later chancellor of France. A Poitevin, Peter of Roches (d. 1238), began as a knight under King Richard, entered orders to become bishop of Winchester in 1205 and in 1213 was England's chief justiciar. Politically active until 1235, he was also an excellent soldier in England, Wales, the Holy Land and, in his last years, the papal states. Not surprisingly, the mores of the martial aristocracy penetrated the clergy. In 1298, the church of St John the Evangelist at Liège allowed its canons to protect family interests in arms.

Regulars tormented seculars and mendicants rarely played fair. At Paris the Dominican master Hannibal Gaetani (d. as cardinal 1327) blocked a secular opponent's degree. When the Picard rector finally yielded, Hannibal allowed him the licentiate, coolly kidding him about his advanced age. Aggressive friars sometimes appalled the cardinals. When Pope Nicholas IV (d. 1292) asked the Austin Eremites' prior general for a penitentiary, he named Augustine (Matthew of Termini, d. 1309), once a chancellor of King Manfred of Sicily. Augustine had joined the order after his Hohenstaufen prince was slain in 1266, and became famed for self-mortification. In the consistory, the cardinals, 'seeing him despicable in dress and austere and rigid in visage, exclaimed to the general, "What woods did you drag him out of?"'[33]

In response, secular clerks looked for the regulars' Achilles heel. Admission into monasteries was normally purchased, a problem especially acute in poor female convents. Celibate or widowed inmates often retained their own property, living there, in fact, as if they had bought a pension. Many, especially canon lawyers, condemned this traditional simony, the Lateran Council of 1215 even pronouncing that 'the crime of simony has so infected the majority of female religious who palliate their crime by the pretext of poverty that hardly anyone is admitted without payment'. Justifying the religious, notably the Clares, the Franciscan general Bonaventure equivocated: 'if money is

---

[33] Jordan of Saxony, *Liber vitas fratrum* 2 7 (ed. Arbesmann and Humpfner) 117.

received for someone who would be freely admitted had a house the means to support her it is not simony'.[34] This casuistry did not appeal to the fervid. Not that the cloisters were abandoned: some still sought to flee the world, and monastic educational and pensioners' contracts for oblates were durably appealing. But the days when Peter Damian hoped to convert the parish clergy and laity to something like monastic brotherhood had passed.

Regulars also fought among themselves. The Franciscan Salimbene clearly implies that Dominic Guzman, the founder of the Dominican order, was a fake. Referring to Francis's canonization of 1228, he made the cardinal promoter of Dominic's later canonization in 1234 say to the brethren: 'Since the Franciscans have a saint, make sure you have one too, even if you make him out of straw.'[35] This hostility partly reflected conflicts over ideals. Although Dominic himself shared much with Francis, his preachers soon advanced in the hierarchy. Eremitic, Francis opposed building churches and was reluctant to encourage his brethren to preach or hear confession. Nor did he want them to be prelates, in spite of a plea attributed to Hugolino, cardinal of Ostia, later Pope Gregory IX:

> In the primitive Church, pastors and prelates were poor and fervent in love and not in cupidity. Why then do we not make your brethren bishops and prelates whose words and deeds would influence others?[36]

Francis favoured leading by example instead of by commanding. The founder lost the argument, however: only two in number in 1245, fifty-six Franciscan bishops attended the council of Vienne in 1311.

The orders were rent by disputes. In the Franciscan, the lay friars fell out with those in holy orders, and the crisis came to a head during the generalate of Elias (d. 1253) from 1232. A layman like the founder, Elias wanted the lay friars to run the order, but was defeated by the clerical friars and replaced by the pope in 1239. In his *On Prelates*, Salimbene describes the general's 'tyranny', repeating stories against the lay brethren. A priestly friar, taking his turn at kitchen duty, was asked to perform the mass for passing travellers. He replied: 'Go sing the mass yourselves! I'm cooking . . . !'[37] The slow exclusion of the lay friars from the First Order changed the Franciscans' basic character: Francis had wanted the friars to work with their hands, but mendicancy won out.

Because of those whom they admitted, the two orders appealed to different audiences. Far less numerous, Dominicans were selective and excluded those without Latin, for example, because, as Humbert of Romans said, they:

---

[34] The two passages in this paragraph are cited in Lynch, *Simoniacal Entry into Religious Life*, 201n–202n.

[35] *Cronica* in *MGH SS* XXXII 72 and 77.

[36] *Speculum perfectionis* 3 43 (ed. Sabatier) I 109–10.

[37] *Cronica* in *MGH SS* XXXII 103.

incur temptation when they see that, in preaching, giving advice and similar duties, they cannot do what their colleagues do. The Law therefore ordained: "You shall not plough with an ox and an ass together", because, owing to his weakness, an ass cannot do what an ox can, and is upset when yoked to him.'[38]

Even after the defeat of the lay friars, Franciscans were more open. According to Salimbene, they were 'fishers of men' whereas Dominicans were 'hunters', richer, more urban and noble and, as will be seen, more inquisitorial. All the same, individuals escape pigeonholes. The first Dominican bishop was Bernard of Le Fauga, bishop of Toulouse from 1232 to 1270. A companion of the sainted founder, his episcopate ended with, at the least, suspension from his see. When excommunicated by the metropolitan of Narbonne, a hundred witnesses, of whom he impugned half, were prepared to testify against him in 1264–65. He was charged with nepotism, dissipation of ecclesiastical property, simony, infamy and even fratricide. He certainly employed family members, but the records of this astonishing suit have been lost.

Clerks and layfolk

To many clerks, layfolk were imperfect. Giles of Rome, for example, said that most people married, and that if they do not it is 'either because they wish to fornicate more freely and hence choose a quasi-bestial life below that of men, or because they wish to study truth and divine works and hence lead a life superior to that of men, that of a quasi-God'. Giles's clergy were the celibate quasi-gods. He also argued that 'if men . . . were not prone to evil, their possessions would be in common because the more property is in community, the more divine it is . . . Things being as they are, however, and men being too imperfect, the world's inhabitants need private property.'[39] To Giles, the regular clergy – and only they – were those who held property in common. As seen above, however, some churchmen believed that active laypersons were as 'religious' as the formally professed.

Churchmen were convinced that they were especially fit to educate humanity to attain heaven. Penitential practices and Church courts claimed jurisdiction over 'moral cases' in the lay world. A council of Toulouse in 1229 ordered that last wills be drafted with clergy in attendance to discourage heresy, encourage restitution for usury and require charitable donations. Endowed commemoratory feasts and masses helped finance parish schools and charity. These were amplified by the indulgence, a remission of the penalties for sin won by good works. This institution grew up in conjunction with the Crusade but soon went beyond it, being sold for any good cause.

---

[38] *Expositio regulae B. Augustini* 144 (ed. Berthier) I 472, and Deuteronomy 22:10.
[39] The two quotations are from his *De regimine principum* 2 1 7 (Rome, 1607) 240 and 2 3 6, 361.

When Maastricht planned to replace a collapsed bridge, her magistrates turned to Rome and, at Orvieto in 1284, forty-day indulgences were sold to help out. For a time, the laity were dazzled by this 'sweet and sour' mixture of coercion and attraction.

Even soldiers had a role to play in this heaven-bent economy. Defence of family and fatherland was enjoined on them, even in Lent; lest, said Bartholomew of Exeter, they tempt God by unpreparedness. However, churchmen also condemned them. John of Salisbury remarked in his *Policraticus* that there had hardly ever been a just war. Bernard of Clairvaux said that soldiers were nothing but murderers seeking booty, even converting self-defence into self-indulgence. 'There is one who slays a man not with zeal for vengeance nor pride in conquest, but only as a means to escape. But I would not call even this a good victory, since of the two evils, it is easier to die in body than in soul.' Not that Bernard was pacific. He cheered crusading Templars on to battle with a perfervid prose appropriate to one whose lance was his pen:

> How gloriously the victors return from battle! How blessed are the martyrs who die in battle! Rejoice, stout champion, if you live and conquer in the Lord, but exult and glory even more if you die and join Him! . . . If those who die in the Lord are blessed, how much more are those who die for Him?[40]

Layfolk were also often of two minds about clerks. Peter, the hermit of Monte Morrone (Celestine V), was the youngest of seven remaining sons of twelve born to his farming family. One was already a monk, and a worldly one, but his mother wanted Peter to be a clerk as well. His brothers opposed it, arguing 'one who does not work is enough'.[41] Thomas Aquinas's noble family put him in the clergy, but wanted him at hand in Montecassino. When, aged around fifteen, he joined the Dominicans, the friars planned to take him to Paris 'so that he should be removed from his relatives'. His mother had him kidnapped and forced to stay at home for over a year.[42]

Salimbene of Parma's entry into the Franciscans reflected adolescent revolt. He never forgave his mother for saving his sisters first in an earthquake. 'I did not love her so much after that,' he reports, 'because she ought to have cared for me, a boy, more than for the girls.' He entered the order at fifteen under the influence of his older brother Guy, who had left the world as a judge and married man. Apart from an illegitimate brother who went away to Toulouse, Salimbene was the last male of the line, and his father fought bitterly against his decision. A Ghibelline, he even enlisted the help of the

---

[40] *De laude novae militiae ad milites Templi* 1 1 and 2 in *Sancti Bernardi opera* (ed. Jean Leclercq and H.M. Rochais, Rome, 1963) 214–15 and Apocalypse 14:13.

[41] *Tractatus de vita sua* in ed. Arsenio Frugoni, *Celestiana* (Rome, 1954) 57.

[42] James of Voragine, *Legenda aurea* (ed. Graesse) 918–19.

emperor, once crying out against the brethren: 'Don't believe these piss-in-skirts!' A Guelf, the youth replied to his parents' final overtures by comparing himself to the harlot Jerusalem: 'My father was an Amorite and my mother an Hittite', but forbore from continuing: 'No eye pitied me . . . but I was cast out in the open field, to the loathing of my person, on the day I was born.' Although proud of his birth, Salimbene enjoyed his parents' defeat: 'I, brother Salimbene, and brother Guy destroyed our family both male and female by entering the order that we might build it in heaven.'[43] Stealing young rebels from their families, monks were harsh. Both Bernard of Clairvaux and the Franciscan radical Angelo of Clarion (d. 1337) repeated a passage written by Jerome:

> 'if your mother's torn clothes . . . show the dugs that fed you and your father lies prostrate on the threshold, push past him, and, with dry eyes, fly off to the banner of the cross . . .' For [continued the Franciscan] their own misery and the judgement they will incur for their sins does not suffice for your parents, because, just as they bear and raise us in sin, so do they love us to remain in sin to have us with them in hell's torments![44]

If monks often hurt layfolk, the laity often exploited the cloister. At Ardres near Boulogne in 1161, the abbot was appalled to find that his Benedictines were mostly lame, blind, deformed or illiterate. They were also almost all noble, showing that the house was a dump for the rich. Boncompagno's manual of love letters has one addressed to a nun:

> The voice of the turtle or rather of the cuckoo has been heard in our land, saying that you have decided to put off the honour of this world and receive the monastic garb to live a cloistered life together with hunchbacks, lame, hooknosed and squinting women.[45]

Families also forced the aged to enter religion. A preacher at Tortosa in the thirteenth century tells that 'we many times see that sons make their fathers monks or hermits because they are annoyed at their living so long and want their inheritances'.[46]

Lay lordship of churches was now rare, but patronage was still very much alive. In 1207, Philip Augustus of France ordered that four priests and four knights settle conflicts over secular patrons' presentations of candidates for rural parishes in Normandy. Lay influence also saw to it that prelates largely

---

[43] These two passages are in his *Cronica* in *MGH SS* XXXII 34, 40 and 56. The harlot in Salimbene's mind was Ezekiel 16:3–5.

[44] Clareno's Letter 11 in Florence, Bibl. Nazionale, *Codex Magliabecchi* XXXIX 75 31r. Bernard's is Letter 322 in *PL* 182 527d–28a.

[45] *Rota veneris* (ed. Friedrich Baethgen, Rome, 1927) 20. Song of Solomon 2:12.

[46] M. Zink, 'Le traitement des "sources exemplaires" dans les sermons occitans, catalans, piémontais du xiiie siècle' in *Cahiers de Fanjeaux* 11 (1976) 177.

came from the well-to-do. Of about 314 German bishops in the thirteenth century, only six per cent were of burgher or peasant origin. Although it could no longer be said, as earlier in Cluny, that, save as a converse, 'no son of a villein will ever be in my cloister', the rich and noble were advantaged.[47] Acquiring office by family influence, clerks owed favours. In his archiepiscopal inspection, Odo Rigaud turned up an abbot who had dowered and married off his nieces and sent a nephew through the university, giving him an expensive copy of the corpus of Roman law.

Privilege, however, was vigorously, if inefficaciously, attacked. Peter Cantor called class 'prejudice' simony. A gloss on John of Garlande's *Scholars' Behaviour* of 1241 notes that 'nobles in spirit and word ought to be preferred to nobles of family'.[48] The Dominican Hugh of St Cheer (d. 1263) castigated his order's bias that allowed gentlemen novices to enter before the canonical age of fifteen. The medical doctor Arnold of Villanova (d. 1311–13) found class prejudice a vice threatening the Church, even asserting that 'those born of vile adulteries, if decorated by mores and cleanliness of life, are more noble than others, even to the degree that their parents gave a clearer example of vileness'.[49] In 1232, Gregory IX was informed that the chapter of Strasbourg refused to admit anyone who was not noble on both sides of his parentage. He disallowed the practice because:

> purity of life and nobility of virtue, not lineage, make a pleasing and suitable servitor of God. God chose for [his Church] not many noble or powerful according to the flesh but instead those who were non-noble and poor, for God is no respecter of persons.[50]

Even lovers of the Church were not disinterested. When Francis of Assisi was near death at Nocera, news of his condition reached home. 'Certain knights hastened to that place to bring him back to Assisi, fearing that he would die there and others would have his most holy body.'[51] Pious confraternities, Boncompagno of Signa wrote, were actuated by more than piety:

> Inspired by charity, confraternities are created . . . for which simple statutes are written, telling how much wine or grain each member is to contribute. 'Inspired by charity,' I say, because folk join such confraternities so as to . . . swell their bellies. In the diocese of Florence, a rustic fraternity exists for the utility of the church. As is usual in such fraternities, the rectors arrange no mean banquets for the members and, after them, render accounts. A rector once rose and said: 'Blessed be the Lord

---

[47] Discussed in Schreiber, 'Cluny und die Eigenkirche' in *Gemeinschaften des Mittelalters* 83n.

[48] *Morale scolarium* 10 (ed. Paetow) 208.

[49] *Apologia de versutiis atque perversitatibus pseudotheologorum et religiosorum ad Magistrum Jacob Albi* in Heinrich Finke, *Aus dem Tagen Bonifaz VIII* clxv, 24.

[50] *Venerabilis frater* in *Liber extra* 3 5 37 in *CICan* II 480–81.

[51] *Speculum perfectionis* 1 22 (ed. Sabatier) I 57; also in Celano's and Bonaventura's lives.

who has performed a miracle in and through us, because nothing of that which we have given was lacking to pay the expenses and nothing remains save a ha'penny!'

Whence, says Boncompagno, comes the Tuscan proverb: 'May what happened to the parishioners of St Hilary's happen to us.'[52]

Although seemingly influencing everything and seen everywhere in secular society, moreover, the Church barely touched much of lay life. If current ideas of love borrowed much of their intensity from religious and especially monastic thought, churchmen cut pitiful figures in love poetry. The most religious of all poems, *Tristan and Iseult*, argues that true love exists only in heaven, not on earth. The God who loves true lovers, moreover, even helps the lovers cheat the queen's husband. The institutional Church is represented only by an old hermit whose hopeless duty is to make the lovers give up love, re-enter society and resume their normal careers. Another example is seen in *Aucassin and Nicolete*. When told that he is buying hell with his unsuitable love, Aucassin avers that he would as soon go there. Hell holds the lovesome, beautiful and brave; heaven a few old Enochs and Elijahs, miserable priests, the decrepit and sick.

To conclude, medieval men and women seem to have felt towards their beliefs as they usually do. They built their Church and applauded its law, yet played with its rules to fit them to their taste. In the age treated here, however, the world seemed so bright that they only took occasional exception to what they had inherited and re-created. Their adherence may be measured: after fortification, churches and cloisters received the largest investment of money and energy.

The beauty of these almost wholly uneconomic buildings was not all gain. Fulk, parish priest of Neuilly, was a great preacher, and along the way determined to replace his church at Neuilly with a sumptuous edifice. But, for all his talk about voluntary poverty, against usury and his plan to finance the poor to go on Crusade, his career fell apart because men saw where the money was going, 'and by the hidden judgement of God his authority and preaching began to diminish remarkably'.[53] Shortly before, Fulk's teacher Peter Cantor tells of Bernard of Clairvaux, he was weeping because he saw:

the thatch-roofed shepherds' huts . . . in which the early Cistercians had lived [now converted] into star-strewn palaces. For this disease of building, these monks . . . are often punished . . . For protection, even their farms are castellated and, lest they lose them, they often hide the truth and leave unmentioned God's justice, fearing to grumble against princes. For this reason they have lost their freedom of which 'tis said: 'An empty-handed traveller will sing before a thief', [and] for the riches of

---

[52] *Cedrus* in *BuF* I 125.
[53] James of Vitry, *Historia occidentalis* 8 (ed. Hinnebusch) 101.

their farms and fields, permitting dormitories and refectories to be built for them by plunderers and usurers as a sign and eternal memorial of their avarice.[54]

Caesarius of Heisterbach reported that when a rich Parisian usurer came to repent, Peter Cantor told him to restore his gains to the poor or those from whom he took them. His bishop, Maurice of Sully, who died in 1196 with the choir and nave of Nôtre Dame of Paris completed, had wanted the money put toward his cathedral. Who was right?

---

[54] *Verbum abbreviatum* 86 in *PL* CCV 257, quoting from Juvenal's *Satires* 10 22.

Part Four

GOVERNMENT

Chapter 13

The Church

Power and Crusade

What most distinguishes medieval Latin Europe from all other societies and cultures throughout the ages is the role of the ecclesiastical order, and especially the leadership of the Roman church. In 1301, Boniface VIII called Rome 'the common court of all the nations of the Christian people'.[1] Even Peter Dubois, Boniface's enemy, seeking European unity under the French king, chose the pope to arbitrate Europe's wars.

Churchmen regarded Christendom as governed by princes or magistrates submissive to the pope. In 1198, Innocent III stated: 'We do not deny that the emperor is superior in temporal matters to those who receive temporal things from him, but the pope is superior in spiritual matters, which, as the soul is superior to the body, are more worthy than temporal ones.'[2] Secular might advanced humankind's earthly good. Higher were eternal life and supernal virtue, attainable only by God's grace through the Church. So highly were sacerdotal functions esteemed that Hostiensis did not blush to state that the sacerdotal dignity was 7,644.5 times greater than the royal, paralleling the difference in the brightness of the sun and moon stated in Ptolemy's *Almagest*.

Lay governments were to serve the Church. Writing in 1301, Giles of Rome avowed that, because the Church could not shed blood, the state must act for it but, in so doing, gained no power of its own. Secular might was like a smith's tongs. Although the tongs touched hot iron, which the smith could not, the smith, symbol of spiritual power, moved them. Suger, abbot of Saint-Denis, urged the kings of France and England to cast themselves at the pontiff's feet, and the emperor to serve as groom for this prince of princes. To John of Salisbury, companion in exile of Thomas Becket, 'all law not bearing the imprint of divine law is . . . inane, and princely enactments not conforming to Church discipline must be considered harmful'.[3] Around 1160,

---

[1] *Rem non novam* in *Extravagantes communes* 2 3 1 in *CICan* II 1256.
[2] *Solitae* in *Liber extra* 1 33 6 in *CICan* II 197.
[3] *Policraticus* 4 3 and 6 (ed. Webb) I 239 and 251.

a canonist remarked that the pope 'is the true emperor, and the emperor is his vicar'.[4]

A source of this power was the 'Constitutum Constantini', the famous *Donation of Constantine*. In 1207, Gerald of Wales congratulated the emperor because his gift of majesty was worth more than one of property, but the document was awkward. Had the emperor really given the Empire to the pope? The civilian Accursius's ordinary gloss (*circa* 1250) observed that, if so, Constantine gave what was not his to give. He was the Empire's administrator, called 'august' from the Latin 'to increase', but the *Donation* had hardly done that. Rising against papal rule in 1152, the Romans wrote to the emperor:

> This lie and heretical fable in which Constantine is alleged to have simoniacally given the Empire to [Pope] Sylvester is so thoroughly exposed in Rome that common workmen and washerwomen silence even the most learned about it.[5]

Besides, he who gives is greater than he who receives. Around 1211, Gervase of Tilbury said that God founded the Empire and Constantine the pope's glory. Papal apologists therefore supplemented the *Donation* from history: had not the popes transferred the Empire from the schismatic Greeks to the Franks at Charlemagne's crowning? Albert Behaim, archdeacon of Passau, went on to ask in 1240: could they not transfer it again if Germany's princes proved delinquent?

Scripture was better than history: the pope had received all power from Christ through St Peter. This magic allowed Gregory VII to ask a council at Rome in 1080: 'Act now, I beg, fathers . . . and let the world know that, if you can bind and loose in heaven, here on earth you can remove from anyone and grant to anyone . . . empires, kingdoms, principates, duchies, marquisates, counties, indeed all men's possessions.'[6] Congratulating John of England because he held his realm of Rome, Innocent III remarked in 1213:

> The king of kings and lord of lords Christ Jesus . . . has so established the kingdom and the priesthood in the Church that the kingdom is priestly and the priesthood royal . . . so that, as body and soul, both kingdom and priesthood should be unified in the single person of the vicar of Christ to the great advantage and augmentation of both.[7]

He also pithily summed up the subordination of the material sword to the spiritual by telling an archbishop of Ravenna in 1198 that 'ecclesiastical

---

[4] The *Summa Parisiensis* on the *Decretum Gratiani* (ed. T.P. McLaughlin, Toronto, 1952) 108.

[5] Wenzel's letter cited in G.W. Greenaway, *Arnold of Brescia* (Cambridge, 1931) 136.

[6] *Registrum* 7 14a in ed. Ph. Jaffé, *Bibliotheca rerum Germanicarum – Monumenta Gregoriana* (Aalen, 1965, rprt.) II 404.

[7] Letter no. 131 in *PL* CCXVI 923–24, and Genesis 14:18, Psalm 110:4, Exodus 19:6 and 1 Peter 2:9.

liberty is never better served than when the Roman Church obtains full power in both temporal and spiritual matters'.[8]

Popes wrote to princes as to children. A form letter for a newly elected German king reads: 'Mothers derive great joy from their sons' excellence and nothing so delights parents as the wisdom and probity of their offspring.'[9] Boniface VIII wrote to Philip IV of France in 1301: 'Hearken, dearest son, to the precepts of your father and bend the ear of your heart to the teaching of the master who, here on earth, stands in place of Him who alone is master and lord.'[10] Knowing that the pope was addressed as 'prince of princes', Boncompagno of Signa told lawyers pleading in consistory to begin with 'I have risen to speak before the father of fathers, who obtains the plenitude of power on earth in place of Simon Peter' or 'before him . . . who yokes the necks of kings and emperors, crowning the worthy and deposing the unworthy'.[11]

Secular princes were thought to hold of the pope. At a diet at Besançon in 1157, two cardinals, irked by imperial support for the see of Hamburg–Bremen against Scandinavia's Lund, asked that, if the emperor did not hold the Empire from the pope, from whom did he? One of the two was Roland Bandinelli, the later Alexander III and, for five years previously, chancellor of the Holy See. The jurist Roffredo of Benevento wrote that 'vassals are those who receive anything from anyone in fief, as the emperor has the kingdom of Sicily from the pope, and many say the same about the Empire', an opinion stated as fact by the papalist Alvarez Pelayo in 1327.[12] His views were widespread, and Thomas Aquinas contrasted Roman times when the emperors persecuted the Church with the present when they defend it. Now, he said, it befits kings to be Church vassals. His secretary, Ptolemy of Lucca (d. 1327), observed that the emperor received the Empire 'from the Church under oath like a vassal getting a fief, which is why the Church can depose him more easily than other princes'.[13]

On Europe's frontiers, kings were papal vassals. Scandinavia, Hungary, Poland, Bohemia and Bulgaria and the British Isles were all at one time or other under papal lordship. Adrian IV may even have given Ireland to England in 1155 to propagate a 'reformed' religion, and in return Rome got one penny annually from each hearth, a tax reminiscent of the Peter's pence revived when England was conquered in 1066. To repulse a French invasion, John placed his realm under Roman protection in 1213, granting a modest

---

[8] Letter no. 27 in *PL* CCXIV, 21.

[9] *Baumgartenberg Formularius de modo prosandi* in *BuF* II 807.

[10] Pierre Dupuy, *Histoire du differend d'entre le pape Boniface VIII et Philippe le Bel* (Paris, 1655, rprt.) 48.

[11] *Rhetorica novissima* 5 in *BIMA* II 262b.

[12] E.H. Kantorowicz, *Friedrich II – Ergänzungsband* (Berlin, 1931, rprt.) 26.

[13] *Determinatio compendiosa de iurisdictione imperii* 30 in *MGH FIG in usum scholarum* 60.

tax of which Ireland paid a third. If papal suzerainty ended with Edward I, Peter's pence lasted until Henry VIII. The Norman kingdom of Apulia–Sicily had been held of Rome since the mid-1050s. Aided by French immigration, the popes intervened in Iberia, taking Portugal in 1179, Aragon and even Leon under their suzerainty. These nations used the papal link to raise crusades against Islam and balance the might of Castile–Leon. In 1198 the pope was titled suzerain of Jerusalem, Cyprus and Armenia, and in 1217 Peter of Courtenay, the second Latin emperor of Constantinople, was crowned at Rome. In 1217–21, a crusade against Egypt, the Saracen strategic base, was actually commanded by a cardinal.

Secular states often resisted: excommunicated, Frederick II crusaded and took both Jerusalem and Cyprus in 1228–29. With the resounding defeat of the Hohenstaufen, however, even imperialists such as Alexander of Roes admitted that at Lyons in 1274, 'not only did the Christian people and ecclesiastical prelates assemble at the feet of the Roman pontiff, but even the kings of the world, together with the Jews, Greeks and Tatars, confessed that world monarchy [belonged] to the Roman priest'.[14] As did others of his faith, the rabbi Todros son of Isaac casually referred to the pope as the 'king of nations'.

The pope had his war, the Crusade. The word 'war' was usually avoided, although one pope, Clement III (d. 1191), did use it. Bernard of Clairvaux even liked it, as when he told the Templars that God 'taught your hands to battle and your fingers to war'.[15] The canonist Hostiensis described Crusades as 'Roman wars' because Rome's Syria, Palestine and Spain had been 'usurped' by Christ's enemies. Nevertheless, Crusaders were not considered soldiers, but instead pilgrims wearing the cross. This meant that Crusaders slain in battle were likened to Bethlehem's Holy Innocents slaughtered by Herod the Great. Not all these 'innocents', however, were voluntary. Penitent heretics were condemned to crusade, and many serving in Spain against Muslims and in 'crusades' against the Hohenstaufen and Catalans in south Italy were even criminals. If some were coerced, others were bought. Crusade indulgences had expanded in conjunction with holy war, but soon went beyond gratifying soldiers: replacing Muslims, Christian settlers in Majorca in 1228 received them.

Hard on non-Christians, crusades helped limit warfare at home. There, wars were to be just, defined, that is, by a good cause such as self-defence, observance of formalities and moderation. As the war between the emperor and the popes and their allies grew in violence, however, domestic combats became more violent. Describing the Guelf crusade against Ezzelino of Romano (1256–59), Rolandino of Padua said of the past:

---

[14] *Notitia seculi* 8 in *Alexander von Roes Schriften in MGH Staatschriften* 154.

[15] *De laude novae militiae* in *Sancti Bernardi opera* III (ed. Leclercq and Rochais) 239 and Psalm 143 (144):1.

Then were wars, if one may say so, good wars . . . A captured man was not forthwith put to death or loaded with chains, nor condemned to be horribly mutilated in his members, but was instead sent where he wished honourably and with praise. But today brutality and fratricide rule.[16]

Ideology embittered the Hohenstaufen wars, and prompted the unprecedented execution of Conradin, the last Hohenstaufen of the male line, by the pope's French allies in 1268.

Once taken, a Crusader's oath was irrevocable. Forced to take the cross in order to be crowned in 1220, Frederick II was excommunicated in 1227 for non-fulfilment while trying to cement his south Italian realm. Popes also controlled marriage and divorce, vital because dynastic marriage affected interstate policy. Unimportant until Rome defeated the old state churches, marital control then became real, confounding princes used to subservient local prelates appointed by themselves. When Philip Augustus of France dissolved his marriage to Ingeborg of Denmark and tried to ally with the Hohenstaufen, a local council at Compiègne annulled the marriage. Times had changed, however, and from 1193 to 1200, the pope intervened and fought Philip to his knees.

Enforcement mechanisms underwent development. Personal excommunication severed the communion of a prince with his subjects, thereby dissolving their allegiance. Interdicts evolved by which all but the last sacraments were withdrawn from subjects whose indifference to 'spiritual' causes led them to live easy under recalcitrant leaders. Although group interdict had long been known, whole peoples were not touched until Alexander III, and Innocent III won great triumphs using it against France in 1200 and England in 1208. Later, stronger stuff was needed and, at the first Council of Lyons in 1245, Innocent IV both anathematized Frederick II as a heretic and launched a Crusade against him. After this fulmination, one that harked back to Europe's civil wars of the Gregorian age, no new weapons were found in the papal arsenal.

Popes and princes

Writing between 1149 and 1152, Bernard of Clairvaux minted arguments that were much repeated thereafter. Like most churchmen, he asserted the supremacy of the pope's spiritual power and right to use secular coercion. Had the material sword not pertained to the Church, 'the Lord would not have replied "It is enough" to those who said "Look, here are two swords," but rather, "It is too much." Therefore both spiritual and material swords are the Church's, but the latter is to be wielded for it and the former by it.'

---

[16] *Cronica . . . marchie Trivixiane* in ed. Muratori *RIS* (1905 edn) VIII i 22.

But the pope's power should not encourage him to wear a crown or ride a white charger surrounded by soldiers, imitating Constantine instead of Peter. Bernard told the pope: 'You err if . . . you think your apostolic power to be the only one instituted by God. If you do, you disagree with him who says, "There is no power but of God." Although said mainly for you, he did not say it for you alone.'[17] All was permitted to the pope, Bernard taught, but not all was expedient.

To clerks still attached to Europe's faded state churches, princes were God's vicars, a title that the popes monopolized by 1200. During the Gregorian fury, proponents of princely authority borrowed late Roman teaching. A monk of Farfa, Gregory of Catina, wrote about 1111 that God alone judged the Empire, which preceded the priesthood. Christ never gave the Church temporal power; Constantine did that, and his action was inane. The Lord had recognized the imperial authority vested in Pontius Pilate. Based on such sources, Jordan of Osnabrück and Alexander of Roes commented in the 1280s that, if the pope's was a royal priesthood, the emperor's was a priestly kingship. Although the pope transferred the Empire from the Greeks to the Germans, this was no human initiative, being instead heaven's unalterable design: 'Before it happened, the deity foreknew that the Roman Empire must be transferred to the Germans', to remain in their hands until the Antichrist's coming. 'Christ Jesus deigned to honour the Roman Empire in the days of his flesh . . . honouring Caesar or the Roman king when entering the world, living in it and departing from it.'[18] The Saviour's coming signalled Rome's era of universal peace. He submitted to the census, paid tribute, and admitted Pilate's jurisdiction over his body, thereby confirming the emperor's material sword. These arguments were summed up anew by Dante Alighieri in the early fourteenth century.

Because effective censure depends on popular cooperation, papal resistance to these ideas reflected the Church's alliance with the nearly sovereign towns and rural lordships that were typical of Europe's political decentralized state. What there was of political liberty within any monarchy at this time was because its subjects had two monarchs – a secular prince and the pope – and shifted allegiance from one to the other as circumstance dictated, thus destroying the pretensions to absolutism of both. With inadvertent accuracy, John Quidort of Paris (d. 1308) described this state of affairs:

> When a king sins in temporal matters, the judgement of which does not pertain to the Church, [the pope] has no right to correct him in the first instance, for this right instead belongs to the barons and peers of the kingdom. If they are unable . . .

---

[17] Bernard's two quotations and appropriate scriptural citations are from his *De consideratione* 4 3 in *Sancti Bernardi opera* III 454, and John 18:11 and Luke 22:38, and ibid. 3 4 in ibid. III 444 and Romans 13:1–2.

[18] Alexander of Roes, *Memoriale* 4 and 36 in *MGH Staatsschriften* I i 94–95 and 147.

to do that, however, they may invoke help from the Church which, as an aid to law, may warn the prince, excommunicating him so that the people can replace him.[19]

The overthrow of tyrants was urged by Manegold of Lautenbach in the Gregorian age and more discreetly by John of Salisbury later on. Manegold (d. *circa* 1103) proposed that princes who breach their contract with the people may be removed. For John, tyranny was to attack ecclesiastical freedom, but he and others reminded their audiences that all were affected. Popes, in fact, responded with alacrity to complaints about tyrannical princes. Condemning Frederick II in 1245, Innocent IV not only adverted to this prince's heresy, but also to the misery of his realms, claiming that the best citizens had been exiled and the rest reduced to indigence and slavery. Being itself electoral, the papacy often favoured elected over hereditary monarchy. The priests of Alexandria, Jerome had said, elected their bishops, 'even as the army raises the emperor or deacons choose one of themselves ... and call him archdeacon'.[20] This seemed a satisfactory way of aligning the interests of the people with those of the supreme pontiff, and Innocent IV was emboldened to say: 'The pope has the Empire from God, and the emperor from the people.'

A weakness of this position was that the divine origin of the office and the election of the officer by the people could also be combined to exclude the pope. Cino of Pistoia wrote: 'Nor is it absurd that [the Empire] should derive from both God and the people. The emperor is from the people but the Empire, called divine, from God.'[21] Cino was not being inventive. Writing around 1302–3 with the French monarchy in mind, John of Paris said the same about royal power, and also used the argument to undermine the historical base of the papal claim, namely the transfer of the Empire from the Greeks to the Franks. The pope had not done this alone, he asserted; the Roman people had, 'for a reasonable and necessary cause, namely defence against infidels and pagans, since no other seemed able to defend them; which action was legal because a people makes the king and an army the emperor'. John also justified hereditary monarchy, saying that royal authority derived not from 'a pope but from God and the people electing the king either in person or in dynasty'.[22]

The popes were never wholly able to impose their will, even in the Empire. That Rome won there cannot be doubted: the electoral tradition of other western monarchies faded in this period, while the reverse was true in the

---

[19] *De regia potestate et papali* 13 (ed. Fritz Bleienstein, Stuttgart, 1969) 138–39.

[20] Gratian's *Decretum* 1 93 24 in *CICan* I 328.

[21] With a good discussion, Innocent's and Cino's comments are found in Kantorowicz, *The King's Two Bodies* 298n and 322n.

[22] *De potestate regia et papali* 10 and 15 (ed. Bleienstein) 113 and 150–51, cited in reverse order.

Empire. Other states increased; the Empire slowly weakened. However, the victory was incomplete. Viewing a German king's election as an episcopal one, the popes tried to intervene if disputes erupted. Partial successes were enjoyed in the conflict between the Welf Otto IV and the Hohenstaufen Philip of Swabia in 1199 and again during the Great Interregnum in 1263, when the electors fell out over Richard of Cornwall and Alfonse of Castile. In 1202, Innocent III claimed the right to refuse to crown as emperor an insufficient emperor-elect or 'rex Romanorum':

> If the princes . . . elected as king a sacrilegious person, an excommunicate, a tyrant or fool, a heretic or pagan, should we then unction, consecrate or crown a man of that kind? Certainly not![23]

Electoral monarchy was, Germans said, a mark of German natural freedom. Not a few also preferred a weak imperial government, but none accepted the rest of the papal programme. Eike of Repkow's *Saxon Mirror* refused to exclude excommunicates from imperial election, because this opened the door to papal intervention, and the electors were certain that their vote alone made the Roman king and that he could rule without papal coronation. This doctrine grew from the Hohenstaufen *Declaration of Speyer* in 1199, through Lewis of Bavaria's edict *Licet juris* in 1338 to full acceptance in the *Golden Bull* of 1356.

To defeat the Empire, the popes reinforced Europe's other princes, who in any case did not applaud Frederick Barbarossa's remark that they were mere kinglets. Some peoples subscribed to the fiction that, like Rome, the Trojans had founded their states. Having never been part of the Carolingian reconstruction of the Roman Empire, England and Castile asserted freedom from imperial sovereignty, and there the germ of the notion that each king was emperor in his own kingdom made its appearance. Castile recalled Visigothic declarations of independence from Rome. Geoffrey of Monmouth in 1147 tells of a fictional English king who requested Roman law from an imaginary pope. The pontiff refused, saying: 'You are God's vicar in your kingdom. The royal psalmist [said] "Give the king thy judgement, O God," etc. He did not say, "the judgement or justice of Caesar".'[24]

Areas once under Carolingian sway went about this differently. During the twelfth century, France's Capetian kings claimed to be Charlemagne's heirs, true rulers of the Franks. Germans such as Alexander of Roes replied by saying that the French were mere by-blows of Frankish soldiers and Gallic women. The popes rescued the French by first applying to them, in the letter *Per*

---

[23] *Venerabilem* in *Liber extra* 1 6 34 in *CICan* II 80. The bull in 1263 was *Qui coelum*.
[24] From the *Leges Anglorum* of c. 1200, a London version of the *Leges Edwardi Confessoris* in ed. Felix Lieberman, *Gesetze der Angelsachsen* (Halle, 1901) 636. Psalm 71 (72):1.

venerabilem of 1213, the idea that kings justly recognize no superiors. This became a commonplace, as in the later Castilian code: 'Kings are vicars of God each in his kingdom placed above his people to maintain them in justice and truth as far as temporal things are concerned, just as the emperor is in his Empire.'[25] This doctrine helped the popes prevent the united front of secular princes that the Hohenstaufen promoted.

Dividing in order to rule, papal action and ideology were partly determined by expediency. In 1310, a hostile witness charged the dead Boniface VIII with having said: 'If between the kings and princes of the world there is no discord, the Roman pope cannot be pope; but if there is, then he is, because each one fears him for fear of the other, and he can rule them and do what he wants.'[26] Boniface himself came close to this in 1296 when he asked the French king, then at war with England and at loggerheads with the Empire, what would happen if he so offended the papacy that Rome joined his enemies. More significantly, local society lent strength to papal leadership. Action by substantial elements of the English nobility and church against 'tyranny' made John Lackland capitulate to Innocent III in 1213. A similar combination of powers allowed Innocent IV, acting as suzerain of Portugal, to depose Sancho II and crown his brother Alfonso in 1245.

This support was sometimes lacking. An example is the Albigensian crusade of 1209, which began as a papal war. From 1210 on, Rome recouped its investment by a hearth tax of three pence in the conquered territory and, in 1215, the pope dictated a settlement. A popular uprising against the Crusaders then forced the popes to beg Capetian intervention in 1226. After the royal victory in 1229, the popes were effectively excluded from the Midi except on the Rhone river. Another example is the revolt of Sicily against the Angevin French in 1282, a recrudesence of Hohenstaufen claims. Once a papal fief, Catalonia–Aragon implemented this attack on the pope's French allies, and tied Sicily to their growing Mediterranean empire.

Local churches

The clergy wanted to be judged only by other clerks, to choose their own officers and to be exempt from secular taxes. The further from France or Italy it was, the less free the Church. In Scandinavia's Carolingian-style state churches, courts Christian were not separate from secular tribunals and, as late as 1247, the clergy's right to trial in their own courts did not exist in Sweden. A pope deposed Sverre of Norway (d. 1202) and laid his land under interdict, but the king's bishops backed his right to select prelates in 1199.

---

[25] *Las siete partidas* 2 1 5 (Madrid, 1807) II 7.
[26] Dupuy, *Histoire du differend* 335.

Layfolk never anywhere fully accepted the Gregorian programme. In 1247, French prelates recalled that Charlemagne had chosen popes, that 'not long ago the kings of France nominated all the bishops in their chamber'.[27]

In principle, clerks were exempt from lay taxes. In practice, since prelates held baronies and counties, they usually, like other vassals, owed both service and taxes. Most princes also retained powers over local churches, among them *regalia*, the revenues of a vacant see. German and Spanish princes were often given shares of the tithe to protect Europe's frontiers. The customs of Milan in 1216 noted that, although canon law prohibited it, layfolk in fact both acquired and collected tithes. Besides, the tithe collectors were laymen who often took the cream.

More threatening were taxes on real and other property. The first signifi-cant legislation, that of Alexander III in the third Lateran Council of 1179, was directed against Italy's city republics. Charged with imitating Pharaoh's plundering of the Jews, towns were told that such taxes were forbidden 'unless the bishop and clergy perceive so great a need . . . that, without coercion and for common purposes . . . when lay resources do not suffice, they esteem that the churches ought to lend aid'.[28] So open to pressure were local clerks, however, that Innocent III made such grants contingent on papal approval in 1216. In 1260, Alexander IV (d. 1261) applied the same legislation to French and other towns, and also forbade the taxes on ecclesi-astical acquisitions that were becoming common. The capstone was Boniface VIII's bull *Clericis laicos* of 1296, which extended the prohibition to all mon-archies. Strong opposition obliged the pope to suspend the bull in 1297 and fall back on Alexander III's position.

After this capitulation, 'voluntary gifts' to local governments became common. Nor could it have been otherwise. Italy's republics, against which papal law was first directed, were Rome's allies in the war against the Hohenstaufen, and had come to rely on these taxes. France, as another of Rome's allies, was also granted clerical taxes from the days of the Albigensian crusade and, by 1300, was used to the income. The crown could count on about £260,000 of Tours from the French clergy's tenth. The revenue from its tallage raised on all properties other than military fiefs gave only a slightly larger sum, about £315,000. In short, as with Jews, the state found it easier to tax the Church than its citizens.

Benefit of clergy, the right of clerks to be tried by peers – other clerks, that is – repeated the Roman law principle: 'Accusers plead their suits in defend-ants' courts.' Criminal cases were the problem, and in 1181 Lucius III stated that 'especially in criminal cases, [clerks] may never be condemned by other

---

[27] *Gravamina ecclesie Gallicane* in the 'additamenta' of Matthew Paris, *Chronica majora* in *Rolls Series* LVII vi 105, dated by Barraclough, *Papal Provisions* 11.

[28] *Liber extra* 3 49 4 in *CICan* II 655.

than ecclesiastical judges'.[29] This was the main issue from 1164 until 1170–72 between Henry II of England and Thomas Becket (d. 1170). The king was willing to let trials be conducted in a church forum, but insisted on his right to punish guilty clerks. Becket argued that this not only invaded clerical immunity but also offended God, who did not wish men punished twice, that is, degraded from orders by the Church and then executed by the state. Becket's position seems forced unless one recalls that clerks hoped to relive the freedom of the apostolic community. Besides, canon courts were gentler than secular and, like John of Salisbury and Peter Cantor, ecclesiastics attacked the violence of secular punishments. Bad in itself, execution was not to be inflicted on clerks, for whom imprisonment amply sufficed.

Churchmen never got their way, partly because some offences also threatened them. In 1222 Stephen Langton, archbishop of Canterbury, usually an exponent of Peter Cantor's views, stripped a deacon of orders for judaizing and gave him to the Crown for punishment – he was burned! – thus obeying a papal decretal of 1184. The clergy also bowed to enraged public opinion. In Padua in 1301, a clerk found guilty of theft, murder and rape by secular judges, but exempt from execution, was put in a cage hung from the top of the Red Tower, expiring after a fortnight. Political cases were also very chancy. The arrest of Bernard Saisset, bishop of Pamiers, in 1301 for treason precipitated the final struggle between Boniface VIII and Philip IV of France, which the former lost.

Churchmen won part of what they wanted by surrendering activities judicable in secular tribunals. Their course was necessarily tortuous. On one hand, except for Pascal II's abortive agreement with the emperor at Sutri in 1111, churchmen refused to surrender secular jurisdictions just because they were held accountable by lay authority. On the other, they legislated against clerks' exercising secular offices. In 1198, Innocent III wrote to Richard Coeur de Lion about Hubert Walter, archbishop of Canterbury and England's chief justiciar, telling the king that 'for the sake of his soul, he should not permit the said archbishop to exercise secular administration any longer nor should he again admit the archbishop or any bishop or priest into secular government'.[30] By 1215, clerks were prohibited from serving as lawyers, judges and public notaries for civil persons and governments, laws that effectively if gradually drove them out of these professions.

This law advertises Rome's inadvertent Italian myopia. The vision suited Italy's urban regions where lay education and professionalism were advanced, but few other places. In the north, lay society did not yet have large enough professional cadres from which to draw state servants, and weak public finance obliged lay power to rely on clerical benefices to pay its officers. In England,

---

[29] Rome's *Code* 3 19 3, and the papal *Liber extra* 2 1 8 in *CICan* II 241.
[30] Hashagen, *Staat und Kirche vor der Reformation* 207.

as noted earlier, the treasurer Richard Fitzneale was a second-generation crown servant who died as bishop of London in 1198. Again, the twelve members of the king's court of 1195 included Hubert Walter, chief justiciar and archbishop of Canterbury, three other prelates, three archdeacons and another clerk who later became bishop of London. One is not surprised that, after Hubert's obedient resignation in 1198, he soon resumed office, holding it until his death in 1205. Still, things were changing north of the Alps. As early as 1259, the composition of the *parlement* of Paris, royal France's highest court, was nearly half lay and if, in 1272, England's king's bench was nearly wholly clerical, it too was half lay by 1307. Although barely begun, secularization was the order of the day.

Lay government's use of clerical personnel and benefices partly explains the importance of clerical appointments. During the period treated here, however, the Church, heir of the Gregorians, increased the freedom of clerical elections. This was especially marked in the Empire, where the struggle between the Welfs and the Hohenstaufen cost the emperors almost all that was left to them after the Treaty of Worms in 1122. From 1201 to Speyer in 1209, Otto IV Welf surrendered taxes as well as the rights to collect income from vacant sees and to appoint to clerical benefices during a vacancy. His representatives were withdrawn from episcopal elections and lost the power to intervene in disputed ones. His rival Frederick II confirmed these losses by the *Golden Bull of Eger* in 1213. Although it was not implemented until after Frederick's death in 1250, *Eger* was decisive: after it, popes and local princes had more to do with German bishops than did emperors.

If secular power diminished, a great deal was retained and, for example, England's kings kept much even after Becket. The biographer of William the Marshal reports that in 1194 Richard Coeur de Lion ordered the archbishop of Rouen to give the marshal's brother the see of Exeter. Still, when John Lackland fought Innocent III from 1208 to 1213, the bishops, usually royalist in the past, sided with Rome, only two of seventeen prelates remaining at home with John. When the dust settled, the king admitted the pope's right to settle disputed ecclesiastical elections. In 1208 when two candidates were elected to Canterbury, Stephen Langton, inimical to the crown and teaching at Paris, was provided by the pope and occupied the see in 1213. In addition, prelates holding fiefs always needed princely consent, and lay patrons of churches and monasteries helped provide persons for offices and livings.

The laity as a whole also had rights. In Gregorian times lay participation (other than princely) in episcopal elections had ended but, paralleling the economic corporatism seen earlier, town and village parish associations appeared. In Venice from *circa* 1150 and Florence from the 1180s, parishioners elected laymen to regulate building and charity in their churches. Parishioners also wanted a voice in setting burial and marriage costs. In 1296, those of a parish in Toulouse accepted an arbitral settlement between themselves and the parish clergy, which, after regulating fees, provided that changes were to require 'the assent of all parishioners or of two-thirds of this body'.[31] Parish organizations were sometimes collective patrons, presenting candidates to bishops or choosing among those whom they nominated. Rolandino Passaggeri provides a model letter showing how parishioners, after inquiry and invocation of the Holy Spirit, 'unanimously and in full accord and consent agreed on Dom Peter . . . among others nominated . . . electing him priest and rector of the said church'.[32] Parish election of rectors was widespread in north and central Italy and southern and eastern Germany, and was known in Scotland. About 1311, William Durand the Younger remarked that 'a bishop should not be installed without the testimony of the clergy nor [a parish priest] without that of the people'.[33]

Laymen were never loath to assert political control over the Church, and always pleaded moral grounds. Although few rallied to him, at Pavia in 1160 and again at Avignon in 1162 Frederick I Barbarossa summoned councils to heal the schism caused by the disputed papal election of 1159. Lay moralizing was also profitable. Louis IX of France eradicated blasphemy so enthusiastically that he was censured by Clement IV (d. 1268). Princes often inspected 'their' clergy. In 1234 Otto I, duke of Brunswick, removed all young nuns from the double monastery of Nordheim and, by prohibiting replacement, converted it into a male house. Ottokar II, king of Bohemia, deputized a parish priest and a layman to visit monasteries in the diocese of Passau in 1259.

Confronting lay power, churchmen were necessarily opportunist, popes, for example, never being able to act everywhere at once. Their prime target was the emperor, and hence other princes escaped their ire. Threatened by the Hohenstaufen, by the disputed papal election of 1159 and by Frederick I's proposed arbitration at Pavia in 1160, Alexander III fled to France, seeking help from Henry II of England. In 1161 he canonized Edward the Confessor, thus confirming the Plantagenet house on England's throne, a gesture countered by the imperialist pope Pascal III's canonization of Charlemagne in 1165. In the 1160s, Alexander muted Becket in the conflict with Henry II, and the archbishop's assassination in 1170 was well timed. Not only did the king's domestic troubles increase during the 1170s, but the Hohenstaufen also weakened. The pope came to an agreement with Henry in 1172, canonized Becket the next year, and turned to devote his attention to the Empire, where the emperor's defeat at Legnano in 1176 led to a temporary settlement. Alexander had dragged his feet in England in order to gain his footing in Italy, but the settlement upset Anglicans who favoured church freedom.

---

[31] R.C. Julien, *Histoire de la paroisse N.-D. la Dalbade* (Toulouse, 1891) 138 and 151.

[32] *Summa artis notariae* 1 5 (Venice, 1583) I 126r–v.

[33] *De modo generali concilii celebrandi* 2 15 2 and 38 3 in *TUJ* XIII 161ra and 165ra.

Local churchmen complained ever louder in the thirteenth century as the popes mobilized everything to defeat Italy's Ghibellines. William Durand the Younger protested that they were surrendering the clergy to English, Aragonese and especially French kings. As England and France gravitated towards war over Flanders and Guienne in the 1290s, clerical taxes became crucial and Boniface VIII tried to recover them. His bull *Clericis laicos* of 1296 was a reason that Robert Winchelsea, archbishop of Canterbury (d. 1313), stood so firmly against King Edward I, but French power made the pontiff compromise. In 1297 he permitted Philip IV the Fair to collect clerical taxes without his consent in case of dire need, a switch that neatly cut off the limb on to which Winchelsea had ventured.

William Durand also complained about appointments. In the appeasement of 1297, Boniface granted Philip the right to provide one canon in every collegiate church of France and the provinces of Lyons and Viviers. This favour reflected how monarchy, whether of popes or of princes, was triumphing over electoral traditions. An example is seen in the Neapolitan kingdom of Charles II. In 1302, a Catalan ambassador reported that Boniface was angered when the Angevin refused to appoint a family member to a church office, and the king had remarked: 'If you look at the matter carefully, Father, I've given your family enough.' Furious, the pope said: 'Don't you know I can take your kingdom from you?' But the king knew better.[34]

Church government

Around 1348, the jurist Lucas of Penna rightly said that the Church was a state. Its territories had long been divided into archiepiscopal provinces and episcopal dioceses. The diocese was usually split into archdeaconries, areas placed under a senior priest, sometimes titled rural dean. Below were the parishes, headed by rectors. Size varied widely: in the diocese of Lincoln the archdeaconry of Stow consisted of four rural deaneries, that of Lincoln itself of twenty-three. There were poor and rich bishops: Rochester, for example, had about a fifth of the income of the bishop of Winchester. Some variations are easily explained: the Mediterranean's ancient dioceses were smaller than those created later in north Europe. The bishop of Cavaillon in Provence ruled a territory scarcely as big as a northern parish, enjoying hardly a hundredth of the bishop of Winchester's revenue. Italy's many petty dioceses explain why papal courtiers often had episcopal grade and why a wealthy prince-bishop from the north, such as Anthony Bek of Durham, seemed a being of a different scale to the Romans in 1302.

---

[34] Lawrence Martini's diary for the bishop of Valencia from January to March 1302 in Finke, *Aus dem Tage Bonifaz VIII* xlv.

Administrative changes created new offices, emptying old ones of authority. Archdeacons had been interposed between bishops and their clergy but,
from the 1170s, were replaced by a new episcopal judge, the official, who, by
the publication of Boniface VIII's decretals in 1298, had become the second
personage of the diocese. Structures also changed: from 1316 to 1334 John
XXII created ten new dioceses and one archdiocese.

Powerful primates were protected by local interests. Toledo's primacy evoked
in Castilian minds Iberia unified as in Visigothic days. Milanese and Palermitan
pretences to freedom from Rome were used by the emperors against the
papacy. The momentary subordination of the see of Lund to that of Bremen
in 1133 reflected German expansion into Scandinavia. Because York was
'royalist' and Canterbury 'Gregorian', the former's vain struggle for equality
with the latter epitomizes the defeat of England's royal church. The papacy
recognized still larger entities, the nations. National identity surfaced at the
council of Vienne in 1311–12 where the clergy from France, Spain, the British
Isles, Germany, Scandinavia and Italy sat separately in preliminary discus-
sions. Showing who led the Church, ten rolls of these records are French,
nine Italian, five Spanish, four German, one English and one Scandinavian.
A papal letter of 1335 imitated antiquity by dividing Europe into four nations:
France, Germany (including Scandinavia and the British Isles), Italy and Spain.

Jurists said that the pope's plenitude of power was analogous, though
superior, to that of the emperor. The papacy adopted secular insignia: the
umbrella of eastern royalty sent by Venice in the 1170s and the superim-
posed coronets that, by the early fourteenth century, made up the triple-
tiered tiara. Ceremonials were borrowed from the emperors, and in 1161–62
Gerhoh of Reichersberg caustically remarked that the 'Roman court' had
previously been called the 'Roman Church'. Meeting in consistory, the pope
and cardinals had replaced the old episcopal synod of the Roman clergy and
become Christendom's highest court, wherein were promulgated the decretals.
At first numbering about twelve but rising to over twenty in the early fourteenth century, these cardinal bishops, priests and deacons formed a true
college by the end of Alexander III's reign in 1181. They were raised above
the rest of the clergy, a process completed by 1245 when they were gratified
with the red hat. The most important legatine missions were normally
entrusted to them but, since papal legates had precedence over all clergy,
lesser affairs were given to others. Papal judicial functions had so expanded
by the mid–thirteenth century that auditor judges hearing cases below the
episcopal grade constituted a tribunal later called the 'Rota'. The consistory
and 'Rota' brought to Rome cases reserved to the Holy See and appeals from
sentences issued locally. The secretariat was under a chancellor, an overmighty
cardinal until 1216 when he was replaced by a vice-chancellor, never a
cardinal. Finances were mainly entrusted to the chamberlain. Curial personnel
totalled about four hundred in the late thirteenth century, not including

servants and soldiers. For postal service the popes used passing clergy and the couriers of Italy's merchant bankers.

Papal letters or decretals contained decisions taken in consistory, which were enrolled as precedents. Some protested that popes should legislate only in council with clergy other than Roman participating. And indeed, much law was issued in the general councils summoned by the popes. These, beginning with the first Lateran in 1123 and ending with Vienne in 1311–12, illustrate the papacy's triumph over the Empire, whose rulers had been wont to call councils in the past. From the third Lateran Council of 1179 to Vienne, a general council met on an average of once every thirty-three years. At the fourth Lateran Council of 1215, metropolitans, bishops, mitred abbots, provosts of cathedral chapters and even university masters of theology and law participated. Nor were general councils the only assemblies where laws were written. By 1215, every unit from the rural deanery to the archbishop's province was urged to hold yearly convocations, and statute books from some are extant. Above these were larger regional councils, the Scottish and English churches, for example. After the Capetian conquest of Normandy, the provinces that, together with the University of Paris, constituted the kernel of the Gallican church were Rheims, Sens and Rouen, joined occasionally by Bourges and Tours. The meetings of national synods, and some provincial ones such as Canterbury and York, often coincided with lay parliaments summoned by princes.

Except for mitred abbots, the regular clergy did not attend councils, but instead sought exemption from episcopal authority and looked to the papacy. Cistercians, for example, were not visited by bishops and, together with Templars and Hospitallers, were exempt from crusade taxes. The later mendicants also won exemption from episcopal control, and were busy in the lay apostolate in spite of secular opposition. Exemptions contributed much to the centralization of authority, making Rome the arbiter of battles between regular and secular clergy.

More and more power accrued to Rome. By 1153, canonization had become a papal monopoly and, by 1215, the same was true of the authentication of relics. During the twelfth century prelates were obliged to visit Rome, and local elections were scrutinized, disputed ones invalidated and rival candidates replaced by papal appointees. The thirteenth century saw the reservation of certain posts by Rome, and by 1215 the papal right to provide was admitted everywhere. In 1265, Clement IV claimed an unequivocal right over all Church posts, but actually reserved only the provisioning of benefices falling vacant when incumbents were serving at, or visiting, the Holy See. Thereafter, papal intervention increased. Of the sixteen promoted to the episcopal grade in France from 1295 to 1301, only one was elected by a cathedral chapter as of old; Rome chose the others. In 1311, the bishop of Angers claimed that, of the thirty-five prebends vacated in his diocese since

1291, he had conferred only five; the rest went to Rome's providees. Provisions and reservations provoked enmity because they overrode local interest and, at the cost of absenteeism, enabled the popes to finance their court personnel, favouring Italians and others wedded to their cause. The system had local advocates, however. The educated favoured it because it enabled university graduates to penetrate the serried ranks of the local clergy. Nor was the polemic of vice or virtue always pertinent. Laws regulating the provision of vicars made pluralism into a kind of rural taxation designed to subvent urban clergy, university teachers and curial officers.

Papal taxation also increased. Providees or those elected, for example, paid fees for confirmation, the amounts varying according to the wealth of the benefice and the litigation involved. Fees usually included common services (about a third of the first year's revenue of a benefice), minor services (fees for curial personnel) and a private audience with the pontiff. Wealthy prelates paid heavily. In 1302, an abbot of St Albans confirmed his election at Rome at a cost of just above 10,000 florins. He borrowed the sum from Italian moneylenders, and consequently had to buy a dispensation for conniving at usury! Although some were exempt, metropolitans and some abbots were required to visit Rome at specific intervals, an obligation that could be commuted to sending a deputy and fixed payment. In 1300, Rouen and Rheims each paid 2,000 florins every second year, Canterbury 1,500 and York 600 every third year.

After 1199 a papal tithe on ecclesiastical benefices and installations was instituted. Initially designed only to subvent the Crusade, it speedily grew. In 1199 it was a fortieth, and in 1215 the Lateran Council authorized a twentieth for three years. In the period from 1247 to 1274, a tenth was raised no less than twenty-one times. Moreover, because the Crusade was internalizing, receipts were increasingly used at home. During the nine years of his pontificate, Boniface VIII encashed about 1,800,000 florins, a sum largely spent against rebels in the papal states and Aragonese Sicily. Secular states were already cutting heavily into this revenue, however, and this figure does not record their share. Regularity made the papal tithe Europe's most advanced tax except for those in urban republics.

Local churchmen complained about growing central government, even about general councils. A bishop of Chartres is said to have exhorted the Lateran Council of 1179 to issue no new law: 'let us rather . . . strive that evangelical teaching be observed, which now only few obey'.[35] Writing around 1150, Bernard of Clairvaux bewailed the frequency of appeals to Rome, attributing their increase to curial avarice. Many deplored papal dispensations allowing clerks to hold several benefices at once. Peter Cantor attacked papal

---

[35] *Verbum abbreviatum* 31 in *PL* CCV 116.

exemptions, whereby abbots were freed from their bishops or bishops from their metropolitans. He even said that the celebrated rivals Bernard of Clairvaux and Gilbert of La Porrée (d. 1154), bishop of Poitiers, agreed on this matter. The latter said that exempt abbots were schismatics, and Bernard complained to the pope that, by granting exemptions, 'you prove you have the plenitude of power, but perchance not that of justice. You do this because you can, but the question is whether you ought', and pictured the Church as a disordered body with fingers attached to its head.[36] Later, William Durand the Younger directed criticism against papal reservations and provisions, citing ancient canons against such practices: 'Bishops from other cities ought not to be elected, nor foreign clerks preferred to those raised in their own churches.'[37] Bernard's *On Reflection* set the critical tone: the apostle Peter gave Rome what the Lord gave him: 'solicitude . . . over the churches. Did he give domination? Hear him! "Not ruling over the clergy, he says, but being examples to the flock" . . . Domination is clearly forbidden.' He concluded that 'your power is therefore not the only one derived from God. So also is that of the middling and the lesser . . . Above all, reflect that the holy Roman Church . . . is not the mistress but the mother of the churches. You are not lord of the bishops but rather one of them.'[38]

Resistance to papal centralization grew only slowly, because local excesses were greater than those of Rome. Before his election to the see of Durham in 1283, Anthony Bek was a pluralist, holding five benefices other than his archdeaconry. Anti-papal diatribes were usually motivated. The protest of the Gallican church in 1247 stated only too frankly that papal provisions were prejudicial 'to the lord king and the nobles of the kingdom, whose sons and friends were accustomed to be promoted in the churches'.[39] Local churches, in fact, often needed papal action to resist the 'armed prayers' of princes and nobles. Criticism was also muted because Rome grew as did clerical liberty. Besides, the Church was a monarchy. Fearing to offend, Peter Cantor worried:

> Am I not allowed to ask the lord pope, "Why do you do that?" It is only sacrilegious to contradict [him] . . . True, I do not see the solution of these problems . . . but I know that divisions and exemptions of this kind in the Church do not derive from its canons, old or new, but rather from the special authority of the apostolic see that God will not permit to err.

The result, he maintained, is that Caesar governs everything and his proconsuls nothing.[40]

---

[36] *De consideratione* 3 2 in *Sancti Bernardi opera* III 442.

[37] *De modo generali concilii celebrandi* 2 15 2 in *TUJ* XIII 161ra.

[38] The first quotation is *De consideratione* 2 6 in *Sancti Bernardi opera* III 418, and 1 Peter 5:3, and the second and longer ibid. 3 4 and 4 7 in ibid. III 444 and 465–66.

[39] Matthew Paris, *Chronica majora* VI 105; and see note 27 above.

[40] *Verbum abbreviatum* 44 in *PL* CCV 139.

Lacking solutions, Peter and others blamed the pope and his court – especially the latter – for the Church's problems. They had made, as the Saviour said in the Temple, 'my house, the house of prayer, into a den of thieves and a house of commerce'.[41] William the Marshal's biographer used the theme of Roman corruption to good effect. When France's 'sly' king wanted to rob 'honest' England at Rome, he sent the necessary relics: money for greasing palms. John of Salisbury told Pope Adrian IV that everyone knew the Roman court was not the mother, but the plundering stepmother of the Church. In reply, Adrian told a story: a body's limbs once complained that the stomach ate what their labour brought in. True, he agreed, but limbs wither without nourishment.

Rome's eminence left it exposed. In the pre-Gregorian days of the state churches, 'reformers' attacked the vices of particular prelates and parts of the Church, but rarely the whole as subsumed in its head. In this age, as a general is blamed for an army's defeats, so was Rome for Christendom's failures. Until after 1300, however, great victories more than compensated for occasional failures.

---

[41] Ibid. 36 in *PL* CCV 123. Matthew 21:13.

Chapter 14

The greater monarchies

The Empire

All Latin Europe's states were beginning to centralize, with one exception. In the late eleventh century the Empire – once the greatest state, reaching into north and central Italy, France and the Low Countries – began to decentralize or, rather, fall apart. This would have been hard to believe around 1150. After the Gregorian wars from the 1070s into the 1120s, when many of the later German princely lines appeared, a period of pacification and renewal began before the death of Henry V in 1125 and continued through the crowning of the Hohenstaufen Frederick I Barbarossa in 1152. Pacification was aided by Germany's churches, now somewhat freed from imperial control and fearing domination by local princely houses. Smaller Italian towns also resisted greater ones, such as Milan, that grew at their expense. The need to stop unremitting civil war by means of regional peace ordinances likewise played a role.

The Hohenstaufens tried to tighten controls. At Würzburg in 1196, Barbarossa proposed replacing the elective monarchy by dynastic succession. In Italy, the diet of Roncaglia in 1158 asserted the Empire's right to tax and govern the towns by imperial lieutenants or *potestates*. In Germany, even great princes were forced to surrender freehold offices and receive them back in vassalage. The ministerial system of quasi-servile knights was extended along major arteries of communication, and the monarch allied with townsmen against local princes and with the ministers against the nobility.

The greater magnates who had profited from the breakdown during the Gregorian troubles nevertheless retained most of their gains. When, in 1138, they elected Conrad III Hohenstaufen, they passed over the Welf Henry the Proud, whose Saxon, Bavarian and Tuscan domains would have built a solid royal power. The ensuing combat of the Welfs and Hohenstaufen, moreover, ensured the monarchy's failure. In Germany, a Rhenish prince-bishop and Saxon notables defeated the emperor's dynastic attempt at Würzburg. In Italy, the imperial renewal and attempt to profit from Italy's commercial and industrial growth announced at Roncaglia in 1158 failed at Legnano in 1176, and the judgement of that battlefield was confirmed by the Peace of Constance in 1183. After helping Frederick I defeat Henry the Lion in 1180, the Saxon magnates distributed the powers taken from the Welf, and set a precedent forbidding the emperor to hold great fiefs for more than a year. Lack of means led to alienation of imperial rights. In 1162 Pisa bought control of its county and Florence gained self-government by 1187.

Imperial hope bloomed anew in 1194. The marriage of Henry VI Hohen-staufen to Constance of Sicily, heiress of the Norman princes of southern Italy, threatened Rome with German–Italian unification.[1] After Henry's death in 1197, this effort collapsed in another war between Welfs and Hohenstaufen, popes and emperors, north and south Italy and north and south Germany. Innocent III helped wreck the Hohenstaufen Philip of Swabia. In 1199, this pontiff appealed to the Germans' conviction that their electoral monarchy proved them naturally free in these words:

> we oppose [Philip] lest, if a brother should immediately succeed a brother just as a son a father, the Empire would seem . . . not to be conferred by election but by [dynastic] succession. Hence what ought to be free would appear to be hereditary.[2]

After Philip's death in 1208, his Welf rival Otto IV adopted the Hohen-staufen programme of uniting the Empire with south Italy and Sicily, but his defeat by the French at Bouvines in 1214 reinforced the popularity of his Hohenstaufen enemy, Frederick II. Thereafter this new prince, called the 'Apulian boy', worked to unify north and south Italy and join it to the Empire and, for a time, seemed about to defeat the popes and their allied city republics.

At the Council of Lyons in 1245, Innocent IV wove the alliance of Italy's republics, dissident German princes and French invaders that brought the Hohenstaufen down. He there issued *Aeger cui levia*, attacking the emperor and claiming – as had Nicholas II in 1059/60 – that Jesus had 'constituted not only the pontifical but also the royal monarchy, granting the blessed Peter and his successors the reins of both the earthly and celestial empires'.[3] Frederick died in 1250 and his attempt to unify Italy under imperial vicars speedily unravelled. The Capetian Angevins invaded south Italy in 1265, killing King Manfred in 1266 and executing Conradin, the last Hohenstaufen, in 1268. Married to a Hohenstaufen heiress, Peter III (d. 1286), king of Aragon, intervened in Sicily's rebellion of 1282, thereby ending south Italian unity.

In Germany, the monarchy continued to weaken. The exclusion of lesser magnates from the electoral college devolved power into the hands of the greater princes. In the *Saxon Mirror*, the Wittelsbach Rhenish count palatine, the duke of Saxony, the margrave of Brandenburg and the king of Bohemia

---

[1] The Norman kingdom was a dynastic union of the kingdom of Sicily, duchy of Apulia and principality of Capua.

[2] Letter No. 29 in *PL* CCXVI 1025.

[3] *Decretum* 1 22 1, and Friedrich von Raumer, *Geschichte der Hohenstaufen* IV 49.

(who first voted in 1237), together with the prelates of Mainz, Trier and Cologne, voted first, while the lesser magnates were reduced to waiting in the wings. Earlier in 1199 at the election of Philip of Swabia, twenty-six magnates voted, a vote confirmed by twenty-four others. By 1256, sign of a failing monarchy, the electors chose foreigners, the candidates for king of the Romans being Alfonse, king of Castile, and the English prince Richard of Cornwall.

One reason for the great defeat was that the Empire's expansionary urges went in disparate directions. In Germany, guided by the flow of her rivers towards the North and Baltic seas and by the eastward-leading reaches of her great plain, growth went north and east. In this period, as Germans turned toward the Slavs and Scandinavians, their intervention in France and Italy lost its earlier strength. In Italy, northern towns pushed toward south Italy and the Mediterranean, and towards the north, they looked up the Rhone valley, the main trade route until 1300. Imperial policies meant little to Italy's greater urban centres. What the schism between the concerns of north and east Germans and the imperialist ideas of south Germans and some Italians meant is shown by what happened at the battle of Legnano in 1176. The emperor was defeated partly because the Welf Henry the Lion had refused support.

The Empire's failing was accompanied by a shift of its centre. In 1281, Alexander of Roes lamented that the Franks and Saxons had surrendered leadership to the 'weak' Swabian Alemanni. He was at least looking in the right direction. If Germans in north and east had little interest in France and Italy, those of Swabia and Austria had much. The need to control the popes who, as in the Gregorian age, helped local German princes and Italian towns gain independence made the Swabian Hohenstaufen look south because, to rule at home, they needed the resources of Italy's cities. By the thirteenth century, the Empire had shifted still farther south. Under Frederick II, although Germany continued to play a major role, the base of imperial power lay in south Italy. The results were unhappy. The Empire had mortgaged wealth in undeveloped Germany to acquire rights in more expensive Italy; selling cheap, in short, to buy dear.

This costly policy resulted in the wholesale loss of imperial rights along the western frontiers and north of the Alps. In the late twelfth century, imperial ministers were being freed or given hereditary rights, a policy pursued with abandon by Otto IV. As noted above, in 1213 and 1220 the emperor surrendered controls over the election of German bishops. The greater secular imperial fiefs – Austria in 1156 and Bavaria in 1180 – were becoming hereditary, and fiscal resources and jurisdictions were alienated to local princes. A final attempt to arrest this course was crushed by Frederick II's defeat of his own son Henry VII in 1232. By the time of Conrad IV's failure and death in 1251, Italian expeditions were financed through massive sales of rights in Germany, and the exercise of most imperial rights was limited to the moment that the emperor appeared in person to exercise them. The prince being absent, the citizens of Bern elected their imperial governors in 1268, 1271 and again in 1291; just as, they said, Roman citizens had elected their rulers. In 1290, Besançon asked the pope to confirm the election of Rudolph of Habsburg as German king before accepting him. Meanwhile, the French intervened in the Lorraines and Rhineland and influenced Franconia, Thuringia and Swabia. Territories along the Rhine and the left bank of the Rhone gradually fell to France, Provence going to the Capetian Charles of Anjou in 1245.

The Empire went into receivership. A modest Dutch princeling was elected in 1245, and in the disputed election of 1257 was replaced by a brother of the king of England and a king of Castile, neither of whom played a role in Germany. By the time Rudolph of Habsburg acceded in 1273, the treasury was empty and, as Humbert of Romans remarked, the Empire was reduced 'almost to nothing'. Alexander of Roes lamented in 1285 that the papal peacock and the French cock had brought the imperial eagle down. The rabbi Meir son of Baruch of Rothenburg remarked that 'now every prince is like a king in his land and nobody dares to tell him what to do'.[4] In 1274, Humbert of Romans recommended that:

> the German king should no longer be elected but instead succeed by dynasty, to be thereafter content with his kingdom . . . Italy should have one or two kings bound by laws and statutes based on the consent of the towns and prelates, one in Tuscany and the other in Lombardy. These should accede by succession but could . . . be deposed by the apostolic see.[5]

In 1280, Nicholas III may have suggested to Rudolph of Habsburg splitting the Empire into four independent monarchies: Germany, Arles, Tuscany and Lombardy.

In fine, to see evidence of the growth of the state, one has to turn from the fading Empire to the German and Italian princely states and urban republics. Not that the Empire was wholly dead by 1300, however. Revivals were seen after that date and, to Dante and others, the memory of Hohenstaufen greatness left a legacy of hope for a universal state. In spite of this and lamentations about the Empire, ones repeated into modern times, its subjects at this time did not view it as a tragedy. Italy was rent by wars in the thirteenth century, but rose to lead Europe's economy, an Italian papacy ruling the Latin and even the Greek communion. The lawyers remarked that the Peace of Constance in 1183 freed Italy's city republics from any temporal superior on earth. Alberic of Rosate of Bergamo opined that, in strict law, only Lombard

---

[4] In Baron, *A Social and Religious History of the Jews* VIII 152.
[5] Hauck, *Kirchengeschichte Deutschlands* V i 49n.

cities, who had won it at Constance, possessed the right to tax, but added that 'in fact, all [Italy's] cities have usurped this right'.[6] In Germany, the Hohenstaufen defeat of the Welf Henry the Lion in 1180 split the Saxon duchy among local magnates, busy expanding frontier principalities. The rulers of Holstein, Meissen and Brandenburg raced to open land for settlement. In 1212 Bohemia became a kingdom, and in 1220 the Teutonic Knights allied with others to subject the Baltic's shores. German town liberty grew, and leagues of all kinds linked towns, princes, rural magnates and even counties. In areas such as Westphalia, nominally ruled by a powerless duke, the archbishop of Cologne, townsmen and rural nobles banded together to maintain the peace.

Although historians raised in the age of the nation-state thought that the imperial failure was irreparable, this period was a happy age of regional and urban liberty marked by great economic, social and intellectual inventiveness in both Germany and Italy.

England

England provided the best contrast with the Empire. Although other centralized governments existed (notably in Bohemia), England was one where the lineaments of a nation-state could be seen before 1300. William I of Normandy took over Saxon unitary institutions, the shires and courts in the subdivisions called 'hundreds'. The conquest of 1066 also gave the crown greater resources with which to remunerate servitors than were found elsewhere. Nor was the invasion a single event. Although the penetration of foreign institutions and population into England gradually lessened, a second invasion ran from about 1135 to 1154, ending with the accession of the Plantagenet Henry II of Anjou. A later one in 1216–17, that conducted by France's Capetians, was repulsed. Early and late, noteworthy leaders of disruptive baronial factions, such as King Stephen of Blois (d. 1154) and Simon of Montfort (d. 1265), came from France, but invasion nevertheless usually enhanced centralization.

England's monarchs were Frenchmen and, from Henry II to John, spent most of their time in France, meanwhile exploiting their island kingdom. Royal justice, in fact, was unusually exploitative: until 1278, even accidental killing involved hanging and confiscation of property unless bought off. In addition, the conquest encouraged French feelings of superiority. The *Exchequer Dialogue* states that, after the conquest, English communities were fined when Normans or French were assassinated. By the time the *Dialogue* appeared in 1174–83, the races had so fused that the fine was collected for

---

[6] *De statutis* 3 19 in *TUJ* II 57va.

the murder of any freeman but, until 1340, this could be avoided by the 'proof of Englishry', if, that is, the murdered man was a serf. One sees why Gerald of Wales called England the home of tyranny.

The monarchy used any tool that came to hand. The Norman connection enabled England to recruit administrators from as far away as Sicily. Although French settlement slowed, Savoyards helped build the offices of the royal court during the reign of Henry III from 1216 to 1272. The Bolognese son of the jurist Accursius, Francis Accursius, served Edward I from 1273 to 1281. More than France or Germany, England was open to the influence of Italy's schools of Roman law, a subject treated later.

England nevertheless shared much with continental states. Her church sought freedom and usually had its way up to the early thirteenth century. Her nobles were restive, building centres of local power, private castles and seizing once-royal courts and offices. In the early twelfth century, about a hundred families possessed palatine counties, monastic advocacies and county administrations in hereditary right. England's frontier barons often disturbed the monarchy, and the Anglo-French of Ireland and south Scotland intervened in England. Palatine counties, those of the prince-bishop of Durham and the earl of Chester, were like little kingdoms. As in Normandy, county or shire administration tended to become hereditary. The magnate Geoffrey of Mandeville (d. 1141) gained hereditary right to the shrievalties of London, Essex, Middlesex and Hertfordshire, a veritable principality close to the monarchy's heart. At the accession of Henry II in 1154, England seemed about to undergo the decentralization seen on the continent.

This did not happen: the reigns of Henry II and his sons brought centralization. That Richard was seldom in England and John was weakened by the loss of his French domains did not halt the process. This was partly because England's church rarely led magnate opposition successfully, a reason being Rome's need for England's friendship while battling the Empire. As seen above, Alexander III dragged his feet at the time of Becket's combat with Henry II over clerical immunity. Initially hard on John because he allied against the French with the Emperor Otto IV Welf, then threatening Rome, Innocent III had moved Langton from Paris to Canterbury. John capitulated in 1213, admitting the suzerainty of the pope over England and Ireland. Langton and his bishops fought on through 1215, but were defeated when Innocent released his royal vassal from his oath to the *Great Charter*, suspending Langton for failing to excommunicate baronial leaders. A similar conflict between pope and local church occurred during Robert of Winchelsea's tenure as archbishop. In 1296, Winchelsea obeyed church law prohibiting lay taxation of clergy even after the pope had withdrawn it. The latter then suspended the primate and aided the king. In return, Italians were provided with English posts and the payment of common services was extended to all England's prelates.

Emerging from those coming to England during and after the conquest, the barons were both the king's principal servitors and opponents. Since they won hereditary title to their fiefs by the early twelfth century, the desire of knights (lesser nobles or gentry) to enjoy similar tenures led to an alliance between the latter and the crown. From the assize of Clarendon in 1166 onward, royal writs provided knights with ways of appealing from baronial courts to the crown to protect their 'rights' or interests, and royal inquests gave them juries of their peers. Prompted by the future King Edward I, knights supported the provisions of Westminster in 1259 that repeated the earlier provisions of Oxford requiring sheriffs to be chosen from the knights of the county where they served. Knights and the rest of what was soon termed the 'commons' began to think of themselves as representing the whole realm.

The commons also included the representatives of cities and boroughs. As the barons attacked Henry II's centralism, his successors Richard and John made money and friends by granting townsmen rights. By 1216, seventy cities and boroughs had gained these, and the care with which London was treated in the *Great Charter* shows that the barons knew how significant they were. Still, the interests of many boroughs, really villages, cannot be separated from those of the barons who often promoted their growth. Of about 160-odd new towns founded in England from 1066 to 1370 (about forty per cent between 1151 and 1250), only twelve per cent were royal foundations and seventy-eight seigniorial, either ecclesiastical or lay. When this figure is considered together with the baronial attack on royal forestry restrictions, villages, small towns and many knights plainly stood to gain as much from the barons as from the crown.

Arbitration of conflicts defined this community. In 1205, John promulgated a sworn commune to defend the realm's peace. The obverse of this was the prince's demand for service, especially fiscal. As early as 1166, Henry II collected scutage in lieu of military service from knights' fiefs held of his tenants in chief. The Saladin tithe of 1188 taxed everyone, although, being for a crusade, did not set a precedent. The wars with the Capetians prompted Richard to demand an aid of five shillings from each hide in 1198. By 1207, John's feudal aid required a shilling on every mark of rent and personal property from everyone, no matter from whom he held his land. Together with custom duties, these taxes illustrate England's precocious centralization.

Like the papacy or the Norman and Hohenstaufen realm in south Italy, English unity built a real central government, most of whose principal bureaux were established in the reign of Henry II. The realm's second officer was the chief justiciar who, like an Islamic vizier, was especially significant under the absentee monarch, Richard. The courts he supervised began to specialize in the early thirteenth century: that of Common Pleas, sitting in Westminster, dealt with suits between private litigants; that of the King's Bench with criminal cases, royal rights and, by the 1260s, faulty justice in magnates' courts. In addition, there were the treasury and chancery offices and the semi-judicial exchequer. As in France and most other monarchies, these offices were usually farmed or were directly venal. Churchmen often bought them, especially the monarchy's central offices, as has been seen in the case of Richard Fitzneale, royal treasurer, frequent judge and bishop of London.

On the local level, viscounts or sheriffs ceased being hereditary and were recruited annually from among local knights. To police the shires, justices were dispatched from the king's court from about 1166. Initially both invest-igative and judicial, analogous judge-visitors were seen before in England and on the continent in Carolingian days. These justices pursued crime without waiting for accusations by a harmed party. This active prosecu-tion weakened local independence and was also profitable, which explains the sour comment by Becket's partisan, John of Salisbury, about justices in eyre: 'And indeed the verb "to err" . . . fits those who wander from the path of equity to follow avarice and rob the people.'[7]

Had not the lesser nobles supported them, these offices would not have flourished. At the assize of Clarendon in 1166, the discovery of crime was put into the hands of four to twelve knights or other worthies, a method that evolved into the jury after the Church's prohibition of ordeals in 1215. A typical example is in the code attributed to Glanville: 'Testate or intestate, a usurer's property is the king's . . . If someone dies in this crime . . . it is to be investigated and proved by twelve legal men of the neighbourhood.'[8] In 1194 and 1195, three shire knights and a clerk assembled the crown's pleas for judgment by the justices in eyre, and local knights pursued infractors of the peace in each county.

The barons fought to curb the crown's growth. Henry II's later years were embittered by rebellions, and a revolt coupled with French invasion battered John and disturbed the first years of Henry III's reign. The barons rose again in the 1250s, initiating civil wars ending around 1267. A renewed time of troubles began late in Edward I's reign, leading to the *Confirmation of Charters* in 1297 and culminating in the 'tyrannicide' of Edward II in 1327. The mag-nates, however, never acted as one. In 1215, for example, central England's baronial families and those of the Welsh marches were not as exercised as the northerners, and only about forty-five barons holding thirty-nine baronies out of a total of 197 forced John to bow at Runnymede in 1215. Although the barons won much, it was costly, and families wore themselves out in the struggle. In the early fourteenth century, only seven of the once twenty-three leading families still remained powerful.

---

[7] *Policraticus* 5 15 (ed. Webb) I 344.
[8] *De legibus et consuetudinibus regni Angliae* 7 16 (ed. Woodbine) 112.

Attempts to control monarchy often led to political decentralization, to splitting unified bodies into independent entities, as in France, where counties had been subdivided into castellanies or baronies. Some of this was seen in England. As royal government invaded seigniorial courts, it itself partly fell into the hands of local magnates. In Wiltshire, for example, about two-thirds of the hundred courts in 1194 were the crown's; by 1275, slightly less than a third were. Decentralization, however, was not the main path that England's barons took. Instead of eradicating the crown's central offices, they tried to run them. As shall be seen below, they created councils to control royal officers and even appoint them. Balanced between crown and magnates, royal judges became more independent. Whereas the early *Exchequer Dialogue* echoed the sentiment that kings were above the law, the later compilation named after Bracton repeated the equally hoary notion that they were under it. Worried by this, the king abolished the chief justiciarship for good after 1268, and his new offices grew out of his personal household. A wardrobe keeper, Peter of Rievaulx, helped remove Hubert de Burgh, the last real chief justiciar, in 1232.

Like judges, barons began to think of themselves as men sworn to uphold the crown, but not necessarily an unsuitable prince. Against Edward II in 1308, they stated their position thus:

> Our homage and oath of allegiance . . . bind us more by reason of the crown than by reason of the king's person . . . Whence, if the king does not behave reasonably . . . his liege men, by the oath taken to the crown, are justly bound . . . to repair it, otherwise their oath is violated.[9]

At the time of Simon of Montfort, some argued that the earls were the king's associates in government, concluding that he who has such associates has a master. This participation had advantages for the crown, if not for the monarch who wore it. Owing to the growth of parliament, the national tax limned in the reign of John had become almost permanent, far more so than in France.

Led by the baronial aristocracy, the well-to-do in parliament failed to grant the monarchy sufficient subsidies to meet domestic and foreign responsibilities, forcing it to rely on external resources. Italian merchant bankers helped carry the burden until the economic crises of the early fourteenth century. Edward I's debts to the Riccardi of Lucca alone aggregated £392,000 from 1272 to 1294, while the crown's ordinary revenue in 1318 was about £30,000 yearly. By collecting customs dues on the trade in wine and raw wool, the monarchy exploited the three-cornered trade between Guienne, England and Flanders, and in 1318 drew slightly more revenue from Guienne than from England. As long as the king was starved fiscally at home, ties

---

[9] Cited in Kantorowicz, *The King's Two Bodies* 365n.

with Flanders and Guienne meant everything to him. From the late thirteenth century onwards, increasing involvement abroad prompted an emigration of the crown from England to the continent that led to the later Hundred Years War. A people wanting centralization may not wish to pay the price.

France

Perhaps prompted, and certainly accompanied, by the spread of both heredity and primogeniture among their barons, both England's and France's once elective monarchies became both hereditary and primogenitous in this time. This institutional change was general throughout western Europe. In Bohemia, the dukes tried in vain to replace election by the primates in favour of hereditary right as early as 1139, but won out by 1172–73. Although strongly in favour of electoral monarchy in regard to the Empire, the popes also often favoured hereditary right. They applauded it in both England and France and had, as early as 1130, accorded the crown of Sicily, Calabria and Apulia in this way to the Norman Roger.

While election was alive, France's kings associated the eldest heir or designated the chosen successor during the life of the incumbent. The system worked there but not in England, where the designation (1155) and association in kingship (1170) of his son Henry by Henry II failed because the young king allied with his father's enemies. Henry III at his accession in 1216 was England's first king not designated by his predecessor; France's was Louis VIII in 1223. The first to assume government immediately on a predecessor's death were France's Philip III in 1270 and England's Edward I in 1272. France still suffered minorities (five years in the eleventh century and ten years after Louis IX's accession in 1226) but, unlike those in the Empire, they passed easily. Popular support enabled the regent, Blanche of Castile, to give her son Louis a stronger government when he took over in 1235 than was hers when her husband died.

Owing to the evolution of local society, the strength of the Capetian house was its weakness: the smallness of the royal domain. Louis VI had put some order into the Ile de France and his son, Louis VII, had married France's greatest heiress, Eleanor of Aquitaine, seemingly starting the monarchy on the way to success. Louis's divorce in 1152 and Eleanor's subsequent marriage to Henry II of England, however, reduced the Capetians to their nadir. Not only were Brittany, Champagne, Flanders and the Midi all but independent, but Henry held Guienne, Anjou, Poitou, Touraine, Maine and Normandy. Even France's church was more Plantagenet than Capetian. Of the seventy-seven prelates in the kingdom, twenty-seven were Plantagenet nominees and twenty-six Capetian. Louis knew where he stood:

Byzantium's emperor and Sicily's king may boast about their gold and silk cloth, but they have no men who can do more than talk, men incapable of war. The Roman emperor or, as they say, the emperor of the Germans, has men apt in arms and warlike horses, but no gold, silk or other wealth . . . Now your king, the king of England, lacks nothing and possesses men, horses, gold, silk, jewels, fruits and wild beasts. We in France have nothing except bread, wine and joy.[10]

Capetians were hard masters of their own churches, towns and baronage, but luckily did not have too big a church, too many towns or too large a baronage in their domains. Louis VII won over France's churches by confirming the liberties of clergy and monasteries ruled by other French princes. Although Philip II Augustus fought Innocent III over his divorce from Ingeborg of Denmark, pope and king made peace between 1200 and 1213. The Capetian emerged as the enemy not only of the Plantagenet John, but also of the threatening Otto IV Welf, whose army was beaten at Bouvines in 1215. Thereafter, although Philip was slow to join the Albigensian crusade and Louis IX refused aid against the Hohenstaufen, the Capetians became the papacy's principal ally in Italy and Germany. The Rhone valley was also the popes' refuge when Italy became too hot for them.

The Capetians always heard the complaints of the subjects of France's other princes. In Plantagenet domains they supported the baronage. In Burgundy, where barons ruled, they favoured the knights. They encouraged towns such as Rheims, Soissons and Dijon to gain freedom at the expense of their lords. Sometimes, as in the region around Laon, the king buttressed villagers seeking liberty. In short, Louis VII and Philip II profited from giving away what was not theirs to give and, by the accession of Louis IX in 1226, the monarchy had come to be viewed as a fountain from which freedom flowed. Resident in Paris on and off from 1165 to 1180, Gerald of Wales polemically compared England's tyranny with France's pacific bliss, saying that Normandy fell into French hands so easily because:

at the time of the dukes, before the kings [of England] had oppressed the Normans as they did the English with . . . insular tyranny, [the Normans] were . . . strong in liberty, undaunted in arms to repel injury. When the necks of the nobles were bowed by the oppression of these tyrants, how could they rise with daring arms and spirits to resist France's freemen? Nothing so excites and raises the hearts of men to virtue as does the joy of liberty; and nothing so depresses . . . them as the oppression of servitude![11]

Aided by the subjects of other princely houses, Capetian power expanded with great rapidity. Shortly after 1200, campaigns with little fighting cost

---

[10] Walter Map, *De nugis curialium* 5 5 (ed. M.R. James, Oxford, 1914) 225 and also in Gerald of Wales, *De principis instructione* 3 30 in *Rolls Series* XXI viii 317–18.

[11] *De principis instructione* 3 12 in *Rolls Series* XXI viii 258.

the Plantagenets Normandy, Anjou and Poitou, leaving only Gascony or Guienne in their hands in 1226. After Bouvines in 1215, royal garrisons were invited into Flanders, whose barons and towns swore loyalty in 1226. Campaigns by Louis VIII made Languedoc prostrate by 1229 when all but Toulouse, Foix and Comminges was surrendered to the crown. By 1245 Charles of Anjou, a Capetian cadet, had taken the imperial territory of Provence and, at the same time, the nominally independent county of Champagne was all but run from Paris. This spurt of growth meant much: the crown's income nearly doubled from 1180 to 1223 and, by Louis IX's death in 1270, France was Europe's richest state. Moreover, the once troublesome nobles of the old royal domain had found empire by becoming the officialdom of an expanding monarchy.

The Capetians initially rested lightly on the lands under their rule. Unlike in England, government was based on the rural or urban lordship. Beaumanoir tells readers that 'where the king is not named, "sovereign" refers to those who hold in barony, for each baron is sovereign in his barony', and, anent towns, said that 'at no time does one strike or push communes as one does a minor child'.[12] It was in these local entities, in fact, that much of the state's development took place. In towns, for example, the first professional lawyers and notaries were seen, initially in a Midi influenced by Italian law schools but, around 1300, in France itself. Professional political leadership also spread north. Much like an Italian *potestas*, the burgher John of Champbaudun began as royal provost of Crépy in Valois in 1246, moved to Paris, and was then successively elected mayor of Montreuil, Compiègne and again Crépy.

The crown penetrated these circumscriptions carefully. The author of *The Book of Justice and Pleas* of around 1259 required a two-thirds majority to permit the election of a royal officer as town mayor. Whereas in England almost all new towns were founded by lords or the crown alone, in France sharing was the order of the day. In Gascony, forty-three per cent of the new towns and villages founded from about 1250 to 1350 were planted by lords aided by princes, such as the count of Toulouse and the kings of France and England. The absorption of the Dauphiny between 1274 and 1333 consisted of the crown's acquisition of two large baronies, sharing in founding two new towns and purchasing part of the lordships of Gévaudan and Viviers from their bishops.

The monarchy often waited for local society to invite it. Because of conflicts between the humble and the wealthy and the pressures of growing centralization, many towns were in financial difficulty after 1250. The humble preferred graduated taxes based on property or income, whereas the rich preferred levies akin to sales taxes. Besides, the reluctance of the rich to

---

[12] *Coutumes de Beauvaisis* 34 1043 and 1524 (ed. Salmon) II 23 and 270.

share government with the people resulted in undeveloped finance based largely on loans or sales of communal property. Appeals to the crown led to auditing: this applied to thirty-five northern towns in 1254, and by 1262 all books were opened. The crown claimed impartiality, but this quality militated against the patricians, under whom the towns had gained liberty. Beaumanoir viewed it thus:

> We have seen many struggles in the good towns, of the poor against the rich ... and the rich seek to put all the expense on the poor ... [Governors must therefore] assess the tallage in the towns by loyal inquiry, on the rich as well as the poor, and from each according to his means.

To effect this, moreover, required changes in government because 'we see many good towns in which poor and middling folk hold no offices, so that the rich have them all and are feared for their wealth or lineage'. Initially, the crown was supported by the people against the patricians.[13]

France was still profoundly decentralized; private war, for example, was far more persistent than in England. Blanche of Castile outlawed it in the royal domain, but Louis IX's attempt in 1258 to extend this to the kingdom evoked wide protest. Provinces such as Brittany paid no heed at all and the crown was obliged to grant exemptions. In 1278, for example, the count of Foix refused to obey the royal seneschal of Toulouse because he had royal letters authorizing him to make war.

What happened on the national level in England happened locally in France. Provincial annual assizes performed judicial and even legislative functions. In the 1250s, the assembly of Agen consisted of town representatives and four persons speaking for the nobility. In 1254, the crown ordered a convocation of prelates, barons, knights and two town proctors to embargo the export of wine from the seneschalcy of Beaucaire. As will be seen, unlike the common law of England, provincial customary law was the basis of French law. It will be recalled that Henry II of England tried to divide his continental domains among his sons. The Capetians did the same, as at the death of Louis VIII in 1226, when the realm was divided into royal France and the appanages of Poitou and Anjou, to the former being added the county of Toulouse in 1249. Luckily, these grants escheated to the crown by 1300.

In basic respects, France's institutions evolved in a similar way to those of England. The crown tried in 1263 to monopolize minting money. A few baronial mints were known in England, but France admitted to no fewer than thirty-odd even after this effort. Still, the spread of the royal coinage of Tours throughout the areas conquered by the Capetians shows the crown's gains. As in England, also, the monarchy tried to bring business into its courts.

---

[13] Ibid. 1520, 1522 and 1525 (ed. Salmon) II 267 269 and 271.

The elder William Durand (d. 1296) claimed that, although many held of barons and not of the king, 'nevertheless all men in the kingdom of France are under the power and principate of the king, who has jurisdiction over them all'.[14] The jurists usually described two categories of cases: those reserved to the crown, such as treason, and appeals from other courts because of faulty judgment or procedure. A litigant, for example, could appeal from trial by battle, a proof forbidden by an ordinance of 1258 that favoured instead witnesses and documents.

Another similarity with England was the crown's attempt in 1181 to require service from all inhabitants, whether or not they were vassals. Here the monarchy disinterred a Carolingian tradition, namely that the defence of the fatherland required service from everyone. A protest by the marshal of Mirepoix in 1272 in the *parlement* of Paris against such service was of no avail. The later Capetians and early Valois therefore tried to force those not serving to pay compensatory taxes and, by the 1290s, the government collected aids and tallage in lieu of service. In spite of feudal and provincial reaction in the early fourteenth century, this idea was so useful that every war was proclaimed to be in defence of the fatherland.

From the mid-twelfth century, when local administration was entrusted to hereditary provosts or offices farmed out to towns such as Paris, the change towards centralized control was spectacular. Similar to Plantagenet itinerant justices, non-hereditary bailiffs were sent to investigate local administration from 1190, and became France's provincial governors in the course of the early thirteenth century. As other regions from Poitou through to the Midi were absorbed, similar functions were given to officers called seneschals in imitation of the Plantagenet administration. From 1229 these governors had judges associated with them who, by 1270, had become almost independent of their chiefs. The investigative functions were now carried on by other officers, clerical and lay inquisitors, sent out from court to report on the provinces after 1247.

France's governors were more highly paid than comparable officers in England, and family traditions soon built up. Son of a provincial governor, Philip of Rémi, lord of Beaumanoir, held governorships in the Beauvaisis, Poitou, Saintonge, Vermandois, Touraine and Senlis. These recruits from the magnate families of the old domain were more than royal servants. Beaumanoir believed that he could judge his king's actions, refusing to record a royal edict in his book because it contravened public interest. A governor must obey his king's commands, he says, save for those 'for which he may lose his soul because the obedience he owes is to be understood as doing right and maintaining loyal justice. Nor will he be excused before God if

---

[14] His *Speculum juris* cited in Lot and Fawtier, *Histoire des institutions françaises* II 220.

he wrongs his own conscience ... It is better for an officer to leave the service than ... wound his conscience.'[15]

Although governorships and high judgeships were not, many French offices were farmed like the shrievalty in England. The republican Brunetto Latini railed against the practice, calling it characteristic of monarchy's corruption. Even those excusing it, such as Thomas Aquinas, told princes to do it only 'if ... those [buying offices] are suitable and if the offices are not sold at so high a price that [the investment] cannot be recovered without burdening your subjects'.[16] All was certainly not bliss, and Louis IX's investigators record many complaints. One example out of many will suffice. In the seneschalcy of Beaucaire, a free farmer named Durand was harassed by a local bailiff and decided, as was his right, to leave. Intercepted by this officer at the gate, he said: 'I'm leaving because I can't live in peace with you who bedevil me night and day.' The officer exploded: 'Wouldn't it be great if your and your brother's mouths were stuffed *de merda* so you couldn't bellow or breathe *nisi per anum*' and, sweeping a cowflop off the ground, suited the action to the word at the expense of the open-mouthed rustic.[17]

Later than England's, but more rapidly, the king's court also grew. Although the 'men of the accounts' began to exercise fiscal judicial powers from about 1285, the treasury was entrusted to the Templars of Paris until 1295. By 1306 this exchequer had sixteen members, more than England's counterpart. By the mid-thirteenth century, the mixed ecclesiastical and lay tribunal called *parlement* had become resident at Paris. In 1296 there were fifty-one judges, by 1319 sixty-nine, far more than the four or five justices of the Common Pleas and the three on the King's Bench across the Channel. The Chamber of Inquiries, the part of the court investigating cases appealed from lesser courts, was just under sixty per cent of the whole in 1319.

For a time, France was a happy monarchy, one reason for Louis IX's canonization in 1297; but the honeymoon was ending. As in England earlier, French society needed the crown's arbitrative and centralizing functions but did not want to pay for them. By the time of Philip IV the Fair, the air resounded with complaints about maladministration and illicit taxes. John of Joinville's 1309 biography of the sainted Louis IX was partly aimed at Philip's monarchy. Joinville argued that the king should live of his own, a pious commonplace even mouthed by the contemporary crown servant and lawyer Peter Dubois. The position was polemic, because it exacerbated the population's dislike of taxes at a time when the old domain and tax structure were insufficient to finance the services demanded of the government. Far richer, the crown was also poorer than before. In 1203 its income is estimated

---

[15] *Coutume de Beauvaisis* 1 18 (ed. Salmon) I 22.
[16] *De regimine Judeorum* 5 in ed. Spiazzi *Opuscula philosophica* 250b.
[17] Michel, *L'administration royale dans la sénéchausée de Beaucaire* 88.

at £179,000 (of Paris) and its expenses at £95,000. In 1292 it took in £589,000 and spent £687,000. The hand-to-mouth financing of the later age of crisis had begun.

Faced with this challenge, the monarchy began to kill the geese laying golden eggs. Repeated expropriations of the Jews and of the Lombards are examples. The Templars, like Lombards creditors of the monarchy, were attacked and their properties held by the crown from 1307 to 1313. The crown tried to float forced loans and, in 1295, began to debase the coinage stabilized by Louis IX. Even the urge towards freedom was exploited by a hungry government and, as seen earlier, farmers were forced to buy freedom at cost of land and movables.

If the reaction against the monarchy by provincial lords and free towns awaited the accession of the Valois dynasty in 1328, the signs were already ominous. Royal taxation succeeded only because local powers shared in the proceeds. In 1296, the princes of large fiefs such as Flanders and Burgundy were given half the subvention raised, around a hundred great barons got a third and lesser lords a quarter. Provinces were also beginning to mobilize against centralization. Languedoc's *parlement* of Toulouse emerged between 1278 and 1303. In 1302, the lords and towns of the Auvergne applauded the attack on the Roman Church, but demanded in exchange confirmation of local customs and local recruiting for all royal officers. The reaction against the monarchy was partly expressed in an estates or parliamentary movement similar to that in England. More typical of France, however, was provincial separatism, which was to revive the appanage with far more detrimental effect than before and invite English intervention in French affairs during the Hundred Years War.

Chapter 15

Princes, senates and assemblies

Popes, cardinals and councils

Churchmen explored styles of self-government, especially the regular clergy. Whereas Benedictines, including Cluny, were monarchical, newer orders were conciliar. The constitution issued by Stephen Harding in 1119 for the Cistercians was a step in this direction, proposing an annual general chapter of elected abbots to issue statutes and judge cases. In the fourth Lateran Council of 1215, similar assemblies meeting triennially in each province or kingdom were imposed on all Benedictines. The Cistercian rule also formed the basis for those of the Templars and most military orders, and influenced those of the regular canons.

Conciliar government, however, culminated in the mendicants. The Franciscans were socially democratic, initially gave lay brethren a great voice and were always relatively open in recruitment. Unstable, theirs was a democracy with overtones of tyranny. Their revolt against the long reign of the Minister General Elias of Cortona from 1226 to his deposition in 1239 inspired Salimbene of Parma to propose abolishing lifetime office, arguing that 'the frequent change of prelates is the preservation of the regular orders'.[1] Elitist but also homogeneous, the Dominicans were the best clerical republicans. Building from 1220, they distinguished three levels: convent, province and order. In convents, members elected priors and voted on laws and actions. Provincial priors were elected by, and responsible to, annual assemblies of conventual priors and another group chosen by the member houses, diffinitors. On the highest level, an annual chapter general, composed of provincial priors every third year and at other times of provincial diffinitors, elected and controlled the master general of the order. Excluding the general, whose tenure was lifetime, all officers were elected for limited terms and all, including the general, could be retired by an assembly. Not being administrative officers, diffinitors preserved the health of this republic. Not that debate was lacking, however. Hugh of St Cher spoke out in 1257 against the annual change of officers; Humbert of Romans pleaded at Lyons in 1274 to make the removal of tyrannical or incompetent ones easier.

---

[1] *De prelato* in his *Chronicon* in *MGH SS* XXXII 156.

The popes were elected and their deposition and resignation were some-times envisaged. Unique in the history of the office, resignation was seen when Celestine V stepped down in 1294. As for deposition, most canonists agreed that a heretical or wholly incompetent pope could be deprived of office. It had also long been recognized that, since the world is larger than Rome, an assembly, not to speak of the whole Christian people, was superior to any one officer, no matter how high. The problem was to find the agency that could control this elected monarch.

There were two such, the cardinals and a general council. As monarchs, popes treated with their senate or consistory, the cardinals. In 1234, Gregory IX ordained that 'there will be no alienation of the papal patrimony without the common advice and consent of the brethren'.[2] In 1262, Urban IV re-scinded his predecessor's recognition of Richard of Cornwall as emperor to be because he had acted without the consent of the cardinals.

The cardinals were also the electors of the popes, but were unable to find a foolproof way of electing them. Of the thirty-five popes and 'antipopes' elected from 1145 to 1334, no more than eight were from outside their college; testimony, one might think, to their solidarity. Europe's conflicts, however, found ways to penetrate. Although its right to elect popes was established in the late eleventh century, there were recurrent disputed elections and schisms until the two-thirds majority in papal elections was imposed by the Lateran Council of 1179. During Alexander III's twenty-two-year reign, no fewer than four 'imperialist' popes reigned, one of whom served for ten years. After that, the problem was to obtain the required majority. Vacancies were frequent, totalling about ten years from 1241 to 1305, one being just under three years. To correct this, the conclave was borrowed from Italian urban elections in 1216. Used intermittently until made obligatory at the Council of Lyons in 1274, the electors were locked up until they decided on a pope. Even this method did not obviate vacancies, however, because the cardinals postponed the conclaves. At the time of the Council of Vienne, William Durand the Younger proposed that, if the see were vacant for more than three months, the cardinals' power should devolve on a general council. Although nothing came of this until 1417, John of Paris also believed that general councils were the ultimate recourse.

Members of the Sacred College also claimed the right of removing popes and, as early as the battles with Gregory VII, had justified that act with his-torical examples. Nevertheless, although they often created rival popes or sabotaged a pope's programme, the notion of deposing a pope was being worked on in the late thirteenth century. The Dominican John of Paris then declared that any college was superior to its elected head, asserting that

---

[2] Bresslau, *Handbuch der Urkundenlehre* II 58n.

'I believe the college of cardinals suffices for a deposition because their consensus, standing for the whole Church, elects the pope, and it therefore seems
likely that it could depose him'.[3] This position, however, won little favour,
even in the Sacred College.

Although Rome's general councils signalled her victory, they also focused
local church opposition to papal centralization. The struggle with the Hohenstaufen made the papacy bow to the prelates in the general councils of Lyons
in 1245 and 1274 and Vienne in 1311. At Vienne, complaints against aspects
of papal centralism make up much of the extant record. At issue were the
mendicants, allies of centralism with papal privileges to preach and hear
confessions. In the first half of the thirteenth century the popes generally
supported them. At First Lyons Innocent IV reversed this policy, and at Second
Lyons and Vienne the prelates got their way. Legislation against expanding
or founding new orders was there accepted by the popes.

At the time of Vienne, William Durand the Younger wrote a tract on
conciliar 'reform'. Himself a bishop of Mende, he expressed episcopal opposition to papal centralism and the mendicants, and recommended a conciliar
'constitutional monarchy'. Counsel, William said, is salubrious for governments. To change earlier law, a pope or secular prince should act only with
the express consent of the cardinals or an equivalent secular group. Indeed,
no prince should dispense with old law without conciliar consent, 'since,
according to the rule of both laws, what touches all should be approved by
all'.[4] William also proposed a system of local councils similar to that already
encouraged by papal legislation, but added 'that the pope should issue no
general laws from now on unless a general council has been convoked, a
body to be called every ten years'.[5]

Nor was William wild. Although guardedly, canonists often held that councils were superior to popes. The canonist Alan taught in Bologna that 'in a
question concerning the faith a synod is superior to a pope . . . Hence for
[heresy] a synod can condemn and judge a pope.'[6] Using similar arguments,
John of Paris proposed that a defective or heretical pope may 'be warned to
step down, and, if he does not wish to, can be removed, a general council
having been summoned and he called before it. If found violently pertinacious, he can be removed by the advocate of the secular arm.'[7] As shall be
touched on later, ideas like these were used to attack both Boniface VIII and
John XXII.

---

[3] *De potestate regia et papali* 24 (ed. Bleienstein) 201–2.
[4] The principle is stated in *De modo generalis concilli celebrandi* 1 4 4 in *TUJ* XIII 155va, Code 5 59
   5 2 and *Sexti decretalium* 5 de regulis juris 29 in *CICan* II 1122.
[5] *De modo* 1 4 4 in *TUJ* XIII 176va.
[6] Tierney, *Foundations of the Conciliar Theory* 67n.
[7] *De potestate regia et papali* 22 (ed. Bleienstein) 192–93.

Conciliarism nevertheless faltered in the early fourteenth century. Although Boniface was defeated, the monarchical principle triumphed in the Church, and no general councils were called after Vienne. Conciliarism, however, was not dead. If general councils were not summoned, those of the regional and national churches continued to meet. Wedded now to the developing secular state, these councils provided the training ground from which came the conciliar fathers of the fifteenth century.

Secular princes and parliaments

As was true in the early Middle Ages, all large states were monarchies. One wonders why. Perhaps the grandeur of ecclesiastical power made it unnecessary for people to seek freedom by replacing monarchies with republics, a replacement that only began after the Reformation when the Church was gradually subordinated to the state. It may be that, as stated earlier, medieval political freedom was found in the space between two mutually antagonistic governments, the Church and the state, whose rivalry limited their implicit totalitarianisms. In any case, nobody envisaged doing away with monarchy, but instead tried to devise means of controlling it.

Early ages had left a rich political tradition. Monarchy was frequently elective and law often issued by a prince with the express consent of the 'people' – a term usually meaning the higher officers – as at Pîtres in 864. In the tenth century, Hincmar of Rheims opined that monarchies were not necessarily divinely founded. Princes had been elected and removed by citizens and soldiers and, echoing Augustine of Hippo, this metropolitan claimed that they were under the law and not above it. During the Gregorian revolution, Manegold of Lautenbach argued that kings and dukes held offices not dynastic possessions, maintaining that they could be removed if they broke their contract with the people. Revolution's child, he likened princes to hired swineherds dismissible for cause.

During the twelfth century, these traditions were enriched by canon and Roman law. Culminating in the translation of Aristotle's *Politics* in 1260, the scholastics added further knowledge. Some, like Brunetto Latini and Roger Bacon, worshipped the ancients Seneca and Cicero. Europe's expansion, moreover, widened Latin horizons. Continuing Aquinas's *On the Rule of Princes* around 1305, Ptolemy of Lucca compared different kinds of government. Divine in origin, the papacy was a type of monarchy; secular monarchy was either electoral and universal, like the Empire, or hereditary and local, like France. Because Aristotle had treated Carthage as well as Greek republics, Ptolemy described Egypt's Mamluk government and its imported slave elite, and praised it for its rejection of tyrants.

In monarchy the people delegated their powers to a man for life, but should he be elected or succeed dynastically? As seen above, ecclesiastics generally favoured election, especially for the office of emperor. Germans also supported electoral monarchy, contrasting their natural liberty with French servility. Gervase of Tilbury spotted another vice of hereditary monarchy, namely that princes' subordinates tend also to be hereditary. He praised Tiberius Caesar for teaching officers that good shepherds shear their sheep but do not flay them, adding:

> Surely the Roman republic was more wisely ruled when the government was obtained by election and not by succession, and its provincial governors acted in a more restrained manner when they ruled for a term . . . But now family succession calls to government immature infants, inconstant, harsh, impious fellows, authors of all sorts of levity, who do not believe themselves to rule as a duty imposed by God, but rather as a right owed them by nature.[8]

The Empire aside, however, electoral monarchies generally failed, and hereditary kingship was normal. The problem was, therefore, how to organize and control this institution. Writing on prelatry, Salimbene of Parma employed Gregory I's familiar passage derived from Roman law: 'Man by nature rules brute animals, but not other men . . . He is to be feared by animals but not by men, because it is a crime against nature to wish to be feared by an equal.'[9] Natural equality suggested government based on contract, and Rufinus, a Bolognese canonist who became archbishop of Sorrento in 1150, therefore wrote: 'When a king is instituted, a certain tacit pact is initiated between him and the people, so that the king governs the people and the people honours the king with traditional tribute and services.'[10]

Princes were to defend the faith and serve the commonweal. If tyrannical, seeking personal gain, they rob their subjects of life, liberty, position and property, thus precipitating a withdrawal of obedience pithily described by Jerome long before: 'Why should I,' said a senator to the Emperor Domitian, 'treat you as a prince when you don't treat me as a senator?'[11] John of Salisbury went further, declaring that it is licit, even glorious, to kill tyrants. Thomas Aquinas spelled it out: revolt against tyrants was seditious only when 'government is so inordinately disturbed that the multitude suffers more from the ensuing disturbances than from the tyrant's government. A tyrant who sews discord and sedition among his people that he may safely rule them is really more seditious.'[12] Speaking of Caesar's assassination, he went on:

> Cicero is talking about an occasion when someone violently seizes the government when the subjects do not want it or when they agree to it only because they are

---

[8] Published by G.C. Leibnitz, *Scriptores rerum Brusvicensium* (Hannover, 1707) 902.

[9] *Cronicon* in *MGH SS* XXXII 120.

[10] *De bono pacis* 2 9 in *PL* 1617c.

[11] *Decretum* 1 95 7 in *CICan* I 334.

[12] *Summa theologiae* II-II 42 2 ad 3.

coerced, and when there is no recourse to a superior . . . then whoever kills a tyrant to liberate the fatherland is to be praised and receive the reward.[13]

There were better ways of limiting princely power than tyrannicide. One was Roman law's trial by a man's peers in his own court, a Roman idea applicable to judicial relations between prince and subject. That a prince should not judge his own case was embodied in England's *Great Charter* of 1215 and was common on the continent. The French *Establishments of St Louis*, a compilation of customary law of 1272–73, for example, asserted a noble's right to be judged by his peers when sued by the king in a royal court.

More suited to the grander stage of politics, another way was to expand old royal or princely courts into assemblies representing society's powerful elements. In Benavente in 1202, the king of Leon reported that 'the case both of my party and that of the knights and others having been heard, judgement was rendered between me and them' by the prelates, vassals and town representatives there assembled.[14] From 1265, the king of Aragon chose a chief justiciar from among the lesser nobles to try cases between the crown and its subjects, an officer removable only by vote of the parliament. By the *Golden Bull* of 1222 in Hungary, the lesser nobles assembled annually to review the actions and decisions of the king and his chief justiciar, the count palatine. Princely objections to such examination led to threats to withdraw allegiance, examples being the final chapter of England's *Great Charter* of 1212 or the thirty-first of Hungary's *Golden Bull*.

The same courts or assemblies also issued new law promulgated by the prince. Centralizing their realms, princes wanted to address their subjects. Meeting his notables at Ariano, Roger II of Naples and Sicily (d. 1154) ordered: 'we therefore wish you to receive faithfully and obey expeditiously the commands we have caused to be shown to the present assembly'.[15] What subjects desired often differed from what princes wanted to hear, and the latter sometimes recognized it. At Foggia in 1225 and 1234, Frederick II invited assemblymen to submit complaints against royal government.

The issue was whose will was superior, that of the prince or the 'people'. William Durand the Younger thought that a prince was merely a person such as Scipio in the Roman republic who, although individually superior, was not as powerful as the whole people. Rome's *lex regia*, on the other hand, asserted that, once surrendered, the people's power was forever the prince's, and that what his heart pleased to find had the force of law, a free product of his will.[16] Earlier on, the Emperor Henry III (d. 1056) contradicted a

---

[13] *Commentarium in quatuor libros sententiarum Magistri Petri Lombardi* 2 44 2 2 ad 5 cited in A. Passerin d'Entrèves, *Scritti politici* (Bologna, 1946) 93–94.

[14] Juan Beneyto Perez, *Testos politicos españoles de la baja edad media* (Madrid, 1944) 202 No. 532.

[15] Cortese, *La norma giuridica* II 235n.

[16] Versions are in *Digest* 1 4 1 1, *Code* 1 17 1 7 and *Institutes* 1 2 5.

Bohemian custom by saying that 'kings are not ruled by law, because law, as is commonly said, has a nose of wax and a king uses his iron and far reaching hand to bend it when he wants'.[17] Jurists disagreed about this, as Cino of Pistoia remarked about Bolognese professors:

> John [Bassiani, d. 1197] said that nowadays the Roman people cannot make law . . . Hugolino [d. circa 1233] said the opposite. The ordinary gloss approves John's opinion . . . Certain moderns hold with Hugolino . . . Now, choose which opinion pleases you, because I don't care.[18]

Other jurists expatiated on the *lex digna* in which the prince confessed himself bound by law.[19] And if the *lex regia* held that was not so, it was usually admitted, as by Frederick II Hohenstaufen to the Romans in 1238, that princes were bound by reason, law's mother.

Consultation was what subjects wanted, either that of a small body, a consistory as in late Rome or the papacy, or a larger one. Writing on day-to-day action, William Durand the Younger remarks that 'it is wise for the republic and its administrators to limit their power reasonably, so that, without the council of the lord cardinals, the lord popes and, without the council of other prudent men, kings and princes' should not use their plenitude of power to abrogate old law or issue new.[20] In the first book of the Castilian *Book of the Laws*, the prince is forbidden to issue new law without the consent of the 'people'. At Barcelona in 1283, the prince confessed that 'if we or our successors wish to issue a general constitution or statute in Catalonia, we will do so with the approbation of the prelates, barons, knights and citizens . . . [of] the larger and sounder part of those summoned'.[21]

The issues were new law, war and peace, new taxes and ordinances dealing with service and status. Alfonse IX of Leon swore at his accession in 1188 not to make war or peace or hear important suits without the consent of his bishops, nobles and townsfolk. In a charter of 1205 addressed to 'all Catalonia' at Gerona, Peter I renounced new taxes, avowing that his vicars will only be Catalan knights chosen 'on the advice of the wise and weighty in the country'. Avid exponents of councils for other princes, the popes had a keen eye in these matters. In 1267, Clement IV castigated the king of Naples and Sicily for raising taxes without the assent of the prelates, barons and notable inhabitants of his cities and towns. Commenting on the *Decretals of Gregory IX*, Innocent IV maintained that a prince should not debase coinage without the consent of the majority of his people. In 1228 the patriarch

---

[17] Janet Nelson, 'Kingship and empire' in ed. J.H. Burns, *The Cambridge History of Medieval Political Thought c. 350–c. 1450* 251, citing Cosmas of Prague.

[18] Cortese, *La norma giuridica* II 130.

[19] *Code* 1 14 4.

[20] *De modo generali concilii celebrandi* 1 4 4 in *TUJ* XIII 155va.

[21] Perez, *Testos politicos españoles* 304 No. 542.

of Aquileia, prince of the March of Friuli, referred to fortifications, public works and roads constructed on the advice of his assembly of prelates, nobles, ministers (knights) and town citizens. When a dynasty became extinct, the matter came before the magnates or the 'people', and hence Styria's ministers (the great nobles) won the right by 1300 to choose a new prince and house.

All these assemblies treated new law. An assembly at Worms before the issuance of the *Statute in favour of the Princes* of 1231–32 was asked the following question: 'Whether any territorial prince can issue constitutions or new laws without the consent of the better or more important people of his land?' With the princes' consent, this question was answered thus: 'that neither the princes nor anyone else may make constitutions or new laws unless the better and more important people of the land have first agreed'.[22] These Germans were not inventive. As courts, regional assemblies or proto-national parliaments made their appearance, clerical and secular lawyers disinterred texts concerning the duty of a ruler to consult interested parties. One was a passage from Rome's *Code* posing the principle that 'what concerns all shall be decided by all'.[23] An even more useful formulation was the imperial constitution *Humanum*, addressed to the late Roman senate in 446. The emperor there proposed that new law requiring consent included statutes, judicial decisions and tax assessments:

> a general formulation not found in previous law will be discussed before all the magnates of our palace and your glorious assembly, conscript fathers, and, if it pleases you and our judges, . . . [will be recited in our consistory] so that the opinion of all shall be confirmed by [our] authority . . . For well we know that what your advice ordains will redound to our empire's happiness and glory.[24]

Quoted a few paragraphs above, the document concerning the assembly at Barcelona in 1283 mentioned not only the 'larger' but also the 'sounder' part of the assembly as the constituent body. Generally speaking, the unanimity or majority of an assembly was considered to be the 'sounder' opinion. Given the significance of monarchy at this time, the term was also used to limit majorities, when, for example, a prelate or prince overrode the choice of a body of electors. Majorities could also be transcended in yet another way, namely by taking the rule 'what concerns all shall be decided by all' in the sense that everybody without exception must concur for a decision, law or election to be valid. In a law of 1234 adverted to above, Gregory IX not only envisaged that certain matters required the advice or consent of the

---

[22] *MGH Legum sectio IV* II 420 No. 305.

[23] 'Quod omnes tangit' in *Code* 1 15 8 for 446 AD and ibid. 5 59 5 2 and in canon law *Liber Sextus* 5 12 5 No. 29.

[24] Addressed to the senate by the emperors Theodosius and Valentinian in *Code* 1 14 8.

Sacred College, but went on to state that each and every cardinal 'also possesses the faculty of freely opposing his veto for a legitimate reason'.[25] Such veto rights were only exercised in small bodies at this time, but were adapted in late medieval times to larger assemblies, such as the Estates of the Netherlands or Poland.

Because of the exiguous records available, much is unclear about these early consistories and regional or proto-national parliaments. Following clerical practice and medieval Roman law advocacy, the idea of representation began to appear, one that obviously did not apply to the higher clergy and the baronage but only to the lesser nobility or knights, the commons and the clergy generally. Representatives' actions came to bind those at home by about 1250. Within these assemblies, furthermore, a vote by a majority or two-thirds counted, but in comparison with republican city councils and ecclesiastical colleges little is known about procedure.

Prelates and great magnates had always been members of princes' courts and naturally took part in the new assemblies. Sometimes, as in Castile and France, all gentlefolk, baronial and knightly, formed one body, but elsewhere the lesser nobility were separated from the greater, presumably because the latter had always attended the prince's court. The author of the *Way of Holding Parliaments* in the early fourteenth century felt that the knights (two per shire by that time) and the representatives of the boroughs and lesser clergy represented England's community, whereas the barons and prelates were there only for their own persons, that is, as petty princes possessing jurisdictions. At the assembly of Barbastro in 1192, Catalonia's knights constituted a separate 'arm', distinct from the magnates and town citizens, something also seen in Aragon and Friuli in Italy. In Aragon the clergy did not constitute an 'arm' until the fourteenth century. There, as in England, the lesser clergy usually met apart in their own synods, while the prelates met with the general assembly. Urban representation varied. In England the two representatives for each borough appeared for the first time in 1265. In Frederick II's parliaments at Foggia the cities and fortified villages each sent two in 1232, and in 1240 each city sent two and each village one. Decentralized France started late and tried to crowd everybody into its early estates, which in 1307–8 contained prelates, nobles and representatives of no fewer than 558 towns and villages in northern France.

Humbert of Romans reported that kings normally held 'great courts' several times yearly to handle business requiring broad advice, recite the crown's fiscal accounts and issue necessary edicts. Paralleling princely courts, town assemblies often met four times yearly, but this was impractical for larger political units. In Catalonia, an assembly at Barcelona in 1283 decreed an

---

[25] Bresslau, *Handbuch der Urkundenlehre* II 58n.

annual great *cort*, but a later meeting at Lerida in 1301 determined that once every third year was enough, except in crises. Enforcing decisions taken in parliament required nominating councillors to sit with the prince in between times. Even before England had a parliament, twenty-five notables (of whom four were to remain permanently beside the king) were elected by the barons at Runnymede to check on the implementation of the *Great Charter*. In the baronial wars from 1258 to 1265, more elaborate arrangements were made. Interlocking councils of four, twelve and fifteen members, partly chosen by the king and partly by the barons, policed the working of the 'reforms' and the issuance of new law. The chief officers of state – the treasurer, chancellor and chief justiciar – were to be chosen jointly by king and barons. These radical arrangements did not last, but they show the way the wind was blowing. In 1287, the king of Aragon conceded that the parliament of Sara-gossa would meet yearly and that it, together with the proctors of that town, would elect commissioners 'with whose council we and our successors will govern and administer the realms of Aragon, Valencia and Ribagorza'.[26] At war with Venice over Trieste in 1283, the patriarch of Aquileia called his parliament of prelates, nobles, ministers and townsfolk together to choose twenty-four members, six from each group, and bound himself to carry out whatever they determined.

The trend towards parliaments was most successful in the smaller or less populous realms of Latin Europe. In France, provincial assizes and assemblies like those of Agen were more systematized than the 'national' one that had hardly begun before 1290, and was not to flourish thereafter. In Italy modest realms, such as Friuli and the Catalan kingdom of Sicily after 1282, were the centres of conciliarism. In Brunswick–Lüneburg, Pomerania, Bohemia and the Austro-Swiss mountains, assemblies of clergy, nobility and townsfolk emerge in the 1280s and 1290s, but the conciliar was only one of the ways in which German towns and rural lords limited regional princes. They else-where claimed to hold directly of the emperor, thus disrupting the forma-tion of local princely states without really reinforcing the imperial one. Like those of Iberia's smaller states, England's grander parliament regularly issued legislation, such as, for example, the *Statute of Westminster* of 1275, which granted taxes and investigated complaints against royal government.

In 1300, although new, the parliamentary trend seemed about to be tri-umphant, but thereafter it faded during Latin Europe's age of crisis. Foreign war and internal social war then required strong governments trammelling people's rights in order to mobilize, police and pacify society. What was needed was a separate estate, the estate royal, coercively to arbitrate social conflict and, empowered by society, a prince's advantage for that function

---

[26] Perez, *Testos politicos españoles* 249 No. 453.

was that he loved only himself and no other class or part of society. Except for the final effort of ecclesiastical conciliarism in the fifteenth century, and except in England, parts of Spain, south Italy, Poland and not a few areas of the old German Empire where assemblies continued, or even grew, to limit monarchies and principates, parliamentary institutions generally weakened.

Unaware of what the future was to bring, most Latins around 1300 would have applauded the sentiment of Marsiglio of Padua when he wrote that, unlike the monarchical tyrannies of the 'servile' peoples of the east, 'royal monarchy is a temperate form of government in which the ruler is a single man deferring to the common good and will or consensus of his subjects'.[27] For a time, regional and quasi-national assemblies seemed a good way of providing such a consensus. Even Giles of Rome, scholasticism's most widely read defender of hereditary monarchy, could not imagine a prince without a council. Although it is generally useful 'for a son to succeed his father, if there is any defect in the royal child to whom the royal charge should come, it can be supplied by wise and good men whom the king should join to himself in a kind of society as his hands and eyes'. Besides, as he had to confess, since one person cannot know as much as many, a prince must associate others with himself in a partnership, thus becoming 'one man with many eyes, many hands and many feet'.[28]

Again, although ecclesiastical and secular conciliarism had not won out and monarchy triumphed in the later Middle Ages, its juristic doctrine was carried forward by lawyers such as Alberic of Rosate. Commenting on Roman law's *Humanum*, this widely read professor noted that:

> The emperor makes law with his magnates' consent . . . a practice opposed by many kings and barons who do not want to follow the advice of counsellors . . . Is a law founded by the emperor without the advice of his magnates or a decretal [by the pope] without the council of his cardinals valid? . . . Cinus [of Pistoia] maintains it is because *Humanum* is not obligatory.

Alberic had nevertheless let conciliar government in by the back door. Talking about a passage in the *Code*, he remarked:

> It is often alleged that a prince has all law written in the briefcase of his heart and is full of philosophy . . . [but this] is not literally true because there were and are many illiterate emperors . . . Again, the pope is said to have all law . . . but [he] can be deceived by forgetfulness . . . One should instead say that all law is in his heart's briefcase which is [constituted by] the magnates and wise of his court . . . by whose advice he ought to act.[29]

---

[27] *Defensor pacis* 1 8 in *MGH SS in usum scholarum* 1 38.

[28] Giles's first reference is from his *De regimine principum* 3 2 5 (Rome, 1607) 237, and the second from ibid. 324, 460; see also 3 1 17.

[29] These texts are in his *In primam codicis partem commentarii* C 1 14 8 *Humanum* #1 (Venice, 1586) 53rb and *Code*. 6 23 19 *Omnium testamentorum* #1–2 28rb.

Chapter 16

Princes, villages and towns

Communities and defence

Profitable and beautiful, towns were loved by princes. Convinced that spiritual advancement required material foundations, a bishop of Meissen waxed poetic when founding a town in 1154:

> Although, with Mary, one must choose the good or, rather, the better part of intimate quiet in the sweetness of the contemplative life, we are nevertheless generally obliged, with Martha, to be busy in the bitterness of the active life . . . For the tabernacle of the covenant and the ark of the Lord's witness would not shine with such brilliance were they not protected from storm and rain with goat's hair and rams' skins dyed red and blue. Whence the Church of God is not only to provide the Lord's flock with a good teacher in things spiritual and eternal, but also sagaciously to succour it as a provident shepherd in things carnal and temporal.[1]

Since a town was also often the 'origin and fountainhead' of a province, as an archbishop of Magdeburg said when founding Jüterbog in 1174, granting it liberties was sometimes advantageous. Under Henry II, Rouen was accorded a measure of self-government. In 1199 and thereafter, her law was given towns in Poitou and Guienne, and these were among the few places loyal to the Plantagenets during the Capetian conquests in the early thirteenth century.

Town seals often had walls and towers engraved on them because all were fortified, and walling was a major preoccupation. The third wall around Florence contained no fewer than fifteen gates and seventy-three towers. Keeping up with population was a problem, and Ghent's walls were enlarged five times between 1160 and 1300. Curiously, the same was true of villages. Those too small or poor to have their own walls often clustered for protection below a lord's castle, but many were also fortified, as is shown by the frequency of the suffix 'bourg/burg' in French and German village names. In Florence's dependent rural county, there were about eleven fortified villages in 1100; by 1200 there were 205. Since Tuscany was decidedly more pacific by 1200 than a century earlier, these figures show that walls were not constructed because society was given over to warfare. Again, although few villages could stand a

---

[1] Kötzschke, *Quellen zur Geschichte der ostdeutschen Kolonisation* 28 No. 10, Luke 10:38–42 and Exodus 25:4–5.

siege, what their walls meant for rural security is obvious. Urban and village fortification and lordly castles were the material counterparts of the institutional restraints on war that gave defence an advantage over offence in this period.

The Church tried to slow war at home in order to project it abroad in the Crusades. The growing freedom of the nobility, townsfolk and even villagers also limited service owed to princes, and hence impeded the employment of their militias for offensive wars. These limitations were reinforced by the community solidarity that was common in this time of increasing liberty and beneficent economic circumstances. That the cohesion necessary for defence was never complete nor the militia always efficacious is obvious, and that they were weakening around 1300 has already been shown, but, for a time, local society joined the Church to limit war.

Liberty cannot exist without a capacity to defend oneself, and the possession of this capacity by both town and countryside reflected the decentralized political structure of this age. Decentralization helps explain why monarchy was so general. Kings and emperors were distant, and real and intense political life took place in town and village. Europe's monarchies were to be limited or destroyed in modern times partly because the rural lordship and the free town had all but vanished.

Village and town

No sharp distinction existed between town and village. Settlers of unoccupied land were not infrequently called 'burghers' because they inhabited burgs, a term originally meaning fortified enclosures. Although this use died out around 1200, well-to-do villagers still often used the term burgher to set themselves apart from lesser inhabitants. The urban distinction between workers and bourgeois also appeared in villages. In Switzerland and Savoy, the neighbours enunciating local custom and judging cases were not only called 'worthy' and 'the better and more ancient parishioners' but also, emulating Rome's ancient law, 'honest' or 'honoured men'. Not that these distinctions were rigid, however. The customs of Villefranche in the Lauragais in 1280 considered that adultery was proved when the male 'was taken naked with a naked woman or clothed with a clothed woman but lying on the ground by any inhabitant . . . having with him two consuls or other worthy men, or indeed any two others, whencesoever they may come, worthy of trust'.[2]

Villagers liked to think they had urban institutions, as two charters of 1159 issued by the archbishop of Magdeburg illustrate. In the village of Pechau, settlers were promised the 'burghers' law', which was in fact Flemish law, the

---

[2] Ramière de Fortanier, *Chartes de franchises du Lauragais* 706.

usual north German settlers' law. In the village of Grosswusterwitz they had the same, but called it the town law of Schartau and, moreover, their market was organized according to Magdeburg law. Titles of office, like mayor and *scabini*, had long been shared by village and town, and villages emulated new town styles as well. One was the term 'consul' (to be defined below), used for elected governors of towns in Italy, southern France and parts of Spain. By the later thirteenth century almost all north Italian villages had consulates. In the Lauragais south of Toulouse, a city with a consulate from 1189, about nine villages used this elevated style in 1256. Sixteen years later, just under a hundred small towns and villages did. This was not so everywhere: the scribal manualist of Baumgartenberg remarked that 'because there are no consuls in cities, fortified villages or open ones in our country, we [Austrians] do not have the habit of writing to them'.[3]

Like towns, some village boards of governors combined knights and commoners. In 1282, the consuls of Cordes near Albi were half knights and half 'good men'. Where lordships were subdivided over time, the lords were reduced to being scarcely more than yeoman farmers themselves. Just after 1150 seven lords, sons of four fathers, held the lordship of Montferrier near Montpellier; and in 1207 no fewer than thirty-five co-seigniors divided the large barony of Mirepoix just north of the Pyrenees mountains. Lordly rights were also often held by patrician townsfolk, an example being the Sienese lords of Cerrato, who in 1216 promised its inhabitants that 'we will choose one of us rector who will govern the castle, inhabit it three days each month and there decide the suits brought to the castle's court'.[4] Like towns, villages also allied together. In the early fourteenth century, the thirteen villages of the bailiwick of Mas Saintes Puelles near Carcassonne customarily acted as one unit in law. In a charter of 1314, the hamlet of Aigne in the same region joined the large village of Cintegabelle to elect one of the eight consuls governing the joint community. The best-known example of all is the Swiss alliance of the small towns and villages of Uri, Schwyz and Unterwald in 1291. Renewed in 1315, it was to last for centuries.

Villager and townsman differed in the degree of liberty attained. In theory, every 'university' could make law, but Italian commentaries show that this freedom was in fact limited by lords or by nearby larger communities. Most village customs merely tried to limit taxation, military or labour service, rents and fines for justice, and sometimes allowed inhabitants the freedom of moving away. Villagers nevertheless usually participated in judging civil cases, and sometimes had jurisdiction over them, especially in newly founded centres. More rarely, as in parts of Italy, Swabia and southern France, their consulates won the right to try criminals, whose punishment involved death,

---

[3] *Formularius de modo prosandi* in *BuF* II 741.
[4] Plesner, *L'émigration de la campagne à la ville libre de Florence au XIIIme siècle* 56n.

confiscation of property and heavy fines, although the costs and fines were usually shared by their lords. Rare were the rights accorded to Villefranche in the Lauragais in 1280, where the consuls had full jurisdiction over theft, homicide, adultery and other crimes. Formal limitation of taxes was also unusual, but villagers frequently regulated collection and shared the amount raised.

Rural consuls in Italy and France were elected, sometimes by all freemen, sometimes through co-optation by an outgoing consulate, thus building village oligarchies. The law of Beaumont in Argonne of 1182 – it eventually spread to 500 towns and villages – gave inhabitants the right to elect officers directing justice and finance. In most southern French or Gascon new founda- tions, the community elected a slate and presented it to the lord, who chose the four or so consuls for the year. In Pasignano, a village outside Florence owned by the Cistercians, the monks chose half the magistrates and the inhabitants the rest. This did not assure subservience, because one of the consuls in 1173 was the village's largest landed proprietor, a contentious man who was busy suing the abbot. Sometimes, as at Vidigulfo near Milan in 1254, consuls were elected by the people and merely confirmed by the lords: 'the inhabitants of this place may choose the consuls, smiths, guards of the fields and swineherds; and the aforesaid lords . . . shall invest and confirm them'.[5]

As in Germany east of the Elbe, villagers had freedom in areas needing settlers. Again, in parts of France, Italy and south and west Germany, particularism made it necessary for lords to buy their subjects' loyalty. England had a 'new-town' movement as vigorous as the Gascon one, but substantial political liberties were rarely accorded to settlers there. Gascons won them probably because, if blocked by the officers of the king of England, they could switch loyalty to those of the king of France, and vice versa.

At best, however, village liberties, especially political ones, were restricted. Save for relatively primitive areas such as Scandinavia, Frisia and Schleswig, the lands of the Baltic Slavs and occasional mountain areas where seigniorial and urban institutions had barely penetrated, villagers were everywhere affiliated with a lord or a town. A charter of 1172 records the subjection of some Swabians to the emperor:

> The inhabitants have unanimously subjected their town of Bernheim, which they have possessed up to now free of all lordship, to our power, on these terms, namely that they and all their posterity will pay the Empire twenty-five measures of wheat each year in order . . . to be free from all tyranny under the protection of our imperial highness.[6]

---

[5] Leicht, *Storia del diritto Italiano – le Fonti* 334.
[6] Gierke, *Das deutsche Genossenschaftsrecht* I 204n.

In an age when the ideal political unit was the barony or free town, villages lacked sufficient industry and commerce to stand alone, but large towns or substantial baronies that united many villages could. Updating Aristotle, Ptolemy of Lucca opined that monarchy was best for large areas with discordant interests and traditions, and that the republican form was ideal for substantial cities. Small communities, however, lacked what cities had, namely 'the community of the multitude, without which a man cannot live decently; and this is much more true of a city than of a village, because cities have many arts and crafts providing a sufficiency for human life'.[7] To crafts and trades may be added legal, scribal, political and military training beyond that of a farmer tilling the fields. The result was that patricians and nobles not only served those functions themselves and trained their sons in them, but also taxed the villages to pay for soldiers, lawyers, bailiffs, clergy and other specialists. Farmers surely wanted freedom and political rights; yet, considering the time at their disposal and the size of the economic units characteristic of the age, it was more profitable for them to buy these functions from lords or townsfolk. The characteristic village political form was therefore the intimate monarchy of the rural lordship. Urban or rural, the rulers of these farmers often confused their sometimes brutally exercised prerogatives with the liberties of 'their subject people'. Great baronial families were convinced that they possessed 'sovereign' fiefs, as Beaumanoir called them, by divine right, and their subjects made this boast meaningful. Rustics sometimes favoured the independence of the little states in which they lived because they sheltered them from the economic power of great towns and the taxes and services demanded by greater princes.

The provision of the services thought necessary by Ptolemy of Lucca for true self-government may be tested by examining small towns, those between city and village. Isle Jourdain in Gascony near Toulouse in 1210 had a stone bridge, a leprosery and two hospitals, one named after its lay founder, just as was customary in its greater neighbour. Before 1200, lay public notaries were instrumenting within its walls, about a half a century after they were seen in Toulouse and a slightly shorter length of time before nearby villages boasted the same. In 1230 or 1232, the community elected thirteen worthies to serve as its consulate, a body having 'with the consent of the university, full and free power of changing, tempering and deleting heavy and onerous customs, written or not, and the right of making and instituting by itself . . . new customs to advance the common utility of the whole university'.[8] These republican rights had been diminished by 1275, when the lord or his vicar and the outgoing consulate together nominated forty worthies, from whom

---

[7] *De regimine principum* 4 2 in ed. Spiazzi, *Opuscula philosophica* 328a.
[8] My 'Village, Town and City in the Region of Toulouse' in ed. J.A. Raftis, *Pathways to Medieval Peasants* (Toronto, 1981) 165 n. 79.

seven consuls were chosen by lot. Monarchy, in short, was normal in rural and small town political life, but oligarchy and even democracy were also seen there.

Town and city

To Ptolemy of Lucca, the natural urban political form was a collective lordship or republic. He observed 'that in every region, whether Germany, Scythia or France, cities are republics, but [other than in Italy] are bound by laws under the power of a king or emperor'.[9] He was surely right about the general principle. Areas marked by urban self-government lay along the frontiers of the principal power blocs. The most important of these were the western and southern marches of the fading Empire, extending from the North Sea through the Lorraines and Burgundies and down the Rhone to Provence, thence traversing north and central Italy. Of these, north and central Italy's cities were the most free, some winning independence in 1183 at the Treaty of Constance, others during the Hohenstaufen collapse in the mid-thirteenth century. Other areas notable for liberty were the Lorraines, the Burgundies and adjacent regions in the Empire along the Rhine valley and its confluents. As the Hohenstaufen fell, towns in Swabia, modern Switzerland and along the upper Rhine and Danube advanced greatly. So also did communities in imperial Provence and on the Rhone until 1250, when Capetian power began to penetrate there.

Cities also profited when local ruling houses were harmed by greater ones. An example was Flanders, a French province. Her towns were almost as free as Italian ones, because, after Philip of Alsace (d. 1191), the French crown intervened to ruin the counts by the time of Guy of Dampierre (d. 1305). With the region's tallest belfry, adjacent Tournai, freed from its bishop in 1188 with French aid, was almost an Italian-style republic. Flanders and north and central Italy had the additional advantage of great industrial and commercial power. Since these regions imported food and raw materials, however, their industry would not have sufficed had not Europe been politically decentralized. Toulouse and other towns of the Midi also did well as long as the local house of St Gilles was being squeezed by the Catalans and the French, both Plantagenet and Capetian. After the Capetian triumph in 1229, town freedom slowly withered.

To have freedom is to vaunt it. From 1212 onwards, Marseilles was led by a patrician Confraternity of the Holy Spirit. This body acquired the lordship of the town's various parts; 1214 saw a town seal, in 1218 the town won the right to mint its own coinage and, in 1220, the counts of Provence recognized the community's right to self-government. Thereafter political

---

[9] *De regimine principum* 4 1 in ed. Spiazzi, *Opuscula philosophica* 326b.

leadership was entrusted to an elected *podestà* or head of state. The period from 1220 to 1230 was Marseilles's age of self-government, and a preamble dated 1218 to a public act read: 'With God's aid, we have gained the liberty of our city, decorated our republic and increased its profit and right... Wherefore, God alone governing our city of Marseilles, we, wishing to provide for its profit in the future' form an alliance with the town of Nice.[10] The legend on the Venetian ducat said as much: 'Be this duchy, which you rule, given to You, O Christ!' To be ruled by the deity is to be ruled by no earthly power.

Town alliances advanced urban independence. In Italy leagues date from the later eleventh century, but the great one was that formed by Lombard cities after Frederick I destroyed Milan in 1161. In 1167 and 1168, ten major towns (including a new Milan) in Lombardy and the Romagna joined with lesser allies to defeat the Empire, and Barbarossa capitulated at Constance in 1183. Thereafter, although leagues were common enough in Italy (Milan headed one of seventeen cities in 1226), oath associations were replaced by something like a modern system of interlocking alliances. During the thirteenth century, Germany became famous for leagues, a manifestation of that realm's decentralization. From 1226 onwards Frederick II, who wanted peace at any price in Germany and supported local princes, tried to ban them by condemning seven Franconian towns fighting the prince-archbishop of Mainz. The Empire's fading made such efforts nugatory. Leagues such as the Rhenish Peace Confederation, founded in 1254 by Mainz, Cologne, Worms, Speyer, Basel and other communities, made political decentralization tolerable. Eventually comprising about a hundred towns as far afield as Zürich and Bremen, seven ecclesiastical princes, the count palatine of the Rhine and many lesser lords, this league called for parliaments to meet four times yearly at Cologne, Mainz, Worms and Strasbourg. Another and more durable association was that of Germany's seaports and allied towns. Eventually known as the Hanseatic League, this began in 1210 when Lübeck and Hamburg granted each other's burghers joint citizenship. Together with local lords, the league smashed Danish Baltic power in 1227, thus forwarding German penetration of Scandinavia. By 1285, the king of Norway was able to observe that the thirteen cities extending from Bremen, Hamburg and Lübeck to Wisby, Riga and Revel constituted a 'university'. A large town like Cologne was a member of several leagues, allied to Franconian and other Rhenish towns, to those of the Netherlands and to Bremen and Hamburg on the North Sea.

Elected boards possessing judicial and executive powers characterized towns. In Italy members, numbering anywhere from four to twenty-four, were initially called consuls. The word 'consul' was borrowed from princes, the counts

---

[10] L. Méry and F. Guindon, *Histoire analytique et chronologique des actes et des délibérations des corps et du conseil de la municipalité de Marseille* (Aix, 1873) I 272.

of Toulouse, for example, and the dukes of Benevento, who, in the twelfth century, found in it a reminiscence of Rome's magistrates. Elected officers bearing this title were widespread in Lombardy by 1100 and were first seen at Florence in 1138. The institution spread throughout south France and penetrated into Germany, even far north. The members of Lübeck's governing board were called consuls in a charter of 1188, and the same was true in Utrecht in 1192. The further from Italy, however, the more this was mere fashion: Lübeck's consuls were ordinary town councillors.

The *podestà* was an office invented in Italy. Originally a title (*potestas* = power) attributed to imperial governors, the post became elective after the Peace of Constance as towns became independent of both the Empire and local lords. The elected *podestà* was accorded the honours given princes and, acclaimed by parades when entering town, was seated on the 'throne of glory'. Initially chosen from a town's inhabitants, as in Pisa in 1190, such officers were later recruited from other communities, as at Pisa in 1208. The motive for electing foreigners was fear of monarchy, the institution being replaced in Italy's towns. A foreign *podestà* was forbidden to marry within a town or dine privately there and was prohibited from summoning general assemblies, lest tyranny be built by working on the passions of the many. Strictly limited by community law and elected town councils, the *podestà* underwent public examination (*sindicatio*) at his term's expiration.

Elected for a year or six months, a *podestà* was a salaried officer who brought with him jurists, notaries and soldiers. Invariably knights to command the militia, they were also professional. In four decades of the thirteenth century, twenty such officers are known to have served in at least six towns each. Writing in 1282, Bonvesino of Riva praised William of Pusterla, a fellow citizen of Milan, because he had been elected supreme magistrate sixteen times in nine cities from 1190 to 1224, no fewer than four times in Bologna. 'When [William was] "podestà" of Bologna, there, among the jurisconsults, these latter, seeing a man without Latin to be so wise, called him antonomastically the "Wise Layman".'[11] The Franciscan Salimbene showed the respect accorded to these officers by complaining that Elias, then general of his order, failed to rise when receiving Gerald of Corrigia, *podestà* of Parma, accompanied by his sons, themselves occupants of many similar offices.

Except in Provence and south Germany, Italian-style podestarial office rarely spread beyond the peninsula, other officers heading towns in the north. The professional mayor was one of these. The difference between the *podestà* and the mayor was that the latter was usually a royal officer elected to serve in this capacity, a reflection of urban subordination to princes. In the laws of Rouen that spread through Plantagenet domains, the mayor was chosen by

---

[11] *De magnalibus urbis Mediolani* 19 in ed. Novati, *Bullettino dell'Istituto Storico Italiano* XX (1898) 147–48.

the king from a slate of three presented to him by the electoral body or the citizens. Another partial analogue to a *podestà* was the burgomaster (president of a town council), seen as early as 1224 in Strasbourg but only widely spread around 1300. Their office differed from the Italian one because the incumbents were natives of the towns where they served their yearly terms and were usually not professional. Well before 1300, Italy's towns boasted professional associations of judges, lawyers and notaries, something not equalled elsewhere in Europe save in the courts of kings.

Ideally, northern towns were capitals of provinces, housing merchants and artisans and the old service cadres that were slowly becoming knightly. Save for a few late foundations, such as Freiburg in the Breisgau (1120) and Lübeck (1157–58), from which ministers or knights were expressly excluded, such groups generally lived in or near towns and initially took part in their political life. Until 1112, for example, ministers led communal activity in Cologne. In Mantes on the Seine as late as 1150, a common council of knights and burghers was formed to maintain peace and protect the poor. This old pattern changed in two ways where princely power was fairly strong: either the knightly or ministerial aristocracy was excluded from active participation in town politics, or town and countryside were separated. In north and central Italy the fading Empire did not prevent knightly participation, and this was also true in Languedoc and Provence until after the 1230s. The participation of knights or ministerial groups was known in Germany as far north as Alsace and Franconia. Cities such as Mainz, Worms, Strasbourg and Zürich had active knightly aristocracies, the town council of Worms, for example, being composed of twelve ministers and twenty-eight burghers in 1198. Elsewhere, as in Cologne and Regensburg, not a few ministerial families, faced with the choice of being knights outside the community or burghers within, simply became burghers, helping to shape a patriciate.

The effect on a town's political structure of the exclusion of knightly elements was unmistakable. It sometimes created double towns. In a Capetian charter to St Quentin in 1195, for example, knights and some clergy were assigned their own court, that of the count. The viscount's court, on the other hand, was to handle the burghers' cases, who in 1215 won the right to elect its judges. The mayor and sworn men of his council exercised the general right of government, other than judicial, over the burghers. A similar pattern may be seen in Liège, where the old town nucleus or 'city' remained in the hands of the archbishop-prince, his knights and their councillors who also exercised criminal justice throughout the town. The 'Port' or new town was ruled by its burghers whose sworn men judged civil cases.

A corollary of division within a town was the separation of town from countryside. In Flanders, for example, councillors often split into two bodies, a town board presided over by the count's bailiff, and another that served as the count's court for the countryside. Starting in 1194 in Arras in Artois and spreading to Flanders in 1209, councillors of the town board were elected yearly by the burghers. Although large Flemish towns dominated the countryside by 1300, such jurisdictional divisions rarely vanished and were sometimes reinforced in later ages. In Italy, towns often ruled whole provinces. Few north of the Alps equalled this, although towns had similar ambitions. From 1202 to 1204, for example, the consuls of Toulouse led expeditions against twenty-three rural lords and communities. Although at first successful, the effort was beaten back by the Albigensian crusade and the subsequent reimposition of princely control. Most northern town jurisdictions, however, extended beyond their walls. Seen above, even modest Provins in Champagne had eight outlying villages, whose inhabitants voted in town.

In Germany, moreover, towns used their link with the Empire to win freedom from the territorial princely states that were just beginning to form. The idea of the later 'imperial free city' was already expressed when Lübeck was described as a 'free city' and an 'imperial place' in 1226. Vienna won similar status in 1237, the emperor recording that 'we have received this city and its citizens into our protection; nor shall they ever be removed from our power or that of the Empire'.[12] Cities of this kind in Germany had extensive rural circumscriptions, especially in Swabia, Burgundy and Lorraine. Metz eventually ruled 150 villages. Great though these towns were, however, they did not equal Italy's republics, whose citizens were inordinately proud of their institutions. Remigio de'Girolami catalogued God's seven gifts to his native Florence: 'the abundance of money, the nobility of the money itself, the multitude of the people, the civility in style of life, the woollens industry, the armaments industry and the command of the countryside in the county or district'.[13]

These small republics were powerful, and not only economically. Although England's crown had done better in the Welsh wars of the late thirteenth century, it assembled a substantial host of 3,000 knights and over 25,000 foot for a campaign in Scotland in 1298. In 1325, the tiny republic of Florence fielded 2,000 knights (three-quarters professional) and 15,000 foot for a war with the famed captain Castruccio Castracani, lord of Lucca. In conclusion, although Europe's larger states and rural and urban lordships were monarchies large and small, significant republican and even democratic elements were to be seen in town and village.

---

[12] Planitz, *Die deutsche Stadt im Mittelalter* 418n.

[13] His *De bono communi* in Davis, 'An Early Florentine Political Theorist: Fra Remigio de'Girolami' in *Proceedings of the American Philosophical Society* CIV (1960) 668a.

Chapter 17

Republics

Republican thought

Although much thought on government was transmitted from the early Middle Ages, real political literature was first seen in the thirteenth century. Italians were especially good at it because they had the strongest lay professions and, living in both republics and monarchies, were inspired to compare constitutions more than others. Some were northerners, however, borrowing from Aristotle's *Politics* available in William of Moerbeke's translation (1260–65). John of Hocsem, a canon favouring the early fourteenth-century revolutions at Liège who had studied at Paris, applauded democracy, decried oligarchy and remarked that 'almost all today's princes are . . . tyrants'.

Two of the significant scholastics who dealt with political thought, Marsiglio of Padua and William of Ockham (d. *circa* 1349), are only touched on here because their careers lie beyond the time treated in this volume. Earlier writers had prepared their way, however, and the most consequential of these were Giles of Rome and Ptolemy of Lucca. Widely circulated and eventually translated into English, French, German, Hebrew, Italian, Portuguese, Spanish and Swedish, Giles's *On Princely Rule* of 1277–79 favoured hereditary monarchy, and was divided into the three parts of 'practical philosophy', ethics or self-government, economics and politics. Composed about 1302, Ptolemy's tract with the same title benefited from the fact that it had been begun by Thomas Aquinas around 1265, under whose name it spread throughout Europe.

Thomas Aquinas shared the reserve of clerical intellectuals: he did not wholly favour any one form of government, that is, monarchy, aristocracy or democracy. Depending on his audience, he shifted: addressing a prince in his *Rule of Princes*, he does not praise electoral government; writing for scholars, however, he does, as when he lauded the ancient constitution of the Jews. These, he thought, had been governed by a prince aided by a group of elders, chosen by and from the people: 'This is the best of all polities, being a mixture of monarchy, in so far as one leads; of aristocracy, in so far as many rule according to virtue; and of democracy, that is, of the power of the people, because the rulers are chosen from the popular elements and the election of these rulers pertains to the people.' This celebrated 'mixed constitution' was to have a long history. Elsewhere in the same book, Aquinas

255

shows that he respected what the fathers of the Church had said about popular government. Everything depends on the people's virtue. As Augustine said in his *On Free Will*:

> if a people is moderate and sober, a diligent guardian of the common good, then the law rightly says that such a people may elect the magistrates by whom the republic is administered. If, however, the same people becomes depraved, sells its vote and commits its government to profligate and vicious persons, the power of giving office is rightly taken from it and given instead to the judgement of a few good men.[1]

Not a few disliked republicanism and, since this polity was widespread among Italians, detested them as well. Dreaming of a unified Europe in 1306, the French judge Peter Dubois complained that the Empire had been wrecked by the German princes and especially the Italian urban republics. He asked: 'because these cities and many princes who recognize no superior on earth . . . will stir up disputes, before whom will they litigate or proceed in law?'[2] He therefore proposed a general council to stop wars and settle disputes by arbitration, final appeals going to the pope. As had his earlier compatriot Beaumanoir, this monarchist believed that the Lombard republics had been spawned by traitorous, forked-tongued rich patricians. More thoughtfully, Alexander of Roes in 1288 believed democracy to be a manifestation of Italian 'materialism':

> The republic of the Christian Faith resides principally in three nations, Italy, Germany and France . . . Italians love to acquire, Germans to rule, and French to learn . . . Because humanity is prone to evil . . . Italians suffer from avarice and envy, Germans from rapacity and discord, and French from pride and lust . . . This is why soldiers rule in Germany, the clergy in France and the people in Italy.[3]

Italy's Ghibellines shared these suppositions. Dante Alighieri worshipped the Romans because they exemplified the discipline needed for world empire and not because of their republican form of government. Freedom, for him, was no mere gratification of appetite's impulse, but instead due subordination to the common good, and he asserted that human free will is best exemplified in those 'who live under a monarchy'. Italian republicans such as Boncompagno of Signa were forever prating about how Italy was the 'mistress of the other provinces', but the poet sourly converted this into the 'mistress of a whorehouse'.[4]

---

[1] These two quotations derive from Thomas's *Summa theologiae I–II* 105 1 c. and *I–II* 97 1 c.
[2] *De recuperatione terre sancte* 12 (ed. C.V. Langlois, Paris, 1891) 10.
[3] *Noticia seculi* 12–14 in *Alexander von Roes Schriften* in *MGH Staatsschriften* 159–60.
[4] *De monarchia* 1 12 and *Purgatorio* 6 78, cited with context in R.B. Benson, '"Libertas" in Italy (1152–1226)' in *La notion de liberté au moyen-âge: Islam, Byzance, Occident* (ed. George Makdisi, Dominique Sourdel and Janine Sourdel-Thomine, Paris, 1985) 191–92.

Although he was an ardent advocate of papal monarchy, Ptolemy of Lucca's vision reflected north and central Italy where republics were everything. Even if there was a tradition of monarchy, 'counts and other princes, unless they tyrannize by violence, must rule in the republican style. Certain titles to office derived from the Empire are found among them, giving them jurisdiction over their subjects, although today this authority is . . . almost wholly eliminated because of the power of the cities.'[5] Ptolemy's republics were communities of citizens and, although heavy with religious overtones, citizenship could be casual. At Pisa in 1286, naturalization required twenty years' residence but, because industry needed labour, this was reduced to three years by 1319. Rural inhabitants with a tax valuation above £50, moreover, were obliged to become citizens.

In theory, all citizens were equal before the law and all could hold office. Discussing Aristotle, Ptolemy rejected Crete's oligarchy in favour of Sparta's way, in which, he thought, the king

> was elected by the wise, chosen from all grades of the citizenry; and it appears reasonable that a king should be raised up to rule the people by the counsel of the whole [population], as the cities of Italy commonly do today. This is what the word 'city' means, being, according to Augustine's *City of God*, 'a multitude of men bound together by a certain bond of society'.[6]

To persons of this commitment, this polity was better than monarchy. The Dominican John of Paris explained, 'Because of the great power conceded to kings, kingdoms easily degenerate into tyrannies.'[7] Monarchy is also inefficient because even excellent subjects, when elevated, are sometimes incapable of ruling and hence must be quickly replaced. Bonaventure asserted that experience, not birth, makes ship captains and, like Ptolemy of Lucca, that Rome had risen under elected leaders and fallen under hereditary emperors. Ptolemy had earlier stated that, according to the ancients and practical experience, the appetite for honours is innate and makes men seditious if it is never sated, and that men best obey a law that they have themselves proposed. In addition, no one, however wise or instructed, is superior to the whole population. The Franciscan Peter John Olivi defended a mixture of electoral monarchy together with powerful councils:

> The regime in which the subjects participate in elections and councils is more acceptable to them and, because of this, is better advised, more honourable and

---

[5] *De regimine principum* 3 22 in ed. Spiazzi, *Opuscula philosophica* 324a–b. The word 'republic' is used here to translate the author's 'polity'.

[6] *De regimine principum* 4 18 in ed. Spiazzi, *Opuscula philosophica* 347a and Augustine's *De civitate dei* 15 8 2.

[7] *De potestate regia et papali* 19 (ed. Bleienstein) 175.

more authoritative because it would be unlikely, indeed incredible, for one acting together with many to err as much as one acting alone.[8]

Monarchist arguments against these positions were perhaps best expressed by Giles of Rome who argued that, as noted above, if an heir is defective, monarchy is more than one person because princes are aided by their councils. Indeed, Humbert of Romans found that counsellors were more vital than princes. Giles also argued that the participation of the many in elections and legislation led to sedition. Nevertheless, even this convinced monarchist knew that, in theory, republicanism was the better form of government. 'Speaking absolutely, it is better to choose a prince by election than by hereditary succession. Nevertheless, because men have corrupt appetites . . . it is better for a realm or city that its lord be chosen by heredity rather than by election.'[9] A reason for this is that it is 'natural' for fathers to want their sons to succeed to their place. As others also said, 'experience' showed that most states were hereditary monarchies.

Giles's and others' use of the argument from history could, however, be subverted. Although he too thought monarchy better in the corrupted state after the Fall (before which mankind had been republican), Ptolemy of Lucca cited significant exceptions. God had ordered the ancient Jews to elect their leaders, and the virtuous Romans had created the paradigmatic republic praised in the first book of Maccabees. Even if corrupt man needed monarchy, God and history found this polity to be beneficial for the Romans and therefore for their heirs, the contemporary Italians!

Ptolemy went on to observe that subordinate officers of princes usually held their charges hereditarily, whereas even lifetime office was viewed with suspicion in republics: 'In the regions of Liguria, Aemilia and Flaminia, which are today called Lombardy, no lifetime government is found except by way of tyranny, with the exception of that of the Doge of Venice who nevertheless has a temperate government. Whence government by short-term office is the one most suitable for these regions.'[10] Writing in the early 1260s, Brunetto Latini summed this all up: monarchies are corrupt and inferior to republics:

> in France and other countries under the government of kings and other lifetime princes, they sell the governorships to those who buy them at the highest price, who then look after their own profit and not that of the citizens. In Italy, on the other hand, the citizens, bourgeois and commons of the town elect their *podestàs* . . . as they wish, and these are more profitable to the common good of the town.[11]

---

[8] *De renunciatione papae* in *Archivum franciscanum historicum* XI–XII (1915–19) 354–55.

[9] *De regimine principum* 3 2 5 (Rome, 1607) 461.

[10] *De regimine principum* 4 5 in ed. Spiazzi, *Opuscula philosophica* 336a.

[11] *Li livres dou Tresor* 3 73 (ed. Carmody) 392.

The Franciscan Salimbene also found the system superior:

> Do we not observe in Italy's cities today that the Captains and *podestàs* are changed twice yearly, and that they give good justice and rule well? When they enter office, they swear to observe the statutes promulgated by the wise of the city to which they have come, and have with them judges and learned men who are governed by ancient [Roman] law ... For if 'the number of fools is infinite', so also 'is the multitude of the wise the health of the earth'. Therefore, if laymen rule their cities well by means of officers elected for short terms, how much more should the religious ... be able to improve their government.[12]

Writing before 1246, John of Viterbo counselled against choosing a *podestà* simply because he was noble or rich. He recommended, however, that if two candidates were otherwise equal, the richer could be chosen, because 'one presumes that [the poorer] might be more easily corrupted. I do not deny, however, that, if diligent ... and tested, the latter may be elected.'[13] Following Aristotle, Ptolemy of Lucca found that those best suited for elected office were 'the middling folk of the city, that is, not those who are too powerful for they easily tyrannize over others, nor yet those of too low a condition for they straightway democratize or level everything'. Still, according to Ptolemy all should have a chance to rule: 'Praiseworthy therefore is that polity in which office and honours are distributed to each in turn according to merit, as did the ancient Romans.'[14] Although Ockham later also favoured the middle range, his *Dialogue* expressed the notion that the ideal polity is that 'in which the many rule for the common good, whether notable or non-notable, rich or poor, so that this polity is distinguished by the multitude from aristocracy'.[15]

Although leading citizens were often nobles, a vision of natural equality marked Italian republics; equality, at least, before the law. In statutes of 1251, a *podestà* swore 'to uphold the people of Viterbo, each and everyone ... in their persons and property'.[16] One result was that some magistrates were of modest origins. John Barixellus, liberator of Parma from the Ghibellines, was a tailor and son of a peasant. The 'people' rewarded him: 'first, they made him, who had been poor, rich. Second, they gave him a wife of noble lineage ... Third he was always, without election, a member of the council because he had common sense and the gift of public speaking.'[17] Gentlemen even became democratic. Bonvesino of Riva told of Hubert of Croce, a

---

[12] *De prelato* in his *Chronicon* in *MGH SS* XXXII 156. Ecclesiastes 1:1 and Wisdom of Solomon 6:24.

[13] *Liber de regimine civitatum* 5 in *BIMA* III 221b.

[14] The two quoted passages are in *De regimine principum* 4 8 and 4 7 in ed. Spiazzi, *Opuscula philosophica* 335a–36a.

[15] *Dialogus* I ii 8 cited by Roberto Lambertini, 'Wilhelm von Ockham als Leser der "Politica"' in *Das Publikum politischer Theorie im 14. Jahrhundert* (ed. Jürgen Miethke) 213.

[16] *Cronache e statuti della città di Viterbo* ed. Ignazio Ciampi (Florence, 1872) 518.

[17] *Cronica* in *MGH SS* XXXII 374–75.

Milanese champion around 1215. This knight was a huge eater, once devouring thirty-two eggs at one sitting with much pasta, and his mistress bore him a daughter of wondrous strength. Still, Hubert was always polite, and never vaunted his strength or injured anyone without reason.

Laws were issued differently in republics and monarchies. Although intellectuals said that kings were bound by law, hence distinguishing between good and despotic royal government, both Giles of Rome and Ptolemy of Lucca noted that princes enjoyed arbitrary power or free will when issuing law, something found in the inmost recesses of their hearts. If limited, Ptolemy found this capacity almost godlike:

> A king, society's artificer or architect, must answer the needs of the realm, those that pertain to the conservation of human social life, and repair society's every defect . . . If needed therefore, princes can impose legitimate exactions or tributes, as long as they do not transcend the bounds of need.[18]

Elected officers were even more bound by the laws of the communities in which they served, and changes were to be made only by the 'people' or their assemblies. Retiring magistrates were often judged by the 'people' in public hearings (*sindicationes*) at term's end.

In republics, Alberic of Rosate said, law was made by assemblies of the people or by elected magistrates, the latter acting 'in two ways, either by executive act or by judicial sentence . . . because what these magistrates do . . . is done by the authority of the people which elected them, and so the people makes the law'. Legislation was issued in three ways. Relatively rarely, all males met in a public parliament and voted on a proposal of the rector or magistrates of the city. More frequently, the elected officers 'are to be convoked [together with the councillors] . . . and among them the proposal, discussion and enactment of statutes take place'.[19] Borrowing from Albert Galeotti (*fl.* 1250s–72), Albert of Gandino described procedure:

> whatever its members think ought to be enacted may be proposed in a council, the *podestà* being present, because resolutions can only be introduced in his presence . . . Second, any councillor may speak to what is proposed. Third, resolutions shall be discussed by the councillors to determine whether or not they wish them made into law.[20]

A third way was that the citizens or their councillors chose experts to formulate statutes, a system naturally favoured by this jurist.

Public assemblies varied in size. The anonymous *Pastoral Eye* notes that princes favour small councils, but that republics

---

[18] *De regimine principum* 3 11 in ed. Spiazzi, *Opuscula philosophica* 311b–12a.
[19] Alberic's two passages are in his *De statutis* 1 3 6 and 1 4 3–6 in *TUJ* II 2va–b.
[20] *Quaestiones statutorum* 2 in *BIMA* III 157–58.

choose many for their councils, adhering perhaps to the rule that 'what touches all
should be agreed to by all' . . . And Authority says that omnipotent God 'sometimes
reveals to the humble what he hides from the powerful' . . . But truth is revealed
more clearly by many [than by few].[21]

As to the size and social composition of such assemblies, Alberic of Rosate
cites a question of the Bolognese doctor Martin Syllimani (d. 1306). To abrogate or change a law, could a *podestà* summon both his own Council of the
600 and the 'people's council' of the Captain of the People? The lawyer
replied 'No!' His reason was: 'if the People's Assembly is mixed together with
the Council of the 600, the people's councilmen, for fear or reverence, will
not dare to speak their minds as freely as they would were they by themselves,
and hence often follow the councilmen of the Council of the 600'.[22]

Magistracy differed in monarchy and republics. Ptolemy of Lucca confessed
that kings were majestic because, since the state was theirs, they shared its
interest. Elected for a year or six months, republican hirelings merely ran the
government for personal profit or salary, no matter what honorifics were
lavished on them. Like the newly rich, however, hired politicians maligned
their rivals, feared losing office and used the public treasury to buy friends.
Dante's lawyer friend Cino of Pistoia speaks of 'a certain People's Captain
who sold himself in the middle of the communal palace like a whore in her
lupanar'.[23] Temporary and mercenary, such officers were sometimes viewed
disrespectfully. A Paduan chronicle in 1302 described one *podestà* as 'mali-
cious' and next year called another an 'imbecile'. As seen above, however,
salaried political officers were both professional and experienced. Moreover,
their governments were more gentle than those of princes. Ptolemy remarked
that 'the way of governing in a republic is usually mercenary because the
lords are hired for a salary; and where salary is the object, the officer does
not concentrate on ruling his subjects, and therefore the rigour of the law is
tempered'.[24] This temperance was why Brunetto Latini, roundly contradicting Aristotle's *Ethics*, claimed that 'seigniories are of three kinds: one is of
kings, the second is of the aristocracy and the third of the commons, which
is the best of all three'.[25]

Not all were equally suited for republican government. Moved by natural
history, Ptolemy of Lucca opined that, because of the influence of the stars,
climate and geography, some peoples were naturally servile; notably, to this
north Italian, Corsicans, Sicilians and Greeks. Reading Vegetius, John of

---

[21] A composite quotation from the *Oculus pastoralis* 6 5 and 2 3 in ed. Muratori, *Antiquitates Italicae medii aevi* IX 856 and 806. See *Code* 5 59 5 2.
[22] *De statutis* I 120 in *TUJ* 17va.
[23] From his *In Codice* cited in Sbriccoli, *L'interpretazione dello statuto* 409.
[24] *De regimine principum* 2 5 in ed. Spiazzi, *Opuscula philosophica* 285a–b.
[25] *Li livres dou tresor* 44 (ed. Carmody) 211.

Hocsem thought he discovered that all southerners were servile, but not the good Walloons of Liège. Still, Ptolemy confessed that 'republican government flourishes best in cities . . . Large regions appear to pertain more to royal government, as is seen in many cases.' But he went on: 'The exceptions are Rome, which governed the world by its consuls, tribunes and senators . . . and certain Italian cities [of today] which, although they rule whole provinces, are nevertheless governed as republics.' Having thrown sociology out of the window, Ptolemy reverted to patriotism:

> Some regions are servile by nature, and are to be governed by despotical government, and I include in 'despotical' royal as well. Those, however, who are virile in mind, bold in spirit and confident of their intelligence, cannot be ruled except by a republic, which term I extend to include aristocracy. This kind of government flourishes best in Italy.[26]

Boncompagno of Signa put it more succinctly. Italians, he said, 'neither can nor ought live under tribute, because liberty has placed its principal seat in Italy'.[27]

The 'people'

With the exception of clerks and military, twelfth-century new towns were democratic because settlers were as yet undifferentiated. Needing solidarity to oppose princes, moreover, older cities veiled social differences. In 1164, the consuls of Pisa forbade knightly clans from erecting towers higher than their neighbours. Revolutions against princes also stirred all social classes, and hence a measure of equality characterized towns seeking freedom.

As towns grew, however, so did social differences. Where ministers resided, the developing idea of nobility gradually separated them from other social groups. Often oligarchies or plutocracies came to monopolize office. At Bruges in 1240, only members of the Hanse of London, the merchants' association, could hold public office. In Rouen in the late twelfth century, the mayor and the twenty-four councillors were chosen from the Hundred Peers. At Freiburg in the Breisgau after 1218, the twenty-four consuls held almost lifetime office and were all patricians or knights. Co-optation was common. At Ghent, three bodies of thirteen members each served in rotation as boards of governors, advisers and electors, their members being termed 'hereditary men'. In Cologne in 1297, the officers of the patricians' association chose the magistrates. In Genoa, all town business was brought before the general assembly

---

[26] Ptolemy's two passages are in his *De regimine principum* 4 2 and 4 8 in ed. Spiazzi, *Opuscula philosophica* 327a and 336a.

[27] From his *Liber de amicitia* in Carl Sutter, *Aus Leben und Schriften des Magisters Boncompagno* (Freiburg im Breisgau, 1894) 5, a polemical use of Italy's tax exemption under Rome.

until 1157, but thereafter a small council monopolized it, even electing the first *podestà* in 1190. Oligarchy, however, served a useful function for a time: it reinforced the solidarity of those fighting for town liberty.

It was noted above that princes were opportunist in regard to towns. They sometimes supported the rich, as the Capetians did in Flanders against their feudatory, the count. At other times they aided the middling and lower classes, as during Stephen Boileau's provostship of Paris from 1261 to 1269. Since town freedom had grown under patrician leadership, princes largely sided with modest elements against the rich until self-government had been weakened. One of the few democratic electoral systems in Languedoc was that of Nîmes, installed by the count of Toulouse when he restored the power of his vicar in 1207: 'The whole people of the city or its larger part shall be summoned . . . to create consuls together with our vicar, and, when assembled, shall elect five good men from each quarter, which twenty electors shall choose four consuls.'[28] Tailored to fit Italy, Hohenstaufen policy was similar: divide in order to rule. Trying to split the rulers of Florence, the emperors supported knightly privileges. Where the rich ruled, as in the March of Treviso when Ezzelino of Romano was imperial vicar from 1239 to 1259, they supported the humble.

In Italy, the attack on oligarchy was sparked by the militia service required by the Hohenstaufen wars. In 1260, the Florentines were defeated at Mont-aperto by the Sienese. The statutes issued by the town officers 'to the glory, triumph, honour, good state and praise of all the militia and people of Florence and to the detriment, confusion and death of all its enemies' fell into the hands of the victors. The papers show that professional and militia formations were backed by pioneers, a siege train, notaries, etc. An order of the day named a doctor 'to visit and cure the sick . . . with fever or other ailments . . . with certain others . . . [and] to treat the wounded'.[29] Apart from the town's lion keeper, millers and a few others, all adult males were called up.

Taxes were almost equally draining. As seen before, sales taxes and import duties were favoured by the rich, but unpopular with the people. At Genoa in 1164 and Venice by 1171, citizens were ordered to lend money to the city, being allotted in return shares based on revenue, which became negotiable and alienable. Although the poor also put in their mites, the well-to-do and monasteries were especially drawn to these loan funds or *montes*. Reorganized in 1274, Genoa's Salt Company, so called because of a tax on that commodity, was managed by officers appointed by two representatives of town government and by the larger shareholders. Often themselves town

---

[28] P.M. Viollet, 'Les communes au moyen-âge' in *Mémoires de l'Académie des inscriptions et belles-lettres* XXXVI ii (1901) 436.

[29] The two cited passages are from the *Libro de Montaperti* (ed. Cesare Paoli, Florence, 1889) 369 and 79, in that order.

councillors, shareholders set the rate of return on such 'forced loans', investments bringing from five to fifteen per cent annually. A similar system (the
'census') involving the sale of 'rents' on town revenue began in northern
Europe about 1300. This was favoured by the rich, but the popular party in
Liège abolished the system when it rose in 1302.

Middling and lesser folk favoured taxes based on property values. Well-
nigh universal was Beaumanoir's attitude, namely that taxes should vary
according to the wealth of the taxed. As early as 1162 in Pisa, a public assembly
determined revenue needs and imposed a public deposition under oath
estimating each household's wealth. At Volterra in 1239, town officers swore
'to impose the tax in good faith and without fraud on those in their quarters,
the rich according to wealth, and the poor according to poverty, by examining equity carefully and each inhabitant's convenience and inconvenience'.[30]
Naturally, true equality was rare. In Pistoia in the mid-1280s, knights were
taxed less because of their military value. In 1240 after much resistance, the
popular party in Milan imposed this kind of taxation both in town and in
rural areas where town patricians and knights had property.

However oligarchic a town may really have been, equality was its public
cult, and hence the 'people' were never entirely forgotten. In Italy, the male
population was assembled three or four times yearly to hear the statutes read.
That 'new law' needed the consent of all was also a tradition that oligarchies
tried to obviate. At Arles around 1200, only 'the better and saner council of
the consuls and the archbishop' may call a general 'public assembly . . . in
which changes in the consulate are to be made, improvements, augmenta-
tions and diminutions in law introduced or taxes for the common utility
raised for a war or reprisals'.[31]

What gave muscle to the humble was the rise of the guilds, because, if
individuals are weak, their collectivities are not. The popular movement
was seen first in Italy where, starting with Milan in 1198, the 'people' gained
a larger voice. New offices appeared, the People's Captains, for example, whose
function was to defend popular legislation and, in the manner of Rome's
tribunes, protect the 'people'. Like a *podestà*, a captain was elected and had
one or more councils but, unlike the former, was often a citizen. Popular
victories began with the Peace of St Ambrose in Milan in 1258 and spread
until the *Most Sacred Ordinance* of Bologna in 1282 and the similar law of
Florence in 1293. By that date, moreover, the state had become corporate,
the electorate being composed of the guilds together with regional representation of town quarters or militia companies. Other officers were elected to
protect the people: Florentine Standard Bearers of Justice, for example, and

---

[30] Enrico Fiumi, 'L'imposta diretta nei comuni medioevali della Toscana' in *Studi in onore di Armando Sapori* (Milan, 1957) I 332.
[31] Kiener, *Verfassungsgeschichte der Provence* 195.

those of the guilds and militia companies. A group of six to twelve 'ancients' or priors chosen by lot or elected by the leading guilds often served brief terms (two months in Florence in the 1290s) and headed the republic, as did Athens' ancient prytany. Corporate structure had made the Italian republic hydra headed.

As seen above, the rise of the people formalized the group of nobles or magnates. The latter sometimes tried to limit the power of the whole. In Pisa during the 1280s, knights of both old lineage and new creation created a nobles' commune with officers to balance the popular one. In the late thirteenth century, Pavia had three *podestàs*, each with his council, one for knights, one for the people and the other for notaries and jurists, all subordinate to the *podestà* of the commune and his council. Such separatism failed in the face of popular attack. In Bologna in 1252, the magnate association (*universitas militum*) was outlawed, carrying sidearms prohibited and family towers demolished. Guilds also tried to limit magnate participation in political life. By 1282 in Bologna and Florence, a citizen 'who has not worked in a craft with his own hands' could not sit in the general council. Excluding patrician families was common. A Bolognese law of 1288 granted the head of the Guelph popular party 'free will to exile magnates . . . and great commoner families, whenever and however often necessary for reason of crimes, rumours or rixation which they may or can commit . . . or which they may be suspected of being able to raise up'.[32] Bologna's *Most Sacred Ordinance* stated that, 'wishing and intending that rapacious wolves and gentle lambs walk with equal step', the popular gentle lambs obliged ninety-two well-to-do persons to put in escrow guaranties of good behaviour.[33] In Florence from 1293 to 1295, seventy-three magnate and great popular families were excluded from political life, just under half of all those in this category.

The 'people', moreover, were themselves divided. Corporations housed both entrepreneurs and crafts- and tradesmen, and some labourers were unable to acquire the right to form guilds. When these workers sought to participate politically, a familiar problem of democracy was posed: should the majority bow to what was a minority in social power and numbers? The exclusion of magnates was also necessarily incomplete because the popular party needed experienced leadership: a knight, Giano of Bella, led the Florentine popular party in 1293. Laws excluding the educated upper classes were therefore subverted. Even after Giano's popular movement failed in 1295, the priors were to be chosen only 'from the more prudent, better and legal artificers . . . continuously exercising their profession or those who are recorded in the

---

[32] The two passages are in Dahm, *Untersuchungen zur Verfassungs- und Strafrechtsgeschichte der italienischen Stadt* 33 and 39n.
[33] Salvemini, *Magnati e popolani in Firenze* 327.

matricule of any profession of the city, as long as they are not knights'.[34] Yet the knightly Florentine Dante was enrolled in the doctors' guild and even served as a prior.

Limitations aside, the popular party triumphed. As seen above, noble magnates petitioned to become commoners and, around 1277–79, Giles of Rome was probably near the truth when he wrote:

> In Italy's cities the many, as the whole people, commonly rule. The consent of the whole people is required in establishing statutes, in electing the *podestà* and correcting him. Although there is always a *podestà* or lord who rules the city, nevertheless the whole people rules more than he does, because it pertains to the whole people to elect him, to correct him if he acts badly and to establish statutes beyond which he is not permitted to go.[35]

In Florence in the 1290s, putting aside the elected Standard Bearer of Justice and the six priors, there were three councils, a financial one with 100 members, a second with 300 to serve with the *podestà* and a third with 150 to sit with the Captain of the People, all elected by and from the twelve major guilds and the twenty-one minor ones. Since councillors' terms were for a half-year without re-election to the same council, and since the councils were elected at different times of the year, well over 1,000 citizens out of a population of under 50,000 helped legislate each year. Nor was Florence extraordinary. Lucca, a city with a population of around 15,000, had a main council of 1,550 members. Oligarchic though these constitutions were, they permitted a measure of political participation exceeding that of today's democracies.

A similar 'democratization' took place in the north, sometimes parallel-ing the Italian experience. The office of the Captain of the People or guild Overmaster first appeared in Basel in 1280 and soon spread to Swabian, Burgundian and Alsatian towns. In Freiburg in the Breisgau, a popular rising against the patricians made the consulate into an annually elected board, basic financial power being given to another annually elected council chosen in 1293 from eighteen trade and artisan guilds presided over by the Over-master. At Liège, sixty governors of the crafts moved into the government beside the two burgomasters and their council of sworn men. The general assembly policed the new constitution, an act of 1311 stating that new law could not be issued or new taxes raised without the consent of all citizens, big, middling and humble. Already weakened in 1297, Ghent's thirty-nine 'tyrants' or 'hereditary men' were replaced by a council recruited from three 'members'. First came the 'portmen' (soon containing no less than twenty-six old patrician lines), second the craftsmen and third the cloth weavers.

---

[34] Dahm, *Verfassungs- und Strafrechtsgeschichte der italienischen Stadt* 33.
[35] *De regimine principum* 3 2 2 (Rome, 1607) 455.

The rise of popular parties prompts one to ask whether these political parties were like those in modern states. During the Hohenstaufen wars, Italian parties had ideologies. Ghibellines favoured monarchy and Italian unity under the Empire and Guelphs decentralization and the republican form of government, and the rise of the 'people' grafted on to them a quasi-democratic ideology. On winning, however, the victorious often tried to exclude their opponents altogether, exiling defeated political leaders and abolishing the rival party. When both parties continued to exist, as at Todi, offices were equally divided between them annually, a practice having little to do with a party system. Victorious parties also often lost their initial ideological bent. In the late thirteenth century, the Florentine Guelphs – once the people's party and still continuing as of old, for example, to force magnates to become commoners – fell into the hands of the wealthy. Dante, although ideologically a Ghibelline, served as a Florentine prior in 1300 in the White Guelph party, and was later exiled by the Black Guelphs.

What stifled the party system is hard to fathom. A guess is that, after the Hohenstaufen defeat, the corporate social organization of the rising guilds eventually englobed society. Citizens participated as guildsmen, members of professional colleges or of a formal social order like the magnates, and politics was reduced to determining what groups were allowed in government and how much representation each was to have. Within republics, therefore, the corporations had largely taken over the party role. These had not wholly disappeared, as they were still useful for describing diplomatic alignments. Florence's rivals in Tuscany were Siena and Pisa, Florence being Guelph, Siena and Pisa Ghibelline. Experience also taught the later jurist Bartolo of Sassoferrato that either party, Guelph or Ghibelline, could promote tyranny, and he therefore proposed that a good man's duty was, if the tyrant was Guelph, to be Ghibelline, and vice versa.[36]

Princes and oligarchs

Although not readily discernible until about 1400, many changes marking the dawn of modern times were previsioned in the late thirteenth century. The political unit was becoming larger and, clearly in England but even in France, the national state was being born. In the German Empire territorial states were consolidating, and in Italy larger centres such as Milan, Venice and Florence were busy absorbing their neighbours. The independence that characterized the medieval town and rural lordship was beginning to wane.

Italy's towns had also attained their closest approach to democracy and those of north Europe began to move towards theirs; but, at that very moment, princely government and stable oligarchy also began to appear. The first was

---

[36] *De Guelphis et Gebellinis* 2 in Quaglioni, *Politica e diritto nel trecento italiano* 135–36.

more general. In France and most of north Europe the building of monarchy, what Ptolemy of Lucca called 'despotical government', took place covertly, by reimposing the power of traditional princes on erstwhile free towns and occasional free villages. This occurred in Italy as well, especially in the south and Sicily under the Angevines and the Aragonese, but, on the whole, this peninsula's peculiar destiny was to invent anew the princely institution.

With the exception of Venice with its lifetime but powerless Doge, Italian magistrates held office for short terms, six months or a year. This began to fail in the combat between democratic and oligarchic elements in the latter thirteenth century. When a party won office, it tried to hold it long enough to effect its aims. Azzo VII of Este was elected *podestà* of Ferrara in 1242, again in 1244, for three years in 1247 and again in 1258. At his death in 1264, his heir Obizzo was elected governor and 'perpetual' or lifetime lord. In Parma, Gilbert of Gente became Captain of the People and of the guilds for a five-year term and took over the office of *podestà* as well. In 1254 he was elected for a ten-year term, with a proviso that if he died in office his son would fill out the remainder of his term. In 1303 a relative, Gilbert of Correggio, was elected Perpetual Defender of the Peace and Protector and Defender of the Merchants, Arts and Guilds.

The powers granted to the new magistrates were also enlarged. Albert of Scala at Verona in 1277 was given full, general and free authority to govern the city, change the statutes, alienate the town's properties, decide all cases, and generally handle all other matters 'by his free will and wish as it appears to him to be useful and better . . . and whatever is done, acted or decreed by him or by his command . . . will persist unchanged as if it had been done, acted or decreed by the *podestà* . . . the ancients . . . and the general and special council and by the whole people of the city of Verona'.[37] A similar grant to Guido Bonacolsi, captain of Mantua, in 1299 added that the captain should make war and peace, choose and remove *podestàs*, judges and other officers, summon councils and general assemblies, refuse permission to summon the same, and generally do anything 'with council or without, at his full, pure and general choice and will, no solemnity of law, custom, reform, decree or statute being observed'.[38] Although true dynastic succession awaited the fourteenth century, the Scaliger of Verona associated heirs in their offices in the 1290s. In fine, 'free will', traditionally a monarch's right, was given to elected officers, terms of office were lengthened and dynastic succession was beginning to be visible.

Ferrara was one of the few larger Lombard towns to have evolved the new magistracy, the basis of the later principate, from the old office of the *podestà*. Elected *podestàs* had appeared when the then aristocratic republics had

---

[37] Salzer, *Über die Anfänge der Signorie in Oberitalien* 173.
[38] Leicht, *Storia del diritto Italiano* 338 No. 30.

recently broken free from imperial power. As noted earlier, fearing renewed monarchy, these heads of state were chosen from outside the communities that hired them, and were allowed no social relationships with their citizens. In addition, unlike the new extraordinary magistrates, a *podestà* was rarely chosen in general assemblies and, at Bologna, that body could not even praise this magistrate or his retinue. His powers were carefully circumscribed. Although always judges of criminal cases, the *podestà* of Bologna in 1250, for example, could only enlarge fines, not reduce them. Nor could such officers summon general assemblies; except, as at Siena, when this action was applauded by a two-thirds vote of the council. Although new towns were sometimes named after a popular *podestà* (Pietrasanta in 1255 after Guiscard of Pietrasanta, *podestà* of Lucca), anything that smacked of the hero on horseback, such as an equestrian statue, excited alarm. At Milan, Verona, Mantua and Padua the later princes exercised the Captaincy of the People, an office generalized by the rise of the popular party. Like John Barixellus of Parma seen above, Captains usually had a special corps of militiamen to serve as the 'people's guards'. Having been given extraordinary powers to enforce the popular will, in short, captains were not quite as limited by the anti-monarchical safeguards as the *podestà* had been.

Stimulated by the Hohenstaufen wars, Salimbene remarked that Italy's little states were like children piling their hands one on top of the other. The one who last slipped his hand out from below and slapped it on top felt happy. As in ancient Athens, the 'people' undoubtedly favoured war to weaken rival towns, exploit the countryside and spread the good word. Under the leadership of the Torre family from the 1240s to the end of the 1270s, Milan's popular party conquered Como, Lodi, Bergamo, Novara and Vercelli. Parties, popular or patrician, were also led by nobles, and the ascendancy of particular families was built on military success. The hero of Milan's resistance after the defeat by the Hohenstaufen at Cortenuova in 1237 was Pagano of Torre, whose fame made his family the leaders of the popular party for the rest of the century. On the other hand, warlike ability does not explain the rise of the princes. War captains, even Roman-style dictators at Milan like Humbert Pallavicini in 1259 and William of Montferrat in the 1290s, had moments of puissance but did not found principates.

Two readings of a Paduan history illustrate the relationship between foreign war and internal violence: 'discord between cities is the joy and security of tyrants' went one version, but the first clause was also replaced with 'discord among citizens'.[39] Because war with a neighbour often expresses internal conflict, the latter was probably more significant. Although Ptolemy of Lucca asserted that despotical or royal government had no place among Lombardy's

---

[39] The *Annales S. Iustinae Patavini* cited in Philip J. Jones, *The Italian City-State from Commune to Signoria* 555.

naturally free men, he added a quiet 'except by way of tyranny'. Bonvesino of Riva warned that division within the city might permit foreign tyrants to establish their sway over the free Milanese. The notion that tyranny derived from oligarchy was an Aristotelian commonplace found in Aquinas's *On the Rule of Princes*. What was harder to explain was how tyranny arose from democracy, but Plato helped out. Aquinas argued that 'the government of the many has almost always ended in tyranny, as was shown in the Roman republic', and added that 'in past and present history one discovers that tyranny has been more frequent in lands ruled by the many than in those governed by one'.[40]

That tyranny or the principate derived from only one part of the population, from either the rich or the poor, is doubtful. When warning the Paduans of the rising tyrant Can Grande della Scala in 1313 by likening him to Ezzolino of Romano, Albertino Mussato (d. 1330) affirmed that Padua had begun as a mixed government of knights and commoners. It then became an oligarchy of the rich, 'the fat people', who oppressed the plebs, after which it became a plebeian democracy from which tyranny arose. Leaning on the astrological determinism of Peter of Abano (d. *circa* 1315), he went on to conjecture that, like the human body, the body politic maintained sobriety into its forties. Thereafter, fat, lustful, envious, insolent, the body sickened for twenty years, until finally freedom died, wasted by tyranny. Another example illustrates further dimensions. Milan's principate was established by the Visconti, whose first assumption of the town's lordship was by Archbishop Otto in 1277. This was followed by repeated five-year terms as Captain of the People granted to Matthew V Visconti from 1310 onwards. Although the Visconti represented the plutocracy or oligarchy, the restraints on the old magistracies had already been weakened by the Torre, who played the role of the Gracchi in the Roman republic. The popular party of St Ambrose had created for Martin of Torre the extraordinary magistracy of the people's *podestà* in 1256, had appointed him lifetime lord in 1259, and granted his brother Philip a lifetime term as head of the party and lord of Milan in 1264.

Having pioneered the battle of Italy's towns against the Empire, Milan epitomized the aspirations of many Lombard and Tuscan towns when it led in developing the principate. A likely reason for the choice of this form of government was that class conflict had become endemic. Because political democracy threatens to promote social levelling, Peter of Auvergne, rector of Paris in 1275, argued that 'where the multitude rules, it does violence to the rich by confiscating their goods in the manner of a tyrant, and the multitude is therefore obviously a tyrant'.[41] Talking about Florence, Remigio de'Girolamo

---

[40] *De regimine principum* 1 6 in ed. Spiazzi, *Opuscula philosophica* 263a.
[41] *VIII libri politicorum seu de rebus civilibus* 3 8 in *Thomae Aquinatis opera omnia* (ed. S.E. Frette) XXVI 234a cited by Gewirth, *Marsilius of Padua* I 200n.

said the republic was being wrecked 'because the artisans speak evil of the rich, namely that they devour them, commit treason, protect the property of their enemies . . . and the rich say that the artisans wish to dominate and do not understand that they are ruining the country'.[42]

Moderates everywhere echoed Ptolemy of Lucca's advice to exclude both the very rich and powerful and the humble poor from the management of the republic, but the centre itself lacked moderation. In Florence, for example, entrepreneurial industrial guilds such as the Calimala both exploited humbler artisans economically and exercised criminal jurisdiction over them. On the other end of the social scale, the attack on magnates and their commoner allies was pushed with great severity. So exacerbated had relationships become that anything harmful to the opposing party was permissible. Although the majority ruled, whenever defeat in war or economic difficulties supervened, its solidarity was cracked, creating breaches through which the excluded groups mounted the stage again, fuelled with the rage of past rejection. The history of these cities also illustrates that, no matter what its social origins or initial party affiliation, a principate, a complex composed of a leader, his family and agents, belonged to no one part of the republic. Until weakened in modern times, the advantage of this form of government was that it permitted no parties and favoured no member or social group at the expense of its neighbours, save only the prince himself. Writing in 1324, Marsiglio of Padua spoke of the sovereign people as the 'legislator' or 'defender of the peace'. In the sense that the people were choosing the principate he was right; but the 'legislator' or 'defender of the peace' turned out not to be the people but instead the prince.

To these reasons may be added another. It was remarked above that political units were becoming larger, thus changing the relationship of cities to the small towns and villages of the countryside. In north Europe, monarchs used rural resistance to urban domination to control, or take power in, their towns, and similarly in Italy rustics sometimes aided the growth of the principate. In times of economic hardship or rapid industrial growth, countryfolk flooded into town, there to swell the disfranchised who were disrupting the political balance of the community, ready for violent action. Princes also derived from families exercising power who were coming not only from town but also from the villages and small towns of the countryside, an example being the Este in Verona, Mantua and Ferrara who beat out the rival family of the Torelli, with whom they had long shared office, to become hereditary *podestàs* in the late thirteenth century. Similarly, south Piedmont and Lombardy saw the rise of the Montferrat family in Alexandria and Acqui, whose leaders held offices in towns as far apart as Ivrea, Como and even

---

[42] Davis, 'An Early Florentine Political Theorist: Fra Remigio de'Girolami' in *Proceedings of the American Philosophical Society* CIV (1960) 667a.

Milan in the 1260s and 1280s. Nevertheless, although villages and small towns helped build principates, the durable ones were created inside large cities such as Milan.

Some Italian republics did not evolve into principates, but into stable oligarchies. In Venice, this process could be clearly discerned around 1300: the cloture in 1297 of the group participating in government, the abolition of the general assembly and the creation of a secret council. The defeat of a popular revolt in 1300 and a patrician rising in 1310 cemented oligarchic power. The problem here is to explain why Venice and, to a lesser degree, Florence and Genoa were able to build stable oligarchies when elsewhere the principate rose. What seems peculiar about these cities was the strength of their international connections. Both Genoa and Venice had maritime empires, and it was the governing cadre of these empires and of the fleets binding them together that constituted their oligarchies. Merchant bankers, richer than those of other cities and closely linked to papal finances, formed the base of Florence's oligarchy. In the long run, however, her financial power was not as stable as the others' maritime empires.

These were surely oligarchies. As noted above, Bartolo of Sassoferrato borrowed from Aquinas, Ptolemy of Lucca and Giles of Rome to argue that large regions were best governed by kings, and the largest, the Empire, by an elected monarch. Cities of modest size, he thought, were best ruled by the multitude, excluding, of course, the magnates and the very poor. Large cities should neither be ruled by a prince nor by the multitude:

> These should instead be ruled by a few, that is, by the rich and wise . . . Both Venice and Florence are ruled in this way . . . and there seditions play no role. For although they are said to be ruled by the few, I say that they are few with respect to the multitude contained in these cities, but many with respect to other cities. Since they are many the multitude does not object to being ruled by them, and also they cannot easily be divided against themselves because of the many middling folk who participate and uphold the law of the city.[43]

A deceit surely, but one required for oligarchic republicanism.

---

[43] *De regimine civitatis* 2 in Quaglioni, *Politica e diritto nel trecento italiano* 164–65.

Chapter 18

Government and law

Scribes and chanceries

Other than the clergy, the largest literate profession in Italy and adjacent regions was that of the scribes. In 1293 Pisa, a substantial but not huge town, had at least 232 public notaries. At first close to judges, notaries evolved to become somewhat like modern solicitors who not only wrote acts for their clients, but also informed them about the law and did private business on the side. As towns gained freedom, princely controls over notaries also diminished, and before 1200, their most significant affiliation consisted in the town magistrates who examined and licensed them. In much-divided Italy, however, notaries were also instituted by imperial or papal authority, thus enabling a town notary to extend the area in which his acts had currency. Although imperial notaries were rare outside the Empire and Italy, papal notaries were found in much of Europe until the Reformation. Licensed by public authority, a notary's signature or 'manual seal' sufficed to authenticate documents. Soon even the abbreviated entry that he made in the register where he first recorded the client's wishes became a valid proof of an action taken. The earliest such register extant is that of the Genoese John the Scribe ('Scriba') of 1155. This book was also made of paper, thus showing that multiplying documentation required materials cheaper than parchment and more durable than waxed sheets, both of which, however, remained in use.

Although Italy's system was quickly imitated in nearby southern France and Catalonia, its implantation was slower in the north. Addressing John Peckham, archbishop of Canterbury, John of Bologna wrote: 'Tracts on instruments are widely diffused in Italy because Italians . . . wish to have a public record of everything, but . . . almost the opposite is true in England, where, unless absolutely necessary, instruments are rarely requested.'[1] The situation was changing, however. By about 1300, town scribes were everywhere. The northern system differed from Italy's because these scribes were tied more directly to government. In England's Ipswich, for example, the town's customary rolls expanded to record private transfers of property in 1255, testaments in 1281 and other personal actions in 1285.

---

[1] *Summa notarie* prologue in *BuF* II 603.

In north Europe, princely, episcopal and even seigniorial courts were also enlarged to accommodate society's need for records. Exercising so-called gracious jurisdiction, these courts sold their seals to authenticate and register private documents. Northern charters were therefore usually sealed, whereas southern ones, unless emanating directly from a prince, prelate or republic, were signed by notaries. A council held in London in 1237 recommended that, 'since the use of notaries is not customary in England and recourse is instead had to authentic seals . . . we ordain that not only archbishops and bishops, but also episcopal judges, abbots . . . [and] rural deans shall have . . . such seals'.[2] The popes accepted both authentications, Alexander III observing that 'if witnesses have died, documents have no authority unless drawn by the public hand [of a notary] . . . or have an authentic seal'.[3] Scribal service expanded enormously. Under Philip the Fair, the Paris Châtelet had sixty notaries for public and private services. The French crown so profited from 'gracious jurisdiction' that it tried to extend the system to south France in 1291, but the flourishing public notariate there fought the project to a standstill within a year. By 1304, royal France was divided into two zones, that of the seal and that of the notarial signature.

Before the Gregorian age, titles to property were mostly housed in ecclesiastical archives. Written by the clerks of the institutions receiving the gifts, the acts were often compiled into cartularies or long rolls. By 1300, cartularies had become rare and documentation laicized, because laymen collected their own records and instruments were written by lay scribes. Although this change was underway in the north, it was slower there. From England through France to Germany, for example, scribes of episcopal officials everywhere registered testaments and other documents for layfolk.

Most public documents originated in ecclesiastical and secular chanceries. The Church provided the model for all these chanceries, and the canon lawyer Stephen of Tournai truthfully wrote that at Rome, 'when a letter about a matter of importance is sent to anyone, a copy is retained, and such copies are compiled into books called registers'.[4] This archive was insecure, however, because the popes often moved about within the Patrimony and even went outside of Italy, and hence, save for some fragments, this once huge collection was lost and the extant series begins only with Innocent III (accession 1198). Loss aside, the papal chancery was Europe's busiest. In the eighteen years of John XXII's pontificate about 65,000 papal letters were registered, and many missives were not so recorded. The *curia* was awash with 'paper'. In 1183, Lucius III restored a decision in favour of the serfs of Rosny sur Bois that he had mistakenly reversed. He told Rosny that 'because of the great

---

[2] In Matthew Paris, *Chronica majora Rolls Series* LVII iii 438.
[3] *Liber extra* 2 22 2 in *CICan* II 344.
[4] Bresslau, *Handbuch der Urkundenlehre* I 121.

quantity of business referred to the apostolic see, it is impossible to recall the contents of all our letters . . . Trickery can therefore circumvent us, and we can unknowingly be induced to write things contradicting what we have written before.'[5]

Prelates imitated the papal court. In north Europe, bishops' registers and those of their officials were common, but this was not the case in Italy where, because of greater lay literacy, episcopal business was inserted into the books of secular notaries. Churchmen registered almost everything. Odo Rigaud, archbishop of Rouen, registered the visitations of his archdiocese, stretching from 1248 to 1269. Less pleasantly, starting in the 1230s, the books of the inquisitors of 'heretical pravity' recorded the interrogations of whole communities in south France.

Princely chanceries begin to be organized in the late twelfth century. The first extant registers or rolls of letters sent from princes were those of John of England (accession 1199) and James I (accession 1213) in Catalonia–Aragon. Before that time, governments and princely courts left the preservation of the privileges and grants that they issued to those who received them and concentrated on recording their own rights and revenues. The tally of what was owed to the king called the *Domesday Book* (1086) was used by the English treasury, and was supplemented by a record of actual income called the *Pipe Rolls*, a series continuous from Henry II's accession in 1154. Catalonia possessed a celebrated *Book of Fiefs* dating from the reign of Alfonse II (accession 1162). This chancery registration sometimes provided a resource that was open to others than the prince. Introducing the *Book of Fiefs*, Raymond de Caldès, dean of Barcelona, stated that his prince had 'often publicly stated that you want all contracts drawn up between your predecessors, yourself and your men . . . recorded for the use of your subjects so that . . . each shall learn his rights, and hence . . . discord arising between you and your men shall be prevented'.[6] Specific governmental offices also began early to produce manuals treating the history, practices and legal implications of their functions. An early example was the *Exchequer Dialogue* of the English treasury, whose author was probably Richard Fitzneale (d. 1198).

As state authority grew during the thirteenth century, moreover, the Roman practice of inserting private documents into public archives was revived, thus supplementing the private repositories of the notaries with public ones. In 1289, 'it was enacted at Bologna that legal instruments are to be inserted in the public registry, if valued at more than twenty-five pounds'.[7] Government

---

[5] Marc Bloch, 'De la cour royale à la cour de Rome' in *Studi in onore di Enrico Besta* (Milan, 1937) II 153.

[6] *Liber feudorum maior. Cartulario real que se conserva en el Archivo de la Corona de Aragòn* (ed. F.M. Rosell, 2 vols., Barcelona, 1945) I 1.

[7] Albert of Gandino's *Quaestiones statutorum* 69 in *BIMA* III 189.

also required public registration of the statutes of business companies and partners' names. In 1303, a suit in Paris charging a firm for the debts of a presumed associate failed when it was found that the debtor was not listed as a partner in the register of the Florentine chamber of commerce. As urban taxation increased, furthermore, registers containing statistics amassed under oath about household or family wealth in real property and income were compiled and kept up to date.

Governments also put together books containing privileges, administrative orders, judicial decisions and legislation. The popes legislated by publishing the canons or laws decided on in council. The *Liber augustalis* of the Emperor Frederick II housed the law or legislation (*constitutiones*) issued in a general assembly of his realm. Statutes were published by town governments. Often called *reformationes*, these embodied the idea that princes or magistrates were restoring the right order of things, applying ancient principles to new circumstances. Collections designed to protect princely prerogatives and possessions or the liberties of towns contained a mass of diverse materials, privileges, judicial decisions and legislative enactments.

Public scribes produced grammars and letter-writing manuals, for which the usual Latin term is *ars dictaminis*. To these were added formulary books, some for general use and others specific to a given chancery or notariate. One written for the papal chancery of around 1270 contained nearly three thousand model letters. Linked to ecclesiastical and princely courts, northern manual writers and some of those in Italy, such as the imperial chancellor Peter of Vinea (d. 1249), favoured ornate Latin. Public notaries were simpler in their tastes, and invented the notarial manual. An example is Boncompagno of Signa, who taught briefly at Bologna and was a famous wit. This Florentine wrote several grammars, two rhetorics, one containing humorous letters on simoniacal elections of abbots and bishops, another addressed to lawyers and public speakers, a tract on how to write statutes and a mildly blasphemous manual of love letters.

The difference between notaries and chancery clerks is exemplified by two careers. In 1167, Peter of Blois (d. 1205) was tutoring a Norman–Sicilian prince and, in 1173, he entered the secretarial service of Henry II of England and his wife. He closed his career as archdeacon of London and chancellor of the archbishop of Canterbury. Peter wrote an elegant letter-writing manual, worldly and amatory Latin poetry, tracts on the Crusades, ecclesiastical discipline and the sacraments, and produced sermons and a spate of letters full of classical allusions. Quite different was the Bolognese Rolandino Passaggeri. A notary in 1234, Rolandino entered the town chancery in 1238, becoming notary of the bankers' guild in 1245. Back in the town chancery in 1249, he penned a celebrated response to the threats against Bolognese liberty contained in a letter of Peter of Vinea, Frederick II's chancellor. In 1255 or 1256 he issued his *Summa of the Notarial Art*, the main textbook for this discipline for several centuries. In the 1280s, he was busy teaching at the university and redacting the legislation of the Guelph party, including the *Most Sacred Ordinance* of 1282, the crowning monument of popular legislation, and he may have still been living in 1297.

Although testaments and court cases are sometimes exciting, private charters, administrative manuals and court records rarely entertain. So much dull work, however, made wit a mark of the legal and scribal professions. King John of England, to name a prince, was witty even in correspondence. Bologna's Bulgarus (d. *circa* 1166), a widower marrying a widow, caused his students to crack up when he resumed his course on Roman law after his bridal night by commenting on *Code* 3 1 14: 'I have entered a thing neither new nor unaccustomed.'[8] And Boncompagno of Signa taught how *not* to use Scripture in this manner:

> A fellow who carnally knew a nun said; 'I have not violated the divine bed, but, because the Lord delighted me by his creature, I have striven to exalt his horn.' Again, a nun might say to her lover; 'Thy rod and thy staff, they comfort me.' Or wives to their lovers; 'Give us of your oil, for our lamps have gone out.'[9]

Laws

Higher than scribes and notaries were lawyers, who generally went to universities in Italy or schools such as England's Inns of Court. These technicians dealt with complex bodies of law embodied in gradually accumulating bodies of law, sometimes huge ones. These were of two kinds: compilations of local customary law, and those of general, or common, law.

One common law was canon law. By 1150, the Camaldolese monk Gratian had compiled the basic collection of conciliar canons, papal letters and patristic sources called the *Concordance of Discordant Canons* or *Decretum*. This collection soon drove earlier ones out and gave rise to commentary, those who glossed it being called 'decretists'. Recent papal letters and conciliar canons were thereafter amassed into collections of *extravagantes* (laws and canons not yet encoded). One of these, immediately regarded as authoritative, was assembled by the Dominican Raymond of Penyafort and published by Gregory IX in 1234. Since there were five books in this text, the next similar publication, that of Boniface VIII in 1298, was called the *Sixth Book*. Boncompagno of Signa sourly described the consequent combat between old and new law:

> A decree is a holy canon promulgated by the authority of the highest pontiff with the assent of a council . . . A decretal is the first born of the decrees, whence 'tis said:

---

[8] An incipit also used by Boniface VIII in *Extravagantes communes* 2 3 1 in *CICan* II 1256.
[9] *Rhetorica novissima* 8 1 in *BIMA* II 284a. 1 Samuel 2:10, Psalm 23:4 and Matthew 25:8.

'A decretal is named from decree and is its diminutive, but now it's trying to be its equal.'[10]

All these basic texts were glossed. The ordinary gloss on Gratian was by John Teutonicus around 1215–17, that on Gregory IX's collection was by Bernard of Parma from 1241 to 1266, and John Andreae did the *Sixth Book* from 1294 to 1303. Canonists also wrote epitomized surveys of the whole field. Among the most celebrated were those of Huguccio of Pisa (d. 1210), Innocent IV and Hostiensis. Certain problems received special treatment, for example a tract on usury by Alexander Lombard written shortly before 1307. The standard manual of judicial procedure was published by Tancred of Bologna in 1216.

Europe's other universal law was Rome's Justinianic compilation, of which a good text save some novels had been reintroduced in the late eleventh century. It was studied in Italy, especially Bologna, where work initially was in the form of exegetical glosses. Azzo, a Bolognese professor, wrote glosses on the *Code* and *Digest*, 'Summae' on the *Code* and *Institutes*, commentaries and questions on the principles of law and much else. Accursius, another Bolognese, wrote the great or ordinary gloss on Roman law, and his and Azzo's contemporaries extracted their treatments of specific problems, such as usury or arbitration, and published them separately. Specialization grew apace: a treatise on criminal law and another on statutes by Albert of Gandino being typical examples. Compilations of the debates of the doctors appeared and judges and professors rendered opinions, thereby creating a large literature, variously called 'counsels' or 'answers' (*consilia* or *responsa*). Like individuals, faculties at Bologna, Toulouse and elsewhere produced collections of opinions.

In politically decentralized Latin Europe, jurisprudence was often based on regional customs. In France, codes of provincial law appeared, the first being in Normandy in 1194, but the main period of such codification was the fourteenth and fifteenth centuries. There and elsewhere, local customary law ranged from village and town customals to monuments of jurisprudence such as Eike of Repkow's *Saxon Mirror* and the *Customs of Clermont* in the Beauvaisis by Philip of Rémi, lord of Beaumanoir, both encyclopaedias of legal and social lore. Although local customs were also found there, what was early celebrated in that relatively unified realm was England's 'common laws and customs', of which an early general collection was attributed to the then chief justiciar Ranulph of Glanville in about 1187. A second was compiled by English judges from 1220 to 1234 and was named after its reviser, Henry of Bracton (d. 1268). The attempt to unify Castile's customs resulted in a code called the *Book of the Laws* (*Siete Partidas*). Written from

---

[10] *Rhetorica novissima* 2 3 in *BIMA* II 255.

1256 to 1263 for the king of Castile, Alfonso X, this compilation won currency only in the next century.

Political decentralization and the relationship between Church and state led to conflicts between canon and civil law. Although some Roman law titles were 'canonized', as churchmen said, and many prelates were themselves jurists, they shared the feeling that law was earthbound and theology heaven directed. This conviction led Honorius III to grant theological study such great advantages at Paris in his *Super specula* of 1219 that law was driven to other centres such as Orléans and Toulouse. William Durand the Elder in his *Judicial Mirror* noted the superiority of canon law over civil and listed the cases reserved to it: marriage, for example, and usury. Secular princes and republics nevertheless insisted on judging cases concerning these topics. Besides, although much canon law was received, some was expressly rejected. English law, confirmed at Merton in 1236, refused to receive legitimization according to canon law, stating that once a natural child, always so. In canon law, in addition, two witnesses sufficed to prove a marriage or a testament, but town statutes and civilian doctors insisted on more. Besides, canon law necessarily borrowed much from Roman jurisprudence. As Boncompagno put it: 'canon law leans on another's staff because it . . . is forced to beg the aid [of Roman law] in incepting and conducting trials and promulgating sentences'.[11]

Roman law attracted the schools because it provided models; although nowhere enforceable, it ruled, as the tag had it, 'not for reason of Empire but because of the empire of reason'. Especially designed for civil jurisprudence and promulgated by a monarch, this law rarely conveyed principles useful for limiting princely power. The *Code* does contain *Humanum* dated 446 AD, wherein the emperors vowed to issue new law with the express consent of their consistory and the senate, but late Rome's elaborate structure of provincial and urban assemblies has to be excavated from references dealing with other subjects. So indifferent to political ideas is this law that the principle 'what concerns all shall be decided by all' is buried in a treatment of inheritance and tutorial rights and is not featured, as it was in canon law, among the 'rules of law'.[12]

The study of Roman law especially flourished in Italy, partly because it expressed Italy's anti-German 'nationality'. Proud of their ancient Italian law, Bologna's jurists often even maligned the Lombard law that had been systematized at Pavia on the Roman model in the late twelfth century. Attributing it to Charlemagne (!), Boncompagno called it the 'German stain' or 'blot', not law but instead dung, the Latin pun being *lex* vs *faex*. Respect for Roman law, however, does not mean that it was considered above local custom or

---

[11] Ibid. in *BIMA* II 290–91.
[12] *Quod omnes tangit* in *Code* 1 15 8 for 446 AD and ibid. 5 59 5 2 and *Liber Sextus* 5 12 5 No. 29.

law. The superiority of the latter over the former was everywhere a common-place in Italy. Using the word 'custom' to refer to local law, lawgivers at Salerno in 1251 and Amalfi in 1274 insisted that 'although [Roman] laws were, are and will be holy, good customs are even more holy and, where custom speaks, there the law ought to be wholly silent'.[13] Boncompagno commented dryly: 'Civil law is of little worth because it does not govern a hundredth part of the earth, and is vituperable because villagers' statutes and popular plebiscites straightway obviate its authority.'[14] Notwithstanding the superiority of statute, the schools' Roman law was a normative jurisprudence harmonizing the laws of the peninsula's many independent states. It was Italy's 'common law', something it later became in the Empire and much of Europe.

Oddly, the Italian customary law mocked by Boncompagno nearly became yet another Europe-wide law. Typical is a Beneventan law of 1202 ordering judges to decide cases first by the statutes of the republic, then, in regard to fiefs, Lombard law and lastly Roman law. In that region, reworked by Roman law jurists, Lombard law regulated the fiefs and service of nobles. Although weakened by the hostility of the popular parties, it persisted in Italy and everywhere encouraged jurists to systematize the system of fiefs in the later Middle Ages. Its derivatives also ruled the duelling field, even in modern Europe.

The north was slower to accept Roman law and even bridled at canon law. Not being as unified, France had no 'common law' like England's but instead provincial laws. As a result, these 'foreign laws' filled up the cracks. The custom of the Orléanais called *The Book of Justice and of Pleas* lifted 195 of its 342 titles from the *Digest* and 31 from the *Decretals of Gregory IX*, but disguised this fact by citing them in or as French enactments or judgments. As stated in a royal edict of 1312, furthermore, Roman law took over the schools:

> Our kingdom is especially ruled by custom . . . not by written law; and although in certain parts . . . written law is used . . . it does not bind as such, but as custom introduced . . . following the model of written law. Just as the study of the liberal arts introduces a student to the science of theology, however, so does the study of . . . written law perfect reason's understanding . . . thus preparing [the mind] for local customs.[15]

By that date, indeed, French Roman lawyers even had something to teach the Italians. The work of James of Revigny (d. 1296) and of Peter of Belleperche, both teachers at Toulouse and then at Orléans, was influenced by the dialectics

---

[13] Cortese, *La norma giuridica* II 139.
[14] *Rhetorica novissima* 7 3 in *BIMA* II 259b.
[15] Chénon, *Histoire générale du droit française publique et privé* I 510n.

of the Parisian scholastics, a method transmitted to Cino of Pistoia, the teacher of the great Bartolus of Sassoferrato.

Oddly, the first northern centre of Roman legal studies was that of Vacarius in Oxford. Since Roman law was widely viewed as supporting monarchy, however, the 'feudal' king Stephen of Blois expelled this Italian after 1149. In spite of repeated prohibitions such as that for London's practical law schools in 1234, Roman law made its way in surreptitiously. Doctrines reinforcing the English monarch, such as the inalienability of royal property, were speedily picked up. The justiciar's manual ascribed to Glanville used Justinian's *Institutes* to define the majesty of England's king, and the author of the lawbook called *Fleta* (1290–1300) copied this earlier source together with the Roman-style panegyrics accorded to Frederick II Hohenstaufen. But more than monarchy was involved. Bracton's case book made extensive use of Bologna's celebrated jurisconsult Azzo, especially when insisting on precedents derived from prior judicial decision. The code of laws bearing the same jurist's name was itself modelled on the *Institutes* in its division into books.

Other examples of this influence are not hard to find. Alfonse X's Castilian *Book of Laws* was freighted with Roman law, and his compilers even incorporated whole sections of Vegetius's late Roman manual on warfare. To turn north, Magdeburg law of 1300 (soon translated into Latin, Czech and Polish) explained servitude's origin and nature in these words: 'All men are either free or servile. Liberty . . . is the natural faculty of a man to do what he wants unless prohibited by force or law. Servitude derives from the positive law in which a man is subject to the rule of another against nature.' What could be more German? But, word for word, this law's source was the *Digest*.[16]

Lawyers and judges

In past ages, most suits were brought against defendants by specific persons who, if they failed to prove their charges, were punished, and free defendants were tried by their peers and often by their own law. One result was that, although a prince or lord presided and was often aided by a legal specialist, court decisions were made by persons of the same status or law as the defendants and were often chosen by the parties. Among the quality, when proof was lacking, oaths were taken by family or social groups favouring defendants, and the military could claim trial by battle or duel. Both conjuration and duel sometimes deteriorated into vendettas or small local wars. Things were different for the lower and the servile classes. When proof was lacking, ordeals such as grasping hot iron were imposed on defendants.

---

[16] *Das Sächsische Weichbildrecht. Jus municipale saxonicum* in ed. A. von Daniels and Fr. von Gruben, *Rechtsdenkmäler des deutschen Mittelalters* I (Berlin, 1858) 66 from *Digest* 1 5 4. 'Positive law' translates *ius gentium*.

The growth of government in both Church and state militated against the magic of earlier modes of proof. Churchmen such as Peter Cantor and his contemporaries among Italian jurists detested oath, battle and ordeal. Oath taking or compurgation was nevertheless durable. In 1262, an archidiaconal court of Rouen established the guilt of a clerk for having relations with his brother's wife. The archdeacon, 'fearing that the said Thomas, appearing in his court with compurgators, would lie, enjoined him to leave the country for two years and busy himself at the university of Paris or elsewhere'.[17] Although trial by battle was gradually exiled from the courts, gentlemen claimed the right to defend themselves by the sword, thus starting the transformation of public judicial battle into private duel. The ordeal was less resistant. A way of condemning one against whom there was much suspicion but insufficient proof, the ordeal – often avoided by exile – was brutal and led to abuses, especially against foreigners. Clerical participation in ordeals was formally prohibited by the fourth Lateran Council of 1215, which helped it fade away.

Barbarisms were discountenanced, slaughtering 'criminous' animals, for example, especially domestic pigs. To Beaumanoir such actions were irrational and to his near contemporary Thomas Aquinas they were blasphemous, but they nevertheless went on to win a huge place in later medieval jurisprudence. Law's punishments, moreover, were neither rational nor gentle. In Burgundy, if a horse or ox killed a person, the beast was sold for the lord's profit. 'But if other beasts or Jews do it, they are to be hanged by their hind feet.'[18] Awful punishments, furthermore, were characteristic of the age's tight little communities. Adulterers and other criminals were normally run naked through the streets of towns before expulsion, and maiming and death were visited on condemned persons with ferocity. Sometime before 1246 in Fanjeaux near Carcassonne, a young man sneaked a look into a house and witnessed the entry into Catharism of a condemned murderer. The murderer had wanted this purification because he was about to be buried alive!

The new-school law prided itself on being more gentle than the old. John Bassiani repeated the old Roman saw: they 'thought it more equitable to release a criminal without punishment than to condemn an innocent person'.[19] As in canon law, imprisonment was sometimes substituted for the death penalty, and exile, already known in German Europe, was remodelled on analogous Roman institutions. Alberic of Rosate remarked that 'to be

---

[17] *Regestrum visitationum archiepiscopi Rothomagensis – Journal des visites paroissales 1245–69* (ed. Th. Bonnin, Rouen, 1852) 432.

[18] *Coustumes et stilles de Bourgoigne (1270–1360)* in Esther Cohen, 'Law, Folklore and Animal Lore' in *Past and Present* 110 (1986) 12 and 20.

[19] In his *De ordine judiciorum* in Rossi, *Consilium sapientis judiciale* 143–44, citing *Digest* 48 2 4 and 48 19 5.

banned is to be ejected from the public good and is a secular excommunication'.[20] Civil courts and prisons were separated from criminal ones, and custodial or pre-trial imprisonment of those suspected of grave crime was distinguished from imprisonment as punishment. A system similar to bail appeared. Albert of Gandino proposed that, if one accused of grave crime denied guilt before trial, he should be imprisoned and the case hurried to its conclusion to limit the custody. If, however, 'the crime is not grave, the accused is to be given to his guarantors'.[21]

Legal personnel became increasingly professional and written procedure replaced verbal. From the mid-twelfth century, the old diocesan boards of laymen and clergy were replaced by episcopal judges, the professional officials. Italy's lay consuls gave way to schooled jurists. Azzo scorned seigniorial judges and jurors and, mocking their lack of Latin and schooling, called them 'laymen and illiterates'.[22] Judges at Verona in 1228 were required to have studied law at school, and Padua's statutes of 1285 insisted on six straight years of study. With increasing complexity, past judicial decisions or opinions became increasingly useful, hence the *consilia* literature referred to earlier in this chapter. Culled from *Digest* 1 3 12 and 13, the system was that, as jurists such as Azzo said, judges should decide cases by precedent, by proceeding 'from like to like'.

Opposition to Romanism was unremitting. The English reaction, seen above, was paralleled by churchmen who lamented the replacement of synodal justice by what they called Justinian's laws. Nor were they merely being obscurantist. Law's literature had become vast and full of contradiction. Boncompagno made fun of the first glossator Irnerius (d. by 1118), concluding that 'when a gloss requires a gloss, the [law's] sense is contemned and drowned in a labyrinth of double meaning'. Jurists and lawyers were also usually upper class in interest if not origin (although Bartolus of Sassoferrato was born a rustic), as is seen in 1239 at Pistoia where the opposition to the popular party was called the 'knights and judges'. Popular parties therefore tried to protect their legislation against being glossed away, and Boncompagno suggests a model: 'this statute is composed for the common good, and we wish that . . . the whole of it be understood literally without any gloss or interpretation'.[23] A similar desire led Francis of Assisi to require that the rule he gave his order be obeyed 'to the letter' without gloss. Casuists, however, always had the last word. Alberic of Rosate quoted the paradigmatic popular legislation:

---

[20] *De statutis* 4 1 8 in *TUJ* II 66ra.

[21] *Tractatus de maleficiis* 4 in Kantorowicz, *Albertus Gandinus und das Strafrecht der Scholastik* II 155.

[22] His commentary on the *Code* in Rossi, *Consilium sapientis judiciale* 34.

[23] The first of Boncompagno's passages derives from his *Rhetorica novissima* 10 1 in *BIMA* II 292 and the second from his *Cedrus* 6 in *BuF* I 123.

Jacob Butrigarius [d. 1348] said that at Bologna, where the Most Sacred Ordinance was to be obeyed literally, anyone shedding blood in the town hall was to be beheaded. A certain barber phlebotomized a judge of the *podestà* there. Was he to be beheaded according to the statute?[24]

Besides, few could question the maxim from *Digest* 50 17 No. 56 that 'in doubtful cases, the kinder interpretation is always to be preferred'.

Professional judges were also controlled in several ways. Entry into their ranks required education and corporate bodies tested aspiring members. Also, by Roman tradition judges usually had to choose trained assessors to sit with them, as William Durand the Elder said about civil procedure: 'If there is no assessor at the trial with whom the judge can deliberate, then, according to general Italian custom, learned men should be elected jointly by the litigants and the judge should pronounce according to their opinion.'[25] A statute at Vicenza in 1264 required judges to swear not to decide cases involving more than 100 shillings without assessors, and ecclesiastical inquisitors invariably chose lawyers or notables to help them. As significant were political controls. In Italy, judges were often elected and their decisions were examined by a council or even a general assembly at the end of their terms. Albert of Gandino reports that at Cremona the *podestà* could not sentence anyone for high crime without the consent of the elected 'ancients' or four councillors.

As the new system grew, the barristers (*advocati*) evolved from those chosen by the litigants as arbitral judges, and came to stand before the bar to speak for their parties. These specialists clearly advantaged the rich. Following Roman antecedents, *Peter's Excerpts* therefore recommended in the twelfth century that counsel be equalized to aid the poor, and John of Viterbo later urged the *podestà* to provide them with advocates. Around 1300, William Durand the Younger recommended that magistrates appoint not only advocates without cost to poor litigants but notaries as well. Good in theory, the principle was usually breached in practice, as jurists such as Azzo knew.

As advocates multiplied, so did critics. Being court officers, lawyers were to instruct clients in the law and help them answer questions truthfully, and judges sought to protect court serenity and stifle their objections. Advocates were to defend justice, theory said, helping only those litigants they thought right, but Boncompagno knew better, asserting that their 'function is to . . . palliate lies, veil falsity under the image of truth, instruct their party in positions and answers and induce witnesses to corroborate whatever he wants proved or confuted'.[26] The justification of the barristers was simple. Even an excommunicate or one banished for treason should be represented by a

---

[24] *De statutis* 1 9 in *TUJ* II 5rb.

[25] His *Speculum juris* 2 2 1 in Rossi, *Consilium sapientis judiciale* 37.

[26] *Rhetorica novissima* 3 2 in *BIMA* II 259.

lawyer in order to protect the law and public interest. In both canon law and Italian urban practice, however, such aid was usually prohibited in trials involving treason, habitual violence and heresy.

Legal change also linked juristic professionalism to social utopianism and encouraged the active eradication of crime. Accusation by an injured party was supplemented by other procedures, especially the inquisition, a judicial inquiry initiated by substantial evidence against a putative wrongdoer. This vigorous sense of individual responsibility prevented the protection of putative wrongdoers by family and local interests, and had the advantage of making all citizens equal, save for differences attached to special functions. The modern nation-state was to favour this procedure, and signs of its future development were already visible in Hohenstaufen southern Italy, Plantagenet England and Capetian France in the late thirteenth century. Typical of the period treated here, however, leadership in developing the inquisition was taken by the ecumenical Church and Italy's urban republics.

Digest 22 3 2 had it that 'proof is incumbent on him who charges, not on him who denies the charge', but a well-conducted inquisition obviated this rule because there was no accuser. Investigations were begun when persistent report reached the ears of a judge, one obtained from many worthy and honest men or, as Hubert of Bobbio (d. by 1245) put it, one 'not doubted by the people or a majority of the people'.[27] One result was that trials of usurers, traitors, violent criminals and heretics were usually initiated by, or based on, public opinion. Once sufficient indications of 'guilt' had been assembled to begin a trial, the report was converted into proof, mainly by means of sworn witnesses or voluntary confession. Strong preliminary indications of guilt made it difficult for lawyers to protect defendants, and a papal law heavily influenced by contemporary Italian criminal law, *Ad extirpanda* of 1252, forbade legal counsel for those charged with heresy. Even when permitted, counsel was limited to giving the defendant general advice.

Two other qualities marked inquisitorial trials. When witnesses needed protection against a defendant who was reputedly violent, as Albert of Gandino states, the latter was not given the names of those testifying against him. Adapted from Roman law, the *quaestio*, as torture was discreetly called, was also introduced into Italian urban law at Verona as early as 1228 and into almost all towns by mid-century. The crime had to be of unusual gravity, usually being restricted to treason (*crimen laesae maiestatis*), but because that crime had long ago been generously defined by Ulpian as an offence 'committed against the Roman people and its security', it soon extended to crimes of unusual violence and, again following Roman law, brought with it confiscation of a family property as well as death.[28]

---

[27] As in Albert of Gandino, *Tractatus de maleficiis* 17 (ed. Kantorowicz) II 100.
[28] *Digest* 48 1 7 and *Codex Theodosianus* 9 14 3 in *Code* 9 8 5.

In the mid-thirteenth century, John of Viterbo recommended that torture was to be used only when a suspect was very probably guilty, and jurists
counselled moderation, that it leave no lesions or broken bones. Once in
place, however, the *quaestio* was easily abused. The *Pastoral Eye* complains
that 'when proof is lacking in a criminal case, you [a *podestà*] turn straightway
to torture . . . nor do you consider how much trust should be put in this
procedure'. Some stand it better than others 'and hence confessions extorted
from defendants should not be considered as evidence of crime unless afterwards, having been free [from torture] for a time, they should persevere in
confession'.[29] Although providing only a partial proof requiring supplementa-
tion, torture seemed so effective in lay criminal cases that *Ad extirpanda*
recommended it in 1252:

> A *podestà* . . . is required to force all heretics . . . short of breaking limbs and danger
> of death . . . expressly to confess their error and accuse all other heretics whom
> they know . . . and their receivers and defenders, just as thieves and robbers of
> temporal things are forced to accuse their accomplices and confess the crimes they
> have committed.[30]

Italian secular courts reflected the rise of the popular parties in the urban
republics. Social utopianism joined democratic hope in accentuating community welfare, making social crime especially heinous. The establishment
of guilt no longer sufficed, and a confession by a 'criminal' was required to
confirm the laws or beliefs of the community from which he or she had
diverged. From being passive and protective, justice had become active and
penitential. So attractive was this law, indeed, that almost all Europe adopted
it, even the *quaestio*. Princes picked it up with enthusiasm. It was incorporated in the Neapolitan *Liber augustalis* of 1231 and constituted a chapter in
Castile's *Siete Partidas* forthrightly called 'De los tormentos'. Employed by
northern French tribunals by about 1300, to offer a partial proof confirming
the results of an inquest, in England it was used to make a defendant submit
to an inquest. The English version was known in France, but only in baronial
courts. Although jurists recommended it earlier, Germany's governments only
began to adopt it early in the fourteenth century.

Percipient though the new law was, it was harsh. The previous chapter
noted that political thinkers thought it wise to exclude the very poor and
very rich from the political community. A partial legal equivalent was the
reintroduction into criminal law of the Roman distinction between the
'honest' well-to-do and the 'humble' or 'vile' poor. Albert of Gandino, a
professional judge and *podestà*, asks the question whether

---

[29] *Oculus pastoralis* 6 5 Invectiva justitiae in ed. Muratori, *Antiquitates Italicae medii aevi* IX 853–54.
[30] Fiorelli, *La tortura giuridica nel diritto commune* I 80.

both rich and poor ought to be given like punishments. I answer that it depends on whether the penalties are pecuniary or corporal. If pecuniary, the law says that the penalty should be diminished for cause of poverty, as we see the *podestà* doing daily . . . If corporal [save for false testimony, forgery, treason and desertion in war], the poor are to be more severely punished.[31]

Nor may one weep only for the humble. At Bologna in 1282 and Pisa in 1286, popular party statutes proposed proceeding against magnates on the basis of rumour or likelihood, even permitting torture and condemnation as if a case 'had been fully proved'. In Parma in 1316, for example, the *quaestio* could be used on commoners only in the presence of the elected 'ancients', the heads of the popular party and those of the guilds:

saving and reserving that the *podestà* and the Captain [of the People] and their judges may torture magnates, nobles and powerful men . . . without the presence of the 'ancients' . . . Against all others of whatsoever condition one must proceed rationally and with such moderation that none fall into danger of death from the severity or damage of torture.[32]

In social war, it seems, anything goes.

---

[31] *De maleficiis* 39 22 8 (ed. Kantorowicz) 253.
[32] Cited in Dahm, *Untersuchungen zur Verfassungs- und Strafrechtsgeschichte der italienischen Stadt* 35.

Part Five

THOUGHT

Chapter 19

Intellectuals

Schools and universities

Around 1300, William Durand the Younger summarized papal legislation dating from 1179 through to 1215 and went on to propose that 'bishops are to provide masters in cathedral churches and major parish churches to teach poor students without cost . . . and a tenth part of all ecclesiastical benefices, both secular and regular, are to be assigned poor scholars in the faculties of the university by whom God's Church will be illuminated'.[1]

Details aside, this system was largely built and was being amplified by the foundation of residential colleges ostensibly for poor pupils, the earliest being created at Paris in 1180. In spite of this effort, most intellectuals came from families whose means bought supplementary or better education than most. Hired tutors taught noble and patrician children, and some young burghers and villagers were instructed by them, entered parish schools or became monastic oblates in order to be educated. The Church attempted to improve lower-school education and so did secular government. Testamentary bequests mention five parish schools in Toulouse between 1234 and 1257 and, in spite of sparse evidence, not a few rural parish schools were seen in the Lauragais south of town at mid-century. John Villani patriotically claimed that up to 10,000 Florentine boys and girls were learning to read and write, and that 1,200 students attended six abacus schools for arithmetic, and four great grammar schools housed up to 600 pupils of Latin and logic. Bonvesino of Riva, a teacher himself, asserts that Milan had about seventy teachers of elementary letters and eight professors of grammar in 1288. In 1253, the town of Ypres settled with St Martin's. The chapter was to provide the rector and masters of the 'great' schools whose costs were regulated. Under town licence, 'small' schools, teaching reading and writing, could be secular. Some communities even ran public facilities. In 1253, Lübeck founded a long-lived municipal Latin school. The division between these schools and universities was not fixed at this time.

The earliest university or 'high school' was the school of law at Bologna, privileged by the emperor in 1158 and confirmed by papal authority. The

---

[1] *De modo generali concilii celebrandi* 2 4 16 in *TUJ* XIII 165rb.

town of Bologna provided the teachers and the students, usually not citizens, and controlled and regulated the service sold to them, eventually winning a decisive hand in choosing instructors. In Paris, where masters were not citizens, the king recognized their association in 1200. Although the pupils also organized, the masters' association, divided into faculties or nations within the large faculty of arts, was the real university. Curiously, it was more disturbed and torn by problems about academic liberty than was the law school at Bologna. Differences aside, the two institutions had much in common. Both came under church law: the Lateran Council of 1179 regulated the licence for teaching, and degree requirements in both were formalized in the 1220s.

The university system expanded rapidly. Masters' associations like that of Paris formed schools at Oxford in 1214 and Cambridge in the 1230s. Montpellier built a faculty of medicine in 1220, and added one of law in the 1230s. In the north, Orléans evolved in the same decade, becoming north France's centre for legal study after the eradication of Paris's law faculty in 1219. In 1229, a school was founded at Toulouse to attack heresy. It faltered before southern hostility but, after the successful repression of Catharism in the early 1230s, it resumed to become France's premier law centre.

Between 1204 and 1248, no fewer than nine high schools appeared in urbanized Italy, six in the north and three from Rome south. Founded and licensed in 1224 by Frederick II, Naples was Europe's first state university, serving the whole of this prince's kingdom, and the same was true of the ancient school of medicine at Salerno, given royal privileges in 1231. Universities hardly existed elsewhere. Although initiatives date from as early as 1208–9 and Salamanca subsisted from 1254 until its collapse in the 1280s, Spain's schools did not get under way until around 1300. Germany lacked universities until after that date also, but the Dominican school at Cologne was famous.

With the exception of Paris and Bologna, these institutions were small and enrolled pupils at rather early ages, thus overlapping the lower schools. Thomas Aquinas had completed six years in the faculty of letters at Naples at the age of sixteen. As to size, a convocation of the liberal arts at Padua included two teachers in physics, one in logic and six in grammar and rhetoric. Alfonse X's unrealized foundation at Salamanca in 1254 was to have two civilian jurists, three canonists, two logicians, two grammarians and two physicists. Academic ceremonies had appeared: in 1215 Boncompagno of Signa read a work before the doctors and students of Bologna, and was then crowned with laurel, or so he reported.

During the thirteenth century, a curriculum of philosophy and theology became traditional. The schedule at Paris for a theology degree began with six years in the arts faculty, the last two as a bachelor attaining the master's degree. To become a theological doctor or 'divine', a student spent eight years in the theological faculty, devoting four years to biblical exegesis and Peter Lombard's *Sentences*, and four more as a bachelor disputant. During that period he also became a teacher, a member of the institution's basic teaching staff. For a time, commentaries on parts of the *Sentences* became the theological dissertation. Academic disputations (*quaestiones quodlibetales* or *disputatae*) embodied syllogistic methods used in such monumental works as Thomas Aquinas's *Theological Summa*. In addition, teachers wrote essays on various topics, as Aquinas's tracts *On Being and Essence* and *On the Rule of Princes*. Subjects requiring practical experience needed different methods. At Salerno, medical students read logic for three years and then devoted five years to Hippocrates, Galen and surgery. They were licensed after a final year of practical experience under a working physician.

Secular clerks usually returned to parish work after a few years of study. In the deanery of Stowe near Lincoln, only nine per cent of the rural priests had been touched by higher education in the 1230s, but by the 1270s twenty-one per cent had. Great careers required much study. Thomas Aquinas studied arts at Naples and, between visits to pick up degrees at Paris, spent over ten years with Albertus Magnus (d. 1280) in the Dominican school at Cologne. Thereafter he taught regularly at Paris, with periods at the papal court, Bologna and Naples. He also counselled popes, princes, bishops and church courts, dying on his way from Naples to attend the second Council of Lyons in 1274.

Although hobbled by officers such as the chancellor at Paris and the arch-deacon at Bologna, the masters' power was their monopoly of the right to examine students and thereby to control access to teaching. In 1231, the *Liber augustalis* defined Salerno's doctorate:

> We order that no one seeking the title of doctor shall dare to practise or otherwise heal unless first approved at Salerno by the judgement of the masters in a public examination. He should then enter our presence . . . with letters . . . from the masters and other doctors, and receive from us . . . the licence to heal.[2]

The power of masters to conduct examinations was admitted even at Bologna, where students chose the teaching staff.

Masters were as devoted to writing as their successors are today. A bio-grapher of Thomas Aquinas claimed that he had written nearly a hundred books. The Franciscan Ubertino of Casale (d. *circa* 1330) defended Peter John Olivi before the pope, saying: 'And your Apostolic Wisdom should know that the number of books by brother Peter . . . is twenty-seven times greater in quantity than Peter Lombard's *Sentences*.'[3] Writing a history of

---

[2] P.O. Kristeller, 'The School of Salerno' in *Studies in Renaissance Thought and Letters* (Rome, 1956) 528.

[3] Douie, *The Nature and the Effect of the Heresy of the Fraticelli* 95.

the Dominicans, Bernard Gui described the accomplishments of his order's scholarly luminaries as well as their holy men. Not that divines were slavishly respected. The distinguished Parisian theologian William of Auxerre (d. 1230) sat on a papal commission examining Aristotle's works, but Salimbene casually remarked that, although perhaps a great professor, he was an incoherent preacher.

Like many artists and architects, academic writers habitually signed their works. Few went as far as a jurist, the first letters of each chapter of one of whose works spelled out 'Roffredo of Benevento, professor of Roman law, author of this work'.[4] This example brings up plagiarism. Because learned pieces were directed to an audience already in the know, and because the sources were authorities whose opinions had to be attacked or relied on, both juristic and scholastic treatises cited authors, ancient and modern, by name. It was different when an audience was broader. Careful in his technical works, Thomas Aquinas did not bother to note his debt to Vegetius in his *On the Rule of Princes*, a work addressed to a non-learned audience. Other motives are also seen. Fearing to set his readers' teeth on edge before his argument had been swallowed, the secular master Henry Goethals of Ghent quoted but did not identify Aquinas when attacking his doctrine of original sin. The Dominicans spotted it anyway, and sprang to the defence of their doctor. Earlier authors were often shaved close. About a third of John Quidort of Paris's *On Royal and Papal Power* came from contemporaries such as Aquinas. Unlike today's authors who are impeded by copyright, medieval ones not only lifted ideas, but copied text as well.

Intellectuals are backbiters, and were so at this time. Roger Bacon claimed that divines such as Alexander of Hales and Albert the Great, who were trained before Aristotle's natural history was studied and had little mathematics, were incapable philosophers. The Franciscan Peter Auriole (d. 1322) was notorious for acidulous views about contemporaries and teachers, and William of Ockham later turned the tables on him, observing (probably falsely) that he had wasted barely a day reading Peter's works.

There was more here than envy, because institutional rivalry made for conflict. When, as shall be seen, the mendicant orders invaded the parishes, they were resisted at Paris by the secular masters. Supported by the popes, however, they forced their way in from 1229, when the first Dominican, Roland of Cremona, began teaching. The battle occasionally erupted as in the 1250s, when the career of the secular doctor William of St Amour (d. 1272) was ruined and he himself rusticated from Paris in 1260. During these combats, moreover, the mendicants split apart. The Franciscans attacked Aquinas, asserting the superior authority of their Bonaventure. Retarded by the Parisian

---

[4] *Quaestiones sabbathinae* in F.C. von Savigny, *Geschichte des römischen Rechts im Mittelalter* (Heidelberg, 1829) 5 186.

condemnation of certain propositions expounded by Aquinas in 1277, the canonization in 1323 and the revocation of the articles attacking this great Dominican in 1325 left no doubt as to the efficacy of his order's pressure. In 1287, a general chapter ordered the Austin friars to defend the opinions of their spokesman, Giles of Rome, against all comers. Divisions aside, the masters constituted an order based on competence in theology and philosophy, but their power was circumscribed by local and general powers. Aided by divines, Bishop Stephen Tempier of Paris condemned a series of Averroist and Aristotelian propositions, some Thomist, in 1277. Chancellor of the university in 1280, Geoffrey of Fontaines called this action scandalous because he claimed (exaggeratedly) that the commissioners were ignorant.

The papal monarch was weightier. Dissent was impermissible, the canonists said, once a pope had made a decision. But to intellectuals lawyers are always servile. Recalling William of St Amour's debates with the mendicants in the 1250s, the poet John of Meung called the university Christianity's guardian, far superior in that function to the popes. When the mendicants' privilege of preaching was again attacked in 1290, the secular masters took up the cudgels under Henry of Ghent. Henry asked why, since masters could discuss scripture, they could not question the privileges. The papal legate Benedict Gaetani (later Boniface VIII) angrily rounded on the masters:

> You sit in your chairs and think that Christ is ruled by your reasons . . . Not so, brothers, not so. Because the world has been committed to us [at Rome], we ought not think about what will humour you clerks, but about what is advantageous to the world . . . You believe you have great glory and commendation at Rome, but we judge you to be fatuity and blather [*fumus* = smoke] . . . I have seen your arguments, and they can be answered, and this is the answer . . .

Let there be no further question of the mendicants' privileges. Warming up, he added:

> And I tell you that before the Roman court will withdraw this privilege, it would sooner confound the University of Paris. We have not been called to be learned or appear glorious, but instead to save souls. Because the said brothers' life and teaching saves many souls, their privileges will always be preserved.

After this peroration, a master sourly observed: 'Lo! So valid and firm were the masters' arguments built up over ten years that they have all been shattered by the statement of one cardinal. What d'you think they'll say at Rome when all the masters seated in their chairs were unable to answer [him]?'[5]

The curial party won this battle because the mendicants and many French bishops stood behind it. It lost a later one because the French had defeated the papacy, the mendicants were divided and the conciliar idea of

---

[5] Finke, *Aus dem Tagen Bonifaz VIII*, Anhänge, V–VII.

ecclesiastical government – often led by the bishops of the Gallican church and the divines of Paris – was threatening papal monarchy. In an attempt to buttress Franciscan conservatives, John XXII supported the opinion of a commission of theologians on the Beatific Vision in 1333, to the effect that those dying in a state of grace would not see God face to face but would repair to Abraham's bosom, there to await the Last Trump. Others had quite different opinions, Aquinas, for example, having gone so far as to propose that both Moses and St Paul had seen God briefly even while they were alive. In 1334, amid much excitement, twenty-nine Parisian masters informed the king that the pope's opinion was purely personal, having no other significance than that he held it. The king then supported 'his' university. During the fray, the usually peppery John XXII was very defensive indeed when he wrote to the king: 'Because someone will perhaps tell you that we are not a master of theology, hear what a wise man says: "Give ear not to who speaks, but rather to what he says."'[6] And this embarrassed sage held an office whose doctrinal infallibility had been asserted at the second Council of Lyons in 1274! John withdrew his opinion before he died.

Learning and freedom

Education, it was thought, prepared humanity for heaven. Because most assumed that human reason was capable of comprehending some part of nature and even of glimpsing the deity, learning was almost idolized. This belief encouraged Latin minds to explore the wealth of ancient and Islamic thought to serve a Church that was busy leading the world and attempting to penetrate the beyond. Human reason, however, was inadequate. It did not obviate death, predict the morrow, explain the cosmos or define eternity, nor tell if behaviour was free or bound by fate. Some therefore favoured a different, non-rational way of looking at the world, one that had marked the Church from its earliest reaction against the thought of Greece and Rome.

Most intellectuals would have denied that they were balancing on a tightrope strung between the naturalism of reason's philosophy and the religion of man's need as expressed by theology. They were instead convinced that philosophy and theology combined together to argue for Christ. Thomas Aquinas put it thus:

> The gifts of grace are added to nature so that they do not do away with it, but instead perfect it. Hence the light of faith freely infused into us does not destroy the light of natural knowledge implanted in us naturally. Although the . . . human mind cannot show us things made manifest by faith, it is nonetheless impossible that that which faith gives is contrary to that implanted in us by nature. Were that the

---

[6] Heinrich Denifle and E. Chatelain, *Chartularium universitatis parisiensis* (Paris, 1889) I 436–37 No. 978.

case, one or the other would be false, and, since God gave both, He would be the author of untruth, which is impossible . . . Just as sacred doctrine is founded on the light of the faith, so is philosophy founded on the light of natural reason, and hence it is impossible that philosophical things are contrary to things of the faith.[7]

Given his bent for natural science, the Franciscan Roger Bacon believed that 'the objective of philosophy is to know the creator by what He has created'.[8] Philosophy, he thought, could help make man understand the Eucharist, which, he said, many deny, many doubt and many receive with repugnance. Writing earlier, before 1230, Roland of Cremona had explained: 'Because many believe that the human soul is corruptible and dies together with the death of man's organs . . . it seemed useful to me . . . to adduce philosophical reasoning.'[9] Even those questioning philosophy really favoured it. Bonaventure reminded his readers that Christians had always used non-Christian sources:

> Read [Augustine's] *On Christian Doctrine* where he shows that Holy Scripture cannot be understood without the skills of the other sciences, and that Israel's sons carried off Egypt's vases, just as [today's] divines appropriate philosophical teaching.[10]

The question, however, was whether reason and philosophy were equal to authority and theology. To those repeating Gregory the Great's (d. 604) assertion that 'faith to which human reason lends proof has no merit', Abelard had long before a ready answer: if someone claims that an idol is the true God, who, without reason, can disprove it? Aquinas was more tactful: reason teaches faith. Certainly, if only doubt is to be removed, authority is to be used, but if auditors are to be persuaded 'then one must lean on reason to investigate the truth and show how what is said is true'.[11]

New knowledge was often non-Christian. Preaching during the prohibition of the study of natural history at Paris, James of Vitry counselled scholars to avoid Plato and Aristotle. Theologians, he said, need no natural science and anyway Plato erred when saying that the planets were gods and Aristotle that the world was eternal. The Dominican general Humbert of Romans complained of ostentatious professors who always cited Plato, Aristotle, Algazel, Averroës, Alfarabi and other 'unworthy' philosophers. Some anti-Aristotelians, however, rejected this extreme. Bonaventure believed that even reading Christ's enemies was useful: 'if studious persons study heretical writings to better comprehend the truth by refuting them, they would neither be idly curious or heretical, but instead Catholic'.[12]

---

[7] *In Boetium de trinitate* 2 3 cited in Chenu, *La théologie comme science au treizième siècle* 88.
[8] *Opus maius* 2 7 (ed. Bridges) III 51.
[9] From his *Expositio in Job* in Chenu, *La théologie au douzième siècle* 28.
[10] *Epistola de tribus quaestionibus* 12 in *Opuscula varia* (Quaracchi, 1898) VIII 336ab.
[11] His *Homiliae in Evangelia* cited in Grabmann, *Die Geschichte der scholastischen Methode* I 144.
[12] *Epistola de tribus quaestionibus* 12 in *Opuscula varia* 336a.

Intellectuals shared few such reservations, and showed it in two ways. First, translations of scientific and philosophical works from Greek and Arabic appeared, including the recent works of Averroës (d. 1198) and Maimonides (d. 1204). The translators from Arabic were Gerard of Cremona (d. 1187) and Michael Scot (d. before 1235), and those from Greek were James of Venice (*fl.* 1140s) and especially the Dominican William of Moerbeke, who died in 1286 as archbishop of Corinth. Substantial segments of Greek theology by John Chrysostom (d. 403) and John of Damascus (d. 749) were also translated. Second, scholastics tried to smooth the rough edges of non-Christian thought. Guessing that the Greek had comprehended the Christian godhead, Abelard likened Plato's 'world soul' to the third person of the Trinity. John of Salisbury thought that Aristotle had awakened the Latin mind. In 1190 Daniel of Morley, worshipper at the Arabic shrine of Toledo, condemned Oxford and Paris for their hostility to natural science. Roger Bacon explained away the polytheism and sacrifices of his Roman favourites by asserting that 'these philosophers busied themselves with this because of the law and the multitude, not because of truth, as Seneca says in the book he composed about superstition'. Excerpting whole sections from Seneca to build his moral philosophy, he distinguished between earth and heaven:

> Although . . . [pagan] philosophers did not know the virtues that lead to grace, that is, faith, hope and charity, we Christians nevertheless . . . do not equal them in elegance of statement about the virtues commonly required for . . . human society . . . Christian philosophers must attentively study the [pagans'] great glory.[13]

Put simply, the divines were syncretist. Alan of Lille proposed first to prove the unity of the Trinity's 'essence by reasoning, second, by the varied authority of gentile philosophers and, third, by the authority of the holy fathers'.[14] He then cited anything that came to hand – ancient philosophers, hermetic writings, Arabs such as the astrologer Albumazar as well as Christian authors, old and new.

Even if contrary to the faith, therefore, non-Christian sources enjoyed authority. This did not rest only in the texts themselves but also in those who explicated them, the masters, a group enjoying a measure of autonomy with regard to the rest of the Church. Autonomy required self-police, however. Albert the Great, for example, did not agree with Peter Lombard on original sin, but said that he would uphold Peter's view out of respect. There were, of course, dissenters. The contentious Roger Bacon wanted the

---

[13] Both passages are in *Baconis operis maioris pars septima seu moralis philosophia* 1 8 and 3 5 proemium (ed. Eugenio Massa, Turin, 1953) 132.

[14] *Quoniam homines* I 1 prologue in ed. Pierre Glorieux, *Archives d'histoire doctrinale et littéraire du moyen âge* XXVIII (1953) 122.

Lombard's book replaced by the study of scripture, history, natural philosophy and mathematics. But in important matters solidarity existed. The revival of Aristotle was pushed just as avidly by Albert and Aquinas as by the Parisian extremists known as the Latin Averroists, after the Arabic commentator Averroës. That the masters thought of themselves as authorities, even church fathers, is shown in a book 'that is all gold, because herein are contained the golden sentences and questions of the holy fathers Augustine, Jerome . . . and of the modern masters William of Champeaux, Yves of Chartres and Anselm of Laon'.[15]

Nor can the measure of intellectual freedom attained be described only as a conflict between authority and reason. Reason's defenders were not disinterested intellectuals, but rather those whose claim to attention rested on their ancient and other non-Christian authorities. Theirs was, in short, the authority of the learned. Nor was authority simple. James of Vitry and others of Peter Cantor's circle were certainly opposed to Plato, Aristotle and natural philosophy, but they were no less revolutionary because of that. By trying to realize here on earth the utopia of the Acts of the Apostles, James and his colleagues tried to turn the world on its ear. The same may be said of the later radical Franciscan Peter John Olivi, who stoutly maintained that Aristotle had nothing to do with Christ. In brief, those who loved authority were often more revolutionary than those who loved reason.

Besides, authority required constant redefinition. Although no one was permitted to doubt, few basic doctrines were not susceptible to interpretation. At the time of the controversy over the Eucharist in the late eleventh century, contemporaries noted that Augustine differed from Ambrose and, to reconcile them, reason was employed, however tortuously. Later, Aquinas perceived that the doctors who preceded the Arian heresy did not speak as clearly about the unity of the divinity as those who followed it. He also noted that Augustine had changed his mind: 'in his books written after the birth of the Pelagian heresy he spoke more cautiously of the power of free will than in those he wrote before the said heresy'.[16] Earlier, Alan of Lille admitted that authority has a nose of wax that can be bent in any direction, an opinion applicable also to scripture, the source of all authority. Around 1324, a manual for preaching friars and parish priests stated that 'Sacred Scripture is a soft wax that takes the impression of every seal', now of the lion, now of the eagle, now of Christ, and now of the devil.[17] Authority, in fine, was like reason, both being traditions interpreted by persons advancing their favoured causes.

---

[15] The *Liber Pancrisis* cited in Chenu, *La théologie au douzième siècle* 358, dated to the second third of the century.

[16] The *proemium* of his *Contra errores Graecorum* in *Opera omnia* (Rome, 1967) XL A 71a.

[17] Prologue of the *Speculum humanae salvationis* (ed. Lutz and Perdrizet) 3.

Mainstream thought oscillated between avowing the usefulness of natural philosophy and reason and the opposing position, an oscillation most marked during institutional crises in Church life. Being static, somewhat anti-historical and inclined to justify whatever was, the naturalist position was not helpful when new institutions were needed. In revolutionary moments, utopians summoned the irrational urges of Christian hope. Once old institutional impediments had been demolished, however, reason's philosophers harmonized conflicting viewpoints. An illustration is seen during the Gregorian revolution, when the Church underwent institutional recasting and rose to lead Latin Europe. The 'rationalist' defenders of the symbolic interpretation of the Eucharist were then defeated by the spokesmen of the miraculous interpretation, and their champion Berengar of Tours was silenced in 1059. The 'irrationalists' won the day by claiming that priests miraculously renew the incarnation, binding God to humanity and its institutions. Still, although condemned, Berengar and his mystical belief in human reason had partly won the day. As he put it in his *On the Holy Communion:* 'to have recourse to dialectics is to have recourse to reason. And a being made in God's likeness who does not resort to it abandons his honour and cannot be daily renewed in God's image.'[18] By 1150, the Church's need for systematic organization led to the victory of the 'rationalists' in most matters. In the great battles about dialectics, Bernard of Clairvaux had momentarily silenced Peter Abelard and Gilbert of La Porrée, but the latter had really won the victory.

A similar crisis occurred around 1200. The repression of the great popular heresies and the opening of the Church to new forms of monasticism led to a general attack on all intellectual frontiersmen. Aristotelianism was assaulted at Paris in 1210 and 1215, and Amalric of Bène's (d. *circa* 1205–6) Platonic or pantheistic naturalism was repudiated there in 1210. Joachim of Fiore's utopian historicism was rebuked at the Lateran Council in 1215, and the Platonism of the Carolingian philosopher John the Scot Erigena's was outlawed in 1225. These traditions, however, were repressed only momentarily, and the mendicant professors of the Dominican order that rose during this crisis became the greatest exponents of the new learning.

The last crisis considered here took place around 1300, when the pullulation of the mendicant orders and their utopian wings was attacked. Divided internally, Church leadership was seriously questioned by lay society and the secular state. Some Thomistic propositions, Aristotelian naturalism, and especially the Averroist interpretation of that philosophy was questioned at Paris in 1270, and again in 1277, by the celebrated commission of Stephen Tempier, bishop of Paris. As exemplified in Olivi's work, Joachitic historical

---

[18] *De sacra cena* 5, cited in Henri de Lubac, *Corpus mysticum* 261.

utopianism was condemned. In Italy, the positions of determinist astrologers such as Peter of Abano, teacher of medicine at Padua, and Cecco of Ascoli, professor of astronomy at Bologna, were assaulted with great vigour. A pacific age followed, however, and the articles against Thomas Aquinas were retracted in 1325.

Intellectuals were sometimes punished for their opinions. Amalric of Bène suffered the obloquy of being anathematized after death, and the sect that his teaching inspired, like that of the later Olivites, was hunted down. William of St Amour was silenced and rusticated. Siger of Brabant (d. 1281–84) was on his way to Rome to clear himself when he died. Olivi had substantial parts of his work condemned from 1284 onwards but, formally submissive, appears to have gone on writing as he saw fit until his death in 1298. In spite of the death penalty so freely imposed on heretics and book burning, however, no teacher in the schools was killed: no master before the astrologer Cecco of Ascoli in 1327, and no theological divine before John Hus in 1415. Mitigation aside, the Church undoubtedly limited intellectual freedom. The famed Dominican Meister Eckhart, teacher at Paris and Cologne, died in 1327 while appealing to the Holy See against a condemnation issued by the archbishop of Cologne. Two years later, John XXII condemned twenty-eight of his propositions, an act that caused the loss of some of his work and vastly diminished his influence.

Hearing about thinkers busy in academe inadvertently introduces bias, because it overlooks another side of intellectual activity that churchmen believed essential. The distinguished Dominican jurist Raymond of Penyafort composed the major penitential manual of the age as well as the *Decretals of Gregory IX* in 1238, and was also busy as an administrator and executive. Four years after publishing the *Decretals*, he was elected General of his order and, two years before that, headed a council at Monzón in his native Catalonia. An inquisitor having been slain at nearby Castellbó, an expedition was launched against the place and here, according to his laudatory biography, Raymond imprisoned for life many Cathars and burnt not a few.

Perhaps because they lacked police unless they called on that of the Christian community, the Jews largely kept their disagreements to themselves, but were nevertheless rent by them. One crisis was precipitated by Maimonides's *Guide to the Perplexed*, an attempt to link revealed religion to the somewhat Platonized Aristotle of Arabic philosophical circles. Europe's rabbinate reacted strongly, especially in north France and Germany. Although less successful than its parallel among Christians, the defence of the new thought was similar. A medical doctor from Barcelona and Rome, Seraiah son of Isaac, grandson of Salathiel, said about a celebrated rabbi of Barcelona: 'Nahmanides was a Talmudist who understood nothing of philosophy and therefore attacked Maimonides . . . He would have done better to be silent because a judge must first understand what he is judging.' Nahmanides had himself actually defended Maimonides, using terms that would have been familiar to Parisians favouring Aristotle and Averroës. He asked the Talmudists: 'Did Maimonides seek to disturb your greatness in Talmudic studies when he wrote a book designed to be a refuge against the Greek philosophers Aristotle and Galen? Have you ever read these books, or have you been seduced by your own arguments?'[19] Led by Rabbi Solomon son of Abraham, Montpellier's Jews denounced the *Guide* to the Dominican inquisitors, who obligingly burned it in 1233.

---

[19] The first cited passage is in Güdemann, *Geschichte des Erziehungswesen . . . der Juden* II 157–8 and the second in ibid. I 72.

Chapter 20

Reason and religion

History and progress

History helps educate mankind towards the good. Gerald of Wales outlined its advantages:

> Careful reading of the histories of the ancients helps princes because it warns of the chancy outcome of war, of difficult and fortunate circumstances, of hidden traps and [needed] precautions. History teaching, princes may examine as though in a mirror past actions to see what is to be done, what avoided, what fled and what pursued.[1]

Godfrey of Viterbo addressed his versified history to the Emperor Henry VI with this monition: 'An emperor cannot attain true glory unless he knows the course and origin of the world.... Learned in philosophy an emperor is thought to stand before other men, but, if ignorant, he appears to err or stray rather than reign.'[2] Specious practicality aside, myth was intertwined with history. Martin of Troppau repeated the fictions that Charlemagne had visited Jerusalem and that Pope Sylvester II (Gerbert of Aurillac, d. 1003) had, like Faust, sold his soul to the devil to get Arabic mathematical and scientific knowledge. And Martin, papal penitentiary, prelate and counsellor of princes, provided historical information for intellectuals of the stature of Marsiglio of Padua and William of Ockham!

History was moralistic and programmatic. Godfrey of Viterbo, for example, repeated the myth that the Trojans had moved to Europe where they founded Rome and the Frankish kingdom. From Carolingian times, Troy was thought to have given the Franks, a people unconquered by Rome, the natural right to govern others. John Quidort of Paris used this history to argue against putting the Church above the state. Among the Franks (that is, the French) royal power had clearly preceded ecclesiastical authority: 'Hence royal power is not from the pope either intrinsically or in terms of exercise, but instead from God and the people electing the king either in person or dynasty... To say then that royal power derives first from God and afterward from the

---

[1] *De principis instructione* 1 11 in *Rolls Series* XXVIII viii 42–43.
[2] *Memoria seculorum* prologue in *MGH SS* XXII 103.

pope is utterly ridiculous.'[3] But there was more to history than myth. Quidort accurately said that in the days of the sainted Emperor Henry III (d. 1056) no pope was elected without imperial assent, and ecclesiastical unction, although mentioned in the Old Testament, is nowhere found in the New. Besides, unction was not applied in the Iberian monarchies.

From Abelard on, those of the rational or dialectical tradition viewed human history as static; great changes were unlikely to take place until the end of time. Times change, but not the faith; small things are mutable, but great ones unchanging. Historian of the early twelfth century, Otto of Freising divided history into three ages: the Old Testament and the law, the present age of the New Testament and the sacraments, and a third age, the end of the world. Today's age chronicled the histories of successive empires and was a time of senescence, awaiting the Antichrist and the Last Days. Thomas Aquinas also likened modernity to senescence:

> The last age is the present, after which there is no further age of salvation's [history], just as there is no further age after old age. Although men's other ages have a determined number of years, that is not so in old age, because it begins at the sixtieth year and some live for 120 years. Hence it is not determined how long this age of the world will last.'[4]

Some found modernity superior to earlier ages. Priscian's ancient tag 'the more recent, the more perspicacious' was often quoted, and John of Salisbury and Peter of Blois stated that, although mere dwarfs on the shoulders of giants, moderns see further than the ancients. In the early thirteenth century, Boncompagno of Signa said that the old saw 'there's nothing new under the sun' was only true in a limited sense. God, after all, daily creates new souls, putting them into new bodies and, working with primordial matter, a common 'artisan shapes it into new forms at will'. Indeed, the Incarnation's renovation of grace proves that man, God's creation, sees things with new eyes, whence the apostle Paul 'ordered him who came first to be silent when something has been revealed to him who comes after'.[5]

Around 1255, Rolandino Passaggeri noted that old manuals on contracts were useless because they were designed for the ancients. Although perhaps more virtuous than moderns, the result was that their authors:

> were ignorant of the subtleties of modern man . . . And 'because the more a thing is modern, the more it is perspicacious', our age brings with it in contract law as in other matters new and more subtle ways of doing things. It is therefore fitting that we should put old laws aside . . . because they are somehow foreign to, or lack congruence with, any or few modern subtleties. As in other things, we should make

[3] *De potestate regia et papali* 10 (ed. Bleienstein) 113.
[4] *In epistolam ad Hebraeos* 9 5 cited in Chenu, *La théologie au douzième siècle* 76.
[5] *Rhetorica novissima* prologue in *BIMA* II 252.

a new law reflecting today's ways and methods . . . in order to improve our way of life.[6]

Borrowing from Aristotle, Aquinas asked whether or not human law can be changed. It could:

because human reason naturally moves step by step from the imperfect to the perfect. Whence we see in the speculative sciences that those who first philosophized provided imperfect results which were afterward made more perfect by their successors. Similarly in practical matters, those who first tried to find something useful for the human community, being unable to understand everything, introduced things in many ways deficient; but their successors replaced these with ones far less faulty.[7]

This moderate idea of man's advancement did not attract enthusiasts who required stronger stuff. This alternative vision was expressed by Joachim of Fiore:

When scripture says, 'the eye is not satisfied with seeing nor the ear filled with hearing', it means that full and unending pleasure is to drink not what has been tasted but instead what is yet to be tasted, nor to hear what has been heard and interpreted by the fathers, but rather to hear something new from God's inexhaustible treasure, something we lack of divine wisdom.[8]

To this was added history. The Parisian canon and teacher Hugh of St Victor distinguished the spiritual character of each age in the faith's history, each of them having within it the prophets of the succeeding one, the men before their time.

The Premonstratensian Anselm of Havelberg, who died as archbishop of Ravenna in 1158, defended the multiplication of new orders by saying that spiritual progress was essential to the Church. Although humanity was living in the last of three ages, that initiated by Christ's coming, he found progress there. Seven seals, or periods, were delineated, of which humankind was in the fourth and, in spite of persecutions, each age was one of fulfilment through which the Church wound its upward course. Praising new orders, Vallumbrosans, Cistercians and others, Anselm said: 'From generation to generation, God's wonderful dispensation causes the youth of the Church to be ever renewed by a new order, just as the youth of the eagle which seeks to fly higher in contemplation.' Nor is it surprising that an unchanging God allows the Church to be changeable 'because it is necessary that, according to time's progression, the signs of spiritual grace should increase and increasingly declare the truth. Thus, together with the desire for it, the knowledge of the truth will grow in the course of time, and so first good things were

---

[6] *Summa artis notariae* I *praefatio* (Venice, 1583) I 2v, and *Code* 3 38 3.

[7] *Summa theologiae* I–II 97 1 c.

[8] *Tractatus super quatuor evangelia* (ed. Ernesto Buonaiuti, Rome, 1930) 195, and Ecclesiastes 1:8.

published, then better, and lastly the very best.'[9] Indeed, scripture revealed itself progressively. Richard of St Victor (d. 1173) glossed the text: 'And when he opened the third seal' – that is, when, according to the progress of time, the effect of the divine promise and the progress of human salvation more and more began to be discerned and known in scripture – 'I heard the third beast saying, "Come and see"'![10]

By the latter part of the century these ideas had been much elaborated. A Benedictine who likened Benedict of Nursia (d. about 747) to John the Baptist, Odo, abbot of Battle (d. 1200), had a scheme of four ages. The 'first testament God gave men's hearts was called natural law and, had they obeyed it, they would not have needed a second. But since men are habitual lovers of novelty, he gave them a second testament, that of circumcision.' A third time, the deity brought them out of indifference with the testimonial of

> baptism which was predestined to remain for all eternity. But because long and inveterate custom began to lead man again bit by bit into neglect, He gave a fourth testament, the monastic cowl, to which . . . novelty's lovers have now gravitated. There will be no fifth testament because, in a new and wonderful way, the blessings of all peoples are contained in [the fourth].[11]

Tied to an unfolding revelation in history of an ever purer morality of brotherhood in the procession of the three persons of the Trinity, varieties of this monastic vision gave enthusiasts something analogous to the fervours of the modern idea of progress. The best example was the teaching of Joachim of Fiore and those who claimed to follow him. This abbot envisaged the successive ages of the Father, Son and Holy Ghost. Advancing from the slavery of the Mosaic law to the lighter burden of Christ's law, humanity was to be fulfilled in the spiritual freedom of the Holy Spirit, when all were to receive and live on earth some part of the monastic calling. As did the nearly contemporary 'children's crusade' and Francis of Assisi's exemplification of childhood's 'innocence', Joachim replaced old age with youth as the mark of the age to come. In Old Testament times, the maturity of the aged taught mankind to shun the transitory and cleave to the lasting. In that of the New Testament, the patience of the young became the teacher. In the third age, leadership was surrendered to childhood's sincerity, uncorrupted by property and the flesh. Joachim not only believed that the Church, including Peter's see, was soon to be replaced and purified by spiritualized monks, but also that it would itself foster the change. 'For just as old Simeon lifted the boy [Christ] in his arms, so the successors of Peter . . . seeing this order following Christ's footsteps in spiritual virtue, will sustain it by [their] authority.'

---

[9] Anselm's quotations are in *Dialogus* I 10 in *PL* CLXXXVIII 1157 and 1160.

[10] Kamlah, *Apokalypse und Geschichtstheologie* 118, and Revelation 6:5.

[11] Letter to a novice in Jean Mabillon, *Vetera analecta* (Paris, 1723, rprt.) 477b.

Indeed, the old order will rejoice in its replacement: 'Nor should it lament its own dissolution since it knows that it will remain in a better succession . . . What order can grieve that it lacks perfection in itself, when a universal perfection succeeds it?'[12]

Although progress was ineluctable, Joachim did not promise an easy victory. Before the angel pope ushered in paradise on earth, an apocalypse complete with Antichrist and Armageddon was to afflict mankind. Even before that, there were to be battles. Joachim attacked the static image of trinitarian unity found in Peter Lombard's *Sentences*, insisting on the historical procession of the three persons. Showing that the old order was not prepared to step down as quietly as the abbot envisaged, this view was roundly condemned by the pope and bishops at the Lateran Council in 1215. Perhaps Joachim suspected this recalcitrance, because he had not infrequently referred to the present Church as the 'great whore', a view warmly espoused by his sectaries. Indeed, although the abbot was vague about details, Joachites in Italy and elsewhere, like the earlier Amalricians at Paris, proclaimed the abolition of the old Church. William the Breton reported that the Parisians had argued

> that the power of the Father lasted as long as the Mosaic law; and, because it is written, 'the old shall be cast out when new things come in', after Christ came, they abolished all the sacraments of the Old Testament, and the new law flourished up to this time. They said that today the sacraments of the New Testament are come to an end and the time of the Holy Spirit has begun, in which confession, baptism, the Eucharist and other sacraments without which salvation cannot be had have no longer any further place, but each man inwardly can be saved without any exterior act merely through the grace of the Holy Spirit.[13]

The Parisian Amalricians believed that the age of the Holy Spirit had begun, or would within five years, but according to the Franciscan Hugh of Digne (d. by 1257), Joachim of Fiore never actually named a time, although it was imminent. Both his enemies and the later Franciscan Spirituals, however, were sure that he had. When Joachitic views were condemned at Anagni in 1255, a judge stated:

> So much for the words of Joachim, by which he strives in a bizarre way to exalt I know not what order that will come, as he says, at the end of the second age, of which there now remain only five years . . . by which, I say, he seeks not only to exalt [his order] over all other orders, but also above the whole Church and the whole world, as is clearly stated in many passages of the above work.[14]

---

[12] *Tractatus super quatuor evangelia* (ed. Buonaiuti) 80, and Luke 2:25ff.

[13] *De gestis Philippi II* in Grundmann, *Religiöse Bewegung im Mittelalter* 365–66, and Leviticus 26:10.

[14] Second article in Heinrich Denifle, 'Das Evangelium aeternum und die Commission zu Anagni' in *Archiv für Litteratur- und Kirchengeschichte des Mittelalters* II (1900) 112.

Explaining why the abbot's doctrines had failed to elicit broad support, Hugh of Digne put his finger on the truth. What prevented 'Abbot Joachim from being believed was that he predicted future tribulations. This was why the Jews had slain their prophets . . . Carnal men do not willingly hear about future tribulations, only about consolations.'[15] Lastly, if Joachim had not named a date, his followers certainly had.

The idea of lost primal bliss also encouraged men such as Robert of Curzon to envisage recovering the apostles' primitive community, and Francis of Assisi and the extremist wing of his order tried to imitate the Saviour or the apostles. Nor did this restoration conflict with the idea of progress, because if humanity had the capacity to reproduce lost perfection it proves that God had made the species perfectible. Obviously, that Francis equalled the Saviour or the Franciscans the apostles could not be claimed, but this impediment could be side-stepped. Borrowing from Peter John Olivi, Ubertino of Casale, a leader of the Spiritual Franciscans, formulated a solution in 1305. Francis and his brethren were certainly not equal to Christ and the apostles, but there had been something unfulfilled about the apostolic age. Because of the synagogue's perfidy and because the gentiles were then incapable of understanding so spiritual an idea, 'the Holy Spirit showed the apostles that the perfection of the evangelical life was not at that time open to the multitude. Whence the apostles did not require perfection to be observed in the churches they ruled, that perfection they themselves accepted when imposed by Christ and which they fully followed.'[16] Referring to Joachim of Fiore, Ubertino observed that the apostolic mission was not to be spread to the multitude until a later time, the sixth seal of the seventh age, by his calculation. As John the Divine had prophesied in Revelation 7:2, that age was to see the coming of the angel ascending from the east, bearing the sign of the living God. To Ubertino and his followers this angel was Francis of Assisi, and he noted in passing that Bonaventure had also asserted this identity when preaching at Paris. In short, Francis was not Christ nor the Franciscans the apostles, but Christ's apostolate was to be made real only by the Franciscans in their own age.

Linked to a utopian view of man's relation to his neighbour, this idea of progress was expressed in attacking usury, aiding economic corporatism and exalting poverty and communal living. The historical vision was also combined with the natural history and moral sociology of the Aristotelians. In Roger Bacon, inventions such as flying machines and optical devices were to be joined to an accurate forecasting of astral and geographical influences, a correct ordering of law and society, the abolition of sexual and moral

---

[15] Recounted in Salimbene's *Cronica* 15 in *MGH SS* XXXII 238.
[16] *Arbor vitae crucifixae Jesu Christi* 5 1 (Venice, 1485, rptd) 422a.

irregularity and educational reform. All were needed to defeat the Tatars, the Saracens and the soon-to-appear Antichrist:

> I do not wish 'to set my mouth against the heavens', but know that if the Church studied Holy Scripture, sacred prophecy, the predictions of the Sibyl, Merlin, Aquila, Joachim and others, and also the histories and books of the philosophers, and ordered astronomy to be studied, a sufficient or even certain estimate of the time of the Antichrist would be discovered . . . All the wise believe that we are not far from that time. Because individuals, cities and whole regions can be changed for the better according to the aforesaid, life can be prolonged as long as necessary, all things managed functionally, and even greater things can be done . . . not only in the natural sciences, but also in the moral sciences and arts, as is evident from Moses and Aristotle.[17]

Intellectuals felt hopeful as they dealt with natural history, because, as seen above, they accepted the notion that, since nature begins with less perfect forms, the later the time, the more perfect the creature or thing. Reinforcing this vision was human success: everywhere forests and swamps were being cleared, architecture and metalwork surpassed in quantity and equalled in quality the achievements of antiquity, and transportation was taking decisive steps forward. Not that this age saw technological innovation on a scale comparable to today, but humankind could nevertheless imagine that nature beneficently welcomed human use. Exploitation is catching: just as the Latins plundered Greek and Muslim society economically, so did they intellectually. The spate of new translations of Arabic, Jewish, Byzantine and classical sources mentioned briefly above attests the Latins' ability to use others' ideas. Albert the Great may not have been inventive, but his encyclopaedic interest in the sciences – indeed, in all kinds of subjects and authors – exemplifies the aggressive confidence of the Latin mind.

Science and determinism

A wide gap lay between the theoretical sciences of the schoolmen and the practical techniques of artisans, architects and others, but its size can be exaggerated. As the occasional act ennobling or granting privileges to architects or masters of works in Italy shows, the higher practical arts were not rigidly separated from the liberal ones. Practice and theory were necessarily distinguished, but their relationship was also recognized in apprenticeship contracts recorded by Rolandino Passaggeri. Neophytes were instructed in both the practice and theory of an art or craft. Anent the medical profession, the translator Dominic Gundisalvo, archdeacon of Segovia (d. after 1190), paraphrased Alfarabi:

---

[17] A composite quotation from the *Opus maius* 4 16 on Mathematics and Astrology (ed. Bridges) I 269 and 402, and Psalms 72 (73):9.

The royal virtue is composed of two virtues, one consisting of the knowledge of universal rules and the other of observation and assiduity in working and testing. A medical doctor does not become a perfect physician unless he knows universal rules or theory and unless he also shows ability in healing the sick with medicines, which is called practice.[18]

Some humanists played with science. Essentially literary, Alexander Neckham, who had taught at Paris and died as abbot of Cirencester in 1213, compiled not only a moralized account of natural history, but also a dictionary of tools and domestic implements. The age's great mathematician, Leonard Fibonacci of Pisa (d. after 1240) – whose own work, although theoretical, was not philosophical or speculative – kept in touch with those who were. He dedicated his manual of geometry to an astronomer and his *Book of the Abacus* to the translator and astrologer Michael Scot.

Nevertheless, the gap was wide and technological lack may well have been its principal explanation. The inability to do much with what knowledge there was led minds interested in natural science towards metaphysical speculation or to play with magic. Their difficulty was not that they postulated a necessary interlinking of all of nature's parts from the stars to the earth and a common quality, or essence, within all its elements. It was rather that neither natural philosophers nor magicians could use their possibly valid vision to transmute metals, predict the course of nature or, save for the most obvious phenomena, show the effects of the heavenly movements on human life. Both common sense and anti-intellectualism therefore lay behind the widespread mockery of such learning, popular though they often were. To Boncompagno alchemy was futile: its adepts never accomplished anything, because, as he put it, their subject contained nothing, and nothing is true about nothing. Moreover, 'intelligent sailors know more about the changes of the weather than learned astrologers'. Mathematicians also excited his scorn: 'you really have little or nothing to boast about because you merely count other people's money, and in this you're like common moneychangers. So don't boast about the science of numbers because there's scarcely anyone so stupid that he can't count his own money.'[19]

The vulgarities of common sense were combated, however, by strong intellectual traditions, Platonic and Aristotelian. Although Aristotle wrote the basic textbook, he was too secular, too narrow to encompass man's moods or inspire utopian hope and feelings of certitude, but Plato added an emotional melodiousness to this monotone intellectualism. The marriage of the two led to useful work, as is exemplified by the study of optics by Robert Grosseteste and his followers, including the famed popularizer Roger Bacon.

---

[18] *De divisione philosophie, de partibus practice philosophie* in ed. Ludwig Baur *Beiträge zur Geschichte der Philosophie des Mittelalters* (Münster, 1903) IV ii–iii 135.

[19] *Rhetorica novissima* 8 3 in *BIMA* II 289b.

Trying to harmonize the illuminate mysticism of Platonic Augustinianism with Aristotelian naturalism, these latter-day Boethians linked dialectics, the experiential side of the natural sciences and mathematics to create something like a scientific method. Bacon summed it up:

> There are two ways of knowing, argument and experience. Argument demonstrates and makes us concede conclusions, but it does not certify or remove doubt . . . until truth is discovered by experience . . . Since arguments do not verify [propositions], abundant experiences are to be carefully examined by means of instruments . . . for everything depends on experience.

And mathematics was the science that lent certainty to experience:

> In mathematics we attain full truth without error and certitude without doubt in all things because mathematics provides a demonstration by means of its own necessary cause . . . In sciences without mathematics, there are so many doubts, so many opinions, so many errors that they cannot be explained . . . since a demon-stration by their own necessary causes is absent in them . . . In natural entities there is no necessity because of the generation and corruption of their own causes and therefore of their effects . . . In mathematics alone is there certitude without doubt.[20]

Natural science, like history, posed the problem of determination. In his *Introduction to Astronomy*, translated by John of Seville around 1133, Albumazar argued that the planets 'show that a man can choose only what they prognosticate because his choice of a thing or of its contrary is made by the spirit of reason which is implanted in the individual's living mind by means of planetary influences'.[21] John of Salisbury apprehended that this emphasis on nature or the stars' role in determining human and natural history subsumed God into nature, thus depriving both God and humanity of free will. John's opposition was nevertheless moderate. Like Aquinas later on, he saw value in astrology:

> Although no faith should be put in auguries, I do not deny the value of those signs which divine disposition has given to educate God's creatures. 'For in many places and many ways, God instructs his creatures' . . . making clear what will happen now by the voices of the elements, now by the evidences of sensible and insensible things.[22]

Accommodation aside, fears inspired by astrological and natural determination helped provoke the assault on Aristotelian naturalism at Paris in the early thirteenth century.

---

[20] *Opus maius* 6 1 and 12 (ed. Bridges) II 166 and 201 and ibid. 4 1 13, I 105–6, the first being a composite quotation.
[21] Lemay, *Abu Ma'Shar and Latin Aristotelianism in the Twelfth Century* 128n.
[22] *Policraticus* 2 2 (ed. Webb) I 417a. See Hebrews 1:1.

In spite of opposition, astral, geographical and climatological theories of determination invented by the ancients and elaborated by the Arabs were accepted among intellectuals. So familiar were these by 1300 that they were used to explain the natural liberty of one's own people, as Peter Dubois did for the northern French, and the slavishness of others, as did Ptolemy of Lucca for Greeks. Much could be accepted if, as did Aquinas, natural determination was restricted to man's lower nature. It was even permissible to find human morals determined by climate or the stars, if these were limited by man's free will, God's grace, the devil and even, as Bacon quaintly added, good or bad advice, especially in childhood. Both Albert the Great and Bacon thought that the practical weakness of astronomical determination could be avoided and its value affirmed by broadening its focus. Bacon said: 'It was not Ptolemy's intention for an astrologer to render sure judgement in specific cases . . . he can, however, render a limited judgement in a general matter, one midway between the necessary and the impossible.'[23]

This muffled advice rarely restrained those whose inclinations were totalitarian or who responded to the human need for predictability. Bacon's own utopianism led him not only to believe in relationships between astronomical conjunctions and historical events, such as the 'children's crusade', but also to predict that astrology would be a useful weapon in the forthcoming war against the Antichrist.

Nature and freedom

At Paris, Henry Goethals of Ghent observed about the relationship of divine and natural law to positive law that 'our design is to live according to nature'.[24] An Augustinian critic of Thomistic Aristotelianism, Henry did not mean what a modern or an ancient would by this phrase, but clearly conceived of a world in which it was meaningful to link God, nature and man. Even stronger were Aquinas's opinions. Philosophy:

> first proves things one needs to know in order to understand the faith . . . things proved by natural reason concerning God, namely, that He exists, that He is one, or similar things concerning Him or his creatures. Second, to make known things of the faith by means of analogy, just as Augustine in his book *On the Trinity* used many analogies taken from philosophy in order to explain the Trinity.[25]

The masters faced real quandaries. Perhaps because of Platonic influence, those who elevated nature claimed that the deity endowed mankind with intellect and matter with individuality and particular form. This was the root

---

[23] *Opus maius* 4 judicia astronomiae (ed. Bridges) I 245.
[24] *Quodlibet* 2 question 17 cited in Lagarde, *La naissance de l'esprit laïque* III 253.
[25] *In Boetium de trinitate* cited in Chenu, *La théologie comme science au treizième siècle* 59.

of the varied pantheisms attributed to Amalric of Bène and David of Dinant early in the thirteenth century, and also of the doctrine described as the unity of the intellect, ascribed to Averroës and the Latin Averroists, especially Siger of Brabant. Such doctrines not only weakened a Christian's conviction of corporeal and personal immortality, but also, by making both individuation and the individual's capacity to think dependent on the emanations of a necessarily uniform divine spirit, threatened individual responsibility. Writing in 1323, Thomas Aquinas's biographer William of Tocco congratulated his hero:

> Quite apart from the said great volumes . . . in which he confuted the ancient heresies, he . . . destroyed the heresies of his own time, of which the first was that of Averroës, who said that there was one intellect common to all men. This error encouraged the crimes of the wicked and detracted from the virtues of the saintly, since, if there is but one mind in all men, there is no difference between men or distinction of merits. This [teaching] even penetrated the minds of the ignorant and spread so dangerously that when a certain knight was asked in Paris if he wished to purge himself of his crimes, he answered: 'If the soul of the blessed Peter is saved, mine will be also, because, since we know everything by one intellect, we share the same fate.'[26]

To defeat Platonizing Aristotelians, Aquinas turned to Aristotle and followed him in locating the source of individuation and cognition in the matter initially created and then enlivened by the divine spirit. Since no two things in nature are exactly alike, this seemed to resolve the problem of individuation and intellection. It required, however, that Thomas play again a game that had been played earlier in antiquity and Islam. The perception given to an individual by his material corporeality had somehow to be linked to the uniform divine intellect that sparked the matter into being. This was done by postulating a series of intermediary intellects, active, possible and so on. Not only was this cumbersome, but it also indicated to some that the Thomistic solution did not differ much from that of the Averroists. From Bonaventure through the condemnations at Paris in the 1270s, the so-called Augustinians tarred the Thomists with the Averroist brush.

The Augustinians also searched for a way out of the quandary. Although retaining much of the apparatus of the active and possible intellects, they simplified matters and based man's intellectual endowment on God's intervention through special illumination. Pushed far enough, the cure was as bad as the malady. On the one hand, the direct application of God's illumination to seemingly random and particular cases had the advantage of freeing a theologian from having to explain the unexplainable by means of reason, but it left him with two worlds, that of divine intellection and that of

---

[26] *Vita S. Thomae Aquinatis* 4 in *AA SS* March 1 664BC.

human or natural perception, linked only by unpredictable divine initiatives. This helped not at all in justifying human institutions: it is lovely when God loves sinners, but ugly when he does not love those who, in human terms, are good. Confounding the regularities of divine illumination with the arbitrariness of grace, this teaching served to comfort only those who believed that they had found in particular institutions – as did Joachite Franciscans – or even in their own lives – as did Francis of Assisi and some heretics – the tracks of divine intervention that had not illuminated other institutions or persons.

The other side of the illuminist argument, however, brought the theologian back to where he had started from. To assert that God had so endowed humanity that all possessed a capacity to understand and live according to moral truths was equally unsatisfactory. This position's weakness was that, since everyone had the capacity to be good and yet only some exercised it, an individual's free will was what enabled him or her to be good. As was later charged against Ockham, this opinion smacked of the Pelagian heresy because it weakened the primal motivating force of divine election or predestination. God endowed mankind with a capacity to be free but, like Aristotle's deity, he had left it up to the individual to make the choice. And what did that choice have to do with grace?

Because God was the source of all loveable things such as freedom, truth and beauty, it was necessary to define His freedom. Divine freedom had always posed insoluble problems, ones so weighty and frightening that they invited playfulness. The Latin father Jerome, Peter Damian, Alan of Lille and Thomas Aquinas all debated whether God could wholly restore a violated woman's virginity. In short, could God undo what He had done? Augustinians of Damian's stripe replied that, although God generally acted predictably, He could do what He wanted because to bow to necessity is offensive to divine omnipotence. Alan of Lille argued the other side:

> Opposing this, I say that God cannot change what has taken place, because, if He did, He would obviate His own will and his orderly arrangement of things. For since He willed that there be a world, if He now wishes that there never had been one, He would go against His own will, which God forbid![27]

God's will, in fine, was so strong that He could not change His mind!

To bind divine freedom to what had been created satisfied some. Writing around 1310–13, Dante Alighieri, who elsewhere praised both Thomas Aquinas and the Averroist Siger of Brabant, overturned Augustine's celebrated denial of a moral foundation for the Roman state. Justifying secular authority, he applauded the virtue of the Romans, the spread of whose empire was,

---

[27] *Quoniam homines* 1 2 4 in ed. Glorieux, *Archives d'histoire doctrinale et littéraire du moyen âge* XXVIII (1953) 233.

in his opinion, divinely ordained. Derived from ancient sources, the notion that God justified the Romans was stated at length by Jordan of Osnabrück around 1281, and Ptolemy of Lucca expounded Roman natural virtue shortly thereafter. Dante copied this idea, but added nature to the equation. For him, God's will was expressed in the world by the principle of right. Rome's capacity to conquer and to govern proved that its empire was in accord with nature's right order:

> It is clear that nature ordains things with respect to their capacities, which respect is the basic right placed in things by nature. From this it follows that the natural order cannot be conserved in things without right, since the fundamental principle or right is annexed to [nature's] order . . . The Roman people was ordained by nature to rule.[28]

What was, then, was right!

This was awkward. Since the past is the precondition of the present, the creator is bound to his creation. As Averroists were said to have put it, God cannot but produce and create, and that creation is necessarily good. Although this description of God and nature could be greeted with complacency when circumstances were happy, it relies on a limited segment of experience. Dualist sectarians such as the Cathars were not alone in believing that everything in creation was not good. Some of the orthodox were also not convinced by the familiar arguments that evil was merely the absence of good and human misery merely a punishment for sin. In a manual of love letters, Boncompagno of Signa repeated a common theme. Writing to a nun unwilling to bow to his suit and who said that she wished to commit adultery at the expense of the Lord of Hosts, the annoyed lover replied that he would 'rather violate the bed of Him who has slain my parents and relatives, and who visits us with storms, hail and tempests, than that of any human who can harm few or none'.[29]

To describe the divine principle, moreover, as bound to its creation and prior ordinances fails to account for the unpredictable and, for each mortal, the unknowable in life. Augustinians such as John Duns Scotus (d. 1308) argued that, since God is the first cause, were He bound by a necessity derived from His own nature or subject to a pressure exerted by His creation, all freedom and judgement would be destroyed among men and women. God must be free for humanity to have a hope of freedom.

Averroist or Thomist, the adherents of Aristotelian thought were aware of the insufficiencies of the teaching that they espoused. Thomists escaped its limitations by emphasizing God's freedom to perform miracles; in short, by insisting on God's magic and man's free will. Their Augustinian critics

---

[28] *De monarchia* 2 6 (ed. Gustavo Vinay, Florence, 1950) 148.
[29] *Rota veneris* (ed. Baethgen) 21–22.

dismissed such exceptions, keeping their eyes glued to the general system. What made it worse for Aquinas and other innovators of what a modern has called 'natural theology' was that Aristotelian teachings were often in conflict with the faith. Opposed to the Christian's historical view, with its creation, its incarnation and other clear demarcations of human and divine history, was the static Aristotelian human and natural history, a teaching insisting on the eternity of the world or cosmos. Having extended an analogy derived from present experience back into eternity, their position was ostensibly the stronger of the two, but it clearly contradicted the faith. Never one to insist on theory to the exclusion of obedience, Aquinas recognized the problem in several debates, where he opined that the creation of the world at a given moment in time must be believed but cannot be proved by human reason. Christians, he went on, who insist on trying to prove otherwise merely make themselves the laughing stock of unbelievers.[30]

That fun could be poked at revelation's historical scheme is shown by John of Jandun (d. 1328). Commenting on the Jewish and Christian creation, he wrote:

> The gentile philosophers did not know this method of creation, and this is not astonishing because it cannot be known from sensible evidence . . . especially because it . . . only occurred once, and it is now a very long time since that happened. Those therefore who understand this kind of creation know it by another way, that is, by the authority of the saints, by revelation and by things of the sort.[31]

Elsewhere, John went on to assert about a similar matter that this kind of belief is best learned in childhood by dint of repetition.

Critics of Averroist Aristotelianism and Thomistic theology hunted for ways to release God from bondage to His own creation. From Augustinians of Bonaventure's persuasion through Duns Scotus to the later Ockhamists, they criticized past attempts to demonstrate the deity's existence and qualities by arguing from analogies seen in the natural world. To cease to argue back from effect to cause was costly, however. What appeared good to man could no longer be said to be necessarily God's good. Only the moral injunctions and ecclesiastical institutions explicitly found in scripture were beyond question. Since the Bible offered only the Deuteronomic code, Christ's laws of love and Paul's recommendations, it directly bolstered few ecclesiastical institutions. How this threatened the institutional structure of the Church and its claimed superiority over the secular state was already clear in John of Paris's tract *On Royal and Papal Power* of 1302.

---

[30] *Quodlibetum* 12 6 1 and *Quodlibetum* 3 15 2 2 in ed. Spiazzi, *Opuscula philosophica* 277b and 68b–69a.

[31] *Quaestiones super libros physicorum* cited in MacClintock, *Perversity and Error: Studies on the 'Averroist' John of Jandun* 91–2 and 173–4n.

Deity and certitude

The excision of the accretions of the somewhat naturalist theology required care. It was impermissible to assert, as did a proposition condemned at Paris in 1277, 'that nothing can be known about God save that He exists or has being', since scripture revealed many of His actions.[32] The proponents of the deity's freedom could get pretty close to this proposition, however, by falling back on orthodox thought. In the Lateran Council of 1215 where Joachim of Fiore and Amalric of Bène were castigated, it was asserted that 'there is no similarity to be discerned between the creator and his creatures that is not overtopped by a discernible dissimilarity'.[33] Even Alan of Lille, a leader among those expanding the role of reason in theology, said that the terms with which God is described differ from those with which mankind is, hence there is no true similitude of God and man. Humans may be rational, but God is reason itself. Although such distinctions also appealed to Aquinas, the Augustinians and Duns Scotus used them to weaken naturalist theology irreparably. If much can be learned from faith and divine illumination, Scotus said, unaided human reason can know no more than the fact that both God and man have being. The analogies derived from humanity's brief life cannot define that wilful, all-perceiving and eternal principle of freedom.

Intellectuals turned back to views such as those with which Bernard of Clairvaux assailed Abelard:

> Since he was prepared to use reason to explain everything, even things which were above reason, he presumed against both reason and faith. What is more hostile to reason than to try to transcend reason by means of reason? And what is more hostile to faith than to refuse to believe what cannot be attained by reason?[34]

To Bernard, as to the later Augustinians, believing derived from direct divine illumination and therefore produced certitude. Against the rationalists' belief that theology had to lean on the crutch of philosophy for its proofs, Bernard asked the question:

> How do we understand [the truth]? Disputation does not understand it; holiness does, if, in some way, the incomprehensible can be understood. But unless it can be comprehended, the apostle would not have said 'that we be able to comprehend with all the saints'. The saints therefore understand. Do you want to know how? If you are holy, you understand and know. If not, be holy, and you will know by experience.[35]

Bernard's opinion that Abelard misused reason attracted others than irrationalists. Describing the debates in the theological faculty of Paris about the

---

[32] Denifle, *Cartularium universitatis Parisiensis* I 553: Error No. 215 of Item No. 473.
[33] *Liber extra* 1 1 2 in *CICan* II 6–7.
[34] *Contra quaedam capitula errorum Abaelardi* 1 1 in *PL* CLXXXII 1055.
[35] *De consideratione* 5 14 in *Sancti Bernardi opera* III 492. See Ephesians 3:18.

character and origin of human intellect and other matters, the Averroist John of Jandun wrote in 1323: 'Of what use these are, and how they advance the Catholic faith, God alone knows. Anyone can see this for himself, anyone, that is, who [honestly] seeks . . . from [these divines] the rationale of their arguing in this way.'[36] Bacon remarked that theologians overstepped their bounds when they discussed such problems as matter, species, being and ways of knowing; they should merely accept philosophers' solutions. John of Jandun said in effect that each discipline, theology and philosophy, was autonomous in presuppositions, methods and results, and would have agreed with the earlier Boethius of Dacia, whose opinions had been questioned in 1277 by Stephen Tempier's commission at Paris. In his *On the Eternity of the World*, Boethius had separated the spheres comprehensible by philosophy or reason from those comprehensible by faith or theology. Debating the familiar difference between the Christian creation in history and the philosopher's eternity of the world, he concluded that 'two things are clear: one is that natural [reason]'s eternity of the world cannot contradict the Christian faith, and the other is that natural reason cannot prove that the world . . . was ever new'.[37] There were, he said in effect, two truths, one in theology, the other in philosophy.

Although double truth was called an Averroist heresy, the separation of the disciplines was going on apace, and even the censure in 1277 of the Parisian Averroists had the inadvertent effect of strengthening it. Some severed the disciplines by finding languages appropriate to each, and by giving to one, theology, the possession of a higher truth. The Parisian Peter of Poitiers (d. 1205) observed that an opinion of the ancient Boethius, a philosopher and not a theologian, reflected probability more than certainty. Earlier, Bernard of Clairvaux had chided Abelard for applying philosophy's probabilities to theology, in which only certitude ruled. The Cistercian's opinion was like that of the later Bonaventure and was used to attack Thomistic theology. Around 1300, the majority of the schoolmen limited natural philosophy to the production of probable propositions.

Natural philosophers, however, refused to be deprived of certitude. Astrologer and medical doctor Peter of Abano was reported as saying that he and others dealt with things describable 'by human certitude' and not, as did theologians, with those held by simple credulity. This view was not devoid of tradition. Alan of Lille earlier wrote that 'properly speaking, there is no science of God. For when it is said that the science of God is known, reference is being made rather to the knowledge of the faith and of credulity than to the knowledge of certitude.'[38] Besides, the results of Robert Grosseteste's

---

[36] Chapter II of his *Tractatus de laudibus Parisius* (ed. Taranne and Leroux de Lincy, Paris, 1856).
[37] MacClintock, *Perversity and Error* 100.
[38] *Quoniam homines* 1 1 in ed. Glorieux, *Archives d'histoire doctrinale et littéraire du moyen âge* XVIII (1953) 136.

repeated experiences in optics gave him a feeling similar to Bernard's illumination by divine light.

Nor could theology do without probability. The rising tide that sought to cut away all authorities, ancient or modern, other than scripture actually encouraged theological probabilism, that is, the weighing of one authority or historical precedent against another. Arguing from scripture against Bernard of Clairvaux's stand that the secular sword was to be used at the behest of the Church, John of Paris blandly remarked that the Cistercian's opinion was of little weight. When the same Dominican's treatise on the Eucharist was being examined by the bishop and doctors of Paris in 1305–6, they reported that John:

> asserted in the presence of the college of the masters of theology that he holds that either way of assuming the body of Christ to be on the altar is a probable opinion, and that he finds both approved by Holy Scripture and the opinions of the saints. Furthermore, he says that nothing [concerning the Eucharist] has been determined by the Church, and that nothing therefore falls under the faith, and that, if he had said otherwise, he would not have spoken correctly. And he who would pertinaciously assert either one of these options of itself to fall under the faith should incur anathema.[39]

The attempt to separate philosophy from theology, 'learning' (*scientia*) from 'wisdom' (*sapientia*), by giving the latter certitude's superiority and the former probability's inferiority was bound to fail. Of course, nobody doubted that the two spheres were distinct. The glosses on Plato's *Timaeus* by William of Conches (d. 1153–54) had long ago distinguished between the creator's and nature's work: the former created 'from nothing' and performed miracles; the latter only according to the rules placed in it at its creation. Albert the Great observed in his commentary on Aristotle's *On the Heavens and the World* that the business of a philosopher was not to discuss God's omnipotence or his miracles, but rather what happens in nature by reason of its inherent causes.

This simple distinction became significant when it touched on moral life here on earth. In his *On Monarchy*, Dante defined humanity's aims:

> Unerring providence has ordained two objectives man must seek: the bliss of this life which consists in the use of his own powers and is configured by the terrestrial paradise, and the bliss of eternal life which consists in the enjoyment of the vision of God to which man's own powers cannot ascend unless aided by divine illumination, and which is made understandable by the celestial paradise.[40]

Like Aquinas, Dante believed that the former objective was attained by the exercise of moral and intellectual virtues and the latter by the theological

---

[39] Denifle, *Cartularium universitatis Parisiensis* I 120 No. 656.
[40] *De monarchia* 3 16 (ed. Vinay) 280–82.

virtues and spiritual teaching transcending human reason. Unlike the heavenly objective, the earthly objective could never be perfectly achieved. Writing shortly before 1310, Engelbert of Volkersdorf, abbot of Admont, said that 'the objective of present felicity in the temporal kingdom is to labour continuously with zeal and joy to build its peace . . . even if it can never really be obtained fully'.[41] The objectives, then, were clear, but the problem was to determine whether moral and political virtues were valid of themselves or only in terms of their relation to celestial ends.

A limited autonomy was traditionally allowed to humankind's natural moral virtues. Ever moderate, Thomas Aquinas felt that political virtues were not morally indifferent but intrinsically good, and were meritorious if informed by God's grace. An anonymous commentary produced in the arts faculty at Paris just after 1277 advances the case that God helps those who help themselves, the author contending that:

> felicity derives from both a divine cause and a human one. It derives . . . originally from God as a primal and remote cause; in an immediate sense, however, this same felicity is from a human cause. Whence happiness is not immediately from God, but instead from God when man works with Him. Whence felicity consists in human actions, because it is necessary for man to labour if he would be happy.[42]

John of Paris reinforced this by affirming that, pagan or Christian, humans are God's 'assistants', and 'it can be said that the moral virtues [they] acquire [on earth] can be perfect without the theological virtues, nor, except for a certain accidental perfection, are they made more perfect by the [latter] virtues'.[43] A secular morality free of Christianity had begun to appear and, with it, the ambition of discovering a firm link between God and humanity, between heaven and earth, began to fade.

Utopians, however, did not retreat easily, and the years around 1300 witnessed the assault of their forlorn hope. Raymond Llull's scheme of universal knowledge lent certitude to natural philosophy and theology by means of mathematics. So did Roger Bacon's: 'Since it is proved that philosophy cannot be known unless mathematics is known, and everybody knows that theology cannot be known unless philosophy is known, it is necessary for theologians to know mathematics.'[44] This unified knowledge will be useful because, by means of it:

> faithful Christians will attain the reward of future blessedness . . . The republic of the faithful shall so dispose its temporal goods that all things useful both to

---

[41] From his *De ortu et progressu et fine regnorum et precipue regni et imperii Romani* 15 in Vinay's edition of Dante's *De monarchia* 284–5n.

[42] A Paris manuscript quoted in MacClintock, *Perversity and Error* 165n.

[43] *De potestate regia et papali* 18 (ed. Bleienstein) 163.

[44] *Opus maius* 4 4 (ed. Bridges) I 175.

individuals and the multitude for conserving bodily health and a wonderful pro-longation of life shall be effected in material and moral goods and in discretion, peace and justice . . . All nations of the infidels predestined to eternal life shall be converted to the great glory of the Christian faith . . . Those foreknown to be damned who cannot be converted shall be restrained by the ways and works of wisdom rather than by civil wars.[45]

But humanity's natural endowment was not up to the task, and direct divine illumination was required. Bacon confessed 'that, through his own industry, man cannot know how to please God . . . nor how to deal with his neighbour or even with himself, but is wanting in those things until the truth is revealed'. What was needed was:

that a revelation should be made to one man only that he is to be the mediator between God and man and the vicar of God here on earth, a man to whom the whole human race should be subject and who ought to be believed without contradiction . . . He is [to be] the legislator and the highest priest, who has the plenitude of power in spiritual and temporal things, a 'human God' as Avicenna says commenting on . . . the *Metaphysics* 'whom it is licit to adore after God'.[46]

This curious fantasy shows how utopians rejected rational theology and philosophy, and instead tried to force God and nature to be one. Others, such as John of Jandun and the Ockhamists, found reason limited, and resigned themselves to thinking that God and nature were worlds apart. From whichever side they approached the problem, however, they had one thing in common. They no longer believed that human reason could construct a Christian synthesis of God, humankind and nature, and hence the confidence that had animated intellectuals from Peter Abelard to Thomas Aquinas was beginning to weaken.

---

[45] *Compendium studii philosophiae* I in ed. Brewer, *Opera Fr. Baconi hactenus inedita* 395.
[46] *Baconis operis maioris pars septima seu moralis philosophia* 1 1 (ed. Massa) 8.

Chapter 21

Enthusiasm and heresy

Doubt and heresy

Quoted by the cardinals at Anagni in 1255 examining the works of Joachim of Fiore, Gratian defined heresy as when 'each man chooses for himself the teaching he thinks best. Whoever understands Holy Scripture in a manner other than is required by the judgement of the Holy Spirit by whom it was written, is to be called an heretic even if he does not leave the Church.'[1] The Holy Spirit had inspired the Church Militant, that is, the popes, hierarchy and 'divines' here on earth. Heresy was to diverge from them. But people did diverge, and scepticism, doubt and simple disbelief were pervasive.

Particular issues precipitated doubt. Since the days of Gregory VII, clerical celibacy had been prized and enforced, for example, but the lively dissent seen around 1100 in such tracts as those of the *Norman Anonymous* was never stilled. It echoed through the Platonic school of Chartres into the thirteenth century, becoming popular among the laity or those who wrote what laymen read. The type of argument employed may be seen in Andrew the Chaplain's *On Love* of 1184–86. Condemned by Stephen Tempier's commission of theologians in 1277, and thereafter enthusiastically translated from Latin into vernacular tongues, Andrew's tract affirmed that, even for clerks, from love comes virtue:

> I believe that God cannot be gravely offended by love, for what is done because nature obliges us to can easily be purged by expiation. Besides, it is unsuitable to call criminal the [act] in which the greatest good in this life has its origin and without which no one on earth can be considered worthy of praise.[2]

In addition, the idea that celibacy was unnatural was widespread, especially among layfolk. A poet of the quality and popularity of the Parisian John of Meung pronounced in his *Romance of the Rose* that almost all the virtues of the religious were unlovely: poverty was ugly, abstinence and chastity unnatural, and humility and obedience refused humanity's high place in nature's order.

---

[1] *Decretum* 24 3 27 in *CICan* I 997–98, from Jerome and Isidore of Seville.
[2] *De amore* 1 6 H (ed. Trojel) 94.

Chronicles and histories propagated a Christian viewpoint and were crowded with references to miracles, but these events evoked ambivalence. Anti-Hohenstaufen, Caesarius of Heisterbach loved telling stories against Philip of Swabia, king of the Romans. According to this Cistercian, Philip, hearing that the Templars were miraculously hidden from the Saracens who surrounded them by singing a verse from Psalm 26, sourly observed that, had he been there, he'd have dropped the psalm and run for it. Salimbene records how Boncompagno of Signa made fun of the Dominican miracle worker and preacher John Schio of Vicenza (d. 1260). At the time of the Alleluia of 1233, a widespread political and religious movement against the Hohenstaufen, Boncompagno announced at Bologna that he would fly. When the crowd assembled, he, having worn wings but not flown, dryly congratulated its members on their credulity. When Florentine wiseacres heard that John was about to visit their town, they said: 'For God's sake, don't let him come here. He raises the dead, and we're already so many that our city can't hold us.'[3]

To scepticism as a source of hostility to miracles may be added dislike of clerical manipulativeness. Joinville tells that Louis IX praised Simon of Montfort, commander of the Albigensian crusaders, because he refused to rush out to witness a nearby miracle whereby the Lord's body had become flesh and blood in the hands of a priest, thus confuting Catharism. His faith being firm, said the king, Simon had no need of proof. Besides, what soldier enjoys the cries of those who both urge him to risk his life and draw attention to themselves? Lastly, a common lament was that miracles were no longer taking place because of the 'corruption' of the Church.

The Franciscan Salimbene exemplifies the age's mixture of credulity and disbelief. Franciscan saints were sound in his opinion, but he happily recounted stories against Dominican ones and against those of the Friars of the Sack. Cults fostered by the secular clergy were invariably frauds, and he was especially hostile to plebeian holy men. Speaking of Albert, the Lion Banner Bearer for the wine-porters' guild of Cremona, he ascribed the spread of his cult to Parma and Reggio around 1279 'partly to the hope of the sick to become well, partly to the desire of the curious to see novelties, partly to the secular clergy's envy of the modern orders and partly to the profit gained by bishops and canons from such a cult'.[4] This Guelph then added politics: exiled Ghibelline nobles hoped to return home during a wave of plebeian good feeling precipitated by the elevation of a worker to sanctity. He was here referring to the kind of social alliance between the top and bottom of society that threatened the mixed rich and middle-class Guelph popular parties that were ruling so many Italian town republics after 1250.

---

[3] *Cronica* in *MGH SS* XXXII 83.
[4] Ibid. 503–4.

The faith itself evoked doubt. Joachim of Fiore likened doubt about predestination to the devil's temptation of Christ during the forty days. This was especially hard on monks, who had surrendered so much: 'If you are not elected, you vainly exhaust yourself by sustaining such labours, for no one can be saved who is not chosen; if, however, you are chosen, even if you spare yourselves so that you are idle when the Lord comes, you will be saved, because no man of the elect can perish.' Joachim's solution was dour. If you seek profit from your faith, you breach the law of Matthew 4:7: 'You shall not tempt the Lord your God.' The abbot then sounded what he thought was a more positive note: 'Although we cannot be certain in this life whether we are reprobate or chosen, nevertheless just as the sign of election is to act strongly and be strengthened, so is the sign of reprobation to fall from rigour with one's power of justice enervated.'[5] This quasi-Calvinist teaching about external signs of salvation required believers to show by a dogged happiness they did not despair. The deity, so to speak, was keeping mum. As a manual for parish clergy put it:

> Nobody should presume to investigate why God wished to create men who he knew would fall or why he wished to create angels whose fall he certainly foreknew . . . These and other works of God are beyond human understanding.[6]

A tract produced between 1184 and 1207, sometimes attributed to Durand of Huesca's Waldensians, attests that the Cathars argued that Catholic teaching on predestination meant that, since God created everything and foreknew what it was, He had created evil. In a work composed between 1241 and 1250, the Lombard Cathars claimed that Lucifer and the fallen angels could not have been good before they fell from heaven, because, if they had been:

> from the very beginning, God [had] knowingly created his angels of such imperfection that they were unable to resist evil. Hence God, who is good, holy, just, wise and fair . . . is the cause and beginning of evil, an opinion which must be wholly rejected. One must instead believe that there are two first principles, one good and the other evil, the latter being the cause of angelic imperfection and likewise of all evil.[7]

Orthodox Christians and moderate dualists countered this argument by asserting that it deprived humanity of free will, thus inducing despair and destroying individual responsibility. Yet dualist doctrines were hardly more

---

[5] The two passages are from Joachim's *Tractatus super quatuor evangelia* (ed. Buonaiuti) 159. In the first, the phrase 'at the moment when the lord comes' translates *ad horam*, because Joachim was thinking of Matthew 24:42–50 and Apocalypse 3:3. The second is from the *Tractatus* 160.

[6] *Speculum humanae salvationis* I prologue (ed. Lutz and Perdrizet) 5.

[7] *Liber de duobus principiis* (ed. A. Dondaine, Rome, 1939) 84.

destructive of human optimism than orthodoxy. Discussing those predestined to salvation, Thomas Aquinas wrote:

> It may be said that a good proportionate to the ordinary state of nature is found in many and is lacking in few, but that a good that exceeds that ordinary state is discovered only in very few. It is evident that there are many who have knowledge sufficient for governing their own lives, and few, who are called fools or idiots, who lack this knowledge, but there are also very few who are able to attain a profound knowledge of intelligible things [that is, of philosophy]. Since, therefore, eternal blessedness, which consists in the vision of God, exceeds the ordinary state of nature (especially because grace has been weakened by the corruption of original sin), there are very few indeed who are saved.[8]

Faced with this vision, some dualists such as the Rhenish Luciferians lauded the fallen angels, proclaiming that Lucifer was God's brother who had been unjustly cast out of heaven, and that the fraternal victor was too cruel to be worshipped.

If philosophical learning was like salvation, damnation was like death. The Luciferians cursed God for damning Lucifer, as did the orthodox Boncompagno of Signa for condemning mankind to death. Caesarius of Heisterbach tells about Landgrave Lewis II of Thuringia (d. 1168). Literate and hard on the clergy, as Caesarius puts it, he loved Psalms 115:16: 'The heavens, even the heavens are the Lord's: but the earth has he given to the children of men', thence arguing that there is no link between heaven and earth. He was wont to say that, if predestined to salvation, no evil deed would cost him heaven; and, if foreknown to damnation, no good one would gain it for him. Urged to repent lest he die in sin, he replied: 'When the day of my death comes, I will die. I cannot delay it by living well nor advance it by living evilly.'[9]

Anti-Christian polemic reinforced natural scepticism. Muslims ridiculed monogyny, clerical celibacy and trinitarian 'polytheism'. Much of the evidence about this kind of thought among Christian princes and prelates comes from the mouths of their enemies. Gregory IX's letter of 1239 condemning Frederick II Hohenstaufen was widely distributed. The pope closed this lengthy missive by asserting that Frederick enjoyed repeating that three impostors, Moses, Jesus and Mohammed, had deceived the world. Nor did he believe in the Virgin Birth, because none is born save of the carnal commerce of man and woman, 'and a man ought not to believe anything he cannot prove by natural means and reason'.[10] According to hostile witnesses deposing before Clement V in 1310–11, when he was a cardinal Boniface VIII observed that,

---

[8] *Summa theologiae I*, 1 23 7 ad 3.
[9] *Dialogus miraculorum* 1 37 (ed. Strange) I 33.
[10] *Historia diplomatica Friderici Secundi* (ed. Huillard-Bréholles) V i 350.

although the mob may think otherwise, no educated person could believe in the Trinity, Virgin Birth or the real presence in the Eucharist. These questions had surfaced when discussing the relative validity of Christian and Muslim law, wherein the cardinal (like a Pre-Socratic) was said to have observed that 'no law is divine; all has been invented by men. Eternal penalties are there included for only one reason, namely that men shall be restrained from evil deeds by fear of punishment. Therefore this law has no truth other than that, because of fear of punishment, men will live peacefully.'[11]

These tales were not fabrications. Anent Frederick II's incredulity, the Muslim historian Sibt ibn al-Jauzi of Damascus (d. 1257) remarked that the emperor was known to be an atheist who poked fun at Christianity. Such scepticism also had a popular base. In 1288, the harangue of a Bolognese statute threatened punishment 'because it often happens that barmen and dice players in the streets and public squares of the commune of Bologna . . . utter truly detestable and horrible words against God and His Mother, and their tumult puts many difficulties in the way of the preachers who announce the word of God in these squares'.[12] In 1299, a student at Bologna told the inquisitors that a farmer from a nearby village said that the proposition that Merlin was God's son was as easily demonstrable as it was about Jesus. The sceptical naturalism of the statements attributed to Frederick II and Boniface VIII is paralleled by Boncompagno of Signa's remark about Tuscans who denied the afterlife. They imitated the ancient Athenians by 'mendaciously asserting that, because it can be shown demonstratively, everything proceeds from the elements and all individual things individually revert into their elements'.[13] Caesarius of Heisterbach speaks of a female recluse who, urged by an abbot to recover her faith in God, asked:

> Who knows if God exists or if he has angels, souls or the kingdom of heaven? Who has seen them? Who has returned thence and told us what he has seen?[14]

He also found a priest who admitted that he had not believed in the real presence in the consecrated host. Academics touched on this as well. No less an intellectual than Siger of Brabant averred that all the world's philosophers could not convince anyone of personal immortality, and Aquinas confessed that unaided human reason could not know what the beatitude of the future life really was. The Parisian condemnations in 1277 also record that university artists asserted that bliss was found only in this life and that bodily death was so awful that it was silly to worry about hell. A little later,

---

[11] Dupuy, *Histoire du différend d'entre le pape Boniface VIII et Philippe le Bel 531* (testimony No. 7 quoted above) and 534 (testimony No. 12).

[12] Charles du F. DuCange, *Glossarium mediae et infimae latinitatis* s. v. incisor.

[13] *Rhetorica novissima* 8 1 in *BIMA* 11 278b.

[14] *Dialogus miraculorum* 4 39 (ed. Strange) I 207.

in 1308, inquisitors at Foix turned up the account of a university student who told another 'that he and almost all students of natural philosophy at Toulouse and Paris believe it impossible and contrary to nature for holy words to convert bread into the body of Christ'.[15]

The Church was powerless against this kind of doubt. Attempts to confront it often leaned on pitiable reasoning. Alexander Neckham praised the efficacy of dialectics, telling about a Parisian scholar who lay dying. The youth asserted that, unless convinced by reason, he could not believe in personal resurrection. A fellow student argued against his position:

> If you believe in the future resurrection, this resurrection will either be or will not be. If you believe it will be and it is not, this belief will not harm you. If you believe it will be and it is, this belief will be of advantage to you. Now, if you do not believe and there should be a future resurrection, eternal woe will fall on you. It is therefore better to believe than not to believe.[16]

According to Alexander, the youth closed his eyes in happy belief. If so, his awakening may have been rude. John of Joinville tells of an old woman of Acre carrying a brazier of coals and a bucket of water. She wished, she said, to burn heaven up and douse hell's fires so that humanity would act not for reward but rather for love of God. The Franciscan Jacopone of Todi (d. *circa* 1306) said he cared not if he were saved or damned, just so long as God would tell what he could do for Him. Jacopone was saying that those who love either love or freedom should love them for themselves and not for any good that they may do them or their world. To both the elegant seneschal of Champagne and the onetime lawyer of Todi, Alexander's Parisian had broken the law: 'You shall not tempt the Lord your God.' With Him, there is no *quid pro quo*.

Some divergent sects almost seem founded on such scepticism. A record dated 1270–1300 from Passau reports that Waldensian rustics condemned obligatory tithes, testamentary charity and church burial, the Crusade and indulgences, as well as the cults of the cross and of all the saints save the apostles. These folk from the Bohemian Forest 'denied purgatory, saying that there were only two paths, that of the elect to heaven and that of the damned to hell, quoting Ecclesiastes 11:3: "there where the tree falls, there shall it remain"'.[17] Other divergent religions were not so thoroughgoing. Although they also expressed such scepticism and usually mocked miracles, the Cathars nevertheless used them. Around 1320, a Cathar preacher tried to prove the

---

[15] Annette Pales-Gobilliard, *L'inquisiteur Geoffroy d'Ablis et les Cathares du Comté de Foix (1308–1309)* (Paris, 1984) 358.

[16] *De naturis rerum* 2 73 in *Rolls Series* XXXIV 297.

[17] Margaret Nickson, 'The "Pseudo-Rainerius" treatise: the final stage of a thirteenth century work on heresy from the diocese of Passau', *Archives d'histoire doctrinale et littéraire du moyen âge* 34 (1967) 301.

truth of metempsychosis, or transmigration of souls, by telling of a Perfect who, 'while standing next to a fountain, declared he recalled that, when he was a horse, he lost one of his shoes in the bed of the said fountain while drinking. He had the said horseshoe looked for and there it was!'[18]

Heretics were often not those who believed too little, but rather those who believed too much, and scepticism helped orthodoxy almost as much as it did heresy. Initially Joachite, Salimbene provides a good example. His ardent friends were persuaded that the new age would begin in 1260, the date on which the death of 'their' Antichrist, Frederick II, was prophesied. When the Hohenstaufen suddenly died ten years before the projected date, Salimbene, already out of his depth among sectaries given to such passion, dropped the teaching, resolving never again to believe anything he had not actually seen – unless it was, of course, safely orthodox.

In fine, what held doubt in check was not the ability of churchmen to prove personal resurrection, man's freedom to make moral choices or similar propositions. Such can be believed, but, as was often then stated, they assuredly cannot be proved. The reason for belief seems to have been twofold. First, church teaching was no less capable of gaining the trust of its adherents than other systems also based on propositions beyond human demonstration that had preceded it or were to follow. Second, the period from 1150 to 1300 was one when the relatively beneficent material conditions of life combined with the newness of the Church's institutional and mental mechanisms to reinforce Latin cultural confidence. Wishing not to disbelieve, many were bemused for a time.

Divergent belief

Several sects showed Judaic influence. One such, the Passagians of around 1200, were clearly judaizers, defending circumcision, the Jewish sabbath and the primacy of the Mosaic law. The partial parallel between Cathar teachings and those of the Kabbalah – strong among Mediterranean Jews at this time, with its metempsychosis and dualism – has often been noted. Since the Kabbalah often reinforced attacks on Maimonidean rationalism, it paralleled the hostility to Aristotelian natural reason so strongly expressed by many Christian utopian enthusiasts, both orthodox and heretic. Of contacts between Jews and Cathars little is known except that the orthodox claimed that there were such. The main outside influence on Latin Cathars was probably Byzantine. Before 1167, for example, they held to the Bogomil or Bulgar doctrine that Lucifer, cast out of heaven by God, founded evil. In that year, however, Niketas, a Cathar bishop of Constantinople, visited the Lombard

---

[18] *Le registre d'inquisition de Jacques Fournier, 1318–1325* (ed. Jean Duvernoy, Toulouse, 1965) III 221.

churches and is said to have assembled a council at St Felix de Caraman near Toulouse. Ordaining bishops in both areas, he persuaded the Cathar clergy to adopt his church's rigorous dualism, whereby Lucifer was regarded as the creator of the material world and co-eternal with God. In spite of the reality of foreign influences, gnostic dualism was undoubtedly an innate part of Latin Christianity and required little external stimulus in order to flower.

Most critical enthusiasts were anti-sacerdotal. Hugh Speroni of Piacenza averred around 1177 that merit and not office gave priests their power, and merit was hard to come by. Writing between 1179 and 1202, Alan of Lille remarked that the Waldensians quoted Pope Gregory I to argue 'that the power to bind and loose was given only to those who preserve and live both the teaching and the life of the apostles'.[19] So far, thought some, had the clergy fallen from the apostolic life that their sacraments were all vitiated. This view turned enthusiasts into heretics: the true believer must cleanse the corrupt Church or secede to found a purer one. According to the ex-heretic Buonacorso of Milan, writing between 1176 and 1190, this was the opinion of the Arnoldists, a pre-Waldensian sect deriving its name from Arnold of Brescia, the companion of Abelard, radical reformer and leader of Rome's revolt against the temporal dominion of the popes, executed in 1155.

Such assaults could be nipped in the bud, the orthodox believed, by insisting that the merit of the officiant was not the basis of sacramental validity. An argument appealing to ordinary penitents came from Alan of Lille:

> All priests have the power of binding and loosing, but those only who adhere to the life and teaching of the apostles use this power justly . . . Absolutely speaking, however, the remission or retention of sins is also performed by those who are not holy, for God gives his blessing to the worthy seeker even by means of an unworthy minister.[20]

This was codified at the time of Innocent III in the doctrine *ex opere operato*, wherein grace was conferred by a sacrament irrespective of the merit of the person administering it.

If the moral quality of the officiant bore no relation to sacramental validity, however, this teaching destroyed individual responsibility and hence society. Reinforcement was needed, and that turned out to be the idea of intention. In the excitements of the Gregorian revolution, this ancient idea had been revived, being expressed, for example, in Peter Abelard's *Ethics*, where he pronounced that an individual's merit or demerit does not lie so much in what they do as in what they intend to do. Hugh of St Victor applied this teaching to the sacraments: for efficacy, a priest must intend to perform them.

---

[19] *Quadripartita editio contra hereticos, Waldenses, Judaeos et Paganos* or *Contra haereticos* 2 6 in *PL* CCX 383.

[20] *Contra hereticos* 2 7 in *PL* CCX 383–84.

By the time of the great scholastics the matter was complex. Some, like Bonaventure, opined that God would supply man's deficiencies; others, like Aquinas, that habitual or virtual intention, that is, the lack of a positively perverse intention, was enough. But few indeed cared to maintain that, even with God supplying, one who did not believe in the faith or was a heretic could perform or receive a valid sacrament. In short, however hard the doctors tried to lock the door, it always came unlatched again: the problem was, as of old, to define what heresy was.

Enthusiasts, both orthodox and heretical, found simony heretical. This attitude derived from the Gregorian age when the 'reformers' had disinterred this ancient weapon to beat the clergy who were loyal to the old state churches. Simony could also be broadly construed, occurring not only when a sacrament was purchased or an office bought, but also when obtained by means of, or exercised under the shadow of, family influence, favour, vice or even hypocrisy. Since simony was heretical, enthusiasts could say that believers should not attend heretical conventicles and sacraments. As Peter Damian reported, had not the Vallumbrosan radicals in Florence in the mid-eleventh century asserted that, because of simony, there was no pope, no king, no archbishop and no priest, and had not thousands of men, deceived by the 'trumpery and incantations' of false sacraments, died without a valid sacrament? In 1218, two branches of the Waldensian movement, the Lombard Poor of Christ and the French Poor of Lyons, met to heal differences at Bergamo. The French accepted the orthodox position on sacerdotal authority; the Lombards refused, alleging that Christians must obey God, not man. Although admitting that God would supply deficiencies, the Lombards cited Gratian, who attributed to Gregory I a statement that simoniacs:

> cannot be priests, whence it is written: damnation of the giver, damnation of the receiver. This is the heresy of simony. In what way, therefore, can they who are not holy and are damned sanctify others? How can they transmit or receive the body of Christ? He who is cursed, how can he bless?[21]

It was but a short step from this to propose that only good men, those predestined to salvation, were true priests; that, in short, there was a priest-hood of all true believers, lay and clerical alike. This view was attributed to the Arnoldists and to later groups among the Waldensians. According to Stephen of Bourbon, an inquisitor in the Rhone valley between 1232 and 1249, some Waldensians held that women could be priests. And at the con-ference of Bergamo in 1218, the Lombard Poor charged that the extreme

---

[21] *Decretum* 2 1 1 12 in *CICan* I 361. Cardinal Deusdedit had attributed this passage to Pope Pascal I. The Waldensian source is the *Rescriptum heresiarcharum Lombardie ad pauperes de Lugduno qui sunt in Alamania* in Giovanni Gonnet, *Enchiridion fontium Valdensium* (Torre Pellice, 1958) I 181–82.

views of their French associates on this point would lead them to admit not only women but even whores to the priesthood.

Lay anti-sacerdotalism was restrained by the fact that enthusiasts lived within a Church in which, until after 1300, lay religious passions were normally channelled into monastic or quasi-monastic groups. Even for the orthodox religious, sacraments were of limited importance; the way of life almost everything. Thus, for example, the French Waldensians at Bergamo accepted the sacerdotal authority of priests ordained by Rome. Vital things – preaching and exemplaristic living in common like the apostles – however, they entrusted to lay rectors and ministers elected by the community. A compromise reached at Bergamo provided that the community 'gathered together in one body . . . may jointly choose provosts for life or rectors for a set term whichever seems more useful to the community or the maintenance of peace'.[22] Hostility to ecclesiastical hierarchy and insistence on the equality of all Christians was a doctrine among the Waldensians at Passau, seen above.

Lay direction usually faltered as time went on. In orthodox movements, this was exemplified by the Franciscan order after the death of the founder and the defeat of his successor Elias of Cortona. Among the deviant, the larger sects seem to have evolved towards hierarchy and sacerdotalism, and would surely have gone further had they been allowed to grow freely. The Cathars were early divided into simple believers and Perfects, and higher officers appeared, bishops, for example, as early as 1164. These were initially elected but, in the thirteenth century, were chosen by the hierarchy. Perfects were celibate, and women, although permitted into this grade, were never admitted to higher office. Among Waldensian sects this evolution did not always take place, but, when Bernard Gui summed up available information in his manual of 1323–24, he claimed that that faith had a self-perpetuating, celibate cadre of bishops, priests and deacons from which women were excluded. Practical need may also have encouraged this tendency. The Latin father Jerome, the Norman Anonymous of the late eleventh century and Marsiglio of Padua all said that the threat of schism had prompted the growth of the hierarchy in antiquity. All divergent movements, including the Cathars, suffered from scission, and hierarchy based on priestly magic and socio-sexual differentiation served to combat this tendency.

Hierarchy and sacerdotalism were, however, braked by the enthusiasts' belief that they had a way of living or knowing that made them superior to others. This elitism derived from the monks who thought of themselves as already citizens of supernal Jerusalem. Significant here was the teaching of Joachim of Fiore and the later Joachites about historical progress. The 'spiritual men' of the third age were to live the contemplative life, enjoying an understanding

---

[22] Ibid. (ed. Gonnet) I 171–73.

of scripture granted by the Holy Spirit, one far above that of the clergy of the second age who, bound by the compromises of the active life, enjoyed only a rational understanding. This gnosis made the theology of such sects somewhat inconsistent. The learned Amalricians crushed at Paris in 1210 were inspired by a Platonic pantheism presumably taught by the Parisian master Amalric of Bène and remotely derived from John the Scot Erigena. Although believing that God was everything, they nevertheless did not conclude that all men were equal, but rather that he who knows with the apostle Paul that 'God worketh all in all' cannot sin. Many sectaries thought of themselves as God's special vessels into which the Holy Spirit or the Saviour had been or was about to be poured.

Deviant gnosticism spiritualized religious conceptions in wonderful ways. The Amalricians held that 'hell is nothing other than ignorance, and paradise nothing but the knowledge of the truth . . . and this full knowledge is the resurrection, nor is any other resurrection to be expected'.[23] It also seems that the clergy initially did not understand quite what they were dealing with. In a synod at Hildesheim in 1224 summoned by the papal legate Conrad, Cardinal Bishop of Porto, the local cathedral provost Henry Minnike was condemned for diabolism. Henry was nevertheless said to have averred that the Holy Ghost was the father of the Son and that Holy Wisdom was higher in paradise than the Blessed Virgin Mary, all of which smacks of views like those of the Parisian Amalricians. The onetime heretic and later inquisitor Rainier Sacconi reported in 1250 that John of Lugio of Bergamo (one of the few Cathar intellectuals known by name) said that:

> 'the primal principle of evil has many names in Holy Scripture: evil, iniquity, cupidity, impiety, sin, pride, death, hell, calumny, vanity, injustice, perdition, confusion, corruption and fornication.' [John] even says that all the aforesaid vices are gods or goddesses deriving from the evil he claims to be the primal cause.[24]

Although orthodox utopians were usually hostile to Muslims and Jews, heretical ones, members of persecuted minorities, were often not. The Amalricians thought that, had Jews their knowledge of the truth, they would need no baptism. Some Joachites shared these views. In 1254, the Parisian divines examined the Eternal Evangel, a compilation of Joachim of Fiore's tracts introduced and glossed by Gerard of Borgo San Donnino. This Franciscan was said to have believed that his book would serve as the New Testament of the age of the Holy Spirit now nearly ushered in. Among the propositions purportedly found, and certainly condemned, was the following: 'However greatly the Lord will afflict the world's Jews, he will nevertheless

---

[23] *Contra Amauricianos* 3 and 7 in Clemens Baeumker, *Beiträge zur Geschichte der Philosophie des Mittelalters* XXIV (1926) 13 and 21.

[24] *De Catharis et Pauperibus de Lugduno* in *Liber de duobus principiis* (ed. Dondaine) 72.

reserve some to whom he will impart benefits at the end, even those who remain Jews, whom he will liberate.'[25] And Prous Boneta of Montpellier, a woman condemned for her version of the Olivite heresy in 1325, added the Saracens as beneficiaries of divine dispensation.

Some gnostic sectaries emphasized nature's inherent goodness and others its malevolence. The Amalricians accented the natural moral purity of those who know or learn the way, linking this to progress: within five years, the world would become a sinless natural paradise. Cathars, especially the rigid dualists among them, contrasted the unalterable sinfulness of the material world with the bliss of the spiritual world, the two being linked by the slow ascension of purified souls to heaven. Both visions went to extremes. The Amalricians said, in effect, that whatever is is good, or is shortly to be so. Writing thirteen years after the eradication of their sect, Caesarius of Heisterbach laughed that their predicted five-year term was long past and matters had not happened as foretold. The Cathars went in the other direction. The material world was all bad: created by concupiscence, meat could not be eaten (fish could!), and sin was so pervasive that some consoled (a ceremony of forgiveness and entry into the ranks of the Perfects) when sick are said to have fasted to death for fear of relapsing. Dour though they may have been, the Cathars were not without heart. Burned in 1321, the Perfect William Belibasta taught that 'it was a good work to give charity to anyone, so much so that, if a man gives charity to the devil because of God, God would remunerate that act', and that, if a man fell away, he should remember that 'God will indulge all men's sins, except desperation, that is, when a man despairs of God's having pity'.[26]

The ideal world

Rome's police maintained that elitist divergences led to moral antinomianism. Garnier of Rochefort wrote in 1208–10 that the Amalricians were wont to say: '"He who knows that God does everything cannot sin even when fornicating because he should not attribute what he does to himself, but rather to God." O shameless opinion! Why do they hold it? In order to persuade girls to fornicate more easily.'[27] Inquisitors at Bologna in 1299 reported that Gerald Segarelli of Parma, head of the Apostles or Poor of Christ, taught that nude necking and even copulation among the unmarried were without sin. The notion that a soul annihilated in God's love may do anything without remorse was among the opinions for which the Beguine Margaret, called

---

[25] Denifle, *Chartularium universitatis Parisiensis* I 273 No. 243.

[26] *Le registre d'inquisition de Jacques Fournier* (ed. Duvernoy) II 481 and 515, in reverse order.

[27] *Contra Amauricianos* 2 in Baeumker, *Beiträge zur Geschichte der Philosophie des Mittelalters* XXIV (1926) v–vi 12, putatively attributed to Garnier.

Porrette, was condemned in Paris in 1310, and a charge of moral antinomianism was also used at the Council of Vienne in 1311 to impugn all Beguines and Beghards.

Variations of sexual expression were also condemned. A Bolognese statute of 1259 directed the *podestà* to assist the Confraternity of the Blessed Virgin's war on sodomy and heresy. These two 'crimes' were frequently linked in polemic, but proof is lacking that homosexuals were more than usually heretical. What the literature indubitably shows is that men saw all crimes or deviations as analogous. The charges against Boniface VIII peddled by the French party after his death in 1303 included heresy, simony, usury, the more common sexual divergences, and a defence of masturbation.

Although the voices are ones inimical to them, some dissidents may well have been libertine, but others were surely not. The Amalricians were perhaps the former, but the Ortliebians, an Italian sect sharing many of their views, were moral rigorists. The Cathars were perhaps those who most rejected nature and the flesh, even calling marriage no better than disguised fornication. This teaching cost the sect adepts. In 1246, a noblewoman from Avignonet, south of Toulouse, told the inquisitors that she quit Catharism because she thought she had heard them say that 'a man could not be saved if he slept with his wife'.[28] Cathar arguments nevertheless appealed to others than moral rigorists. According to Alan of Lille, 'they even say that marriage contradicts nature's law, because natural law dictates that all should be in common, and marriage appropriates to one what ought to be shared'.[29] Besides, theory and life overlap only partially. A hidden advantage of the sharp separation between the believers and the Perfects who headed the Cathar cult was that the former were not expected to eschew marriage, usury or the other 'faults' of ordinary living, save that, when dying, they were to forgive their enemies. In short, although hard on their clergy, theirs may have been an easy religion for believers because they lacked orthodoxy's penitential police.

Like the orthodox monks of Fontevrault, Cathars and Waldensians placed women higher than did most Catholics. The former, for example, emphasized the spiritual equality of women and men, the Perfect William Belibasta saying that 'the souls of men and women are the same and without difference, and the whole difference between men and women is in their bodies which Satan made'.[30] In divergent belief, also, women could lead and are known to have attracted followings. Such a one was Willelma of Milan, whose cult was supported by the monks and aged pensioners of the Cistercian monastery of Chiaravalle near Milan, but whose followers – this annuity set included a Visconti! – were charged with heresy after her death in 1281.

---

[28] My *Men and Women at Toulouse in the Age of the Cathars* 42.

[29] *Contra hereticos* 1 63 in *PL* CCX 366.

[30] *Le registre d'inquisition de Jacques Fournier* (ed. Duvernoy) III 223.

Another was the Olivite Prous Boneta, who was, she said, the spiritual Mary through whom God would send the Holy Spirit to humanity. A study in woman's inferiority overcome, she reported that 'just as Eve, the first woman, was the beginning and cause of the damnation of all human nature and of all the human race through the sin of Adam, so', the Lord had told her, ' "you will be the beginning and cause of the saving of human nature and the human race by means of the words I make you say, if they are believed".'[31]

Enthusiasts, in fact, often believed that the world was upside down, certain that contemporary Christian life was far from noble. William Pelisson, the Dominican inquisitor, reported that a Toulousan weaver in the late 1220s, who later hereticated and was burned, cried out when first arrested: 'Sirs, hear me! I'm not a heretic because I have a wife, lie with her, have children, eat meat, lie and swear, and am a faithful Christian.'[32] The sectaries blamed the corruption of the Church and, within the Church, the attack on heresy evoked campaigns in which churchmen, starting at the top, condemned other ecclesiastics for deserting Christ's path and falling into avarice and lubricity. The problem is to discover what all the shouting was about.

Self-criticism among churchmen was one way in which the Church mobilized itself to combat heresy. By blaming individuals for falling short, churchmen allayed anxiety about the inherent impossibility of attaining the ideal. A result was that much polemic was misdirected or untruthful. Polemists said that the clergy of Languedoc, beset by Catharism, were luxurious and rich. Some were, but their church was a poor one. In the diocese of Toulouse, the bishop was so indigent that, in 1206, he was hounded by lay creditors and even by his own cathedral's canons. Papal letters and even public opinion claimed that heresy was victorious there because Languedoc lacked Christian devotion. But the rise of deviating belief everywhere paralleled the growth of orthodox enthusiasm. A rector of the Dalbade alleged that the parish revenues had fallen off 'both because of the heretics whose perverse sects abound in the area of Toulouse and because of the newly built churches in the parish to which everybody goes on festivals'.[33] Nor could the Church expect to meet its critics' objections, since their demands were contradictory. On one hand, for example, the clergy were often condemned for failing to live up to clerical celibacy. On the other, many sectarians, especially Waldensians, were sure that to obey the requirement perverted scripture.

These polemics reflected inherent contradictions, because it was hard to agree on what the Christian republic should be. Some were convinced that humanity was neither perfect nor perfectible. They accepted the endowment

---

[31] W.H. May, 'The confession of Prous Boneta' in *Essays in Medieval Life and Thought Presented in Honor of A. P. Evans* (eds. J.H. Mundy, R.W. Emery and B.N. Nelson, New York, 1955, rprt.) 29.
[32] *Chronicon* (ed. Charles Molinier, Aniché, 1880) 17.
[33] In my 'Charity and Social Work in Toulouse' in *Traditio* 11 (1966) 237n.

of the Church with wealth and power to enable it to rule men for their good. Worrying about this, Gerhoh, provost of the Augustinian chapter of Reichersberg, in 1155 or 1156 saw Jesus standing before Pontius Pilate clad in both the white robe of the priesthood and imperial purple. He then sadly observed: 'It would indeed please me if Caesar's things could be rendered to Caesar and God's things to God, but with this caution, that the Church be not ravaged or stripped of its white robe if the purple is taken off too rashly.'[34]

Some spoke out against such voices, trying to free the Church from the world's contamination. Peter Cantor praised Bernard of Clairvaux for his dislike of expensive churches and lauded Peter Abelard for insisting that the gifts given by the count of Champagne to his monastery called The Paraclete not come from money tainted by usury or violence. Others – like Peter Waldes, who converted in 1173 and died in 1216, and Francis of Assisi – comprised the utopian wing of the Christian republic. Naked to follow the naked Christ and, like the apostles, having all in common, they wanted to live the communism described in the Acts of the Apostles. Having no property and not saving for the morrow, they were to earn their bread by preaching, begging and working. Clergy and laymen were inspired by grand visions of this kind. One sect, the Amalricians, was led by secular clergy from in and around Paris. Of its thirteen leaders, at least three were masters at the university, and all but two had studied arts or theology there. Among them were four parish priests, and all the others were clerks in minor orders. The monastic or mendicant orders also frequently provided leadership for both enthusiastic and deviant movements. Many, however, such as Waldes and Francis mentioned above, were layfolk, inspired by texts and ideas from the clergy, but layfolk nonetheless.

Clerk, monk or laymen and laywomen, those who diverged from orthodoxy were to change the character of the Church. The next chapter will discuss how these enthusiasts or disbelievers were either won back to orthodoxy, suppressed or driven underground.

---

[34] *De novitatibus huius temporis* 12 in *MGH Ldl* III 296–97.

Chapter 22

Repression

Divergence and society

Most radical ideas had been heard before 1100, especially during the Gregorian revolution. At that time, however, radical spirits seemed orthodox, because they participated in the new monastic orders and types of life in which the religious and associated layfolk brigaded themselves for war against the old state churches. The alliance disintegrated afterwards. Remembering the earlier Gregorian disorders, the clergy wanted to claustrate the monks again and limit lay participation in preaching. Once established, religious orders themselves prized 'stability', and tried to prevent members going off to found or join more exciting ones. Formulated in the third Lateran Council of 1179 and again in the fourth of 1215, restrictive legislation voiced this worry. The aristocracies of the Church, so to speak, combined to muzzle the people, and secession from the Church therefore swelled in the late twelfth century.

But the prince of the Church came to the aid of 'his' people and derived much profit therefrom. Although insisting on episcopal control, Alexander III embraced Peter Waldes in 1179 and, in 1181, the latter swore loyalty. Innocent III opened the gates wider. Negotiations starting in 1198 led to a papal rule for the Lombard Humiliati in 1201. Some Waldensians, Durand of Huesca's Poor Catholics and Bernard Prim's Poor Lombards, were legitimated in 1208 and 1210, and thereafter fought the Cathars. In 1216, James of Vitry persuaded Honorius III to license Mary of Oignies's Beguines, a group begun at Liège around 1207. The Franciscans received verbal approval in 1209 and a rule in 1223, followed by the Dominicans in 1216. Rome privileged these orders to perform sacramental, penitential and preaching services. They opened the way for lay enthusiasm and helped divert the flood from the threatening popular heresies.

The expansion continued until the counterattack of the secular clergy and the older orders clamped the lid on again from 1245 to 1311. Before that, however, divergent persons and their opponents in lay devotional groups associated with the new orders had created a lay religious competence, equalled again only during the Reformation of the sixteenth century. Anent the Lombard Humiliati whom he visited in 1216, James of Vitry praised their preaching, remarking that many male members were 'literate', meaning that they had some Latin. Those limited to the vernacular also knew much religion. The humble Prous Boneta of Montpellier, for example, commented on the earthly paradise soon to come, then briefly held up by 'her' Antichrist, Pope John XXII. She noted that Franciscans and Dominicans had prepared the way for a new church, a spiritualized Eve, whose fabric was, however, temporarily rent asunder. From Eve, God, a spiritualized Adam, had had two sons, Cain and Abel, the latter being the Franciscan Peter John Olivi, and the former the recently canonized Dominican Thomas Aquinas. 'Just as Cain slew his brother Abel in the flesh, so did this brother Thomas slay his brother, namely the said brother Peter John, spiritually, that is, in his writings.'[1]

Much of this was related to a battle over language. Most sectarians used only the vernacular and, although not to flourish until the Reformation, the notion that Latin slavery was opposed to vernacular freedom was already known. Waldes employed a priest to translate scripture, and translations of commentaries by Jerome, Augustine, Gregory I and Bernard of Clairvaux were seen. The context of this effort was that, as noted above, vernacular poetry and literature were invading the world of ideas and, after an initial period when lay scribes and notaries revived and popularized a vulgarized Latin, vernacular legal documents were penetrating into law and contract. This change portended the subordination of the clergy to secular magistrates and princes in later modern nation-states. In the meantime, the clergy reacted vigorously. In 1178, a cardinal examining heretics at Toulouse was horrified at having to discuss the faith in the vernacular and not in Latin, the language of the western clergy, of its liturgy and thought since antiquity. By the end of the 1230s, papal letters, local conciliar legislation and the inquisitors had begun to prohibit translations because sectarian biblical interpretations combated orthodox ones. All the same, churchmen were obliged to use the vernacular to spread their teaching, thus also helping to popularize religious culture immensely by 1300.

As long as monasticism expanded to admit new devotions and functions, lay utopians could express their hopes by entering religion without too greatly disturbing civil society with its many necessary but unhappy institutions. Churchmen often said that they alone could live according to natural and divine law, that is, sharing property communally in apostolic communism's true freedom and equality. In the world, laymen were obliged to live by the civil law, the law that instituted slavery and private property. Perhaps because they could exist alongside and not within secular society, also, the Humiliati, Beguines and mendicants were able to build relatively durable institutions; durable, at least, when compared to short-lived ancient or modern utopian settlements.

---

[1] W.H. May, 'The Confession of Prous Boneta, Heretic and Heresiarch' in *Essays in Medieval Life and Thought* (eds. Mundy, Emery and Nelson) 24.

However, there were limits to the discreteness of the social orders, which were, in fact, already breaking down. As seen above, the spread of the monastic calling to layfolk began to empower men and women to live in the cloisters of their hearts while inhabiting the world and going about its business. Although its full weight was not felt until nearly two centuries had passed, secularism or the lay spirit was therefore already alive. Ecclesiastical visions necessarily shared similarities with secular ones. Although churchmen insisted on distinguishing between ecclesiastical and secular matters, some went pretty far in the other direction. When discussing the sin or heresy of simony, Peter Cantor said that princes derive their authority from consecration: 'When someone is too young, as a boy to whom as heir a kingdom falls, or someone is insufficient in life and merit, does not the prelate sin who grants him consecration? It seems so. For does he not consent? He can and ought to resist.'[2] Since justice is sacred, it is simony to sell it or buy its exercise, just as it is simony to buy a kingdom or a duchy because princes have the care of souls:

> One wonders whether the royal dignity should be conferred by election. It appears iniquitous that, as though forced by necessity, men should be obliged to receive unjust princes by reason of succession. Jerome says: 'Joshua the son of Nun is chosen from another tribe that it may be known that the government of the people is to be conferred not because of blood but because of life.'[3]

Is hereditary monarchy then heretical?

That enthusiasts' beliefs reached into political and social realms is not surprising. War and coercion were to be abolished. Both the Waldensian sects and the Passagians, for example, urged Christians to beat their swords into ploughshares and nations not to learn war any more, and most assuredly not the Crusade: 'That for which kings were created, namely to wage war, to wield the material sword and administer punishment, has no further place among Christians.'[4] Exploitation was condemned and economic brotherhood prized: all must labour honestly and not live by others' sweat. The primitive communism of the apostles was the model for Christian organization.

Robert of Curzon's utopian message and the propaganda against usury of his contemporary Stephen Langton provided arguments for economic brotherhood that were useful to guildsmen when attacking exploitative entrepreneurs and rich masters. It will be recalled that craft and trade guilds were only beginning to be organized after 1150, and that the full flood of this

---

[2] *Liber casuum conscientiae* 185 in *Summa de sacramentis et animae consiliis* III 2a (ed. Dugauquier) 102.

[3] *Liber casuum conscientiae* 185 (ed. Dugauquier) 101. Jerome in *Decretum* 2 8 1 6 in *CICan* I 591.

[4] *Summa contra haereticos* ascribed to Praepositinus of Cremona 21 (ed. J.N. Garvin and J.A. Corbett, Nôtre-Dame, 1957) 225–26. See Micah 4:3.

movement was not attained until the late thirteenth century. Although few guilds were directly affiliated with the Church, the spectacular growth in the number of hospitals and confraternities offering burial and hospital care shows how close the explosion of religious passion was to the emergence of a guild economy. Although useful for all classes, these services were especially needed by working-class people, and charitable institutions evoked less resistance from the rich than did economic ones. Although often founded by nobles or patricians, early Beguine settlements in the Low Countries and Rhine valley attracted female workers in the cloth industry, women who continued to work after conversion. Widespread in north and central Italy, the Humiliati were initially industrial workers, and craftsfolk exploited by entrepreneurs had an unusual affinity for religious enthusiasm. Among these were weavers, whose very name became a popular synonym for 'heretic'.

Christ's or the apostles' poverty had a natural appeal to such groups because it asserted the moral superiority of the poor. William Cornelis, a secular canon of Antwerp, resigned his prebend, preached poverty and died in the odour of sanctity in the early 1250s. On his demise, his followers were charged with heresy because they were said to maintain that the poor were automatically saved and the rich damned. Being in a state of grace, indeed, the poor could fornicate and commit prostitution without sin. Working-class commitment to enthusiasm emphasized labour's purifying force, an idea exemplified by the Waldensians, Humiliati and Beguines. Although begging, or mendicancy, taught the virtue of humility, Francis of Assisi's rule of 1221 urged his friars to work at the trades they knew and, using all the New Testament passages on manual labour, James of Vitry reported in 1216 that the early Franciscans worked with their hands.[5] Utopian ideas die hard. Later on, Bishop Robert Grosseteste of Lincoln preached to the Franciscans at Oxford and, after praising mendicancy, went on to observe that there was a higher calling, 'namely, to live from one's own labour. Whence he observed that the Beguines are the most perfect and holy of religious because they live of their own labour and do not burden the world.'[6]

For several reasons, however, labour was minimized and, in the case of the Franciscans, replaced with mendicancy. Not all churchmen were happy about this replacement. Aiming his shots at the Beguines and Beghards, William of St Amour, a secular master at Paris, complained that the world was crowded with unproductive people:

> What I have said above concerning mendicity I have said especially because . . . of youths called Good Workers and young women called Beguines, who are spread

---

[5] See *Lettres de Jacques de Vitry* (ed. Huygens) 76, and, in Letter No. 1, Ephesians 4:28, 1 Thessalonians 4:10–21 and 2 Thessalonians 3:7–12.

[6] Thomas of Eccleston, *Tractatus de adventu fratrum minorum in Angliam* 15 (ed. Little) 99.

throughout the whole kingdom. They are all perfectly capable of work but instead wish to do little or no labour and live from alms in bodily sloth under the pretext of praying.[7]

But his was a lost cause. Early on, some argued against the Waldensian requirement of manual labour by noting that the Lord had exempted his apostles from it because he wanted them instead to preach, pray and save souls. The decline of religious economic utopianism also coincided with the political and economic triumph of artisan guilds. Fearing competition once they had won their place in the world, they no longer needed utopian aid, and turned against celibate workers.

Utopian enthusiasm was also linked to society's assault on usury. Just as the religious mind joined sodomy to heresy, so it did usury, the offence against economic brotherhood. The attack on these two 'crimes' by the White Confraternity, established in Toulouse in 1209 under Bishop Fulk of Marseilles mentioned earlier, is an example of this ecclesiastical propaganda and action. Caesarius of Heisterbach reports that around 1200 heretics from Montpellier came to preach in Metz, and were there protected by patricians who hated the bishop because he had refused burial to one of their usurious relatives. But usurers were not necessarily inclined towards heresy. At Toulouse Pons of Capdenier, whose testament of 1229 included restitution for usury, was described by none other than Bernard Gui as the 'patron' of the newly founded Dominican order. As with sodomy, so with usury: it was risky enough without adding heresy. Heretics, moreover, answered orthodox charges by charging churchmen with profiting from usury. In Bologna in 1299, they claimed that the Dominicans buried usurers for a share of their filthy lucre, all to keep their concubines in style!

As noted above, usury had class connotations. Usurers were not merely those who lent money at interest, but those who became infamous doing so. Because the poor were preserved for virtue by incapacity to be evil and the old rich by lack of need or antipathy to the counting house, usurers denominated infamous were usually new men making their fortunes. Especially in the twelfth century, when episcopal lords of cities were charging the proponents of urban liberty with heresy, it is sure that some of them were inclined to deviant thought. In Languedoc, however, middle-class burghers were relatively few among those listed in the inquisitor's registers.

Nobles and patricians, the great bourgeois of Metz, for example, or the merchant bankers of Tuscany, were more involved. An example is Hugh Speroni, a consul of Piacenza and schoolmate of the jurist Vacarius at Bologna, who wrote against the Church around 1177 and whose sect was still alive

---

[7] Alphandéry, *Les idées morales chez les hétérodoxes latins au début du XIIIe siècle* (Paris, 1903) 12–13n. 'Good workers' translates *boni valeti*, meaning journeymen.

in the 1220s. Another was Peter Maurand of Toulouse, who confessed and underwent penance in 1178, involving a trip to the Holy Land, restitution of usury and surrender of tithes to the Church. A patrician whose family was unusually Cathar, Peter owned a towered town house and large rural properties including a castle or fortified village. An inquisitorial register of 1245–47 shows that the mixed rural and urban aristocracy of the area in and around Toulouse was deeply implicated in this belief. These wealthy folk were surely attracted to divergent thought for many reasons. One may have been that, being used to having their way, to have a variant spiritualism to set against the authority of orthodoxy was naturally appealing. In the Midi, also, they may have worried about the rise of new wealth and popular parties threatening their leadership. The latter possibility tinctures with truth the common Guelph charge that Italian Ghibellines were heretical. Still, all that can be said is that the imperialist party in Milan, Brescia and Bologna had heretical overtones, and that Ghibelline chiefs in Lombardy, like Humbert Pallavicini and the proto-tyrant Ezzelino of Romano in his lordships of Treviso, Padua and Vicenza, actively protected heretics against the inquisitors.

Urban or rural?

Deviating belief or heresy, it is rightly reported, was strongest and most inventive where urban life was vigorous. North and central Italy were its most vibrant centres, and Milan, the very symbol of industry and self-government, was often described as heresy's capital. Other lively areas were western Languedoc, the Rhone valley, the Rhine with its western confluents and the relatively heavily urbanized region extending from Liège through Brabant to Flanders. These were also, however, the same regions where Gregorian enthusiasm had been liveliest, where most monastic innovations were first introduced, where the mendicant movements had their initial success and where orthodox learning flourished most brightly. In other words, regions marked by relatively heavy urbanization were in the forefront of everything, orthodox or heterodox.

Not that rural populations were untouched by divergent thought. Rural Flanders and the villages of Champagne, whose fairs were visited by Italians and other foreigners, were influenced by Catharism. Languedoc and adjacent regions offer the best examples of rural heresy, where it followed a pattern later repeated in the Protestant movement. Catharism flourished among nobles in the early thirteenth century, and even penetrated the local princely houses of Foix, Béziers-Carcassonne and possibly St Gilles-Toulouse. The Crusade of 1209–29 and the repression by the inquisitors through the decades prior to 1250 drove heresy out of the well-to-do, both rural and urban, and confined it to the humbler classes. Nobles and patricians were too visible and exposed and more attracted by careers in civil and ecclesiastical office than were ordinary folk. Oliver of Termes, member of a heretical family and militant opponent of the Crusade and the inquisitors in Narbonne during the 1230s, gave up, went on crusade with Louis IX in 1248 and entered royal service.

When attacked, deviant belief lost its hold first in rich areas. In Languedoc, for example, Catharism was strongly implanted in both town and country-side in the early thirteenth century. By about 1230, it was irreparably damaged in Toulouse, western Languedoc's capital. Even before 1250 it had weakened rapidly in the more populous and cultivated plains, being driven into the foothills of the Pyrenees. Impoverishment affected its intellectualism. The historian Matthew Paris reported that Lombard and Tuscan Cathars had sent members to study at the University of Paris, and three such students were condemned in 1241 and 1247. By 1300, Catharism had ceased to grow intel-lectually and was being reduced to a somewhat primitive dualism. In Italy, dissent was also pushed out of the towns and plains into isolated geographic pockets: the Piedmont, the Alps above Lake Como and the Apennines. An example is Gerald Segarelli's sect called the Apostles, who distilled a mixture of Franciscan poverty, Joachitic optimism and dualism. Starting in Parma and the Romagna about 1260, the sect spread throughout Lombardy. By 1308, when its leaders were executed, it was strong only in a few villages in the mountain piedmont above Vercelli.

The fact that a local lord hostile to the town of Vercelli initially aided the Apostles shows that there was more to this than mere flight. Inhabitants of marginal lands, especially uplands, seem to have favoured secession. Waldensians spread from the Rhone valley to the hills of Dauphiny, Savoy and Piedmont. In 1210, the bishop of Turin launched against them the first of a series of small punitive expeditions that lasted throughout the century. In the meantime, these sects spread through the Alps to Austria, Moravia and Bohemia (where Peter Waldes died in 1216). In the early fourteenth century they began moving down the Apennines to southern Italy. The endemic social conflict between hill and plain seen in much of Italy in the later Middle Ages was already emerging, a reflection of the combat between town and countryside and between crop agriculture and herding. Hillfolk resisted ecclesiastical and secular government, tax collectors and the repres-sion of smuggling designed to protect a corporatized economy. A primitive version had earlier been seen in the northern German forests and marshes around the Weser River. Rural 'Stedingers' were charged with heresy and defeated in 1234 by a holy war launched by nearby towns, rural lords, bishops and papal pronouncements. Vestigially pagan, perhaps, and surely reluctant to pay tithes, the Stedingers were resisting commercial penetration and centralizing government.

Divergent belief also demarcated cultural frontiers. An example was Bogomil Catharism, proselytized from Byzantium through Bulgaria into the south-east marches of Latin Christendom. Having become the religion of a Bosnian local prince, Innocent III condemned it in 1199, an anathema repeated by Honorius III in 1221. In spite of campaigns launched by Hungarians and Venetians, this ineradicable cult continued into modern times.

To conclude this brief section on the regional history of heresy or divergent belief, although rural populations rarely invented or developed it to its highest intellectual pitch, they were as much given to it as urban ones. It is clear, moreover, that urban growth does not wholly explain its incidence, because it was stronger in lightly urbanized Languedoc than in heavily urbanized Flanders. One also notes that the Low Countries, the Rhine and the Rhone valleys, Languedoc and north and central Italy generated most new enthusiasm for orthodoxy as well as for heterodoxy. These were also the regions where the devolution of political power into small principalities and urban republics was most marked. Areas in which the older monarchies held on better or were renewing their power, such as England, royal and Plantagenet France, Aragon, Castile and Norman and Hohenstaufen southern Italy, were famed neither for heresy nor (save for academic) inventive orthodoxy. Although ecclesiastical liberty had everywhere increased since Gregorian days, the greater princes of these regions had retained much power over their local churches, and hence were interested in defending institutions in which they still enjoyed presidency. Where the link between secular power and the Church was weaker, religion was both more inventive of new forms of orthodoxy and more liable to heretical secession.

Force and repression

Ecclesiastics were terrified or infuriated by divergence. Although some detested the practice – Peter Cantor, for example, cited Abelard, Bernard of Clairvaux and Gilbert of La Porrée as though all opposed it! – schoolmen often charged that their rivals' opinions smacked of heresy. In spite of this, from 1150 to 1300 no ecclesiastical intellectual was more than censured, rusticated or briefly imprisoned for deviant opinions. This contrasts sharply with the burning or perpetual immurement frequently meted out to the members of heretical sects. Although, therefore, the charge of heresy was thrown about loosely, ideological divergence on the part of single individuals or intellectual groups rarely invited serious repression. John of Joinville reports that a bishop of Paris consoled a university teacher who doubted the sacraments by likening him to a soldier at the front and himself to a man back home where it was safe.

Dissent by individuals differs from mass secession, and how extensive that could be is seen in western Languedoc. In 1207 at Montréal near Carcassonne, a papal legate was obliged to debate publicly with a group of Cathars, his performance being 'judged' by four laymen, knights and burghers. In the same year Pons Ademar of Roudeille, a 'wise knight', told Fulk of Marseilles, bishop of Toulouse, that he could not act against the Cathars 'because we have been raised with them, have kindred among them and see them live virtuously'.[8] Although these were minorities amidst (passive?) orthodox majorities, such large-scale secession was threatening.

The Church defeated popular divergent belief mainly by opening its arms to the initiators of new devotions, enthusiasms and utopianism. However dangerous these were, their success in undermining heresy is evident. When Bishop Fulk of Toulouse visited the Low Countries in 1212 to raise money and men for the Albigensian crusade, he was impressed by the success against heresy of the Beguines, a group introduced to him by Robert of Curzon and James of Vitry. Four years later James, on his way to Rome – where he had the Beguines approved – and the Holy Land, stopped off in Milan:

> which is the womb of heresy, where I remained for some days and preached . . . One can scarcely find anyone in the whole city who resists the heretics save for certain holy men and religious women called Patarines by the malicious and worldly, but Humiliati by the pope who gave them the right to preach to fight the heretics, and who confirmed their order. These people leave all for Christ, assemble in communities, live by manual labour and preach God's word . . . So greatly has this order multiplied in the diocese of Milan that they have founded 150 conventual congregations, men in some and women in others, without counting those who remain in their own homes.[9]

The Church, in short, defeated the popular heresies partly by means of persuasion, that is, by preaching or providing seemingly attractive alternatives.

Many believed that coerced belief was not true belief, and therefore hoped that persuasion would succeed. Bernard of Clairvaux preached in Languedoc in 1145 and, although his effort was much lauded, he was hooted down at Verfeil near Toulouse and his tour had no lasting effect. Later Cistercian missions reinforced preaching by coercion. The third Lateran Council of 1179 asked laymen to help, promising Crusaders' protections, and two years later Henry of Marcy, abbot of Clairvaux, cardinal and papal legate, raised a small force while preaching in Languedoc and captured the town of Lavaur. In 1209 the Albigensian crusade was launched, at first under the command of the legate Arnold Amalric, abbot of Cîteaux.

A similar change took place among the Dominicans, whose founder, Dominic Guzman, had preached in Languedoc without much success from 1206 to 1208. In 1221 the pope instructed the order to combat heresy. Ten years later they were referred to as inquisitors in a law applicable in Rome that passed into imperial legislation the next year. Thereafter the Dominicans (and occasionally the Franciscans) produced not only famed preachers but also inquisitor-judges. From the 1230s onwards, Dominican lay associates

---

[8] *Guillaume de Puylaurens Chronique* 8 (ed. Jean Duvernoy, Paris, 1976) 48–50.
[9] *Lettres de Jacques de Vitry* (ed. Huygens) 72–73 No. 1. *Patarin* meant heretic in Lombardy.

or tertiaries were brigaded into confraternities of Jesus Christ or the Blessed Virgin to hunt heretics, and the Dominicans denounced as unprofitable the public debates with heretics that had been common around 1200.

During the battle against dissent, teaching and preaching were not what a modern might imagine. Roland of Cremona has been mentioned as the first Dominican to teach in France, for a time, in fact, at the new university in Toulouse. In 1231, he led a mob there on Christmas day that burst into a house where a Waldensian had died, tore it down, converted it into a latrine, disinterred the body and dragged it off to be thrown on the town dump. And preaching was similar to what was seen in yesterday's one-party states. In 1247, the count of Toulouse repeated ecclesiastical injunctions by ordering his subjects to assemble and hear the preaching of mendicant friars not only on feast days and Sundays, but whenever they came to town. Churchmen had clearly come to believe that persuasion without coercion was inefficacious.

And the ultimate coercion was judicial. The penalties visited on those designated heretics were found in Roman law and, since heresy was a crime against the state, an entity defended by war, the death penalty for pertinacious heretics and confiscation of property were recommended. In regard to the requisite publication and enforcement, local princes took the lead. Other than profiting from the confiscation of property, their motives were various. Some fought to protect their profitable local churches; others desired to appear more catholic than the pope. England was off to an early start. In 1165–66, a group of Flemish or German Cathars was condemned by a local synod at Oxford, 'relaxed' to the secular court and there branded and exiled. One of Henry II's attempts to impose a settlement on Thomas Becket, the *Constitutions of Clarendon* of 1166, ordered punishment for those aiding heretics. The kings of Aragon then moved ahead, imitating Roman law by ordering exile, confiscation and, in 1197, death by fire. In edicts issued from 1224 to 1239, Frederick II Hohenstaufen extended the death penalty from Lombardy to all his dominions. His laws were 'canonized' by Innocent IV in 1254, thus making ecumenical what had been local.

Not all were happy about this revival of old law, but it won out. An example of changing attitudes is seen in comments on the execution of Arnold of Brescia at Rome in 1155. At the time, this act was attributed to the civil prefect of Rome and not to the pope, but contemporaries knew that this was mere legalism. Gerhoh of Reichersberg wept:

> How I wish he had been punished for his admittedly evil doctrine by exile or imprisonment or by any other penalty than death, or, at least, that he had been killed in such a way that the Roman Church or its court should not bear the responsibility for his death.[10]

---

[10] *De investigatione Antichristi* in *MGH Ldl* III 347–48.

By the time the canonist Huguccio of Pisa (d. 1210) wrote, Arnold's fate was no longer bewailed, but instead praised as an example. To be tried, degraded, hanged and then burned on order of the pope, as Huguccio describes it, was justifiable and shows that 'when incorrigible, [heretics] are to suffer the extreme penalty, as was done in the case of Arnold of Brescia'.[11]

Some wanted to mitigate the severity. Before heresy became widespread, they could afford to be tolerant, largely because the people and princes almost thoughtlessly slew those who diverged from the Church. About such a lynching, Bernard of Clairvaux said that 'we approve the [people's] zeal, but do not persuade them to do it because faith is a matter of persuasion not to be imposed by force'.[12] Long before Innocent IV, this disingenuous position became untenable, and moderates such as Peter Cantor were reduced to insisting on due process and easier punishment. Peter blamed a prelate for condemning as Cathars women who had refused the advances of a priest. He may have had in mind an event in the late 1170s, when Gervase of Tilbury precipitated the extirpation of a sect in Rheims because a maiden refused his overtures by rashly asserting that the loss of her virginity would be tantamount to immediate damnation! Still, the Chanter did not want heretics to circulate freely and corrupt others. Imprisonment was best but, if death was to be imposed, a heretic should be given time to think it over. The Romans, he thought, were gentler than the judges of his own day:

> Even the infidels used to allow Christians a thirty-day delay . . . to think over whether or not they wished to sacrifice to the idols . . . Why then does the Church presume to examine men's hearts with this strange and uncouth judgement? Why are Cathars immediately burned and not given legitimate delays to think the matter over?[13]

In the past, deviance had been pursued and punished by episcopal and secular authorities. Reliance on the latter was insufficient because it gave laymen power over the clergy, and because laymen were either indifferent or excessively severe, action against heretics, for example, often being like lynching. Episcopal action was slow because prelates were recruited from local society and reflected local moods, something obviously harmful to the Church in Languedoc, where the well-to-do were often heretical or indifferent. Local ordinaries continued to be active, but were soon stiffened by inquisitors appointed by the popes in the 1230s.

These latter were usually chosen from among the new mendicants, especially Dominicans. Armed with papal letters instructing them 'to reform the Church' as well as purge heretics, their missions initially enjoyed popular support but soon awakened opposition. Aided by mendicants and fortified

---

[11] Maisonneuve, *Etudes sur l'origine de l'Inquisition* 88.
[12] Ibid. 105n.
[13] *Verbum abbreviatum* 72 in *PL* CCV 320.

by papal authority, Conrad of Marburg, a canon of Mainz, spread fire and death in much of western Germany from 1227 but, having taken on a rich landed notable, he and three companions were assassinated in 1233. The Dominican Robert the Bugger (so called because he was a converted Cathar or Bulgar) was active from Flanders to Champagne. The apex of his career was reached in 1239, when he is said to have burned just under two hundred inhabitants of the village of Montwimer in one day. He was shortly thereafter sentenced to life imprisonment as mad. Occasional excesses, however, were not the principal reason for opposition. What provoked resistance was simply that the heretical minority resisted being rooted out and the relatively orthodox majority wearied of the disruption caused by probing investigations. After reading an inquisitor's register, one understands why local Cathar lords slew no fewer than ten inquisitors at Avignonet south of Toulouse in 1242. The history of Peter of Verona also illustrates the ambivalence with which this problem was fraught. The first inquisitor at Milan (from 1233), this Dominican was assassinated in 1252. Within ten months of his death, he, who had saved souls by slaying bodies, was canonized as St Peter Martyr.

Although accepting help against heretics, local clergy were rarely enthusiastic about the inquisitors or speedily tired of them. Meeting in councils, French and German bishops arrested the missions of Conrad of Marburg and Robert the Bugger. The papacy, however, generally had its way, and the mendicant inquisition was introduced along with mendicant preaching and teaching. Princes and self-governing communities also often resisted the papal inquisition. Frederick II Hohenstaufen promulgated harsh laws against heresy, but his Ghibelline supporters actively impeded inquisitors. Where heresy was weak and the state's power over the local church strong, the papal inquisition never penetrated. This was the case in Castile, England and much of central, north and east Germany. Inquisitors were to be found in France, but were especially busy in frontier provinces such as Flanders, Champagne and Languedoc.

What was happening was that, in spite of a failed attempt to centralize by appointing in 1262 an inquisitor resident at the papal court, the actual inquisitors were gradually bowing to the secular state. An early example about Catalonia–Aragon illustrates this. King Peter III had issued the severe law of 1197 threatening heretics with fire adverted to above, but was nevertheless slain by the Crusaders when leading his southern allies at Muret in 1213. Facing papal pressure, his successor's parliament at Tarragona in 1234 adopted a provision issued by the council of Toulouse of 1229 favouring the inquisition, but changed a vital provision. In Toulouse bishops were to appoint sworn priests or other clerks and two or three laymen to investigate suspect communities; in Tarragona the king or his local officer chose the layfolk. Another example is seen in 1255, when Alphonse of Poitiers, the first Capetian to rule in Toulouse, replaced south French Dominicans by ones from Paris.

Similar to that of his largely northern civil officers, this recruitment was evidence of the French absorption of Languedoc.

The repression of heresy was necessarily tied to politics. Around 1250, the inquisitor Rainier Sacconi estimated that there were about 2,500 Cathar Perfects in northern and central Italy as against some 200 in southern France, but the crusade was launched against Languedoc, not Lombardy. The pope had proposed a crusade against Milan in 1213, but dropped it because this Lombard capital headed the towns who were the papacy's allies in the struggle against the Empire. By 1236 when the emperor resurrected the idea, the popes would have nothing to do with it. Although townsfolk everywhere fought the first introduction of the inquisitors in the 1230s (and as late as 1256 in Genoa and 1289 in Venice), the frequency with which their advent was hailed by the Guelph, or popular, parties (as in Milan in 1233) implies that the citizenry of Italy's urban republics favoured them. As long as Ghibelline or Hohenstaufen power balanced that of the Guelphs, Lombardy remained the home of toleration for those of divergent religious commitment. A farmer from Ax near Pamiers confessed in 1321 that a mercer had told him six or seven years ago 'that heretics, Jews and Saracens – indeed all good workers – were not harmed in Lombardy, and that to hurt those who earned their living by work was criminal'.[14] The inquisition penetrated slowly elsewhere, as in Spain. It took time to eradicate the commitment of Catalonian and Pyrenean nobles to Catharism. Only after the Peace of Corbeil between France and Aragon of 1258 was confirmed in 1262 did the crown break the opposition of the nobles so that the parliament of Ejea in 1265 admitted 'its' inquisition.

Inquisitors also needed technical information. In 1178, it was still possible for a council at Toulouse headed by a papal legate to make a Cathar recant by repeating the oath exacted from Berengar of Tours in 1059 in favour of the real presence in the sacramental host. This worked because Cathars also did not believe in the real presence, but was rough and ready. Inquisitors needed guides, and special books were speedily added to the already vast literature against heresy. Partial ones appeared in the 1240s, but the first large one was written around 1256, an anonymous work later expanded by the Franciscan David of Augsburg (d. 1272). With manuals came sophistication: the basic beliefs of each sect were described and lines of interrogation suitable for each suggested. The surgical tenor of this literature is illustrated by Bernard Gui's discussion of what to do about a heretic who wants to retract when being led out to execution. Unless a recidivist, he or she is to be received into penance, for two reasons: mercy is to be preferred to rigour and, adds the policeman, the fainthearted would be scandalized were a

---

[14] *Le registre d'inquisition de Jacques Fournier 1318–1325* II p. 157: Petrus de Fonte de Vayshis.

penitent refused. The sincerity of the penance, however, is to be demonstrated by a prompt confession of the names of all associates.

Resistance enraged these policemen. Inquisitors were sometimes onetime heretics, and some, like the Bugger, went mad at work. Even Bernard Gui, perhaps provoked by the Franciscan Bernard Délicieux's (d. 1320) attacks on Dominican inquisitors, abandoned judicial calm to record with joy the slaughter of Dolcino of Novara and Margaret, the last leaders of the Italian Apostles, in 1307. Margaret was cut to pieces before Dolcino's eyes, and he was himself chopped up immediately after. These punishments should not leave the impression that inquisitors were uniquely brutal. As seen above, awful corporal punishments were normal in Latin jurisprudence, and this savagery was reinforced by the educational publicity given to public executions. By partially replacing the death penalty with imprisonment, moreover, the inquisitors were even progressive. All the same, their underfinanced prisons were infamous.

The Catharism of western Languedoc was eradicated by bishops and inquisitors in three stages. A vehement attack initially close to lynching rooted it out of the capital city of Toulouse by the mid-1230s. Two better-organized inquisitorial campaigns, those of 1245–46 and 1256–57, then broke the back of the heresy in rural districts around town. The first was directed against a heresy still widespread and was more gentle than the second, which pursued stubborn remnants. In the year 1246, 945 heretics were sentenced. None was killed; eleven per cent were imprisoned, and eighty-nine per cent were given various penances, including pilgrimage and Crusade service. In 1256–57 about fifteen per cent of 306 sentences were levied against those previously dead in heresy or in flight, seven per cent were death penalties and there were seventy-eight life sentences. Even after the back of heresy was broken, the inquisitors found many victims, especially in the hills and mountains. Aided by others including James Fournier, bishop of Pamiers (later Pope Benedict XII, d. 1342), from 1308 to 1323 the Dominican Bernard Gui sentenced 638 persons, largely Cathars, but also some Waldensians, radical Franciscan Beguines, other sectarians and relapsed Jews. Although this harvest seems rich, these officers were scraping the barrel: Gui's celebrated *Manual* had a section on witches, the inquisitors' future market, so to speak.

Weighing heavily on society, inquisitorial professionalism had 'reformed' apprehension, investigation and punishment of divergent belief. Summed up in a series of titles in the *Sexts* 5 2 published by Boniface VIII, the judicial inquiry against putative wrongdoers began with obligatory depositions by witnesses drawn from the community, insisted on the secrecy of witnesses and denied counsel to defendants so as to expedite judgement 'without lawyers' din'. Its design was to elicit proof, ideally culminating in a voluntary confession by these 'murderers of souls and thieves of Christ's sacraments'. Imitating Italy's republics (as early as 1233 in Parma), torture was introduced by the papal letter *Ad extirpanda* in 1252. The reputation of these tribunals was not benign. When the Franciscan Bernard Délicieux was tried and condemned in 1319, he was charged with saying among other things that 'the inquisitors would have so mistreated Saints Peter and Paul had they been tried that they would have confessed heresy'.[15]

Inquisitorial brutality always excited opposition. Upset by protests against a blanket condemnation of 156 inhabitants of Limoux south of Carcassonne in 1248, Innocent IV intervened and precipitated the resignation of the inquisitors. But, once repression became habitual, bishops could be as harsh as the mendicant specialists. From 1280 to 1329, the bishop of Albi Bernard de Castanet violently attacked the town's patricians, alleging Catharism. To speak of only one family, the Pumets, the pursuit caught the senior male, his son, two of his brothers and four other persons both male (one a canon) and female bearing the family name. This campaign involved lifetime prison sentences, disinterring and burning deceased family members, destroying houses and confiscating property. A result was that civil opposition was unremitting.

The king of France Philip the Fair, responding to petitions from Languedoc in 1301, complained to the bishop of Toulouse about the pursuit of the Spiritual Franciscans, charging the Dominicans with committing 'abhorrent crimes' under the guise of protecting the faith. Both the offence and the protests prompted the popes, sometime after mid-century, to employ both inquisitors and bishops together. This eventually became obligatory, the crowning legislation being issued by Clement V at the council of Vienne in 1311, where his *Multorum querela* forbade either a bishop or an inquisitor acting alone to assign suspects to 'hard and straight prisons, which seem designed for punishment rather than custody, or to torture or indeed sentence them'.[16]

In spite of the failure to organize a real papal inquisition, the popular heresies of 1200 had been broken by the Church, some, like the Cathars, nearly extirpated, and others, like the Waldensians and illuminist sects, gravely weakened. This victory should not encourage readers to believe that whole populations were massacred. Awful though the repression was – patrician and noble families in Toulouse and its area, for example, lost not a few members and property – but wealth and power enabled them, after surrendering the freedom to think about the deity as they saw fit, to survive and even flourish. As to Toulouse's humbler families, two observations may be made: the powerful early repression inadvertently aimed high, socially speaking, and they were therefore afforded time to duck out. Besides, as was the case of the women in every class, weak evidence veils the fate of the poor far more than it does that of the rich, or, rather, that of rich males.

---

[15] Michel de Dmitrewski, 'Fr Bernard OFM, sa lutte contre l'inquisition de Carcassonne et d'Albi, son procès, 1297–1319', *Archivum Franciscanum Historicum* 17 (1924) 480.

[16] *Clementines* 5 3 1 (Friedberg 2 1181).

Deviant or secessionist belief, moreover, was changing. Impossible to camouflage, the dualism of the Cathars – who, it is worth recalling, thought of themselves as true Christians – never again played much of a role and, of these early groups, only the Waldensians (and the remote Bosnian Cathars) persisted into modern times. The inquisitor Bernard Gui said that Waldensians were 'foxy', and he was right: they were hard to nail down because they had so much in common with orthodoxy. Later divergent thought, moreover, had the advantage of being less immediately popular. The theological probabilism of the schools disguised the dangerous thrust of new ideas. The academic or sacerdotal grades of the spokesmen of what seemed a 'reforming' orthodoxy made it possible to build a party before the police broke it up. In the post-monastic age of the later Middle Ages, Waldes's true successors were John Wycliffe, John Hus and Martin Luther, all important ecclesiastics. The final chapter of this book will attempt to describe the start of the great transition, one in which the lay and clerical constituencies of the later Reformation were first beginning to identify themselves.

This said, it is wise to recall what was said before, namely that twelfth-century popular heresy was beaten not only by force but also by opening the Church to new devotions and orders and by preaching and teaching. One without the other, force or persuasion, would surely not have worked. Also, great though it seemed, the victory did not arrest the spread of divergent thought for long.

Part Six

1300

Chapter 23

Church, state and society

Lay and papal authority

The secular state always strove to appoint, control, judge and tax the clergy, and the Church, especially the papacy, attempted to regulate secular governments. The first combat after the Hohenstaufen defeat was between King Philip IV of France and Pope Boniface VIII. It started in 1296 and continued intermittently until the election of Clement V in 1305 and the removal of the papacy from Italy to Avignon on the Rhone river in 1309. The second began in the teens of the fourteenth century, involved a civil war in Germany and resulted in the election of an imperialist antipope. It reached its peak in the 1320s, but dragged on until 1347. The two principal protagonists were John XXII and the emperor (or, rather, king of the Romans) Lewis of Bavaria. This second combat exceeds the period treated in this volume.

To turn back, Alexander of Roes had said that the Empire fell victim to Rome and France. When Conradin was executed in 1268, the Hohenstaufen cause seemed obliterated, but it had left a legacy: Frederick II's polemics, for which the curialists invented the verb 'to frederize'. One lively centre of 'frederization' was the court of Philip IV the Fair. The French were especially dangerous heirs of the Hohenstaufen because, from Philip Augustus's latter years, France had been Rome's principal ally. The alignment of the Capetian cadet house of Anjou–Provence with the popes and the Guelph popular parties of Italy enabled the French to conquer south Italy and Sicily and spread their influence throughout the peninsula. Although second thoughts abounded as Angevin power was cemented, most Italians admired the French, their manners, arts and institutions. Medieval France was at its peak. The Plantagenets were defeated and Louis IX even arbitrated England's civil troubles at Amiens in 1264. Although suffering one severe defeat and gaining no territory, his expeditions bore the burden of the Crusades and helped stabilize the frontier with Islam from the 1240s until his death at Tunis in 1270. Louis exemplified monarchy's glory for all Europe. Noted above, the Florentine Remigio de'Girolami stated that, in comparison with France's king, all other western princes were mere kinglets. Even northern French heretics were loyal, Caesarius of Heisterbach remarking that the Amalricians believed that Latin Europe would be ruled by France's king in the forthcoming age of the Holy Spirit.

So useful were the French that the pontiffs converted Capetian and Angevin wars into crusades financed by clerical taxes. The popes also helped convince this nation that it was special. Although the title 'Most Christian King' was liberally bestowed, Innocent III declared in 1215 that this honorific was a special mark of France's kings. Alexander III told the archbishop of Rheims in 1171 that French kings had always helped St Peter in his hour of need and possessed unshatterable faith. In 1239, Gregory IX glorified the people of that nation by writing that, on earth as in heaven, 'the son of God . . . according to the divisions of tongues and of races . . . has constituted diverse kingdoms, among which, just as the tribe of Judah was granted the gift of a special benediction among the sons of the patriarch, so the kingdom of France is distinguished from all other peoples on earth by a privilege of honour and grace'.[1] As a pacific gesture between the already embroiled monarchy and papacy, Boniface VIII canonized Louis IX in 1297.

As France aided Rome, the number of cardinals representing French and Angevin south Italian interests gradually increased. Of the thirteen reigning popes from the accession of the French Urban IV in 1261 until that of Clement V in 1305, four were French, the first breach of the Italian monopoly of that office since 1159. For years – since the decretal *Per venerabilem* of 1213 referring to a king of France, as seen above – the popes argued that a king is emperor in his own kingdom, thereby contradicting Frederick I Barbarossa's observation that Europe's kings were mere 'kinglets' under the emperor. In 1303, Rome abruptly reversed its long-held position. Shortly before he was seized at Anagni by France's Roman allies, Boniface VIII remarked anent his tentative alliance with the German king Albert I of Habsburg that all kings, and especially the 'vainglorious' and untruthful king of France, were really subject to the emperor.

This attempted diplomatic revolution had no morrow. The brief pontificate of Boniface VIII's Italian successor was followed by Clement V, who moved the papal court from Rome – actually from the Patrimony, because the court had spent most of its time in Viterbo, Orvieto and elsewhere – to Avignon. There new troubles began. The renewed marriage of French and papal policies helped precipitate the battle between John XXII and Lewis of Bavaria. French influence had long been penetrating south and west Germany, and the Capetian court was dreaming of having its king elected emperor. Although with reservations, John XXII advocated that policy.

French power did not precipitate these conflicts; because, in fact, the reverse was true. The loss of Constantinople in 1261, the collapse of the union of

---

[1] Huillard-Bréholles, *Historia diplomatica Friderici secundi* V i 457–8.

the Byzantine and Roman churches in 1282, the fall of Acre in the Holy Land in 1291 and the shrinking of Europe's 'first colonial empire' in the face of Islamic and Byzantine attacks affected the French with peculiar intensity. They had led the Crusades and their language was implanted in the Near East and Aegean. They sought scapegoats, not only blaming the Templars, the first military order and a French foundation, but also their Roman ally. Much that exacerbated relationships between France and Rome was due to the arrest of French expansion, as well as the domestic crises foreshadowing France's internal breakdown in the later Hundred Years War. In 1296, the issue between Boniface VIII and Philip (as well as the king of England) was the secular government's right to tax the clergy without papal approval. The crown needed money to suppress the revolt of the Flemish cities and battle their English ally. Its penury was worsened by the refusal of its own well-to-do, rural and urban, to finance the government adequately.

The rivalry of France and England threatened Boniface VIII because it drew church revenue away from causes dearer to his heart. Foremost was the hope of resuming crusades against the infidel, a cause still believed in, at least formally, by many. But priorities differed. The pope wanted to get on with crusades, but first had to settle Italy; the French wanted the same, but first had to settle the Anglo-Flemish question. Another issue was Catalonia–Aragon. The revolt of the Sicilians against the Angevin French in the Vespers of 1282 had established a Catalan–Aragonese dynasty in that island. By the early fourteenth century, Catalan fleets and armies penetrated an Aegean Sea once ruled by the French and Italians and weakened Angevin Marseilles's commerce. The rise of this Iberian kingdom encouraged the still lively separatism of the recently absorbed provinces of the Midi, especially Languedoc and the adjacent Pyrenean principalities.

Catalonia–Aragon's emergence as a main player in Europe's affairs encouraged Boniface VIII to try to escape the French alliance. The repulse of repeated Angevin attempts to reconquer Sicily and the failure of the Capetians against King Peter III of Aragon led the pope (who had earlier assisted these efforts because of the link between Peter and the Sicilian Hohenstaufens) to think of allying with Barcelona. At least one Catalan spokesman, Raymond Llull, had plans for renewing the crusades that were more attractive to the pope than French ones. Whereas French and Italians usually proposed conquering Egypt or Syria as a start, Llull preferred to begin at Granada in Spain, and thence move through North Africa to Egypt and Syria. More appealing was the institutional side of Llull's scheme. While the French talked about uniting the military orders of the Church under their king, Llull proposed unifying these shock troops under Rome. Even more enticing was his notion 'that the pope and cardinals should assign the tithe of the Church to the Crusade until the Holy Land is conquered, the tithe which they now give to Christian kings. This tithe has its origin in, and is contributed by, those who labour so that the Church be honoured and sustained, but kings wickedly divert it to secular causes.'² The pope's attempt to work something out with Catalonia–Aragon, together with the unrest in Languedoc, precipitated Philip IV's attack on the papacy. In 1301 he arrested Bernard Saisset, bishop of Pamiers and papal legate. He also asked Rome to degrade the bishop and hand him over to his court, to be charged with treason and collusion with Catalonia and dissident southern French elements. The pope refused and issued the famous bull *Unam sanctam*, on which more anon.

At the time of Lewis of Bavaria, in addition, the pope's adhesion to French policies hurt the papacy. Even before the 1290s, Franciscan radicals from south France shared politics earlier seen in Italy, where, as the Hohenstaufens failed and the Angevins rose, utopians viewed the Franco-papal alliance as wicked. Hostile to the Crusade as an irruption of naked force into religion, they had prayed for the defeat of Louis IX's crusades. When the Catalans revived the Hohenstaufen dream in 1282, Franciscan radicals joined them, along with other sectaries. In south France this ideology was linked to regional separatism. Franciscans such as Bernard Délicieux intrigued with Catalonia–Aragon, and were consequently pursued by both the pope and the king of France in the 1320s. One result was that the Franciscan 'left' sided with Lewis of Bavaria.

France experienced more intensely what happened to all Europeans affected by the cessation of expansion and the Saracen counterattack. Because the German frontier continued to expand and the full extent of the Turkish threat was not yet apparent, it was hard to read the signs. Men still followed the same old roads, blaming others when they led nowhere, as Boniface blamed the French who, in turn, blamed him.

Ecclesiastical divisions

Although the clerical order had often split during past struggles with secular authority, it was unusually lacking in solidarity around 1300. Fearfully, France's prelates adhered to their king against the pope in the north French assembly of 1302. The secular clergy and the older regular orders had fought for nearly a century against the invasion of their parishes and prerogatives by the mendicant orders fostered by the popes. They were also linked to local interests, and had long resisted Rome's appointment of university-trained clergy or Italian absentees. Cardinal Matthew of Aquasparta's statement in consistory that the French had no grounds for complaint because only two French prelates were Italian, and these were famous men (one was Giles of Rome) who had spent much of their lives in France, was not heard over the Alps. The abbots of older orders, bishops and provosts of cathedral chapters traditionally

---

² *Disputatio Raymundi christiani et Hamar saraceni* 2 in *Beati Raymundi Lulli opera* IV 477b.

summoned to general councils also favoured a conciliar constitution, whereas the pope stood for monarchy.

The secular clergy's shaky loyalty would not have been decisive, however, had not the mendicants failed to help. A reason for this was that the growth of these new orders was being slowed by the clergy assembled in the general councils to which the popes were being forced to bow. Although represented by members who had been elevated to prelacies, the mendicants had no direct conciliar representation. The squeeze was already felt at the first Council of Lyons in 1245, but the legislation of second Lyons in 1274 was more drastic. Several recent orders of friars were there abolished, one being the Friars of the Sack, an order founded in Provence in 1248 and granted a rule in 1251, which boasted about eighty houses at its abolition. The culminating legislation was the canon *Cum de quibusdam mulieribus* at the Council of Vienne in 1311, which cut off further expansion by the Beguines. By that time, what had been viewed as progressive was seen as disorderly and dangerous. This opinion, moreover, was not foolish: monasticism was laicizing with a vengeance. In 1310 Augustine Trionfo, an enemy of Peter John Olivi, inveighed against the world of the lay enthusiasts, having in mind perhaps the Franciscan tertiary, philosopher and missionary Raymond Llull and the medical doctor and lay theologian Arnold of Villanova:

> When we see these fellows mobile in their status, now married, now continent, now secular, now monks, now overseas, now at home, now spurning the world, now belonging to it, this is a sign that their visions are not divine revelations but rather diabolical illusions.[3]

Nor could the conciliar fathers have had their way had not the mendicants themselves been divided. There were conflicts between the orders, especially between Dominicans and Franciscans, and also an increasingly intense battle within the latter order. By far the largest mendicant order, it was also the most tumultuous, partly because it was the major orthodox equivalent of the Waldensians described above. Francis and his early companions differed from other extremists because they obeyed bishops and popes, thereby playing a 'counter-revolutionary' role. The initial lay leadership of the order and the express desire to imitate Jesus' life and poverty enabled it to attract utopian spirits who would otherwise have leaned towards divergent thought. They hoped to rebuild in the Franciscan order a world modelled on the supernal Jerusalem.

In its early days, the principal conflict in the order concerned lay leadership. Francis was a layman and so was Elias of Cortona who, having served as the practical Martha to Francis's spiritual Mary until the latter's death in

---

[3] *Tractatus contra divinatores et sompniatores* 1 in Richard Scholz, *Unbekannte kirchenpolitischen Streitschriften aus der Zeit Ludwigs des Bayern* (Rome, 1914) II 483–84.

1226, assumed the office of minister general at that date. Elias tried to maintain lay predominance but as he slowly lost out to the clerical brethren,
he became increasingly arbitrary, especially during his second generalate
beginning in 1232. The lay principle protected him in Italy, but the opposition was led by friars from ultramontane houses where there was no mass lay
recruiting. This foreign pressure obliged or enabled the pope to depose him
in 1239. Although Francis and his companions provided an example of the
eremitical life and personal fulfilment, only the brethren in orders could provide the sacramental services necessary for Franciscan success in the lay world.

As in early Christianity, moreover, spontaneity and equality were lost
in emphasizing the mission. Francis, for example, suspected that education
created invidious distinctions between equals. His rule of 1223 therefore stated
that the brethren should not busy themselves with learning or even with
Latin. How this anti-intellectualism failed is seen in a statement of the general
Bonaventure. When discussing the origin of the order, this famous and learned
doctor asked:

> Does it not move you that the brothers were simple and unlearned in the
> beginning? . . . I confess that what has made me love the life of Francis is that it is
> like the beginning and perfection of the Church, which first began with simple
> fishermen and afterward advanced to famous and learned doctors . . . [Our order]
> was not invented by man's prudence, but instead by Christ . . . because learned men
> did not disdain to descend into the company of simple ones, bearing in mind the
> apostle's message: 'If there is a wise man among you, let him become a fool, that he
> may be wise.'

Francis's *Testament* of 1226 had also insisted that the rule that God had given
him should not be glossed away, but instead obeyed 'to the letter, to the
letter, to the letter'! Bonaventure glossed it:

> The rule does not prohibit study for those with letters, only for the unlettered and
> lay. Following the apostles, [Francis] wants each one to remain in the vocation to
> which he has been called so that no one should ascend from the laity into clerical
> orders, but he did not want clerks to become laymen by refusing to study.[4]

Although lay rule vanished with Elias's fall, the tertiary lay brethren were
often truculently radical in the late thirteenth century.

Few layfolk espoused the eremitical life of a Francis, but instead wanted
the preaching, sacramental, burial and charitable services that the order could
offer. To provide these, the Franciscans invaded the secular clergy's parishes,
battled with rival mendicants and acquired bishops' mitres and cardinals'

---

[4] Bonaventure's two cited passages are in *Opusculum XII: Epistola de tribus quaestionibus ad magistrum
innominatum* 13 in *Opera omnia: Opuscula varia ad theologiam mysticam et res ordinis fratrum minorum
spectantia* VIII (Quaracchi, 1898) 336a–b and 334b, in that order. Both refer to scripture, the first
to 1 Corinthians 3:18 and the second to ibid. 7:24.

hats. This had angered the founder, but it is fair to say that his friend Cardinal Hugolino of Ostia, the later Gregory IX, was of real value to him, and that he himself revealed a talent for manipulating others. He stilled the opposition to his *Second Rule* by having God speak to him directly, so that he appeared like another Moses on Sinai. Unlike the founders of other orders – including the Dominicans, who settled for a version of the so-called Augustinian rule – Francis's insistence on promulgating his own rule served to foster an aggressive sense of his order's peculiar fitness. This led later brethren to use papal privileges to get their way with the parish clergy, thus disobeying Matthew 10:23: 'when they persecute you in this city, flee into another', a passage repeated in the founder's testament of 1226. Again, the more the Franciscans defeated the popular heresies, the more vehemently they pursued their mission.

Missions require sustenance. Ideally, the Franciscan was to acquire, by begging or working, only enough for the day with no accumulation for the morrow, and neither member nor order was to have property. Even before mid-century, the idea of Franciscan poverty split into rigorous and lax interpretations: the poverty of the *usus pauper* as against moderate use. The austerity demanded by John of Parma, general from 1247 to 1257, or by the later Spiritual Franciscan Ubertino of Casale, was beyond the capacity of most brethren, and alienated them by favouring the ascetical minority. However moderate, use required property.

Property held in trust by other than the friars offered a way of both avoiding poverty and endowing the mission. The mission required the predictable use of economic means. It also needed cult centres, and the convents and churches erected in Francis's name, starting with the basilica raised over his tomb in Assisi by Elias, were costly. Without predictable use, libraries, scheduled preaching, sacramental services or charity could not be maintained. Missions also needed specialists whose training required time, time bought by property's fruits. Working men were sometimes wise and inspired, but had little time to learn and teach. Behind Prous Boneta stood Olivi, whose work on the Apocalypse she had read (or had read to her) in a vernacular translation. Behind Salimbene's stammering day labourer of Parma, Master Benvenuto, stood those who had translated or read him sections from the Bible, Joachim of Fiore, Michael Scot and anonymous prophetic works of the time.

The Franciscan quandary, in brief, was how to reconcile an aggressive mission with an ideological unwillingness to endow it. Starting with Gregory IX's *Quo elongati* of 1230, the pontiffs provided ways around the rigour of Francis's rule and testament. While the predictable use of the fruits accrued to the Franciscans, the ownership of the property from which the fruits derived was vested in a cardinal protector at Rome, two proctors in each province and associated layfolk. Writing shortly after 1312, the conservative

Bonagratia of Bergamo argued that, 'since by natural and divine law the use of all things pertaining to human life ought to be common to all men, and, since it came about by iniquity that this is said to be mine and that yours', the Franciscan's right to use nature's fruits fulfilled the communism of the apostolic community.[5] After Nicholas III issued the decretal *Exiit qui seminat* in 1279, moreover, which declared that Christ and his apostles owned nothing severally or in common, some believed that the Franciscans fulfilled Christian utopian hope.

Poverty became an obsession among Franciscans, perhaps because the defeat of their lay brethren had made them so similar to other mendicants. It became their special claim to attention, a substitute for the early order's social radicalism, and a way of beguiling its eremitical and laic wings. Although there were serious battles about poverty as early as the 1240s, the split between the minority radicals, soon to be called Spirituals (and, when they really diverged, Fraticelli), and the majority or Community awaited the end of the generalate of Bonaventure in 1272. Following the *usus pauper* guideline, the radicals first charged that the majority was not as austere as the founder wished. They then moved to a more telling point: the distinction between use and ownership was deceitful, because one who enjoys a predictable use of the fruit of a good is surely the 'moral' owner of the good in question. Composing his letter *Sanctitas vestra* just after 1312, the Spiritual Ubertino of Casale observed:

> Surely the blessed Francis did not wish that the possession would be the pope's and the use ours. Quite the contrary, he wanted ownership to be vested in the hands of prelates, donors or communities, so that no tenure be given the brethren . . . In his testament and legend he says that the brothers should not inhabit their poor homes as their own, but live as pilgrims and strangers in others' homes.[6]

Under Boniface VIII and John XXII, the popes' usual policy was to aid the Community against the Spirituals, sometimes with inquisitorial prosecution. The spirit of this effort is seen in a phrase from John XXII's bull *Quorundam exigit* of 1317: 'Great is poverty, but greater still is blamelessness and the greatest good of all is obedience.' John here quoted an ancient tradition urging the religious to remember that 'nothing so pleases God in a monk as obedience, and one obedience is worth more than all the other virtues'.[7]

---

[5] Douie, *The Nature and Effects of the Heresy of the Fraticelli* 158. Bonagratia used Gratian's paraphrase from Augustine and a letter attributed to Clement I in *Decretum* 1 8 1 and 2 and 2 1 2 in *CICan* I 12–13 and 676.

[6] Leff, *Heresy in the Later Middle Ages* I 148, partly derived from Bonaventure's *Legenda Sancti Francisci* 7 2 in *Opera omnia* VIII 523b.

[7] *Extravagantes Johanni XXII* 14 1 in *CICan* II 1223. The source passage is cited in Jordan of Saxony, *Liber vitas fratrum* 2 2 (ed. Arbesmann and Humpfner) 78. Jordan had it from Hugh of St Victor, who in turn used pseudo-Augustine, *Sermo de obedientia et himilitate*.

The radical Franciscans were therefore hostile to Boniface VIII in his French troubles and actively sided with Lewis of Bavaria against John XXII, and both the secular clergy, the Dominicans and some other mendicants, none of whom enjoyed the privilege of poverty, united to oppose them. In addition, the Community's position on use and ownership obliged the papacy to uphold a dubious case at the cost of some bloodshed and much disturbance. Spurred on by the Dominicans, the same pontiff declared in his *Cum inter nonnullos* of 1322 that to aver that Christ and the apostles did not own and have free use of property was heretical. In the decretal *Ad conditorem canonum* of the same year, he cut the Gordian knot and used the Spirituals' argument to weaken the Community's position. He there denied that there was any substantial difference between the predictable use of fruits and the ownership of the property whence they derived. With minor exceptions, therefore, Franciscans were to hold property as other orders did. Following Thomas Aquinas, John asserted that not poverty but charity or love was the basis of a perfect life. Having thus been stripped of their order's claim to attention, the Community's leaders went over to the side of the Bavarian, there to rest in uneasy proximity to their brothers of the radical wing. In brief, the largest and most popular order actively harmed both the papacy and ecclesiastical liberty in the struggle with the secular state.

The loss to the Church was more than tactical. Bonaventure reports that when Francis asked Innocent III for the right to be poor, Cardinal John Colonna said that he could not 'refuse the request of this poor man as being too hard and unheard of . . . If anyone should say that the observance of evangelical perfection or the vow of this man is strange, irrational or impossible, he blasphemes against Christ, the author of the Gospel.'[8] Nor did this failure merely involve the way of life. As poverty's partisans became aware of the resistance facing them, they began seeking assurances that their cause was inevitably going to win, and that shortly. In the 1240s, the Joachitic idea of spiritual progress penetrated radical Franciscan circles, and consequently each crisis over poverty was accompanied by one over Joachitic historicism. The first of these occurred during the generalate of John of Parma, when Gerard of Borgo San Donnino's *Introduction to the Eternal Evangel*, a glossed compilation of Joachim's works, was published. Gerard thought that these texts would replace both the Old and New Testaments in the forthcoming age of the Holy Spirit. The storm provoked by this publication resulted in a hasty condemnation of Joachim's teaching by a papal commission at Anagni in 1255, the resignation of John of Parma in 1257 and repression under Bonaventure. In the general chapter of 1266, that general even attempted to suppress all other lives of the order's sainted founder in favour of his own.

---

[8] *Legenda S. Francisci* 3 9 in *Opera omnia* VIII 512a.

The lid on the radicals was lifted when Raymond Gaufridi became general in 1289, and hope bloomed again until Celestine V resigned in 1294 and was replaced by Boniface VIII. Thereafter things worsened. Languedoc's Olivites were wiped out in the 1320s and Olivi's *Apocalypse* was condemned in 1326. This Franciscan's enemies claimed he said that Francis and his twelve companions had founded the church of the final age. The constitution of this new evangelical church was the several rules dictated by Francis, his testament and the bull *Exiit qui seminat* on the poverty of Christ. So infallible were these precepts, they said, that no authority, of pope or general and ecumenical council, could ever change them. If the Dominican Bernard Gui's understanding of what they had to say is correct, this self-designated elite asserted that they could reject the opinions of the Church in the name of spiritual progress. Anent *Exiit*, they may also have reinforced the already born notion of papal infallibility: so infallible was this bull that no successor on Peter's throne could change its teaching.

Some churchmen reacted by denying that the radical Franciscans were the vehicle of spiritual progress, and by questioning the idea of progress itself. John of Anneux, a secular clerk silenced in 1279 at the time of *Exiit*, sprang up to defend the pope in 1328, tripping over his tongue in his anger:

> How could this witless fellow Francis discover a new way of living which so many doctors, Augustine, Gregory and other saints inspired by the Holy Spirit didn't know, and which the Church that lasted before him for a thousand years didn't have, which was then more perfect, just as the men of that time were a hundred times more perfect than they are now; nor can this Francis's way of life be lived except by hermits in the desert.[9]

Others said the same with moderation, and hence it seems that the Franciscan failure marked a recession of the hope of spiritual progress that had fired the Church from the Gregorian period until Avignon. That hope had not vanished, however, but instead became attached to the secular state – as in the time of Cola di Rienzo (d. 1354) – to flower again in modern times as an obsession of secular dreamers.

The Franciscan failure also served to advance secularization, to bring nearer the moment when all true Christians, whatever their worldly vocation, equalled the religious. In his *Ad conditorem canonum*, John XXII argued that, without charity, a monk or friar derived no spiritual advantage from his vow of poverty unless he was free from the solicitude or care incumbent on those who seek to use property. Such was clearly not the Franciscan case or, indeed, that of any monk. Later on in 1334, Ockham angrily responded:

> This error opposes the religious who profess to live without their own property. According to it, if monks . . . are solicitous to acquire, conserve and dispense temporal

---

[9] Douie, *The Nature and Effects of the Heresy of the Fraticelli* 170.

goods after taking their vow of poverty ... their [personal] surrender of goods ... confers no advantage so far as [spiritual] perfection is concerned. From this error there follows a certain ancient error ... namely, that it is not better to do good works with the vow than without it.[10]

Ockham was right: John XXII had taught that there was no spiritual or moral advantage to being in a religious order. The doctrine of charity or love, moreover, could be treated similarly. A later defender of John's position, John of Celle, a Tuscan gentleman who retired to a hermitage in 1351, told the Fraticelli that they had made poverty their idol and lost sight of mercy and love. In urging the elders of Ephesus to be charitable, Paul had reminded them of Christ's injunction: 'It is more blessed to give than to receive.' John drew from this the corollary: 'And if this is true, and it surely is, the rich who give deserve more than the poor who receive'![11] Rich lay donors were therefore more blessed than poor monks who received. A utopian hope that had seemed about to penetrate all society at the time of the Humiliati, Robert of Curzon and others had been channelled into the Franciscan order, and had there failed once again.

Lay pressures

Clerks would not have vacillated had not layfolk pressed so hard, and they did so because, although at its apogee, Latin society was in difficulty. Overpopulation had led to the cultivation of marginally productive land. By 1300, social and economic corporatism had maximized rights and profits in agriculture, industry and commerce, and society was divided into interest groups flying at each other's throats in efforts to realize their ambitions. Men responded with anger and utopian fancies to this *rallentando* of their dreams' realization. The potentiality of social and economic corporatism for mobilizing larger units of production and government was known, but had yet to win support. To give that, people had to be convinced by the harsh experience of domestic and foreign war that private right and property should be diminished and the liberties and privileges of individuals, localities and social groups restricted. They were not yet ready to surrender these in order to erect the unitary monarchies or principates that were to harness and police their passions in early modern times.

Real princely government was already emerging around 1300. The idea of the 'arbitrary power' or 'free will' that empowered princes to act without the constraints of prior law or public assemblies was already well defined. Princely prerogatives were nevertheless still everywhere impeded by particularist

---

[10] *Tractatus contra Johannem 23* in H.S. Offler, *Opera politica* (Manchester, 1956) III 89.
[11] Felice Tocco, 'L'eresia dei fraticelli e una lettera inedita del beato Giovanni delle Celle' in *Studi francescani* (Naples, 1909) 460, and Acts 20:35.

elements and, indeed, were not to be freed – and then never wholly so – until ecclesiastical conciliarism had been defeated and secular parliamentarianism weakened in the fifteenth century and even after. Still, the restraints on the powers of princes and their unitary states were already visibly fading. Before 1300 Latin Europe had been ruled by an alliance of the ecumenical Roman Church with the local rural and urban well-to-do. At the time of Boniface VIII this combination faltered and these leading classes, hard pressed by the rise of the plebs beneath them and by the growth of princely power above, sought escape by sacrificing Rome.

Layfolk reacted for many reasons: they spoke of resistance to ecclesiastical domination, and how heavily the Church weighed on them. It did. The attack on usury, the exercise of controls over marriage and the family and the regulation of just war in the forum of conscience paralleled the Church's attempt to police Europe's states, to call for service against heretics and for participation in the Crusades. The Church's call also inadvertently summoned lay magistrates and princes to examine, and intervene in, its workings. Layfolk were not merely meretricious in their desire to control the behaviour, services and appointments of the clergy. Having been called to serve, their consciences or fears were as deeply involved in the affairs of the Church as those of the clergy. To witness executions was normal in the thirteenth century, but to light the fire, as inquisitors asked them to do, was different. Laymen were also more capable. The growth of lay literacy and professionalism had begun to give them the ability to intervene in the clerical sphere, and the spread of the monastic vocation to those living in the world was convincing them that they were the spiritual equals of churchmen.

Human conscience is related to interest. It was noted above that, in 1301, Philip the Fair complained to the bishop of Toulouse about the inquisitors' pursuit of the Spiritual Franciscans. The king later changed his tune on learning that the Spirituals were in touch with his enemies in Catalonia–Aragon. In 1308, the same prince mounted his campaign against the Templars and asked the theologians of Paris if lay magistrates could proceed against heretics without ecclesiastical permission. They said 'No!' – 'except when evident and notorious danger threatened, in which case secular power could [intervene], if it had a sure hope of ecclesiastical confirmation'.[12] The king's hope soon became sure, because the Templars collapsed under torture and he leaned on the pope at Avignon. Nor were princes unique. All kinds of groups tried to limit ecclesiastical power and direct the Church. Typical was the clergy's lament at a synod held in 1258 at Ruffec (between Poitiers and Angoulême) about leagues of 'knights, communities and barons, farmers and townsmen' combating ecclesiastical jurisdiction.[13]

---

[12] Denifle, *Chartularium universitatis Parisiensis* I 126 No. 664.
[13] Lagarde, *La naissance de l'esprit laïque* I 169n.

Quarrels between towns and churchmen reflected the issues that embroiled Rome and larger states. An extreme but revealing example is a complaint against the knights and citizens of Eichstätt brought before an archiepiscopal council held at Mainz. It was there reported that the townsmen, aided by some rural lords, had remained almost a year under excommunication, plundered the church's treasure, continued burial services and 'with heretical and diabolical presumption and perversion, cruelly and violently expelled the bishop together with the clergy who supported him, and chose laymen to serve as bishop, provost and dean', thus continuing the church's administrative services.[14] Everyone went to extremes. Describing the divisions rending Florence in the early fourteenth century, Remigio reported that the clergy called laymen 'traitors, usurers, perjurers, adulterers, robbers. . . . And laymen say that clerks are fornicators, gluttons and idle and the religious vainglorious thieves.'[15]

Apart from the clergy's right to trial in its own courts, what angered the laity was the enlargement of the papal right to appoint to posts in local churches, the increased control of Church courts over testaments, the consequent appeals to Rome and Rome's taxation of local churches. The bone of contention was partly gold. That Rome was avaricious had long been a commonplace. In 1245, Louis IX protested about the taxes paid by the Gallican church to Rome, claiming that his kingdom was being impoverished and foreigners enriched by its spoils. A dispatch in 1301 from an Aragonese ambassador at Rome said that Philip the Fair's embargo was bringing the pope to his knees. France had ordered, he reported, that:

> no one shall take from the kingdom gold, silver, cloth, wool, horses and money even in letters of exchange or deposit contracts. Thus have the French prelates summoned by the pope been wholly prevented from coming. Whence you should know, famous lord, that fear and tremors have gripped not a few, especially if the way of gulping down the gold of France should be closed to them.[16]

The pope combated the charge. Boniface VIII remarked in consistory that Capetian revenues had more than doubled since the days of Philip Augustus because of favours granted by the Holy See. An argument that might have also carried weight – but did not – was that the communities and lords who protested over losing business to ecclesiastical courts were losing far more to royal tribunals. In regard to taxes, the French crown had been assigned substantial ecclesiastical subsidies by the popes in every year from 1284 to 1296, and Boniface's attempt to stop this haemorrhage precipitated the first crisis

---

[14] *Annales erphordenses fratrum praedicatorum* in the *Monumenta Erphesfurtensia, MGH SS in usum scholarum* 44 97.
[15] Davis, 'Remigio de'Girolami' in *Proceedings of the American Philosophical Society* CIV (1960) 667a.
[16] Finke, *Aus den Tagen Bonifaz VIII* lv.

between him and Philip. As seen above, a reason for this was that the monarchy had not yet been able to impose regular taxation on France's nobles and communities; nor did it, in fact, until the latter part of the Hundred Years War. Even so, what can be said of that later time may probably be said of 1300: the fiscal demands of the secular state were growing more rapidly than those of Rome. Unused to the costs and constraints required and threatened by the quasi-democratic urgings of the plebs, the well-to-do of town and countryside did not wish to pay for the growing central state, but were nevertheless obliged by circumstances to favour the growth itself. For a time, then, they willingly joined prince and people in making the Church pay.

Arising from natural solidarity, the idea of the nation provided an alternative focus of loyalty. In the letter of Gregory IX of 1239 cited above, the idea was twofold: a people was defined by language and race. When Edward I summoned the archbishop of Canterbury to the Model Parliament in 1295, this French-speaking prince cited the threat of the French, whose king, he said, intends to obliterate the 'English tongue'. Racist notions are seen in the Rhinelander Alexander of Roes. To him, as noted above, Italians were ruled by the love of gain, Germany by that of ruling and Frenchmen by the desire to know. These natural qualities determine their different governments: in Italy the people rule, in Germany the soldiery and in France an arrogant and lustful clergy. The word 'Gaul' derives from cock, and Frenchmen share that bird's qualities, being 'handsome of body, but more handsome feathered than plucked, that is, when clothed not naked'. The French erroneously say that 'Gaul' comes from the Greek *galla* which means milk, and that they are so called because their colour is white. 'It is true that, when compared to Spaniards or Moors [variant: Greeks], they are white, but . . . their whiteness cannot compare with that of the Saxons and English.'[17]

France naturalized the same ideas. Peter Dubois insisted that, by geographical and astral determination, north France was the cradle of those naturally capable of ruling others. Stealing his text from the Hohenstaufen propaganda of Godfrey of Viterbo (who had taken it indirectly from Carolingian Frankland), John of Paris found that the French, heirs of ancient Troy, had never been subject to Rome and hence were naturally free. Assembled in 1247 to protest about Church policies, the French baronage, headed by the magnates of Burgundy, Brittany and St Pol, used arguments prefiguring those of the largely Calvinist Monarchomachs of the late sixteenth century. Proclaiming Roman servility and Frankish liberty – the liberty, that is, of the French nobility – they stated that the Gallo-Roman plebeians was servile.

Because the superstition of clerks does not consider that the kingdom of France was converted from the error of the gentiles to the Catholic faith by the wars and blood

---

[17] *Memoriale* 15 in *MGH Staatsschriften* I i 107.

of not a few under Charlemagne and other princes . . . [and that clerks have by now] so absorbed the secular jurisdiction of the magnates that sons of slaves judge by their law the children of freemen; and because they ought rather to be judged by us according to the laws of the original victors, our ancestors' customs ought not to be superseded by [their] constitutions . . . therefore we, barons of the kingdom, perceiving with attentive mind that the kingdom was not acquired by the written law nor by the arrogance of clerks, but by the sweat of soldiers, declare . . .

that, except for usury, marriage and heresy, no case may go to an ecclesiastical tribunal.[18]

In France for a time the monarchy embodied the sentiments of the nation. The ideas of the king as emperor in his kingdom and as most Christian and ever orthodox were repeated again and again in the manifestos issued by Philip's ministers William of Nogaret and William of Plaisans. So faithful was this prince that a sermon delivered at court during the Flemish war congratulated the enemy on the opportunity of being defeated, thus to be brought back to the ways of Jesus and right reason. Indeed, to this perfervid preacher, the king's interests were identical to those of the faith: 'Whoever inveighs against the king combats the whole Church, Catholic doctrine, sanctity, justice and the Holy Land.'[19]

Addressing the French clergy in 1303, Nogaret contended that his prince's duty was to reform the Church. He had borrowed the idea from Frederick II Hohenstaufen, who in 1239 proposed to emend the Church 'to the better', a phrase taken from the canon of the mass. Repudiating his condemnation at the Council at Lyons in 1245, Frederick's *Illos felices* of 1246 declares that he 'most especially intends that the prelates and clergy should be returned to that state of poverty in which they were at the time of the primitive church . . . [when] clerks contemplated the angels and, coruscate with miracles, cured the sick, raised the dead and subjected kings and princes by sanctity and not by arms'.[20] By 1247, north French barons were borrowing this rhetoric to justify reducing clerical power. They acted, they said, so that:

our jurisdiction thus revived should breathe again, and that [churchmen], up to now enriched by our impoverishment . . . should be reduced to the state of the primitive church, so that, living in contemplation while we, as is fitting, lead the active life, they will again perform miracles, those miracles that have so long departed from this earth.[21]

---

[18] Matthew Paris, *Chronica majora* in *Rolls Series* LVII iv 595–98. See Lagarde, *La naissance de l'esprit laïque* I 161 and Wieruszowski, *Vom Imperium zum nationalen Königtum*, especially Verzeichnis 222ff.

[19] In Kantorowicz, *The King's Two Bodies* 254.

[20] Huillard-Bréholles, *Historia diplomatica Friderici secundi* VI 393 and Eduard Winkelmann, *Acta imperii inedita* II (Innsbruck, 1880) 50.

[21] Matthew Paris, *Chronica majora* in *Rolls Series* LVII iv 593.

Everybody loved the Christian republic, but each protagonist wished to defend it after first purging the others. In 1301 Boniface VIII issued two bulls, *Ausculta, fili* and *Ante promotionem*, in which he summoned a council of French prelates and masters of law and theology. To reconquer the Holy Land, he proposed, royal policies, such as the debasement of coinage, were to be rescinded and much was to be done 'for the augmentation of the Catholic faith, the conservation of ecclesiastical liberty, the reformation of the king and kingdom, the correction of past excesses and the good government of the kingdom'.[22] French anger may be gauged from a passage in a tract by Peter Dubois, probably of 1303: 'You, noble king, by inheritance above all other princes defender of the faith and destroyer of heretics, can, ought and are obliged to require . . . that the said Boniface be held and judged as an heretic.'[23] In June 1303, the court adopted and publicized a plan suggested long before in 1239 by Frederick II: convene a general council to judge the crimes attributed to the pope. Even with the split among the cardinals, the adhesion of the French clergy to the crown, and France's power, it is unlikely that this council would have carried more weight than the one summoned later at Rome against John XXII by Lewis of Bavaria, but, in the meantime, Boniface had been seized at Anagni by France's Italian allies. He was shortly thereafter released by his friends, although he died suddenly in October 1303. Before his end, however, the pontiff had issued in November 1302 *Unam sanctam*. It is to this great bull and the polemics around it that attention will now be turned.

---

[22] *Ante promotionem* in *Les registres de Boniface VIII* III 336 No. 4426.

[23] *La supplication du peuple de France* cited in Wilks, *The Problem of Sovereignty in the Later Middle Ages* 236.

Chapter 24

Unam sanctam

Polemics

During this threatening time, the enthusiast Roger Bacon dreamed that an angel pope would mobilize the Latins against the Antichrist, launch crusades again and convert infidels, Jews and pagans. Fearing that the vast realms of the Tatars would fall to Islam or Judaism, Raymond Llull wanted them converted, asserting that '[God] has given the Latins power to acquire the whole world, if they wish to'.[1] The opinions of another Catalan, Arnold of Villanova, sometime medical doctor of Boniface VIII, were close to Llull's and his politics were vehemently anti-French. He believed in an early version of the secular idea of progress, in which a new church or spiritual order of a Franciscan type was joined to mystic medicine and natural science. Yet another scheme was that of the Norman Peter Dubois. This lawyer and judge proposed reforming and financing the Church by entrusting its property to lay management. Latin Europe was to unify under France's king, who was to direct the 'reconquest' of the Holy Land and the Near East. As a first step, the pernicious freedom of the Italian city republics and the resistance of King Peter of Aragon and the Sicilians to the Angevin French were to be crushed.

These schemes were contradictory: some favoured clerical leadership, others secular; some favoured the French, others their enemies. Although Llull's work was approved at Paris in 1310 and later influenced so reputable a thinker as Nicholas of Cusa (d. 1464), some thought him mildly mad. Suspected of being a Joachite, Roger Bacon was shunted aside in his later years, perhaps imprisoned. An ardent defender of the losing cause of the Spiritual Franciscans, Arnold of Villanova was convinced that the clergy had it in for him because, although a married medical doctor, he wrote about theology. He was probably correct, but the reserve greeting him is understandable. Responding to attacks on his tract proclaiming the immediate coming of the Antichrist, Arnold warned churchmen that:

> just as they rejected John [the Baptist] and Christ . . . so do they now defame these two modern messengers. For they said of him whom [God] first sent, namely, Master

---

[1] *Disputatio Raymundi Christianiet Hamar Saraceni* 3 in *Beati Raymundi Lulli opera* IV 477a.

Raymond Llull, that he was an illiterate ignorant of grammar. Then he sent them the second messenger [Arnold himself], not only a true and splendid expert in the Latin language, but admirably competent in many subjects, and they said he was a rash fantast, a magician and necromancer.[2]

Utopia aside, there were two main issues. The first was the conflict between monarchism and conciliarism. It was noted that both Boniface VIII and Philip IV tried to summon councils in which to condemn the other. This conflict of political ideologies has been rehearsed in the chapters of Part Four above and will be referred to here only in so far as it concerns the second. The second issue is the familiar one: the relationship of Church to state, the prospects of the independence of the latter from the former, and its insistence on the subordination of the laity to the clergy. Of those who addressed this problem, the two greatest, Marsiglio of Padua and William of Ockham, escape the scope of this volume. Those on whom attention is centred are Giles of Rome, whose *On Ecclesiastical Power* was issued in 1301, and John Quidort of Paris, whose *On Papal and Royal Power* appeared in 1302.

Before examining Giles of Rome, one recalls that, in the opinion of curialists, those who questioned papal authority hardly differed from those who preached popular heresy. In the battle against the emperor Otto IV in 1210 and again against Frederick II, the popes invoked a passage used by Gregory VII saying that a person 'incurs the sin of paganism who, while claiming to be Christian, refuses to obey the Holy See'. And Hostiensis in his *Summa aurea* asserted that 'he who strives to remove the privilege of the Roman church . . . and who transgresses the precepts of the Apostolic See is to be considered an heretic'.[3] And these teachings were widely accepted among local clergy. Basing his argument on Matthew 16:19 in 1281, John Peckham, archbishop of Canterbury, averred that:

> perchance an enemy of the church will say that the highest pontiff may not impose [the] yoke on a secular prince whereas we together with the universal church and all the saints and wise of this world affirm the contrary. . . . [The] determination of all conflicts which cannot be settled by lesser judges belongs to the highest pontiff. . . . [And] those who disobey the church, especially when assembled in council, are to be thought heretics.[4]

---

[2] *Tractatus quidam in quo respondetur obiectionibus que fiebant contra tractatum Arnaldi de adventu Antichristi* in M. Batllori, *Analecta sacra Tarraconensia* XXVIII (1955) 68.

[3] The text of the first passage is in [*Decretum*] D. 81 15 and that in the *Summa aurea ad X. 5 7 'De hereticis'* 1 was cited in Helmut G. Walther, 'Häresie und päpstliche Politik: Ketzerbegriff und Ketzergesetzgebung in der Übergangsphase von der Dekretistik zur Dekretalistik' in *The Concept of Heresy in the Middle Ages (11th–13th Century)* ed. W. Lourdaux and D. Verhelst, 143.

[4] Cited in Janet Coleman, 'The Intellectual Milieu of John of Paris OP' in ed. Jürgen Miethke, *Das Publikum politischer Theorie im 14. Jahrhundert* 186.

Whistling in the dark, the archbishop had gone on to say that he recalled that Constantine, a king of England as well as emperor, had confessed that only clerks judge clerks.

Although theories about ecclesiastical autonomy and papal power reached the peak of their development just about the time they were dismissed, the claims were rooted in a vision of the Church in the world. Cardinal John Lemoine, for example, defended the bull *Unam sanctam* because there were four ends in life: physical health, personal moral virtue, the good of the multitude or society and the good of the eternal soul. These ends are in ascending order but, without the last, the others are of no consequence. Giles of Rome was more subtle. He followed Thomas Aquinas in admitting that human and natural goods – health, a sufficiency of means, education and peace – were intrinsically good. Following Augustine, however, he argued from experience that things beneficial in themselves are not necessarily good for humanity because by itself humankind is incapable of using them to advantage. Without God's grace, they are of no value, and he therefore concluded: 'If therefore neither our end nor our bliss is to be found in temporal things but only in spiritual ones, it follows that temporal things are good only in so far as they are directed toward spiritual objectives.' Also, although the secular state is needed to provide a peace in which Christians may be educated toward blessedness:

> we say with Augustine that true justice cannot be found except in that republic whose founder and governor is Christ. Now, the pagan Romans talked much about justice and pontificated about the republic, but that republic, as Augustine says, . . . was not alive in behaviour but merely painted in colours . . . Hence Augustine asserts that the Roman republic was not a true republic because true justice never ruled there.[5]

In 1302, James of Viterbo not unfairly epitomized his master Giles: 'No community can be called a true republic save the ecclesiastical one, because true justice, utility and community exist in it alone.'[6]

It is true, says Giles, that secular power derives from God, and that directly. But then so do fire, water, human bodies and human learning – indeed, everything in the natural world. Since good things may be put to evil use, however, the thing itself is not the same as the use made of it. The search for salvation is the only justification of all natural things and, for that, the sacraments of the Church are required. It is therefore true that:

> since none are worthy of honour, dominion, power, or indeed of any good except by ecclesiastical sacraments through the Church and under the Church, what our

---

[5] Giles's two passages are in *De ecclesiastica potestate* 2 4 (ed. Richard Scholz, Leipzig, 1929, rprt.) 49, and ibid. 2 7, 73. See also Augustine, *De civitate dei* 2 21 and 19 21.
[6] *De regimine christiano* 1 4, cited in Wilks, *The Problem of Sovereignty* 18.

chapter heading said was well said, namely that, even if there is no power except that derived from God, no one is worthy of having any power unless he becomes worthy under the Church or through it.

Although John of Paris appears not to have known it, Giles contradicted one of the Parisian's practical objections to ecclesiastical power (one later much developed by Ockham) by stating that secular princes or laymen should not grumble about the yoke placed on their necks by the Church, because this yoke is not servitude, but instead liberty:

> Because faithful Christians are redeemed by the Church from the power of the devil, they ought confess themselves to be ascript slaves of the Church . . . This servitude is meritorious because it is more of love than of fear, of devotion than of coercion. By this servitude nothing is lost, but much is gained because what is given by the faithful to the Church will be returned a hundred times over, and they will possess eternal life.[7]

As Ockham and Marsiglio were to point out, to Giles and his followers the Church Militant was not merely an institution of divine foundation but also a godlike one.

So immense is ecclesiastical power in this view that one wonders what was left to laymen. According to Giles, however, the Church has obeyed the injunction to render to Caesar what is Caesar's by attributing to the laity a particular and lower form of lordship or ownership, while reserving to itself a superior and universal one. He also applauds the view that, since all power is really vested in the spiritual sword, it was percipient to have invented the material sword, because 'a certain dignity in government should be given to the laity lest laymen perceive themselves to be wholly contemptible. This would cause murmurs and quarrels between the laity and the clergy in the Church.' Here, glossing over Bernard of Clairvaux's earlier caveats, Giles asserts that the Church exercises both the lord's 'jurisdictional' right and the tenant's 'use' right in all temporal things. Still, as is evident, the Church grants laymen the tenant's right, that is, the right to raise fruits from temporal things, and this for good reason: as payment for their souls' care, the laity will support the clergy. This is especially advantageous because scripture teaches us that, in order to occupy themselves with spiritual solicitude, the apostles were enjoined to avoid earthly care. 'It was therefore the glory of the apostles that they possessed nothing at all as far as responsibility or anxiety are concerned, but everything as far as lordship', and the clergy are the apostles' heirs.[8]

---

[7] Giles's two passages are in his *De ecclesiastica potestate* 2 9 (ed. Scholz) 85 and ibid. 2, 10 95.

[8] The two quotations are from Ibid. 2 15 (ed. Scholz) 136 and ibid. 2 1, 37–38. Note also 1 Corinthians 7:32.

Without a general, an army is nothing and vowed to defeat. By analogy, the good of the Church is embodied in the pope. 'The Church must be feared and its commands obeyed, and the highest pontiff, who holds the apex of the Church and who verily can be called the Church, must be feared and his commands obeyed, because his power is spiritual, celestial and divine, and is without weight, number and measure.' Lay or clerical, all other offices have weight, number and measure but, like God, the papal plenitude of power cannot be weighed or measured.[9] This vision of the pope as a quasi-God or 'image of Christ' infuriated both Marsiglio and Ockham, and had already elicited much opposition. In 1295 Olivi, although a moderate defender of practical papal authority, remarked: 'They say that he is uncreated, immense, impeccable, infallible and prescient in all things, like Christ, an opinion which no one would state or even hint at, except a lunatic.'[10]

Giles tried to circumvent this objection by separating office and person. A truly spiritual man may judge all others and never himself be judged, and there are two kinds of spiritual men. One is spiritual because of personal perfection; another, like the pope, because of office. 'He who is spiritual according to his status and perfect in the highest degree according to the jurisdiction and plenitude of his power will be the spiritual man who judges all things and cannot be judged by anyone.'[11] To believe otherwise, as was said in *Unam sanctam*, by John Lemoine and others, is to substitute a heretical Manichaean duality for a divinely ordained unity. It is therefore, as Giles says, 'indeed well said that the power of the supreme pontiff is that sublime power to which every soul should be subject', or, as the princely Boniface VIII put it in *Unam sanctam*: 'We declare, state, decide and pronounce that it is altogether necessary for the salvation of every human creature to be subject to the Roman pontiff.'[12]

Appealing to some, this teaching was anathema to many. To John of Paris, a Dominican divine, the Church was instead to keep the mean between the Waldensians and the Herodians. The former wished it to surrender all property and coercion. The latter – Herod had mistakenly thought that Christ was an earthly king – wanted the Church to rule the world. Following Bernard of Clairvaux, John argued that the pope is not a master of souls, but rather a steward. Just as Jesus ruled men's hearts and not their possessions, so the pope accepts 'the keys of the kingdom of heaven, not because of power over [material] possessions but because of power over [moral] crime'. Whatever temporal authority the Church enjoys was given to it by the people or their governments. The very fact that Constantine gave the Church the 'Italian

---

[9] Ibid. 3 12 (ed. Scholz) 209, and Wisdom of Solomon 11:21.
[10] *Epistola ad Conradum de Offida* in *Archivum franciscanum historicum* XI–XII (1918–19) 368.
[11] *De ecclesiastica potestate* 1 2 (ed. Scholz) 6.
[12] Ibid. 1 4 (ed. Scholz) 11 and *Extravagantes communes* 1 8 1 in *CICan* II 1246.

empire' and that the Church accepted the gift proves that it did not have civil dominion of its own right. Like Marsiglio later, John denied Henry of Cremona's allegation of 1302 that 'those saying that the pope lacks power in temporal matters are heretics because they are saying that the Church cannot coerce heretics by the secular arm'.[13]

The Church has powers, John says: the power to consecrate, the medicinal power of the keys in the forum of conscience and the power to teach or to preach. Although great, the power to teach relies only on persuasion, not on coercion. The Church can also punish spiritually: it can exclude, for example, heretics from its community. Unless the secular state freely lends its coercive force, however, this capacity to punish is devoid of earthly sanctions. 'An ecclesiastical judge cannot impose a . . . penalty for a crime as can a secular judge, unless the criminal wishes to accept it. If he does not, an ecclesiastical judge can compel by excommunication or other spiritual penalty, which is the most he can do: he cannot do anything more.'[14] Unless there is firm scriptural precept, especially in the New Testament, moreover, the Church may not even render judgements about moral matters. Usury can be judged, for example, but the larger issue of private property cannot. Although both moral and natural law clearly favour the common possession of property, John says, practical experience teaches that it leads to civil strife among sinful humans. The Church is therefore not to interfere here, following Augustine's recommendation: 'Remove', the African had said, 'the law of the emperor and one cannot say that this thing is mine, because in natural law there is one liberty for all and the common possession of all things.'[15] After the Fall, both the coerciveness of the state and private property became necessary: heaven, the monastic communism of the apostles, is not for this earth. But, to John, there was an advantage here: the divinely imposed sanctity of private property protected layfolk against tyrannical efforts by either Church or state to impose unwanted solutions on them.

John's separation of the spheres is not as daring as it seems. Many had justified secular authority, even that of pagans or infidels, and John never tried to equal the earlier Peter Damian. Enraged by a summons to arms to protect the Church, Peter had insisted on the difference between the spiritual and the material:

> If therefore for the faith by which the universal Church lives it is impermissible to take up arms of iron, how then do armoured hosts rage with their swords for the earthly and transitory riches of the Church? Indeed, when the saints prevail, they

---

[13] The two passages are from John's *De potestate regia et papali* 10 (ed. Bleienstein) 110 (derived from Bernard's *De consideratione* 1 6) and ibid. 11 126.

[14] Ibid. 13 (ed. Bleienstein) 138.

[15] Ibid. 13 (ed. Bleienstein) 136, a rough quotation from *Decretum* 1 7 1 in *CICan* I 13.

will surely not destroy heretics or worshippers of idols, but will instead not flee being slain by them for the Catholic faith.[16]

An Aristotelian moderate, John allows an exception to the Church's abstention from the employment of coercion described above: the case of dire need, when good people can transcend their normal roles to act for equity or epiky. The pope may never dispose of lay properties 'except in the ultimate need of the Church, in which case he acts not as a dispensator [with ordinary jurisdiction], but rather as one who declares the law [of epiky].'[17] And so can any good person!

The secular state, then, is independent of the Church. Although the Church is more worthy, the state preceded it in history. 'Whence the Empire is from God alone . . . As the pope does not have the [spiritual] sword from the emperor, so the emperor does not have the [temporal] one from the pope: "For the army makes the emperor".' Corresponding to their different ends, the organization of Church and state differed. Contradicting the tradition that led Dante to favour universal monarchy, John maintains that, although God's ordinance made the faith one and unified, the same is not true of civil society:

> Laymen do not have it from divine law that they must be subject in temporal matters to one supreme monarch. By the natural instinct implanted by God, it is instead recommended that they live in a civil community, and, as a result, choose diverse kinds of governors in order to live well according to the diversity of their communities.[18]

This difference partly derived from nature: religion is naturally more unified than civil dominion because the word of persuasion travels faster than coercion's sword. Borrowing an idea of Augustine's, also, John argued that Rome's experience and that of other empires did not show that a universal state is necessarily beneficial. He concluded that, although the rule of one man is probably the best for any people (a point later contradicted by Marsiglio, who argued that true unity was the oneness of a community and not the number of its magistrates), 'it is nevertheless better that many should rule in many realms than that one should rule the whole world'. Again, although ecclesiastical unity best protects Church property that is held in community, the existence of private property in secular society pleads rather for diversity than unity. The basic reason that John took this position, however, was that, in the natural sphere where the state operates, varieties of tongues, peoples

---

[16] Book Four, Letter 4 in *PL* CXLIV 316a.

[17] *De potestate regia et papali* 7 (ed. Bleienstein) 96.

[18] John's first passage is in ibid. 10 (ed. Bleienstein) 111 and *Decretum* 1 93 24 and 96 11, and his second in ibid. 3 82.

and climates make it obvious that 'what is virtuous in one people is not so in another'.[19]

Ideally, for John, each nation is possessed by its inhabitants who, following the Roman law applauded by jurists such as Innocent IV, are capable of entrusting government to elected or permitted magistrates – an example of the latter being the hereditary monarchs of France. So also is the Church an assembly of the faithful who continue to possess its government while attributing its exercise to ecclesiastical magistrates. Although, for example, the papacy is of divine foundation, the person holding the office is not divine. God's rule of the world does not exclude our work, for we are his co-workers. Although the papacy is from God, it is nevertheless placed in this or that person through human co-operation, namely by the consensus of the electors and the elected, and, as a result, it can cease to be vested in this or that particular person by human consensus.[20]

A pope or other magistrate can therefore be removed, and the question boils down to how and for what reasons. Everyone agreed that the reasons should not be minor. Writing in 1295, Peter John Olivi stated that one must defer somewhat to princes: 'minor mistakes or frauds may be committed by a monarch as long as he is obliged to use the advice of the many and the good in important matters'.[21] Real monarchists went in for wilder thought. In about 1308, an unknown defender of Boniface VIII reported that the pope had asserted that he, theoretically both emperor and pope, could not commit simony because everything was anyway his. Taking this as a probable proposition, the author argued that, if Boniface had said it, 'he should be understood in the good sense and not the bad, especially because, when we do not know with what intention things are done, we ought always give the benefit of the doubt'![22] Ever moderate, John's position was simply that a pope could be removed if he were mad, heretical or wholly inept.

He then spelled out such a removal. Like Olivi, he thought that if, for good cause, a pontiff were willing to resign, the cardinals could stand for the people and accept the decision. Were he unwilling, his deposition required a larger 'consensus of the people', and he therefore followed Gratian 'where it is said that a general council was convoked to depose Pope Marcellinus' (a pope suspected of capitulating to the pagans during Diocletian's persecution).[23] And if a pope violently resists, a secular prince may be called in, 'nor does he act against the pope as pope, but against . . . the enemy of the

---

[19] The first passage is in ibid. 21 (ed. Bleienstein) 190 and the second in ibid. 3, 83.

[20] Ibid. 25 (ed. Bleienstein) 202.

[21] *De renunciatione papae* in *Archivum Franciscanum historicum* XI–XII (1918–1919) 354–55.

[22] Cited in Finke, *Aus den Tagen Bonifaz VIII* lxxiv.

[23] *De potestate regia et papali* 201 (ed. Bleienstein) 201. See *Nunc autem* in *Decretum* 1 21 7 in *CICan* l 71.

republic'. John went on to praise the emperor Henry III for removing three rival popes and replacing them with another at Sutri in 1046 – an action that had infuriated the Gregorians. John also opined that the cardinals could invite secular intervention if a pope were notoriously heretical or simoniac. Then, 'as an aid to law . . . the emperor, requested by the cardinals, ought to proceed against the pope and depose him', an idea that was to enjoy adhesion among the conciliar fathers in 1415.[24]

Employed together with the idea of the king as emperor in his own kingdom, John's doctrine was obviously useful to France's monarch. The difficulty was that the Church was made dependent on the secular sword, and history was to show that those who wielded that weapon subordinated the Church in return for their service. Unlike the far more secular Marsiglio, however, John tempered his advocacy. He viewed the accidental power 'in aid of law' as a double-edged sword, one that could be employed by the Church as well as by the state. Just as a prince invited by the clergy could act against a pope, so could a pope requested by the barons act against a prince. In John's imagination, everything depended on the people:

> I also say . . . that the pope acts *per accidens* because, if a prince is heretical, incorrigible and a contemner of ecclesiastical censures, the pope can do something among the people so that the prince will be deprived of his office by the people and be deposed. The pope does this for ecclesiastic crimes, which cases pertain to him, by excommunicating those who obey the prince as a lord, and thus the people deposes the prince [directly] and the pope indirectly.[25]

Wise about princes, this Dominican did not perceive that the people's affections were shifting. From the Gregorian age until about 1300, the people and the popes had together judged and limited princes. From 1300 onwards, the people together with their princes and magistrates were to judge the popes and clergy. In that context, Boniface VIII's remark in 1301 that 'we have both spiritual and material power!' elicited a truthful rejoinder from a Frenchman: 'Indeed so, sir, but your power is verbal; ours is real.'[26] His views paralleling his contemporary Dante, John also provided a justification for laymen. Observing that temporal ends and virtues were distinct from spiritual ones and good in themselves, he averred that 'moral virtues acquired [on earth] can be perfect without theological ones', and went on to draw the corollary that on earth, 'without Christ governing, there is true and perfect justice', that is, true and perfect government.[27]

---

[24] The last two quotations are in ibid. 22 (ed Bleienstein) 196, and ibid. 13, 140.

[25] Ibid. 13 (ed. Bleienstein) 138.

[26] Dupuy, *Histoire du Differend* 130.

[27] *De potestate regia et papali* 18 (ed. Bleienstein) 163.

Conclusions

It has long been known that there was little original in *Unam sanctam*, and often observed that both John of Paris and Giles of Rome drew heavily on Thomas Aquinas. Yet from that central teaching, two very different doctrines were derived to feed the fires of institutional conflict. One, that of John of Paris, was to lead to Ockham's endless doubting questions and to the outright secularism of Marsiglio of Padua. It thus served to open the way for secular magistrates and lay philosophers to replace churchmen and theologians as the vessels holding the basic religion of western man. The other, that of Giles of Rome, so hardened a once somewhat flexible doctrine that, in spite of its occasionally perceptive cynicism about laymen, it no longer rang true to life. To use the monk's image, Giles's clerical Marys were to be supported by unnaturally subservient lay Marthas. As seen in the order of Grandmont, the attempt to deprive the Marthas of some exercise of leadership had never really worked even among the religious. When applied to monarchies and republics and to their subjects and citizens (all fired by the spread and laicizing of the monastic vocation), this deprivation did not fare half as well.

Perhaps the problem should be put differently. Perhaps the people only support intellectual or religious leaders who sing the tunes they wish to hear; and that, as the lay spirit became more powerful and capable, layfolk cast their priests and monks aside. Against this, one may argue with Jean-Jacques Rousseau that there is a true religion of intellectual and spiritual freedom, and that its levites can raise humanity above its mundane concerns, even against its will; and that, because of their vices, the clergy failed to do that. There are difficulties here, however. When discussing voluntary poverty, Aquinas remarked that he who seeks to live virtuously with no means of his own and who depends on the generosity of others has a problem:

> Freedom of the mind is most especially required for the attainment of perfect virtue, for, if this is weakened, men very easily become 'partakers of other men's sins' either by expressly agreeing, being adulatory or hiding their true feelings. Hence this way of living is prejudicial to freedom because there is no man who does not fear to offend him from whose kindness he lives.

Aquinas's answer was that those who give themselves to voluntary poverty are of such perfection that they would not be suborned by 'the little' they need in order to live.[28] But 'little' is a relative term, and it seems from the history of the Church in this period that the objection of which the saint thus hastily disposed was the more probable or safer opinion. Even among the best, even among the Franciscans and their radical offshoots, few or none were perfect and, consequently, few or none were free.

---

[28] *Contra gentiles* 3 132 4 4 and 3 135 4 4 (Rome, 1934) 386b and 391b, and 1 Timothy 5:22.

The quandary was much discussed at the time. A solution had twice been tried, once at the time of the attack on heresy and usury around 1200 and once again among Franciscan rigorists around 1300: the utopian solution. When discussing 2 Thessalonians 3:7–12, Peter Cantor urged the clergy to follow Paul:

> When preaching in Achaia, the apostle accepted no charity from [the people], partly because they were covetous and hated him to whom they gave . . . and partly because he did not want the idle – who, seeing him labour with his own hands and eat the bread of his own labour, were no longer able, as had been their wont, to eat the bread of sloth [the bread, that is, of others' labour] – to have bought impunity by thinking: 'We have filled Paul's hands, and now we can do what we want.'[29]

But the history of the Church and indeed of society had shown that the ascetic's or utopian's solution, although momentarily possible for individuals, was impossible for the many. The attempt to realize this ideal had twice failed, once in the world at large and once within the narrower confines of the Franciscan order, and with this failure the solidarity of the Christian republic and its leadership had begun to crumble.

It serves no purpose to declare – in the moralizing language so often employed by today's historians – that churchmen failed because they were corrupt. Such views overlook the fact that the clergy, although seeming to rule, was only one group or one 'nation' in the Christian republic whose citizens permitted or created their leadership. They are also untruthful because they encourage one to forget that, although Christian ideals were useful because they helped men both develop their talents and reconcile themselves to their misery, they could not be attained. To dilate only on the beauty of the hope of living the 'apostolic life' or of creating here on earth a perfect society on the model of the supernal Jerusalem obscures a function of espousing impossible social and religious ideals. That function is to give ideologues a way of condemning their neighbours for failing to live up to what they cannot reasonably be expected to. An aspect of this social idealism is, then, an instrument for both personal aggrandizement and social warfare, because it deprives one's neighbours of rectitude and therefore of rights. Not tinged by resignation, utopian dreams soon become nightmares. A historian should therefore eschew judgement and instead try to understand, viewing those neighbours of the past not as those others, but rather as brothers. Concerning a special aspect of utopian hope, Peter Cantor once remarked: 'In nature's law, all things are in common: earth for treading, air for breathing, water for drinking and bathing. Why then do princes and clergy hold as private goods what should be in common?' But in spite of his utopian hope,

---

[29] *Liber casuum conscientiae* 3 50 in *Summa de sacramentis et animae consiliis* 3 2a (ed. Dugauquier) 342.

a thousand experiences echoed in Peter's mind and finally made him say: 'It is difficult to advise princes on this matter and hard indeed to condemn the whole Church.'[30]

However truthful it may be, the above runs ahead of history's schedule. To go back to the battles between Church and state in the early fourteenth century, Philip the Fair undoubtedly defeated Rome: a quasi-French party in the Roman court triumphed and brought the papacy to Avignon. In spite of this, little institutional power was surrendered to the secular state, and even the effect of the papacy's move to the Rhone valley was soon dissipated by the French collapse in the Hundred Years War. The later battle with the Empire was almost a papal victory. When Lewis of Bavaria died in 1347, the emperor's pope had long since disappeared, while the pope's imperial candidate remained on the throne. Such being the case, who, in 1300 or 1330, would have believed that, following Europe's diplomatic alignments, the Church was to split into two or more obediences during the Great Schism and that, in the Conciliar Age, it would begin to surrender institutional power to the state? What contemporaries did see, however, was that a pope had stumbled badly in his attempt to control the Capetian king, and could compare this with Innocent IV's earlier resounding victory over the Hohenstaufen emperor.

To close, that their world had begun to fall apart was not because the churchmen were corrupt, but rather because they, like their lay fellow citizens of the Christian republic, were not perfect. In judging them, one had best follow Gaius's rule in *Digest* 50 17 56:

Semper in dubiis benigniora praeferenda sunt.

---

[30] Ibid. *Liber casuum conscientiae* 3 2 (ed. Dugauquier) 162 Para. 208.

Bibliography

INTRODUCTION: SOURCES

1 Guides to translations

C.P. Farrar and A.P. Evans, *Bibliography of English Translations from Medieval Sources* (New York, 1946).

M.A.H. Ferguson, *Bibliography of English Translations from Medieval Sources, 1943–1967* (New York, 1974).

2 Collections of translations

Columbia University's *Records of Civilization.*

Nelson's Medieval Texts.

Les Classiques de l'histoire de France au moyen-âge.

Much is translated: nearly all of Thomas Aquinas and key figures such as Bonaventure and Roger Bacon are available in English. Paperback versions abound. Almost all poems and romances and not a few histories are translated. Much of English law is translated, but the same is not true of Roman, canon or continental European law.

*　*　*

The bibliography published below is arranged according to the chapters of the volume. The authors and titles preceded by an asterisk are those from which quotations from original sources have been taken and used in this book.

PART ONE: LATIN EUROPE

1 Social orders and Crusade

*David Abulafia, *A Mediterranean Emporium: the Catalan Kingdom of Majorca* (Cambridge, 1994).

Alois Dempf, *Sacrum Imperium: Geschichts- und Staatsphilosophie des Mittelalters und des politischen Renaissance* (Munich, 1929).

*Peter W. Edbury, *Crusade and Settlement* (Cardiff, 1985).

*Justus Hashagen, *Staat und Kirche vor der Reformation: Eine Untersuchung der vorreformatorischen Bedeutung der Laieneinflüsses in der Kirche* (Essen, 1931).

*E.H. Kantorowicz, *The King's Two Bodies: A Study in Medieval Political Theology* (Princeton, 1957).

*Georges de Lagarde, *La naissance de l'esprit laïque au déclin du moyen âge* (5 vols, 2nd edn, Louvain, 1962).

Jacques Le Goff, *The Birth of Purgatory* (Chicago, 1984, a transl. of the French of 1981).

Colin Morris, *The Discovery of the Individual 1050–1200* (London, 1972).

*John Hine Mundy, *Society and Government at Toulouse in the Age of the Cathars* (Toronto, 1997).

Jean Rivière, *Le problème de l'église et l'état au tenps de Philippe le Bel* (Louvain, 1926).

Eugen Rosenstock-Huessy, *The Driving Power of Western Civilization: The Christian Revolution of the Middle Ages* (Boston, 1950; from his *Out of Revolution: The Autobiography of Western Man* of 1935).

Gustav Schnürer, *Kirche und Kultur in Mittelalter* (3 vols, Paderborn, 1924–30. One vol. transl. as *Church and Culture in the Middle Ages*, Patterson, 1956).

Gerd Tellenbach, *Church, State and Christian Society at the Time of the Investiture Contest* (Oxford, 1940, transl. of his *Libertas* of 1936).

2 The Jews

*S.W. Baron, *A Social and Religious History of the Jews* (Vols III to XII, 2nd edn, New York, 1957–67).

Vittore Colorni, *Gli Ebrei nel sistema del diritto comune fino alla prima emancipazione* (Milan, 1956).

*R.W. Emery, *The Jews of Perpignan in the Thirteenth Century: An Economic Study* (New York, 1959).

*Moritz Güdemann, *Geschichte des Erziehungswesens und der Cultur der abendländischen Juden während des Mittelalters und der Neueren Zeit* (2 vols, Vienna, 1880–84).

Guido Kisch, *The Jews in Medieval Germany* (Chicago, 1949).

Maurice Kriegel, *Les Juifs à la fin du moyen-âge dans l'Europe meditérranéen* (Paris, 1979).

Gavin Langmuir, 'The Jews and the Archives of Angevin England: Reflections on Medieval Anti-Semitism', *Traditio* XIX (1963) 183–244.

H.G. Richardson, *English Jewry under the Angevin Kings* (London, 1960).

Zephira Entin Rokeah, 'Money and the Hangman in late thirteenth century England: Jews, Christians and coinage offences alleged and real', *Jewish Historical Studies* 31 (1990) 83–109 and 32 (1993) 159–218.

J.E. Scherer, *Die Rechtsverhältnisse der Juden in den Deutsch-Österreichischen Ländern* (Leipzig, 1901).

*Gershom Scholem, *Jewish Mysticism* (New York, 1967).

Joseph Shatzmiller, *Recherches sur la communauté juive de Manosque au moyen âge, 1241–1329* (Paris and The Hague, 1973).

Joshua Trachtenberg, *The Devil and the Jews: The Medieval Conception of the Jew and its Relation to Modern Antisemitism* (New Haven, 1943).

3 The Crusades and Europe's frontiers

Paul Alphandéry and A. Dupront, *La chrétienté et l'idée de croisade* (2 vols, Paris, 1954–59).

*Peter W. Edbury ed., *Crusade and Settlement* (Cardiff, 1985).

Carl Erdmann, *The Origin of the Idea of the Crusade* (Princeton, 1977, transl. of German of 1955).

*René Grousset, *L'empire du Levant: histoire de la question d'orient* (Paris, 1946).

Norman Housley, *The Italian Crusades: The Papal–Angevin Alliance and the Crusades against Christian Lay Powers, 1254–1343* (Oxford, 1982).

Steven Runciman, *A History of the Crusades* (3 vols, Cambridge, 1951–54).

A History of the Crusades, ed. K.M. Setton (2 vols, 2nd edn, Madison, 1969).

Michel Villey, *La croisade – Essai sur la formation d'une théorie juridique* (Paris, 1942).

PART TWO: ECONOMY

1 Population and technology

K.J. Beloch, *Bevölkerungsgeschichte Italiens* (3 vols, Berlin, 1937–61).

Josef Kulischer, *Allgemeine Wirtschaftsgeschichte des Mittelalters und des Neuzeit* (Vol. I, Munich, 1955).

Roger Mols, *Introduction à la démographie historique des villes d'Europe du XIVe au XVIIIe siècle* (3 vols, Gembloux, 1956).

Henri Pirenne, *Histoire économique de l'occident médiéval*, ed. Emile Coornaert (Paris, 1951).

Cambridge Economic History of Europe, Vol. II: *Trade and Industry in the Middle Ages*, ed. Michael Postan and E.E. Rich (1952), and Vol. III: *Economic Organisation and Policies in the Middle Ages*, ed. Michael Postan, E.E. Rich and Edward Miller (1961).

J.C. Russell, *British Medieval Population* (Albuquerque, 1945).

Lynn White, *Medieval Technology and Social Change* (Oxford, 1962).

2 Agriculture, industry, trade and urbanism

*Heinrich Büttner, 'Frühmittelalterliches Städtewesen in Frankreich' in *Studien zu den Anfängen des europäischen Stadtewesens* (Lindau, 1958).

E.H. Byrne, *Genoese Shipping in the Twelfth and Thirteenth Centuries* (Cambridge, MA, 1930).

Philippe Döllinger, *The German Hanse* (London, 1970, transl. from the French of 1964).

Georges Duby, *Rural Economy and Country Life in the Medieval West* (London, 1968, transl. of French of 1962).

R.L. Lopez and Irving Raymond, *Medieval Trade in the Mediterranean World* (New York, 1955).

Yves Renouard, *Les hommes d'affaires Italiens du moyen-âge* (Paris, 1949).

Fritz Rörig, *Mittelalterliche Weltwirtschaft* (Jena, 1933).

Armando Sapori, *The Italian Merchant of the Middle Ages* (New York, 1970, transl. from the Italian of 1952).

Adolf Schaube, *Handelsgeschichte des romanischen Volkes des Mittelmeergebiets bis zum Ende des Kreuzzüge* (Munich, 1906).

Germain Sicard, *Aux origines des sociétés anonymes: les moulins de Toulouse au moyen-âge* (Paris, 1953).

B.H. Slicher van Bath, *The Agrarian History of Western Europe: 500–1850* (London, 1963 from a Dutch original of 1960).

Max Weber, 'Zur Geschichte der Handelsgesellschaften im Mittelalters', *Gesammelte Aufsätze zur Sozial- und Wirtschaftsgeschichte* (Tübingen, 1924, pp. 312–443, first publ. in 1889).

3 Economic corporatism and usury

J.W. Baldwin, *The Medieval Theories of the Just Price* (Philadelphia, 1959).

J.W. Baldwin, *Masters, Princes and Merchants: The Social Views of Peter the Chanter and his Circle* (2 vols, Princeton, 1970).

Emile Coornaert, *Les Corporations en France avant 1789* (Paris, 1941).

*Joel Kaye, *Economy and Nature in the Fourteenth Century: Money, Market Exchange, and the Emergence of Scientific Thought* (Cambridge, 1998).

T.P. McLaughlin, 'The teaching of the canonists on usury XII, XIII, and XIV centuries', *Mediaeval Studies* 1 (1939) 81–147 and II (1940) 1–22.

Gunnar Mickwitz, *Die Kartelfunktionen der Zünfte und ihre Bedeutung bei der Entstehung des Zunftwesens* (Helsinki, 1936).

B.N. Nelson, *The Idea of Usury: from Tribal Brotherhood to Universal Otherhood* (2nd edn, Chicago, 1969).

J.T. Noonan, *The Scholastic Analysis of Usury* (Cambridge, MA, 1957).

Fr. Olivier-Martin, *L'organisation corporative en France d'ancien régime* (Paris, 1938).

Franz Schaub, *Der Kampf gegen den Zinswucher, ungerechten Preis und unerlautern Handel im Mittelalter von Karl dem Grossen bis Papst Alexander III* (Freiburg, 1905).

PART THREE: SOCIETY

1 Women and men

Wilhelm Behagel, *Die gewerbliche Stellung der Frau im mittelalterlichen Köln* (Berlin, 1910).

*R.R. Bezzola, *Les origines et la formation de la littérature courtoise en occident* (3 vols, Paris, 1944–63).

John Boswell, *Christianity, Social Tolerance and Homosexuality: Gay People in Western Europe from the Beginning of the Christian Era to the Fourteenth Century* (Chicago, 1980).

James A. Brundage, *Law, Sex, and Christian Society in Medieval Europe* (Chicago and London, 1987).

Karl Bücher, *Die Frauenfrage im Mittelalter* (Tübingen, 1910).

*Ch.-V. Langlois, *La Vie en France au moyen-âge* (4 vols, Paris, 1926, rprt).

Emanuel Le Roy Ladurie, *Montaillou: The Promised Land of Error 1294 to 1324* (New York, 1979, partial transl. of French of 1975).

Laurent Mayali, *Droit savant et coutumes. L'exclusion des filles dotées – XIIème–XVème siècles* (Frankfurt, 1987).

*J.H. Mundy, *Men and Women at Toulouse in the Age of the Cathars* (Toronto, 1990).

F.X. Newman, ed., *The Meaning of Courtly Love* (Albany, 1969).

L.L. Otis, *Prostitution in Medieval Society: The History of an Urban Institution in Languedoc* (Chicago, 1980).

*Helmut Wachendorf, *Die wirtschaftliche Stellung der Frau in den deutschen Städten des späteren Mittelalters* (Quakenbrück, 1934).

Georg Weise, *Die geistige Welt der Gotik und ihre Bedeutung für Italien* (Halle, 1939).

2 Farmers and townsmen

Maurice Beresford, *New Towns of the Middle Ages* (New York, 1967).

*Thomas N. Bisson, *Medieval France and her Pyrenean Neighbours – Studies in Early Institutional History* (London, 1989).

*Marc Bloch, *Rois et serfs: un châpitre d'histoire capétienne* (Paris, 1920).

* Pierre Bonnassie, *From Slavery to Feudalism in Southwestern Europe* (Cambridge, 1991).

*Wolfgang Braunfels, *Die Staatsbaukunst in der Toskana* (Berlin, 1959).

Philippe Döllinger, *L'Evolution des classes rurales en Bavière* (Strasbourg, 1949).

*Georges Duby, *La société aux XIe et XIIe siècles dans la région Mâconnais* (Paris, 1959).

*Edith Ennen, *Frühgeschichte der europäischen Stadt* (Bonn, 1953).

*Wolfgang H. Fritze, *Früzeit zwischen Ostsee und Donau. Ausgewählte Beiträge zum geschichtlichen Werden im Östlichen Mitteleuropa vom 5. bis zum 13. Jahrhundert* (Munich, 1982).

*Roger Grand, *Les 'paix' d'Aurillac* (Paris, 1945).

*Paul Hyams, *Kings, Lords and Peasants* (Oxford, 1980).

*Philip Jones, *The Italian City-State from Commune to Signoria* (Oxford, 1997).

Walter Kuhn, *Siedlungsgeschichte Oberschlesien* (Würzburg, 1954).

*Emile Lousse, *Société d'ancien régime* (Louvain, 1943).

John Hine Mundy, *Toulousan Society in the Age of the Cathars* (Toronto, 1997).

Niccolà Ottokar, *Le città francesi nel medio evo* (Florence, 1927).

Charles Petit-Dutaillis, *Les communes françaises: caractères et évolution des origines au XVIIIe siècle* (Paris, 1947).

Henri Pirenne, *Medieval Cities* (New York, 1925).

*Hans Planitz, *Die deutsche Stadt im Mittelalter von der Römerzeit bis zu den Zunftkämpfen* (Graz-Cologne, 1954).

*Johann Plesner, *L'Emigration de la campagne à la ville libre de Florence au XIIIe siècle* (Copenhagen, 1934).

J.A. Raftis, *Tenure and Mobility: Studies in the Social History of the Medieval English Village* (Toronto, 1964).

*Zvi Razi, *Life, Marriage and Death in a Medieval Parish – Economy, Society and Demography in Halesowen 1270–1400* (Cambridge, 1980).

Fritz Rörig, *The Medieval Town* (London, 1967, transl. from the German of 1955).

Geoffroi Tenant de la Tour, *L'homme et la terre de Charlemagne à Saint Louis: Le Limousin* (Paris, 1942).

*Leo Verriest, *Institutions médiévales* (Vol. 1, Mons, 1946).

Max Weber, *The City* (Glencoe, 1958, transl. Pt. II, Chap. 8 of *Wirtschaft und Gesellschaft*, 2nd edn, Tübingen, 1925).

3 Nobles and patricians

Marc Bloch, *Feudal Society* (2 vols, Chicago, 1961, from the French of 1949).

Yvonne Bongert, *Recherches sur les cours laïques du Xe au XIIIe siècle* (Paris, 1949).

*Karl Bosl, *Die Reichsministerialität der Salier und Staufer* (2 vols, Stuttgart, 1950–51).

Otto Brunner, *Land und Herrschaft* (Baden bei Wien, 1939).

*Emilio Cristiani, *Nobilità e popolo nel commune di Pisa dalle origini del podestariato alla signoria dei Donoratico* (Naples, 1962).

Georges Duby, *La société aux XIe et XIIe siècles dans la région Mâconnaise* (Paris, 1953).

*Hermann Fitting, *Das castrense peculium in seiner geschichtlichen Entwicklung und heutige gemeinrechtlichen Geltung* (Halle, 1871).

*Léon Gauthier, *La chevalerie* (Paris, 1884).

Léopold Génicot, *L'Economie rurale namuroise au bas moyen âge*, Vol. II: *Les hommes – La noblesse* (Louvain, 1960).

*P. Guilhermoz, *Essai sur l'origine de la noblesse en France au moyen âge* (Paris, 1902, rprt).

Walter Kienast, *Untertaneneid und Treuvorbehalt in Frankreich und England* (Weimar, 1952).

Heinrich Mitteis, *Lehnrecht und Staatsgewalt* (Weimar, 1933).

Sidney Painter, *French Chivalry* (Ithaca, 1957).

Michael Powicke, *The Military Obligation in Medieval England* (Oxford, 1962).

*J.-P. Ritter, *Ministerialité et chevalerie: Dignité humaine et liberté dans le droit médiéval* (Lausanne, 1955).

*Gaetano Salvemini, *La dignità cavelleresca nel comune di Firenze* (Florence, 1896, rprt).

4 Ecclesiastics

G.G. Coulton, *Five Centuries of Religion* (4 vols, Cambridge, 1929).

*Johann Haller, *Vier Kapitel zur Geschichte des ausgehenden Mittelalters: Papsttum und Kirchenreform* (2 vols, Berlin, 1903).

David Knowles, *The Monastic Order in England* (2nd edn, Cambridge, 1963).

Gabriel Le Bras, *Institutions écclésiastiques de la Chrétienté médiévale* (Books 1 to 6, 2 vols, Paris, 1959–64).

H.C. Lea, *A History of Auricular Confession and Indulgences* (3 vols, Philadelphia, 1896).

Joseph H. Lynch, *Simoniacal Entry into Religious Life from 1000 to 1260: A Social, Economic and Legal Study* (Columbus, 1976).

E.W. McDonnell, *The Beguines and Beghards in Medieval Culture* (New Brunswick, 1954).

Odorico Rinaldi, *Annales ecclesiastici ab anno MCXCVIII ubi desinit Cardinalis Baronius auctore Odorico Raynaldo* (Vol. I ed. J.D. Mansi, Lucca, 1747).

*Georg Schreiber, *Gemeinschaften des Mittelalters – Recht und Verfassung: Kult und Frömmigkeit* (Münster, 1948).

Luigi Zanoni, *Gli umiliati nei loro rapporti con l'eresia, l'industria della lana ed i communi nel secoli XII e XIII* (Milan, 1911).

PART FOUR: GOVERNMENT

1 The Church

Geoffrey Barraclough, *Papal Provisions: Aspects of Church History: Constitutional, Legal and Administrative* (Oxford, 1935).

R.L. Benson, *The Bishop-Elect: A Study in Medieval Ecclesiastical Office* (Princeton, 1968).

Pierre Dupuy, *Histoire du differend d'entre le pape Boniface VIII et Philippe le Bel* (Paris, 1655, rprt).

J.M. Ferrante, *The Political Vision of the Divine Comedy* (Princeton, 1984).

*A. Hauck, *Kirchengeschichte Deutschlands* (8th printing, Berlin, 1954).

Friedrich Heiler, *Altkirchliche Autonomie und papstliche Zentralismus* (Munich, 1941).

Michele Maccarrone, *Chiesa e stato nella dottrina di Innocencio III* (Rome, 1940).

Victor Martin, *Les origines du Gallicanisme* (2 vols, Paris, 1939).

Kenneth Pennington, *Pope and Bishops: The Papal Monarchy in the XIIth and XIIIth Centuries* (Philadelphia, 1984).

*Brian Tierney, *Foundation of the Conciliar Theory: The Contribution of the Medieval Canonists* (Cambridge, 1955).

Walter Ulmann, *Medieval Papalism – the Political Theories of the Medieval Canonists* (London, 1949).

*Helene Wieruszowski, *Vom Imperium zum nationalen Königtum* (Munich, 1933).

2 Monarchies and parliaments

Frank Barlow, *The Feudal Kingdom of England – 1042–1216* (2nd edn, London, 1961).

Geoffrey Barraclough, *The Origins of Modern Germany* (2nd edn, New York, 1947).

*Wilhelm Berges, *Die Fürstenspiegel des hohen und späten Mittelalters* (Stuttgart, 1958).

* J.H. Burns ed., *The Cambridge History of Medieval Political Thought c. 350–c. 1450* (Cambridge, 1988).

Marcel David, *La souveraineté et les limites juridiques du pouvoir monarchique du IXe au XVe siècle* (Paris, 1954).

Robert Fawtier, *The Capetian Kings of France – 987–1328* (London, 1962, transl. from the French of 1955).

*Ch. Giraud, *Essai sur l'histoire du droit français* (2 vols, Leipzig, 1846).

J.C. Holt, *Magna Carta* (Cambridge, 1965).

J.E.A. Joliffe, *Angevin Kingship* (New York, 1955).

E.H. Kantorowicz, *Frederick II* (Princeton, 1957, transl. from the German 1927–31).

Fritz Kern, *Kingship and Law in the Middle Ages* (Oxford, 1945, transl. from *Gottesgnadentum und Wiederstandsrecht im früheren Mittelalter* of 1914 and *Recht und Verfassung im Mittelalter* of 1919).

*Fritz Kiener, *Verfassungsgeschichte der Provence* (Leipzig, 1900).

Ferdinand Lot and Robert Fawtier eds, *Histoire des institutions françaises au moyen âge* (3 vols, Paris, 1957–64).

Emile Lousse, *La société d'ancien régime: Organisation et répresentation corporatives* (Vol. I, Louvain, 1943).

Antonio Marongiu, *L'istituto parlamentare in Italia dalle origini al 1500* (Rome, 1949).

Antonio Marongiu, *Medieval Parliaments: A Comparative Study* (London, 1968).

Ernst Mayer, *Deutsche und französische Verfassungsgeschichte* (2 vols, Leipzig, 1891).

Geoffrey Barraclough, *Medieval Germany: Essays by German Historians* (2 vols, Oxford, 1935).

*Robert Michel, *L'administration royale dans la sénéchausée de Beaucaire* (Paris, 1910).

Heinrich Mitteis, *The State in the Middle Ages: A Comparative Constitutional History of Feudal Europe* (New York, 1975, from German 3rd edn of 1948).

Charles Petit-Dutaillis, *The Feudal Monarchy in France and England* (London, 1936, transl. from the French of 1933).

F.M. Powicke, *The Thirteenth Century* (Oxford, 1962).

P.E. Schramm, *Der König von Frankreich* (Weimar, 1960).

3 Villages, towns, republics and political thought

K.S. Bader, *Studien zur Rechtsgeschichte der mittelalterlichen Dorfes* (2 vols, Weimar, 1957–62).

R.W. and A.J. Carlyle, *A History of Medieval Political Theory in the West* (Vols II to V, Edinburgh, 1902–36, rprt).

M.V. Clarke, *The Medieval City State: An Essay on Tyranny and Federation in the late Middle Ages* (Cambridge, 1926, rprt).

Alan Gewirth, *Marsilius of Padua* (2 vols, New York, 1951–56).

*Otto Gierke, *Political Theories of the Middle Ages* (Cambridge, 1913, transl. by F.W. Maitland of part of his *Das deutsche Genossenschaftsrecht,* 3 vols, Berlin, 1861–81).

C.H. McIlwain, *The Growth of Political Theory in the West* (New York, 1933, rprt).

Jürgen Miethke ed., *Das Publikum politischer Theorie im 14. Jahrhundert* (Munich, 1992).

Sergio Mochi Onory, *Fonti canonistiche dell'idea moderna dello stato* (Milan, 1951).

Niccolà Ottokar, *Il comune di Firenze alla fine del dugento* (Florence, 1933).

Henri Pirenne, *Early Democracies in the Low Countries: Urban Society and Political Conflict in the Middle Ages and Renaissance* (London, 1915, transl. from the French of 1910).

*Gaines Post, *Studies in Medieval Legal Thought: Public Law and the State, 1100–1322* (Princeton, 1964).

Nicolai Rubinstein, 'Some ideas on municipal progress and decline in the Italy of the communes' in D.J. Gordon ed., *Fritz Saxl 1890–1948: A Volume of Memorial Essays* (Edinburgh, 1957, pp. 165–83).

*Gaetano Salvemini, *Magnati e popolani in Firenze dal 1280 al 1295* (Florence, 1899, rprt in 1960 without published documents).

*Ernst Salzer, *Über die Anfänge der Signorie in Oberitalien* (Berlin, 1900).

*Pasquale Villari, *I primi due secoli della storia di Firenze* (Florence, 1905).

Daniel Waley, *The Italian City Republic* (London, 1969).

*Michael Wilks, *The Problem of Sovereignty in the Later Middle Ages* (Cambridge, 1963).

4   Scribes, lawyers and society

A. de Boüard, *Manuel de diplomatique française et pontificale* (2 vols, Paris, 1929–48).

*Harry Bresslau, *Handbuch der Urkundenlehre* (3 vols, Berlin and Leipzig, 1912–60).

*Emile Chénon, *Histoire générale du droit français publique et privé* (2 vols, Paris, 1926–29).

M.T. Clanchy, *From Memory to Written Record, England 1066–1307* (Cambridge, MA, 1979).

*Ennio Cortese, *La norma giuridica: spunti teorici nel diritto comune classico* (2 vols, Milan, 1962–64).

*Georg Dahm, *Untersuchungen zur Verfassungs- und Strafrechtsgeschichte des italienischen Stadt in Mittelalter* (Hamburg, 1941).

*Piero Fiorelli, *La tortura giuridica nel diritto commune* (2 vols, Milan, 1953).

Hermann Kantorowicz, *Studies in the Glossators of the Roman Law* (Cambridge, 1938).

Paul Koschaker, *Europa und das römische Recht* (Munich, 1953).

*Guido Rossi, *Consilium sapientis judiciale* (Milan, 1958).

*Mario Sbriccoli, *L'interpretazione dello statuto: Contributo allo studio della funzione dei giuristi nell'età. comunale* (Milan, 1969).

A.M. Stickler, *Historia iuris canonici latini* (Turin, 1950).

PART FIVE: THOUGHT

1 Intellectuals

Henry Adams, *Mont-Saint-Michel and Chartres* (constantly rprt since publication of 1905).

*M.-D. Chenu, *La théologie au douzième siècle* (Paris, 1957).

*M.-D. Chenu, *La théologie comme science au treizième siècle* (Paris, 1957).

F.C. Copleston, *A History of Philosophy* (Vols II and III, London, 1950–53).

A.C. Crombie, *Medieval and Early Modern Science*. Vol. I: *Science in the Middle Ages* (2nd edn, New York, 1959).

S.C. Easton, *Roger Bacon and his Search for a Universal Science* (New York, 1952).

André Forest, F. van Steenberghen and M. de Gandillac, *Le mouvement doctrinale du XIe au XIVe siècle* (Paris, 1951).

*Martin Grabmann, *Die Geschichte der scholastischen Methode* (2 vols, Freiburg, 1900–10).

Herbert Grundmann, *Studien über Joachim von Floris* (Leipzig, 1927).

Herbert Grundmann, *Neue Forschungen über Joachim von Fiore* (Marburg, 1950).

C.H. Haskins, *The Renaissance of the Twelfth Century* (Cambridge, MA, 1927).

*Wilhelm Kamlah, *Apokalypse und Geschichtstheologie: Die mittelalterliche Auslegung der Apokalypse vor Joachim von Fiore* (Berlin, 1935).

*Richard Lemay, *Abu Ma'Shar and Latin Aristotelianism in the Twelfth Century* (Beirut, 1962).

*Stuart MacClintock, *Perversity and Error: Studies on the 'Averroist' John of Jandun* (Bloomington, 1956).

Johan Nordström, *Moyen-âge et Renaissance* (3rd edn, Paris, 1933).

Erwin Panofsky, *Gothic Architecture and Scholasticism* (New York, 1957).

Hastings Rashdall, *The Universities of Europe in the Middle Ages* (3 vols, ed. Powicke and Emden, Oxford, 1936).

Marjorie Reeves, *Influence of Prophecy in the Later Middle Ages* (Oxford, 1969).

Beryl Smalley, *The Study of the Bible in the Middle Ages* (Oxford, 1952, rprt).

2 Enthusiasm and repression

*Paul Alphandéry, *Les idées morales chez les hétérodoxes latins au début du XIIIe siècle* (Paris, 1903).

Arno Borst, *Die Katharer* (Stuttgart, 1953).

Norman Cohn, *The Pursuit of the Millennium* (2nd edn, New York, 1961).

*Herbert Grundmann, *Religiöse Bewegungen im Mittelalter: Untersuchungen über die geschichtlichen Zusammenhänge zwischen der Ketzerei, Bettelorden und der religiösen Frauenbewegung im 12. und 13. Jahrhunderts* (2nd edn, Hildesheim, 1961).

Gottfried Koch, *Frauenfrage und Ketzertum im Mittelalter. Die Frauenbewegung im Rahmen des Katharismus und des Waldensertums und ihre sozialen Wurzeln* (Berlin, 1962).

Lothar Kolmer, *Ad capiendas vulpes: Die Ketzerbekämpfung in Südfrankreich in der ersten Hälfte des 13. Jahrhunderts und die Ausbildung des Inquisitionsverfahrens* (Bonn, 1982).

Malcolm Lambert, *Medieval Heresy: Popular Movements from the Bogomils to Hus* (New York, 1976).

H.C. Lea, *A History of the Inquisition of the Middle Ages* (3 vols, New York, 1888).

R.E. Lerner, *The Heresy of the Free Spirit in the Later Middle Ages* (Berkeley and London, 1972).

*W. Lourdaux and D. Verhelst eds, *The Concept of Heresy in the Middle Ages (11ᵗʰ–13ᵗʰ Century)* (Leuven and The Hague, 1976).

*Henri Maisonneuve, *Etudes sur l'origine de l'Inquisition* (Paris, 1960).

Taddeusz Manteuffel, *Naissance d'une hérésie: les adeptes de la pauvreté volontaire au moyen âge* (Paris, 1970, from the Polish of 1968).

J.H. Mundy, *The Repression of Catharism at Toulouse: The Royal Diploma of 1279* (Toronto, 1985).

Christine Thouzellier, *Catharisme et Valdeisme en Languedoc à la fin du XIIe et au début du XIIIe siècle* (Paris, 1966).

Walter Wakefield, *Heresy, Crusade, and Inquisition in Southern France* (Berkeley and Los Angeles, 1974).

Ernst Werner, *Pauperes Christi* (Leipzig, 1956).

PART SIX: 1300

Ernst Benz, *Ecclesia spiritualis: Kirchenidee und Geschichtstheologie der franziskanischen Reformation* (Stuttgart, 1934).

*D.L. Douie, *The Nature and the Effects of the Heresy of the Fraticelli* (Manchester, 1932).

*Henrich Finke, *Aus dem Tagen Bonifaz VIII* (Münster, 1902).

M.D. Lambert, *Franciscan Poverty: The Doctrine of the Absolute Poverty of Christ and the Apostles in the Franciscan Order, 1210–1323* (London, 1961).

*Gordon Leff, *Heresy in the Later Middle Ages: The Relation of Heterodoxy to Dissent* (Vol. I, part 1, New York, 1967).

Jean Rivière, *Le problème de l'église et l'état au temps de Philippe le Bel* (Louvain, 1926).

J.R. Strayer, *The Reign of Philip the Fair* (Princeton, 1980).

Maps

1. Europe's languages and patterns of settlement *circa* 1300

2. The Latins in the eastern Mediterranean in the 1230s

3. Spain *circa* 1310

Areas taken from Islam 1150–1300

4. The British Isles *circa* 1300

5. The Empire and Italy *circa* 1300

The following map labels are visible:

NAPLES ANGEVIN 1266

Naples

CARNIOLA

AQUILEA

VENETIAN POSSESSIONS

Treviso

Venice

Padua

Bologna

STATES OF THE CHURCH (Affiliated towns and seigniories)

PATRIMONIUM

Rome

Bergamo

Crema

Como

Lodi

Cremona

Piacenza

Milan

Parma

Pistoia

Florence

Arezzo

Siena

Lucca

Volterra

Pisa

Novara

Vercelli

Pavia

Tortona

Bobbio

Alessandria

Genoa

CORSICA Genoa and Pisa

Bern

LUCERNE

USU

SAVOY

PROVENCE

Lyons

Marseilles

Arles

Avignon

PROVENCE ANGEVIN 1246

Allies and dependencies of Guelph Milan (della Torre) c.1310: Pavia, Vercelli, Bergamo, Crema and Tortona

Allies and dependencies of Ghibelline Milan (Visconti) c.1313. The above and Novara, Como, Piacenza, Bobbio, Lodi, Cremona, Parma and Alessandria

The March of Brandenburg

USU = The forest cantons: Uri, Schweitz and Unterswald

The frontier of the Hohenstaufen Empire

The frontier of the Empire in the early fourteenth century

The Welf duchy of Saxony (dismembered in 1180)

Habsburg holdings about 1291

Later imperial territories and Hohenstaufen holdings (Rhenish Palatinate becomes Wittelsbach in 1214)

Areas of strong French penetration up to 1310

The Bavarian duchy of the Wittelsbachs

Bruges
Ghent
FLANDERS
Arras
Cambrai
Amiens
Rouen
Beauvais
Rheims
Bayeux
NORMANDY
Paris
Chalons
CHAMPAGNE
BRITTANY
MAINE
Troyes
Sens
Le Mans
Orleans
Angers
Tours
Nantes
ANJOU
Bourges
BURGUNDY
POITOU
Poitiers
MARCHE
Angouleme
Lyons
AQUITAINE
AUVERGNE
Le Puy
Bordeaux
TOULOUSE
GASCONY
Albi
Avignon
Montpellier
PROVENCE
Toulouse
Arles
Marseilles
Narbonne
NAVARRE
ARAGON
CATALONIA

Direct royal (Capetian) government	Plantagenet house lands	Catalonia-Aragon
Northern episcopal domains closely linked to the monarchy	Plantagenet dependencies and aquisitions	French and imperial dependencies of Catalonia-Aragon
Cambrai: Area of French preponderance within the Empire	House of Toulouse-Saint Gilles	Frontier of the Kingdom of France

6. France in the 1180s

Bruges
FLANDERS
Ghent
Arras
Ponthieu
Cambrai
Amiens
Rouen
Rheims
Bayeux
Beauvais
Paris
Chalons
NORMANDY
CHAMPAGNE
MAINE
Troyes
BRITTANY
Sens
Le Mans
Orleans
Angers
Tours
Nantes
ANJOU
Bourges
BURGUNDY
Chalon
POITOU
Poitiers
Angouleme
PERIGORD
Le Puy
Bordeaux
Lyons
GUIENNE
PROVENCE
TOULOUSE
Albi
Avignon
Montpellier
Arles
Toulouse
Marseilles
Narbonne
NAVARRE
ARAGON
CATALONIA

Direct Royal (Capetian) government	Areas in dispute between England and France	Royal French expansion into the Empire
Dynastic union of Champagne, Navarre, France in 1284	Areas with strong Gascon-English influence	Angevin cadet line of Capetians in Provence
To King of England in Treaty of Paris of 1259	Ponthieu, by marriage to King of England in 1279	Papal Avignon
		Montpellier (part of Majorcan-Catalan kingdom until 1349)

7. France *circa* 1310

405

Index